2013

# ON THE ROAD

YOUR COMPLETE DESTINATION GUIDE
In-depth reviews, detailed listings
and insider tips

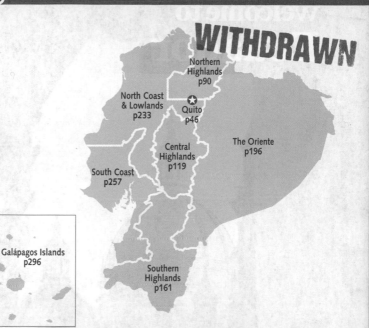

WITHDRAWN

Northern
Highlands
p90

North Coast
& Lowlands
p233

Quito
p46

Central
Highlands
p119

The Oriente
p196

South Coast
p257

Galápagos Islands
p296

Southern
Highlands
p161

# SURVIVAL GUIDE

VITAL PRACTICAL INFORMATION TO
HELP YOU HAVE A SMOOTH TRIP

**Language**

THIS EDITION WRITTEN AND RESEARCHED BY

## Regis St Louis

## Greg Benchwick, Michael Grosberg, Tom Masters

# welcome to Ecuador

## Cultural Splendor

The historic centers of Quito and Cuenca – both Unesco World Heritage Sites – are lined with photogenic plazas, 17th-century churches and monasteries, and beautifully restored mansions. Wandering the cobblestone streets amid architectural treasures from Spanish colonial days is a fine way to delve into the past. You can travel further back by contemplating great pre-Columbian artworks at museums across the country.

Beyond the cities, the Ecuadorian landscape unfolds in all its startling variety. There are Andean villages renowned for their colorful textiles and sprawling markets, Afro-Ecuadorian towns where days end with meals of fresh seafood and memorable sunsets, and remote settlements in the Amazon where shamans still harvest the traditional rainforest medicines of their ancestors.

## Andean Adventure

Setting off on a trek into the Andes can seem like stepping into a fairy tale: there's the patchwork of small villages, gurgling brooks and rolling fields, with a slowly wheeling condor overhead. Then the mists clear, a view of those towering snow-covered peaks comes into view, and the adventure begins – the challenging climb to the summit of a 5000m-high volcano.

Although the view from the top is sublime, you don't have to scale a mountain to

*Picturesque colonial centers, Kichwa villages, Amazonian rainforest and the breathtaking heights of the Andes – Ecuador may be small, but it has a dazzling array of wonders.*

(left) Cuenca's Catedral de la Inmaculada Concepción (p168)
(below) Flower sellers at the Otavalo market (p93)

enjoy the Andes. These verdant landscapes make a fine backdrop for mountain-biking, horseback-riding or hiking from village to village, overnighting at local guesthouses along the way. Ecuador's other landscapes offer equally alluring adventures, from surfing tight breaks off the Pacific coast to white-water rafting Class V rivers along the jungle-clad banks of the Oriente.

## Wildlife-Watching

The famed Galápagos Islands, with their volcanic, otherworldly landscapes, are a magnet for wildlife lovers. Here, you can get up close and personal with massive lumbering tortoises, scurrying marine iguanas (the world's only seagoing lizard), doe-eyed sea lions, prancing blue-footed boobies and a host of other unusual species both on land and sea.

The Amazon rainforest offers a vastly different wildlife-watching experience. From a remote lodge tucked away in the jungle, you set out on the rivers and trails snaking through the undergrowth in search of monkeys, sloths, toucans, river dolphins, anacondas and other creatures. Some lodges also have canopy towers offering magnificent views (and a better chance to see birdlife).

Speaking of birds, premontane cloud forest is yet another biologically rich area, and home to a fantastic array of avian life. Indeed the Mindo area, with more than 350 recorded bird species, is one of the best bird-watching sites in all of South America.

# ❯ Ecuador & the Galápagos Islands

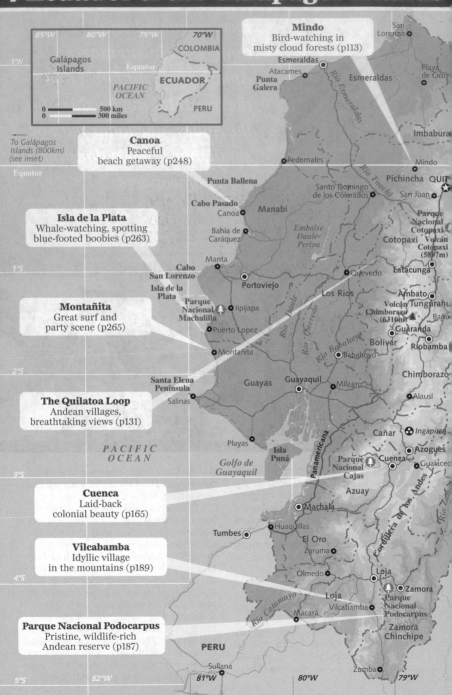

**Mindo**
Bird-watching in misty cloud forests (p113)

**Canoa**
Peaceful beach getaway (p248)

**Isla de la Plata**
Whale-watching, spotting blue-footed boobies (p263)

**Montañita**
Great surf and party scene (p265)

**The Quilatoa Loop**
Andean villages, breathtaking views (p131)

**Cuenca**
Laid-back colonial beauty (p165)

**Vilcabamba**
Idyllic village in the mountains (p189)

**Parque Nacional Podocarpus**
Pristine, wildlife-rich Andean reserve (p187)

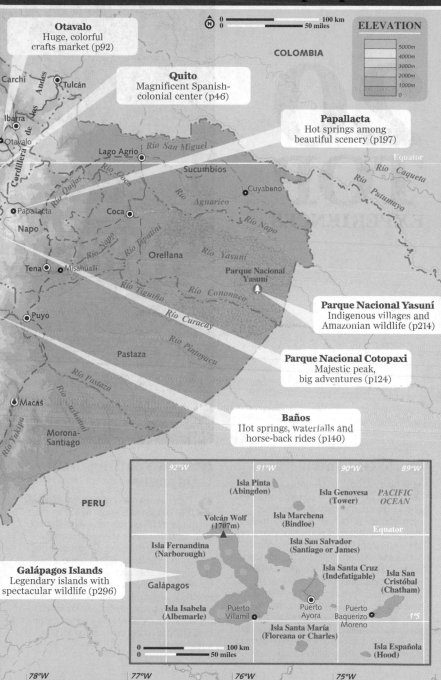

**Otavalo**
Huge, colorful
crafts market (p92)

**Quito**
Magnificent Spanish-
colonial center (p46)

**Papallacta**
Hot springs among
beautiful scenery (p197)

**Parque Nacional Yasuní**
Indigenous villages and
Amazonian wildlife (p214)

**Parque Nacional Cotopaxi**
Majestic peak,
big adventures (p124)

**Baños**
Hot springs, waterfalls and
horse-back rides (p140)

**Galápagos Islands**
Legendary islands with
spectacular wildlife (p296)

**ELEVATION**

5000m
4000m
3000m
2000m
1000m
0

0 — 100 km
0 — 50 miles

COLOMBIA

Carchi
Tulcán
Ibarra
Otavalo
Lago Agrio
Río San Miguel
Sucumbíos
Cuyabeno
Río Caqueta
Río Putumayo
Equator
Papallacta
Coca
Río Aguarico
Río Napo
Napo
Orellana
Río Yasuní
Parque Nacional Yasuní
Río Coca
Río Quijos
Río Napo
Río Tiputini
Tena
Misahuallí
Río Tiguiño
Río Cononaco
Puyo
Río Curaray
Pastaza
Río Pintoyacu
Río Pastaza
Macas
Morona-Santiago
Río Yakupa
Río Pastaza

PERU

Isla Pinta
(Abingdon)
Isla Genovesa
(Tower)
PACIFIC
OCEAN
Volcán Wolf
(1707m)
Isla Marchena
(Bindloe)
Equator
Isla Fernandina
(Narborough)
Isla San Salvador
(Santiago or James)
Isla Santa Cruz
(Indefatigable)
Isla San
Cristóbal
(Chatham)
Galápagos
Isla Isabela
(Albemarle)
Puerto
Villamil
Puerto
Ayora
Puerto
Baquerizo
Moreno
1°S
Isla Santa María
(Floreana or Charles)
Isla Española
(Hood)

92°W  91°W  90°W  89°W

0 — 100 km
0 — 50 miles

78°W  77°W  76°W  75°W

# 20
# TOP
## EXPERIENCES

## Quito Old Town

**1** A Spanish-colonial stunner, Quito's vibrant Centro Histórico (p49) is packed with elaborate churches and mournful monasteries (some centuries in the making), people-packed plazas and looming bell towers. History lurks around every corner of this well-preserved center. Delve into the past by stepping off the cobblestones and entering beautifully maintained museums, historic mansions and jaw-dropping sanctuaries. Afterwards, have a meal in one of El Centro's old-world restaurants or join the festivities on lively La Ronda street before retiring to one of the many charming guesthouses in the neighborhood.

## Iguana Spotting in the Galápagos

**2** There aren't many places that can beat the Galápagos Islands (p296) for close encounters of the prehistoric kind. Rather than scurrying away when approached, the unique lizard species of iguanas found throughout the archipelago go about their slow-moving business with little concern for the clicking cameras. The dark gray or black marine iguanas pile on top of one another like a messy pyramid of cheerleaders basking in the sun, whereas the imposing yellow land iguanas nibble on cactus plants for sustenance.

## Local Crafts at Otavalo Market

**3** Every Saturday the world seems to converge on the bustling indigenous town of Otavalo (p92) in the Andes, where a huge market (which goes on in a rather redacted form every other day of the week, too) spreads out from the Plaza de Ponchos throughout the town. The choice is enormous, the quality immensely changeable and the crowds can be a drag, but you'll find some incredible bargains here among the brightly colored rugs, traditional crafts, clothing, striking folk art and quality straw hats.

## Parque Nacional Yasuní

**4** This vast tract of protected rainforest (p214) contains a simply dazzling biodiversity matched almost nowhere else on earth. Excitement-filled canoe trips through tiny overgrown creeks and hikes across the jungle floor with experienced guides reveal all manner of flowers, plants and creatures, many of which you'll not even have heard of before, let alone seen in real life, while several populations of indigenous peoples continue to resist contact with the outside world here. This natural wonder remains, at present, unspoiled.

LEE FOSTER/LONELY PLANET IMAGES ©

ALICE GRULICH-JONES/LONELY PLANET IMAGES ©

PER-ANDRE HOFFMANN/ALAMY ©

## Cuenca

**5** The fairy-tale colonial center of Cuenca (p165) is a Unesco World Heritage Site that's been charming visitors since the 16th century. And while the cobblestone streets, polychrome building fronts and remarkably well-preserved cathedral will have you snapping a photo on nearly every corner, it's the town's laid-back feel, friendly locals and bohemian spirit that will truly fill your heart and soul. Top that off with great nightlife, plenty of museums and galleries, and some of Ecuador's best eateries, and there's no doubt why this is the bar-none top highlight of southern Ecuador.

## Beaches of the Northeast Coast

**6** Don't associate Ecuador with sun and sand? Well think again, because the northeast of the country is packed with fishing villages, resort towns, surfer hang-outs and totally pristine areas of golden sand, so head down or up the coast and take your pick. Top choices include the huge stretch of sand at charming Same (p244), the vast and still undeveloped beach at the tiny fishing village of Mompiche (p247) and the surfer-favored waves and golden sands at funky little Canoa (p248). Same beach

DAVID LITSCHEL/ALAMY ©

## Quilotoa Loop

**7** Adventure begins at 3000m along the popular Quilotoa Loop (p131), a rough travelers' route that takes you through indigenous villages and painters' colonies to a deep-blue crater lake and into the heart of Ecuador's central highlands. The best thing about the loop is that you can custom-build your adventure to fit your needs. Want to volunteer in a sustainable agriculture project? No problem. Or would you like to hike and bike from village to village on forgotten trails? Yep, they've got that, too.

## Riding the TeléfériQo

**8** Proving there's more than one way to summit the Andean peaks, the TeléfériQo (p56) whisks you up by aerial tram to breathtaking heights (4100m) over Quito. In a city of sublime views, Cruz Loma offers the finest of all – assuming you go on a clear day. Here, Quito spreads out across the Andean valley, with majestic peaks (including Cotopaxi) visible in the distance. At the top, you can extend the adventure by hiking (or taking a horseback ride) to the 4680m summit of Rucu Pichincha.

## Soaking in the Steaming Waters of Papallacta

**9** The beautifully maintained public baths just outside the Andean village of Papallacta (p197) offer one of Ecuador's best natural highs: move between baths of thermally heated water surrounded by mountains all around, swim in the fantastic pool, enjoy a bracing jump into the icy plunge pool and then get right back into those steaming baths. It's even more magical at night, when you can lie back and watch the stars come out in the giant black sky above.

## Whale-Watching off Isla de la Plata

**10** In terms of sheer awe-inspiring natural power, experiencing first-hand the breaching of a humpback whale is hard to equal. From June to September every year nearly 1000 of these majestic creatures migrate to the waters off the coast of Ecuador. The prime base for organizing boat trips, during which you might also spot dolphins and killer, pilot and beaked whales, is the fishing town of Puerto López (p261).

## Parque Nacional Podocarpus

**11** Down by the Peruvian border, Parque Nacional Podocarpus (p187) is one of the southern highland's least-visited reserves. With elevations ranging from 900m to 3600m, Podocarpus is home to an amazing array of plant and animal life. There are an estimated 3000 plant species here (many of which you will see nowhere else in the world). For bird lovers, an astounding 600 unique types of feathered friends await. Top that off with trails, highland lakes and sweeping views and you have one of Ecuador's most unique off-beat attractions.

10

SOLEDAD CONTRERAS /CORBIS ®

11

GLENN BARTLEY/CORBIS ®

## Parque Nacional Cotopaxi

**12** Home to Ecuador's best known volcano, Parque Nacional Cotopaxi (p124) offers quick adventures from the capital with million-dollar views and some of the best mountainside lodging options around. Climbing the 5897m peak of Volcán Cotopaxi will no doubt be a Grade-A highlight for the lucky few who make it to the top. Otherwise, you can skip the crampons and ice-axes, opting instead for life-affirming snapshots from the edge, or hikes, bikes and horseback rides around high Andean lakes and up to nearby volcanic peaks.

## Vilcabamba

**13** The air in Vilcabamba (p189) just feels right – not too hot, not too cold; mountain fresh with just a hint of incense on its fleeting skirts – giving this southern highland draw a mystical quality that many travelers find inescapable. Perhaps that's why you'll find more foreigner-owned businesses here than almost anywhere else in Ecuador. And who can blame them? The hiking is great, there's a national park nearby for backwoods adventures on horseback and mountain bike, and the pitch-perfect spa resorts will cater to your every need, whim and desire.

## Surfing at Montañita

**14** A dependable year round beach break and a welcoming community of experienced surfers and mellow dreadlocked travelers make this coastal village (p265) an ideal stop for those looking to ride some waves. Beginners unafraid to take a little pounding and swallow some salt water can easily find willing locals for lessons and there are smaller breaks north of here in Olón. Even if you're not looking to get air on gnarly overheads, watching the exploits from the beach while stunning sunsets provide the backdrop is not a bad alternative.

## Punta Suárez

**15** Looking out over the dramatic cliffs on the western tip of Isla Española (p325) you'll feel like you're standing at the edge of the known world. Wide-open sea stretches to the horizon and a spectacular blowhole erupts rhythmically in the foreground. Waved albatrosses and their fluffy young nest in the bushes and tiny finches hop along the rocky path. Nazca and blue-footed boobies gather along the precipice and red-billed tropicbirds and Galápagos hawks soar over the ledge in beautiful displays of aerial virtuosity.

## Hiking & Bird-Watching in Mindo

**16** Word is well and truly out about this friendly town set amid gorgeous cloud forest in a dramatic valley between Quito and the Pacific coast. While Mindo (p113) may no longer be an undiscovered off-the-beaten-track destination, its twin attractions, world-class bird-watching and wonderful scenery to hike through, remain as dazzling as ever. The biodiversity here means that bird-watchers can happily spend days with one of the village's guides seeing a wide variety of avian life, while walkers will love exploring the nearby waterfalls, thick cloud forest and soaring cliffs.

## Guayaquil's Malecón

**17** There's nowhere more emblematic of Guayaquil's rejuvenation and civic pride than its riverside promenade (p273). It's a veritable parade of kissing couples, lunching office workers and strolling families. This once neglected and maligned waterfront now combines the often conflicting virtues of a park and town plaza. Historic monuments abut landscaped gardens, a top-flight museum and art-house movie theater are only a short walk from a contemporary kids' playground, and outdoor restaurants and cafes looking out on the river make downtown seem far away.

## Baños

**18** Caught between the Andes and the Amazon in a magical little valley complete with its own waterfall and numerous natural springs, Baños (p140) is an adrenaline junkie's paradise. Gearheads and naturalists alike will love the mountain-bike descent down to the remote outpost of Puyo in the Amazon Basin. For paddlers, there are a handful of white-water trips and flat-water floats. It's also the most popular backpacker spot in the central highlands, meaning that for better or worse, you'll never be alone in Baños.

ALFREDO MAIQUEZ/LONELY PLANET IMAGES ®

## Meeting Indigenous Tribes in the Rainforest

**19** Humbling, fascinating and unforgettable: just a few words to describe a visit to an indigenous village in the Oriente (p196). You'll be introduced to customs that have remained unchanged for centuries, learn about indigenous trapping, hunting and cooking techniques, see how *chicha* is made, watch some local dancing and singing and perhaps witness a shamanistic soul-cleansing ritual. If you've got a good guide, the locals you visit shouldn't be too used to seeing foreigners: the best interaction is normally when it's equally interesting for both sides. Huaorani man making poisonous darts

## Climbing Volcán Cayambe

**20** Climbers are spoiled for choice with the range of volcanoes and mountains in Ecuador's northern Andes, but Volcán Cayambe (p92) is definitely the most impressive of all. Soaring majestically over the town of the same name, its snow-dusted peak shimmering in the sunlight year round, this extinct volcano is Ecuador's third-highest peak and the highest part of the equator anywhere on earth. Ascents are tough, but manageable for anyone with a few days' training, and views from the climb are breathtaking!

# need to know

**Currency**
» US dollar ($)

**Language**
» Spanish

## When to Go

Puerto Ayora
GO Jan–May

Quito
GO Jun–Sep

Canoa
GO Dec–Feb

Coca
GO Dec–Mar

Cuenca
GO Jun–Sep

Warm to hot summers, mild winters
Tropical climate, rain year-round
Dry climate
Desert, arid climate

### High Season
(Jun–Sep)

» Sunny, clear days in the highlands; less rain in the Oriente.

» December to April is high season on the coast: expect warm temperatures and periodic showers.

» January to May is high season in the Galápagos.

### Shoulder Season
(Oct–Nov)

» Cooler temperatures, more showers (usually sun in the morning and rain in the afternoon) in the highlands.

### Low Season
(Dec–May)

» Cooler, rainier days in the highlands.

» June to December is low season in the Galápagos with cooler, drier weather and rougher seas.

» Low season is April to July in the Oriente, when heavy rains are common.

## Your Daily Budget

### Budget less than
# $30

» Dorm beds: $7–10; budget guesthouses: $10–15 per person

» Shopping at markets, set lunches: $2–3

» Travel by bus; forget the Galápagos

### Midrange
# $30–100

» Double room in midrange hotel: $40–60

» Dinner in good restaurant: $15–20

» Climbing, cycling and bird-watching tours: $40–80 per day

» Jungle lodges: from $250 for four days

### Top end over
# $100

» Galápagos tour with a respected operator: from $300 per day

» Top Amazon lodges: around $250 per day

» Haciendas on Cotopaxi: from $100 per day

## Money

» ATMs available in cities and bigger towns. Credit cards accepted (with commission) at high-end hotels, restaurants and shops.

## Visas

» Visitors from most countries don't need visas for stays of less than 90 days.

## Cell Phones

» GSM phones operating at 850MHz (GSM 850) will work on Claro and Movistar networks. Alegro uses 1900MHz (GSM 1900).

## Transportation

» Buses are plentiful and cheap (about $1 per hour of travel).

## Websites

» **Lonely Planet** (www.lonelyplanet. com) Destination information, hotel bookings, travel forum, photos.

» **Hip Ecuador** (www. hipecuador.com) Good general information site on Ecuador.

» **Ministry of Tourism Ecuador** (http://ecuador.travel) Handy overviews of highlights, cuisine and travel tips countrywide.

» **Latin American Network Information Center** (http://lanic. utexas.edu/la/ecuador) Scores of useful links about everything Ecuadorian.

## Exchange Rates

| Australia | A$1 | US$1.06 |
| --- | --- | --- |
| Canada | C$1 | US$1 |
| Europe | €1 | US$1.31 |
| Japan | ¥100 | US$1.23 |
| New Zealand | NZ$1 | US$0.81 |
| UK | UK£1 | US$1.57 |

For current exchange rates see www.xe.com.

## Important Numbers

To call any regular number, dial the area code, followed by the seven-digit number.

| Ambulance | ☏ | 131 |
| --- | --- | --- |
| Directory Assistance | ☏ | 104 |
| Emergency (major cities only) | ☏ | 911 |
| Fire | ☏ | 102 |
| Police | ☏ | 101 |

## Arriving in Ecuador

» **Quito**
Quito's Aeropuerto Mariscal Sucre (scheduled to close by 2013) is about 10km north of the old town. Taxis charge $8 to the new town and $10 to the old town.
A new airport, 20km east of the city, is due to open in 2013. Check www.quitoairport.com for the latest info.

» **Guayaquil**
Taxis to downtown: $4–5
Bus 2 Especial (to downtown, under an hour): $0.25

## Don't Leave Home Without...

» The proper vaccinations and insect repellent (containing 30% DEET)

» Travel insurance, photocopies of your passport and essential travel documents

» A waterproof, windproof jacket – it will rain and the wind will blow (especially in the highlands)

» Ear plugs – often essential for sleeping and a good novel for those long bus rides

» A universal sink plug for hand-washing clothes and a few meters of cord – makes a great clothesline

» Dental floss – sews your clothes, laces your shoes and more!

» Duct tape – make your own mini-roll around a pencil stub or a lighter

» A flashlight (torch), travel alarm clock, ziplock bags, hat, sunglasses and sunscreen

» A Swiss Army–style pocket knife – but don't forget to pack it in your checked baggage

# if you like...

❯

## Colonial Splendor

Ecuador has a treasure chest of architectural wonders, with magnificent churches, cathedrals and convents looming above photogenic plazas – some of which date back to the 16th century. Two colonial centers are Unesco World Heritage Sites and archrivals in terms of beauty.

**Quito** Wandering the buzzing streets of the *centro histórico* (aka old town) presents stunning scenes at every turn. Step inside the atmospheric churches, house museums and colonial-art galleries for a journey into the past (p49)

**Cuenca** Smaller and more laid-back than the capital, Cuenca is no less impressive, with soaring bell towers looming over cobblestone streets and a gurgling river down below (p165)

**Loja** Boasts a small, picturesque colonial center with centuries-old streets and plazas (p181)

**Riobamba** The bustling city can't detract from its photogenic cathedral or its beautifully restored 16th-century convent (p153)

## Dramatic Scenery

Home to dramatic mountain peaks, misty cloud forests, Amazonian verdure and the otherworldly Galápagos Islands, Ecuador has countless places to stop and savor the scenery.

**Laguna Quilotoa** This topaz lake set deep in a volcanic crater is a magnificent setting for a hike (p132)

**San Rafael Falls** Ringed by rainforest, Ecuador's highest falls are well worth a detour when heading into the Oriente (p201)

**Lagunas de Mojanda** At eagle's-nest heights, these alpine lakes glimmer like jewels way up in the northern highlands (p99)

**Parque Nacional Cotopaxi** You can climb it, hike around it or simply savor the view of 5897m-high Volcán Cotopaxi from one of the historic haciendas on its flanks (p124)

**Isla Isabela (Albemarle)** Wildlife is only part of the equation when it comes to the Galápagos allure, particularly when gazing out over Darwin Lake or Volcán Sierra Negra on Isla Isabela (p316)

## Outdoor Adventures

Adrenaline junkies can get their fix in this wild and wondrous Andean nation, where snow-capped peaks, rushing rivers and pounding surf provide the perfect backdrop to a long day's outing. For other ways to get your heart racing, see p30.

**Zip-lining** In the cloud forest of Mindo, you can blaze through the canopy at breakneck speeds on one of two high-octane zip-lines (p114)

**White-water rafting** Head to Tena in the Oriente for one of Ecuador's best white-knuckle rides, with something for everyone – Class III to Class V (p216)

**Mountain-biking** There are loads of great cycling trips, but a perennial favorite is racing down the flanks of 6310m-high Chimborazo – best arranged in Riobamba (p155)

**Surfing** You'll find decent breaks all along the coast, and even out on Galápagos, but a great place to learn (and enjoy a bit of nightlife besides) is in Montañita (p265)

» Traditional Ecuadorian crafts

# Craft Markets

Leave plenty of extra space, or plan on buying an extra bag while you're down: Ecuador is a fantastic place for market-lovers. Woolly sweaters, hand-woven bags, pottery, panpipes, elaborate weavings: you'll find all this and more...

**Otavalo** The mother lode of markets, Otavalo's sprawling market is a must for first-time visitors. It's biggest and best on Saturdays (p93)

**Mercado Artesanal La Mariscal** If you can't make it out of Quito, hit this daily market in the Mariscal, with a decent selection of clothes and handicrafts (p82)

**Saquisilí** Bustling with mostly local shoppers, this Thursday market is a fascinating slice of highlands life (p135)

**Gualaceo, Chordeleg & Sigsig** Just outside of Cuenca, this trio of small, specialized towns hosts charming Sunday markets where local artisans sell their fine works, including hats, jewelry, woodcarvings and weavings (p179)

# Wildlife Encounters

An astounding variety of animals have made their home in Ecuador's rainforests and cloud forests, high-altitude grasslands, tropical dry forests and on its islands. You'll find world-class bird-watching, and superb opportunities for animal encounters – both in the Amazon and in the Galápagos.

**Bird-watching** With over 400 recorded bird species in the area, Mindo's cloud forests are a mecca for birders (p114)

**Amazonian jungle lodges** Spy monkeys, toucans, caiman, river dolphins and more from one of a handful of jungle lodges in the pristine Lower Río Napo (p210)

**Parque Nacional Podocarpus** This massive but little-known park in the southern highlands is home to a staggering number of animal (and plant) species, including tapirs, bears and nearly 600 bird species (p187)

**The Galápagos** Needing little introduction, these fascinating islands are home to creatures so tame, you'll practically be tripping over all the sea lions you come across (p296)

# Climbing, Hiking & Trekking

Strap on crampons and make your way up a 5000m volcano, blaze through endangered forests or plot a route between villages in the highlands. Whether you're out for a short day's hike or a multiday trek, Ecuador has you covered.

**Quilotoa** Avid walkers shouldn't miss this scenic highland journey, hiking from Quilotoa to Chugchilán to Isinliví, overnighting at simple village guesthouses along the way (p131)

**Cotopaxi** Only about one in two succeed in summiting this massive volcano, but it's still one of Ecuador's most popular climbs. Arrange guides in Quito (p125)

**Camino del Inca** This three-day, 40km hike to Ingapirca follows the original Incan royal road and takes in picturesque views over the highlands (p164)

**Parque Nacional Machalilla** There are great day and overnight hikes at this coastal national park near Puerto López (p259)

**If you like... speaking (better) Spanish**
Quito and Cuenca both have excellent, affordable schools offering one-on-one instruction (p62 & p170)

**If you like... white-sand beaches**
Deserted Los Frailes near Puerto López is one of the country's prettiest (p260)

# Pre-Columbian History

A land of many cultures, Ecuador has seen thousands of years of human habitation, with the ancestors of today's indigenous peoples living in every corner of the country. Museums are the best place to see relics of this rich past.

**Casa del Alabado** A beautiful new addition to the old town, this atmospheric museum showcases pre-Columbian works of art and explores the mystical side of ancient beliefs (p53)

**Museo Nacional** Delve into the past inside the nation's largest collection of pre-Columbian artifacts. Don't miss the darkened rooms of stunning gold jewelry (p61)

**Ingapirca** See Inca stone masonry up close at the wall of the Inca, Ecuador's best-preserved archaeological site (p164)

**Agua Blanca** In this coastal indigenous community, local guides lead tours around a fascinating archaeological museum and nearby ruins, once a key site of the Manta people (p260)

# Festivals

Ecuador's festivals, especially traditional fiestas in the highlands, are worth planning a trip around. Each city, town and village has its local celebrations, which feature a generous dose of fireworks, alcohol, music and dancing

**Fiesta del Yamor** Held in honor of the fall harvest, this September bash brings two weeks of merriment to Otavalo (p95)

**Mamá Negra** Processions, witches, whole roast pigs, a man dressed up as a black woman and plenty of *aguardiente* (sugarcane alcohol) – it's all part of the picture in this wild highland festival (p130)

**Fiestas de Quito** In the days leading up to the anniversary of the city's founding on December 6, the capital lights up with live bands, beauty queens, flamenco dancing, nightly street parties and bullfights (p47)

**Fiesta de Frutas y Flores** In late February, Ambato celebrates the sweet life, with processions, parades and plenty of fruits and flowers (p137)

# Indigenous Culture

With more than three million indigenous people hailing from at least a dozen distinct groups, the country offers numerous ways to interact with native Ecuadorian culture. Community-run ecotourism projects often provide memorable travel experiences.

**Tsáchila** Near Santo Domingo, you can learn all about the traditions and beliefs of the 3000-strong Tsáchila community (p235)

**Cofán** Deep in the Amazon, the Cofán people run one of Ecuador's oldest community-run ecotourism projects; seeing the forest through their eyes can be a profound way to experience the Amazon (p202)

**Shuar** Head to Macas in the Oriente to arrange a guided visit to traditional Shuar villages, where you can overnight and learn about traditional lifestyles in the rainforest (p229)

**Saraguro** South of Cuenca, this a great spot to immerse yourself in a Kichwa-speaking indigenous community. Nearby natural attractions – waterfalls, scenic hikes and horse rides – abound, and you can also arrange a community homestay (p180)

## Top Events

1 **Carnaval**, February

2 **Semana Santa**, March

3 **Inti Raymi**, June

4 **Fiesta de la Mamá Negra**, September

5 **Fiestas de Quito**, December

# month by month

## February

Cooler, wetter days are common in Quito and the highlands, while dry, sunny skies rule the Oriente. Blazing sunshine mixed with heavy downpours is common along the coast.

 **Carnaval**
Held during the last few days before Ash Wednesday, Carnaval is celebrated with water fights – sometimes dousing passers-by with all manner of suspect liquids. Guaranda is famous for its Carnaval, with dances and parades.

**Fiesta de Frutas y Flores**
Held in Ambato, the fruit and flower festival coincides with Carnaval and features fruit and flower shows, bullfights, parades and late-night dancing in the streets. Unlike in other parts of Ecuador, water-throwing here is banned.

## March

The highlands' rainy season is still in full swing (running roughly October to May), but March is a fine time to visit to beat the crowds. Expect plenty of sun in the Oriente and storms and sunshine along the coast.

 **Semana Santa**
Beginning the week before Easter Sunday (in late March or early April), Semana Santa (Holy Week) is celebrated with religious processions throughout Ecuador. The Good Friday procession in Quito, with its purple-robed penitents, is particularly colorful.

## April

The highlands continue to have the rainy season pattern of morning sunshine and afternoon showers; the Oriente and coast remain generally sunny but with periodic rainstorms.

**Founding Day, Cuenca**
The anniversary of Cuenca's founding runs over several days near April 12 and is one of the biggest events in the southern highlands. Locals celebrate with live bands, parades and elaborate fireworks-laced floats, while food stalls along the river draw daytime crowds.

 **Independence Battle of Tapi**
Riobamba's biggest night out, April 21, revolves around the historic 1822 battle. Expect an agricultural fair, with the usual highland events: street parades, dancing and plenty of traditional food and drink.

## May

The highlands head toward the dry season with fewer showers and sunnier days, while rain picks up in the Oriente. In the Galápagos, the warmwet season (January to June) prevails, with warmer days and periodic showers.

**Chonta Festival**
Held during the last week in May in Macas, the Chonta Festival is the most important Shuar celebration of the year. It culminates in a dance to help ferment the *chicha* (a fermented corn or yuca drink).

 **Corpus Christi**
This religious feast day combines with a tradit-

ional harvest fiesta in many highland towns, and features processions and street dancing. Particularly good fests are in Cuenca. It takes place in late May or early June.

# June

**The highlands' dry season coincides with Ecuador's peak season, when more North Americans visit the country. It's generally rainy in the Oriente, and cool and dry in the Galápagos (with rougher seas through August).**

## ⭐ Inti Raymi
This millennia-old indigenous celebration of the summer solstice and harvest is celebrated throughout the northern highlands, including Otavalo, where it is combined with celebrations of St John the Baptist (on June 24) and SS Peter and Paul (on June 29).

# July

**Clear, sunny highland skies make this an excellent time to visit, while rain is more prevalent in the Oriente. The Galápagos and the coast remain dry and cool (though sometimes overcast).**

## ⭐ Founding of Guayaquil
Street dancing, fireworks and processions are all part of the celebration on the nights leading up to the anniversary of Guayaquil's founding (July 25). Along with the national holiday on July 24 (Simón Bolívar's birthday), the city closes down and celebrates with abandon.

(above) Indigenous dancers and musicians parade through the streets of Quito during Carnaval

(below) The Fiesta de la Mamá Negra in Latacunga combines Catholic, pre-Columbian and civic rituals in a colorful procession of costumes

# August

It's still warm and dry in the sierra, while the Oriente sees a brief respite from the heavy rains. It's a busier time to visit, with holidaying North American and European visitors.

###  La Virgen del Cisne

In the southern highlands, thousands of pilgrims take part each year on August 15 in the extraordinary 70km procession to Loja carrying the Virgen del Cisne (Virgin of the Swan).

# September

The highlands remain sunny and clear, while a mix of rain and heat marks the Oriente. September is a lively time to visit, with important traditional fests under way.

###  Fiesta del Yamor

Imbabura province's biggest festival celebrates the fall equinox and Colla Raimi (festival of the moon) with bullfights, dancing, cockfights, partying, feasts and lots of *yamor* (a non-alcoholic drink made from seven varieties of corn).

###  Feria Mundial del Banano

In the third week of September, Machala celebrates its favorite yellow fruit with music, parades and fireworks. One of the biggest events is a beauty pageant to select the Reina del Banano (the Banana Queen).

###  Fiesta de la Mamá Negra

Latacunga hosts one of the highlands' most famous celebrations, in honor of La Virgen de las Mercedes. La Mamá Negra, played by a man dressed as a black woman, pays tribute to the 19th-century liberation of African slaves

# December

Despite the cooler temperatures and rainier skies in the highlands, December to mid-January brings a fair number of holidaying North Americans and Europeans to Ecuador.

###  Fiestas de Quito

Quito's biggest bash is a much-anticipated event, with bullfights, parades and street dances throughout the first week of December. Open-air stages all across town fill the capital with music.

###  End-of-Year Celebrations

Parades and dances starting on December 28 culminate on New Year's Eve with the burning of life-size effigies in the streets, plus fireworks. You'll see the most celebrating in Guayaquil and Quito.

# itineraries

*Whether you've got six days or 60, these itineraries provide a starting point for the trip of a lifetime. Want more inspiration? Head online to lonelyplanet. com/thorntree to chat with other travelers.*

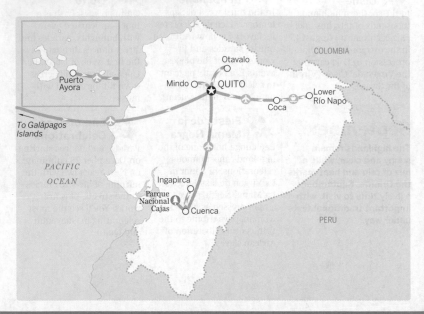

## Two Weeks
# Best of Ecuador

> Colonial treasures, cloud forests, rainforests, teeming markets and wondrous wildlife are all on the menu of this action-packed journey around Ecuador. Begin the trip in **Quito**. Spend two days soaking up the architectural gems of the old town, then fly to the **Galápagos** for a four-day cruise of wildlife-watching and island-hopping. On day seven, fly back to Quito and go two hours north to **Otavalo** for its famous market (best on Saturdays). Spend the night there; then on the eighth day, head back early to Quito for a flight to **Coca**, gateway to the Amazon. Spend three nights at one of the beautifully sited jungle lodges on the lower **Río Napo**. Catch the early morning flight back to Quito, and take a bus two hours west to the lush cloud forests of **Mindo**. Overnight in a riverside lodge, then return to Quito for a round-trip flight to **Cuenca**, the colonial jewel of the south. Spend two days exploring 500-year-old churches and visiting the fairy tale-like setting of **Parque Nacional Cajas**, 30km to the west. If time allows, visit the Inca ruins of **Ingapirca** before returning to Quito at journey's end.

QUITO

Volcán Cotopaxi
(5897m)

Quilotoa Loop

Latacunga

Volcán
Chimborazo
(6310m)

Baños

Puyo

Riobamba

Nariz
del Diablo

Alausí

Ingapirca

Cuenca

PERU

Three Weeks
# Exploring the Andes

Traveling along the spine of the Andes, you'll take in sublime alpine scenery, laid-back villages and a mix of colonial and pre-Columbian wonders. Opportunities for hiking, trekking, mountain-biking and climbing are superb. Start the highland adventure in **Quito**, where you can acclimatize to the altitude while exploring one of South America's most fascinating capitals. After two nights in the capital, head south for a night or two in a historic hacienda on the flanks of **Volcán Cotopaxi**, where you can horseback ride and hike; avid climbers can tackle one of Ecuador's iconic peaks. Around day four, travel south to **Latacunga** and journey into the mountainous landscape of the **Quilotoa Loop**. This is a great place to hike between high-up indigenous villages, overnighting in simple guesthouses along the way.

After two days spent in the clouds near Quilotoa, head to a slightly lower elevation to the delightful subtropical town of **Baños**, where you can soak in natural spring baths, book in to a charming inn with views, and take a fabulous downhill bike ride past refreshing waterfalls to **Puyo** in the Oriente. After Baños, move on to **Riobamba**, an ideal base for setting out on a high-adrenaline mountain-bike ride or hike around **Volcán Chimborazo**. From Riobamba book passage on the train to Alausí, then on to the famed **Nariz del Diablo**, with its dramatic views of Chimborazo, El Altar, Laguna de Colta, and other vistas dotting the Avenue of the Volcanoes. Alight in **Alausí**, and continue by bus to the marvelous colonial city of **Cuenca**. There enjoy a few days taking in the colonial churches, peaceful plazas and idyllic river setting before striking out for the Inca ruins of **Ingapirca**. You can visit by bus, organized day trip, or on a more challenging three-day hike along the **Camino del Inca** (Inca Trail), with gear and guides available in Cuenca. Afterwards, make your way back to Quito for a final night out (Zazu is a good choice, followed by drinks/dancing at La Juliana) and a big send-off to the great Andean experience.

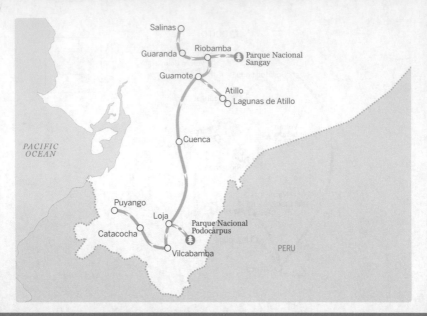

Two Weeks
# Southern Ecuador

Heading south of Quito, you'll soon find yourself in bustling market towns, remote indigenous villages and pristine national parks far from the touring crowds. Start your journey in the gateway town of **Riobamba**, a rather workaday mid-sized settlement that's at its liveliest on Saturdays, when a sprawling market takes over. From here, take a detour west to **Guaranda**, a scenic town that's the gateway up to **Salinas**, a fascinating and charming country village where you can visit cooperatives producing chocolate, cheese, mushrooms and wool products; or you can just take a walk or horseback-ride through the pretty countryside. Stay overnight in the village before heading back through **Riobamba** and continuing east to **Parque Nacional Sangay**, a setting of magnificent volcanoes and diverse flora and fauna. Head back to Riobamba then south to the lovely Kichwa town of **Guamote**. Spend the night in the cozy community-run Inti Sisa, which is also a good place to arrange mountain-biking, horseback-rides or hikes in the pristine countryside surrounding. If possible, try to time your visit for Thursday, when a massive, indigenous market takes over the town.

After Guamote, continue south to Atillo for a couple of days of spectacular hiking around the crystalline **Lagunas de Atillo**. Afterwards, head back to Guamote, then south to **Cuenca**. After days of rugged traveling, indulge in a bit of pampering with a stay in one of the city's many fine guesthouses and a meal at one of its eclectic eateries. Recharged and refreshed, continue south to **Loja**, where you can sample one of the city's specialties, *cuy* (guinea pig) – or, if you're squeamish, try its famous corn- and plantain-based delicacies.

From Loja head east to the **Parque Nacional Podocarpus**, a massive park that's home to astounding biodiversity and offers hikes through mesmerizing landscapes of *páramo* and cloud forest. Afterwards, go back through Loja and continue south to **Vilcabamba**. This pretty village offers some fine walks or bike or horseback-rides, although it's also a perfect spot to simply enjoy the peaceful scenery. Next work your way down the western side of the Andes to **Catacocha**. Spend a day here, then head to **Puyango** to visit one of South America's largest petrified forests.

» (above) Locals sell their wares,
Otavalo craft market
» (left) Canoeing down the Río Napo in
the Amazonian Basin

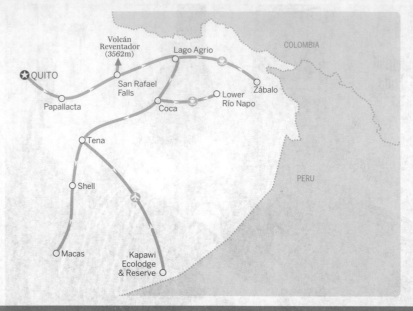

Three Weeks
# Adventure in the Oriente

The Oriente is Ecuador's slice of the Amazon, one of the world's most biologically diverse regions. For adventurers, wildlife lovers and budding anthropologists, there's much to discover here, from indigenous reserves to jungle lodges with an incredible array of plant and animal life. Start in **Quito**; pre-book jungle lodges you plan to stay at and load up on any needed supplies, then catch a bus southeast to **Papallacta**, a sparkling complex of thermal baths with magnificent mountain views on a clear day. With both high-end and budget options, this is a fine place to overnight before heading north to the thundering drama of photogenic **San Rafael Falls** – Ecuador's highest. Next to the falls is a small guesthouse and restaurant where you can hire a guide to make the trek up the active volcano of nearby 3562m-high **Volcán Reventador**.

Continue on to the gritty oil town of **Lago Agrio**; from here you can rendezvous with a Cofán guide (arranged in advance in Quito) and take the long trip along the Río Aguarico by motorized canoe to **Zábalo**, home to a small, remote Cofán community amid pristine rainforest. One of the oldest community ecotourism projects in Ecuador, this is a great place to see the riches of the rainforest and learn about the deep traditions of these Amazonian forest people. After a few days here, travel back to Lago Agrio and catch a bus down to **Coca**, another tiny river settlement turned oil boom town. Take a stroll along the river, then hook up with a jungle guide (again, best arranged beforehand in Quito) for a trip out to the **Lower Río Napo**, home to some of Ecuador's finest jungle lodges. Here you'll find superb wildlife-watching on hikes, canoe rides or climbs to the top of the jungle canopy.

Get your fill of piranha-fishing, caiman-spotting and bird-watching, then head back to Coca and down to **Tena**. This river town is an ideal spot to take in a different perspective of the rainforest: namely, rushing past on a white-water-rafting trip on spectacular class IV rapids. If time allows, you can tack on a trip to the less visited southern Oriente, via **Macas**. The Achuar-run **Kapawi Ecolodge & Reserve** (reachable by chartered aircraft from **Shell**) is a wonderfully remote piece of Amazonia.

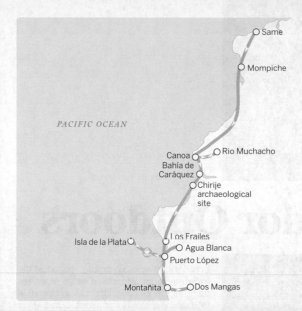

PACIFIC OCEAN

## 10 Days
# Surf & Sun

> Ecuador's charming coastal villages and attractive beaches draw a wide mix of travelers, including sun-seekers, surfers and seafood lovers. Start your trip in the laid-back beach spot of **Same** (*sah*-may) on the north coast. To get here, take a bus from Quito to Esmeraldas, and change there. After the long journey, book into a beachfront cabaña (cabin), enjoy a long walk on the beach, and get your fill of a decadent seafood feast (Seaflower is a good bet). On day two, catch a bus down to **Mompiche**, a tiny fishing village with palm-fringed sands. Once well off the radar of most visitors, Mompiche is being developed, to enjoy its subdued ambience, the time to go is now!

On day three, continue south to **Canoa**, a slow-moving beach town with a long sandy stretch backed by forested cliffs. Canoa is an easy place to linger for a while. You can take surf lessons, study Spanish or go horseback-riding or biking to deserted beaches nearby. There are some fine beachfront guesthouses and decent restaurants. While in Canoa, leave time for a visit to the **Río Muchacho**, a working organic farm, which you can tour, stay overnight on and enjoy the fantastic food grown right on-site.

On day six, continue south to **Bahía de Caráquez** and take a tour (best arranged in advance) through the fascinating **Chirije archaeological site**; you can also explore mangroves, look for frigate birds and take an eco-city tour. Spend the night, then continue on day seven to **Puerto López** (you'll have to transfer at Manta). This sleepy town is the gateway to the **Isla de la Plata**, a fine place to see blue-footed boobies if you're not heading to the Galápagos. In season (mid-June to early October), there's also good whale-watching. Other attractions in the area include the stunning beach of **Los Frailes**, the indigenous community of **Agua Blanca**, and surrounding rainforest with some memorable hiking or horseback-riding.

Spend your last two days in **Montañita**, a laid-back surf town that's a major draw among beach lovers from all parts. If time allows, make a detour to **Dos Mangas**, where you can arrange hikes or horse treks to waterfalls and remote coastal villages.

# Ecuador Outdoors

## Best Climb

The majestic heights of Volcán Cotopaxi (5897m) provide a fantastic view for those fit enough to make the summit.

## Best Trek

The multiday Camino del Inca follows the Inca royal road for 40km to the striking ruins of Ingapirca.

## Best Bird-Watching

The biologically diverse cloud forest of Mindo is home to hundreds of colorful species.

## Best Mountain-Biking Trip

Descend 61km from the crisp highlands town of Baños to steamy Puyo in the Amazon.

## Best White-Water Rafting

In the Oriente, both Tena and Macas offer fantastic full-and multi-day rafting trips past jungle-clad scenery.

## Best Surfing

Montañita, Mompiche and Canoa on the mainland offer good breaks; while Isla San Cristóbal on the Galápagos has more challenging waves.

Ecuador's diverse geography provides the backdrop to an astounding range of adventures, and its compact size makes it possible to combine a number of activities in a short time. You can go bird-watching in misty cloud forests on the Andean slopes, plot multiday treks through lush national parks, climb the peaks of the country's towering volcanoes, and snorkel with giant manta rays, turtles and sea lions off the Galápagos Islands. There's also some excellent surfing and mountain-biking, along with world-class rafting.

# Hiking

The opportunities for hiking are practically limitless. Stunning scenery is a guarantee wherever you go, with snow-covered peaks, cloud forests and verdant lowland jungle setting the stage for hiking and wildlife-watching. Most of the best independent hiking is in the national parks.

## Top Destinations

» **Parque Nacional Cotopaxi** (p124) This 330-sq-km national park is home to the snowcapped peak of the active Volcán Cotopaxi, Ecuador's second-highest point (5897m). There are great opportunities for hiking here and in the surrounding countryside, but few established trails so you'll need to blaze your own.

» **Parque Nacional Cajas** (p177) Amid the picturesque *páramo* (high-altitude Andean grasslands), there are a number of trails (some better signed than others), which take in great views

## HIKING SMARTS

A few tips on navigating Ecuadorian trails:

» **Private property** Some hikes pass through private property, and you may need to pay to visit (never much more than $1). If walking through private lands, always ask the landowner if it's all right to pass.

» **Horse sense** Many trails are cut for horses, and you may end up hiking in small gullies with a fair bit of horse dung to contend with. Good boots are essential!

» **Safety** There have been attacks on popular trails – including paths outside Vilcabamba and Baños. Enquire locally about current security risks. Only bring what you need for the day, and unless you are a professional photographer, you may prefer to leave the digital SLR at home.

» **Resources** An excellent guide for hikers is *Ecuador: Climbing and Hiking Guide* (2009) by Rob Rachowiecki and Mark Thurber. It includes dozens of hikes across the country, from easy jaunts to multiday treks, and covers essentials like where to rent gear and hire guides and porters.

of pretty alpine lakes. Be prepared for rain (the driest months are August to January).

» **Quilotoa Loop** (p131) Near the dramatic topaz crater lake of Quilotoa, there are some excellent hikes here, including village-to-village trips and a few shortcuts through high-altitude canyons. One excellent DIY route goes from Quilotoa to Isinliví, overnighting in Chugchilán along the way.

» **Parque Nacional Podocarpus** (p187) Across lush tropical lowlands and chilly, mountainous highlands, Podocarpus offers several memorable hikes including a day hike through cloud forest and a multiday hike to Andean lakes.

» **Parque Nacional Machalilla** (p260) The country's only coastal national park covers 400 sq km, with trails through tropical dry forest as well as cloud forest. The park also includes Isla de la Plata, which has several loop hiking trails and has been called 'the poor man's Galápagos' because of its wildlife, which includes red-footed boobies.

» **Camino del Inca** (p164) For a fascinating journey along part of the royal road that linked Cuzco (Peru) to Quito, take the Inca trail to the archaeological site of Ingapirca; it's a popular 40km hike that most travelers do in three days.

# Bird-Watching

Nowhere else in the world has such incredible avian diversity been crammed into such a small country. Some 1600 species, including a number of unique species, have been spotted in mainland Ecuador and on the Galápagos. Scope is one of the biggest challenges for bird-watchers – with rainforest, cloud forest and islands all offering allure.

For more information about the colorful birdlife in Ecuador see p336.

## Cloud Forest

One recommended place to start exploring is just north of Quito. The cloud forests around **Mindo** (p113) and **Tandayapa** (p112) are a bird-watcher's paradise. During the Audubon Society's Christmas Bird Count, more than several hundred species are typically spotted in a single day. Highlights include the Andean cock-of-the-rock, scaled fruiteater and golden-headed and crested quetzals. Mindo itself boasts over 400 recorded bird species and has become a major bird-watching center, with excellent guides and lodges in the area.

In the same area is the 700-hectare **Reserva Bellavista** (p113), which has 8km of well-marked trails – along which some 320 bird species have been recorded.

## Amazon

Another excellent destination is the lower **Río Napo** (p210) region of the Amazon, where more than 500 bird species have been logged. Some of Ecuador's best jungle lodges are in this area, some with their own canopy towers and biologist guides.

## Galápagos Islands

The **Galápagos Islands** (p296) is another mecca for bird-watchers, owing to its 28 endemic species that have evolved in extraordinary ways. Isla Santa Cruz boasts the highest bird count overall, and it's a good place to begin to find the 13 species of

Darwin's finches. Various large species are easily seen around Puerto Ayora harbor, including blue-footed boobies, magnificent frigate birds and herons.

# Horseback-Riding

Ecuador has some great horseback-riding opportunities, especially in the highlands. Unfortunately, many of the horses used in tourist hikes are not properly looked after, and several travelers have written to say that their horses were old, overworked and underfed. There are, however, some agencies that take proper care of their animals, and they're worth seeking out, even though they charge more for tours. Haciendas throughout the highlands generally use good horses and offer some of the best opportunities for riding. **Vilcabamba** (p189) offers some fine rides in the surrounding mountains. Trips range from a few hours to three days. **Baños** (p143) is also a good place to sign up for a casual half- or full-day ride.

Another great place for riding is inside the **Reserva Geobotánica Pululahua** (p87) near Quito. Located inside a volcanic crater, this reserve boasts cloud forests and a fascinating microclimate. You can arrange daylong or even multiday horseback rides from there.

An expensive but fully reputable company is RideAndes (www.rideandes.com). It offers day tours, multiday tours and custom-made tours for both experienced and inexperienced riders. One of its most popular excursions is the seven-day hike around Volcán Cotopaxi. Horses and guides are top-notch.

# Mountaineering

The towering Andes sweeping through Ecuador set the stage for serious adventure. The country has 10 peaks over 5000m, eight of which are in the central highlands (p119). This is where you'll find Ecuador's most impressive summits. Keep in mind that many of Ecuador's most impressive peaks are volcanoes, and their status can change quickly. Some are climbable one year and not the next. Those looking to climb a peak where no equipment is required might consider **Volcán Imbabura** (4609m; p108) in the northern highlands. It's a challenging and highly rewarding climb just outside of Ibarra.

## Climbing Essentials

Mountaineers will require standard snow and ice gear: rope, crampons, ice axe, high-altitude sun protection and cold-weather clothing as a minimum. Unless you are very experienced, hiring a guide from Quito (p62) or Riobamba (p155) is recommended. The weather can turn bad quickly in the Andes, and even experienced climbers have been killed. Several agencies offer both rental gear and guides: expect to pay $65 to $90 per person per day to climb a major peak. The best guides have a card accrediting them to the Ecuadorian Mountain Guides Association (ASEGUIM).

You can climb year-round, but the best months are considered to be June to August and December to February.

## Major Peaks

» **Volcán Chimborazo** (p152) Ecuador's highest peak is an extinct volcano that tops at 6310m. It's a relatively straightforward climb for experienced climbers, but ice-climbing gear is essential. From the climbing refuge, most climbers take the Normal Route, which takes eight to 10 hours to the summit and two to four on the return. Riobamba is the best place for arranging a guided hike, hiring equipment and unwinding when the climb is done.

» **Cotopaxi** (p124) The country's second-highest peak is an active volcano and one of the most popular summits in the Andes for serious climbers. Cotopaxi can be climbed in one long day from the climbers refuge, but sane people usually allow two days. Climbers must acclimatize for several days before attempting an ascent. Lodges in and around Cotopaxi (p126) are great for acclimatization.

» **Ilinizas** (p123) The jagged sawtooth peak of Iliniza Sur (5248m) is Ecuador's sixth-highest peak and one of the country's most difficult climbs. It's suitable only for experienced climbers. Iliniza Norte (5126m), on the other hand, is a rough scramble and can be climbed by acclimatized, experienced hikers. It's the country's eighth-highest peak. The small village of El Chaupi is a good base for acclimatizing climbers and hikers, with a handful of simple but pleasant guesthouses.

» **El Altar** (p150) This long-extinct 5319m volcano is widely considered the most beautiful and most technical of Ecuador's mountains. December to March is the best time to visit this area. In July and August El Altar is frequently socked in with clouds.

# Mountain-Biking

Mountain-biking has grown increasingly popular, especially the adrenaline-charged downhills on the flanks of Cotopaxi and Chimborazo. The best mountain-biking operators (with the best bikes, guides and equipment) can be found in Quito (p62) and Riobamba (p155).

Baños is also awash in midrange mountain bikes, thanks to the popular and excellent downhill ride (by road) to Puyo. Nicknamed 'La Ruta de las Cascadas' (Highway of the Waterfalls), it follows the Río Pastaza canyon, dropping steadily from the highlands town of Baños at 1800m to the jungle settlement of Puyo at 950m. It's a 61km ride, with some refreshing dips in waterfalls along the way. For more details see p147.

If you're doing any serious cycling, bring all your own gear and replacement parts, as specialty parts are only available in Quito. Also remember the threat of dehydration; in Ecuador you're either riding at altitude or in the extreme heat of the lowlands, so always carry plenty of water.

## ALTERNATIVE ADVENTURES

Ecuador has much more than volcanoes and rainforests up her sleeve. Wondrous caves, pretty rivers and the fortuitous proximity of the continental shelf all create opportunities for uncommon adventures.

» **Caving, Cueva de los Tayos** Located on the eastern slopes of the Andes, the Cueva de los Tayos (Cave of the Oil Birds; p231) provides a fascinating wonderland for cave lovers. The entrance is located within rainforest at the bottom of a valley – but it's no easy entrance. The journey starts with a 70m drop into the caves – from which you could then spend a week (or a lifetime?) exploring the stalactite-filled caverns. A guide is recommended.

» **Tubing, Mindo** While some prefer kayaks and rafts, in Mindo (p114) there's nothing quite equal to the joy of gliding down the fern-lined Río Mindo, bottom securely planted in a rubber inner tube. Keep in mind this is white water (and all the livelier in the rainy season), and helmets and life jackets are essential.

» **Whale-watching, Puerto López** With an annual population of humpback whales of around 400, Puerto López (p262) is considered the epicenter of whale breeding grounds. Numerous boat operators ply the waters in search of the magnificent mammals, with excellent sighting opportunities from June to September (July and August are peak months).

» **Puenting, Baños** In Baños (p141) visitors with a rock-solid life-insurance policy might consider the freefall excitement called *puenting* (think bungee jumping without the bounce). It roughly translates as 'bridging' but it's really leaping, then swinging pendulum-style on a rope tethered underneath a bridge.

» **Canyoning, Baños** Another Baños-based activity growing in popularity, canyoning (p143) involves rappelling (abseiling) down waterfalls, swimming in rivers and taking short hikes through canyons.

» **Sport-fishing, Salinas** Some 13km offshore from Salinas (p269) the continental shelf drops off, providing an ideal setting for deep-water fishing. Swordfish, sailfish, tuna, dorado and black marlin all frequent the waters, with the best fishing from September to December. Salinas is the place to charter a boat.

# Diving & Snorkeling

The Galápagos Islands is one of the world's great dive destinations, offering dramatic underwater wildlife: sharks, rays, turtles, penguins, sea lions, moray eels, sea horses, fish of many kinds and, if you're very lucky, dolphins or even whales. Conditions are difficult for beginners, with strong currents and cold water temperatures. There are dive operators based in **Puerto Ayora** (p301).

Experienced divers can opt for a week's tour aboard a dive-dedicated boat, stopping at the aquatic hot spots around the archipelago. Those looking for less commitment can usually arrange single- or multi-tank dives for a day from Puerto Ayora. The Galápagos is also a good place for snorkeling as the marine life doesn't often require great depths to access.

Diving has become popular out of the coastal town of **Puerto López** (p261). The sea bottom here mixes rock with coral reef patches and sand. Aquatic life includes angelfish, trumpet fish, puffer fish, morays, parrot fish, manta rays, guitar rays and white-tip sharks. The occasional sea turtle is also spotted.

The water temperature is around 22°C (72°F) from January to April and about 18°C (64°F) the rest of the year, so consider bringing a spring-suit (shorty) with you.

# Surfing

Ecuador isn't a huge surf destination but has some excellent breaks if you know where to go. The season is generally November to April, with peak months in January and February. Localism is generally minimal; Ecuadorians and foreigners mix it up pretty peacefully.

The classic mainland break is **Montañita** (p265), a fast, powerful reef-break that can cough up some of the mainland's best barrels. The break is best from December to May, when swells of 2m to 3m are common. It also has some tolerable beach-breaks nearby. Near Muisne, in Esmeraldas province, **Mompiche** (p247) is a world-class left point-break offering rides of up to 500m on top days. **Canoa** (p248) is a fun spot for left and right beach-breaks, if only because the town here is a great little hangout and the beach is beautiful.

In the Galápagos, Isla San Cristóbal is home to three world-class reef-breaks, all near the town of **Puerto Baquerizo Moreno** (p312). They're extremely fast and best for experienced surfers. The high price of getting there keeps the crowds down. Optimal surf season on the islands is from December to May.

# White-Water Rafting

Ecuador boasts world-class river rafting and kayaking year-round. Some of the rivers offer up to 100km of continuous Class III to Class IV white water before flattening out to flow toward the Pacific on one side of the Andes and into the Amazon Basin on the other. Wherever you go, the best time for rafting is from October to February.

Ecuador's river-guide association is called Asociación de Guías de Águas Rápidas del Ecuador (AGAR; Ecuadorian White-Water Guides Association). Only reputable companies are listed in this book. When shopping around for an outfit, make sure they have decent life jackets, professional guides, first-aid kits and throw bags. Some outfitters also offer wet-suit rental on several of the longer runs (recommended).

## Top Rafting Spots

» **Tena** This is Ecuador's de facto white-water capital, with the nearby upper Río Napo (Class III+) and the Río Misahuallí (Class IV+) among the country's best-known rivers (p216).

» **Macas** Further south, the Río Upano (Class III to IV+) near Macas is excellent for multiday trips and outrageous jungle scenery, including the spectacular stretch along the Namangosa Gorge, where more than a dozen waterfalls plummet into the river. See p229.

» **Río Blanco** On the western slopes of the Andes, about 2½ hours west of Quito, the Río Blanco (Class III to IV), is a year-round possibility and a favorite day trip from the capital, with wildest conditions from February to about June. There are approximately 200km of maneuverable white water here, including the challenging Upper Blanco. There are several Class II to III runs for complete beginners and families near Quito as well. See p62 for operators in the capital.

» **El Chaco** On the eastern slopes of the Andes, El Chaco (p201) is the gateway to the Río Quijos, a Class IV to V river with verdant scenery.

» **Río Pastaza & Río Patate** These are two of the country's most popular rivers due to their proximity to the tourist mecca of Baños (see p143). The Patate, unfortunately, remains very polluted.

# Planning Your Galápagos Adventure

### Best Snorkeling
Devil's Crown off Floreana
Los Túnneles off Isabela

### Best Bird-Watching
Punta Suárez on Española
Prince Philip's Steps on Genovesa

### Best Diving
Isla Wolf
Isla Darwin

### Best Hiking
Volcán Alcedo on Isabela
Cerro Crocker on Santa Cruz

### Best Mountain-Biking
San Cristóbal highlands
Santa Cruz highlands

### Best Sunbathing
Tortuga Bay outside Puerto Ayora
Cerro Brujo on San Cristóbal

### Best Surfing
Puerto Baquerizo Moreno
Isla Isabela

## When to Go

There really isn't a bad time to visit. However, there are several factors to keep in mind in determining when to go. The islands have two distinct seasons, though the tourism high season is generally December to April, and July and August.

» **Warm & Wet Season (January to May)** Generally sunny and warm (average air temperature is 25°C) with strong but short periods of rain. Coincides with vacation periods in the USA such as Christmas and Easter, which means more boats and more groups. The hottest month is March (average 31°C) and water temperatures average 25°C from February to April. Flowers bloom, bringing more color to the landscape; sea turtles nest; and many bird species mate.

» **Cool & Dry Season (June to December)** Often known as the *garúa* for the misty precipitation that affects the highlands. While the air temperature is extremely pleasant (average is 22°C), the water is colder (18°C to 20°C) as a result of the dominant Humboldt Current, and the seas can be rough during overnight passages between islands. There are somewhat fewer visitors; however, it's also the season preferred by divers (6mm-to-7mm thick wetsuits with hoods are worn). Penguin encounters are more common, waved albatrosses arrive on Española and blue-footed boobies mate.

## WHAT TO PACK

☐ binoculars
☐ camera with underwater casing
☐ small backpack
☐ wide-brimmed hat
☐ motion-sickness pills
☐ light cotton clothing
☐ cash for park fee and cruise staff tips
☐ sturdy hiking shoes or boots
☐ sunglasses
☐ rain jacket
☐ light sweater
☐ refillable water bottle
☐ swimming gear
☐ flip-flops (thongs)

The Galápagos Islands is one of the few places on earth where you can encounter animals up close and in the wild, both on land and in the sea – so visiting here can be a life-changing adventure, one that's on many people's bucket lists.

Visit independently or on a tour? Take a two-week cruise or day trips from an island base? Arrange ahead of time or try your luck when you show up? The options can be confusing and overwhelming; this chapter will help you plan your ultimate Galápagos adventure.

# Types of Tours

There are basically three kinds of tours in the Galápagos: the most common and most recommended are boat-based trips with nights spent aboard – this is because of their relatively low environmental impact and the sheer exposure to a variety of wildlife and geography. There are also day trips returning to the same island each night, and hotel-based trips staying on different islands.

Once you decide on the kind of tour you want, you can either fly to the islands and find a tour there, or make reservations in advance on the mainland or through a travel agency in your home country. There is public transportation only between Isla Santa Cruz, Isla San Cristóbal and Isla Isabela, and the crossings can sometimes be uncomfortably rough.

# Boat Tours

Most visitors tour the Galápagos on boat tours, sleeping aboard the boat. Tours can last from three days to three weeks, although five- to eight-day tours are the most common. It's difficult to do the Galápagos justice on a tour lasting less than a week, but five days is just acceptable. If you want to visit the outlying islands of Isabela and Fernandina, a cruise of eight days or more is recommended. On the first day of a tour, you arrive from the mainland by air before lunchtime, so this is really only half a day in the Galápagos, and on the last day, you have to be at the airport in the morning. Thus, a five-day tour gives only three full days in the islands.

## Itineraries

You can find boats to go to almost any island, although it takes more time to reach the outlying ones. Boats have fixed itineraries, so think ahead if you want a tour that visits a specific island. Make sure the tour doesn't include more than one night or half a day in either Puerto Ayora or Puerto Baquerizo Moreno, since you can always tack on a few days (or weeks, for that matter) at the beginning or end on your own.

The daily itinerary on almost all boats includes taking a morning *panga* (small boat used to ferry passengers from a larger boat to shore) to a site on land to observe birds and other wildlife, followed by snorkeling nearby. Lunch and snacks are served while the boat motors to another island or site for a similar combination in the afternoon. There's usually a few hours of time to rest or socialize before dinner, and there's a post-meal briefing of the next day's schedule. While the standardized routine may irk those accustomed to the flexibility of independent travel, it's exceedingly comforting to have everything preplanned, and in the end it's a surprisingly tiring trip. Most people retreat to their cabins before 10pm, hoping to get enough sleep for the early morning starts.

## Boat Types

Tour boats range from small yachts to large cruise ships. By far the most common type is the motorsailer (a medium-sized motor boat), which carries eight to 20 passengers. It might be worthwhile spending an extra few hundred dollars to go on a more comfortable, reliable boat and getting a decent guide (although more-expensive boats can have problems, too). For about $1500 to $2400 you can take a more comfortable tourist-class tour for eight days – the usual extra costs (airfare, fees and tips) apply. Many companies in Quito offer tours at about this price.

## Tipping

It's customary to tip the crew and guide at the end of a trip. On exceptionally good and higher-end boats, a tip amount is usually suggested and you aren't responsible for dividing up the amount among the crew members, as you might on the cheaper boats – on the latter, the guide generally gets the bigger tip, then the cook and captain, and then the other crew members.

## Hotel-Based Tours

These tours go from island to island, and you sleep in hotels on three or four different islands: Santa Cruz, San Cristóbal, Isabela and Santa María. Tours typically last five days and four nights and cost $500 to over $1500 per person, plus airfare and park fee. Several of the travel agencies in Puerto Ayora and Puerto Baquerizo Moreno book these – **Red Mangrove Aventura Lodge** (p304) in Puerto Ayora; **Tropiceo** (☑02-222-5907; www.tropiceo.com), a tour agency based in Quito; and **Sharksky Tours** (p312) are recommended for these trips.

The problem with most tour companies is that they use a mix of boats, hotels and guides, so the quality of all three is difficult to guarantee and there's little consistency from one trip to the next. The camaraderie between guests and guides that adds to the enjoyment of Galápagos boat trips is lost when there's often a new guide for every stop.

## Day Tours

Boat-based day trips depart from either Puerto Ayora or Puerto Baquerizo Moreno. Several hours are spent sailing to and from the day's visitor sites, so only a few central islands are feasible destinations. Some trips may involve visiting sites on other parts of Isla Santa Cruz or Isla San Cristóbal.

One of the downsides of this kind of tour is that there is no chance of visiting the islands early or late in the day. The cheapest boats may be slow and overcrowded; their visits may be too brief; the guides may be poorly informed; and the crew may be lacking an adequate conservationist attitude. Nevertheless, day trips are useful for severe seasickness sufferers and/or if your time and budget is extremely limited. Generally, higher priced high-end operators are feasible and enjoyable alternatives.

Companies in Puerto Ayora and Puerto Baquerizo Moreno charge $75 to $175 per person per day, depending on the destination on offer and the quality of the boat and guides.

| CAMPING |
| --- |
| There are only a few sites in the Galápagos Islands where camping is allowed – and in those cases, a permit is required. On Santa Cruz head to Garrapatero; on San Cristobal try Puerto Grande and Puerto Chino; and on Isabela there's Campo Duro. |

# Booking Your Trip

Most visitors arrange tours before arriving at the islands. You can do this in your home country (it tends to be more expensive, but it's efficient), or you can arrange something in Quito, Guayaquil or Cuenca. Booking in Ecuador is generally cheaper, but you sometimes have to wait several days or weeks during the high season (which could eat into your traveling time). One other word of caution if planning a Galápagos trip while in Ecuador – the default security protocols of some banks and credit-card companies make it difficult to pay for such relatively large amounts without hassle while you're abroad.

## Shopping for a Smooth Sail

There are five boats (*Explorer II, Endeavour, Galápagos Legend, Santa Cruz* and *Polaris*) that carry up to 98 passengers each, and four boats (*Isabela II, Eclipse, La Pinta* and *Islander*) that carry up to 48 passengers each; all are considered luxury or first-class ships. The majority of the other 75 or so boats or yachts carry up to 20 people or fewer. There are also several catamarans. Groups that book far in advance are often able to negotiate prices that are just as good as last-minute rates. Almost every boat operator charges 15% to 20% less in the low season.

## LIVE-ABOARD DIVING TOURS

Not surprisingly for a place with an underwater habitat resembling a well-stocked aquarium, scuba diving in the Galápagos is world class. The conditions aren't suitable for beginners because of strong currents, sometimes cloudy visibility and cold temperatures. When the water is warm (January to March) there's not much of a current so it's also a little murky; from July to October there's better visibility but the water is colder. Besides an array of tropical fish, there are plenty of whale sharks, hammerheads, manta rays and even sea horses to be seen.

Standard overnight boat tours (called 'naturalist trips' in tour-agency vernacular) are not allowed to offer scuba diving as an option. Only seven boats are currently available for diving – Ecoventura's *M/V Galápagos Sky* and *Deep Blue*; Aggressor's *Albatross* (I) and *Jesus de Gran Poder* (II) (☑800-348-2628; www.aggressor.com); *Wolf Buddy* and *Darwin Buddy* (☑866-462-8339; www.buddydive-galapagos.com); and *Humboldt Explorer* (☑in Guayaquil 04-234-5446; www.humboldtexplorer.com). Because there are so few options, these boats are usually booked as far as six months in advance. The average cost of one week on a live-aboard is from $4000/4500 low/high season and includes up to four or five dives a day, plus stops at some visitor sites on land.

Most live-aboard boats go to Wolf and Darwin, northwest of the major islands, where there's a large number of different species of sharks. July is the best month to dive with whale sharks, but they're around from May to October.

The majority of divers take day trips from either Puerto Ayora (p303) or Puerto Baquerizo Moreno (p312).

The airfare, $100 park fee and bottled drinks are not included in fare quotes. Boats are divided roughly into the following categories (prices per day except for live-aboards):

» **Economy-class yachts** up to $199

» **Tourist-class yachts** (tourist superior or standard tourist) $200 to $300

» **First-class yachts** $300 to $400

» **Luxury ships** from $400

To avoid disappointment, the following questions should always be asked before booking:

» **'Is the guide a freelancer?'** Guides affiliated with one company or boat are more likely to feel responsible for their passengers' satisfaction and not to take a *laissez faire* approach to complaints.

» **'What is the itinerary?'** Refer to the map and text of the Galápagos Islands chapter (p296) to understand the wildlife and activities common at each site. Joing boats that spend half-days in Puerto Ayora, Puerto Baquerizo Moreno and/or Puerto Villamil might seem like too much civilization.

» **'Is snorkeling equipment in my size guaranteed?'** Masks, snorkels and fins are generally supplied; however, some boats may lack enough fins and wetsuits in certain sizes for all passengers.

» **'What's the refund policy?'** Read the fine print and clarify how much money you can get back in case of a mechanical breakdown or other unforeseen circumstance that results in the cancellation or alteration of your trip.

» **'How would you rate the food?'** This can be difficult to determine since chefs come and go and some agencies may be less than forthcoming in assessing their own product. Nevertheless, it's worth asking if this is an important issue for you.

» **'One bed or two?'** Couples be warned: all the boats have a limited number of cabins with matrimonial beds. Unless you reserve early, you may be stuck with two narrow single beds.

It's quite common for boats and companies to receive favorable reviews from some people and unfavorable reviews from others. Expectations and standards differ and sometimes things go wrong on one trip but smoothly on another. The quality of your sailing experience will depend on a few things, including the chemistry between you and your fellow passengers; the smaller the boat the more important it is that you get along. However, the larger boats with more passengers can feel impersonal, and the trip and islands may lose some of their unique aura.

There are a number of boats and companies that are worth checking out. There are many more boats that service the islands, so, besides the list below, refer to the travel agencies sections in both Guayaquil (p288) and Quito (p62) for other recommended options:

**Adventure Life** (☑in the US 800-344-6118; www.adventure-life.com) Books a wide selection of boats in all categories.

**Columbus Travel** (☑02-254-7587, in the US 877-436-7512; www.columbusecuador.com) Excellent customer service; can book range of boats depending on budget and dates of travel.

**Cormorant Galapagos** (☑in the US 877-987-4040; www.cormorantgalapagos.com) One of the most up-to-date boats, this catamaran has private balconies and a Jacuzzi.

**Detour Destinations** (☑in the US 866-386-4186; www.detourdestinations.com) Multisport trips for active types, including stand-up paddle board excursions in the islands.

**Ecoventura** (☑02-290-7396, in the US 800-633-7932; www.ecoventura.com) One of the pioneers in conservation and sustainable tourism. All of its four boats, including its diving live-aboards, are highly recommended.

**Ecuador Adventure** (☑02-604-6800, in the US 800-217-9414; www.ecuadoradventure.ec) Specializes in hotel-based and multisport tours including mountain-biking and kayaking.

**Ecuador Travel** (www.ecuador-travel.net/Galapagos.htm) Dependable and honest broker for a wide range of boats, which range from economy to luxury.

**Explorer's Corner** (☑in the US 877-677-9623; www.explorerscorner.com) Offers an 11-day tour cruising long distances on a catamaran and then exploring the nooks and crannies by kayak – one of the only tours of its kind.

**Galapagos Odyssey** (☑in the US 646-415-7758; www.galapagosodyssey.com) This luxurious 16-passenger yacht includes a Jacuzzi.

**Happy Gringo Travel** (☑02-290-6077; www.happygringo.com) Recommended for those looking for last-minute deals on a range of boats.

**Lindblad Expeditions National Geographic** (☑in the US 800-425-2724; www.expeditions.com; 1-week cruise from $4700) Offers *National Geographic Islander* (48 passenger) and *Endeavour* (96 passenger) yachts.

**Metropolitan Touring** (☑02-298-8200, in the US 888-572-0166; www.metropolitan-touring.com) Affiliated with the Finch Bay Hotel in Puerto Ayora; books the luxury yacht *Isabela II*.

**Row Adventures** (☑in the US 800-451-6034; www.rowadventures.com) Luxury camping and kayaking tours.

**Sangay Touring** (☑02-222-1336; www.sangay.com) An experienced outfit that books over 60 boats.

## Local Bookings

Most people arrive in the islands with a pre-arranged tour, although it's usually cheaper to arrange a tour in Puerto Ayora or Puerto Baquerizo Moreno. As a general rule, the cheaper boats are more available for booking once you're in the Galápagos. Don't fly to the Galápagos counting on getting a really good boat for less money. Arranging a tour from the Galápagos can take several days – sometimes a week or more – and is therefore not a good option for people with a limited amount of time. Finding boats both in August and around Christmas and Easter is especially difficult. The less busy months have fewer travelers on the islands, but boats are often being repaired or overhauled at this time, particularly in October. By the time you pay for hotels and meals in Puerto Ayora or Puerto Baquerizo Moreno, you may end up saving less than hoped.

The most important thing is to find a good captain and an enthusiastic naturalist guide. You should be able to meet both and inspect the boat before booking. Agreeing on a quality itinerary is also paramount. For last minute four-day and eight-day tours, expect to pay at least $550 and $1200.

# Dangers & Annoyances

There are some common pitfalls and hassles with Galápagos boat tours. It's sometimes the case that the cheaper the trip, the more likely you are to experience problems. That's not to say that costlier boats are glitch-free, but the companies are often more attentive and quick to respond to complaints.

Some of the recurring complaints involve last-minute changes of boat (which the contractual small print allows), cancellations if not enough passengers, poor crew, lack of bottled drinks, changes in the itinerary, mechanical breakdowns, insufficient and poor-quality snorkeling gear, hidden charges ($5 per day for wet suits is common), bad smells, bug infestations and overbooking. There have also been reports of new arrivals being solicited by less-than-trustworthy

## TIPS FOR THE BUDGET-MINDED

Regardless of the corners you cut, a trip to the Galápagos takes a significant chunk of change. Travelers touring the continent usually bypass it, since a week in the islands may cost as much as a month or two backpacking elsewhere.

There are, however, some strategies for cutting costs, though these may reduce the pleasure involved in a trip. For boats in the lower price range, owners, captains, guides and cooks all change frequently; in addition, many boats make changes and improvements from year to year. Generally speaking, a boat is only as good as its crew. You can deal with a great crew member or boat representative during your search for a cheaper boat, but you may not always end up with a great crew on the boat itself – also, these boats often don't employ naturalists (even though they're supposed to) and may not have English-speaking guides. Also, ask about washing facilities – they can vary from deck hoses and cramped and primitive communal showers on the cheapest boats to private showers on the majority of the better boats.

A few budget-friendly ideas:

» Talk to the ship owners directly to avoid having to pay commission to an agency.

» Keep in mind that Ecuadorian agencies are at least 30% cheaper than agencies that book trips in the USA and Europe.

» A little back-and-forth negotiation is a good idea; indicate that you've been offered a cheaper deal elsewhere, or simply that your budget will only allow you to spend such and such amount of money.

» Individuals and couples (but not larger groups) have a good chance of grabbing a last-minute discounted spot (often outside the high season), even on luxury boats.

» All cabins are not the same size; book the smaller ones to save money.

» Single travelers usually have to pay a supplement to have a room alone. If you're happy to share with someone, partner up with a roommate and avoid paying the supplement.

» Inquire about water – on the cheaper boats, you may need to bring your own large containers of water.

» Alcoholic drinks are usually not covered in any boat tour's rates. One way to keep costs down is to stock up on wine, beer, etc from supermarkets in Puerto Ayora or Puerto Baquerizo Moreno.

---

freelance travel agents at the airports – avoid these and inquire at offices in town.

Passengers share cabins and are sometimes not guaranteed that their cabin mates will be of the same gender. Always ask to see a photograph or layout of the boat, including those of the cabins before booking.

It's frustrating but not uncommon to discover shipmates have paid substantially less than you for the same services, especially if you've booked abroad and they've arranged things locally and at the last minute – there's little recourse, so it's best not to ask and to simply enjoy the trip.

When things go wrong, a refund is difficult to obtain. If you have a problem, report it to the *capitanía* (port captain) in Puerto Ayora and contact the agency where you booked the boat. You should also report problems (in person or by email) to the **Cámara de Turismo**

(tourist information office; www.galapagostour.org) in Puerto Ayora, which keeps a database of complaints to share with agencies and tourists. Reports are taken seriously, and repeat offenders get their comeuppance.

There have also been reports of crew members of tourist boats (and, more commonly, small fishing boats) illegally fishing and killing wildlife. Complaints of this kind should be reported to the Natural Reserve office, a green building just to the left of the information booth at the entrance to the Charles Darwin Research Station in Puerto Ayora.

With all the boats cruising the islands, it's easy to forget that these are remote, inhospitable and dangerous places to be marooned. Seventeen people have disappeared since 1990 – most were found alive, though a few have died after straying from the designated paths.

# regions at a glance

## Quito

**Art & Architecture** ✓✓✓
**Nightlife** ✓✓✓
**Scenery** ✓✓

### Art & Architecture
Steeped in history, Quito's old town is a magnificent Unesco World Heritage Site of elaborate churches, cobblestone streets, picturesque plazas and sun-baked Spanish colonial roofs. You can wander the cloisters of 16th-century monasteries, gaze at masterpieces of the Escuela Quiteña and ponder the ancient past at museums showcasing Ecuador's finest pre-Columbian carvings. Afterwards, take in the staggering artworks of 20th-century luminary Oswaldo Guayasamín, then flash forward to the present at the beautifully designed Centro de Arte Contemporáneo.

### Dining, Drinking & Dancing
Home to Ecuador's best restaurants, Quito spreads a wide array of temptations when it comes to eating out. Tangy ceviche, delicately marinated *corvina* (sea bass), tender *seco de chivo* (goat stew), fresh-squeezed juices and rich Ecuadorian coffee are just a few of the hits; there's also great Italian, Peruvian, Japanese, Indian and more: Quito's palate is truly global. Afterwards, you can work off those calories at one of the city's simmering *salsatecas* (salsa nightclubs) or go bar-hopping in the nightlife-loving Mariscal.

### Scenery
At 2850m and flanked by a massive volcano named Pichincha, this Andean city does not lack for breathtaking views. There are scores of great places to admire the panorama, whether at a rooftop restaurant in the old town (such as Vista Hermosa), at a lush park (perhaps the Parque Itchimbia) or from the ridges of Pichincha itself (catch the TelefériQo).

**p46**

## Northern Highlands

**Scenery** ✓✓✓
**Bird-Watching** ✓✓
**Shopping** ✓✓

### Scenery
The soaring peaks of the Andes make for some of the country's best scenery: the snow-topped Volcán Cotacachi, the stunning views from the Panamericana as you head north, and the mesmerizing Lagunas de Mojanda near Otavalo should not be missed!

### Bird-Watching
One of Ecuador's most diverse regions for birdlife, the northern highlands is a mecca for bird-watchers, who particularly love the tiny town of Mindo for the sheer variety of avian life to be seen in its extraordinarily beautiful cloud forest.

### Shopping
Otavalo's massive clothing and handicrafts market is a feast for the eyes: colorfully woven textiles, *tagua* carvings, primitivist folkloric paintings and alpaca blankets, scarves and shawls in every color of the rainbow. For leather goods of all sorts, don't miss Cotacachi.

**p90**

# Central Highlands

**Outdoor Adventure** ✓✓✓
**Culture** ✓✓
**Dramatic Scenery** ✓✓✓

## Outdoor Adventure

For adventure at full-throttle, head just about anywhere in the central highlands. There are volcanoes to be climbed, rivers to be rafted, bridges to be jumped off and mountains to be biked.

## Cultural Exploration

In the heart of the Andes, age-old cultural traditions remain a mainstay of everyday life. Culturally curious visitors will be rewarded with vibrant festivals, thriving crafts markets and remote indigenous villages that have stood the test of time.

## Dramatic Scenery

There's a snapshot on nearly every corner. The spine of South America has glacier-capped volcanoes and high-altitude grasslands, precipitous canyons that rush white water down to the Amazon, and centuries-old haciendas cut from Incan stone.

**p119**

# Southern Highlands

**Outdoor Adventure** ✓✓
**Art & Architecture** ✓✓
**Cuisine** ✓✓

## Outdoor Adventure

Several national parks in the region provide intrepid explorers with splendid vistas, wild encounters and adventures aplenty. It takes some effort to truly get into the backcountry here, making the views, animal sightings and journey back all the more rewarding.

## Art & Architecture

The colonial city of Cuenca is a veritable open-air museum with amazing architecture, historic center and plenty of artsy folks to get you in the mood.

## Cuisine

The south serves up some of Ecuador's best-loved dishes, from Cuenca's magnificent *fanesca* (bean-and-codfish soup), served during Holy Week, to Loja's corn-loving delicacies of tamales, *quimbolitos* (corn dumplings) and *humitas* (like tamales), served anytime. For the avant-garde foodie, there's always *cuy* (roast guinea pig).

**p161**

# The Oriente

**Wildlife-Watching** ✓✓✓
**Adventure** ✓✓✓
**Indigenous Culture** ✓✓

## Wildlife-Watching

Caimans, sloths, anacondas, howler monkeys, parrots... these are just some of the amazing creatures you can expect to see while staying at a jungle lodge deep in Ecuador's dense rainforest. You can even swim (safely) with piranhas.

## Adventure

If being deep in the rain forest isn't adventure enough for you, then the Oriente has no shortage of additional thrills to offer: white-water rafting, kayaking, tubing, climbing, horseback-riding and *ayahuasca* (psychtropic drug) should you really want to walk on the wild side.

## Indigenous Culture

Sensitively organised community visits to indigenous villages can be a great means of cultural interaction and hugely enjoyable. Learn how to cook, trap animals, build boats, pan for gold and have your soul cleansed by a shaman deep in the rainforest.

**p196**

# North Coast & Lowlands

**Beach Towns** ✓✓
**Cuisine** ✓✓
**Ecotourism** ✓✓

## Beach Towns

Ecuador may not be synonymous with beaches, but the north coast has an enchanting assortment of laid-back beach towns, from sleepy Same to captivating Canoa, with great surf spots (especially forest-ringed Mompiche) along the coast.

## Food

*Cocina manabita* and *cocina esmeraldeña* are considered two of the best cuisines in Ecuador, which makes the north coast a great place to sample the spicy, coconut-infused local cooking. Don't miss the very best ceviche in the country in Esmeraldas province.

## Ecotourism

This area boasts some of the country's best community-run ecotourism destinations, including the jungle reserve of Playa de Oro and the wildlife-rich Reserva Biológica Bilsa. Other highlights: exploring mangrove forests around Muisne and taking an ecocity tour in Bahía de Caráquez.

**p233**

# South Coast

**Beaches** ✓✓✓
**Wildlife-Watching** ✓✓
**Cuisine** ✓✓✓

## Beaches

The Santa Elena Peninsula has strings of resort towns for *guayaquileños,* lined with condominiums and soft white sand. North of here, all the way to Puerto López, beachfront villages with kilometre after kilometre of beach breaks beckon, especially at chill Montañita.

## Wildlife-Watching

Migrating humpback whales share the waters with pods of porpoises, and first-rate birdlife can be observed in several nature reserves and the coastal mountain-range cloud forests.

## Food

The region's long coastline means freshly caught seafood is in plentiful supply. Piles of shellfish, ceviche, *cazuelas* (seafood stew) and lobster are on the menu of even the most casual eateries. Guayaquil's culinary scene, centred in the northern burbs, offers an eclectic choice of cuisine.

**p257**

# The Galápagos Islands

**Wildlife-Watching** ✓✓✓
**Snorkeling & Diving** ✓✓✓
**Landscapes** ✓✓✓

## Wildlife-Watching

Get up close and personal with prehistoric-looking reptiles and a menagerie of birdlife, from vast colonies of endemic seabirds, mating albatrosses and flightless cormorants to tiny mockingbirds flitting around birds of prey.

## Snorkeling & Diving

The variety of aquatic life is so astounding – sea turtles, rays, sharks, whales, tropical fish, to say nothing of frolicking sea lions, speedy penguins and swimming marine iguanas – that donning a mask and snorkel feels like jumping into an aquarium. Divers have spectacular options, with a stunning array of pelagics.

## Landscapes

The Galápagos chain is an archipelago of volcanic islands; its scenic drama comes in the form of massive fumaroles, fantastic rocky escarpments, tropical highlands and lunar-like views.

**p296**

Every listing is recommended by our authors, and their favourite places are listed first

Look out for these icons:

 **TOP CHOICE** Our author's top recommendation

A green or sustainable option

**FREE** No payment required

See the Index for a full list of destinations covered in this book.

# On the Road

# Quito

## Includes »

## Best Places to Eat

## Best Places to Stay

## Why Go?

High in the Andes, amid dramatic, mist-covered peaks, Quito is a beautifully located city packed with historical monuments and architectural treasures. It's Ecuador's most dynamic city, with a vibrant civic scene and a fascinating collection of neighborhoods. Dining, drinking and merrymaking are all part of the equatorial experience in the world's second-highest capital.

Quito's jewel is its historic center, or 'old town'. A Unesco World Heritage Site, this handsomely restored neighborhood blooms with 17th-century facades, picturesque plazas and magnificent churches that blend Spanish, Moorish and indigenous elements. It's also home to the presidential palace. The other draw for travelers is the Mariscal Sucre, a compact area of guesthouses, travel agencies, diverse eateries and a pulsing nightlife scene. This is indeed 'gringolandia', though plenty of *quiteños* (Quito residents) frequent the bars and restaurants here.

## When to Go

### Quito

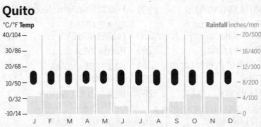

**Year-round** Mild days and cool nights, with sunshine typically in the morning and rain by afternoon.

**Jun–Sep** Best weather for visiting with less rain and warmer, clearer days.

**Oct–May** Slightly cooler and rainier; fewer crowds.

# Food & Drink

Ecuador's culinary capital is a great place to explore the classic dishes from the Andes and beyond. *Seco de chivo* (braised goat stew) is an Ecuadorian classic typically served with yellow rice and *patacones* (plantain fritters). Potatoes, of course, originated in the Andes and are put to imaginative use in dishes like *llapingachos* (fried potato-and-cheese pancakes) often served under grilled steak or fried eggs. A few places also serve *cuy asado* (roasted guinea pig), an indigenous specialty dating back to Inca times.

Seafood specialties include ceviche, uncooked seafood marinated in lemon juice and seasoned with thinly sliced onion and herbs. You can order it as *pescado* (fish), *concha* (shellfish), *camarones* (shrimp), *calamares* (squid) or *mixto* (a combination). Only shrimp is cooked before being marinated.

## FIESTAS DE QUITO

Quito's biggest annual event, on December 6, commemorates the founding of the city by the Spanish. The festivities, however, start much earlier. In late November, Quito chooses a queen, and the evenings are dominated by colorful *chivas* (open-topped buses) maneuvering through the streets, packed with dancing revelers. In the week leading up to the big day, bullfights are held at the Plaza de Toros, located about 2km north of Parque La Carolina on Avenida Amazonas, and flamenco dancing is staged throughout town as *quiteños* connect with their Spanish roots. Momentum builds as the day draws near, with DJs and popular local bands taking to open-air stages set up all over town. Business in Quito comes to a near standstill on December 5, when everyone comes out to party.

# Best Old Town Sights

» **La Compañía de Jesús** (p55) This fantastically elaborate church blends Spanish, Moorish and indigenous elements.

» **Museo de la Ciudad** (p51) Explores the city's development and social history through engaging interactive exhibits.

» **Cathedral** (p49) Curious paintings from the Escuela Quiteña are on display at this iconic church on Plaza Grande.

» **Basílica del Voto Nacional** (p50) The top of Quito's largest church, reached via rickety ladders, has magnificent views.

» **Casa del Alabado** (p53) This small atmospheric museum explores the mystical side of pre-Columbian art.

» **Centro de Arte Contemporáneo** (p55) Cutting-edge gallery showcasing 20th- and 21st-century art.

» **Casa Museo María Augusta Urrutía** (p51) A beautifully preserved house museum offering a window into the 19th century.

## MAIN POINTS OF ENTRY

**Aeropuerto Mariscal Sucre** (old airport) 10km north of old town.

**Quito Airport** New airport 20km east of the city.

**Quitumbe** Big bus station in the south of Quito.

**Carcelén** Smaller bus station in the city's north.

QUITO

# Fast Facts

» Population: 1.8 million

» Area: 324 sq km

» Telephone code: 02

# Resources

» **Lonely Planet** (www.lonelyplanet.com/ecuador/quito) Loads of info on sights, lodging and restaurants, plus the Thorn Tree forum.

» **Quito Tourism** (www.quito.com.ec) City's official tourism portal.

» **El Comercio** (www.elcomercio.com.ec) Quito's major daily.

# Top Tips

» **Altitude** Take it easy on arrival: 2850m is nothing to scoff at!

» **Surprise showers** Always have a rain jacket handy (lovely sunny mornings can quickly cloud over and bring afternoon rain).

» **Vigilance** Pickpockets are highly skilled: on buses, keep your bag on your lap (it's not safe between your legs or over your head).

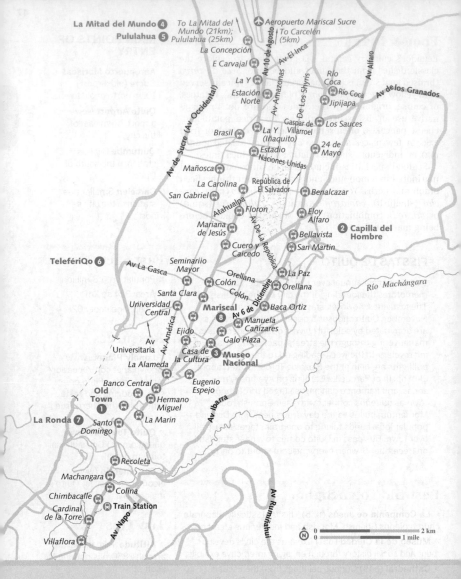

## Quito Highlights

**1** Explore the cobblestone streets of **old town** (p49), crisscrossing one of Latin America's finest colonial centers

**2** Gaze at the evocative works of Oswaldo Guayasamín at the **Capilla del Hombre** (p57)

**3** Discover the vastness of Ecuador's pre-Columbian treasures at the **Museo Nacional** (p61)

**4** Get close to earth's belly button at the kitschy museums surrounding **La Mitad del Mundo** (p87)

**5** Hike into the Middle-earth-like **Pululahua** (p87)

**6** Take the **TelefériQo** (p56) aerial tram up Volcán Pichincha for a magnificent view over the Andean capital

**7** Sip *canelazo* (sugarcane alcohol with hot cider and cinnamon) and hear live bands in the festive **La Ronda** (p54)

**8** Join the party scene in the nightlife-crazed **Mariscal** (p80)

## History

The site of the capital city dates from pre-Hispanic times. The early inhabitants of the area were the peaceful Quitu people, who gave their name to the city.

By the time the Spanish arrived in Ecuador in 1526, Quito was a major Inca city. Rather than allowing it to fall into the hands of the Spanish conquerors, Rumiñahui, a general of Atahualpa, razed the city shortly before their arrival. There are no Inca remains. The present capital was founded atop the ruins by Spanish lieutenant Sebastián de Benalcázar on December 6, 1534. Colonists arrived, along with a host of religious orders (Franciscans, Dominicans and Augustinians, among others), building churches, monasteries and public works, often with the labor of indigenous people. Quito grew slowly during the 17th and 18th centuries but remained a backwater in comparison to Lima.

Revolutionary fervor swept through the city in the 19th century, and Quito became the capital of the newly formed Republic of Ecuador in 1830. Population growth and building projects transformed the city over the following century, with a new astronomical observatory (the first in South America) a key rail line to Guayaquil boosting commerce, and other works. The colonial center remained the commercial heart of the city until the post–WWII years, when the city experienced (as it does now) rapid growth and expansion, fueled in large part by work-seeking immigrants arriving from all parts of Ecuador.

## ◎ Sights

Quito spreads along the floor of a high Andean valley in a roughly north–south direction. The Centro Histórico (historical center) holds nearly all of Quito's famous colonial architecture; locals call it El Centro, and English-speakers the 'old town.'

North of the old town is modern Quito, with major businesses and services. Most hotels and restaurants are found here, especially in the travelers' ghetto of the Mariscal Sucre (aka the Mariscal), which is packed with guesthouses, restaurants and bars.

### OLD TOWN

With its narrow streets, restored colonial architecture and lively plazas, Quito's Centro Histórico is a marvel to wander. Built centuries ago by indigenous artisans and laborers, Quito's churches, convents, chapels and monasteries are cast in legend and steeped in history. It's a bustling area, full of yelling street vendors, ambling pedestrians, tooting taxis, belching buses and whistle-blowing police officers trying to direct traffic in the narrow one-way streets. The area is magical and one where the more you look, the more you find.

Churches are open every day (usually until 6pm) but are crowded with worshippers on Sunday. They regularly close between 1pm and 3pm for lunch.

### PLAZA GRANDE

The heart of the old town is the **Plaza Grande**, a picturesque, palm-fringed square surrounded by historic buildings.

**Palacio del Gobierno**　NOTABLE BUILDING
(Presidential Palace; Map p52; García Moreno; ⊙guided tours 10am, 11:30am, 1pm, 2:30pm & 4pm) The white building on the plaza's northwest side is the seat of the Ecuadorian presidency. Visitors can enter by guided tours (in Spanish and sometimes English), which offer a glimpse of the brilliantly hued mosaic depicting Francisco de Orellana's descent of the Amazon. You'll also peer into a few of the staterooms. The president carries out business in this building, so sightseeing is limited to rooms not currently in use. On Monday, the changing of the guards takes place on the plaza at 11am.

**Cathedral**　CHURCH
(Map p52; admission $1.50; ⊙9:30am-4pm Mon-Sat, services 7am Sat & Sun) On the plaza's southwest side stands Quito's cathedral. Although not the most ornate of the old town's churches, its interior has some fascinating religious works from artists of the Quito School (see p355). Don't miss the painting of the Last Supper, with Christ and disciples feasting on *cuy asado* (roast guinea pig), *chicha* (a fermented corn drink) and *humitas* (similar to tamales). The Nativity painting includes a llama and a horse peering over the newborn Jesus. You'll also see the ornate tomb of Mariscal Sucre, the leading figure of Quito's independence. Behind the main altar is a plaque showing where President Gabriel García Moreno died on August 6, 1875. He was slashed with a machete outside the Palacio del Gobierno and was carried, dying, to the cathedral. Admission includes a free guided tour in Spanish.

## QUITO IN...

### Two Days

Start your day off in the **old town** with coffee at **El Cafeto**. From there, stroll the picturesque streets, taking in **La Compañía de Jesús**, the **Museo de la Ciudad** and **Casa del Alabado**. In the evening, drink or dine at the rooftop setting of **Vista Hermosa**.

On day two, ride the **TelefériQo** up to Cruz Loma. Visit the **Capilla del Hombre** and nearby **Museo Guayasamín** before heading to the Mariscal for souvenir-shopping at **Galería Latina** and coffee at **Kallari**. Close the night with dinner and live music at **El Pobre Diablo**.

### Four Days

On your third day take an excursion to **La Mitad del Mundo**, followed by lunch with a stunning panorama at nearby **El Crater**. That evening, hear live music and join the festive crowds in **La Ronda**.

On the last day, look for hummingbirds in the **Jardín Botánico**, delve back in time at the **Museo Nacional** and see the latest exhibition at the **Centro de Arte Contemporáneo**. In the evening, treat yourself to a decadent meal at one of Quito's best restaurants, like **Zazu** or **Theatrum**.

### Centro Cultural Metropolitano
CULTURAL BUILDING

(Map p52; cnr García Moreno & Espejo; admission free; ☺9am-5pm Tue-Sun, patio to 7:30pm) Just off the plaza, this cultural center houses temporary art exhibitions, an intriguing museum, rooftop terraces and a pleasant (but pricey) cafe on the interior patio. The beautifully restored building is rich in history, supposedly the pre-Hispanic site of one of Atahualpa's palaces. A Jesuit school from 1597 to 1767, it became an army barracks after their expulsion in the late 1700s. In 1809, royalist forces held a group of revolutionaries here, murdering them a year later. Get a glimpse of Quito's early colonial history (and some rather lifelike wax figures) in the onsite **Museo Alberto Mena Caamaño** (admission $1.50; ☺9am-4:30pm Tue-Sun).

### Palacio Arzobispal
NOTABLE BUILDING

(Archbishop's Palace; Map p52; Chile) On the northeast side of the plaza, this former archbishop's palace is now a colonnaded row of small shops and restaurants, located between García Moreno and Venezuela. Concerts are often held on the covered patio on weekends.

#### NORTH OF PLAZA GRANDE

### La Merced
CHURCH

(Map p52; cnr Cuenca & Chile; admission free; ☺7am-noon & 2-5pm) Two blocks northwest of the Plaza Grande, this 18th-century church boasts the highest tower in colonial Quito. Legend says that the tower, the only unblessed part of the church, is possessed by

the devil. Supposedly the only person strong enough to resist the devil was a bell-ringer named Ceferino, and no one has dared enter the tower since he died in 1810.

Myth aside, La Merced has a wealth of fascinating art, including paintings that show volcanoes erupting over the church roofs of colonial Quito and the capital covered with ashes.

### Museo de Arte Colonial
MUSEUM

(Map p52; Mejía Oe6-132, cnr Cuenca; admission $2; ☺9am-5pm Tue-Sat) This museum, in a handsomely restored 17th-century building, houses an excellent collection of colonial art. On display are famous sculptures and paintings of the Quito School, including the works of Miguel de Santiago, Manuel Chili (the indigenous artist known as Caspicara) and Bernardo de Legarda.

### Museo Camilo Egas
MUSEUM

(Map p52; Venezuela 1302, cnr Esmeraldas; admission free; ☺9am-1pm Tue-Fri) Inside a restored colonial home, you'll find a small but iconic collection of work by painter Camilo Egas, Ecuador's first *indigenista* (indigenous movement) painter.

### Basílica del Voto Nacional
CATHEDRAL

(off Map p52; cnr Venezuela & Carchi; admission church/tower $1/2; ☺9am-4:30pm) High on a hill in the northeastern part of the old town looms this massive Gothic church, built over several decades beginning in 1926. Rather than gargoyles, however, turtles and iguanas protrude from the church's side. The highlight is the basilica's **towers**, which you can climb if you have the nerve – the ascent requires crossing a rickety wooden plank inside the main roof and climbing steep stairs and ladders to the top. You can also climb the spiral staircase and three sets of ladders into and above the clock tower.

### EAST OF PLAZA GRANDE

### Monastery of San Agustín
MONASTERY

(Map p52; Chile & Guayaquil; admission $2; ⊗9am-12:30pm & 2:30-5pm Mon-Fri, 9am-1pm Sat) Two blocks from the Plaza Grande, this monastery is another fine example of 17th-century architecture. Many of the heroes of the battles for Ecuador's independence are buried here, and it is the site of the signing of Ecuador's declaration of independence on August 10, 1809.

### Monastery of Santa Catalina
MONASTERY

(Map p52; Espejo 779, at Flores; admission $1.50; ⊗8:30am-5pm Mon-Fri, to 12:30pm Sat) Due south of San Agustín stands this fully functioning convent and monastery, founded in 1592. To this day, entering nuns (who remain cloistered for five years) have only one hour each day to talk to each other or watch TV. But they make all sorts of natural products (shampoos, wine, hand cream, elixirs and more), which you can purchase from a rotating door that keeps the nuns hidden.

A free tour (in Spanish) of the monastery's museum takes in 18th-century religious paintings, some of which are downright gruesome.

### Teatro Sucre
THEATER

Built in 1878, this stately building hosts Quito's best theater, dance and music performances; there's also a top-notch restaurant on the second floor. It sits on the lively **Plaza del Teatro** at the junction of Calles Guayaquil and Manabí.

### CALLES GARCÍA MORENO & SUCRE

### Casa de Sucre
HISTORIC BUILDING

(Map p52; Venezuela 573, cnr Sucre; admission $1; ⊗9am-5:30pm Mon-Fri, from 10am Sat) A block and a half southeast of La Compañía is the beautifully restored former home of Mariscal Antonio José de Sucre, the hero of Ecuadorian independence, and now a small museum full of early-19th-century furniture.

### Casa Museo María Augusta Urrutía
HISTORIC BUILDING

(Map p52; García Moreno N2-60; admission $2; ⊗10am-5:30pm Tue-Sun) Of Quito's house museums, this is the one not to miss: it's a splendidly preserved, 19th-century house, once the home of the city's best-loved philanthropist, María Augusta Urrutía, and sprinkled with period furnishings, stained-glass windows, European artwork and a lush courtyard. Free guided tours are in Spanish and English.

### Museo de la Ciudad
MUSEUM

(Map p52; García Moreno near Rocafuerte; admission $3; ⊗9:30am-5:30pm Tue-Sun) Just past the 18th-century arch, **Arco de la Reina**, this first-rate museum depicts Quito's daily life through the centuries, with displays including dioramas, model indigenous homes and colonial kitchens. The 1563 building itself (a former hospital) is a work of art. Admission includes free guided tour in Spanish. Guides also available in English and French (an extra $4).

### PLAZA SAN FRANCISCO & AROUND

### Plaza San Francisco
PLAZA

(Map p52) Walking from the old town's narrow colonial streets into this open plaza reveals one of the finest sights in all of Ecuador: a sweeping cobblestone plaza backed by the mountainous backdrop of Volcán Pichincha, and the long, whitewashed walls and twin bell towers of Ecuador's oldest church.

### Monasterio de San Francisco
MONASTERY

(Map p52; Cuenca near Sucre; admission free; ⊗7-11am daily, 3-6pm Mon-Thu) Construction of the monastery, the city's largest colonial structure, began only a few weeks after the founding of Quito in 1534, but the building was not finished for another 70 years. The founder was the Franciscan missionary Joedco Ricke, credited with being the first man to sow wheat in Ecuador.

Although much of the church has been rebuilt because of earthquake damage, some is original. The **chapel of Señor Jesús del Gran Poder**, to the right of the main altar, has original tile work. The **main altar** itself is a spectacular example of baroque carving, while much of the roof shows Moorish influences.

### Museo Franciscano
MUSEUM

(Map p52; Cuenca near Sucre; admission $2; ⊗9am-5:30pm Mon-Sat, to 12:30pm Sun) To the right of the church's main entrance, this museum contains some of the church's finest artwork including paintings, sculpture and 16th-century furniture. Some of the furniture is fantastically wrought and inlaid

# Old Town

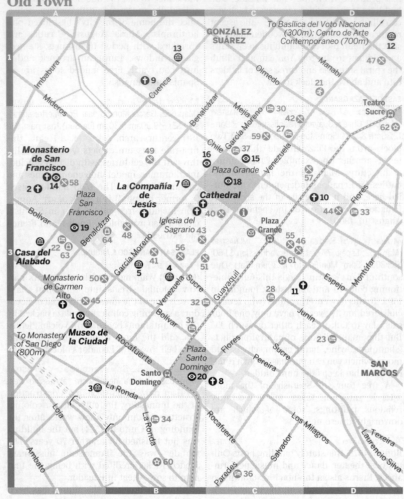

GONZÁLEZ
SUÁREZ

To Basílica del Voto Nacional
(300m); Centro de Arte
Contemporaneo (700m)

Teatro
Sucre

Monasterio
de San
Francisco

Plaza
San
Francisco

La Compañía
de
Jesús

Cathedral

Plaza Grande

Plaza
Grande

Iglesia del
Sagrario

Casa del
Alabado

Monasterio
de Carmen
Alto

To Monastery
of San Diego
(800m)

Museo de
la Ciudad

SAN
MARCOS

Plaza
Santo
Domingo

Santo
Domingo

La Ronda

with thousands of pieces of mother-of-pearl. The admission fee includes a guided tour in English or Spanish. Good guides will point out *mudejar* (Moorish) representations of the eight planets revolving around the sun in the ceiling, and will explain how the light shines through the rear window during the solstices, lighting up the main altar. They'll also demonstrate an odd confessional technique, where two people standing in separate corners can hear each other while whispering into the walls.

**Capilla de Cantuña**                    CHAPEL

(Map p52; Cuenca near Bolívar) To the left of the monastery stands the Cantuña Chapel, which houses a small art collection from the Quito School. It's also shrouded in one of Quito's most famous legends, that of the indigenous builder Cantuña, who supposedly sold his soul so the devil would help him complete the church on time. But just before midnight of the day of his deadline, Cantuña removed a single stone from the structure, meaning the church was never completed. He duped the devil and saved his soul.

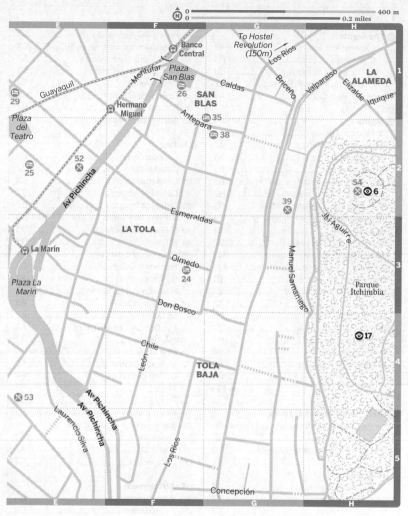

## Casa del Alabado

MUSEUM

(Map p52; Cuenca 335; admission $3; ⊙9am-5pm Tue-Sat, to 12:30pm Sun) Half a block from the plaza, this new, thoughtfully designed museum displays an exquisite collection of pre-Columbian artworks. Dramatic lighting and fine works in stone, metal and ceramic (with some English signage) explore ancient indigenous beliefs about life and death, the spirit world, the role and power of the sha-man, and ancestors. To get more out of your visit, pay the extra $2 for an audio guide (available in English).

## PLAZA & IGLESIA DE SANTO DOMINGO

**Plaza Santo Domingo** (Map p52), near the southwest end of Calle Guayaquil, is a regular haunt for street performers. Crowds of neighborhood *quiteños* fill the plaza to watch pouting clowns and half-cocked ma-gicians do their stuff. The plaza is beauti-ful in the evening, when the domes of the 17th-century **Iglesia de Santo Domingo** (Map p52; cnr Flores & Rocafuerte; admission free; ⊙7am-1pm & 5-7pm), on the southeast side of the plaza, are floodlit. Next door, a **museum** (admission $2; ⊙9am-5pm Mon-Fri, to 2pm Sat),

# Old Town

has a pretty garden cloister and a fine assortment of colonial religious art.

### LA RONDA & SOUTH

One of the most recent areas to undergo restoration in the old town is the handsome street known as 'La Ronda'. This narrow lane is lined with picture-book 17th-century buildings, with placards along the walls describing (in Spanish) some of the street's history and the artists, writers and political figures who once resided here. A new crop of restaurants and colorful shops has opened in recent years, though La Ronda remains a delightfully local and unpretentious affair. The street is at its liveliest on Friday and Saturday nights, when *canelazo* vendors keep everyone nice and cozy and live music spills out of restaurant windows.

### Casa de las Artes GALLERY

(Map p52; La Ronda, Casa 989; admission free; ⊙10am-7pm Tue-Thu, to 10pm Fri & Sat, 11am-3pm Sun) One of many beautifully restored buildings on this atmospheric street, this cultural center showcases small but well-curated temporary exhibitions. In addition, sometimes on display are the finely wrought polychromatic miniatures of 18th-century master sculptor Toribio Ávila, whose work also adorns the sacristy of the Church of San Francisco. (Ávila lived briefly on La Ronda, at No 158, in the late 1700s.)

### El Panecillo HILL

The small, ever-present hill to the south of the old town is called El Panecillo (the Little Bread Loaf) and is a major Quito landmark. It is topped by a huge statue of **La Virgen de Quito** (Virgin of Quito), with a crown of stars, angelic wings and a chained dragon atop the world. *Quiteños* proudly claim she is the only Madonna in the world depicted with wings.

From the summit, there are marvelous views of the sprawling city and the surrounding volcanoes. The best time for volcano views (particularly in the rainy season) is early morning, before the clouds roll in. Definitely don't climb the stairs at the end of Calle García Moreno on the way to the statue – they're unsafe due to muggings. A taxi from the old town costs about $4, and you can hail one at the top for the trip back to town.

### Monastery of San Diego MONASTERY

(off Map p52; Calicuchima 117 & Farfán; admission $2; ⊙9:30am-12:30pm & 2:30-5:30pm) Northwest of El Panecillo, this beautiful 17th-century monastery sits in a quiet courtyard behind thick walls above the old town. Inside, you'll find outstanding colonial works from both the Quito and Cusco schools including one of Quito's finest pulpits, carved by the notable indigenous woodcarver Juan Bautista Menacho.

There's also a fascinating 18th-century painting by Miguel de Santiago of the Last Supper. The oddest piece of work here is an unidentified **painting by Hieronymus Bosch**, titled *Passage from this Life to Eternity*: no one can explain how it got here. At the end of the tour, you can climb narrow stairs to the bell tower and walk along the rooftop.

## AROUND THE OLD TOWN

### Centro de Arte Contemporáneo MUSEUM

(off Map p52; Calles Luis Dávila & Venezuela; admission free; ⊙9am-5:30pm Tue-Sun) Inside a beautifully restored former military hospital, this excellent new museum showcases cutting-edge multimedia exhibits as well as top modern art shows that travel to the city (a Picasso show was a big hit in 2012). There's a cafe on site.

### La Cima de la Libertad MONUMENT

(Av de los Libertadores s/n; admission $1; ⊙8:30am-4:30pm Tue-Fri, 9am-1:30pm Sat & Sun) Further up the flanks of Volcán Pichincha, this monument offers one of the finest views of the city. It was built at the site of the Batalla de Pichincha (Battle of Pichincha), the decisive battle in the struggle for independence from Spain, which was led by Mariscal Antonio José de Sucre on May 24, 1822. There is also a military museum

---

**DON'T MISS**

## LA COMPAÑÍA DE JESÚS

Capped by green-and-gold domes, **La Compañía de Jesús** (Map p52; García Morena & Sucre; admission $3; ⊙9:30am-5:30pm Mon-Fri, to 4:30pm Sat) is Quito's most ornate church and a standout among the baroque splendors of the old town. This marvelously gilded Jesuit church was begun in 1605 and not completed for another 160 years. Free guided tours in English or Spanish highlight the church's unique features, including its Moorish elements, perfect symmetry (right down to the trompe l'oeil staircase at the rear), symbolic elements (bright-red walls are a reminder of Christ's blood) and its syncretism (Ecuadorian plants and indigenous faces hidden along the pillars). *Quiteños* proudly call it the most beautiful church in the country and it's easy to see why.

on-site and a tiled mural by Eduardo Kingman. The best way to get to the site, which lies a few kilometers northwest of the Monastery of San Diego (and roughly 4km from the heart of the old town), is by taxi.

### Parque Itchimbia                                PARK
(Map p52) High on a hill east of the old town, this grassy park boasts magnificent views of the city. It's the perfect spot to spread out a picnic lunch, soak up the sun and take in the views. The park's centerpiece is the **Centro Cultural Itchimbia** (Map p52; admission free; ⊘vary), in a large glass-and-iron building modeled after the city's original Mercado Santa Clara, which hosts regular art exhibitions and cultural events. The park is a popular destination for runners.

Buses signed 'Pintado' go here from the Centro Histórico, or you can walk up (east) Elizalde, from where signed stairways lead to the park.

### TelefériQo                                VIEWPOINT
(Av Occidental near Av La Gasca; local/foreigner $5/9; ⊘8am-8pm) For spectacular views over Quito's mountainous landscape, hop aboard this sky tram that takes passengers on a 2.5km ride up the flanks of Volcán Pichincha to the top of Cruz Loma. Once you're at the top (a mere 4100m), you can hike to the summit of Rucu Pichincha (4680m), about a three-hour hike for fit walkers. You can also hire horses (per hour $10), which are about 500m from the upper station (follow signs to 'paseos a caballo'). Don't attempt the trip to Rucu Pichincha until you've acclimatized in Quito for a couple of days. There's also a children's amusement park at the base station. Try to visit in the morning, when the views here are best; the clouds usually roll in by noon. A taxi here costs about $4 from the Mariscal.

### NEW TOWN
### Quito Observatory                                MUSEUM
(Map p58; Parque la Alameda; admission $2; ⊘10am-5pm Tue-Sun) Opened by President García Moreno in 1864, this four-sided observatory is the oldest on the continent. It houses a museum of 19th-century pendulums, sextants, chronometers and other historic instruments, and opens for stargazing on Thursday and Friday nights (with sessions at 6pm and 7:30pm, admission $3) – but only go if the sky is clear. It sits inside the small Parque La Alameda.

### Parque El Ejido                                PARK
(Map p58) Northeast of La Alameda, the pleasant, tree-filled Parque El Ejido is a popular spot for impromptu games of soccer and volleyball. The north end of the park teems with activity on weekends, when **open-air art shows** are held along Avenida Patria. Just inside the north end of the park, artisans and crafts vendors set up stalls and turn the sidewalks into Quito's largest handicrafts market.

### Museo de Arte Moderna & Instrumentos Musicales                                MUSEUM
(Map p58; cnr Av Patria & Av 12 de Octubre; admission $2; ⊘9am-5pm Tue-Sat) In the same building (but next to) the Museo Nacional, this rambling collection begins with a curious collection of musical instruments from Ecuador, greater South America and beyond. Highlights include pre-Columbian anthropomorphic pipes and whistles and swollen 17th-century harps. Other rooms contain poorly displayed canvases by some of Ecuador's most famous artists, including Oswaldo Guayasamín, Eduardo Kingman and Camilo Egas.

### Legislative Palace                                NOTABLE BUILDING
(Map p58; Montalvo near Av 6 de Diciembre) Between Parque Alameda and Parque El Ejido stands the Palacio Legislativo, the equivalent of the houses of parliament or congress. A huge frieze depicting the history of Ecuador spans the north side of the building.

### Museo Amazónico                                MUSEUM
(Map p58; Av 12 de Octubre 1436; admission $2; ⊘9am-1pm & 2-5:30pm Mon-Fri) Above Abya Yala bookstore, this museum houses a small but worthwhile display of indigenous artifacts, including Quito's only exhibit of *tzantzas* (shrunken heads), plus feather headdresses, a rough-hewn dugout canoe, stuffed wildlife (condor, sloth) and disturbing photos of petrocontamination in the Amazon.

### Mindalae – Museo Etnográfico de Artesanía de Ecuador                                MUSEUM
(Map p58; www.sinchisacha.org; Reina Victoria N26-166 & La Niña; admission $3; ⊘9am-5:30pm Mon-Sat) Just north of the Mariscal, this small but worthwhile museum exhibits the artwork, clothing and utensils of Ecuador's indigenous people, with special emphasis on the peoples of the Oriente. It's run by the outstanding Fundación Sinchi Sacha, and there's an outdoor cafe on-site (open 7am to midnight).

**QUITO** SIGHTS

### Parque La Carolina    PARK

(Map p58) North of the Mariscal lies the giant Parque La Carolina. On weekends it fills with families who come out for paddleboats, soccer and volleyball games, and exercise along the bike paths. A few unusual attractions include an old DC3-Douglas that kids can check out, horse rides and several museums, including a **Vivarium** (Map p58; www.vivarium.org.ec; adult/child $3/2; ☺9:30am-5:30pm Tue-Sun), where you can glimpse (and even handle a few) reptiles and amphibians. Nearby is the snoozy **Museo de Ciencias Naturales** (Map p58; adult/child $2/0.60; ☺8am-1pm & 1:45-4:30pm Mon-Fri, 9am-1pm Sat), full of dead insects and stuffed creatures (condor, tapir, harpy eagle, and uh, Bengal tiger, among others).

### Jardín Botánico    BOTANICAL GARDENS

(Map p58; www.jardinbotanicoquito.com; adult/child $3.50/2; ☺9am-5pm) Parque Carolina's most popular attraction is this peacefully set botanical garden with native habitats covering *páramo* (high-altitude Andean grasslands), cloud forest, wetlands and other areas, plus an *orquideario* (orchid greenhouse), ethnobotanical garden (exploring the plants used by indigenous groups) and Amazonian greenhouse. There's also a kid's play/discovery area.

### Museo Guayasamín    MUSEUM

(off Map p58; Bosmediano 543; admission $4; ☺10am-5pm Mon-Fri) In the former home of the legendary painter Oswaldo Guayasamín (1919–99), this wonderful museum houses the most complete collection of his work. Guayasamín was also an avid collector, and the museum displays his outstanding collection of pre-Columbian ceramic, bone and metal pieces. The pieces are arranged by theme – bowls, fertility figurines, burial masks etc – and in the geometric designs and muted color schemes you can see the influence on Guayasamín's work.

The museum also houses Guayasamín's collection of religious art, including works by highly skilled indigenous artists from the Escuela Quiteña; there's even a collection of bloody crucifixes (although Guayasamín was agnostic, he incorporated tortured and Christlike images in his own work). The highlight is a tiny crucifix with a pendulum heart inside that ticks against the chest cavity when touched (or breathed on, according to the caretaker).

### GUÁPULO

If you follow Avenida 12 de Octubre up the hill from the Mariscal, you'll reach the Hotel Quito at the top. Behind the hotel, stairs lead steeply down the other side of the hill to the historic neighborhood of Guápulo. The views all the way down here are magnificent: ramshackle houses stand interspersed among colonial whitewashed homes with terracotta-tile roofs, and the odd bohemian cafe makes for a welcome break.

---

DON'T MISS

## CAPILLA DEL HOMBRE

A few blocks away from the Museo Guayasamín stands the **Capilla del Hombre** (Chapel of Man; off Map p58; www.guayasamin.com; Mariano Calvache at Lorenzo Chávez; admission $4, with purchase of entry to Museo Guayasamín $2; ☺10am-5pm Mon-Fri), one of the most important works of art in South America. The fruit of Guayasamín's greatest vision, this giant monument-cum-museum is a tribute to humankind, to the suffering of Latin America's indigenous poor and to the undying hope for something better. It's a moving place, and the free tours departing regularly (in Spanish, sometimes in English and French) give depth to the works on display.

The collection itself, which has numerous murals, is superb. One of the most impressive works is *Los Mutilados*, a meditation on the Spanish Civil War; Guayasamín studied da Vinci for eight years and did 470 sketches to get it right.

Another innovative work is the sculptural *El condor y el toro*, which represents the forced fight between a condor and a bull during *Yaguar raimi* (blood festival). During the festival, a condor was tied to the bull's neck – if the condor won, it prophesied a good harvest.

The museum and chapel are in the residential district of Bellavista, northeast of downtown. You can walk uphill, or take a Florestal bus from the Centro Histórico or the Mariscal labeled Bellavista. A taxi from the Mariscal costs about $2.

# New Town

0.5 miles
1 km
0 0

To San Telmo (400m)
To San Telmo (800m)

Eloy Alfaro
Nóñuga
Checosoyaquia
Bosmediano

To Museo Guayasamín (400m);
Capilla del Hombre (800m)

BELLAVISTA

Bellavista

Quebrada El Batán

Av Eloy Alfaro

González Suárez

San Martín

Corinto

Camino de Orellana

Av de los Shyris

2

To Centro Comercial
Quicentro (1km)

Severino
Martín

La Paz
44

Jardín Botánico

5

Parque La Carolina

C Tobar

Apallana

Av de la República

Diego de Almagro

Barón de Humboldt

Whymper
48
49

LA PAZ

10

7

52

46
Mariano Aguilera

67

Orellana

43

Y Pinzón

To Centro Inaquito (1km);
Multicines (1km); Plaza de Toros (2km)

Av de la República

Av Amazonas

Grecia
La Granja
Huigra
Mariana de Jesús

Polonia
Italia
Vancouver

45

La Pradera

27
32
La Pinta

35

La Rábida

Mindalae - Museo Etnográfico de Artesanía de Ecuador

To Cinemark (1km)

Florón

Av Atahualpa

Mariana de Jesús
Mariana de Jesús

Cuero y Caicedo

Inglaterra

Av Eloy Alfaro

LA PRADERA

Acosta

Colegio Militar
Orellana

50
La Niña

21
La Rábida

COLÓN

Santa María

Av América

C Ruiz de Castilla

Tomebamba Méndez

Uvilla
Versalles

Javier Ascázubi

Colón

Av Cristóbal Colón

Cordero

Carvajal

San Gabriel

Bartolomé de las Casas

Selva Alegre

Seminario Mayor

Morán

Marchena

39

Cuero y Calcedo

José Valentín

Humberto Albornoz

To Toa Bed & Breakfast (1km)

Av La Gasca

MIRAFLORES

Universidad Central

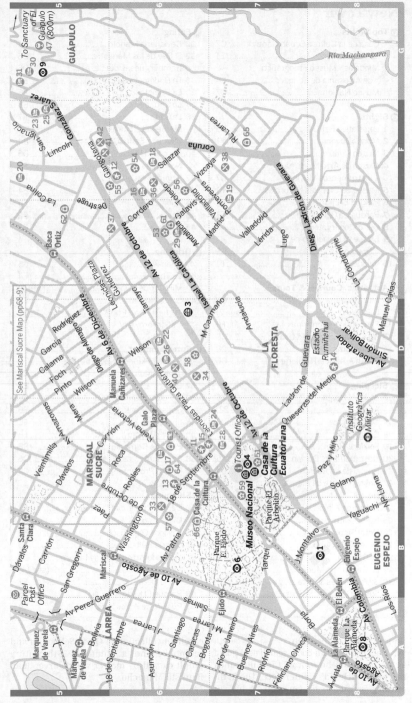

# New Town

**Sanctuary of El Guápulo**          CHURCH
(off Map p58; ⏰9am-6pm, sometimes closed for lunch) At the bottom of the hill stands the neighborhood's centerpiece, the 17th-century Santuario de Guápalo. It has an excellent collection of Quito School art and sculpture, and a stunning 18th-century pulpit carved by master wood-carver Juan Bautista Menacho.

### Statue of Francisco de Orellana  LOOKOUT

(Map p58; Calle Larrea) The best views of Guápulo are from the lookout behind the Hotel Quito, next to the statue of Francisco de Orellana. It depicts the Spaniard looking down into the valley, marking the beginning of his epic journey from Quito to the Atlantic – the first descent of the Amazon River by a European.

##  Activities

Those seeking a bit more adventure can spend the day rock climbing, hiking and cycling – all within city limits.

### Climbing

For information on climbing operators, see p62.

### Rocódromo  ROCK CLIMBING

(Map p58; Queseras del Medio s/n; admission $2; ⊙8am-8pm Mon-Fri, to 6pm Sat & Sun) Climbers can get a serious fix here, with a 25m-high climbing facility with over a dozen routes on the main walls. Gear is available for rental.

### Cycling

Local mountain-biking companies rent bikes and offer excellent tours, including one-day rides through the *páramo* of Parque Nacional Cotopaxi as well as downhill descents, trips incorporating a stop at Papallacta hot springs, and two-day trips to Cotopaxi and Chimborazo and to Cotopaxi and Laguna Quilotoa. Single-day trips cost about $50, not including park-entrance fees. Compare prices and trips at the following operators:

### Biking Dutchman  CYCLING

(Map p68; ☑256-8323; www.bikingdutchman.com; Foch E4-283 near Amazonas; one-day tours from $49) Ecuador's pioneer mountain-biking operator has good bikes and guides and an outstanding reputation, and it offers one- to four-day tours.

### Arie's Bike Company  CYCLING

(☑238-0802; www.ariesbikecompany.com) Also receives positive reports.

### Hiking

Quito's TelefériQo takes passengers up to Cruz Loma (4100m), from where you can hike to the top of jagged Rucu Pichincha (about 4680m). Beyond the rise of Cruz Loma, and past a barbed-wire fence that no one seems to pay any attention to, trails lead to Rucu Pichincha – it's approximately three hours to the top, and some scrambling is required. Don't attempt this hike if you've just arrived in Quito – allow a couple of days to acclimatize.

Before the TelefériQo went in, climbing Rucu Pichincha was dangerous due to armed robberies. There have been attacks in recent years, and it's well worth assessing the security situation with local authorities before heading out.

QUITO ACTIVITIES

---

**DON'T MISS**

## MUSEO NACIONAL

Located across from Parque El Ejido, the **Museo Nacional** (Map p58; cnr Av Patria & Av 12 de Octubre; admission free; ⊙9am-5pm Tue-Fri, 10am-4pm Sat & Sun), located in the circular, glass-plated, landmark building of **Casa de la Cultura Ecuatoriana**, houses one of the country's largest collections of Ecuadorian art, with magnificent works of pre-Hispanic and colonial religious art.

The **Sala de Arqueología** showcases more than 1000 ceramic pieces dating from 12,000 BC to AD 1534. The mazelike exhibit begins with arrowheads from Ecuador's first nomadic hunter-gatherers, then continues with the Valdivia culture (Ecuador's first settled agriculturalists) and ends with the Inca. En route are magnificent pieces, including 'whistle bottles' from the Chorrera culture, figures showing skull deformation practiced by the Machalilla culture, wild serpent bowls from the Jama-Coaque, ceramic representations of *tzantzas* (shrunken heads), 'coin axes' from the Milagro-Quevedo culture and the famous ceremonial stone chairs of the Manteños.

The second room is the **Sala de Oro** (Gold Room), which displays, among other pre-Columbian gold pieces, a magnificent radiating, golden sun mask. Upstairs, the **Sala de Arte Colonial** (Colonial Art Room) showcases masterful works from the Quito School of Art, including several pieces by Ecuador's most famous indigenous sculptor Manuel Chili (Caspicara).

Admission is free, but bring ID.

## Courses

Ecuador is a great place to study Spanish, with homestays, organized activities and volunteer opportunities typically on offer. Private lessons cost from $7 to $10 per hour.

Quito is also a good place to hone (or learn) those salsa moves.

### Yanapuma Language School
LANGUAGE COURSE

(Map p68; 254-6709; www.yanapuma.org; Veintimilla E8-125, 2nd fl) Excellent foundation-run school with opportunities to study while traveling or volunteering, both in Quito and in remote villages in the jungle, the coast and the mountains.

### Quito Antiguo Spanish School
LANGUAGE COURSE

(Map p52; 228-8454; www.quitoantiguospanish. com; Venezuela N7-31; ) The old town's only language school offers a wide range of study options (including courses for older learners), volunteer opportunities, inexpensive apartment rentals and homestays. Excellent setting with interior courtyard and cafe.

### Ecole Idiomas
LANGUAGE COURSE

(Map p68; 252-0850; http://ecoleidiomas.com; García E6-15 near Reina Victoria) Well-organized, Dutch-run school in the Mariscal, occupying a lovely space complete with open courtyard. There are sister schools in Montañita and Puerto Quito and openings on volunteer projects.

### Vida Verde
LANGUAGE COURSE

(Map p68; 222-6635; www.vidaverde.com; Leonidas Plaza Gutiérrez near Wilson) A well-recommended Ecuadorian-owned school, with opportunities to travel and study in the rainforest (near Tena or Coca) and on the coast (at Puerto López and at Rio Muchacho Organic Farm near Canoa). Offers one-on-one online courses through Skype – a great way to brush up pre- or post-trip.

### Academia Salsa & Merengue
DANCE

(Map p68; 222-0427; Foch E4-256; private/group lessons per hr $10/6; 10am-8pm Mon-Fri) Run by Sylvia Garcia, a pro dancer with over 20 years' experience, this place offers lessons in a wide variety of styles.

### Ritmo Salvaje
DANCE

(Map p68; 222-4603; García E5-45; private lessons $10; 10am-8pm Mon-Fri) This small, well-liked dance space offers a free introductory lesson on Thursday nights at 8pm. Friday and Saturday nights, it becomes a popular salsa spot (admission $3; free if you take lessons).

### Ritmo Tropical
DANCE

(Map p68; 255 7094; www.ritmotropicalsalsa. com; Av Amazonas N24-155 near Calama; private/group lessons $10/6; 9am-8pm Mon-Fri) Offers tango and capoeira in addition to its very popular salsa classes.

### Candeias
CAPOEIRA

(Map p58; 224-4314; www.candeiasecuador.com; Mundo Juvenil, Parque La Carolina) One of Ecuador's top capoeira schools offers regular group classes. Call or check online for the schedule.

## Tours

Conventional travel agencies offer all sorts of standard tours to places such as Mitad del Mundo, Pululahua, rose plantations and more.

Quito is one of the easiest places in Ecuador to arrange a guided tour, be it a Galápagos cruise, climbing trip or jungle tour. For mountain-biking tours near Quito, see p61. Be sure to stop by on weekdays; many offices close on weekends.

### Quito Bus Tours
BUS TOUR

(www.quito.com.ec; adult/child $12/6; 9am-7pm) Run by the city tourism authority, this hop-on hop-off bus tour stops at 12 key locations, including La Compañía, the Basílica, Parque La Carolina, El Panecillo and the TelefériQo. You can purchase tickets and pick up a schedule at tourist offices in the old town or the Mariscal, or on the bus.

### Alta Montaña
ROCK CLIMBING

(Map p58; 252-4422; Washington 8-20) Owner Ivan Rojas has been on the Ecuadorian mountain scene for years and is an invaluable resource for adventurers. Courses, guide recommendations and equipment rental are available.

### Compañía de Guías de Montaña
ROCK CLIMBING

(290-1551; www.companiadeguias.com; cnr Av 9 de Octubre N21-170 & Roca) A top-notch mountain-climbing operator, with guides who are all Asociación Ecuatoriana de Guías de Montaña (ASEGUIM; Ecuadorian Association of Mountain Guides) instructors and who speak several languages. Handily located in the Mariscal.

**START** PLAZA GRANDE
**END** PARQUE LA ALAMEDA
**DISTANCE** 3KM
**DURATION** FOUR HOURS

## Walking Tour
# Old Town

This walk takes in the sights of the Centro Histórico as it meanders along cobblestone streets and past 18th-century churches and picture-perfect plazas.

Start at the lively **1 Plaza Grande**, with its shoeshine boys, singsong vendors and well-worn benches. After checking out the **2 Palacio del Gobierno** (and changing of the guards on Monday), head inside the **3 cathedral** for a look at paintings from the Quito School. Head down García Morena to **4 La Compañía de Jesús**, Quito's most staggering church. Then walk northwest along Sucre to the impressive **5 Plaza and Monastery of San Francisco**, with majestic Pichincha visible behind it on a clear day.

From the plaza, cut down Bolívar and turn right on García Moreno. Pass under the arch at Rocafuerte to the **6 Museo de la Ciudad**, an excellent place to learn about Quito's development. Continue on García Moreno toward the historic street of **7 La Ronda**, which is lined with colonial balconied houses, galleries and shops. By evening, live music makes this the liveliest place in the old town. From La Ronda, turn left on Calle Guayaquil, and you'll pass the **8 Plaza and Church of Santo Domingo**, its 17th-century domes making a nice backdrop to yet another picturesque snapshot.

From the Plaza Santo Domingo, head north along Flores to the attractive **9 Plaza del Teatro** and peek inside the theater foyer to see what's on while you're in town. From here, walk north to Esmeraldas and turn left, then right at Venezuela and continue north to the looming **10 Basílica del Voto Nacional**. Climb to the top of the clock tower for superb views over the old town. From the church, walk east along Caldas to busy Guayaquil. Glimpse the pretty **11 Plaza San Blas** before continuing on to the **12 Parque La Alameda** and the handsomely restored **13 Quito Observatory**, where you can peruse 19th-century instruments and return by night for a look at the (often fog-shrouded) sky.

### Eos Ecuador
ECOTOUR

(Map p68; 601-3560; www.eosecuador.travel; Av Amazonas N24-66 at Pinto) Eos specializes in off-the-beaten-path trips where visitors stay in indigenous communities, either with the Santiak community on the Rio Pastaza or the Intac community near Otavalo. Five-day trips run from $400 to $750 per person.

### Fundación Golondrinas
ECOTOUR

(Map p58; 222-6602; www.fgolondrinas.org; Católica N24-679) Located inside the small budget guesthouse La Casa de Eliza, this conservation project organizes hikes in the *páramo* and forests west of Tulcán.

### Gulliver
OUTDOORS

(Map p68; 252-9297; www.gulliver.com.ec; cnr Mera & Calama; 8am-8pm) Well-regarded operator offering hiking, climbing, mountain-biking and horseback-riding trips in the Andes. Excellent prices, daily departures.

### Tierra de Fuego
TOUR

(Map p68; 250-1418; www.ecuadortierrade fuego.com; cnr Amazonas N23-23 & Veintimilla) Full-service agency that receives positive feedback.

### CarpeDM Adventures
TOUR

(Map p52; 295-4713; www.carpedm.ca; Antepara E4-70) CarpeDM earns high marks for its excellent prices and wide range of tours, though it's the excellent service (and follow up) that makes this agency run by the kind-hearted Paul Parreno stand out from many others.

### Happy Gringo
TOUR

(Map p68; 222-0031; www.happygringo.com; Foch near Reina Victoria) One of the best places to go when planning a Galápagos trip, Happy Gringo is an excellent, professionally run outfit that can help demystify the island experience. Also offers day tours (Otavalo, Cotopaxi, Quito) and other excursions.

### Neotropic Turis
TOUR

(Map p68; 252-1212; www.neotropicturis.com; Pinto E4-360) Neotropic runs the wonderful Cuyabeno Lodge in the Reserva Producción Faunística Cuyabeno (p204). A four-day trip costs per person $220 to $395.

### Latin Adventures
TOUR

(Map p52; 316-1568; www.latinadventures.ec; Plaza San Blas) Offers many tours, with a particular focus on experiencing indigenous cultures – in Santo Domingo, the Oriente and elsewhere. Next door to Hostal San Blas.

### Tzanza World
TOUR

(254-6348; www.tzanzaworld.com) Multilingual Danish-Ecuadorian run agency offering smaller group tours. Local guides are available for around $50 per day.

### Ecole Idiomas
ECOTOUR

(Map p68; 223-1592; info@ecotravel-ecuador. com; García E6-15 near Mera) This language school and tour agency offers island-hopping trips in the Galápagos, visits to

## FREE WHEELING IN QUITO

Every Sunday, the entire length of Avenida Amazonas and most of the old town closes to cars (from 8am to 2pm) as thousands of cyclists take to the street for the weekly **ciclopaseo**. The entire ride (some 30km), which you can cycle part or all of, stretches past the old airport, through the old town and into the southern reaches of Quito. It's a marvelous way to experience the city.

Those seeking a bit more adventure might want to join up for one of the weekly **night rides** that take place in the city. Every Monday around 8pm, a group – ranging in size from 20 to 50 – of intrepid cyclists meets in front of **El Rey** bike shop (see p87) on Amazonas (near Cordero) in the Mariscal and heads off into the night. Itineraries vary from week to week (El Panecillo is a favorite), with leisurely rides lasting about three hours. It's a well-organized outfit, with guides in front and back, making sure no one gets left behind. At the end of the ride, the group reconvenes over a bite and a drink. There's no charge, though donations are suggested to help keep the group in business. Bikes are available for hire ($8 for the evening).

You can also inquire about joining one of the group's rides out of town. Periodic outings see them head out to the cloud forests, ride down the coast or take on more challenging rides among the Andes.

Another good place for cyclists to check out is the bicycle-loving cafe La Cleta.

the Tsáchila community in Santo Domingo and other unique offerings; you can also tie in volunteer work to a trip (including the Galápagos).

### Nuevo Mundo Expeditions
BOAT TOUR
(Map p58; ☎250-9431; www.nuevomundotravel.com; 18 de Septiembre E4-161, at Mera) Professional outfit with top-end tours and guides. Organizes four- to five-day Río Napo cruises aboard its comfy *Manatee Amazon Explorer* (see p213).

### Rainforestur
ADVENTURE TOUR
(Map p68; ☎223-9822; www.rainforestur.com; Av Amazonas N21-108 near Robles) Offers well-received rafting trips on the Río Pastaza near Baños, and trips to Cuyabeno, Yasuní and elsewhere. Also offers hiking trips (Cotopaxi) and Quito city tours.

### Safari Tours
TOUR
(☎255-2505; www.safari.com.ec; 11th fl, Reina Victoria N25-33 near Av Colon) Excellent reputation and long in the business. Offers all range of tours and trips, from volcano climbs and jungle trips to local jeep tours and personalized off-the-beaten-track expeditions. Located in the Mariscal.

### Sangay Touring
OUTDOORS
(Map p68; ☎222-1336; www.sangay.com; Av Amazonas N23-31 near Veintimilla) Offers a variety of standardized day tours, including jeep trips, hiking excursions and visits to cloud forests and volcanoes. Also arranges economically priced Galápagos tours.

### Surtrek
TOUR
(Map p68; ☎250-0530; www.surtrek.com, www.galapagosyachts.com; Av Amazonas near Wilson) Top-end company with years of experience in hiking and climbing. Personalized tours available. Also offers island-hopping Galápagos tours.

### Tropic Ecological Adventures
TOUR
(☎222-5907; www.tropiceco.com; Rodrigues E8-34 near Diego de Almagro) Long-standing agency offering numerous three- to six-day tours to the Oriente, Andes and cloud forest. Good rates.

### Yacu Amu Rafting/Ríos Ecuador
ADVENTURE TOUR
(☎223-3922; www.yacuamu.com; 2nd fl, Lasso N32-113 near Las Guayanas) Excellent river-rafting operator with daily departures to the Río Toachi and Río Blanco and several other Class III to IV options.

### Zenith Travel
TOUR
(Map p68; ☎252-9993; www.zenithecuador.com; cnr Mera & Cordero) This gay-friendly agency has a full spectrum of tours, including city tours, Otavalo market, Cotopaxi, the Amazon and the Galápagos.

### Adventure Edge
ADVENTURE TOUR
(☎254-5938; www.adventuredge.com; Office 306, Pinto R4-385 near Mera) Recommended agency in the Mariscal offering a wide range of adventure-minded tours, including mountain-biking, trekking, rafting and kayaking.

### Dracaena
TOUR
(Map p68; ☎254-6590; www.amazondracaena.com; Pinto E4-353) Offers tours of Cuyabeno (p204), based out of the Nicky Amazon Lodge. Five-day tours are $240 per person.

### Kem Pery Tours
TOUR
(☎250-5599; www.kempery.com; Dávalos 117 near Av Amazonas) Kem Pery does trips to Bataburo Lodge, on the edge of Huaorani territory.

### Condor Trek
ADVENTURE TOUR
(Map p68; ☎222-6004; Reina Victoria N24-295) Reputable climbing operator offers guided climbs up most of Ecuador's peaks.

### Sierra Nevada Expeditions
ADVENTURE TOUR
(Map p68; ☎255-3658; www.hotelsierranevada.com; Pinto near Cordero) Long in the business, Sierra Nevada offers climbing and river-rafting trips. Owner Freddy Ramirez is well established and a very reputable mountain guide.

### Freedom Bike
GUIDED TOUR
(Map p68; ☎250-4339; www.freedombikerental.com; Mera N22-37) Offers guided motorcycle tours (both on- and off-road) ranging from four to 12 days with a bilingual guide. You can also do a self-guided tour, with a programed GPS. These range from one-day tours around Quito to three-day trips taking in a bit of the Andes and the Oriente.

## ☆ Festivals & Events

### Carnaval
RELIGIOUS FESTIVAL
Held the weekend before Ash Wednesday (usually in February), Carnaval is celebrated by intense water fights – no one is spared.

### Semana Santa
RELIGIOUS FESTIVAL
Colorful religious processions are held during Easter Week, the most spectacular being the procession of *cucuruchos* (penitents wearing purple robes and conical masks) on Good Friday.

## QUITO FOR CHILDREN

Keeping the kiddos happy in Quito might require a bit of effort, but there's definitely plenty to do. **Parque La Carolina** has loads of fun stuff: after taking them to one of the playgrounds or pedaling them around the lake in a paddleboat, walk them through the natural history museum or (even better) the **Vivarium**, where the snakes, turtles and lizards will surely interest and/or frighten them. Nearby, the **Jardín Botánico** has a hands-on area for kids. The park is also home to the **Mundo Juvenil** (Map p58; ☑246 5846; www.mundojuvenil.ec), with a tiny planetarium, kids shows and changing exhibits (life-size dinosaurs were a big hit in 2012). Another museum that will likely go over well is the **Museo Amazónico**.

Puppet shows are usually held on Sunday in the **Plaza Grande** and are occasionally staged at **Centro Cultural Itchimbia** and other theaters.

At the base of the TelefériQo there's a theme park, **Vulqano Park** (rides from $0.50 to $2; ⊙8am-8pm), complete with bumper cars and other rides.

Tourist-oriented babysitting services are difficult to find in Quito unless you're staying at one of the city's top-end hotels, in which case the hotel will arrange for a sitter.

### Founding of Quito festival
CITY FESTIVAL

By far the biggest event of the year is held in early December (see p47).

### New Year's Eve
CITY FESTIVAL

As throughout Ecuador, people ring in the new year by burning elaborate, life-size puppets in the streets at midnight, launching explosives into the sky and otherwise throwing general public safety to the wind.

## 🛏 Sleeping

Most travelers tend to stay near the Mariscal, which is packed with guesthouses, hostels, bars and eateries. For a more traditional side of Quito, head for the old town, which offers unrivaled beauty and historic streets that make for some great exploring.

The quiet and increasingly artsy neighborhood of La Floresta is a pleasant (and safer) alternative to the Mariscal, and it's only a few blocks away.

Wherever you stay, it's always wise to take a taxi after dark.

### OLD TOWN

TOP CHOICE **Casa San Marcos** GUESTHOUSE $$$

(Map p52; ☑228-1811; www.casasanmarcos.com; Junín 655; r incl breakfast $170-300; 🛜) This beautifully restored colonial mansion has just six rooms, which are set with antique furnishings, 18th- and 19th-century oil paintings and luxurious fittings. There's also an art gallery and antiques shop here, and a breakfast room with picturesque views of El Panecillo.

### Casa Gangotena
HOTEL $$$

(Map p52; ☑400-8000; www.casagangotena.com; Bolivar Oe6-41; r from $375; @🛜) Overlooking Plaza San Francisco, the Casa Gangotena offers Quito's finest accommodation, with first-rate service and elegantly designed rooms set in a beautifully restored mansion that blends art nouveau with contemporary modernism. Common areas include a wood-paneled library, covered patio and roof terrace. Excellent restaurant.

### Plaza Grande
LUXURY HOTEL $$$

(Map p52; ☑251-0777; www.plazagrandequito.com; cnr García Moreno & Chile; ste from $672; @🛜) One of Quito's finest hotels, the Plaza Grande offers gorgeously decorated rooms (all suites) with carved-wood details, chandeliers and marble bathrooms with Jacuzzi tubs. Some rooms have small balconies. There's a small spa, several restaurants (including one in the wine cellar) and world-class service.

### Hostal San Blas
GUESTHOUSE $

(Map p52; ☑228-1434; Caldas 121, Plaza San Blas; r per person $6-8) This friendly, family-run hotel on the attractive Plaza San Blas is a good deal if you don't mind small rooms. Rooms are dark (windows open on to a small interior or patio) but clean, and there's a roof terrace. Discounts to use the small gym next door.

### Hostel Revolution
GUESTHOUSE $

(off Map p52; ☑254-6458; www.hostelrevolutionquito.com; Los Rios N13-11; dm/s/d $9/14/25; @🛜) For an escape from the Mariscal circus, this Australian-Ecuadorian-owned colonial is an excellent, laid-back option with comfy rooms, shared kitchen, terrace with views and colorful bar/lounge where you can meet other travelers.

**Colonial House** GUESTHOUSE **$**
(Map p52; ☎316-3350; www.colonialhousequito.com; Olmedo 432 near Los Rios; dm $10, r with shared/private bathroom $20/24; @☎) True to name, this guesthouse is set in a sprawling colonial with 16 colorfully decorated guestrooms, various lounges and common areas, and a rustic back garden sprinkled with fruit trees. The vibe is friendly, bohemian and easygoing and there's a laundry and guest kitchens.

**La Casona de La Ronda** GUESTHOUSE **$$$**
(Map p52; ☎228-7538; www.lacasonadelaronda.com; La Ronda Oe1-160; r from $200; @☎) Situated along one of the old town's liveliest (and refreshingly automobile-free) streets, this handsome 22-room guesthouse has inviting rooms with wood floors, hand-carved wooden furniture and high-end bedding. Discounted online rates often available (around $120).

**Hostal La Casona** GUESTHOUSE **$**
(Map p52; ☎257-0626; Manabí Oe1-59; s/d $10/12) This family-run place has a dimly lit interior patio watched over by three floors of small rooms with low ceilings and wide-plank floors.

**Secret Garden** HOSTEL **$**
(Map p52; ☎295-6704; www.secretgardenquito.com; Antepara E4-60; dm $11, d with shared/private bathroom $32/39; @☎) The highlight of this perennially popular hostel is the rooftop terrace with magical views over the old town. You'll also find simple but clean rooms, nightly dinners (mains $4 to $5), Spanish lessons, volunteer opportunities, regular events (quiz nights, Aussie-style BBQs) and a first-rate tour agency on-site.

**La Guayunga** HOSTEL **$**
(Map p52; ☎228-3127; www.laguayungaquito.com; Antepara E4-27; dm $9-10, d with shared/private bathroom $28/35; @☎) La Guayunga is an easygoing, family-run guesthouse with simple, wood-floored rooms, an open-sided terrace with views and decent amenities (laundry, guest kitchen, parking).

**Hotel Viena Internacional** HOTEL **$$**
(Map p52; ☎295-9611; www.hotelvienaint.com; Flores N5-04; s/d $24/44; ☎) Aside from the '70s-style wallpaper, the Viena Internacional has few shortcomings, with clean, wood-floored rooms (some with balcony) and a cheerful interior patio.

**Hotel San Francisco de Quito** HOTEL **$$**
(Map p52; ☎228-7758; www.sanfranciscodequito.com.ec; Sucre Oe3-17; s/d $32/51) This historic, converted house boasts spotless rooms with wood floors and cozy furnishings. Because it's a colonial building, most rooms lack windows, but doors open onto a balcony ringing a pretty interior courtyard.

**Hotel Real Audiencia** HOTEL **$$**
(Map p52; ☎295-2711; www.realaudiencia.com; Bolívar 220; s/d incl breakfast $45/72; @☎) The Real Audiencia offers nondescript but nicely kept rooms with either carpeting or wood floors. The service is friendly, and there's a top-floor restaurant with views. Ask here about evening walking tours.

**Hotel El Relicario del Carmen** GUESTHOUSE **$$$**
(Map p52; ☎228-9120; www.hotelrelicariodelcarmen.com; Venezuela 10-41; d incl breakfast $130; @☎) This delightful 18-room guesthouse is set in a converted colonial mansion sprinkled with colorful paintings and stained-glass windows. Rooms are even sweeter, with polished-wood floors and beamed ceilings (but small bathrooms); most face an interior courtyard.

**Hotel Flores** HOTEL **$**
(Map p52; ☎228-0435; Flores 355; s/d $15/20; ☎) A decent and efficient option for cheap lodging in the old town. Rooms have tiled floors and beamed ceilings, and open on to an interior courtyard.

**Hotel Patio Andaluz** HOTEL **$$$**
(Map p52; ☎228-0830; www.hotelpatioandaluz.com; García Moreno N6-52; d $300; @☎) Inside a remodeled 16th-century home, the plush rooms of this elegant hotel have interior wooden-floor balconies. Beautiful woodwork fills the rooms and common areas, service is top-notch and a peaceful air pervades the place. Excellent restaurant serving Spanish and Ecuadorian cuisine in the covered courtyard.

**Hotel Internacional Plaza del Teatro** HOTEL **$**
(Map p52; ☎295-9462; Guayaquil N8-75; r per person $12-15) Across from Plaza del Teatro, this grand old dame has seen better days, but offers value for its rooms, the best of which have wood floors and flower-strewn balconies.

# Mariscal Sucre

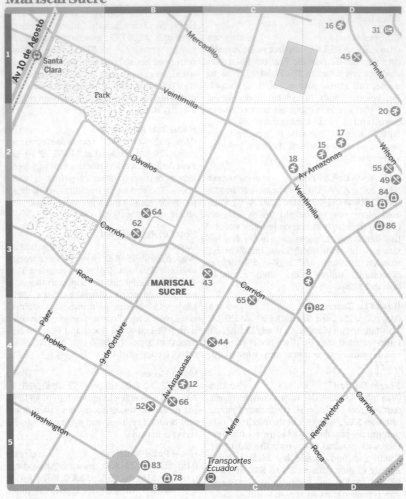

**La Posada Colonial**  GUESTHOUSE $
(Map p52; ☑228-2859; Paredes S1-49 near Rocafuerte; r per person $6-12; ☎) This friendly,
family-run place is one of the old town's
best-value accommodations. Rooms are
bright with wood floors, although the bathrooms are tiny and only some rooms have
them. The rooftop patio is a bonus.

## LA MARISCAL

**Anahi**  BOUTIQUE HOTEL $$$
(Map p58; ☑250-1421; www.anahihotelquito.com;
Tamayo N23-95 near Wilson; ste incl breakfast $130-
160; @☎) The stylish Anahi brings high-

end design to the neighborhood, with sun-
drenched, artwork-filled rooms (some with
balconies) and high-end fittings. Stone walls
in corridors (and in some rooms) resemble
an Inca temple. There's a top-floor veranda
with superb views.

**Casa Foch**  GUESTHOUSE $$$
(Map p68; ☑222-1305; Foch E4-301; s/d $89/102;
☎) In a restored mansion near the heart of
the Mariscal, Casa Foch has attractive rooms
with high ceilings, polished wood floors,
heavy wooden wardrobes and small cast-
iron fireplaces. Some rooms have balconies.

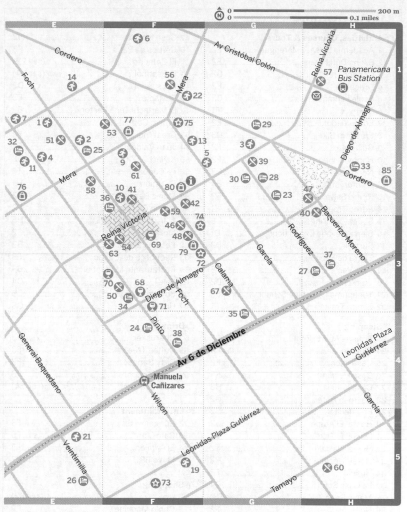

There's a small outdoor area with fireplace and a pleasant lounge/breakfast room. Noise is a major problem on weekends.

### Cayman Hotel
GUESTHOUSE $$

(Map p68; ☎256-7616; www.hotelcaymanquito. com; Rodriguez E7-29; s/d $40/62; @☎) Cayman has 11 rooms, which are generally bright and cheery, with wood floors, shuttered windows and fluffy white duvets, and the best overlook the garden. Some rooms (like No 9) are too cramped to recommend. There's also a lounge and a grassy outdoor space/parking area.

### Vibes
HOSTEL $

(Map p68; ☎255-5154; http://vibesquito.com; Pinto near Av 6 de Diciembre; dm $7-8, d $25; ☎) Set in a converted colonial, this seven-room hostel attracts a laid-back crowd, and it's a good spot to meet other travelers for nights out in the Mariscal. There's a bar with a pool table for starting off the evening. Santiago, the friendly owner, is a good source of local info.

### Blue House
GUESTHOUSE $

(Map p68; ☎222-3480; www.bluehousequito. com; Pinto E8-24; dm $7-8, d without/with private bathroom $24/30; @☎) This friendly guesthouse has eight pleasant rooms (four dorm

# Mariscal Sucre

rooms, with six to eight beds, and four private rooms) with wood floors in a converted house on a quiet street. There's a grassy yard in front for occasional barbecues, a comfy lounge with fireplace and a kitchen for guest use.

### Hostal El Arupo GUESTHOUSE $

(Map p68; ☎255-7543; www.hostalelarupo.com; Rodríguez E7-22; s/d with breakfast $30/45; @🛜) One of several good guesthouses on the quietest street in the Mariscal, El Arupo is a spotless and homey converted house with a lovely front patio. Some rooms are small and a little dark, but all are spotless, with dark wood floors and firm beds. There's an immaculate communal kitchen.

### Hostal Fuente de Piedra GUESTHOUSE $$

(Map p58; ☎252-5314; www.ecuahotel.com; Wilson 211; s/d incl breakfast $57/68; @🛜) In an attractive colonial house, the Fuente de Piedra has whitewashed rooms with wood or terracotta-tile floors and sizable windows (great views from some). The open patio doubles as a restaurant.

### Hotel Sierra Madre GUESTHOUSE $$

(Map p58; ☎250-5687; www.hotelsierramadre.com; Veintimilla 464; s/d $61/75; @🛜) In a handsomely restored colonial building, the Sierra Madre has 21 rooms of varying size. Most have wood floors, excellent beds and a warm color scheme, while the best quarters have vaulted ceilings and verandas. There's a restaurant below.

### Hotel Los Alpes GUESTHOUSE $$

(Map p58; ☎256-1110; www.hotellosalpes.com; Tamayo 233; s/d/tr incl breakfast $68/80/92; @🛜) Italian-owned Los Alpes has wild wallpaper, decorative plates and gilded knickknacks that somehow don't detract from the alpine charm of the place. Accommodation ranges from spacious, airy quarters with wood floors to smaller, cabin-style rooms with carpeting. Very friendly.

### La Cartuja GUESTHOUSE $$

(Map p58; ☎252-3577; www.hotelacartuja.com; Leonidas Plaza Gutiérrez 170; s/d/tr incl breakfast $69/82/98; @🛜) In a stately colonial house on a quiet street, La Cartuja has 12 nicely designed rooms, many of which open onto a grassy courtyard. Framed prints, old-fashioned details and friendly service add to the appeal.

### Antinea Apart Hotel HOTEL $$

(Map p68; ☎250-6838; www.hotelantinea.com; Rodríguez E8-20; s/d from $68/80; @🛜) Bestowing a touch of luxury on the Mariscal, Antinea is a warmly remodeled mansion with somewhat baroque rooms, decked with artwork, gilt mirrors and a warm color scheme. The priciest rooms have fireplaces.

### La Casa Sol GUESTHOUSE $$

(Map p68; ☎223-0798; www.lacasasol.com; Calama 127 near Av 6 de Diciembre; s/d with breakfast $58/72; @🛜) This friendly midrange guesthouse has a warm, inviting lobby with a colonial color scheme and cheerfully painted rooms that face an interior courtyard. There are nice touches throughout, as well as artwork and photos lining the corridors and in the rooms.

### Hotel Sebastián HOTEL $$$

(Map p68; ☎222-2400; http://hotelsebastian.com; cnr Diego de Almagro & Cordero; s/d $85/96; @🛜) Many of the Sebastián's 50 rooms have balconies, and some have great views. The sizable, carpeted rooms have dark-wood trim, big windows and king-size beds (in the doubles). There is a small gym and a cozy bar with a fireplace.

### Hostal de la Rábida GUESTHOUSE $$$

(Map p58; ☎222-2169; www.hostalrabida.com; La Rábida 227; s/d $73/93; @🛜) Doting service, inviting common areas and elegant rooms make a fine combination in this Italian/English-owned guesthouse. Rooms are bright with crisp white sheets and wood floors, and artwork (botanical prints and the like) adorn the walls. Several have terraces. The fireside lounge is a welcome retreat on chilly afternoons.

### Café Cultura GUESTHOUSE $$$

(Map p68; ☎222-4271; www.cafecultura.com; Robles 513; s/d $100/121; @🛜) This atmospheric old mansion-turned-guesthouse has a garden, crackling fireplaces, a first-rate cafe-restaurant and handsome, mural-filled bedrooms.

### Casa Helbling GUESTHOUSE $

(Map p68; ☎222-6013; www.casahelbling.de; Veintimilla 531; s/d with shared bathroom $19/28, with private bathroom $30/40; @🛜) In a homey, colonial-style house in the Mariscal, Casa Helbling is clean, relaxed and friendly; and it has a guest kitchen, laundry facilities and relaxing common areas.

**Nü House**                                    HOTEL $$$
(Map p68; ☎255-7845; www.nuhousehotels.com;
Foch E6-12; r weekday/weekend $158/116) Nü
House offers a touch of modernism in a
Scandinavian-style, wood-and-glass build-
ing rising over Plaza Foch. Its 57 rooms
have dark-wood floors, large windows and
an overly dramatic color scheme (red velvet
curtains).

**Huaukí**                                    GUESTHOUSE $
(Map p68; ☎255-3981; Pinto E7-82; dm $8-9, d $30;
@🛜) This simple but popular hostel has
three dorm rooms (three to six beds) and
a few clean, somewhat dark private rooms
(some with bathroom). There's a small bar
on-site.

**Magic Bean**                                GUESTHOUSE $$
(Map p68; ☎256-6181; Foch E5-08; dm/s/d
$14/28/36; 🛜) Better known for its lively
restaurant, the Magic Bean has just four
rooms – all very tidy and nicely designed.
Light sleepers beware: it can get noisy on
the weekends.

**Casa Kanela**                               GUESTHOUSE $$
(Map p68; ☎254-6162; www.casakanela.mamey.
org; Rodriguez E8-46; s/d with shared bathroom
$15/30, with private bathroom $23/36; @🛜)
Kanela offers minimalist but stylish rooms
(just nine in all) in a pleasant converted
house on pretty Rodriguez. It's a welcoming
place, there's a book exchange and guests
can use the kitchen. Good cooked breakfasts
included.

**Hotel Vieja Cuba**                         GUESTHOUSE $$$
(Map p58; ☎290-6729; www.hotelviejacuba.com;
Diego de Almagro 1212; s/d incl breakfast $64/88;
🛜) In a former colonial home, Vieja Cuba
is an attractively designed guesthouse with
a Cuban theme, inviting rooms (wood floors
are polished to a sheen) and a colorful flair.
There's also a small garden.

**Posada del Maple**                          GUESTHOUSE $
(Map p68; ☎254-4507; www.posadadelmaple.com;
Rodriguez E8-49; dm $10, s/d with shared bath-
room $23/30, with private bathroom $25/41; @🛜)
Maple is a friendly place with comfy lounge
areas, outdoor space and a guest kitchen.
Rooms are simple and comfortable, though
several have worn carpets (others have wood
floors). It's well liked by many travelers.

**El Cafecito**                                   HOSTEL $
(Map p68; ☎223-4862; www.cafecito.net; Cordero
E6-43; dm $7, r per person with shared/private bath-
room $15/25) Inside a yellow colonial house,
this is an eternally popular budget choice,
mostly for its mellow vibe and charming
cafe-restaurant. Rooms are small and well-
worn and could use an update.

**Hostal Nassau**                            GUESTHOUSE $
(Map p68; ☎256-5724; www.nassauhostal.com;
Pinto E4-342; s/d with shared bathroom $10/20,
with private bathroom $15/25; 🛜) Nassau is
a clean and well-run place, with friendly
hosts, tidy rooms and a small, shared kitch-
en. Upstairs rooms have wood floors and are
brighter than the downstairs quarters.

**Hostal El Taxo**                           GUESTHOUSE $
(Map p68; ☎222-5593; www.hostaltaxo.com;
Foch E4-116; dm/s/d $7/12/18; @) Friendly and
modest, El Taxo occupies a converted '70s
house with pleasant, colorful rooms. There's
a small front patio, a lounge with fireplace
and a tidy guest kitchen.

**Toa Bed & Breakfast**                           B&B $$
(off Map p58; ☎222-4241; www.hostaltoa.ec; Lizarazu
N23-209 near La Gasca; s/d $35/42) Although
slightly out of the way (about a 15-minute
walk from the Mariscal), Toa is a wonder-
ful B&B with cheery, comfy rooms adorned
with handicrafts, a common area with a fire-
place, a big communal table and a spotless
kitchen. There's a sunny back patio and a
fully equipped apartment to boot.

### LA FLORESTA & AROUND

**Stubel Suites & Café**                        HOTEL $$$
(Map p58; ☎601-3499; www.stubel-suites.com;
Pasaje Stubel 1 near León Larrea; d from $100; @🛜)
Perched high above Guapulo, this high-end
place has attractive, modern rooms with
luxury fabrics, huge windows and decent
amenities (sauna, fitness center, massages).
Pricier rooms offer great views; the priciest
also have verandas. The restaurant also offers sweeping views.

**Aleida's Hostal**                          GUESTHOUSE $$
(Map p58; ☎223-4570; www.aleidashostal.com.ec;
Andalucía 559; s/d with shared bathroom $17/34,
with private bathroom $24/43; @🛜) This friend-
ly, family-run guesthouse in La Floresta has
comfortably furnished rooms with wood
floors. The best (like No 15) have fine views;
others are dark with internal windows.

**Hostal Villa Nancy**                       GUESTHOUSE $$
(Map p58; ☎255-0839; www.hotelvillanancy.com;
Muros N27-94; s/d incl breakfast $45/65; @🛜) In
a well-to-do residential neighborhood, this
large, pretty house with wooden shutters
has attractive rooms with sponge-painted

walls, big windows, framed artwork and a trim, neat design. There's a sundeck, sauna and small garden.

### Hostal Charles Darwin
GUESTHOUSE $$

(Map p58; ☎223-4323; www.hostalchdarwin.com; La Colina 304; s/d incl breakfast $40/50; @☜) This intimate hotel sits on a quiet street and has 12 comfortable rooms with carpeting and homey furnishings. Extras include a small garden, kitchen facilities and laundry service. Needless to say, the owners are Darwin fanatics.

### Casa Aliso
GUESTHOUSE $$$

(Map p58; ☎252-8062; www.casaliso.com; Salazar E12-137 near Toledo; s/d incl breakfast $140/170; ☜) This charming 10-room guesthouse receives high marks for its friendly service, cozy sitting rooms (where you can sit fireside and enjoy a glass of wine or a cup of tea) and comfortable, classically appointed rooms (some with garden views). It's on a peaceful street, in a converted 1930s home.

### La Casona de Mario
GUESTHOUSE $

(Map p58; ☎254-4036; www.casonademario.com; Andalucía N24 115; r per person $10 12; ☜) In a lovely old house, La Casona de Mario is outstanding value, with homey rooms, shared bathrooms, a flower-filled garden, TV lounge and guest kitchen.

### Folklore Hotel
GUESTHOUSE $$

(Map p58; ☎255-4621; www.folklorehotel.com; Madrid E13-93 near Pontevedra; s/d/ste with breakfast $29/39/45) This delightfully converted blue-and-yellow house with small garden has carpeted rooms, some with murals adorning the walls; others are a little dark (with no outside windows). There's also a minisuite with fireplace.

### Suites González Suárez
HOTEL $$

(Map p58; ☎223-2003; www.hotelgonzalezsuarez.com; cnr San Ignacio & González Suárez; ste incl breakfast $73-123; @☜) This hillside hotel has 11 carpeted rooms with cheery yellow walls and outstanding views over Guápulo. Some rooms have balconies, and the best has a sauna and Jacuzzi.

### Hotel Quito
HOTEL $$$

(Map p58; ☎396-4900; www.hotelquito.com; González Suárez N27-142; s/d $146/160; @☜☲) A Quito landmark, this huge, 215-room hotel sits high on the hill above Guápulo. Recent renovations have given a modern, attractive touch to the rooms, which all have balconies and superb views. The services are extensive, with a heated swimming pool and a 7th-floor bar and restaurant with memorable views.

## ✖ Eating

Quito's rich and varied restaurant scene offers a fine mix of traditional and international fare. All budgets and tastes are catered for, and you'll find everything from modern, sushi restaurants to old-fashioned dining rooms serving up Andean classics.

The historical center is where you'll find Quito's most traditional eateries, some of which have been perfecting family recipes for generations. For broader choices, head to the new town: the Mariscal has the densest concentration, with ethnic and international eateries. For more high-end dining, look to La Floresta, La Pradera and neighboring areas: home to the city's best restaurants.

Many restaurants close on Sunday.

### OLD TOWN

TOP CHOICE **San Agustín**
ECUADORIAN $$

(Map p52; Guayaquil N5-59; mains $6-9; ☺9:30am-6pm Mon-Fri, 10:30am-4pm Sat & Sun) Decorated with oil paintings and elegant light fixtures, San Agustín is a two-story 1858 gem, serving classic Ecuadorian fare to bustling workaday crowds. Opt for first-rate *seco de chivo* (goat stew), *corvina* (sea bass) or *arroz marinero* (seafood rice) followed by old-fashioned *helados de paila* (ice cream handmade in big copper bowls).

### Cafetería Fabiolita
ECUADORIAN $

(El Buen Sanduche; Map p52; Espejo Oe4-17; sandwiches $2; ☺9am-6pm) For more than 40 years, Fabiola Flores and her daughter Monica have been serving up the city's favorite *seco de chivo* ($4) in this immaculate little shop beneath the cathedral, still the most authentic place to try this dish (9am to noon only). Its famous *sanduches de pernil* (ham sandwiches) even humble city politicians.

**Mercado Central**                    MARKET $
(Map p52; Pichincha; full meals $1-3; ◷8am-4pm Mon-Sat, to 3pm Sun) For stall after stall of some of Quito's most traditional (and cheapest) foods, head straight to the Mercado Central, between Esmeraldas and Manabí, where you'll find everything from *locro de papas* (potato soup served with avocado and cheese) and seafood, to *yaguarlocro* (potato and blood-sausage soup) and *fritada* (fried chunks of pork, served with hominy). Fruits and veggies are available too.

**Corvina Don 'Jimmy'**             SEAFOOD $
(Map p52; Mercado Central, Pichincha; mains $4-6; ◷8am-4pm, to 3pm Sun) Open since 1953, this is the Mercado Central's most famous stall, serving tender, meaty portions of *corvina* as well as ceviche.

**El Buen Sandwich**             ECUADORIAN $
(Map p52; Pasaje Amador, Venezuela N3-49; mains $2-5; ◷11am-3pm Mon-Sat) In a secret spot inside a shopping gallery, the unassuming El Buen Sandwich has just three things on the menu: *seco de chivo*, ceviche and *sanduches de pernil*. All are quite good, and the garrulous owner has many talents – his artwork fills the restaurant.

**La Colmena**                    ECUADORIAN $$
(Map p52; Benalcázar 619; mains $4-8; ◷9am-7:30pm Mon-Sat, to 5pm Sun) For over 50 years, this old-town landmark has been serving Ecuadorian classics like conch ceviche and *guatita,* a tripe-and-potato stew in a seasoned, peanut-based sauce.

**Tianguez**                       ECUADORIAN $
(Map p52; Plaza San Francisco; mains $4-9; ◷9:30am-6pm Sun-Wed, to 7pm Thu, to 8:30pm Fri & Sat) Tucked into the stone arches beneath the

Monastery of San Francisco, this cafe–crafts shop prepares tasty appetizers (tamales, soups) as well as heartier mains. Tables on the plaza are perfect for an evening *canelazo* or an afternoon *té de coca* (coca-leaf tea).

**Café del Fraile**               ECUADORIAN $$
(Map p52; Palacio Arzobispal, Chile Oe4-22, 2nd fl; mains $6-10; ◷10am-10pm) Country-rustic charm (cast-iron lanterns, wood-beam ceilings) and balcony seating set the stage for a tasty selection of grilled dishes, sandwiches and cocktails. Recent favorites include vegetable soup, *trucha a la plancha* (grilled trout) and *corvina*.

**Vista Hermosa**               INTERNATIONAL $$
(Map p52; ☎295-1401; Mejía 453, 5th fl; mains $10-13; ◷1pm-midnight Mon-Sat, to 9pm Sun) A much-loved spot in El Centro, Vista Hermosa (Beautiful View) delivers the goods with a magnificent 360-degree panorama over the old town from its open rooftop terrace. Live music on Thursday to Saturday (from 8pm onwards) adds to the magic. Arrive early to beat the crowds.

**Café Mosaico**                        CAFE $$
(Map p52; ☎254-2871; Samaniego N8-95; mains $10-12; ◷11am-11pm) Serving up a mix of Ecuadorian and Greek fare near Parque Itchimbia, vine-covered Mosaico is famed for its magnificent views. The open-sided terrace is great for a sundowner.

**Frutería Monserrate**          ECUADORIAN $
(Map p52; ☎258-3408; Espejo Oe2-12; mains $3-4; ◷8:30am-8pm Mon-Fri, 9am-6pm Sat & Sun) A tall ceiling, brick walls and concrete pillars give an industrial feel to this popular and casual eatery, where filling breakfasts, sandwiches, ceviche and scrumptious fruit salads are among the offerings.

**Mea Culpa**                   INTERNATIONAL $$$
(Map p52; ☎295-1190; Palacio Arzobispal, Chile Oe4-22; mains $13-23; ◷12:30-3:30pm & 7-11pm Mon-Sat, noon-5pm Sun) With a lovely setting

---

### ANDEAN HIGH

Did the hotel stairs make you breathless? Is your head spinning or achy? Having trouble sleeping? If so, you're probably suffering the mild symptoms of altitude sickness, which will disappear after a day or two. Quito's elevation of about 2850m can certainly have this effect if you've just arrived from sea level. To minimize symptoms, take things easy upon arrival, eat light and lay off the smokes and alcohol. For alleviating symptoms, some swear by the benefits of *té de coca* (coca-leaf tea), which some cafes, such as Tianguez, have on hand.

above the Plaza Grande, Mea Culpa is an elegant – if often empty – restaurant serving up nicely prepared grilled meats and seafood to a mostly foreign crowd.

**Theatrum** ECUADORIAN $$$
(Map p52; ☏257-1011; www.theatrum.com.ec; Manabí N8-131; mains $14-24; ☺noon-3:30pm Mon-Fri, 7-10:30pm daily) On the 2nd floor of the historic Teatro Sucre, creative dishes (crab and mascarpone ravioli, oven-roasted sea bass with wild mushrooms) are served in a theatrically set dining room with heavy curtains and red and black velvets. For pure decadence, try the tasting menu (five courses for $52).

**Octava de Corpus** INTERNATIONAL $$$
(Map p52; ☏295-2989; Junín E2-167, mains $13-19; ☺12:30-10pm Mon-Sat) For a completely different dining experience, head to this little-known restaurant hidden inside a colonial home on lovely Junín. Artwork covers every surface of the place, and Jaime, the friendly owner (and host) is also an avid wine collector who can recommend one of more than 300 vintages on hand. The menu features classic meat and seafood (all grilled or steamed). Reservations essential.

**Pim's** ECUADORIAN $$
(Map p52; Iquique; mains $10-16; ☺noon-10pm Mon-Sat, to 6pm Sun) Inside the Parque Itchimbia, this popular, slightly upscale chain has fantastic views over the city. Enjoy tasty traditional Ecuadorian fare, plus sandwiches, pastas, and cocktails in the elegant dining room, or on the outside patio.

**Los Cebiches de la Rumiñahui** CEVICHERÍA $
(Map p52; cnr García Moreno & Bolívar; mains $5-7; ☺8am-4:30pm) Part of the growing ceviche chain, this casual, order-at-the-counter spot serves ceviche and seafood dishes.

**Pizza SA** PIZZA $$
(Map p52; Espejo Oe2-46; pizzas $8-16; ☺noon-9pm Mon-Sat, to 8pm Sun) On a pedestrian lane dotted with restaurants facing the Teatro Bolívar, this casual spot with sidewalk seating bakes up satisfying medium-crust pizzas. You can also enjoy sandwiches, salads and calzones.

**Restaurante Vegetariano Ari** VEGETARIAN $
(Map p52; Sucre Oe4-48; mains $3; ☺8am-5pm Mon-Sat; ☺) Hidden on the 2nd floor of a commercial center, Ari is a colorful, if boxy, space serving vegetarian versions of Ecuadorian classics, like ceviche, as well as juices and fruit salad.

**Cafetería Modelo** ECUADORIAN $
(Map p52) Modelo (cnr Sucre & García Moreno; mains around $2; ☺8am-7:30pm) Modelo II (Venezuela N6-19; ☺8am-8pm Mon-Sat, to 6pm Sun) Opened in 1950, Modelo is one of the city's oldest cafes and a great spot to try traditional snacks such as *empanadas de verde* (empanadas made with plantain dough), *quimbolitos* (sweet, cakelike corn dumplings) and tamales. **Cafetería Modelo II** offers the same trappings of old-world style (plus live music some weekend nights) on Venezuela.

**El Cafeto** CAFE $
(Map p52, Chile 930 near Flores; mains $4-6; ☺8am-7:30pm Mon-Sat) This cozy and welcoming Ecuadorian-owned coffee shop serves rich coffees made from 100% organic Ecuadorian beans. Omelets, sandwiches, salads and desserts (cheesecake) are available.

**El Kukurucho del Maní** SWEETS $
(Map p52; Rocafuerte Oe5-02 at García Moreno; snacks $0.50-1; ☺8am-7pm Mon-Sat, 9am-6pm Sun) This delightful snack stand cooks up kilos of nuts, corn kernels and *coquitos* (coconut sweets) in a giant copper kettle.

**Magda** SUPERMARKET $
(Map p52; Venezuela N3-62; ☺8:30am-7pm Mon-Sat, 9am-5pm Sun) A conveniently located and well-stocked supermarket.

**Hasta La Vuelta, Señor** ECUADORIAN $$
(Map p52; ☏258 0887; Palacio Arzobispal, Chile Oe4-22, 3rd fl; mains $7-12; ☺10am-10pm Mon-Sat, to 9pm Sun) Ecuadorian cuisine is prepared with panache at this excellent restaurant with balcony seating. Reliable favorites include ceviche, *seco de chivo*, tilapia and sea bass.

**Govindas** VEGETARIAN $
(Map p52; ☏296 6844; Esmeraldas 853; mains $1.50; ☺9am-3pm Mon-Sat; ☺) Proudly serving 100% vegetarian cuisine, the Krishna devotees here whip up tasty, fresh lunch plates from a changing menu, plus yogurt and granola, juices and sweets.

## LA PRADERA & LA CAROLINA

**TOP CHOICE Zazu** FUSION $$$
(Map p58; ☏254-3559; Mariano Aguilera 331 near La Pradera; mains $18-33; ☺12:30pm-midnight Mon-Fri, 7pm-midnight Sat) One of Quito's best

## PANORAMAS OVER QUITO

High up in the Andes and ringed by mountains, Quito does not lack for memorable views. Here are a few of our favorite spots to take in the sweeping panoramas while having a drink or a bite:

**Vista Hermosa** The aptly named 'beautiful view' is a top spot to take in the scenery without even having to leave the old town.

**Café Mosaico** Nosh on Greek fare while taking in the sunset.

**Pim's** Peacefully set inside Parque Itchimbia.

**Hotel Real Audiencia** This midrange hotel boasts a top-floor restaurant with sweeping views over Plaza Santo Domingo and beyond.

**Santa Espuma** Go early to snag a table with a view over the city.

**Z(inc)** Sip cocktails at the bar while admiring the twinkling lights of Quito through oversize windows.

**El Crater** Outside Quito, this restaurant and guesthouse overlooking a verdant caldera has the most magical view of all – well worth the long trip out.

**Ananké** In bohemian Guápulo, a splendid setting for a night out.

**Mirador de Guápulo** Laid-back spot for taking in those sweet views over Guápulo.

restaurants, Zazu serves beautifully prepared seafood dishes, grilled meats and ceviches in a stylish setting of light brick, ambient electronica and an inviting, backlit bar. The Peruvian chef seamlessly blends east with west, with dishes like pistachio-crusted tuna, Wagyu tartar with gorgonzola mousse and seafood bouillabaisse.

**Zao**                                    ASIAN **$$**
(Map p58; ☑252-3496; Eloy Alfaro N10-16 near San Salvador; mains $8-10; ☺12:30pm-3:30pm Mon-Sun, 7-11:30pm Mon-Sat) Adorned with carved wooden screens, statues resembling samurai and glowing paper lanterns, Zao is a buzzing spot serving up samosas, rich noodle dishes, vegetable stir-fries, sushi and other flavors from Asia. A DJ on weekend nights adds to the festive vibe.

**San Telmo**                         STEAKHOUSE **$$$**
(off Map p58; ☑333-1944; cnr Portugal & Cassanova; mains $20-30) One of Quito's top steakhouses, San Telmo is an elegant, multilevel, mostly gents affair with a sizzling grill firing up a wide range of cuts, the best imported from Argentina. There's a good wine selection and options for non-meat-eaters (pastas, seafood).

### LA FLORESTA

**Z(inc)**                                 FUSION **$$**
(Map p58; Rivet near Coruña; mains $10-16; ☺noon-4pm & 7pm-midnight Mon-Sat) A creative addition to Quito's night spots, Z(inc)

is equal parts restaurant and bar, with a multilevel industrial-chic interior of untreated timber, dark metals, exposed brick and flame-lit walls. Sip a lychee-infused cocktail on the front patio before heading inside for brick-oven flatbread pizza, mini sirloin burgers, tempura prawns and other dishes ideal for sharing.

**Segundo Muelle**                    PERUVIAN **$$$**
(Map p58; Isabel La Católica N24-883; mains $15-20) Yet another sign the Peruvians are taking over (at least when it comes to cooking), this innovative modern dining restaurant is a good place to sample mouth-watering ceviches, nicely spiced risottos and flavorful sharing plates.

**La Cleta**                                CAFE **$$**
(Map p58; Lugo N24-250; pizzas $4-12; ☺3-11pm Mon-Sat; ☎) Bicycle-lovers shouldn't miss this small, cleverly designed cafe-restaurant, where everything (chairs, bar stools, tables, hanging lamps) is fabricated from bicycle parts. The staff cooks up tasty pizzas and lasagnas, and there's coffee, wine and other drinks.

**La Briciola**                           ITALIAN **$$**
(Map p58; ☑254-5157; Toledo 1255; mains $10-13; ☺12:30-3pm & 7:30-11pm Mon-Sat) This long-time favorite has an outstanding and varied menu. The portions are large, and the wine is fairly priced. Reservations recommended.

## LA MARISCAL

### La Union
BAKERY $

(Map p68; cnr Reina Victoria & Colón; mains $2-3; ☺6am-10pm) Bustling La Union always packs a crowd, with its glass displays of croissants, berry tarts and ice cream, plus filling sandwiches.

### Azuca Beach
SEAFOOD $$

(Map p68; Foch near Reina Victoria; mains $10-14; ☺closed Sun; ☏) Overlooking buzzing Plaza Foch, Azuca Beach brings a touch of the coast to landlocked Quito. *Encocado de camarones* (shrimp and coconut stew), *sopa marinera* (seafood soup) and various ceviches are among the hits. Tropical cocktails, a bamboo-trimmed bar, and potted palms add to the loungelike space, which becomes a popular drinking spot at night.

### Sakti
VEGETARIAN $

(Map p68; ☏252-0466; www.sakti-quito.com; Carrión E4-144; mains $3-5; ☏) This simple vegetarian restaurant serves up tasty lasagnas, soups and salads; it also runs an inexpensive guesthouse behind the restaurant.

### República del Cacao
CAFE $

(Map p68; cnr Reina Victoria & Foch; sandwiches $4.50; ☺9am-10pm) Temptations come in many forms at this chocolate-loving cafe and sweets shop. Decadent cakes and truffles are matched by decent coffees, rich hot chocolate and even chocolate martinis – best enjoyed on the front veranda.

### La Canoa
ECUADORIAN $$

(Map p68; Cordero E4-375 near Mera; mains $6-10; ☺24hr) This respectable restaurant from Guayaquil is a good place to try Ecuadorian classics: there's *fritada con mote y chicharrones* (slow-cooked pork with white corn), *caldo de morcilla* (blood-sausage soup), *bandera* (a mixed seafood plate) and other treats.

### Mama Clorinda
ECUADORIAN $$

(Map p68; ☏254-4362; Reina Victoria 1144; mains $9-13; ☺11am-10pm Mon-Sat) This modest, friendly restaurant serves tasty national specialties to a mostly foreign clientele. Try the *llapingachos* (fried pancakes of mashed potatoes with cheese) with steak or, for the adventurous, *cuy* (guinea pig).

### Petit Pigalle
FRENCH $$$

(Map p68; ☏252-0867; 9 de Octubre & Carrión; ☺prix fixe lunch/dinner $15/38; ☺12-3:30pm Mon-Sat & 7-10pm Mon-Fri) In a small, intimate space just off the beaten path, Petit Pigalle

serves classic French cuisine with a twist. Recent highlights from the small changing menu included crab salad with caviar and oysters, duck with sweet potato and rhubarb and pistachio crème brûlée.

### El Rey de Las Menestras
GRILL $

(Map p58; 18 de Septiembre near Amazonas; mains $4-6; ☺10am-8pm Mon-Sat, to 6pm Sun) This bustling spot where you order at the counter grills up satisfying plates of BBQ pork, chicken and ribs in a hurry and always packs a lunchtime crowd.

### Crêpes de Paris
FRENCH $

(Map p68; Calama E7-62; mains $3-5; ☺12:30-9:30pm Tue, to 11pm Wed-Sat) Amid oversize posters of the Eiffel Tower, Montmartre and Saint Michel, this small eatery serves up a satisfying selection of sweet and savory crepes – a good pit stop while pub-crawling along bar-lined Calama.

### Achiote
ECUADORIAN $$

(Map p68; cnr Rodriguez & Reina Victoria; mains $9-15; ☺noon-10pm) A colorful new addition to the Mariscal, Achiote prepares Ecuadorian dishes with a twist in a warmly int contemporary setting. Empanadas, ceviches, rich seafood stews and *llapingachos* are all first-rate. Live music Thursday to Sunday nights (from 7pm).

### Naranjilla Mecánica
INTERNATIONAL $$

(Map p58; Tamayo N22-43; mains $4-12; ☺noon-9pm Mon-Wed, to midnight Thu, to 2am Fri & Sat) This art-loving restaurant-bar attracts a festive crowd who gather over inventive salads, pastas and sandwiches. The menu comes in comic-book form (the graphic images may kill your appetite), and the decor is bohemian chic. There's an art gallery upstairs.

### Boca del Lobo
INTERNATIONAL $$

(Map p68; Calama 284; mains $8-14; ☺5pm-1am) Beneath the soundtrack of ambient grooves, a mix of stylish Ecuadorians and neatly dressed foreigners mingle over raclette, crepes, open-face sandwiches, baked desserts and sugary sweet cocktails. The ambience is pure kitsch, with colored-glass globes, empty birdcages and psychedelic paintings.

### Canoa Manabita
CEVICHÉRIA $

(Map p68; Calama 247; mains $4-7; ☺11am-2:30pm Tue-Sun) This casual and unassuming place is popular with locals (and virtually unknown to many tourists, despite its Mariscal location). Mouth-watering servings of ceviche and seafood plates bring in the crowds.

### Cevichería Manolo
CEVICHÉRIA $

(Map p58; cnr Diego de Almagro & La Niña; mains $4-6; ☺8am-5pm or 6pm) Join the locals at this excellent and affordable seafood restaurant, with several types of Ecuadorian and Peruvian ceviches on the menu, plus great seafood dishes, including *camarones al ajillo* (shrimp in garlic sauce) and *sopa marinera*.

### Mare Nostrum
SEAFOOD $$

(Map p68; ☑223-7236, 252-8686; cnr Foch 172 & Tamayo; mains $12-28; ☺noon-4pm & 7-10:30pm) In a castle-like building complete with suits of armor and giant wood tables and chairs, Mare Nostrum serves decadent seafood dishes with both Spanish and Ecuadorian influences.

### Ethnic Coffee
ECUADORIAN $$

(Map p68; cnr Amazonas & Robles; mains $6-12; ☺9am-9pm Mon-Fri) Equal parts cafe and handicrafts shop, Ethnic Coffee is a colorfully decorated spot serving snacks (tamales, empanadas, *quimbolitos*) as well as heartier mains (grilled fish with shrimp). There's outdoor seating among ferns and potted plants, and live music on Fridays (6:30 to 8:30pm).

### Suvlaki
GREEK $

(Map p68; Amazonas N21-108; mains $3-4; ☺8:30am-7pm Mon-Fri, to 4pm Sat) The go-to spot for skewers of tasty grilled meat (the eponymous souvlaki), this casual spot has a growing following for its speedy service, cheery interior (complete with photos of Greek icons) and outdoor seating.

### Cosa Nostra
ITALIAN $$

(Map p68; cnr Baquerizo Moreno & Diego de Almagro; mains $9-13; ☺12:30-3pm & 6:30-10:30pm Tue-Sun) Italian-owned Cosa Nostra has a pleasant front patio, cozy dining room and excellent pizzas piled with generous toppings and fired up in a brick oven. Tiramisu and good espresso for dessert.

### Restaurante Manantial
VEGETARIAN $

(Map p68; 9 de Octubre N22-25; mains $2-3; ☺9am-4pm Mon-Fri; ☑) Manantial is a simple, unfussy spot serving meatless Ecuadorian classics like *llapingachos* (here, veg meat over potato patties) as well as tofu sandwiches, soups of the day and juices.

### La Bodeguita de Cuba
CUBAN $$

(Map p58; Reina Victoria 1721; mains $7-8; ☺noon-11pm Mon & Tue, to 1am Wed-Thu, to 2am Fri & Sat)

With its warmly lit interior, graffiti-covered walls and outdoor seating, this is a great place for Cuban food and fun. Live bands perform here on Wednesday and Thursday nights and at neighboring Veradero on Fridays and Saturdays (all from about 8:30pm).

### Great India
INDIAN $

(Map p68; Calama E4-54; mains $4-6) Amid photos of the Taj Mahal, Indian film stars and Bollywood films, this ever popular outpost serves filling lamb or chicken masala, veggie curries, lassis and chicken shawarmas and falafel sandwiches. The food is good but lacks heat.

### Mongo's
MONGOLIAN $$

(Map p68; Calama E5-10; mains $8-9) With a vaguely yurt-like interior, Mongo's fires up grilled meats, seafood and all-you-can-eat (and drink!) specials to a buzzing pre-party crowd.

### El Mariachi Taco Factory
MEXICAN $$

(Map p68; Foch near Mera; mains $7-9) Colorfully woven tablecloths, Mexican mariachi posters and adobe-esque walls conjure a faint impression of Old Mexico in this rather sedate Mariscal eatery. Sizzling plates of fajitas go nicely with frozen margaritas.

### Uncle Ho's
VIETNAMESE $$

(Map p68; Calama E8-29; mains $7-10; ☺noon-10:30pm Mon-Sat) This colorful spot (perhaps you've spotted their 'I love Ho's' flyers about the Mariscal) serves up bowls of *pho* (noodle soup), pad thai and other dishes from Asia.

### Noe Sushi Bar
JAPANESE $$$

(Map p58; ☑322-7378; Isabel La Católica N24-827; 2-person dinners $50-80; ☺12.30-4pm & 6.30-10pm) This stylish, minimalist restaurant offers tender, fresh sushi and sashimi, teppanyaki, Kobe beef and a range of other Japanese delicacies.

### Aladdin's
MIDDLE EASTERN $

(Map p68; cnr Diego de Almagro & Baquerizo Moreno; mains $3-7; ☺11am-11pm Mon-Thu, to 1am Fri & Sat, to 4:30pm Sun) Aladdin's is a souk-themed restaurant with covered front patio serving satisfying falafel and shawarma sandwiches, as well as heartier main courses. This is also a fine place to indulge in a bit of hookah action.

### Café Amazonas
ECUADORIAN $$

(Map p68; cnr Av Amazonas & Roca; mains $5-9; ☺7am-9pm Mon-Sat, to 7pm Sun) A Quito classic, Amazonas gathers a mix of old-timers and upstarts who come for *seco de chivo*, *locro de papas* and other comfort fare. There's good people-watching at the outdoor tables.

**Café Colibri**  CAFÉ **$**
(Map p68; Pinto 619; mains $2-5; ☺8am-6pm) Amid big windows, skylights and a garden-like front patio, German-owned Colibri is a fine spot for breakfasts, crepes, sandwiches and coffee.

**El Cafecito**  INTERNATIONAL **$**
(Map p68; Cordero 1124; mains $3-7; ☺8am-11pm) On the ground floor of the popular guest-house of the same name, this charming cafe and restaurant serves tasty, inexpensive dishes and snacks all day long. On a warm day, dine in the pleasant front garden. Good breakfasts.

**Cactus**  ECUADORIAN **$$**
(Map p68; Carrión E4-74; mains $4-9; ☺8am-10pm Mon-Sat) Just off busy Amazonas, Cactus is a hidden spot serving tasty, authentic *otavaleño* dishes, plus live folkloric music on Friday nights (from 7pm). This is a fine spot to sample *cuy*.

**Kallari**  CAFÉ **$**
(Map p68; www.kallari.com; Wilson E4-266; breakfasts $3.50, lunches $4.30; ☺9am-7pm Mon-Sat) This Kichwa coop serves up satisfying breakfasts and lunches, and stocks its famous chocolate bars.

**El Español**  SPANISH **$**
(Map p68; cnr Mera & Wilson; mains $4-6; ☺8am-9pm Mon-Fri, 8:30am-6pm Sat & Sun) This delightful Spanish delicatessen stocks a range of old-world provisions, including olives, *jamón Ibérico* (Iberian ham), cheeses and wine, as well as sandwiches made to order. El Español has a second location on Plaza Foch.

**Magic Bean**  INTERNATIONAL **$$**
(Map p68; Foch E5-08; mains $6-12; ☺7am-11pm; ☎) The prices are a bit steep, but Magic Bean nearly always packs a crowd with its ample American-style breakfasts and lunches, plus frothy juices, coffees and desserts, best enjoyed on the covered front terrace.

**Hamburguesas del Sesé**  HAMBURGERS **$**
(Map p58; cnr Tamayo & Carrión; mains $3; ☺11am-9pm Mon-Wed, to midnight Thu, to 2am Fri & Sat) One of many student hangouts in the area, Sesé serves hearty burgers (including

veggie, salmon and chicken burgers), and it's a favored option post-salsa dancing at nearby Seseribó.

**La Choza**  ECUADORIAN **$$**
(Map p68; ☎223-0839; Av 12 de Octubre N24-551; mains $7-12; ☺noon-4pm & 6:30-10pm Mon-Sat, noon-4pm Sun) One of Quito's best restaurants for traditional Ecuadorian cuisine, La Choza serves up hearty plates of *llapingachos*, grilled *corvina* and steak with all the fixings in an airy setting with colorfully woven tablecloths and Andean music.

**El Maple**  VEGETARIAN **$**
(Map p68; Pinto E7-68 near Diego de Almagro; mains $5-8; ☺noon-9pm Mon & Tue, to 10:30pm Wed-Sat, to 6pm Sun; ☎) This well-loved restaurant serves good vegetarian food with global influences (Tex-Mex-style burritos, Asian noodle dishes, creamy pastas). The four-course set lunches are good value, and the juices are tops.

**Mercado Santa Clara**  MARKET **$**
(Map p58; cnr Dávalos & Versalles; ☺8am-5pm) This is the main produce market in the new town. Besides an outstanding produce selection, it has cheap food stalls.

**Supermaxi**  SUPERMARKET **$**
(Map p58; cnr La Niña & Pinzón; ☺daily) Biggest and best supermarket near the Mariscal.

**Mercado La Floresta**  MARKET **$**
(Map p58; cnr Galavis & Andalucía; ☺9am-4pm Fri) A small but delightful fruit market set in the peaceful Floresta neighborhood.

## 🍷 Drinking

Bars, nightclubs and other drinking establishments are closed on Sundays.

**Le Thé**  CAFÉ
(Map p58; Whymper 2958; tea cups/pots $3/8; ☺10am-8pm Mon-Fri, to 2pm Sat; ☎) A peaceful spot for a recharge, this modern tea shop and cafe has just four tables and a sizable assortment of teas brewed perfectly (egg timer included).

**Juan Valdez**  CAFÉ **$**
(Map p68; Foch near Pinto; coffees $2-3; ☺8am-9pm Sun-Thu, to 1am Fri & Sat; ☎) A landmark of Plaza Foch, this buzzing Colombian coffee chain has good cappuccinos, desserts and breakfasts, plus outdoor seating that's perfect for taking in the passing people parade.

**Finn McCool's**                                    IRISH PUB

(Map p68; Diego de Almagro near Pinto; ⊘5pm-2am) Proudly flying the orange and green, this Irish-owned bar gathers a mix of locals and expats who come for games of pool, table football, pub grub and theme nights (pub quiz on Tuesdays, live bands or open-mic Thursdays, game nights whenever there's football on).

**Sports Planet**                                        BAR

(Map p68; 3rd fl, cnr Reina Victoria & Foch) You can watch sports till your eyes glaze over on the many screens scattered around this modern pub and restaurant, or grab a seat by the window and watch the endless sea of revelers streaming across Plaza Foch. Burgers, burritos, wraps and other pub grub on hand.

**Coffee Tree**                                          BAR

(Map p68; cnr Reina Victoria & Foch; ⊘24hr) A good place to start the night off is this outdoor bar anchoring lively Reina Victoria. There's great people-watching from the tables on the plaza (and numerous other eating/drinking spots nearby).

**Cherusker**                                            BAR

(Map p68; cnr Pinto & Diego de Almagro; ⊘1pm-1am Mon-Thu, to 3am Fri & Sat) In a red, two-story colonial house, Cherusker has earned a loyal following for its tasty microbrews, warm bohemian ambience and buzzing front patio. Occasional live bands play on weekends.

**Ananké**                                            LOUNGE

(Map p58; Orellana 781, Guápulo) Well worth the trip out here, Ananké is a stylish and warmly lit bar/pizzeria with small colorfully decorated rooms spread out among an old two-story house. It has a small terrace (complete with fireplace) and several good nooks for hiding away with a cocktail and a few friends. When the fog clears, the views over Guápulo are superb.

**Mirador de Guápulo**                                  CAFE

(Map p58; Larrea & Pasaje Stübel, Guápulo) This cozy cafe-cum-bar sits on the cliffside overlooking Guápulo. The views are unbeatable, and the food – Ecuadorian specialties (empanadas, *sanduches de pernil* and the like) – are tasty, although there isn't much ambience apart from the view. Live music, however, adds to the appeal on Wednesday through Saturday nights (around 8pm).

**Santa Espuma**                                  MICROBREWERY

(Map p58; Whymper N29-02) Santa Espuma (which means Holy Foam) has a dark wood interior, meaty pub grub and three specialty beers brewed on-site: a *rubio* (golden ale), *negro* (porter) and our favorite, *puka* (Scottish ale). Go early to get a front table with views over the city.

**Dirty Sanchez**                                      LOUNGE

(Map p68; Pinto E7-38 near Reina Victoria) The cheekily named Dirty Sanchez is a small art-filled lounge with a bohemian vibe. Decent cocktails (and coffee), better music and a more laid-back crowd make this expat-owned place a standout.

**Turtle's Head Pub & Microbrewery**         BAR

(Map p58; La Niña E4-451) Scottish-owned pub serving decent microbrews and pub grub; table football, pool table, and occasional bands.

**Jugos de la Sucre**                              JUICE BAR $

(Map p52; Sucre Oe5-53; drinks $0.75; ⊘9am-5pm Tue-Fri, 10am-2pm Sat) For a freshly squeezed serving of vitamins, this juice stand is hard to beat. Try *tomate de arbol* (tamarillo), *maracuya* (passion fruit) or *guanábana* (soursop).

## ☆ Entertainment

Most of the *farra* (nightlife) in Quito is concentrated in and around the Mariscal, where the line between 'bar' and 'dance club' is blurry indeed. Mariscal bars, for better or worse, are generally raucous and notorious for 'gringo hunting,' when locals of both sexes flirt it up with the tourists (which can be annoying or enjoyable, depending on your state of mind). Bars with dancing often charge admission, which usually includes a drink. Remember to always take a cab home if you're out in the Mariscal at night.

For something more relaxed, sans the pickup scene, head to La Floresta or Guápulo, where drinking is a more cerebral affair.

For movie listings and other events, check the local newspapers *El Comercio* and *Hoy,* or pick up a copy of *Quito Cultura,* a monthly cultural mag available free from the tourist offices.

### Nightlife

Hitting the dance floor of one of Quito's *salsatecas* (nightclubs where dancing to salsa music is the main attraction) is a must. If you don't know how to salsa, try a few classes first (see p62).

**TOP CHOICE** **El Pobre Diablo**                    LIVE MUSIC

(Map p58; ☎223-5194; www.elpobrediablo.com; Isabel La Católica E12-06; ⊘noon-3pm & 7pm-2am

Mon-Sat) Locals and expats rate El Pobre Diablo as one of Quito's best places to hear live music. It's a friendly, laid-back place with a well-curated selection of talent (jazz, blues, world music, experimental sounds) performing most nights. It's also a great place to dine, with delectable fusion fare, a solid cocktail menu and a great vibe.

### Bungalow 6                              CLUB
(Map p68; cnr Calama & Diego de Almagro; ⏰7pm-3am Wed-Sat) The best-loved Mariscal nightspot among both foreigners and locals, Bungalow 6 plays a good mix of beats, with a small but lively dance floor and a warren of colorfully decorated rooms (with table football, pool table and small outdoor terrace) upstairs. Weekends are almost as packed as the ever-popular ladies' night on Wednesday (gals drink for free from 8pm to 10pm). Arrive early to beat the long line.

### El Aguijón                              CLUB
(Map p68; Calama E7-35; www.claguijon.com.ec; admission $5-10; ⏰9pm-3am Tue-Sat) Attracting a mix of locals and foreigners, El Aguijón is open and somewhat industrial, with video art playing on a large screen above the dance floor. DJs spin a little of everything on weekends, with live bands on Thursday and popular salsa nights on Wednesday.

### Seseribó                               CLUB
(Map p58; Edificio Girón, Veintimilla & Av 12 de Octubre; admission $5-10; ⏰9pm-2am Thu-Sat) Quito's most popular *salsateca* is a must stop for salsa fans. The music is tops, the atmosphere is superb and the dancing is first-rate.

### La Juliana                             LIVE MUSIC
(Map p58; Av 12 de Octubre near Coruña; admission $15; ⏰10pm-2am Thu-Sat) In an old converted house, La Juliana is a colorfully decorated space with a good mix of bands (rock, salsa, merengue) lighting up the dance floor most weekend nights.

### Blues                                  CLUB
(Map p58; www.clubblues.com; Av de la República 476; admission $7-20; ⏰10pm-6am Thu-Sat) Quito's only late-night club, Blues is the place party-goers head at 3am. DJs spin electronica and rock (with live rock bands playing on Thursday nights) to a style-conscious *quiteño* crowd.

### Café Libro                             LIVE MUSIC
(Map p68; ☎223-4265; www.cafelibro.com; Leonidas Plaza Gutiérrez N23-56; admission $3-20; ⏰noon-2pm Mon-Fri, 5pm-midnight Tue-Thu, 6pm-2am Fri & Sat) Live music, poetry readings, contemporary dance, tango, jazz and other performances draw an arts-loving crowd to this long-running venue.

### Mayo 68                                CLUB
(Map p68; García 662) This popular salsa club is small and conveniently located in the Mariscal and has a local following.

### House of Rock                          LIVE MUSIC
(Map p58; Isabel La Católica 1160 near Coruña) A rockin' club that hosts some of Quito's best up-and-coming bands, with live music Thursday to Saturday nights.

## Cinemas
Most Quito cinemas show popular English-language films with Spanish subtitles. Tickets cost about $5.

### Ocho y Medio                           CINEMA
(Map p58; www.ochoymedio.net, in Spanish; Valladolid N24-353 & Vizcaya; ⏰cafe 11am-10:30pm) This Floresta film house shows great art films (often in English) and has occasional dance, theater and live music. There's a cafe attached.

### Cinemark                               CINEMA
(off Map p58; www.cinemark.com.ec, in Spanish; Naciones Unidas & Av América) The most recent Hollywood blockbusters are shown here.

### Multicines                             CINEMA
(off Map p58; www.multicines.com.ec, in Spanish; Centro Comercial Iñaquito) Another top multiscreen.

## Theater & Dance
### Teatro Sucre                           PERFORMING ARTS
(Map p52; ☎228-2136; www.teatrosucre.com, in Spanish; Manabí N8-131; admission $5-20) Beautifully restored and looking smart over the Plaza del Teatro, this is the city's most historical theater. Performances range from jazz and classical music to ballet, modern dance and opera.

### Teatro Bolívar                         PERFORMING ARTS
(Map p52; ☎258-2486/7; www.teatrobolivar.org; Espejo) Likely the city's most illustrious theater and definitely one of its most important, the Bolívar was still under restoration at research time. Performances and tours are still given, everything from theatrical works to international tango-electronica gigs. It's between Flores and Guayaquil.

### Humanizarte                            DANCE
(Map p52; www.humanizarte.org.ec; La Ronda, Casa 707; admission $5; ⏰9pm Fri & Sat) This

excellent theater and dance group, currently in La Ronda on weekend nights, presents Andean dance performances. You can also enquire about taking Andean folk-dancing classes.

**Ballet Folklórico Nacional Jacchigua** DANCE
(Map p58; ☑295-2025; www.jacchiguaesecuador.com, in Spanish; cnr Avs Patria & 12 de Octubre; admission $30 ⊙7:30pm Wed & Fri) This folkloric ballet is as touristy as it is spectacular. It is presented at the Teatro Demetrio Agilera in the Casa de la Cultura Ecuatoriana (p61) and is quite a show. You can reserve tickets online.

**Teatro Prometeo** PERFORMING ARTS
(Map p58; ☑290-2272; http://cce.org.ec; Av 6 de Diciembre N16-224) Affiliated with the Casa de La Cultura Ecuatoriana (p61), this inexpensive venue often has modern-dance performances and other shows that non-Spanish-speakers can enjoy.

**Patio de Comedías** PERFORMING ARTS
(Map p58; ☑256-1902; www.patiodecomedias.org; 18 de Septiembre E4-26) Presents plays and performances Thursday through Sunday nights, usually at 8pm. It's near the Mariscal between 9 de Otubre and Amazonas.

## 🛍 Shopping

There are loads of excellent crafts stores in the new town along and near Avenida Amazonas. If buying from street stalls, you should bargain; in the fancier stores, prices are normally fixed, although bargaining is not out of the question. Note that souvenirs are a little cheaper outside Quito, if you have the time and inclination to search them out.

Quito's gallery scene is pretty limited, with just a handful of places exhibiting and selling local work.

*Centros comerciales* (shopping malls) are nearly identical to their North American counterparts, and sell international brands. Most stores are closed Sunday, but the malls included here are open every day from about 10am to 8:30pm. They all have restaurants and fast-food places inside.

**TOP CHOICE Galería Latina** HANDICRAFTS
(Map p68; Mera N23-69) One of the finest handicraft and clothing shops in the city, Galería Latina has a huge selection of beautifully made pieces: tagua carvings, colorful Andean weavings, textiles, jewelry,

sweaters and handmade items from across Latin America. Prices are higher, but so is the craftsmanship.

**Galería Ecuador Gourmet** ARTS & CRAFTS
(Map p68; Reina Victoria N24-263 near Lizardo García) This sparkling new complex run by the Ministry of Tourism has a small selection of skin products and soaps, handicrafts, clothing, CDs, coffee-table books and chocolates, wine and liqueurs (including a smooth chocolate elixir). There's an on-site cafe, and an upstairs gallery with changing exhibitions. Everything sold here is made in Ecuador.

**Mercado Artesanal La Mariscal** HANDICRAFTS
(Map p58; Washington btwn Mera & Reina Victoria) Half a city block filled with crafts stalls, with good prices and mixed quality. It's great for souvenirs. There's talk of this market closing and moving elsewhere (nearby) in the future.

**Folklore Olga Fisch** HANDICRAFTS
(Map p58; Colón E10-53) The store of legendary designer Olga Fisch (who died in 1991) is a good place to go for high-quality crafts. Fisch was a Hungarian artist who immigrated to Ecuador in 1939 and worked with indigenous artists melding traditional crafts with fine art.

**Ari Gallery** JEWELRY
(Map p52; Bolívar Oe6-23) This small jewelry shop sells unique, beautifully made works, incorporating pre-Columbian designs, semi-precious stones and rare materials native to Ecuador (such as Spondylus shells).

**Parque El Ejido Art Fair** ARTS & CRAFTS
(Map p58; Avs Patria & Amazonas; ⊙9am-dusk Sat & Sun) The most popular place to purchase paintings is during the weekend art fair. The work here consists mostly of imitations of established Ecuadorian artists, but it's cheap and colorful.

**La Bodega** HANDICRAFTS
(Map p68; Mera N22-24) In business for 30-odd years, La Bodega stocks a wide and wonderful range of high-quality crafts, both old and new.

**Ag** HANDICRAFTS
(Map p68; Mera N22-24) Ag's selection of rare, handmade silver jewelry from throughout South America is outstanding. You'll also find antiques.

**Tianguez** HANDICRAFTS
(Map p52; Plaza San Francisco) Attached to the eponymous cafe, Tianguez is a member of the Fair Trade Organization and sells outstanding crafts from throughout Ecuador.

**Homero Ortega P & Hijos** HATS
(Map p52; www.genuinepanamahat.com; Benalcázar N2-52) One of Ecuador's biggest sellers of Ecuadorian straw hats (aka panama hats), offering a small but versatile selection of its famous Cuenca brand.

**Posada de Artes Kingman** GALLERY
(Map p58; ☏222-2610; 1st fl, Diego de Almagro N29-54; ⊙9am-1pm & 3-7pm Mon-Fri) This small gallery is dedicated to the works of Ecuadorian painter Eduardo Kingman, the teacher and primary influence on the better known artist Guayasamín.

**Mono Dedo** OUTDOOR EQUIPMENT
La Floresta (Map p58; www.monodedo.com; Rafael Leon Larrea N24-36; ⊙11am-9pm Mon-Fri, 10am-1.30pm Sat); Rocódromo (Map p58; Queseras del Medio s/n; ⊙11am-7:30pm Mon-Fri, 9:30am-5pm Sat & Sun) Outstanding climbing store with rock and ice gear, clothing, tents, bags and more. The Rocódromo branch has more gear.

**Latino Americana** HANDICRAFTS
(Map p68; Av Amazonas N21-20) Boasts a huge selection of handicrafts, plus panama hats, ceramics, jewelry and alpaca wear. Check the quality carefully.

**✿ Productos Andinos** HANDICRAFTS
(Map p68; Urbina 111) This sweet artisans' cooperative is crammed with reasonably priced crafts.

**El Aborigen** HANDICRAFTS
(Map p68; Washington 614) More like an arts-and-crafts supermarket! Huge selection and good prices, too.

**Cienfuegos Galería** GALLERY
(Map p58; Galavis & Andalucía 614; ⊙11am-5pm Mon-Fri, 10am-2pm Sat) A small gallery next to the Mercado La Floresta that carries work from Ecuadorian artists.

**Cholo Machine** CLOTHING
(Map p68; Wilson 712 at Mera) Pop into this hipster boutique for a look at some eye-catching graphic T-shirts by local urban designer Cholo Machine.

**Galería Beltrán** ART GALLERY
(Map p58; Reina Victoria N21-30; ⊙9:30am-7pm Mon-Fri, 10am-2pm Sat) With more than 30 years in the art business, this art gallery sells paintings by well-known Ecuadorian artists.

**Tatoo** OUTDOOR EQUIPMENT
(Map p68; Mera N23-54) Stocks good-quality climbing, rafting and other gear for outdoor adventures.

**Explorer** OUTDOOR EQUIPMENT
(Map p68; ☏255-0911; 1st fl, cnr Foch & Reina Victoria) Above the cafe El Español overlooking the Plaza Foch, this small new store sells pricey but name-brand outdoor gear.

**Libri Mundi** BOOKSTORE
(Map p68; Mera 851) Quito's best bookstore, with a good selection of titles in English, German, French and Spanish.

**Confederate Books** BOOKSTORE
(Map p68; cnr Calama & Mera) Ecuador's largest selection of secondhand books in English and several other languages.

**English Bookstore** BOOKSTORE
(Map p68; Calama 217) Good selection of used books in English.

**Centro Comercial El Jardín** MALL
(Map p58; Avs Amazonas & de la República) A sparkling mall near the Parque La Carolina.

**Centro Comercial Iñaquito** MALL
(off Map p58; CCI; Av Amazonas & Naciones Unidas) On the north end of Parque La Carolina.

**Centro Comercial Quicentro** MALL
(off Map p58; Av 6 de Diciembre & Naciones Unidas) Another popular mall on Naciones Unidas.

# ❶ Information

Excellent topographical maps and various tourist-highlight maps are available for sale (when in stock – which isn't always) in the map-sales room at the **Instituto Geográfico Militar** (IGM; Map p58), located on top of a hill southeast of Parque El Ejido. There are no buses, so you have to either walk or take a taxi, and you'll need to leave your passport at the gate. Aside from the giant map of Quito for sale, city maps are limited.

## Dangers & Annoyances

Quito has its share of robberies and petty crime, though the city's dangers can be minimized by taking a few precautions.

The area with the most guesthouses, restaurants and nightlife, the Mariscal Sucre, remains a target for muggers and pickpockets. Plaza Foch has a police presence, but a few streets away, robberies are common. Take a taxi after dark – even if you have only a few blocks to walk; it's not worth the risk. Sunday, when no one else is around, is also a dodgy time to wander the empty streets of the Mariscal.

The old town is relatively safe as late as 10pm during the week and until around midnight on Friday and Saturday. Muggings are less common here but pickpocketing, the old-fashioned mustard scam, and snatch-and-run robberies still happen so keep your wits about you.

The trolley system is plagued with pickpockets – keep an eye out while riding, and avoid taking it during rush hour and after dark. Always keep your bag close (on your lap); the slicing open of bags (even while between your legs/under your seat, or on your back) is common practice.

The steps of García Moreno, heading from Ambato to the top of El Panecillo, are notoriously dangerous, with continued reports of muggings. Take a taxi to the top and flag another to return.

If you get robbed, file a police report (denuncio) at the **police station** Mariscal (Servicio de Seguridad Turística; cnr Reina Victoria & Roca; ☺24 hr) Old Town (cnr Mideros & Cuenca).

## Emergency
**Ambulance** (☎131)
**Emergency** (☎911)
**Fire** (☎102)
**Police** (☎101)

## Internet Access
The Mariscal area is dotted with internet cafes, many with inexpensive international calling rates. There are fewer options in the old town, although there's an internet cafe in the Palacio Arzobispal facing Plaza Grande. Most charge around $1 per hour. **Monkeys** (Mera N24-200, 2nd fl; ☺8am-11pm) is a popular, traveler-recommended internet cafe.

## Internet Resources
**Corporación Metropolitana de Turismo** (www.quito.com.ec)
**Gay Guide to Quito** (http://gayquitoec.tripod.com)

## Medical Services
The following individual doctors have been recommended, many of whom have offices in the Centro Meditropoli near the Hospital Metropolitano.

**Dr John Rosenberg** (☎252-1104, 09-973-9734; Foch btwn Av 6 de Diciembre & Diego de Almagro) Internist specializing in tropical medi-cine; speaks English and German, makes house calls and is available for emergencies nearly anytime. On Foch, look for Medcenter sign.

**Hospital Metropolitano** (☎399-8000; Mariana de Jesús & Av Occidental) The best hospital in town.

**Hospital Voz Andes** (☎226-2142; cnr Villalengua Oe2-37 & Av 10 de Agosto) American-run hospital with an outpatient department and emergency room near the Iñaquito trolley stop.

## Money
There are several banks and a few *casas de cambio* (currency-exchange bureaus) in the new town, along Avenida Amazonas between Avenida Patria and Orellana, and there are dozens of banks throughout town. Banks listed here have ATMs and change traveler's checks. If you need to change money on a Sunday, head to the Producambios at the airport: the *casa de cambio* in the international arrival area is open for all flight arrivals.

**Banco de Guayaquil** Av Amazonas (Av Amazonas N22-147 at Veintimilla); Colón (Colón at Reina Victoria)

**Banco del Pacífico** New Town (12 de Octubre & Cordero); Old Town (cnr Guayaquil & Chile)

**Banco del Pichincha** (Guayaquil btwn Olmedo & Manabí)

**Producambios** (Av Amazonas 350, Mariscal)

**Servicio Cambios** (Venezuela N5-15)

**Western Union** La Pradera (Av de la República); Colón (Av Colón 1333) For money transfers from abroad.

## Post
**Central post office** (Espejo 935) In the old town.

## Tourist Information
**South American Explorers** (SAE; ☎222-5228; www.saexplorers.org; Washington 311 & Plaza Gutiérrez) For more information on this travelers' organization, see p378.

**Tourist Office** (Corporación Metropolitana de Turismo; www.quito.com.ec); Mariscal (Map p68; ☎255-8440; Reina Victoria N24-263 near Lizardo García; ☺10am-8pm Tue-Sun); Old Town (Map p52; ☎257-2445; cnr Venezuela & Espejo, Plaza Grande; ☺9am-6pm Mon-Fri, 9am-5pm Sat) The old town branch is well located and helpful for general questions, directions and maps; a selection of handicrafts is on sale. The two-story Mariscal branch has a cafe, shops and a gallery on-site.

## Travel Agencies
**Ecuadorian Tours** (☎256-0488; www.ecua doriantours.com; Av Amazonas N21-33 near Washington) This is a good, all-purpose travel agency near Washington.

**Metropolitan Touring** (☑250-6650/1/2; www.metropolitan-touring.com; Av Amazonas N20-39 near 18 de Septiembre) Ecuador's biggest travel agency.

## ⓘ Getting There & Away

### Air

As this book went to press, Quito's new, larger airport, 20km east of the city, was in the final stages of construction, with a projected opening in 2013. Visit www.quiport.com for the latest info. Quito's soon-to-be obsolete airport, **Aeropuerto Mariscal Sucre** (www.quitoairport.com; Av Amazonas at Av de la Prensa) is located about 10km north of downtown. For domestic and international flight and airline information, see p381 and p383.

### Bus

Quito has two new bus terminals and they are both a long way from the center (allow at least an hour by public transit, 25 minutes or more by taxi).

**Terminal Quitumbe** (☑398-8200), southwest of the old town, handles the Central and Southern Andes, the coast, and the Oriente (ie Baños, Cuenca, Guayaquil, Coca and – aside from Otavalo – most destinations of interest to travelers). It can be reached by Trole bus (C4) to the last stop. A taxi to/from here costs about $8 to $12.

**Carcelén Bus Terminal** (☑396-1600), in the north, services Otavalo, Ibarra, Santo Domingo, Tulcán and other northern destinations. To get here, you can take the Trole bus north to La Y Terminal and transfer to a 'Carapungo'-bound bus; tell the driver where you're headed as this bus passes about a block from the terminal, where you can continue on foot. A taxi costs about $6 to $10.

Several bus companies have their own stations in the center of town:

## BUSES FROM QUITO

| DESTINATION | COST ($) | DURATION (HR) |
| --- | --- | --- |
| Ambato | 2.50 | 2½ |
| Atacames | 8 | 7 |
| Bahía de Caráquez | 10 | 8 |
| Baños | 3.50 | 3 |
| Coca | 10 | 10 |
| Cuenca | 10–12 | 10–12 |
| Esmeraldas | 7.25 | 6 |
| Guayaquil | 7 | 8 |
| Huaquillas | 9 | 11 |
| Ibarra | 3 | 2½ |
| Lago Agrio | 8 | 7-8 |
| Latacunga | 1.50 | 2 |
| Loja | 14–17 | 14-15 |
| Machala | 10 | 10 |
| Manta | 10 | 8–9 |
| Otavalo | 2 | 2 |
| Portoviejo | 9 | 9 |
| Puerto López | 12 | 10 |
| Puyo | 6 | 5½ |
| Riobamba | 4 | 4 |
| San Lorenzo | 7 | 6½ |
| Santo Domingo | 3 | 3 |
| Tena | 6 | 5 |
| Tulcán | 5 | 5 |

**Panamericana** (Map p68; ☑255-7134; Av Colón btwn Reina Victoria & Diego de Almagro) Guayaquil, Machala, Cuenca, Manta, Esmeraldas.

**Transportes Ecuador** (Map p68; ☑222-5315; Mera N21-44) Guayaquil.

**Transportes Occidentales** (☑250-2733; 18 de Septiembre Oe2-142) Lago Agrio, Esmeraldas, Huaquillas.

**Flota Imbabura** (☑256-5620; cnr Manuel Larrea & Portoviejo) Cuenca, Guayaquil, Manta.

**Cooperativa Flor de Valle/Cayambe** (www. flordelvalle.com.ec) Goes daily to Mindo from Quito's Terminal Terrestre La Ofelia, reachable by taking the Metrobus line to the last stop. Departs several times daily to Mindo. Confirm times with guesthouses in Mindo.

Approximate fares and travel times are shown in the table (p85). There are daily departures for each destination and several departures per day to most of them, as well as numerous buses per hour to popular places such as Ambato or Otavalo.

### Car & Motorcycle

Car rental in Quito can be pricey – taxis and buses are much cheaper and more convenient than renting a car. Car-rental companies:

**Avis** (☑244-0270) At the Mariscal airport.

**Budget** (☑223-7026; www.budget-ec.com; cnr Amazonas & Colón)

**Ecuacar** Mariscal Airport (☑224-7298; Av Amazonas at Av de la Prensa); Av Cristóbal Colón (☑252-9781, 254-0000; Av Colón 1280 near Av Amazonas)

**Hertz** Mariscal Airport (☑225-4257; Av Amazonas at Av de la Prensa); Swissôtel (☑256-9130; Av 12 de Octubre 1820)

For motorbike hire, contact conveniently located **Freedom** (☑250-4339; www.freedombikeren tal.com; Mera N22-37; bike/motorbike per day from $15/39), which also rents bicycles.

### Train

Although most of Ecuador's train system is in shambles, you can still ride the rails if you're determined. A newly restored tourist **train** (www.trenecuador.com) normally heads south from Quito for about 3½ hours to the Area Nacional de Recreación El Boliche, adjoining Parque Nacional Cotopaxi. The train departs Thursdays through Sundays at 8:15am ($15 round-trip). Inquire at the tourist office about purchasing tickets.

The newly remodeled **Quito train station** (☑800-873-637; Sincholagua & Vicente Maldonado) is about 2km south of the old town.

## ⓘ Getting Around

### To/From the Airport

Quito's new airport is scheduled to open in 2013; visit www.quiport.com to check if it's operational before you depart. Until it opens, all flights use the old airport at the north end of Avenida Amazonas, about 10km north of the old town. A taxi is the best way to get into town. Current charges are $8 into the new town and $10 to the old town.

### Car

With one-way streets and heavy traffic, driving in Quito can be hectic. Don't leave a vehicle on the street overnight. There are private garages throughout town where you can park overnight for around $12.

### Public Transportation

#### BUS

Local buses all cost $0.25. They are convenient but plagued with pickpockets, so keep a close watch on your bags and pockets.

Buses have destination placards in their windows (not route numbers), and drivers will (usually) gladly tell you which bus to take if you flag the wrong one.

#### TROLE, ECOVÍA & METROBUS

Quito has three electric bus routes: the Trole, the Ecovía and the Metrobus. Each runs north–south along one of Quito's three main thoroughfares, and each has designated stations and car-free lanes, making them speedy and efficient.

The Trole runs along Maldonado and Avenida 10 de Agosto. It terminates at the Quitumbe bus terminal, southwest of the old town. In the old town, southbound trolleys take the west route along Guayaquil, while northbound trolleys take the east route along Montúfar and Pichincha.

The Ecovía runs along Avenida 6 de Diciembre, between Río Coca in the north and La Marin in the south.

The Metrobus route runs along Avenida América from the Universidad Central del Ecuador (northeast of Parque El Ejido) to north of the old airport.

### Taxi

Most cabs are yellow and are plentiful, but rush hour, Sundays and rainy days can leave you waiting 10 minutes for an empty cab. A few taxi companies include **Urgentaxi** (☑222-2111), **City Taxi** (☑263-3333) and **Río Coca** (☑334-2727).

Cabs are legally required to use their *taxímetros* (meters) by day, and most drivers do; many, however, charge a flat rate of $2 between the old and new towns, about $0.25 to $0.50 more than if the meter was on. When a driver tells you the meter is broken, flag down another cab. At night, most taxi drivers turn off their meters, and $2 is the minimum going rate.

The minimum fare by day is $1. Short journeys will start at that and climb to about $4 for a longer trip. You can also hire a cab for about $8 per hour, which is a great way to see outer-city sights. If you bargain hard and don't plan on going very far, you could hire a cab for a day for about $60.

### Bicycle

You can hire bicycles from **El Rey** (📞222-1884; Amazonas near Cordero; bicycles per half/full day $12/15; ☺9am-7pm Mon-Fri, 9:30am-2pm Sun). Meet here for the Monday night rides around the city at 8pm.

# AROUND QUITO

🎵02

Quito makes a great base for exploring the striking geography and biodiversity of the region, with a number of excellent day trips from the capital. As well as the destinations covered in this section, Otavalo (p92) can be visited on a long day trip from Quito. The train ride to El Boliche recreation area in Parque Nacional Cotopaxi also makes for a spectacular outing (see p127), as do the magnificent hot springs of Termas de Papallacta (p197).

### ❶ Getting There & Away

Destinations in this section can all be reached by public bus in less than two hours. Taxis are an option if you have between $30 and $60 to spare. Travel agencies in Quito also offer day trips to most of the places covered here.

## La Mitad del Mundo

Ecuador's biggest claim to fame (and name) is its location right on the equator. **La Mitad del Mundo** (The Middle of the World City; www.mitaddelmundo.com; admission $2; ☺9am-6pm Mon-Fri, to 7pm Sat & Sun) is the place where Charles Marie de La Condamine made the measurements in 1736 showing that this was indeed the equatorial line. His expedition's measurements gave rise to the metric system and proved that the world is not perfectly round, but that it bulges at the equator. Today the site is a bit of a circus, with food and handicraft stalls, bustling crowds (at least on weekends) and an assortment of sights and attractions (some with separate admission charges), few of which of relate to the equator.

At the center of La Mitad del Mundo stands a 30m-high, stone trapezoidal **monument** (admission $3) topped by a brass globe. It is the centerpiece of the park, containing a viewing platform and an ethnographic museum, which provides a fine introduction to the indigenous groups of Ecuador through dioramas, clothing displays and photographs.

**Calima Tours**, located inside the complex, arranges short hikes ($8 per person) around the crater rim of nearby Pululahua.

Continue east, a few hundred meters from La Mitad del Mundo, to the amusing **Museo Solar Inti Ñan** (adult/child $3/1.50; ☺9:30am-5pm), supposedly (but again not actually) the site of the true equator. More interesting than the official complex next door, it has a meandering outdoor exhibits of astronomical geography and explanations of the importance of Ecuador's geographical location. One of the highlights is the 'solar chronometer,' a unique instrument made in 1865 that shows precise astronomical and conventional time, as well as the month, day and season – all by using the rays of the sun. The real reason to come, of course, is for the water and energy demonstrations, but you'll have to decide for yourself if it's just a smoke-and-mirrors funhouse.

### ❶ Getting There & Away

La Mitad del Mundo is 22km north of Quito, near the village of San Antonio. From Quito, take the Metrobus ($0.25) north to the last stop, Ofelia station. From there, transfer to the Mitad del Mundo bus (another $0.25) – they're clearly marked, and they currently leave from the far-right platform as you roll up. The entire trip takes one to 1½ hours.

## Reserva Geobotánica Pululahua & Around

This 3383-hectare reserve lies about 4km northwest of La Mitad del Mundo. The most interesting part of the reserve is the **volcanic crater** of the extinct Pululahua. This was apparently formed in ancient times, when the cone of the volcano collapsed, leaving a huge crater some 400m deep and 5km across. The crater's flat and fertile bottom is used for agriculture.

The crater is open to the west side, through which moisture-laden winds from the Pacific Ocean blow dramatically. It is sometimes difficult to see the crater because of the swirling clouds and mist. The moist winds, combined with the crater's steep walls, create a variety of microclimates, and the vegetation on the fertile volcanic slopes is both rampant and diverse. There are many flowers and a variety of bird species.

The crater can be entered on foot by a steep trail from the **Mirador de Ventanillas** viewpoint on its southeast side (easily reached by bus from La Mitad del Mundo). The steep trail is the best way to see the birds and plants, because most of the flat bottom is farmed. There is also an unpaved road on the southwest side via Moraspungo.

Near the Mirador de Ventanillas, you'll pass the castle-like **Templo del Sol** (admission $3; ◷10am-5pm Tue-Sun), a re-creation of an Incan temple, complete with pre-Columbian relics and stone carvings. The guided tour (in Spanish) is a bit gimmicky, led by a heavily decorated 'Incan prince' who touches on presumed ancient beliefs and rituals. The tour ends with a painting demonstration by Ecuadorian artist Cristóbal Ortega Maila, who paints rapidly and adroitly using only his hands (no brushes). There are fine rooftop views.

## 🛏 Sleeping & Eating

### 🏠 Pululahua Hostel                    HOSTEL **$$**
(☏09-946-6636; www.pululahuahostal.com; cabana s/d with shared bathroom $20/30, with private bathroom from $30/40) This ecologically friendly guesthouse is located inside the crater. Pululahua Hostel offers a handful of simple, comfortable rooms in a pristine setting. The owners cook tasty meals (lunch or dinner $10 each) using ingredients from their organic farm whenever possible. Guests can use the Jacuzzi ($3.50), hire bikes ($5 per hour) or horses (from $10 per hour) and do volunteer work. English and German are spoken.

### El Crater                            HOTEL **$$$**
(☏239-8132, www.elcrater.com; r incl breakfast $112; 🗐) Near the Ventanillas viewpoint, peacefully set El Crater has 12 spacious, attractively designed rooms with king-size beds, atmospheric stonelike walls and picture windows overlooking the volcanic

---

## MYSTERIES FROM MIDDLE EARTH

The idea of standing with one foot in each hemisphere is an intriguing one, and the closer you get to the equator, the more you hear about the equator's mysterious energy. But what is fact and what is fiction?

There's no point in starting softly, so let's debunk the biggest myth first. La Mitad del Mundo is not on the equator – but it's close. Global Positioning System (GPS) devices show that it's only about 240m off the mark. And no one who sees the photos of you straddling the equator has to know this, right?

Another tough one to swallow is the myth of the flushing toilet. One of the highlights of the Museo Solar Inti Ñan is the demonstration of water draining counterclockwise north of the equator and clockwise 3m away, south of the equator. Researchers claim it's a crock. The Coriolos Force – which causes weather systems to veer right in the northern hemisphere and left in the southern hemisphere – has no effect on small bodies of water like those in a sink or a toilet. Draining water spins the way it does due to plumbing, eddies in the water, the shape of the basin and other factors.

How about some truth: you do weigh less on the equator. This is due to greater centrifugal force on the equator than at the poles. But the difference between here and at the poles is only about 0.3%, not the approximately 1.5% to 2% the scales at the monument imply.

It is true that the spring and autumn equinoxes are the only days when the sun shines directly overhead at the equator. In fact, that's what defines an equinox. But that doesn't mean the days and night are equal in length, as many would have you believe – this happens just before the spring equinox and just after the autumn equinox, and the day depends on where you are on the planet.

More fascinating than any of the hoaxes perpetuated by Inti Ñan and La Mitad del Mundo, however, is the fact that the true equator (0.00 degrees, according to GPS readings) resides on a sacred indigenous site constructed more than 1000 years ago. The name of the site is Catequilla, and it sits on a hilltop on the opposite side of the highway from the Mitad del Mundo.

crater on one side and Quito on the other. The restaurant (mains $10 to 14; open noon to 4:30pm) serves good Ecuadorian dishes to equally impressive vistas.

## ℹ Information

The official entrance fee for the reserve is $2, which you must pay before you hike down into the crater or as you enter by car via Moraspungo. See p87 for information on inexpensive tours. On weekends, you can also hire horses near the lookout (per hour $10).

## ℹ Getting There & Away

The easiest way to reach the lookout is by inexpensive organized tour from La Mitad del Mundo.

# Volcán Pichincha

Quito's closest volcano is Pichincha, looming over the western side of the city. The volcano has two main summits – the closer, dormant **Rucu Pichincha** (4680m) and the higher **Guagua Pichincha** (4794m), which is currently very active and is monitored by volcanologists. A major eruption in 1660 covered Quito in 40cm of ash; there were three minor eruptions in the 19th century. A few puffs of smoke occurred in 1981, but in 1999 the volcano rumbled into serious action, coughing up an 18km-high mushroom cloud and blanketing the city in ash.

Climbing either of the summits is strenuous but technically straightforward, and no special equipment is required. Rucu Pichincha is now easily climbed from the top of the TelefériQo.

Climbing the smoking Guagua Pichincha is a longer trip. It is accessible from the village of Lloa, located southeast of Quito. From the village, it's about eight hours by foot to the **refugio** (hikers' refuge; dm $5). It is then a short but strenuous hike from the *refugio* to the summit. Reaching the summit will take you two days if you walk from Lloa. There are numerous agencies in Quito (Safari Tours is a good one, p65) that offer this as a day trip from town.

### Dangers & Annoyances

Before the TelefériQo was built, Rucu Pichincha was plagued with crime. Things were safer for a while, but unfortunately there have been several armed robberies recently along the main trail. The TelefériQo management is aware of this problem and it's hoped that they and the Ecuadorian police will beef up security. Hikers are advised to check with SAE (p84) for an update on conditions before heading out. As for Guagua Pichincha, stay up to date on the volcano's activity either by dropping into SAE or checking the website of the **Instituto Geofísico** (www.igepn.edu.ec).

# Northern Highlands

## Includes »

## Best Places to Eat

- » Hostería La Mirage (p103)
- » Shanandoa Pie Shop (p98)
- » La Hacienda (p107)
- » Yolanda's Chicha de Yamor (p98)
- » El Quetzal (p117)

## Best Places to Stay

- » Ali Shungu Mountaintop Lodge (p101)
- » Hostería La Mirage (p103)
- » Hacienda Pinsaquí (p101)
- » Arashá Rainforest Resort & Spa (p118)
- » Caskaffesu (p115)

## Why Go?

Following the snaking Panamericana – through the awe-some scenery of the Andes to the vibrant indigenous town of Otavalo – is a must-do Ecuador experience. As the spine of the Andes bends north from Quito, volcanic peaks punctuate valleys blanketed by flower farms and fields of sugarcane. This is Ecuador's beating heart and a cradle of Andean culture: artisans produce their wares using meth-ods unaltered for generations, and visitors find some of the country's best deals here, on everything from leather goods to traditional carpets.

High-altitude landscapes surrender to the steamy lowlands in the west, a rich transitional zone where coffee plantations flourish amid the spectacular scenery of the Intag Valley. Fur-ther south, the cloud forests of Mindo, one of Ecuador's fast-est-growing destinations, harbor hundreds of bird species: a rich destination for bird-watchers, hikers and anyone looking to retreat deep into nature at one of many jungle lodges.

## When to Go
### Otavalo

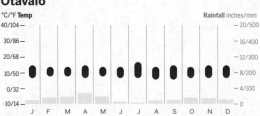

**Jun** Don't miss Otavalo on June 24, when locals celebrate Inti Raymi, a colorful pagan festival.

**Early Sep** Try to make it to Otavalo's Fiesta del Yamor, an in-digenous harvest festival.

**Late Sep** Expect music, danc-ing and lots of food at Ibarra's popular annual fiesta.

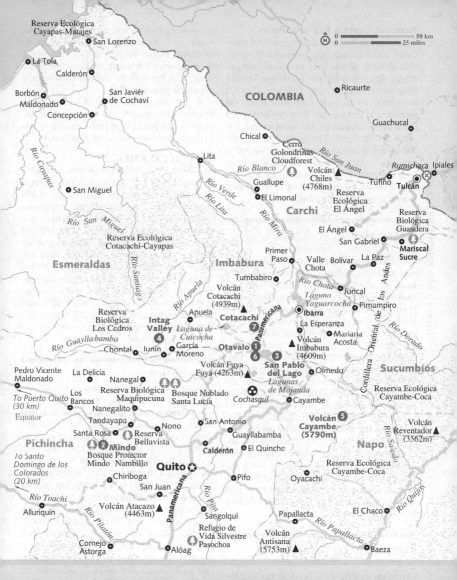

# Northern Highlands Highlights

**1** Browse the dazzling array of goods in Otavalo's colorful **crafts market** (p93)

**2** Hike into the cloud forests around **Mindo** (p113) to glimpse hundreds of bird species

**3** Ride through the countryside on horseback starting from a historic **colonial hacienda** (p101) on the outskirts of San Pablo del Lago, near Otavalo

**4** Take in the spectacular scenery in the dramatic **Intag Valley** (p104)

**5** Summit the massive, glacier-covered **Volcán Cayambe** (p92)

**6** Drink the fermented corn drink *chicha de yamor* during the **Fiesta del Yamor** (p95)

**7** Buy yourself great quality leather goods at bargain prices in the shops and markets of **Cotacachi** (p102)

## National, State & Regional Parks

At 4031 sq km, **Reserva Ecológica Cayambe-Coca** encompasses an enormous territory that spreads across four provinces and includes alpine tundra and rainforest. Volcáns Reventador (3562m) and Cayambe (5790m) sit within its bounds. Also straddling the rainforest is 2044-sq-km **Reserva Ecológica Cotacachi-Cayapas**; its most accessible point is Cotacachi. The comparatively tiny 160-sq-km **Reserva Ecológica El Ángel** is a *páramo* (high-altitude Andean grassland) treasure harboring condors, foxes and the rare, hairy-leaved *frailejones* (gray friars; local name for the *Espeletia* plant).

# Cayambe

📞 02 / POP 39,000 / ELEV 3011M

The snow-dusted peak of Cayambe looms over the rolling farmland surrounding the town of the same name, 64km north of Quito along the Panamericana. The region is considered Ecuador's flower capital (see the boxed text, p102). Enormous white tents packed with rows of blooms blanket the hillsides.

About 2km north of town on the Panamericana you'll find the very cute **Las Cabañas de Nápoles** (📞236-1388; s/d $16/20; 🅿🛜), where you can stay in comfortable brick cabins, with cable TV, that surround a volleyball court and are overlooked by the soaring Volcán Cayambe.

The hotel also has an excellent **restaurant** (mains $8-18; ⊘noon-9pm), which makes for a great stop if you're driving along the Panamericana. You can try the specialty *cuy* (guinea pig) or order the excellent meat grill for two, and wash it all down with delicious homemade lemonade.

# Cayambe to Oyacachi

📞 06

On a clear day, the road north from Cayambe to Ibarra, which passes through the village of Olmedo, provides excellent views. Heading south, you'll encounter the little village of Oyacachi, known for its indulgent community-run **hot springs** (admission $2.50). Some basic hostels and camping by permission are your options for overnighting.

On the road to Oyacachi, **Hacienda Guachala** (📞236-3042; www.guachala.com; s/d $44/59; 🛜🏊) dates back to 1580, making it the oldest hacienda in Ecuador. The sprawling property has whitewashed rooms, a sunny stone courtyard anchored by an old fountain, horse stables and a restaurant. Seven kilometers south of Cayambe, it's a great base for visiting the hot springs, hiking or horseback-riding.

A popular **hike** from Oyacachi goes through the Reserva Ecológica Cayambe-Coca to Papallacta (see p197) and takes two to three days, depending on conditions.

### VOLCÁN CAYAMBE

At 5790m, the extinct **Reserva Ecológica Cayambe-Coca** is Ecuador's third-highest peak and is the highest point in the world through which the equator directly passes – at 4600m on the south side. There is a **mountain refuge** (per person $20), but you need a 4WD to reach it. The seven-hour climb is more difficult than the more frequently ascended Cotopaxi (p124). **Safari Tours** in Quito (p65) offers a three-day glacier school and guided trips to the summit, as does **World Bike** (📞in Quito 290-6639; www. bikeclimbecuador.com; Pinto E4-358 & Amazonas, Quito). Guide services average $100 per day and usually include all equipment.

# Otavalo

📞 06 / POP 39,000 / ELEV 2550M

For hundreds of years, Otavalo has hosted one of the most important markets in the Andes, a weekly fiesta that celebrates the gods of commerce. In the colorful open-air marketplace, vendors hawk everything from handmade traditional crafts to an ever-increasing number of slyly disguised imports. The tradition of swapping money for goods here stretches back to pre-Incan times, when traders would emerge from the jungle on foot, ready to conduct business.

These days the market has morphed into a broader cultural crossroads – a place where packs of tourists from around the globe roam alongside Ecuadorians on a shared hunt for bargains, and so while Otavalo is extremely well set up for tourism, it feels some way from the tiny indigenous town that was discovered by backpackers in the early 1990s.

*Otavaleños* are known for their exquisite weavings and have been exploited for their textile-making skills by the Incas, Spanish and eventually, Ecuadorians. Life improved for many of the *indígena* (indigenous) people after the Agrarian Reform of 1964, which abolished the long-standing tradition of serfdom and permitted local land ownership. Still, many villagers struggle to profit from their crafts. That said, *otavaleños* are the wealthiest and most commercially successful *indígena* people in Ecuador, an achievement that has allowed many to live in relative comfort.

The *indígena* people wear traditional clothing and take extreme pride in their appearance. Women wear white blouses embroidered with flowers, long wool skirts, *fachalinas* (headcloths), woven belts, canvas sandals and strands of beads. Men wear felt hats, blue ponchos and calf-length pants, and braid their hair in one long strand.

Otavalo has become a must-see destination for most tourists who visit the country, but don't let its extreme popularity keep you away. Instead, witness – and let your pocketbook participate in – one of the most successful entrepreneurial stories in the Andes. But don't stop there. To truly appreciate the handcrafted items, visit nearby villages to see artisans at work.

## ◎ Sights

### Markets
MARKET

Every day, vendors hawk an astounding array of goods in the Plaza de Ponchos, the nucleus of the **crafts market**. But the real action happens on Saturday, official market day, when the market swells into adjacent roads and around half of the town center is a sea of brightly dyed carpets, clothing and other trinkets. The aptly named Plaza de Ponchos offers mostly artisan crafts – in particular, woolen goods, such as rugs, tapestries, blankets, ponchos, sweaters, scarves, gloves and hats – as well as embroidered blouses, hammocks, carvings, beads, paintings, woven mats and jewelry made from tagua nut (also known as vegetable ivory).

The options can be dizzying, similar and yet different all at once. Take your time. Browse the tables and check out pricing at a few stalls. Bargaining is expected, especially with multiple purchases. Don't be shy about asking for a deal, but don't be ruthless either.

Food stalls set up at the northern end proffer vats of chicken or tripe soup boiling on portable stove tops; crispy whole fried fish; scraps of flop-eared suckling pigs served with *mote* (hominy); and scoops of *chicha* (a fermented corn or yuca drink) from plastic buckets.

Between June and August, arrive on Fridays to shop before tour groups choke the passageways.

The markets are not free of pickpockets. While shopping, leave valuables at the hotel and keep your money in a safe spot.

The **daily market** (cnr Jaramillo & Montalvo; ◷7am-1pm) is stuffed with everything from exotic highland fruits and baggies of ground spices to mops, weaving tools and bootleg CDs. On Saturdays, this market also explodes with even more raw foods. It also offers an indoor 'food court,' a chance to belly up alongside locals and slurp soups.

You no longer have to get up before the sun to catch Saturday morning's fantastic **animal market** (Panamericana; ◷6am-1pm). While you might have little use for screaming piglets, bags of guinea pigs or a lethargic cow, it's certainly worth visiting this market for the unbeatable atmosphere and general chaos. Observe the subdued bargaining over a fresh *empanada de queso* (cheese turnover) from a hillside vendor. Cross the bridge at the end of Colón and follow the crowds to get to the market, which is just west of the Panamericana.

### El Lechero
HEALING TREE

The Lechero is a famous magical tree outside of Otavalo known for its healing powers. It's worth the 4km walk if you want some fresh air, great views of town or a little magic. But be careful. Readers have reported some robberies. Taxis also visit the spot; ask the driver to wait if you don't want to walk back.

To get there take Piedrahita out of town going south. The road quickly steepens. Look for arrows painted along the way. Hike some unpaved switchbacks and go past a fragrant eucalyptus grove to the crest of a hill where you'll see a lone, stubby tree. You can continue north another 1km to get to Parque Cóndor.

### Parque Cóndor
BIRD SANCTUARY

(www.parquecondor.org; admission $3.75; ◷9:30am-5pm Tue-Sun) A Dutch-owned foundation that rehabilitates raptors, vultures and other birds of prey, this excellent place offers a great opportunity to see an Andean condor up close, as well as eagles, owls, falcons and hawks. Don't miss the free flight demonstrations at 11:30am and 4:30pm. The center is perched on the steep hillside of Pucara Alto, 2km from town. Parque Cóndor is on top of a hill

# Otavalo

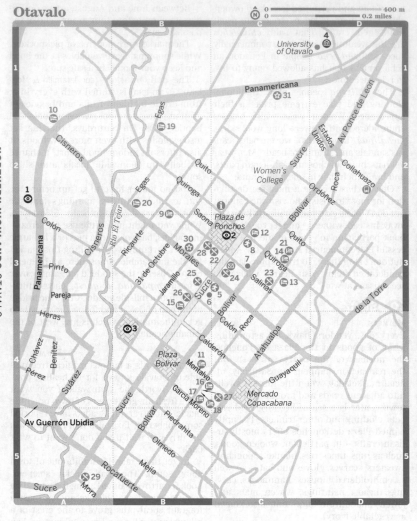

between Otavalo and the Lago de San Pablo. You can access it from any direction – it's about an hour's walk from Otavalo

### Instituto Otavaleño de Antropología
MUSEUM
(admission free; ☉8:30am-noon & 2:30-6pm Tue-Fri, 8:30am-noon Sat) This institute houses a small exhibit of ancient artifacts from the region. It's located inside the University of Otavalo, one block north of Sucre and Panamericana.

## ☜ Courses

Otavalo is a popular place to learn Spanish and has a couple of good language schools.

### Mundo Andino
LANGUAGE COURSE
(☎292-1864; www.mandinospanishschool.com; cnr Salinas & Bolívar 4-04; individual/group lessons per hr $6/4.50) This excellent language school offers a huge range of educational possibilities, including classes Monday through Friday, homestays with local families and long-term volunteer opportunities where your Spanish will really get a workout.

# Otavalo

**Instituto Superíor de Español** LANGUAGE COURSE
(📞299-2424; www.instituto-superior.net; Sucre btwn Morales & Colón; courses per week from $94) Based in Quito, but with a popular Otavalo outpost, this place receives high marks from readers. It can also arrange family homestays.

🎯 **Tours**

**Diceny Viajes** CULTURAL TOUR
(📞269-0787/0460, 09-705-4295; zulayviajes@hotmail.com; Quinchuquí) Native *otavaleña* Zulay Saravino began one of Otavalo's first tour agencies and has been guiding for three decades now. Knowledgeable, bilingual guides lead tours to various villages to learn about crafts, music and local traditions. The company currently does not have an office in Otavalo itself, but is based in the nearby village of Quinchuquí, 4km north of town. Organization can all be done by phone or email, though it's also possible to stay in guest rooms in Zulay's own home for a true taste of indigenous life.

**Runa Tupari Native Travel** CULTURAL TOUR
(📞292-2320; www.runatupari.com; cnr Sucre & Quiroga, 3rd fl) Renowned for its approach to community tourism, Runa Tupari has partnered with 44 indigenous, mestizo and Afro-Ecuadorian rural communities to offer sightseeing, hiking, horseback-riding and biking trips. Rural homestays are $25 per night, while various volunteering options cost $15 per day and include room and board. Offbeat options include a bumpy 2000m mountain-bike descent into the Intag's tropical cloud forest ($85 per person) and a round-trip 10-hour hike up 'Mama' Volcán Cotacachi (4939m; $70 per person).

**Ecomontes Tour** ADVENTURE TOUR
(📞292-6244; www.ecomontestour.com; cnr Sucre & Morales) This Quito-based agency has an office in Otavalo and offers day trips, including biking, climbing, horseback-riding, canyoning and rafting tours. Homestays with indigenous families are also offered.

🎉 **Festivals & Events**
Some small surrounding villages still celebrate pre-Columbian rituals that can last up to two weeks. For dates and info, visit www.otavalo.gov.ec.

**Fiesta del Yamor** HARVEST FESTIVAL
Otavalo's best-known celebration occurs during the first two weeks of September in honor of the fall harvest. An elected queen oversees processions, live music and dancing, fireworks displays and cockfights.

## A TIGHTLY WOVEN CULTURE

Behind the bountiful woolens stalls at the Otavalo market is a living, breathing industry with a culture unto itself. Small indigenous villages outside Otavalo are home to weaving families. The activity starts before dawn in many households. Weavers gather in a small dirt-floor room to do their swift, silent work. Production starts with washing, carding, spinning and dyeing the wool. Children play with yarn instead of toys, practicing to one day join in.

Four thousand years ago, the ancestors of *otavaleño* weavers started using the back-strap loom, which can still be seen in some homes today. They sat on the cold ground, holding the loom between their bare feet, and interlaced threads to make complex and dazzling designs.

The tradition faces its own challenges as the use of electric looms continues to rise. And as trade beyond borders has shot up, so has the incursion of foreign products. Visitors who travel the length of the Andes begin to spot the same stuff everywhere and stop buying. Otavalo addressed this problem by placing stricter controls on goods sold in its market. These days 80% to 90% of the artistry sold is local. If you want to support the traditional industry, purchase handmade goods, even though their bulk is murder on the luggage.

Revelers consume copious amounts of *chicha de yamor*: seven varieties of corn are slowly simmered together to produce the unusual nonalcoholic drink (longer-fermented versions are alcoholic). It's available only during fiesta time from Yolanda's Chicha de Yamor.

**St John the Baptist Day** RELIGIOUS FESTIVAL
June 24 is known locally as La Fiesta de San Juan, or by its pagan name, Inti Raymi. It is said that local *indígenas* live and die to celebrate this event, saving money year-round for costumes, food and drink. The festivities continue through June 29, the **Day of St Peter & St Paul**. Look for the bullfight in Otavalo and the boating regatta on Laguna de San Pablo, as well as celebrations in nearby Ilumán.

### 🛏 Sleeping

Otavalo's perennial popularity has created a good selection of well-priced accommodation. At the lower end, ensure your hotel has hot water and adequate bedcovers for the cold nights, and always reserve in advance, even in budget hotels, for the weekend rush.

There are several excellent options outside the city; see p99.

**Hotel Riviera-Sucre** GUESTHOUSE $
(⌨292-0241; www.rivierasucre.com; cnr García Moreno 380 & Roca; s/d $15/26; @📶) This Belgian-owned hotel in a large, old home has high-ceilinged rooms, endless nooks, a garden, fireplaces, courtyard hammocks, a library, laundry facilities and a small cafe. It offers a communal kitchen, the use of a computer for $1 per hour and friendly staff to make you feel right at home.

**Rincón del Viajero** GUESTHOUSE $
(⌨292-1741; www.hostalrincondelviajero.com; Roca 11-07; r per person incl breakfast with shared/private bathroom $11/13; 📶) A great choice for its warm hospitality and homey, snug rooms, the 'traveler's inn' has a lounge with a cozy fireplace, a sunny rooftop terrace peppered with hammocks and a TV room. English is spoken.

**Hostal Valle del Amanecer** GUESTHOUSE $
(⌨292-0990; www.hostalvalledelamanecer.com; cnr Roca & Quiroga; r per person incl breakfast with shared/private bathroom $11/14; 📶) The tropical-themed decor and pebbled courtyard filled with hammocks creates a popular choice for travelers. Small rooms mean that communal spaces are busy and friendly, as is the on-site restaurant. Rent bicycles for $8 a day.

**Hotel Otavalo** HOTEL $
(⌨292-0416; Roca 504-758; r incl breakfast per person $22; 📶) This simple colonial hotel is decked out with polished hardwood floors and a bright covered courtyard. The high-ceilinged, spacious rooms tucked away from the street are some of the quietest in town and have modern bathrooms and Technicolor bedspreads. It's popular with groups, though, so time breakfast in the restaurant to avoid the crowd.

### Cabañas El Rocío
GUESTHOUSE $

(292-4606; rocioe@hotmail.com; Barrio San Juan; r per person $10; P) Don't be put off by the faded sign and the roadside location: this charming place belies its uninviting exterior and has a range of vaguely alpine rooms and cabins just a short walk from the center of Otavalo. It's great value for this standard of accommodation.

### Hostal Doña Esther
GUESTHOUSE $$

(292-0739; www.otavalohotel.com; Montalvo 4-44; s/d/tr $28/40/48; ) This small, Dutch-owned colonial-style hotel is cozy, with attractive rooms surrounding a courtyard ornamented with ceramics and ferns. The service is personable, and there's a popular book exchange.

### La Posada del Quinde
GUESTHOUSE $$

(292-0750; www.posadaquinde.com; Quito & Egas; s/d incl breakfast $45/68; P) Once the popular Ali Shungu guesthouse and now rebranded by new owners, the Posada del Quinde has gorgeous gardens and attractive rooms in an airy and well-designed space. However, some of the rooms are showing their age and could do with an airing and a repaint.

### Acoma
HOTEL $$

(292-6570; www.hotelacoma.com; Salinas 7-57; s/d incl breakfast with shared bathroom $18/25, with private bathroom $30/40, ste $63; P) The decor in this modern Santa Fe–style hotel may make you crave chili stew and desert views. But who needs the Southwest when you've got beautiful cedar floors, mosaic tiles and skylights surrounding a sleek bar in Ecuador? A detached building in the back offers less luxury; small rooms with shared bathrooms inspire main-building envy.

### Residencial El Rocío
HOSTEL $

(292-4606; Morales 11-70; r per person with shared/private bathroom $8/9) Friendly, clean accommodations on the quieter side of downtown. Modest rooms vary in size. A rooftop strewn with laundry lines offers great views of the hilltops.

### Hotel Santa Fe
HOTEL $

(292-3640; www.hotelsantafeotavalo.com; Roca btwn García Moreno & Montalvo; r per person $13; P) Lovers of wooden interiors will find this Southwestern-style place very much to their liking, even if the kitschy rooms are rather on the small side and those not on the street are a little dark. It has cable TV and an upstairs restaurant.

### Hostal Runa Pacha
HOTEL $

(292-5566; Roca 10-02; r per person with shared/private bathroom $6/8; P) Looking pretty impressive from the outside, the Runa Pacha won't overwhelm you with charm inside, but the rooms are clean and some come equipped with narrow balconies for the very thin to enjoy some fresh air. Bathrooms are in need of a spruce-up, but at these prices, who's complaining?

### Hotel Flores 2
HOTEL $

(292-1826; Sucre btwn Colón & Calderon; r per person $12; P) Located in the heart of the action, shady hallways lead to basic rooms with some welcome daylight. Balconies offer prime people-watching, but the views are over a car park and it can be noisy here.

### Hostal Internacional
HOTEL $

(08-803-3167; Sucre & Quiroga; s/d incl breakfast $10/14) There may be no wireless, but if you want to be right in the heart of the action, this budget-priced but comfortable enough place has views over the Plaza de Ponchos. The management appears overly fond of air freshener, however, which makes you wonder what smells they are covering up.

## Eating

Restaurants are plentiful, even if you're craving international fare.

---

## THOSE RANDY PEAKS

As if it weren't enough that all Spanish nouns have a gender, apparently volcanoes do too. The locals refer to Volcán Imbabura (4609m) as Taita (Daddy) Imbabura and Volcán Cotacachi (4939m) as Mama Cotacachi. These two extinct volcanoes can be seen from Otavalo on clear days: the massive bulk of Taita to the east and the sharper, jagged peak of Mama to the northwest. When it rains in Otavalo, they say that Taita Imbabura is pissing in the valley. Another legend suggests that when Mama Cotacachi awakes with a fresh covering of snow, Taita Imbabura has paid her a conjugal visit. What happens when snow falls on Imbabura? Or when drought dries the valleys? You'll have to ask a local.

### Shanandoa Pie Shop
BAKERY $

(Plaza de Ponchos; pie slices from $1.50; ⊘10am-9pm; ☑) The perfect place to take a break from buying indigenous handicrafts, this bakery on the Plaza de Ponchos does out-of-this-world crusty pies in a selection of flavors (strawberry is amazing) accompanied by ice cream.

### Green Coffee Shop & Diner
ORGANIC $

(Sucre near Salinas; mains $3-7; ⊘10am-9pm Mon-Fri, from 8am Sat; ☑) Located in an eclectic, disheveled courtyard, this spot serves up 100% organic salads, grills, pasta dishes, sandwiches and breakfasts and makes for a great refuge from the chaos outside on market days.

### Mi Otavalito
ECUADORIAN $$

(Sucre 11-19; mains $6.50-8; ⊘11.30am-9pm) This cute place on Otavalo's main street has a sweet rustic decor and lots of cow heads mounted on its yellow walls. Some of the best Ecuadorian dishes in town attract locals and tourists alike. Fresh ingredients shine in grilled meats, trout and hearty soups.

### Yolanda's Chicha de Yamor
ECUADORIAN $

(Sucre & Mora; meals $3-8; ⊘late Aug–mid-Sep, during festival time) Yolanda Cabrera has become famous (see the clippings on the wall) for delicious local fare such as *tortillas de maíz* (corn tortillas), *mote* (hominy), *empanaditas* (Spanish pies) and the local favorite of *fritada* (fried chunks of pork, served with *mote*). Of course, the real attraction is her *chicha de yamor* (see p95), which Yolanda stirs out back in large bubbling cauldrons over smoky fires. Look for the green house.

### Oraibi
VEGETARIAN $

(Sucre & Colón; mains $3-10; ⊘11am-7pm Wed-Sat; ☑) Right in the heart of town you'll find this charming vegetarian oasis in an old hacienda. The menu consists of pizza, sandwiches, salads and tortillas, while the decor is rustic-chic. Outside there's a spacious garden complete with white tablecloths, plenty of shade and live Andean music from 1pm to 4pm daily.

### Buenavista
INTERNATIONAL $

(Plaza de Ponchos; mains $3-6; ⊘10am-10pm Wed-Mon; ☑) This bar and restaurant's name refers to the great panorama of tarpaulin-covered market stalls you'll see from the balcony every day of the week. Service can be brusque, but there's a full menu of good international fare running from trout and beef dishes to a range of breakfasts. If you're looking for a place to drink, there's a full cocktail list to boot.

### Quino
SEAFOOD $$

(Roca near Montalvo; mains $6-11; ⊘noon-11pm Tue-Sun) This popular eatery offers up the town's best seafood offerings within its dimly lit walls. This is the place to come for a good dinner, but not if you're in a rush: all main courses are cooked from scratch, so expect to wait around half an hour.

### Árbol de Montalvo
PIZZA $$

(Montalvo 4-44; mains $7-9; ⊘6-9pm Mon-Thu, noon-10pm Fri-Sun; ☑) Make your way to the back of the Hostal Doña Esther for Otavalo's only wood-fired oven pizza. Also on the menu are organic salads, seasonal vegetables and Mediterranean-inspired pastas.

### Chifa Ming Zhu
CHINESE $

(cnr Roca & Salinas; mains $3-5; ⊘10am-11pm) Tucked inside a colorful house, plates of steaming noodle dishes and gleaming vegetables draw crowds on weekends. Portions are huge.

## ☆ Entertainment

*Peñas* are lively venues (bars or clubs with live folkloric music) common to the high Andes, and Otavalo has a few good ones. It's not a party town per se, but on weekend nights the disco scene can simmer into something sweaty and festive.

Cockfights are also popular with the locals.

### Amauta
PEÑA

(Morales 5-11 & Jaramillo; ⊘8pm-4am Fri & Sat) An absolutely typical Otavalo *peña*, this place shouldn't be missed. Music here is Andean through and through, unlike the salsa and merengue played increasingly elsewhere in town.

### Peña La Jampa
PEÑA

(cnr 31 de Octubre & Panamericana; ⊘7pm-3am Fri & Sat) This more contemporary spin on a *peña* is wildly popular and showcases a mix of live salsa, merengue, rock en español and *folklórica* (folk music).

## ℹ Information

**Dr Leonardo Suarez** (☑09-779-1206) Locally recommended doctor who speaks some English and makes house calls.

**Hospital** (☑292-0444/3566; Sucre) Some 400m northeast of downtown.

## BUSES FROM OTAVALO

| DESTINATION | COST (US$) | DURATION |
| --- | --- | --- |
| Quito | 2 | 3hr |
| Apuela | 1.95 | 2½hr |
| Cotacachi | 0.25 | 15min |
| Cayambe | 0.75 | 45min |
| Ibarra | 0.45 | 30min |

**Police Station** (☑101; Av Ponce de Leon)
**Post Office** (cnr Sucre & Salinas, 2nd fl)
**Tourist Office** (iTur; ☑292-7230; cnr Quiroga & Jaramillo; ☻8:30am-1pm & 2:30-6pm Mon-Fri, 9:30am-1pm Sat & Sun) Helpful staff here speak some English and can recommend tours, hotels and other activities. The building also houses art, photography and history exhibitions.

### ① Getting There & Away

Otavalo is well connected to Quito as well as being a major transport hub for smaller towns and villages in the northern highlands. The busy and chaotic bus station is on Atahualpa and Collahuazo, a few blocks from the Plaza de Ponchos.

To get to Tulcán and the Colombian border, travel to Ibarra and change buses there.

Old local buses, with fares of roughly $1 per hour of travel, go south to San Pablo del Lago (20 minutes) and Araque (30 minutes). Co operativa Imbaburapac has buses to Ilumán (30 minutes), Agato (one hour) and San Pablo del Lago (15 minutes). All buses leave from the same station.

---

## Around Otavalo

☑06
Green-checkered farmland creeps up the steep flanks of the mountains surrounding Otavalo, a rewarding combination for visitors seeking heart-pounding exercise and long views. Hikers shouldn't miss the spectacular Lagunas de Mojanda, southwest of Otavalo.

Hidden haciendas, once-grandiose epicenters of colonial society, now invite travelers to enjoy the sprawling grounds and fascinating history. Then there's Ecuador's largest lake, Laguna de San Pablo, a more domesticated setting with paddleboats and groomed shoreline hotels. Each September an international swimming competition has competitors swimming 3800 cold meters across the lake. Visitors can reach all these places within a short bus or taxi ride from downtown Otavalo.

The Panamericana heads northeast out of Otavalo, passing by the indigenous villages of **Peguche**, **Agato** and **Ilumán**. Explore them by bus, taxi or with a tour. The villages southwest of Laguna de San Pablo manufacture fireworks, mats made of *totora* (straw made from reeds) and other reed products. Other *otavaleño* villages are nearby. Consult the tour operators in Otavalo, as tour prices are not much more than a long taxi rental.

**Las Palmeras** (☑292-2607; www.laspalmerasinn.com; r/ste from $74/122; ☎) offers colorful cottages set in the rural hills, with cozy rooms furnished in colonial style. Rent a bike, go horseback-riding, take Spanish lessons or just enjoy the scenery. Meals at the restaurant are excellent.

### LAGUNAS DE MOJANDA
A crumbling cobbled road that seems almost to defy gravity leads high into the *páramo* to three turquoise lakes set like gemstones into the hills. Located 17km south of Otavalo, the area acquired protected status in 2002 and has since become better protected by police, too, discouraging muggers who at one point quite commonly targeted hikers. If you have come to camp, set up on the south side of the biggest lake, **Laguna Grande**, or in the basic stone refuge (bring a sleeping bag and food). The jagged peak of **Fuya Fuya**, an extinct volcano (4263m), looms nearby.

Taxis from Otavalo charge extra (about $20 each way plus $10 per hour to wait) for wear and tear. To save a few bucks, stay at a nearby inn and hike, or else taxi out early from Otavalo and hike back the same day. If you want to hoof it from the closest lodgings, bring lots of water. Runa Tupari Native Travel in Otavalo offers guided hikes that include transportation.

# Around Otavalo

An extended scenic walk across the *páramo* will drop you into the archaeological site of Cochasquí, 20km due south. Bring a 1:50,000 topographical map of the Mojanda area, numbered ÑII-F1, 3994-III, available from the Instituto Geográfico Militar (IGM) in Quito (p83).

If you're looking to combine budget accommodation with spectacular scenery, **Rose Cottage** (☎09-772-8115; www.rosecottageecuador.com; Mojandita; dm/tw/d $12/17/27) is a great choice. Located 3km from Otavalo up a steep hill, this place packs in awesome views and offers a wide range of accommodation options that allow you to enjoy the Andean scenery while still being within easy reach of Otavalo.

**Casa Mojanda** (☎08-033-5108; www.casamojanda.com; s/d incl breakfast & dinner $110/183; ☎) Consummate relaxation can be found at this lovely inn, 4km south of Otavalo. It's on the road to Lagunas de Mojanda, with views of steep Andean farmland. Cheerful cottages are equipped with electric heaters and hot-water bathrooms; some have fireplaces. Slip into the outdoor hot tub after a long day of hiking, go horseback-riding, take a Spanish class or organize mountain-biking or rafting. Rates include breakfast and dinner made from fresh garden ingredients, and a short, guided hike to waterfalls.

Visit **La Luna** (☎09-315-6082, 09-829-4913; www.lalunaecuador.com; campsites $4, dm $8, s/d with shared bathroom $15/25, with private bathroom $17/28; ☎) for a low-key, low-budget getaway with beautiful views. Located 4.5km south of Otavalo on the way to Lagunas de Mojanda, it's a great haven for hikers. Guests dine in the main house, where the fireplace games are the nexus of evening activity. Showers are hot and four of the doubles have a private bathroom and fireplace. The owners speak English and will arrange hikes (with lunchboxes) or Spanish lessons with advance notice. Walk an hour from town or grab a taxi for $4.

## LAGUNA DE SAN PABLO

A popular stop for weekenders who want to escape the hectic pace of Otavalo but stay within reach of the market. Houses, farms and the paved road encircling the lake are never far from sight, but great views of Volcán Imbabura (see the boxed text, p97) compensate.

**TOP** CHOICE **Hacienda Cusín** (☎291-8013/8316; www.haciendacusin.com; s/d $90/120; set lunch/dinner $18/22; ☎) is a fairy tale 17th-century hacienda. It's located on the southern outskirts of San Pablo del Lago, 10km from Otavalo. Tall cedar trees shade the garden paths linking the cottages and old buildings. Impressive carved wooden doors, oil paintings from Europe, and South American textiles and antiques create museumlike interiors. Guests can play squash, ride horses or mountain bikes, lounge in the reading library then cozy up to the bar, where a roaring fire cuts the highland chill. There are two exclusive craft shops, including one run by the Andrango family from Agato (see p102). The formal, proper dining room serves delicious meals. Packages offer everything from overnight horseback-riding expeditions and Spanish-language lessons to weaving courses. Book well in advance for weekends.

**Cabañas del Lago** (☎291-8108; www.cabanasdellago.com.ec; r $85, cabañas $100-135; ☎) caters to families, with 27 cabins of various sizes and lots of activities: it has a *fútbol* field, minigolf, jet skis and all manner of watersports on the east side of the lake. The on-site restaurant fuels the fun.

**Hostería Puerto Lago** (☎292-0920; www.puertolago.com; s/d/ste $74/86/128; mains $8-20; ☎) is just off the Panamericana 5km southeast of Otavalo. An immaculate, green lawn groomed by grazing llamas surrounds austere cabins that look out onto the lake. The popular, white-linen restaurant offers traditional cuisine on the waterfront, and guests can laze the day away in a paddleboat, kayak or on the tennis court.

## NORTH ALONG THE PANAMERICANA

**Hacienda Pinsaquí** (☎294-6116; www.haciendapinsaqui.com; s/d/tr/q incl breakfast $112/144/155/175, set meal $27; ☎) offers a taste of old-world Ecuador, housed as it is in a former colonial textile hacienda. Wooden-beamed ceilings, grand grounds and refined decor, including antique French washbasins and gaunt portraits, channel the past. Constructed in 1790, parts of this purebred hacienda survived the disastrous earthquake of 1857, and the whole place oozes history: Simón Bolívar used to stay here on his route north to Bogotá. Some of the 30 rooms and suites have Jacuzzis and fireplaces, bringing them very stylishly into the modern age. Check out the chapel or the cozy low-lit bar, an ideal place to sip *canelazo* (sugarcane alcohol – *aguardiente* – with hot cider and cinnamon) and hatch revolutionary plans. Guests can go horseback-riding with a pick from the renowned stables.

## PEGUCHE

In this tiny weaving village, sheep traipse past clotheslines draped with dyed wool drying in the breeze. While electric looms occupy many homes here, it's the traditional, handmade products that deserve attention. Ask locals for directions to sites listed below.

**WORTH A TRIP**

## ALI SHUNGU MOUNTAINTOP LODGE

Gushing isn't really our thing, but we can't recommend this superb mountain retreat more enthusiastically. Run by two American expats who have made Otavalo their home for almost two decades, **Ali Shungu** (☎08-950-9945; www.alishungu.com; Quinchinche; r per person incl breakfast & dinner $95; ☎☎) is a collection of four self-contained hillside villas 5km outside of town with jaw-dropping views of the mountains surrounding the town. Each enormous villa can accommodate up to eight people in two bedrooms, and have full kitchens, glorious living rooms with huge picture windows, a regularly stoked fireplace, private garden and sumptuous decor made up of folk art, crafts and carpets from the surrounding area. What's more, the food is excellent, with both breakfast and dinner being a delightful multicourse affair. The location out of town means that it's only really convenient for people with their own transport, although taxis are cheap, so it's perfectly possible to stay even if you're not driving.

## A ROSE BY ANY OTHER NAME

Flower farms are considered to be the star industry of the highlands, employing 76,600 people in small communities that have few other job opportunities. Only at the equator do roses grow completely straight, and so as a result Ecuador exports one-third of roses grown annually to the US for Valentine's Day alone. The flower boom has brought prosperity to many Ecuadorians, but this has come at a cost to the environment and workers.

In order to grow plump, flawless roses in Ecuador's tropical climate, a number of growers use chemical pesticides and fungicides, some of which are listed as extremely or highly toxic by the World Health Organization. Not all farms provide safety equipment such as fumigation suits, which can lead to serious health consequences ranging from rashes to cancer. Many employees receive substandard wages, and sometimes work 70 to 80 hours a week.

The German-based **Flower Label Program** (www.fairflowers.de) is working to reform the industry by rewarding flower producers that meet environmental and social standards with FLP-certification labels for their products. Equivalent US-based programs include **VeriFlora** (www.veriflora.com) and **TransFair USA** (www.transfairusa.org). To qualify for these schemes, farmers must use natural pesticides, such as chili and chamomile extract, and offer their workers fair wages and conditions.

Start at **Tejidos Mimahuasi**, the home of weavers José María Cotacachi and Luz María Fichabamba, who demonstrate various weaving processes. Then visit **Taller de Instrumentos Andimos-Nañda Mañachi**, where a family crafts traditional musical instruments including panpipes and *charangos*, 10-stringed mandolin-like instruments traditionally made from armadillo shells.

On the central plaza of Peguche, **El Gran Condor** (www.artesaniaelgrancondor.com; ◷8am-7pm Mon-Fri, 11am-4pm Sun) is the place for textile fanatics who didn't find what they wanted in Otavalo. The shop sells high-quality textiles made locally, including sweaters, scarves and wall hangings. Call ahead to arrange for demonstrations of dyeing and weaving techniques.

From the abandoned railway line in Peguche, a trail leads about 2km southeast to the waterfalls **Cascadas de Peguche**. These falls are sacred to the locals and visitors should stay away during Inti Raymi (p96), June's festival of the sun, when men conduct ritual cleansing baths.

Guests come to **Hostal Aya Huma** (☎269-0333; www.ayahuma.com; s/d $18/30) for a quiet village retreat. Rooms are basic but clean, and the cafe serves hearty breakfasts and good vegetarian food. If you're lucky there's live music.

Some Cooperativa Imbaburapac buses go through Peguche en route to Agato from Otavalo.

### AGATO

Take a road uphill 2km east of Peguche to the **Tahuantinsuyo Weaving Workshop**, where master weaver Miguel Andrango demonstrates traditional weavings on old looms and sells his products on-site. The Andrango family runs an outlet at the Hacienda Cusín on weekends (see p101).

### ILUMÁN

Weavers work in this village off the Panamericana about 7km northeast of Otavalo. It is also famous for its shamans; the local shamans' association has around 120 members. Members advertise by scrawling their name in large letters on their homes. Feel free to try it out, but remember that cleansings, involving raw egg and spittle, can get messy. From Otavalo, take an Imbaburapac bus.

### COTACACHI

☑06 / POP 10,500 / ELEV 2560M

Cotacachi has become synonymous with its leather workers, who produce beautiful and incredibly good-value products, which in turn bring discerning bargain-hunters from around the world to the small Andean town. Known as the 'City of Peace,' Cotacachi enjoys an easygoing tranquility that has inspired a recent influx of foreigners, who are snatching up property. With Laguna de Cuicocha and Volcán Cotacachi close by, Cotacachi may some day give Otavalo a run for its money. In the meantime it's certainly managing its development in a far more measured way than its neighbor.

## ◉ Sights & Activities

Most people come to Cotacachi for the shopping: you can get some superb bargains, especially for leather jackets, luggage, wallets, handbags, gloves and shoes. Sunday is market day, but any day of the week the town's main strip, 10 de Agusto, makes for a great place to load up on purchases. Nearly all shops will offer discounts if you pay in cash. There's an ATM on 10 de Agosto.

For information about community tourism, horseback-riding and hiking, go to the municipal tourism office in the **Casa de las Culturas** (🖉291-5140; cnr Bolívar & 9 de Octubre; ⊙9am-1pm & 2-6pm Mon-Fri, 9am-5pm Sat & Sun). The spacious building has an exhibit of Guayasamín paintings, an internet center and a coffee shop.

The **Museo de las Culturas** (Moreno 13-41; admission $1; ⊙9am-noon & 2-5pm Mon-Fri, 2-5pm Sat, 10am-1pm Sun), located in the neoclassical, former municipal palace, presents the ethnohistory of the region, from 8500 BC through colonial and republican periods. Don't miss the costumes and photos from indigenous religious festivals.

## 🛏 Sleeping & Eating

TOP
CHOICE **Hostería La Mirage**　　　HOTEL $$$
(🖉291-5237; www.mirage.com.ec; Calle 10 de Agosto; r incl breakfast & dinner $427-976; P🐾🛜🏊) The unpaved entry road belies one of Ecuador's finest hotels. Beyond the locked iron gates, peacocks stroll the green, past white cupolas and columned entrances. The decor is Louis XIV-exquisite, with original paintings, canopy beds, flower bouquets and luxurious linens. If you can pull yourself away from your room, head to the rose petal-strewn indoor swimming pool and Jacuzzi. The attached spa is a throwback to Roman decadence, featuring treatments ranging from milk-and-rose-petal baths to shamanic cleansings in a stone-slab candlelit nook. Tennis, horseback-riding, bird-watching and mountain-biking are offered. The stylish restaurant guarantees a memorable experience in international fusion; think oxtail consommé, *cuy* off the bone, duck à l'orange and New Zealand lamb chops. Overall, this place is hard to beat if you're looking for some serious pampering in a beautiful Andean setting. It's at the town's edge, just 500m northeast from the main square.

**Land of the Sun**　　　HISTORIC HOTEL $$
(🖉291-5264; www.landofthesun.org; Moreno & Sucre; s/d incl breakfast $60/72, mains $4-10; P@🛜)

This colonial hotel right in the heart of town has an attractive tiled courtyard around which the rooms are arranged; the best have balconies with views of the convent. Additional services include a sauna, which is free for guests, and an excellent courtyard restaurant (open 7am to 9pm), which does an excellent *locro de papas* (potato soup served with avocado and cheese).

**Veraneante**　　　ECUADORIAN $$
(Bolívar & Calle 9 de Octubre; mains $6-10; ⊙8.30am-10pm) With white tablecloths and attentive service, this upmarket spot is between the cathedral and the shopping street and specializes in fresh trout cooked a dozen ways.

**Restaurante Doña Ceci**　　　ECUADORIAN $
(Bolívar near 10 de Agosto; set meals $3; ⊙10am-8pm) This popular no-frills joint is handy for a filling and supercheap lunch after a long morning's shopping. Delicious three-course meals include soup, dessert and fresh juice.

## ❶ Getting There & Away

Cotacachi is west of the Panamericana and 15km north of Otavalo. From Otavalo's bus terminal, buses leave at least every hour ($0.25, 25 minutes) for Cotacachi's bus stand, which is by the market at the far end of town.

In Cotacachi, *camionetas* (pickups or light trucks) can be hired from the bus terminal to take you to Laguna de Cuicocha (round-trip $12, including a half hour of waiting time). A more economical option for Laguna de Cuicocha is to take a Transportes Cotacachi bus (from Otavalo or Cotacachi) to Quiroga, where you can grab a taxi from the plaza.

# Reserva Ecológica Cotacachi-Cayapas

This **reserve** (lake admission $1, entire park $2) protects a huge swath of the western Andes. The range of altitudes, from Volcán Cotacachi to the coastal lowland rainforests, means an abundance of biodiversity. Travel from the highland to lowland areas of the reserve is nearly impossible due to the density of the vegetation, so most visitors either visit the lowlands from San Miguel on Río Cayapas (see p239) or the highlands around Laguna de Cuicocha. From Cotacachi, just before arriving at Laguna de Cuicocha, a rangers' booth serves as the entrance to the reserve.

## ◉ Sights

### Laguna de Cuicocha
LAKE

Head 18km west from Cotacachi and you'll come upon this eerily still, dark lagoon cradled in a collapsed volcanic crater. Some 3km wide and 200m deep, the lagoon features two mounded islands that shot up in later eruptions. The islands look like the backs of two guinea pigs, hence the name: 'cuicocha' means 'guinea pig lake' in Kichwa. Hike the trail skirting the shore, where hummingbirds feed on bright flowers and the occasional condor circles over the glassy expanse. The trail begins near the reserve's entrance booth, a circuit of five or six hours. If the clouds clear, you'll see Volcán Cotacachi. Boats for hire ($2) make short trips around the islands. There have been robberies here in the past; never go alone and check the current situation with the local guards at the park entrance.

A two-day hike goes from Laguna de Cuicocha to Lagunas de Mojanda via a southern trail through the village of Ugshapungu. The 1:50,000 Otavalo map, numbered ÑII-F1, 3994-IV, is recommended and available at the IGM in Quito (p83).

## 🛏 Sleeping & Eating

### Hostería Cuicocha
GUESTHOUSE $$

(📞09-147-4172; www.cuicocha.org; s/d/tr incl breakfast & dinner $40/70/105, mains $4-9) It's possible to stay by the lake in this beautiful and remote spot, where clean rooms with lake views are good value for money. The on-site restaurant (mains $4 to $9) is open to the public and serves filling meals such as fresh grilled trout and empanadas.

## ❶ Getting There & Away

A group can hire a taxi or pickup in Cotacachi for about $20 round-trip; be sure to pay after returning so you don't get ditched. One-way fares by taxi or truck cost about $8 from Cotacachi.

## Intag Valley

Hang on for the dramatic descent into Intag. After chugging to dry and scrabbled heights, the road plunges downward, only to crawl out of mountain gutters and climb again. Sometimes mudslides block this road, but drivers, who may cross themselves before embarking, seem to have an uncanny talent for its narrow dimensions and ghastly conditions. The valley is famous not only for its coffee, but also for its activism.

The **Andean Bear Conservation Project** (www.andeanbear.org) trains volunteers as bear trackers. Hike through remote cloud forest to track the elusive spectacled bear, whose predilection for sweet corn is altering its wild behavior. Other jobs here include working with local farmers to replenish cornfields ravaged by bears (to discourage bear hunting) and maintaining trails. Volunteers can come for as little as a week but a month ($700) is recommended.

Get off just before Santa Rosa for the two-hour walk into **Siempre Verde** (📞404-262-3032, ext 1460 in the US; www.siempreverde.org), a small community-run research station supporting tropical-conservation education with excellent hiking and bird-watching. Students and researchers are welcome with prior arrangement.

An hour's walk from Santa Rosa you'll find the **Intag Cloud Forest Reserve** (📞299-0001; www.intagcloudforest.com; r per person incl all meals $50), a primary cloud forest reserve run by the founder of Defense and Ecological Conservation for Intag (DECOIN). Visitors (in groups of eight or more, booked in advance only) stay in rustic cabins with solar-heated hot water and hike, bird-watch and eat vegetarian meals.

### APUELA
📞06

The tiny town of Apuela hugs the Río Intag, which has carved a vast slit through the mountains as it roars toward the Pacific. On Sundays locals flood the center to play soccer and browse the market for provisions and blue jeans. Coffee addicts should visit Café Río Intag, a cooperative coffee factory. The beans are produced by **Asociación Río Intag** (📞264-8489; aacri@andinanet.net), near the plaza, a group of local farmers and artists. It also sells handbags woven with agave fibers, soaps, and handicrafts made by local women.

There are several places to stay here, all around 3km beyond the town (cross the river and turn left). The best option is **Cabañas Río Grande** (📞264-8296; r $30; ⛲) where you'll find a complex of tidy, four-person wood cabins right next to the rushing Río Intag, where there's also a large and well-maintained pool under the looming hillsides. Meals (mains $4 to $6) can be arranged with a few hours' notice.

Almost next door are the **Nangulví Thermal Springs** (admission $3; ⊙7am-9pm), a

## INTAG ACTIVISM

In the rural Intag Valley, trees are weighted with tropical fruit and kids ride horses bridled with a scrap of rope – an unlikely hotbed of activism. And yet residents have successfully curbed copper mining (www.decoin.org), started a community newspaper (www.intagnewspaper.org) and organized coffee cooperatives.

In 2012 the reintroduction of native crops began, in a large program designed to get farmers who've stopped to once again plant the crops that have been grown in the Andes for hundreds, if not thousands, of years. The project aims to restore over 100 varieties of indigenous crops and medicinal plants, including tree tomatoes, hot peppers, root crops, seven species of potato, and quinoa.

Another goal of the scheme is to increase agricultural biodiversity and maintain culinary traditions, and as such it is run in part by the **Union of Peasant and Indigenous Organizations of Cotacachi** (www.unorcac.org, in Spanish). It's possible to see and taste the results by booking a stay in a rural, family-run lodge through Otavalo's Runa Tupari Native Travel. You'll eat meals alongside your hosts, who prepare dishes using ingredients grown in their gardens.

complex of tiled pools, which, while admittedly having seen better days, remains a gorgeous place to unwind, especially at sunset as the valley grows dark around you. There's also a cluster of **cabins** (r per person $12) and a restaurant with $2 set meals to maximize on-site soaking.

Pass through town to Cuellaje to reach **Finca San Antonio** (☎264-8627; www.intag tour.com; r per person $8). The farm houses guests in basic cabins or dorm rooms or arranges for stays with families. Meals cost extra, although there's a kitchen if you want to bring and prepare your own food. Guests can pay extra for guided hikes, a visit to a nearby cheesemaker and trout fishing.

Buses from Otavalo ($3, 2½ hours) run to Apuela at least four times daily. Some roads can become impassable during the rainy season.

### JUNÍN
☎06

Continue further into remote Andean hills on the road to Junín, taking in the view near the farming village of García Moreno, where a narrow ridge fringed with banana trees drops to hills rolling toward the horizon.

The highly recommended **Junín Community Reserve** (☎08-149-1654, 08-887-1860; www.junincloudforest.com; r per person incl meals $35, volunteers $25) operates a three-story bamboo lodge that's popular with birdwatchers. Relax in a hammock on the terrace, peruse the orchid collection, then hike to waterfalls with attentive Spanish-speaking guides. Bunkrooms are plain but snug, and

vegetarian meals come with robust cups of Intag coffee.

Contact the center in advance to visit or volunteer (the work varies from teaching English and computer skills to maintaining trails and working on the farm). In the rainy season bus services are limited on the muddy roads; arrange for transportation or a guide with the reserve.

## Reserva Biológica Los Cedros

This fantastic, remote reserve is set in 64 sq km of primary forest contiguous with the Reserva Ecológica Cotacachi-Cayapas. It is one of the only access points to the Southern Chocó, a forest ecosystem considered to be one of the most diverse bioregions on the planet. Living treasures include more than 240 species of birds, 400 types of orchids and more than 960 nocturnal moths.

Guests of **Los Cedros** (☎286-5176; www. reservaloscedros.org; r per person $50) arrive at the village of Chontal and undertake a rugged four- to six-hour hike through the Magdalena river valley into the Cordillera de la Plata. Contact the reserve in advance to arrange for a guide, pack animals and accommodations. Facilities include a scientific research station, dining and cooking facilities, accommodations in dorms or private rooms, hot water and electricity. The price includes all meals and guide services, but a three-night minimum stay is required. Volunteers are accepted ($450 per month, two week minimum).

There is a bus to Quito's La Ofelia bus station ($4, 3½ hours) several times a day, as well as painfully slow daily buses to Apuela ($2, three hours) and Otavalo ($4, eight hours).

## Ibarra

📍 06 / POP 132,000 / ELEV 2225M

Packed with a large and bustling population, Ibarra feels appropriately cosmopolitan, but despite its size the city still feels connected to the surrounding mountains. It's the patient, observant visitor who reaps the rewards of spending time in *la ciudad blanca* (the white city). Beautiful palm-lined parks and plazas modestly reveal fine colonial architecture, and friendly residents are happy to share these pockets of peace with outsiders.

The town seems uninterested in courting tourists, so infrastructure is lacking. But the hotels fill up quickly during the last two weeks of September during Ibarra's annual fiesta, a lively event with food, music and dancing.

## 👁 Sights & Activities

### Parque La Merced                        SQUARE
Also known as Peñaherrera, the city's main plaza was built at the beginning of the 19th century. The main feature of the **Iglesia de la Merced** is a gold leaf–covered altar for the Virgen de la Merced, patron saint of the armed forces. The church holds a special mass in remembrance of the victims and survivors of the devastating 1868 earthquake.

### Parque Pedro Moncayo                    PARK
This gorgeous palm-filled plaza is dominated by the baroque-influenced **cathedral**. The altars are covered in gold leaf, and Troya's paintings of the 12 apostles adorn the pillars. The park itself is named after locally born

## Ibarra

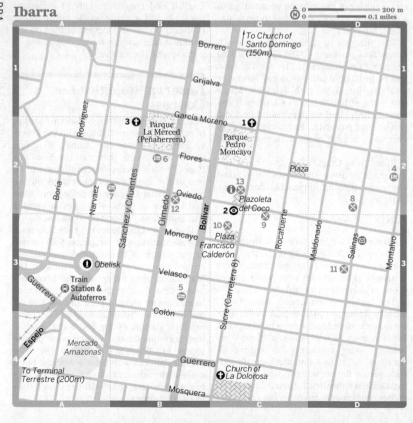

Pedro Moncayo (1807–88), a journalist and diplomat.

### Iglesia de Santo Domingo          CHURCH
At the north end of Bolívar you'll find the quaint **Parque Santo Domingo**. The Dominican church behind this small park houses *La Virgen del Rosarío*, a painting by famous artist Diego de Robles, on its altar.

### Plazoleta del Coco          PLAZA
On the corner of Oviedo and Sucre is this little plaza. Here you'll find the tourist office.

### Centro Cultural          MUSEUM
(admission $1; ⊙8:30am-6pm Mon-Fri, 10am-5pm Sat) The cultural center houses an archaeology museum featuring prehistoric ceramics and gold artifacts from Pimampiro, with signs in English. There's also a local historical archive and library.

## 🛏 Sleeping

While you'll find plenty of budget options in town (make sure there's hot water), the larger, pricier hotels are west of town, near the Panamericana. They're often booked in advance, particularly on weekends.

### Hostal del Río          GUESTHOUSE $
(📞261-1885, 08-006-4163; cnr Montalvo 4-55 & Flores; r per person $20-30; 🅿🛜) Fusing modern art deco with regional colonial style, this excellent option starts with a curved staircase leading to rooms with red hardwood floors, snug fluffy beds and bright balconies. Some rooms have Jacuzzis ($30 per night). Located in a quiet neighborhood a few blocks east of downtown.

### Hostería Chorlaví          HISTORIC HOTEL $$$
(📞293-2222; www.haciendachorlavi.com; Panamericana Sur 4½; s/d incl breakfast $72/82; 🅿🛜🏊) Weekenders flock to this classic, converted hacienda to enjoy the swimming pool and tennis courts. It's a charming place, with rooms stuffed full of antiques, yet remains pleasantly understated. It's best avoided on weekends when live music draws tour groups and shoppers from Otavalo, creating a less-than-peaceful getaway. To get here, drive 4.5km south of Ibarra on the Panamericana and the hotel is signed off to the right.

### Hotel Imbabura          HOTEL $
(📞295-8522; Oviedo 9-33; r per person $7) The revamped courtyard of this 100-year-old-plus colonial hacienda oozes history and character. However, rooms aren't quite as grand as the entrance might lead you to believe: all share bathrooms and are fairly bare – if clean – with drop ceilings and peeling walls. The talkative owner loves to show guests his collection of mini spirits bottles.

### Hotel Barcelona          HOTEL $
(📞260-0871; Flores 8-51 btwn Olmedo & Sánchez y Cifuentes; r per person without/with private bathroom $8/10; 🅿🛜) Spacious rooms in this old colonial building circle a light, central courtyard. Rooms themselves are rather worn. Ask for one that faces the park for an inspiring view and plenty of light.

### Hostal El Ejecutivo          HOTEL $
(📞295-6575; Bolívar 9-69; s/d $7.50/14) Despite the rather dingy lobby area, the rooms at this still rather misnamed place are good: spacious, comfortable and, on the street side, with balconies. It also has cable TV and friendly staff.

## 🍴 Eating

### 🔝 CHOICE La Hacienda          DELI $
(cnr Oviedo & Sucre; sandwiches $3; ⊙7:30am-10:30pm) Pull up a hay-stuffed bench at this friendly, barn-themed deli. Baguette sandwiches are the specialty, but if you've got dining companions, try the multiperson tapas plates ($15) for two to three people. It also offers a full breakfast menu and some of the only decent coffee in town.

### Café Arte
DELI $

(Salinas 5-43; mains $5-8; ⊗5pm-midnight Mon-Sat) This dark, candlelit space adorned with rotating contemporary-art exhibitions is a cozy spot for mingling with locals over drinks. Munch on nachos and beer or opt for a sandwich and espresso.

### Donde el Argentino
ARGENTINE $

(Plaza Francisco Calderón, at Sucre; mains $5-10; ⊗noon-9pm Tue-Sun) Transport yourself south in this matchbox-size cafe packed with ambience. Go for the excellent steaks and fries. Outdoor tables on the square expand the space on sunny days.

### Degloria
CAFE $

(⊘295-0699; Oviedo 5-45; desserts & mains $3-6; ⊗8:30am-8pm) Happy cooks in white chef hats create sweet treats in this dessert cafe's open kitchen. Creamy *tres leches* (milk cake) and fruit pies are the main event, but crepes and salads shouldn't be ignored.

### Entretenedores
CAFE $

(Moncayo 2-13; set meals $2.75; ⊗8am-5pm Mon-Sat) You'll find a surprisingly cheap four-course lunch of home-cooked *comida típica* (traditional Ecuadorian food) here at this charming place with a sunken main floor and plenty of rustic decoration.

## ☆ Entertainment

Ibarra is a quiet city, but Café Arte (Salinas 5-43; ⊗5pm-3am Fri & Sat) is one of the best live-music venues in Ecuador and is well worth checking out while you're in town. Bringing bands from as far as Cuba and Spain, the club's music varies from jazz and flamenco to rock. Shows start Fridays and Saturdays around 10pm. Films, dance les-sons and art shows are also regularly on the program.

##  Information

**Tourist office** (iTur; ⊘260-8489; cnr Oviedo & Sucre; ⊗8:30am-1pm & 2-5pm Mon-Fri) Helpful English-speaking staff can organize community tourism and advise on other activities, including mountaineering and hiking.

**Post office** (Salinas 6-64)

## ⓘ Getting There & Around

Ibarra's modern bus terminal, Terminal Terrestre, is located at the end of Avenida Teodoro Gomez de la Torre, near Espejo. You can grab a taxi to/from downtown for $1.

Buses to the village of La Esperanza ($0.25, 25 minutes) leave from the north side of Parque German Grijalva in the center of town.

# La Esperanza
⊘06 / ELEV 2992M

This picturesque village is set against the sloping flanks of **Volcán Imbabura** (4609m), 7km south of Ibarra. The village is a respite for the roadweary as well as the best spot to climb Imbabura. To climb the peak, start in the early morning and follow the escalating ridge 2000m to the summit, 8km southwest. The last stretch is a scramble over loose rock. If you're not experienced, hire a local guide. Allow for 10 hours round-trip. Those of middling ambition can try the easier three-hour climb to **Loma Cubilche** (3886m), a hill south of La Esperanza with lovely views.

Rest up for your adventure at the affable **Casa Aida** (⊘266-0221; www.casaaida.com; Calle Gallo Plaza; r per person $7; ⊛). Brightly

---

## THE CONE OF ETERNAL YOUTH

Teenage boredom inspired Rosalía Suárez to invent ice creams in the kitchen back in 1897, when she was just 17. Her experimentation led to a discovery – the best ice cream had no cream at all. Rosalía decided to share the sweet treat, and her shop, **Heladería Rosalía Suárez** (Oviedo 7-82; ⊗9am-5pm), has been a sensation for more than a century. *Helados de paila* are actually sorbets stirred with a wooden spoon in a large copper bowl (the *paila*) and cooled on a bed of straw and ice. The shop, now run by her grandson, claims the recipe requires pure juice from tropical fruits and egg whites. It's not entirely possible to imitate, though: ice for the first versions was brought down from the glacier of Volcán Imbabura, which has since disappeared.

Doña Rosalía lived until the age of 105, which speaks something to the restorative qualities of a good *helado*. It's a theory worth testing, anyway. *Guanábana* (similar to soursop) is the shop's most popular flavor. The tart *naranjilla* (a tropical fruit) – known as *lulo* – and *maracuyá* (passion fruit) are also worth a lick.

## BUSES FROM IBARRA

| DESTINATION | COST (US$) | DURATION (HRS) |
| --- | --- | --- |
| Quito | 3 | 2½ |
| Guayaquil | 10 | 10 |
| San Lorenzo | 4 | 4 |
| Ambato | 5 | 5 |
| Tulcán | 2.70 | 2½ |
| Otavalo | 0.45 | 30 |
| Cuenca | 14 | 12 |
| El Ángel | 1.25 | 1½ |
| Santo Domingo | 5 | 6 |

painted rooms are simple but clean and comfortable. Aida is a great source of local information and will make you feel at home with her famous hearty pancakes, box lunches and dinners. She can help arrange a guide for an Imbabura summit.

You can walk here from Ibarra, take one of the frequent buses ($0.25, 25 minutes) or get a taxi for about $5.

## North of Ibarra
☑06

The smooth Panamericana snakes north, offering plenty of pavement to spandex-clad cyclists, who pound up this punishing route on weekends. Entering the **Río Chota valley** at 1565m, the road drops sharply. Round, dry hills covered with cacti surround a lush green valley floor fed by the chocolaty river. Within an hour's drive from Ibarra, this always-warm valley is within arm's reach for day trips.

One place worth checking out is **Grutas de la Paz**, where you'll find a famous grotto converted to a chapel as well as **thermal springs** (☉Thu-San) and waterfalls within easy reach by foot. Other notable sights off the Panamericana include the waterfalls at **Las Cascadas de Paluz**, 3km north of San Gabriel, and the palm-lined hotels with swimming pools in and around Ambuquí.

Sugarcane thrives here, and the valley's inhabitants, Afro-Ecuadorians descended from 17th-century plantation slaves, grow and harvest the crop. Stop at any roadside stand for a juicy sugarcane stick. Farmers here also produce a variety of fruits, beans, yuca and tomatoes.

A token of the unique Afro-Andean culture is *bomba* music, a blend of driving African drums and plaintive highland notes. At bus stops and fruit stands, children dance to the beat in their heads. Fiestas and concerts are irregular, but are sometimes advertised in Ibarra.

## El Ángel
☑06 / POP 3900 / ELEV 3000M

Tufts of ocher grasses ripple along the hillsides surrounding the stark, still Andean village of El Ángel. The village is the entry point to Páramos El Ángel, a misty wilderness favored by foxes and condors. It's part of the 160-sq-km **Reserva Ecológica El Ángel** (admission $2), which is home to *frailejones* – rare, otherworldly plants with fuzzy leaves and thick trunks. You can arrange *páramo* visits with local hotels. The village springs to life with a Monday market.

**El Ángel Hostería** (☑297-7584; Panamericana Norte & Av Espejo 1302; r per person $18) has snug high-ceilinged cabins with comfortable beds and modern bathrooms. The well-run *hostería* (small hotel) offers guided hikes to the reserve and city tours in English or German. It's a 10-minute walk to town.

There are a few restaurants on the town's main plaza, which is full of inventively manicured hedges. Simplest of all is **Cevichería El Golosito** (mains $3-5) where you'll find locals crowding in to enjoy bowls of delicious ceviche. Slightly more upmarket is **Restaurante Doña Mary** (mains $5-8), which is a classier place for a traditional Andean meal.

Transportes Espejo, on the main plaza, goes to Quito ($3.70, four hours) via Ibarra ($1.25, 1½ hours) every hour. There's also a daily bus to Tulcán ($1.50, 1½ hours). At the plaza you'll find shared taxis going to and from the Bolívar crossroads ($1), from where frequent buses go north to Tulcán and south to Ibarra and Quito. Private 4WD vehicles can also be rented on the plaza for excursions into the reserve.

## Reserva Biológica Guandera

This 1000-hectare, tropical, wet, montane forest reserve was founded in 1994 by Fundación Jatun Sacha. The reserve lies between 3100m and 3600m on a transitional ridge (forest to *páramo*) 11km east of San Gabriel. Projects include reforestation and finding alternatives to chemical-intensive potato production. Andean spectacled bears (rarely glimpsed), high-altitude parrots and toucans are among the attractions. Jatun Sacha operates a **refuge** (dm $15). Reservations are required and fees must be paid in advance at the **Jatun Sacha office** (in Quito 02-243-2240; www.jatunsacha.org; cnr Eugenio de Santillán N34-248 & Maurián, Urbanización Rumipamba) in Quito. The reserve takes volunteers for a minimum two-week visit.

From the village of San Gabriel it is 1½ hours on foot to the reserve, but the office can arrange a ride with prior notice.

## Río Mira Valley

06

Ditch your highland woolen clothing for the twisty, scenic ride to the steamy tropic lowlands abutting the northern coast. Farmers tend crops of sugarcane, bananas and tropical fruits on the steep slopes of the 1000m valley.

**Bosque de Paz** (264-8692; www.bospas.org; dm/r incl breakfast per person $13/18, volunteers per day/month $18/235) on the outskirts of **El Limonal**, is run by a friendly Ecuadorian/Belgian couple. Comfortable lodge accommodations are in a lush setting, a 15-minute walk from the bus stop. The food is wonderful (tending toward coastal specialities; mains $4 to $7), and guided hikes are offered. Owner Piet enthusiastically imparts his knowledge of tropical plants and preservation. The farm promotes reforestation and organic pest-control in this highly deforested area. Located 1½ hours from Ibarra.

## Tulcán

06 / POP 53,500 / ELEV 3000M

The busy highland city of Tulcán is the last Ecuadorian stop for visitors headed overland to Colombia. The high altitude creates a constant chill, even among the narrow streets packed with pedestrians, and there's a seedy feel overall. This provincial capital of Carchi used to attract Colombians bargain-hunting with the Ecuadorian sucre (Ecuador's currency before dollarization), but these days Colombian imports are the more coveted deals. Overall, it's a pretty grim place with little to recommend it, but as the first or last major town in Ecuador it gets quite a few visitors passing through.

### ⊙ Sights & Activities

**Cementerio de Tulcán**　　　　CEMETERY
Tulcán is well known for its quiet cemetery and topiary garden. A maze of cypress trees – sculpted into bulbous, pre-Columbian totems, mythological figures, animals and geometric shapes – lines graves and mausoleums ornamented with candles and plastic flowers. Bushes and hedges take shape as they're trimmed by the son of the original topiary master and another artist.

On the weekends, behind the cemetery, locals play an Ecuadorian paddleball game called *pelota de guante*, which requires a soft ball and large, spiked paddles.

**Museo Arqueologico**　　　　MUSEUM
(admission $0.50; 9am-4pm) Walk one block south from the cemetery to this mural-covered museum, which houses pre-Columbian artifacts, ceramics, and modern and contemporary art.

**Aguas Hediondas**　　　　SPRINGS
Literally 'stinking waters,' these hot, high-sulfur thermal springs 16km from Tulcán and 6km beyond the town of Tufiño certainly live up to their name. Many of the pools are on the Colombian side of the border; you can cross the border on a day pass, but those who want to stay overnight must enter via the Tulcán border crossing. Get there before 4pm when the springs take on extra stench; go on weekdays to avoid crowds.

### Volcán Chiles
VOLCANO

Beyond the baths on the main road, this impressive peak (4768m) offers a challenging six-hour summit on the border of Colombia. The peak offers spectacular views; locals say that on a clear day you can see the ocean. Take a bus or taxi to Tufiño and hire a guide in the town's main square. Ask locally about the safety of travel in this remote border region due to ongoing instability in Colombia.

## 🛏 Sleeping

Tulcán has no shortage of hotels, but most fall short on charm. Most travelers coming from Colombia continue directly on to Ibarra or Otavalo where there are far more pleasant places to spend the night.

### Hotel Sara Espindola
HOTEL $$

(☑298-2043; cnr Sucre & Ayacucho; s/d/tr incl breakfast $31/42/53; 🕸) The fact that this is supposedly the town's best hotel is a statement in itself: this modern monolith has seen far better days. Still, comfortable rooms and an eager staff aren't found elsewhere. It also has a sauna and restaurant on-site.

### Hotel San Francisco
HOTEL $

(☑298-0760; Bolívar near Atahualpa; r per person $7) While comparisons with the Bay City are scant, this vertical hotel is probably the best budget option in town. Outer rooms are brighter and airier than those next door at Hotel Azteca Internacional, and have TV.

### Hotel Azteca Internacional
HOTEL $

(☑298-0481; cnr Bolívar & Atahualpa; r per person $7) Dark-paneled, cavernous, carpeted rooms create a '70s feel. It has a sauna and rooms have firm beds and a TV, but charm is not exactly a salient feature.

## 🍴 Eating

Tulcán's eating scene is decidedly unexciting, despite lots of Colombian influence on the street food. By the border, there are plenty of snack stalls and fast-food carts.

### Fritadas Mama Miche
ECUADORIAN $

(cnr Bolívar & Junin; mains $2-5; 🕘9am-9pm) Serving up *fritadas* (pork fried in spices and pork fat – popular with dieters) for over 50 years, Mama Miche's is the most popular place in town to eat this northern Ecuadorian speciality.

### San Francisco
ECUADORIAN $

(cnr Junín & Bolívar; mains $4-8; 🕘9am-10pm) This rather sterile place is nonetheless very popular with locals and a good bet for a filling meal. It has an enormous menu and a reliable *plato del día* (daily special; $3.50). Don't miss the fresh berry desserts and ice creams.

### Mama Rosita
ECUADORIAN $

(Sucre near Chimborazo; mains $2-4; 🕘9am-7pm) Famous for its *fritada* and other *comida típica*, this friendly but unassuming place also excels at pork dishes.

## ℹ Information

Exchanging money (between US dollars and Colombian pesos) is slightly better in Tulcán than at the border. If the currency-exchange centers are closed, try the street money changers in front of the banks. They are associated and wear ID numbers you can record in case of later problems.

**Clínica Metropolitana** (cnr Sucre & Panamá; 🕘24hr) A better hospital is in Ipiales, 2km north of the border.

**Colombian consulate** (☑298-0559; Bolívar & Ayacucho; 🕘8am-2pm Mon-Fri)

**Tourist office** (iTur; ☑298-5760; Cotopaxi; 🕘8am-6pm Mon-Fri) At the cemetery entrance. Staff are friendly and helpful.

**Post office** (Bolívar near Junín)

## ℹ Getting There & Away

### Border Crossings

Entering Colombia via the Panamericana north of Tulcán is currently the only recommended crossing between the two countries. All formalities are taken care of at the Ecuador–Colombia border crossing, Rumichaca, 6km away. The border is open between 6am and 10pm daily. Even day-trippers to Ipiales will need their passport stamped.

Fourteen-seat minibuses to the border leave as soon as they are full, about every 10 minutes, between 6am and 7:30pm, from Tulcán's Parque Isidro Ayora. The fare is $0.80 (Colombian currency is also accepted). Taxis to the border ($3.50) leave from the same location.

On the Colombian side, entrance formalities are straightforward. Check with the Colombian consulate to make sure your nationality doesn't require a visa. Visas are good for 30 to 90 days.

From the border, there is frequent taxi transportation to Ipiales, the first town in Colombia, 2km away, for $1. There you'll find plenty of hotels and connections; see Lonely Planet's *Colombia* or *South America on a Shoestring* for more information.

## Bus

Buses traveling to Ibarra ($2.50, 2½ hours), El Ángel ($1.50, 1½ hours) and Quito ($4.80, five hours) leave from the bus terminal. Note that there can be a thorough customs/immigration check between Tulcán and Ibarra.

### ℹ Getting Around

The **bus terminal** (cnr Arellano & Bolívar) is inconveniently located 2.5km southwest of downtown on the road to Ibarra. City buses ($0.20) run southwest from downtown along Bolívar and will deposit you at the terminal. To get downtown from the terminal, take a taxi for $1 or cross the street and catch the city bus.

# WESTERN ANDEAN SLOPES

The old road to Santo Domingo wends atop dramatic drop-offs while descending through lush, misty cloud forests. Within just a few hours of Quito, visitors can experience a welcome climate shock in the cool, humid hills. The area is known for its bird-watching, but the landscape inspires mountain-biking, horseback-riding and hiking, as well. Mindo is the big draw here: a sleepy village that has in the past few years developed significantly and is now full of charming lodging options for the large number of nature-lovers who flock here. Elsewhere in the region small villages, including Nanegalito and Nanegal, serve as gateways to remote lodges and reserves for those seeking to get way off the beaten track.

## Cloud Forest Lodges

 02

### TANDAYAPA

**Tandayapa Bird Lodge** (☎244-7520, 09-923-1314; www.tandayapa.com; s/d incl meals $126/213) is a serious bird-watcher's paradise, with such highlights as the Andean cock-of-the-rock, scaled fruiteater and golden-headed and crested quetzals. With just 12 bedrooms (two of which are pleasantly isolated on the grounds), the feel is intimate and laid-back here, with a very definite emphasis on bird-watching. The lodge offers multilingual bird-watching guides, comfortable accommodation in the cloud forest with a great viewing balcony, a canopy platform and an enormous number of trails for day trips. Well-placed fruit feeders increase sightings from the lodge. Prices do not include bird guides, who must be booked well in advance, though volunteer guides are often available and there is no charge for going on bird-watching walks with them. To get here from Quito, turn at the 32km point, down the road branching south, and continue 6km to the town of Tandayapa. A pickup from Quito costs $85 per car.

### BOSQUE NUBLADO SANTA LUCÍA

A foray into **Bosque Nublado Santa Lucía** (☎215-7242; www.santaluciaecuador.com; dm/r with shared bathroom per person incl meals $35/56, cabins per person incl meals $75) inspires wonder. This is a trip for the adventurous. The rustic lodge, a steep one- to two-hour hike from the road (mules carry the luggage), rests on the tip of a peak with commanding 360-degree views of lush hills and valleys. Bird-watching and hiking opportunities are excellent. Rooms in the lodge are basic but comfortable, with mostly twin beds, and there are shared bathrooms, composting toilets and solar-powered electricity. New and comparatively luxurious cabañas with impressive views over the cloud forest sleep two to three people and have private bathrooms. You'll get local flavor from the friendly administrator and chef, who cooks up excellent meals that include salad, potato pancakes and hearty soups.

The reserve is owned and run by a cooperative of 12 families who, looking for a more sustainable future, stopped farming *naranjilla* with pesticides to work with tourism and preservation. Considered one of the country's best examples of community tourism, Santa Lucía has won numerous awards for sustainability and reducing poverty. Volunteers are welcome.

A minimum stay of three days is recommended, with entry into the reserve and guide service for the first and last day included in the price. Certified guides from the local families speak basic English and know the scientific names for plants and birds. Transportation by 4WD from Nanegal to the base of the trail is $20 for the trip (for singles or groups), while it's a further $20 if you want to ride a mule up to the lodge instead of hiking. Transportation from Quito is $70 one-way.

### RESERVA BIOLÓGICA MAQUIPUCUNA

Preserving a large swath of the important Chocó-Andean bioregion, this 60-sq-km reserve offers opportunities for hiking, bird-watching and relaxing. Its territory covers a variety of premontane and montane cloud forests in the headwaters of Río Alambi at elevations ranging from 1200m to 2800m. The area, about 80km northwest of Quito, is truly wonderful and is home to a lodge and research station.

About 80% of the reserve is primary forest; the remainder is secondary growth. The reserve has 370 species of birds, including 30 species of hummingbirds (a bird list is available); 240 species of butterflies; and 45 species of mammals, including the spectacled bear, which can regularly be seen here during the fruiting season of a small avocado-like fruit called *aguacatillo*. The nonprofit Fundación Maquipucuna administers the reserve, which it purchased in 1988.

*Maquipucuna Lodge* (www.maqui. org; r with shared/private bathroom per person incl meals $55/65) Offers guests great deck views from the hammocks and tasty, healthy meals at the restaurant, which serves its own shade-grown coffee. In addition to a variety of lodge rooms, there's a family cabin with two bathrooms and a private deck. Day guests pay a $10 entry fee and can hire a guide for $25, though it's well worth taking the time to spend at least one night here. Trails range from an easy 1km walk to a demanding 5.5km hike, while specialized guided tours of the coffee-growing process or wild orchids are also available. The Fundación can arrange a private vehicle from Quito for $80. If you're driving, you'll need a 4WD for the 7km from the main road.

**RESERVA BELLAVISTA**
This 700-hectare reserve is in the same western Andean slopes as Maquipucuna at about 2000m above sea level. About 25% is primary forest, and the rest has been selectively or completely logged but is regenerating. Various conservation projects are under way. There are 8km of well-marked trails, and the area is highly recommended by bird-watchers (320 species of birds have been recorded).

*Bellavista Lodge* (211-6232, 09-416-5868; www.bellavistacloudforest.com; dm $32, s/d incl meals $120/205) is a wooden geodesic dome with a jaw-dropping panoramic view. There's a library/restaurant/bar on the ground floor, over which are five small rooms topped by a two-story dormitory area with a shared bathroom, restaurant and balcony. Light pours into these cozy rooms, but if you prefer privacy, larger private cabins are a short walk from the lodge. About a kilometer away is a research station with a kitchen for self-catering and a 12-bed dormitory for travelers on a budget. For an extra charge meals can also be catered for those staying in the dorm.

Guided hikes and horseback-riding are offered, as are multiday packages. Trucks in Nanegalito, 56km along the Quito–Puerto Quito road, charge $15 to the lodge; they're lined up on the western side, where a small sign reads 'Bellavista transport.'

# Mindo

♪02 / POP 2000 / ELEV 1250M

With its breathtaking setting surrounded on all sides by steep mountainsides of cloud forest, tiny Mindo has become something of a backpacker buzzword in Ecuador and now lives and breathes tourism. Helpfully located just off the main road between Quito and Esmeraldas, Mindo is entered by a dramatically steep and curvy hillside descent that takes you down past dozens of hotels and lodges to a rather ramshackle yet immensely likable town center. Bird watchers, hikers and weekenders from Quito and beyond all flock here, and friendly locals have created an impressive range of activities for enjoying the cloud forest: butterfly farms, zip lines over the treetops, mountain-biking, tubing and orchid collections.

## ◉ Sights & Activities

**Tarabita**                         CABLE CAR
(Rd to Cascada de Nambillo; cable car per person $2, entrance to falls $3; ⊙8:30am-4pm, closed Mon) This unique hand-powered cable car takes you soaring across a lush river basin over thick cloud forest to the Bosque Protector Mindo-Nambillo, where there's a number of waterfalls you can hike to along well-signposted trails. The perfectly safe wire basket on steel cables glides 152m above the ground and, though certainly not for the vertiginous, is a superb way to get above the forest and enjoy incredible views. Your ticket includes a map with routes shown on it; while the Cascade Nambillo is the closest (15 minutes' walk), it's the series of five waterfalls (one hour's walk) that's really worth making the effort to see. The *tarabita* is a 4km taxi ride ($2) from town.

## THE EARLY BIRD GETS...THE MATE

While most birds preen and strut to attract members of the opposite sex, the Andean cock-of-the-rock *(Rupicola peruvianus)* takes top prize for persistence.

Every day, rain or shine, male cocks-of-the-rock, with their bulbous coif of blood-red or orange feathers, gather at 6am and squawk loudly, dance on branches and dive and wrangle with each other, hoping to win some female attention. This all-male revue is called a 'lek' for any bird species. If they're lucky, a drab-brown female will dive into the crowd and choose a mate, but more often than not, females don't show.

How can the plainer sex resist the impressive display? Maybe they're too busy single-parenting; alone, females build nests and care for their offspring while males remain focused on the daily possibility of mating.

Cock-of-the-rock leks are prevalent around Mindo. If you're interested in the flirting behavior of the dashing crimson cock-of-the-rock, grab a local guide or inquire at your hostel about tours. Witnessing the spectacle requires a predawn wakeup call.

**Mariposas de Mindo**    BUTTERFLY FARM
(☏224-2712; www.mariposasdemindo.com; admission $5; ☺9am-4pm) Mindo has several butterfly farms, but this is the best of them. Visit in the warmest part of the day, around 11am, when butterflies are most active. It also has a restaurant and lodging.

**Armonía Orchid Garden**    GARDENS
(www.birdingmindo.com; admission $2; ☺7am-5pm) Check out the blooms at this impressive collection of more than 200 orchids.

**Zip-Lining**    ADVENTURE SPORT
Halfway up the road to the *tarabita,* two dueling zip-line companies compete for adrenaline seekers. Fly over the canopy in a harness attached to a cable strung above the trees, an activity that gets faster in the rain: this is Mindo's most high-adrenaline adventure and it's very popular. The original company, **Mindo Canopy Adventure** (☏09-453-0624; www.mindocanopy.com; 2½hr circuit per person $15), has 13 different cables ranging from 20m to 400m in length. **Mindo Ropes & Canopy** (☏09-172-5874; www.mindoropes canopy.com; 2½hr circuit per person $15) offers a similar experience on 12 cables.

**Tubing**    ADVENTURE SPORT
(per person with 4-person minimum $5) This is a very popular activity around Mindo, with places that rent inner tubes lining Avenida Quito. The price should include a guide, which is essential for safety, as tubing the rapids on the Río Mindo is extremely dangerous unless you know what you're doing. This was tragically evidenced by a spate of deaths in 2008 and 2009, when tubers drowned during the rainy season. Therefore,

err on the side of extreme caution and don't go tubing after heavy rains.

##  Tours

**La Isla**    ECOTOUR
(☏217-0181, 09-743-4667; Av Quito & 9 de Octubre) This outfit certainly lives up to its slogan – 'nature and adventure' – offering horseback-riding, canyoning, tubing and bird-watching excursions. The activities can be combined into one- or two-day trips. English is spoken.

### Bird-Watching Guides

With more than 400 species of birds recorded, Mindo has become a major center for bird-watchers. Locally there are many competent, professional guides. Although many speak only Spanish, guides still know the bird names in English and can easily guide non-Spanish speakers. Most charge between $80 and $220 per day.

**Fernando Arias**    BIRD-WATCHING
(☏08-388-3865; tntedoblef@yahoo.es) A knowledgeable bird-watcher who cut his teeth at El Monte and is now based at Mindo Gardens Lodge.

**Irman Arias**    BIRD-WATCHING
(☏09-170-8720, 217-0168; www.mindobirdguide. com) An excellent English-speaking local bird guide.

**Marcelo Arias**    BIRD-WATCHING
(☏09-340-6321; marceloguideofbirds@yahoo. com) This guide comes highly recommended by many readers.

**Juan Carlos Calvachi**    BIRD-WATCHING
(☏09-966-4503, 286-5213; calvachi@uio.satnet. net) A top guide from Quito who speaks

perfect English; $220 per day for three people including transportation.

**Danny Jumbo**                    BIRD-WATCHING
(☏09-328-0769) Highly recommended local guide who speaks English.

**Nolberto Jumbo**                 BIRD-WATCHING
(☏08-563-8011) An experienced and knowledgeable guide.

**Julia Patiño**                   BIRD-WATCHING
(☏390-0419, 08-616-2816; juliaguideofbird@ya hoo.com) A highly recommended guide. The first woman to guide in town.

**Sandra Patiño**                  BIRD-WATCHING
(☏09-935-9363) Provides excellent guiding in English and comes highly recommended locally.

**Jorge Pilco**                    BIRD-WATCHING
(☏08-296-4705; jorpian17@hotmail.com) A licensed and experienced guide who speaks some English.

## 🛏 Sleeping

Mindo's accommodation scene has exploded in the past few years, with scores of places offering accommodations for all budgets. In general, the smarter places are out of town and have plenty of green space for guests to relax in, while those in town are more budget or midrange. Don't be shy about asking locals for directions since there are no street signs.

### IN TOWN

TOP CHOICE **Caskaffesu**           GUESTHOUSE $
(☏217 0100, 09 386 7154; www.caskaffesu.com; Sixto Duran Ballen & Av Quito; r per person $16; ☏) Supremely popular among readers who continually write to praise this chilled-out and friendly spot, Caskaffesu is run by American expat Susan. Among her other virtues, she considers instant coffee to be a cruel and unusual punishment and makes sure that only the good locally-grown stuff goes to her guests. The two stories of brick and rock rooms are brightly painted, and all have private bathrooms, although rooms are fairly Spartan otherwise. Downstairs you'll find a popular restaurant and a charming garden courtyard. Highly recommended!

**Dragonfly Inn**                  GUESTHOUSE $$
(☏217-0462, 09-238-2189; www.dragonflyinn -mindo.com; s/d incl breakfast $27/46; ☏) An attractive wooden structure by the bridge in the middle of town with spotless wood-paneled rooms, comfy beds and balconies in each room, and a small garden where hummingbirds flit.

**La Casa de Cecilia**             HOSTEL $
(☏217-0243, 09-334-5393; lacasadececiliamindo@ hotmail.com; camping per person $2, dm/r $6/7.50; ☏) Cecilia's warm reception spruces up this maze of bunk beds. You'll find an outdoor fireplace on the hammock deck and an open-air kitchen on the river. On nice days take advantage of the lovely swimming hole and sunbathing platform. Ask staff about long-term discounts and work exchanges.

**Mindo Real**                     GUESTHOUSE $$
(☏217-0120, 09-766-3845; www.mindoreal.com; r incl breakfast per person $25; ☏☏☏) Just far enough out of town to be tranquil but an easy 500m walk to all of Mindo's amenities, the Mindo Real is a two-building guesthouse with spacious, modern rooms and a friendly owner.

---

## PROTECTING THE CLOUD

Mindo is full of foundations and charities working hard to protect the incredibly biodiverse cloud forest and its plants, trees and animals.

The **Mindo Cloudforest Foundation** (www.mindocloudforest.org) operates two superb bird sanctuaries nearby: the **Milpe Bird Sanctuary**, a 250-acre reserve with a network of trails located 15km west of the 'Y,' and the **Río Silanche Sanctuary**. Entry is $9 per day for Milpe, $6 per day for Río Silanche, or $15 for a three-day pass with access to both. This nonprofit also produces shade-grown coffee, which converts cattle pasture into bird habitat.

**Mindo Animal Rescue** (www.mindoanimalrescue.com) is a superb organization that has been helping the victims of animal trafficking in the area for the past 10 years. The center, based in the middle of Mindo, also has a popular volunteer program that allows you to work for a very noble cause without being stuck in the middle of nowhere.

**Las Tangaras**  HOTEL **$$**
(☎217-0166, 08-567-6049; www.lastangaras.com.
ec; r per person incl breakfast $32-45; P@≋)
This sprawling place by the bridge in the
center of Mindo is popular with weekend-
ers from Quito, who come here to relax by
the pool and enjoy the sauna. It's a large ho-
tel, with contemporary rooms in the main
building and slightly more rustic ones out
the back around the pool.

**Rubby Hostal**  GUESTHOUSE **$**
(☎09-340-6321, 09-193-1853; rubbyhostal@yahoo.
com; r with shared/private bathroom per person
incl breakfast $9/15; ☜) At press time, this
well-loved hostel was building a new struc-
ture just beyond the main plaza. The new
building will have six rooms with private
bathrooms and three with shared facilities.
Owner Marcelo is a known bird-watching
guide with his own bird-watching tower in
the forest.

**Jardin de los Pájaros**  GUESTHOUSE **$**
(☎09-422-7624, 390-0459; Barrío El Progreso; r
per person incl breakfast $13-15; ☜≋) Take the
first right after you cross the bridge to find
this family-run guesthouse. The rooms are
large and comfortable and have cable TV.
The large, shaded deck makes for a pleasant
place to relax, as does the heated swimming
pool.

**Cabañas Armonía**  GUESTHOUSE **$$**
(☎217-0131, 09-943-5098; www.birdingmindo.
com; dm/r per person incl breakfast $15) Tucked
away in tousled, unkempt gardens, accommodations here are in quiet, rustic cabins
or dorm-style rooms in the main house. Attached is Armonía Orchid Garden.

**OUTSIDE OF TOWN**

🍃**El Monte Sustainable
Lodge**  JUNGLE LODGE **$$$**
(☎217-0102, 09-308-4675; www.ecuadorcloudfo
rest.com; cabins per person incl meals & activities
$118; ≋) Run by a warmhearted and knowl-
edgeable young American/Ecuadorian cou-
ple, El Monte is a lush retreat with three
lovely, private riverside cabins. The aesthetic
is contemporary and comfortable, with lots
of wood and natural tones. Three cabins
sleep up to four people and have bathtubs.
Located 4km south of Mindo along a wind-
ing dirt road, it's reached by the *tarabita*
over the Río Mindo (reservations are es-
sential). The communal lodge has rustic
furniture, fire pits, a library and some solar-
powered electricity. The food is delicious
and mostly vegetarian: candlelit dinners in-
clude pastas, empanadas, curries and salads
from the organic garden. Guided activities
include bird-watching, hiking and tubing,
but guests can also wander the on-site trails
or swim in the river-fed pool. Reserve ahead
so the owners can arrange transport from
Mindo. A two-night minimum is suggested.

🍃**Séptimo Paraíso**  JUNGLE LODGE **$$$**
(☎in Quito 02-317-1475, 09-368-4421; www.septi
moparaiso.com; r/ste incl breakfast $114/154, mains
$6-12; P☜≋) On the steep hillside descent
from the main road and 2km from Mindo
proper, this hidden-away yet super elegant
collection of wooden buildings is one of
Mindo's best hotels. Thoroughly ecologically
minded, 'seventh heaven' recycles 95% of
its waste. It also operates the Green Mindo
Foundation, which conducts cloud forest
research and bird counts; educates locals
on conservation efforts; reforests old pas-
tureland; and oversees a 420-acre reserve.
Rooms are rustic and understated, with
wood-paneled walls, splashes of color and
some wonderful antiques. The lodge also
has an excellent restaurant, Lo Chorrera,
a heated pool and Jacuzzi. Wireless access
costs $10 for your stay.

**Casa Divina**  CABINS **$$$**
(☎09-172-5874, 09-050-9626; www.mindocasadi
vina.com; s/d incl breakfast & dinner $110/195;
☜) Located 1km outside of town, this small
complex of three two-story luxurious wood-
en cabins makes for a perfect nature retreat
against a quiet, forested hillside. Porches
with hammocks provide comfortable roosts
for bird-watching, and short on-site trails
expand the observation territory. The own-
ers, a woodworker and baker, are extremely
welcoming hosts at this family-friendly loca-
tion. Highly recommended for seclusion and
tranquility with a splash of luxury.

**Mindo Gardens Lodge**  LODGE **$$**
(☎09-722-3260; www.mindogardens.com; s/d incl
breakfast $55/74) Owned by an Ecuadorian
hotel company, this place feels small and
personal. Pathways wind through wooded
gardens to a main lodge and cozy cabins.
The dining room has patio seating, and two-
story cabins have bright bedspreads. The
best rooms have river views. A trail on the
property leads to the *tarabita*. The lodge is
4km beyond Mindo on the road that passes
the butterfly farm.

### La Roulotte
CABINS **$$**

(📞08-976-4484; www.la.roulotte.ec; r per person incl breakfast $28; P) This innovative addition to Mindo's accommodation is 2km beyond the town itself on the road past the butterfly farm. Here five horse coach–shaped rooms manage to pack in quite a bit despite their small size: each comes with bunk beds, a fire place, a private bathroom and lots of color. Those craving space can enjoy the grounds of the hotel, where the friendly Ecuadorian–Swiss owners will whip you up a full meal or help you organize activities in the area.

### El Carmelo Hostería
CABINS **$$$**

(📞in Quito 02-222-4713; www.mindo.com.ec; cab ins per person incl breakfast from $61; P🛜❄) This complex of 29 cabins and three pools is popular with families, although it's looking rather worn these days. The most interesting thing here are the rather cool cabins on stilts, which allow you to live up high with the birds. Some rooms have Jacuzzis, and nature tours and horseback-riding are offered.

## ✗ Eating

Cheap and cheerful dining options line Av Quito and offer plenty of choice. If you're looking for something a bit special, try one of the following, or reserve for dinner at one of the smarter out-of-town lodges, which are nearly all open to nonguests for meals.

### TOP CHOICE⟩ El Quetzal
ECUADORIAN **$**

(www.elquetzaldemindo.com; Calle 9 de Octubre; mains $4-8; ⊙8am-11pm; 🛜) This wonderful, laid-back coffee shop and restaurant does it all right: there's excellent coffee as well as locally grown beans and chocolate for sale, a great selection of breakfasts and sandwich es, and a daily changing Ecuadorian main course. However, the real reason to visit is to try the locally famous (and enormous) brownie, the American owner's proud specialty.

### Caskaffesu
ECUADORIAN **$$**

(www.caskaffesu.com; Sixto Duran Ballen & Av Qui to; mains $5-10; ⊙8am-8pm; 🛜🍴) Dine in the spacious dining room near the fireplace or on the shady streetside patio at this highly recommended restaurant. The large menu is wonderfully varied and includes such Ecua dorian favorites as steamed trout and even a novel vegetarian take on ceviche (using lupin beans instead of fish). You'll also find good coffee here, and full breakfasts.

### Fuera de Babylonia
ECUADORIAN **$**

(Calle 9 de Octubre; mains $3-7; ⊙8am-10pm) The earthy jungle ambience at this curiously pre sented wooden restaurant attracts chilled out backpackers in search of Bob Marley and beer (*cerveza*). It can get raucous on the weekend. Try the pastas, steamed trout or beet soup. Located one block off the plaza.

### El Chef
STEAKHOUSE **$**

(Av Quito; mains $3-8; ⊙9am-7pm) A popular spot for set meals, this basic steakhouse siz zles and is a reliable choice. Try the *lomo a la piedra* (steak cooked on a 'stone') or a hearty burger.

## ❶ Information

There is one **ATM** (Plaza Grande) in Mindo and it's not always reliable, so be sure to bring cash with you. The nearest alternative ATM is in Los Bancos.

**Centro Municipal de Información Turística** (Av Quito & Plaza Grande) is a helpful, if rather erratically open, tourist office that gives out maps and advice on hiking, tours and lodging.

## ❶ Getting There & Away

We have had consistent complaints from readers about robberies on the Quito–Mindo bus route, so make sure your valuables are kept with you at all times during the journey.

There are several daily buses to Quito ($2.50, 2½ hours), run by **Cooperativa Flor de Valle**, which leave from the main plaza. From the same place **Cooperativa Kennedy** runs seven daily buses to Santo Domingo ($3, three hours), where it's possible to connect to services all over the coast. Many other buses between Quito and the coast can be picked up at the 'Y' at the top of the hill.

## ❶ Getting Around

A taxi cooperative runs from the plaza. Prices are higher than in other areas. A trip to the 'Y' costs $3. Drivers with private cars provide trans port around town and to Quito (one-way, $50).

# West of Mindo

This beautiful and out-of-the-way route links Quito to the western lowlands and coast. The town of **Los Bancos** provides ac cess to bird-watching in the **Milpe Sanctu ary**. Heading west, the landscape changes quickly, from cool cloud forest to hotter, lush lowlands as the road drops and flattens near **Puerto Quito**. Soon after, you'll hit the main road between Santo Domingo de los Colorados and the north-coast port of Esmeraldas.

## PEDRO VICENTE MALDONADO

This village is a strip of squat cement buildings fringed by steamy, lowland jungle. At the far edge of town you'll find **Arashá Rainforest Resort & Spa** (02-390-0007, 02-239-2150; www.arasharesort.com; r $149-390; ) nuzzling visitors in the lap of cloud forest luxury. The poshest spot on the western Andean slope, the resort is popular with nationals and families. Accommodations are in stilted thatched huts of different levels of luxury set among beautifully manicured grounds. The simplest rooms are the Eco Rooms, which are quite reasonably priced, while the deluxe bungalows are truly superb. In addition to bird-watching, hiking and wildlife-watching excursions, the resort offers an excellent spa, restaurant, pool, disco, a kids' swimming area and miniature golf. Package rates include transport to and from Quito, three meals a day, a spa treatment and guided tours. The hotel is 3km outside of Pedro Vicente Maldonado, on the old road to Santo Domingo, and about 200m off the main road to Puerto Quito.

## PUERTO QUITO

Not much goes on in Puerto Quito – and that's the charm. It's a relaxing place to see birds and waterfalls and swim in lazy rivers. There are frequent buses from Quito's bus terminal and Santo Domingo. There are a few budget hostels downtown, but better options are found outside town.

**Itapoa Reserve** (09-478-4992, 09-314-5894; www.itapoareserve.com; r per person incl breakfast $12; ) is a nonprofit reserve of lowland tropical rainforest, both the most endangered type of forest in Ecuador and the most biodiverse. By charging tourists to stay here and selling their excellent 'Chocolate to Save the Rainforest,' the reserve funds its project and gradually buys more jungle for conservation. All the plants produced on the reserve are donated to local people to encourage the growth of endangered plants, while volunteers who come here are not charged – one of the few instances of this in the whole of Ecuador.

It's a fantastic project, and passionate owner Raul is an affable biologist who gives engaging presentations about flora and fauna, which makes for a wonderful introduction to the unique biology of lowland tropical forest. Accommodation is in an old farmhouse, simple but comfortable and in a wonderfully tranquil setting.

Activities include tubing and making chocolate and tagua rings. English, French and Italian are spoken here, as well as Spanish. Volunteers are needed for native plant reintroduction. Call ahead for transport from town.

**Hostal Cocoa** (215-6233, 252-9297; r per person incl meals $12) is a quiet, family-run spot with a gorgeous setting on a tropical river bend. Rooms are basic, which draws guests outdoors to enjoy the hammocks. Packages can include visits to a waterfall and an organic fruit farm, or tubing and chocolate-making. Located 2km outside of town; a taxi costs $3.

# Central Highlands

## Includes »

## Best Places to Eat

» Restaurant Roka Plaza
(p138)

» La Posada de Tigua (p132)

» Café Mariane (p146)

» Mercado La Merced
(p157)

## Best Places to Stay

» Hostería La Ciénega
(p126)

» Hostal Tiana (p129)

» Hotel Roka Plaza (p137)

» Posada del Arte (p144)

» Refugio Whymper (p153)

## Why Go?

Cut from fire and ice, the rooftop of Ecuador offers up more adventure per square meter than most places on earth. There are glaciered mountains and active volcanoes, high-arching plains perfect for biking and trekking, surprisingly quaint colonial cities, bucolic haciendas and bustling crafts markets, and precipitous green valleys that take you from the Andes down past waterfalls and indigenous villages to the heavy-aired environs of the Amazon Basin.

Most trips to the area will include a couple of days in the region's exceptional national parks and reserves, including Los Ilinizas, Cotopaxi, Llanganates, Chimborazo and Sangay. The Quilotoa Loop brings hiking and biking travelers through traditional indigenous communities to an impossibly deep crater lake. There are rail adventures on a preposterously steep line known as the Devil's Nose, and plenty of tropical hikes, bikes and boats in the verdant valley leading down to the ever-popular town of Baños.

## When to Go
### Riobamba

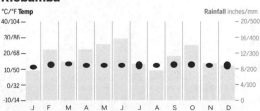

**Jun–Sep** The dry season is the top time for climbs, bikes and treks.

**Sep or Nov** Hit up the Mamá Negra festival in Latacunga.

**Dec–Jan** A dry spell gives way to adventure – plus everything is green!

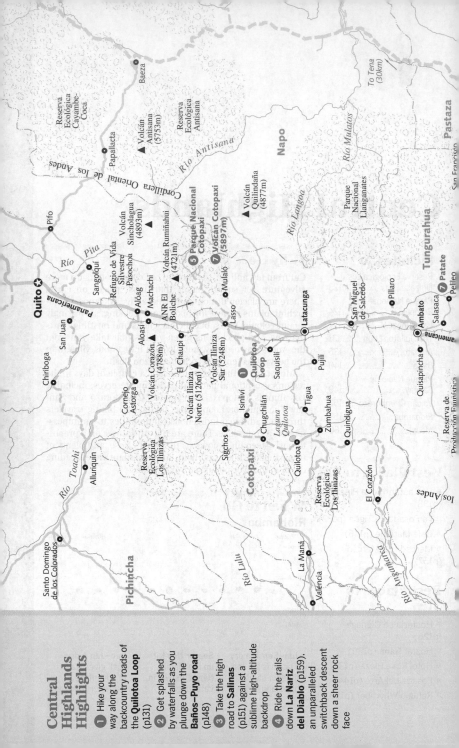

# Central Highlands Highlights

**1** Hike your way along the backcountry roads of the **Quilotoa Loop** (p131)

**2** Get splashed by waterfalls as you plunge down the **Baños–Puyo road** (p148)

**3** Take the high road to **Salinas** (p151) against a sublime high-altitude backdrop

**4** Ride the rails down **La Nariz del Diablo** (p159), an unparalleled switchback descent down a sheer rock face

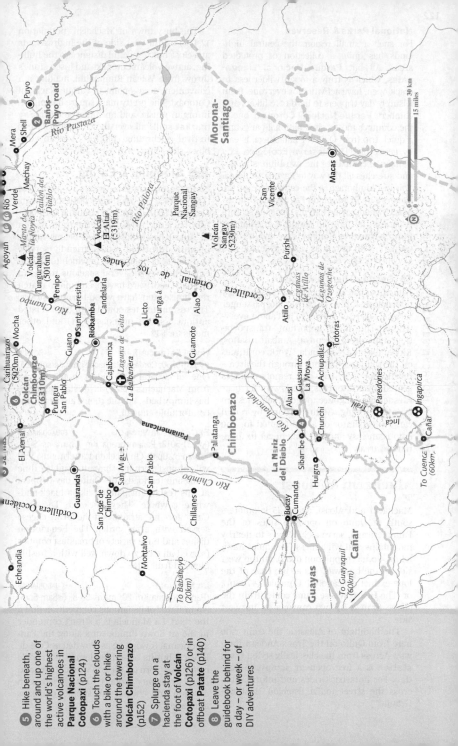

**5** Hike beneath, around and up one of the world's highest active volcanoes in **Parque Nacional Cotopaxi** (p124)

**6** Touch the clouds with a bike or hike around the towering **Volcán Chimborazo** (p152)

**7** Splurge on a hacienda stay at the foot of **Volcán Cotopaxi** (p126) or in offbeat **Patate** (p140)

**8** Leave the guidebook behind for a day – or week – of DIY adventures

30 km
15 miles

## National Parks & Reserves

For such a small region, the central highlands has quite a collection of protected areas. All but **Parque Nacional Llanganates**, which is truly a tough wilderness to crack open, have activities for everyone, from leisurely day-trippers to hard-core hikers and climbers. **Parque Nacional Cotopaxi**, one of the country's most visited national parks and a quick trip from Quito or Latacunga, is easily accessible. The **Reserva Ecológica Los Ilinizas** encompasses the two Ilinizas peaks, and stretches all the way to Laguna Quilotoa. Volcán Chimborazo is the centerpiece of the **Reserva de Producción Faunística Chimborazo**, where roving harems of vicuña scamper across the *páramo* (Andean grasslands). **Parque Nacional Sangay** is the region's largest park, with terrain as varied as jungle and glaciated peaks.

### ❶ Getting There & Around

Latacunga has an airport that is technically international, but so far has no passenger service. Buses, of course, go just about everywhere. The most important transportation hubs are Latacunga, Ambato, Baños, Riobamba and Guaranda. Work continues on the rail lines that run through the area – mostly for day trips to remote villages geared toward tourists; check www.ferrocarrilesdelecuador.gov.ec to see which lines are up and running. Getting around by rental car, tour operator or a taxi (rented for the day) is an easy and safe way to get to more remote areas.

# Machachi & Aloasí

🎵02

Machachi and Aloasí, about 35 kilometers south of Quito on opposite sides of the Panamericana, serve as gateways to nearby mountains and wilderness. The quiet hamlet of **Aloasí** (population 6855), on the west side of the highway, sits at the base of the long-extinct volcano El Corazón (4788m), or 'The Heart,' whose name comes from the shape formed by two canyons on its west side.

The highlight of Aloasí is the train ride here from Quito on the Trans-Andean Railway. Across from the classically styled **train station** is a free open-air **sculpture garden**. For horseback rides and information, cross the street to La Estación Hostería-Granja.

The busy town of Machachi (population 12,470) on the east side of the highway sits at a close but respectful distance to the hulking, active Volcán Cotopaxi and just a stone's throw from Volcán Rumiñahui, making it a convenient access point to Parque Nacional Cotopaxi. The pretty main square has piped-in organ music, and an important **Sunday market** spills all over the city. A boisterous festival celebrating *chagras* (Andean cowboys) rides into town every July 23.

## 🛏 Sleeping & Eating

**La Estación Hostería-Granja**     HACIENDA $$
(🎵230-9246; www.hosteriagranjalaestacion.com; Aloasí; s/d $50/60; 🔊) This rambling 19th-century hacienda across from the train station in Aloasí has exposed wood beams in the quaintly furnished rooms, friendly service and plenty of open areas in which to sit and enjoy the views. Several spacious rooms in the back courtyard have been built to match the house and have wood-burning stoves. The restaurant, festooned with farm-related antiques, serves breakfasts ($4) and other meals for $12.

**Hotel Estancia Real**     HOTEL $
(🎵231-5760; Cordero, Machachi; r per person $10) One of several low-budget hotels across from Machachi's Plaza Mayorista, this place has lumpy beds, but the rooms are clean and comfortable enough.

**El Café de la Vaca**     ECUADORIAN $$
(🎵231-5012; Panamericana Km 23; mains $4-8; ☺8am-5:30pm) On weekend afternoons, you will almost certainly have to wait to dine alongside carloads of Quito day-trippers at this restaurant painted like a black-and-white cowhide. They flock to 'The Cow Cafe' for its straight-off-the-farm cheese served with every order. The Ecuadorian dishes and huge variety of breakfast combos (served all day) go down well with a freshly blended fruit juice.

**La Manuela**     ECUADORIAN $$
(Panamericana Km 20; mains $4-8; ☺8am-5pm) An imitator of its famous competition down the road, La Manuela is a strong contender in the sit-down dining wars along the Panamericana. It won't be as crowded as Café de la Vaca, but its old-school items, like *choclo con queso* (corn on the cob with cheese) and *locro de papas* (potato soup served with avocado and cheese) are simple, delicious and large.

## ℹ Getting There & Around

Buses departing from Quito's bus terminal for Latacunga can drop you in Machachi ($1, one hour) along the Panamericana. To get back to Quito or Latacunga, wave down a bus on the Panamericana.

The **Ferrocarril Transandino** (Trans-Andean Railway; ☑1-800-873-637; www.ferrocarriles delecuador.gov.ec; round-trip adult/child $15/8) runs between Aloasí and Quito from Thursday through Sunday. Trains leave Aloasí at 9:30am, and Quito at 8am and 6pm. Some confusion stems from the fact that the Machachi train station is actually located in Aloasí, and the line is called the Quito–Machachi line.

From Machachi, brightly painted old school buses leave at least every hour during the day to nearby Aloasí. Stay on until the end of the line to reach the train station, approximately 3km from the Panamericana.

# Reserva Ecológica Los Ilinizas

☑02

The Los Ilinizas Ecological Reserve is named for the twin peaks of **Iliniza Norte** (5126m) and **Iliniza Sur** (5248m), respectively the sixth- and eighth-highest mountains in Ecuador. Once part of a single volcanic cone, the two spires are now separated by a narrow, sloping saddle. Although they're close in height, Iliniza Sur has a permanent glacier due to greater humidity and so is a highly technical climb requiring training, a guide and a slew of ice-climbing tools. Extremely popular as an acclimatization hike, Norte is a more approachable, but still demanding, ascent, with scree, rocky scrambles near the top and sometimes snow. Guided trips and volunteer opportunities can be arranged at the Hostal La Llovizna or the Hostería PapaGayo in El Chaupi. La Llovizna also rents climbing gear, sleeping bags and mountain bikes.

Most hikers and climbers kick off their adventures with a night in the small village of **El Chaupi**. From there, you can continue on foot (or by hired pickup) about 3km, first to the staffed **Control** (☺8am-4pm), where you must pay a $2 entrance fee, and then another 6km to the parking lot at La Virgen shrine. From there, it is a roughly three-hour hike to the **Refugio de los Ilinizas** (4650m; ☑09-796-3514; ilinizas_refuge@yahoo.com; dm $15). Bring a sleeping bag and food (basic cooking facilities are available), and be prepared for low nighttime temperatures.

## PLANNING AHEAD

It can be hot, cold, wet or dry anytime of year in the central highlands, so bring a jacket, hat, gloves and maybe even a quick-drying bottom layer. During major national holidays, you'll need to book your room well in advance, and popular hotels fill up quickly year-round.

## 🛏 Sleeping & Eating

**Hostería PapaGayo**     HOSTERÍA $$

(Map p124; ☑231-0002, 09-946-2269; www. hosteria-papagayo.com; Panamericana Sur Km 26; dm $10, s $20-35, d $30-60; @) This 150-year-old converted hacienda is a backpacker's favorite and a convenient base for playing around the Ilinizas, Corazón and Cotopaxi. Dorm beds and private rooms, some with fireplaces, are available, as are a nice restaurant, an ark's worth of friendly farm animals and even-friendlier hosts, who arrange tours, guides and horseback-riding. It's located 500m west of the Panamericana, down a turnoff 1km south of the Machachi tollbooth; call ahead for a pickup from Machachi or El Chaupi village.

**Hostal La Llovizna**     HOSTEL $

(☑09-969-9068; iliniza_blady@yahoo.com; r per person incl breakfast $12) About 500m from El Chaupi on the road to Ilinizas, Llovizna has big, warm rooms with firm beds downstairs and cozy, hobbit-sized garret rooms. The owner is Bladimir Gallo, the manager of the Ilinizas climbers' refuge and a great source of information about the area.

**Hostería Nina Rumy**     HOSTEL $

(☑367-4088; r with shared/private bathroom per person incl breakfast $12/13) This basic wood bunkhouse is quieter than the nearby Llovizna, meaning less traveler interaction but more peace. It is located right at the crossroads of the main drags in the village – you can't miss it.

## ℹ Getting There & Away

Blue-and-white buses signed 'El Chaupi' ($0.36, 40 minutes) leave Machachi about hourly until dark from Amazonas at 11 de Noviembre, returning from the El Chaupi town square on the same schedule.

If you are driving from Machachi, a sign indicates the El Chaupi turnoff from the Panamericana,

CENTRAL HIGHLANDS RESERVA ECOLÓGICA LOS ILINIZAS

about 6km south of Machachi. The cobbled road continues another 7km to El Chaupi. From El Chaupi, the road turns to dirt and continues another 9km to the Ilinizas parking area, identified by a small shrine to the Virgin.

You can also hire a pickup in Machachi (ask around the plaza) to take you directly to the parking area for $25. Trucks from El Chaupi cost around $10.

## Parque Nacional Cotopaxi

📷03

Although you can see **Volcán Cotopaxi** from several provinces, its majestic bulk and symmetrical cone take on entirely new dimensions within the bounds of its namesake national park. Covered in a draping glaciated skirt that gives way to sloping gold and green *páramo*, the flanks of Cotopaxi are home to wild horses, llamas, foxes, deer, Andean condor and the exceedingly rare spectacled bear.

Morning views are the best, making a stay in the park a desirable option. There's nothing like waking up to Cotopaxi during a crisp dawn, when you can appreciate the contours of the glacier and see the Yanasacha 'Forest,' which is not really a forest but a large, exposed rock face near the peak.

Zooming out to Cotopaxi from Quito or Latacunga for a day trip is also feasible. Hiking and mountain-biking to pre-Columbian ruins around the area's lakes and along the park roads can be done with guides or on your own.

Bird-watching in the park is excellent. Keep your eyes peeled for the giant, soaring Andean condor and the Ecuadorian hillstar, one of the world's highest-altitude hummingbirds. Shorebirds and ducks are common visitors to Laguna Limpiopungo.

Infrastructure is better than in most Ecuadorian parks but still limited. *Ganados* (livestock) are raised here, and it is not

## Parque Nacional Cotopaxi Area

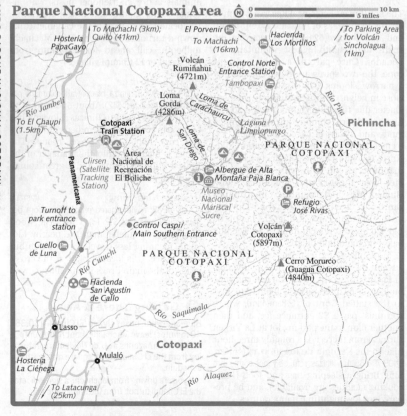

unusual to see SUVs off-roading over bird nesting grounds or visitors toying with the wild horses. To deal with heavy deforestation, environmental groups have planted large stands of conifers – while these non-native trees have helped prevent erosion, they have only partially solved the problem of restoring habitat, and their symmetrical rows are certainly not as beautiful as Cotopaxi's native forests. According to a recent study, Cotopaxi's glaciers shrunk by 40% between 1976 and 2010.

Among the hazards here are the serious threat of altitude sickness and bulls. These problems can be avoided, the first by acclimatizing in Quito for a couple of days, the second by keeping your distance.

The park entrance fee ($2) does not include the overnight refuge fees or camping fees. The main entrance is officially open 7am to 4:30pm, but drivers can get out until about 6:30pm. Hikers can get in or out at any time.

If you plan to take a guided tour or climb, you're best off doing so from Quito, Latacunga or Riobamba, which have the best climbing operators.

## ◉ Sights & Activities

FREE Museo Nacional
**Mariscal Sucre**     MUSEUM
Nine km into the park from Control Caspi (main southern entrance), this basic museum explains the natural history of the area.

TOP
CHOICE **Mountain Climbing**     CLIMBING
Summit attempts can be arranged in Quito and Latacunga. Although the climb is not technical – save for a few basic crevasse crossings and heart-pounding shimmies up fallen seracs – it is physically demanding, freezing, and for some people, vertigo-inducing. The ascent starts around midnight from **Refugio José Rivas** (4800m; dm $22), where you can cook and get a bunk (bring a sleeping bag and a padlock to store your gear). Even experienced, fit and acclimatized climbers can only reach the summit at dawn about one of every two tries (no guarantees, baby!). The reward for those who make it to the top (on a clear day!) are awesome views of other mountains and a peek at the crater's smoking fumaroles.

Even people with no mountaineering experience can make it safely to the top. Be sure you have a competent guide, good gear (rip-free ropes and harnesses, ice ax and crampons, warm double boots and jackets – no cotton please, as it doesn't stay warm when it's wet like synthetics and wool – sunglasses, water, food, headlamp and emergency gear). Your guide should teach you to self-arrest and use your ice ax, travel roped-in on glaciers, and put on your crampons the afternoon before the climb. It's important to meet with your guide before you head up. Ask them how many times they've climbed the mountain, what you need to climb the mountain, if they are certified with the Ecuadorian Mountain Guides Association (ASEGUIM). If your harness is ripped, demand it be replaced, if you're not comfortable with your guide, ask for a new one from the tour operator. It's your life; be your own advocate. And keep in mind that all the expedition shops use the same guides, so go with the shop that has the best gear. For more information on climbing volcanoes like Cotopaxi, see p32.

**Laguna Limplopungo**     HIKING
This shallow, reedy lake at the base of Rumiñahui is home to local and migrating waterfowl. An easy-as-pie trail (one hour) circumnavigates the lake, but keep a safe distance from the bulls that like to sip at the shore. Several campsites in the lake area have fire pits and outstanding morning views of the mountains. North of the lake a trail takes you to the top of the 4721m **Volcán Rumiñahui**. South of the lake, there's a trail that takes you past the 4286m saddle at **Loma Gorda** and on down to the train station. Both are long day hikes.

**Refugio José Rivas**     HIKING
For a fun lung-buster, climb up the final 200m of dirt trail from the Refugio José Rivas parking lot to the refuge itself (it will take you at least an hour at this altitude). You can spend the afternoon playing on the nearby snowfields. Don't go onto the glacier (200m up from the refuge) without a guide, as there are crevasses.

**Mountain-Biking**     MOUNTAIN-BIKING
Cruising around the park's circuit of relatively flat, dirt roads is popular. The Quito-based tour group, Biking Dutchman (p61) transports riders up to the *refugio* (mountain refuge) parking lot, where you can peer up at the awesome glacier before bombing down the western slope of Cotopaxi. Helmets, lunch and transfer from Quito are included.

CENTRAL HIGHLANDS PARQUE NACIONAL COTOPAXI

## 🛏 Sleeping

Most area lodges arrange day trips and horseback rides, and have restaurants onsite. There are campsites in the park ($2 per person), and $22 gets you a bunk in the rustic Refugio José Rivas.

**TOP CHOICE** **Hostería La Ciénega**  HACIENDA $$$
(☏271-9182; www.hosterialacienega.com; s/d/tr incl breakfast $74/89/107; 🛜🍽⊠) This 400-year-old hacienda has hosted some illustrious guests, including the French Geodesic Mission, Alexander von Humboldt and Ecuadorian presidents. A hotel since 1982, it still has hacienda charm: a long, eucalyptus-lined drive, meter-thick walls and an old chapel. The modern annex is less attractive (but priced the same), so confirm that your reservation is in the original house. The restaurant/bar serves classic (but expensive) Ecuadorian fare, done very well. La Ciénega is 2km west of the Panamericana, about 1km south of the village of Lasso. Bus drivers will drop you at the hotel's archway along the Panamericana, and you can walk from there.

**Hacienda Los Mortiños**  LODGE $$
(☏334-2520, losmortinios@hotmail.com; dm/r per person $20/30, breakfast $7, mains $12; 🛜) The best place to stay on the north side of the park, this modern adobe dwelling has beautiful new bathrooms, pitched ceilings, comfortable private rooms and dorms that sleep between six and 16 people, and jaw-dropping views of the neighboring volcanoes. It definitely has a homey feel, and the friendly Fernandez family can offer info on excursions to the park. Call ahead to custom-build your stay. Meals are cooked in the beautiful open kitchen.

**Tambopaxi**  CABIN $$$
(☏09-944-8223; www.tambopaxi.com; camping per person incl breakfast $7, dm/d/tr/q incl breakfast $24/103/133/184; 🛜) About 25km along the main road from the park's south entrance, this certified sustainable-tourism project is involved in wildlife conservation and watershed protection, and hires local workers. The rustic, stove-heated main lodge offers views of llamas and wild horses. In the morning, look through the telescope in the dining room to watch climbers push for Cotopaxi's summit. The dorm rooms have fluffy down comforters and outrageous views of Cotopaxi. A new, separate structure has private rooms.

**El Porvenir**  HACIENDA $$$
(☏09-498-0115; www.volcanoland.com; dm/r/ste incl breakfast $40/100/150; 🛜) Just 4km from the north entrance to the park, El Porvenir mixes the rustic comfort of an authentic hacienda experience with a strong ecological slant and tons of outdoor activities, such as horseback-riding and mountain-biking. The setting, high in the *páramo* with nothing but views of Cotopaxi for company, is spectacular. A wood-burning fire keeps the cozy common area warm and the rooms are loaded with amenities. Call ahead for transport to the lodge.

**Albergue de Alta Montaña Paja Blanca**  CABIN $
(☏231-4234; cabins per person incl breakfast $12.50) For the most budget-conscious, the shared A-frames here have beds and fireplaces but no electricity at night. Next door, the restaurant of the same name serves good local trout ($5) and cold beers. The Albergue is adjacent to the museum.

**Cuello de Luna**  CABIN $$
(☏09-970-0330, 03-271-8068; www.cuellodeluna.com; dm/s/d incl breakfast from $18/40/50) The 'Neck of the Moon' is a convenient midrange option, located 1.5km down a turnoff across from the south entrance of Parque Nacional Cotopaxi. Dorm beds are available and standard rooms have wood stoves or fireplaces. The dinners ($7 to $10) are pretty good.

**Hacienda San Agustín de Callo**  HACIENDA $$$
(☏271-9160; www.incahacienda.com; s/d/ste $219/382/437; 🛜) This hacienda has seen a lot of history over the last five centuries. Originally an Inca fortress, it later served as an Augustinian monastery. The French Geodesic Mission used it as a triangulation point to measure the equator in 1748, and Alexander von Humboldt stayed here in 1802, as did climber Edward Whymper in 1880. The distinctive, mortarless Incan stonework that forms many of the walls makes this hotel unique and mysterious. And the meticulously rustic rooms all come with fireplaces, plush spreads and hand-painted walls. This said, for the price, we still expect more, and most people will be happier at the Ciénega.

# ❶ Getting There & Away

## Car

All of the haciendas provide transportation from Quito, often at an additional cost.

There are three entrances to the park. The main southern entrance, **Control Caspi**, is via a turnoff about 22km south of Machachi (or roughly 30km north of Latacunga). From the turnoff, it's 6km northwest over dirt roads to Control Caspi and another 9km to the museum. Any Quito–Latacunga bus will drop you at the turnoff.

It's possible to reach the park through the northern entrance, known as **Control Norte**, via Machachi, but you'll need to hire a pickup or rent a car. The 21km-long route is well-signed and easy to follow.

The third, rarely used entrance is the turnoff road to **Área Nacional de Recreación El Boliche**, about 16km south of Machachi. The road passes the Clirsen Satellite Tracking Station (once operated by NASA), about 2km from the Panamericana. Just beyond Clirsen is the Cotopaxi train station. Here the road is closed to vehicles but eventually reaches the unattended entrance to Cotopaxi.

On weekends, local tourists visit the park and there is a good chance of getting a lift from the turnoff to the main entrance and on to Laguna Limpiopungo (solo gals are better off going with a guided tour from Quito or Latacunga). Midweek, the park is almost deserted, and you'll probably end up walking if you don't arrange transportation.

## Taxi

You can hire taxis or pickups to take you to the Refugio José Rivas from Latacunga ($40), Machachi ($25) or Quito ($40). Be sure to bargain and be specific if you want to go all the way to Refugio José Rivas. You can arrange for the pickup to return for you on a particular day for another $30 to $40, depending on the pickup location. It is almost an hour's walk uphill from the parking lot to the refuge.

## Train

The **Ferrocarril Transandino** (Trans-Andean Railway; ☑1-800-873-637; www.ferrocarrilesdelecuador.gov.ec; round-trip adult/child $15/8) runs trains Thursday through Sunday, leaving Quito at 8:15am. The train leaves Boliche for Quito at 1:30pm. From Latacunga, the train leaves at 9am, returning at 12:30pm.

---

# Latacunga

☑03 / POP 87,417 / ELEV 2800M

Many travelers end up passing through Latacunga to access either the Quilotoa Loop, the Thursday morning market in Saquisilí or Parque Nacional Cotopaxi. But for those who stick around, Latacunga also offers a quiet and congenial historic center that has partially survived several Cotopaxi eruptions. You'd never know that such a charming city lies behind the loud and polluted section that greets visitors on the Panamericana.

**Volcán Cotopaxi**, which dominates the town on a clear day, erupted violently in 1742 and again in 1768, destroying much of the city both times. The indomitable (or foolhardy) survivors rebuilt, only to have an immense eruption in 1877 wreak havoc a third time. Not to be outdone by Mother Nature, the townspeople were compelled to try again, and they have been spared Cotopaxi's wrath ever since.

To celebrate this good luck and revel in their rich indigenous and Catholic history, the people of Latacunga put on one of the most famous and magnificent parties in all of Ecuador, the Mamá Negra festival.

# ◉ Sights & Activities

### Markets                    MARKET
Latacunga's huge and completely untouristy markets are quite utilitarian, but that's what makes them interesting. The three sweeping market plazas around the intersection of Echeverría and Amazonas are busy every day, but especially on market days, Tuesday and Saturday.

### Parque Vicente León            PARK
Most action tends to center on this main plaza. At the southeast corner of the plaza stands the republican-era **town hall**, topped by a pair of stone condors. On the south side stands the colonial-style **cathedral**; on an exterior wall to the left of the main entrance is an interesting descriptive mural of Cotopaxi erupting over the city. A 17th-century arcaded building houses the provincial government offices on the west side.

### Casa de la Cultura            MUSEUM
(☑281-3247; Vela 3-49; admission $1; ☺8am-noon & 2-6pm Tue-Fri) This cultural center is built on the site of a former Jesuit watermill known as **Molinos de Monserrat** and houses a small ethnography and art museum. The stone steps above the river are a nice retreat from Latacunga's busy sidewalks. Check out its schedule for free dance and theater events.

# Latacunga

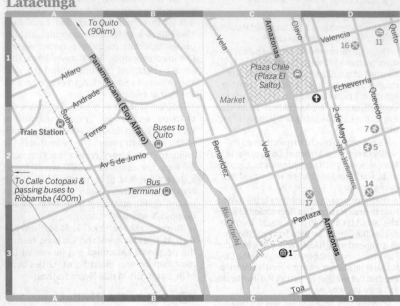

## Latacunga

### ◎ Sights

### ✇ Activities, Courses & Tours

### 🛏 Sleeping

### ✗ Eating

### ✇ Drinking

FREE **Casa de los Marqueses de Miraflores** MUSEUM
(Orellana & Echeverría; ⊘8am-noon & 2-6pm Mon-Sat) Take a break in this archaeological and religious museum housed in a surviving colonial-era mansion. It has good background on the Mamá Negra festivals.

**Mirador de la Virgen del Calvario** VIEWPOINT
(Floreana at Oriente) On a clear day, this lookout east of town offers views of several distant volcanic peaks. Follow Maldonado up the stairs, go left on Oriente and follow it up to the statue of the Virgin.

## ⌲ Tours

A number of tour operators have sprung up in recent years, offering excursions to Volcán Cotopaxi. Day trips cost around $40 per person, with the price varying depending on the size of your group. You'll pay the $2 park entrance fee separately. Two-day climbing trips

change, funky mural, clean rooms and bathrooms, free luggage storage, good information and a free breakfast. The old colonial atmosphere lends an air of cool, while the old pipes will leave you wanting come hot shower time. Dutch, English and Spanish are spoken.

### Hotel Central                    HOTEL $
(📞280-2912; hotelcentrallatacunga@hotmail.com; Orellana, near Salcedo; r per person $12; 🛜) In the same building as Hotel Cotopaxi, the family-run Central outdoes its neighbor when it comes to decor, kitschy finishing touches (such as 1960s ceramic ashtrays) and, best of all, friendliness.

### Hotel Rodelu                    HOTEL $$
(📞280-0956, www.rodelu.com.ec; Quito 16-31; s/d $18/32; 🛜) Popular with the tour groups but still down-home enough to attend to independent travelers, the Rodelu has highly fragranced Andean-style business digs.

### Hotel Rosim                    HOTEL $
(📞280-0853; www.hotelrosim.com; Quito 16-49; r per person $12; 🛜) With lots of emphasis on cleanliness, this budget alternative has high ceilings and original floors. All the beds are firm and extra long. Cable TV and wi-fi are included in the price, making this a top budget bet for the nonhostel crowd.

### Hotel Makroz            BUSINESS HOTEL $$
(📞09-503-4148; Valencia 8-56; s/d $35/50; 🛜) Not quite up to Rodelu standards, this modern and clean hotel is oriented toward business travelers. The spacious rooms have cable TVs, fridges, blow-dryers and nice, big bathrooms.

### Hotel Cotopaxi                    HOTEL $
(📞280-1310; Salcedo 5-61; r $12 per person; 🛜) Cotopaxi offers spacious, comfortable rooms with TVs. Some rooms have giant windows and pretty views of the central plaza. They can be a bit noisy.

to Volcán Cotopaxi cost about $170 per person (see p125 for more information on the climb). Excursions to Laguna Quilotoa and other mountains are also available. Hostal Tiana is a good spot to form groups for your trip. The following outfitters are all licensed by Ecuador's department of tourism.

**Volcán Route Expeditions**    ADVENTURE TOUR
(📞281-2452; www.volcanroute.com; Guayaquil & Quevedo)

**Tierra Zero Tours**            ADVENTURE TOUR
(📞09-779-9916; www.tierrazerotours.com; Guayaquil & Quevedo)

**Tovar Expeditions**            ADVENTURE TOUR
(📞281-1333; www.tovarexpeditions.com; Orellana & Vivero)

## 🛏 Sleeping

Hotels fill up fast on Wednesdays, with people staying over for the Thursday-morning market at Saquisilí. Prices can double during the Fiesta de La Mamá Negra.

### Hostal Tiana                    HOSTEL $
(📞281-0147; www.hostaltiana.com; Vivero 1-31; dm/s/d $12/25/30, with shared bathroom $9/16/22; @🛜) This good-vibes hostel has everything a good hostel should: cool common area to swap tales, kitchen, free internet, book ex-

## 🍴 Eating & Drinking

The classic dish of Latacunga, the *chugchucara* (say that 10 times fast!), is a tasty, heart-attack-inducing plate of *fritada* (fried chunks of pork, served with *mote*, or hominy), *chicharrón* (fried bits of pork skin), potatoes, fried banana, *tostado* (toasted corn), popcorn and cheese empanadas. It's suitable for sharing.

The Latacunga area is also famous for its *allullas* (pronounced 'azhiuzhias'), dry biscuits made of flour, pork fat and a local

## LATACUNGA'S MAMÁ NEGRA

One of the biggest celebrations in the highlands, the Mamá Negra (Black Mother) parade is a combination of Catholic, pre-Columbian and civic rituals that fill the streets of Latacunga with hundreds of costumed and dancing revelers.

Traditionally staged on September 23 and 24, and again on November 8, Mamá Negra now occurs on the closest weekend to those dates. The November occasion also includes a bullfight, but locals say the September revelries are more authentic.

At the head of it all is a statue of the Virgen de las Mercedes, Latacunga's protectress from volcanic eruptions. Believing that the relic has saved the city from Volcán Cotopaxi's wrath many times, people from Latacunga have great faith in her image. (Apparently they overlook the three times that the city *has* been destroyed by Cotopaxi.)

The Mamá Negra, represented by a local man dressed up as a black woman, is said to have been added to the festivities later on. According to one of several legends about him/her, a priest that wanted to earn favor by hosting the Virgin's procession failed to provide sufficiently grand quantities of food and drink, and during the night an apparition of a black woman berated his negligence. She terrified the priest and the rest of the town, so they introduced a new figure to the procession, that of the black mother astride a horse.

Politically incorrect as it might seem, Mamá Negra is an event loved by all. No one – especially foreign tourists! – can escape the *huacos* (witches), who execute a ritual *limpieza* (cleansing) by blowing smoke and *aguardiente* (sugarcane alcohol) on spectators. Most impressive are the *ashangueros*, the men who carry *ashangas*: whole roast pigs, flayed open and flanked by dozens of *cuy* (guinea pigs), chickens, bottles of liquor, and cigarettes. The *ashangueros* stop now and then to rest while their friends ply them with more *aguardiente*.

Players representing *yumbos* (indigenous people from the Oriente), *loeros* (African slaves), *camisonas* (colonial-era Spanish women) and many more all have a role in this grand street theater.

unpasteurized cheese, as well as its *queso de hoja*, unpasteurized cheese wrapped in banana leaves. Head to Quijano y Ordoñez, two blocks south of Tarqui, to eat your fill.

Many cheap *leñadores* (wood-burning ovens) roast chicken along Amazonas between Salcedo and Guayaquil.

**El Copihue Rojo**  ECUADORIAN **$**
(Quito 14-38; mains $3-5, set lunches $2; ⊙12:30-3pm & 6-9pm Mon-Sat) If you're looking for a local recommendation, the Copihue Rojo is it. Their daily *almuerzo* (set-lunch) service is always busy, and meats and soups are popular with families during the dinner hour.

**Restaurant Rodelu**  ITALIAN **$$**
(Quito 16-31; mains $4-10; ⊙7:15am-9:30pm Mon-Sat) In its namesake hotel, Rodelu also serves early breakfast as well as wood-oven, medium-crust pizzas, sandwiches and pasta.

**Chugchucaras La Mamá Negra** ECUADORIAN **$**
(Quijano y Ordoñez 1-67; chugchucaras $5.90; ⊙10am-7pm Tue-Sun; ⊛) There are several chugchucara restaurants on Quijano y Ordoñez, a few blocks south of downtown – they're all family-friendly. La Mamá Negra is one of the best.

**Pollos Jimmy**  LATIN AMERICAN **$**
(Quevedo 8-85 near Valencia; mains $3.25-6; ⊙10am-10pm) Pop in for delicious rotisserie chicken served with rice, potatoes and chicken soup. The place stays busy for a reason.

**Chifa Dragón II**  CHINESE **$**
(2 de Mayo & Salcedo; mains $4-6; ⊙10am-9pm; ⏴) When you tire of chicken and *chugchucaras*, or if you are a vegetarian, enter the dragon for mean stir-fries and other Chinese classics.

**Café Sausalito**  PUB
(cnr Av Quijana de Ordoñez & Luis F. Vivero; ⊙8am-10pm) Quiet spot to share snacks and a beer.

### ⓘ Information

**Banco de Guayaquil** (Maldonado 7-20) Bank with ATM.

**Banco del Pichincha** (Quito near Salcedo) Bank with ATM.

**Discovery Net** (📞280-6557; Salcedo 4-16 near Quevedo; per hr $1) Internet access and telephone booths.

**Hospital** (Hermanas Páez near 2 de Mayo)

**Post office** (Quevedo near Maldonado)

## 🛈 Getting There & Away

### Bus

From Quito, buses will drop you at the **bus terminal** (Panamericana) if Latacunga is their final destination. If the bus is continuing to Ambato or Riobamba, it'll drop you on the corner of 5 de Junio and Cotopaxi, about five blocks west of the Panamericana and 10 minutes' walk to downtown.

Buses to Quito ($1.50, two hours) and Ambato ($1, 45 minutes) leave from the bus terminal and from the corner of 5 de Junio and Cotopaxi. For Riobamba, it's easiest to catch a passing southbound Cuenca bus from the corner of 5 de Junio and Cotopaxi.

Interminably slow Quito-bound buses leave from the terminal, while faster long-distance buses can be flagged on the Panamericana near 5 de Junio.

Transportes Cotopaxi has hourly buses to Quevedo ($3.75, 5½ hours) in the western lowlands, one of the most spectacular bus trips around.

For buses to villages along the Quilotoa Loop, see p135.

### Taxi

You can hire taxis and pickup trucks in Plaza Chile (also called Plaza El Salto) for visits to Parque Nacional Cotopaxi ($40 round-trip to park interior, $15 one-way to the Control Caspi entrance). Shared taxis run to Quito ($10, one hour).

### Trains

From the **train station** (📞1-800-873-637; www.ferrocarrilesdelecuador.gov.ec; Subia & Andrade; round-trip adult/child $15/8; ⊙Thu-Sun), trains run to the El Boliche station in Cotopaxi, leaving Latacunga at 9am and returning at 12:30pm.

# The Quilotoa Loop

📷03

The Quilotoa Loop is a bumpy, ring-shaped road that travels from the Panamericana far into the backcountry of Cotopaxi province. Along the way you'll encounter colorful indigenous markets, a crystal-blue lake that the local people believe has no bottom, a community of painters who are preserving the legends of the Andes and ancient trails that meander in the shadow of snow-capped volcanoes. The isolation of the

**CENTRAL HIGHLANDS** THE QUILOTOA LOOP

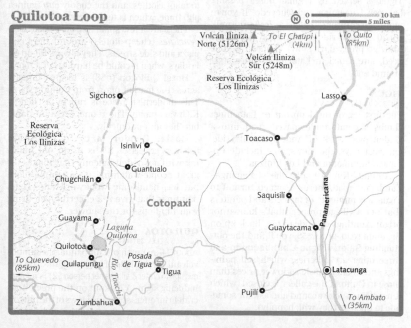

**Quilotoa Loop**

0 ─── 10 km
0 ─── 5 miles

Volcán Iliniza Norte (5126m)
To El Chaupi (4km)
To Quito (85km)
Volcán Iliniza Sur (5248m)
Reserva Ecológica Los Ilinizas
Sigchos
Lasso
Reserva Ecológica Los Ilinizas
Isinliví
Toacaso
Guantualo
Chugchilán
Cotopaxi
Saquisilí
Guayama
Laguna Quilotoa
Guaytacama
Quilotoa
Posada de Tigua
To Quevedo (85km)
Quilapungu
Río Toachi
Tigua
Latacunga
Panamericana
Pujilí
Zumbahua
To Ambato (35km)

loop brings you into contact with lots of Kichwa-speaking indigenous people and their centuries-old way of life.

Several villages offer lodgings, and most travelers go from one place to the next by bus, hired truck or their own two feet. The hiking is fantastic, and although guides are inexpensive (and a good way to support the local economy), many *hostales* (small, reasonably priced hotels) and inns have maps for solo wanderers.

Transportation is infrequent, so it takes some planning if your time is limited, and it's wise to travel the loop with rain gear, water and plenty of snacks for long waits and hikes. It's worth spending at least two nights, but it's easy to get sucked in for days. Many travelers have reported problems with dogs along the way. If they charge you, don't run away. Stand your ground, grab a rock and pretend to throw it.

The loop is covered in this section in clockwise order, starting in Latacunga and taking the southern route through Zumbahua, although traveling in reverse also works.

No buses go all the way around the loop. From Latacunga, they only travel as far as Chugchilán, either taking the southern road through Zumbahua and Quilotoa or the northern road via Saquisilí and Sigchos. Tigua is served by regular buses passing between Latacunga and Quevedo. If you're more adventurous, catch a *lechero* (milk truck) or even ride on the roof of the bus (they go pretty darn slow). If speed is your need, hire a taxi in Latacunga; rates start around $60.

### TIGUA
POP 3000 / ELEV 3500M

The first leg of the loop out of Latacunga climbs a comfortable, paved road into a golden patchwork of Andean countryside. On clear days, the views may include Cotopaxi, Rumiñahui and Los Ilinizas.

Around Km 49 on the Latacunga–Zumbahua road, there's a signed turnoff to Tigua, a community of farmers and painters (but not a village proper) that's known for bright paintings of Andean life. Back up on the main road, at Km 53, you'll find the outstanding Galería Tigua-Chimbacucho and three other art galleries, which sell paintings and wooden masks at lower prices than those in Quito. If the gallery is closed (which it usually is), poke around and ask for someone to open it (they will, happily).

La Posada de Tigua (☑281-4870,09-161-2391; posadadetigua@yahoo.com; Vía Latacunga–Zumbahua Km 49; dm/r per person incl breakfast & dinner $25/$35) is part of a working dairy ranch. The farmhouse dates to the 1890s and is now a rustic and delightfully cozy inn. The rooms, with meter-thick walls, have modern bathrooms and meals include cheese and yogurt made on the farm. Having lived among the local indigenous people most of their lives, the warm and helpful Ecuadorian couple that owns the posada know the area well and have great stories to tell. They can set up horseback-riding and guides. The place is about 500m down the signed road to Tigua – tell the bus driver to drop you at the turnoff.

From the posada, there's a six-hour hike up the Cañon del Toachi to Quilotoa. A guide will cost you $35, and there's a decent map at the posada.

### ZUMBAHUA
POP 3000 / ELEV 3800M

Some 15km southwest of Tigua, the small town of Zumbahua is surrounded by high bluffs and agricultural fields that soon give way to *páramo*. The village has a wonderfully authentic Saturday market that draws indigenous vendors from the mountains. Check out the men on the south side of the market, who use old Singer sewing machines to tailor clothes, and the cuddly *cuy* (guinea pig) trade, which is fun to watch.

There are a few small and very basic *residenciales* (cheap hotels) around the main plaza and side streets. They always fill up on Fridays, when it could be hard to get a room.

Hotel Quilotoa (r $8) is located directly across the market plaza from Condor Matzi. This modernish place is run by a friendly Kichwa woman. The rooms are a bit dank, but they air out quickly.

Hostal Condor Matzi (r with shared bathroom per person $7) is in an old building with a wooden balcony that makes for great people-watching. It's a simple place but has handsome woodwork and Tigua paintings that give it a cheerful feel. Bring your flip-flops for the shower.

### QUILOTOA
POP 150 / ELEV 3914M

About 14km north of Zumbahua, the famous volcanic-crater lake of Laguna Quilotoa (admission to crater & village per person $2) is a gasp-inducing sight. A lookout on the precipitous crater rim offers stunning views of the mirror-green lake 400m below and the snowcapped

# TIGUA PAINTINGS

One of Ecuador's homegrown art forms (and a worthy collector's item) is a style of painting called Tigua that originated near the shores of Laguna Quilotoa. The name comes from the small community of Tigua, where indigenous people had decorated drum skins for many generations. During the 1970s, Julio Toaquiza, a young indigenous man from the area, got the idea to turn those skins into canvases and paint colorful scenes from Kichwa legends. The artist, who spent his days growing potatoes and tending llamas, depicted these legends against the beautiful Andean scenery where he lived. He painted the condor wooing a young girl and flying over the mountains in a red poncho, the 'bottomless' Quilotoa lake with spirits hovering over its waters, and Volcán Cotopaxi, a sacred place that highland indigenous people called 'Taita' (Father).

Originally working with enamel paints and chicken-feather brushes, Toaquiza taught all of his children and neighbors how to paint. They began to incorporate new themes, such as Catholic processions, interiors of indigenous homes and even important political events. Today they use acrylic and oil paints.

Toaquiza's art has brought fame to Tigua, and today more than 300 painters are at work in the highlands, with about 20 studios in Tigua itself. The pieces are exhibited at the community galleries in Tigua, in selected galleries in Quito and in exhibitions around the world.

peaks of Cotopaxi and Iliniza Sur in the distance. When you ask the locals how deep it is, they inevitably say it has no bottom, which seems entirely plausible given its awesomeness (the geologists say 250m).

Fit walkers can hike the crater rim trail in about six hours; another path leads down to the water, where canoes and kayaks can be rented (per hour $5). The hike down takes about half an hour and over twice that to return (you can ride a donkey back up for $5 an hour). The alkaline lake water is not potable.

Dozens of excellent Tigua painters live in Quilotoa and finding a place to buy their work involves little more than having your eyes open.

## Sleeping & Eating

**Princesa Toa II** HOSTEL $
(r with shared bathroom per person incl 2 meals $15) The only lakeside lodging choice, this community-run place has basic thatch-roofed rooms and shared outdoor toilets. Bring a sleeping bag for the cold nights.

**Hostería Alpaca Quilotoa** HOSTERIA $
(☎09-212-5962; www.alpacaquilotoa.com; r per person $10; @) Located about 200m toward the lake from the entrance to Quilotoa, this new upscale option has great views, quiet rooms with wood stoves and a large restaurant area. Add another $10 a day, and they'll cook two meals for you.

**Kirutwa** ECUADORIAN $
(☎in Quito 02-267-0926; mains $3-8; ☺8am-5pm) A big, new, comparatively swanky restaurant right up on the crater rim. Offering classics like *locro de papas* and *choclo con queso*, Kirutwa is run by a foundation that returns much of the revenue back to the local community. It also offers tours to a nearby cave ($20) and the crater ($20).

## CHUGCHILÁN
POP 100 / ELEV 3200M

The dirt road winds down 22km of breathtaking scenery to Chugchilán, a tiny Andean village that has been greatly enriched by ecotourism but that maintains its age-old ways. From here you can hike to nearby villages, visit a cooperatively run cheese factory (see the boxed text, p152) or ride horses into the nearby cloud forest. Two excellent places to stay on the northern edge of town arrange well-priced horseback-riding trips, provide local hiking information, and can help set up private transport in and out of the loop.

**Hostal Cloud Forest** (☎270-8181; jose cloudforest@gmail.com; r per person incl breakfast & dinner $12; @☎) The least expensive and simplest of Chugchilán's accommodations has wood-accented rooms and clean bathrooms. The nice Ecuadorian owners serve tasty meals, and guests can chill out in the fireplace-heated common area.

**Hostal Mama Hilda** (☎270-8005; www. mamahilda.com; r per person incl breakfast &

## TRANSPORTATION ON THE QUILOTOA LOOP

Bus seats on the loop are in demand. Arrive 30 minutes to an hour early for departures, and be prepared for the bus to run late. Rainy season can increase travel times.

### Latacunga–Chugchilán (via Zumbahua; $2.50, three to four hours)

A Transportes Iliniza bus via Zumbahua departs daily at noon. It passes Zumbahua around 1:30pm, reaches Quilotoa around 2pm and arrives in Chugchilán around 3:30pm.

### Chugchilán–Latacunga (via Zumbahua; $2.50, three to four hours)

Buses via Zumbahua leave Chugchilán weekdays at 4am, passing Quilotoa around 5am, Zumbahua around 5:30am and arriving in Latacunga around 7:30am. On Saturday, it leaves at 3am and on Sunday at 6am, 9am and 10am.

### Latacunga–Chugchilán (via Sigchos; $2.50, three to four hours)

Transportes Iliniza buses via Sigchos depart daily at 10:30am, 11:30am and 1pm, passing Sigchos around 2pm.

### Chugchilán–Latacunga (via Sigchos; $2.50, three to four hours)

Buses leave Monday to Saturday at 3am, passing Sigchos around 4am, Saquisilí around 7am, and arriving at Latacunga around 7:30am. On Sunday the service leaves at 4am and noon, but you must switch buses in Sigchos. You can also return via Zumbahua (see above).

### Latacunga–Zumbahua ($1.50, 1½ to two hours)

Transportes Cotopaxi buses bound for Quevedo depart hourly from Latacunga's bus terminal and drop passengers just above the town of Zumbahua.

### Zumbahua–Latacunga ($1.25, 1½ to two hours)

Transportes Cotopaxi buses return to Latacunga from Quevedo just as frequently.

### Zumbahua–Quilotoa (30 minutes)

Trucks can be hired for $5 to $7 per person. The Latacunga–Chugchilán bus passes Zumbahua around 1:30pm ($1).

### Quilotoa–Zumbahua (30 minutes)

Unless you want to take the 4am bus to Latacunga ($0.50 per person), you'll need to hire a truck to get to Zumbahua ($5 per person). On Sunday the Latacunga-bound bus leaves Chugchilán at 6am, 9am and 10am, passing Quilotoa at 7am, 10am and 11am.

---

dinner $23; 🤶) Worth the extra money, this cozy place has brick-walled rooms with lofts and spotless bathrooms. You could spend an entire afternoon lounging in a hammock on your private porch.

### SIGCHOS
POP 2259 / ELEV 2800M

From Chugchilán, it's a journey of 23 muddy, bumpy kilometers to the growing town of Sigchos. You'll likely stop here to catch a bus or while hiking from Chugchilán or Isinliví; otherwise it's not much of a destination.

In a pinch, head to the **Hostal San Miguel** (☑271-4193; cnr Amazonas & Juan Sagastivoelsa; r per person $5), with clean tile-floor rooms.

### ISINLIVÍ
POP 3310 / ELEV 2900M

Some 14km southeast of Sigchos and just off the Quilotoa Loop, the beautiful village of Isinliví makes a good hike from either Sigchos or Chugchilán. A woodworking/cabinetry shop makes high-end furniture and locals can direct you to nearby *pucarás* (pre-Incan hill fortresses).

A popular day hike is to the Monday-morning market at nearby Guantualo. A bus leaves Guantualo ($3.50, 3½ hours) at 1:30pm for Latacunga through Sigchos.

### Sleeping

TOP CHOICE **Llullu Llama** GUESTHOUSE $
(Little Llama; ☑281-4790; www.llullullama.com; dm/r per person incl breakfast & dinner from $18/21) Llullu Llama is an enchanting old farmhouse with thick adobe walls, colorful and comfortable rooms and a wood-burning stove. The biggest attraction here is the good time vibes, friendly hosts and cool surroundings. Check here for volunteer opportunities.

### Quilotoa–Chugchilán (one hour)

Take the Latacunga–Chugchilán bus between 2pm and 2:30pm ($1), or hire a truck for about $25.

### Chugchilán–Quilotoa (one hour)

If you don't want to leave at 4am (on the bus to Latacunga; $1), you'll need to hire a truck to get to Quilotoa ($20 to $25). Additionally, on Wednesday there's a bus at 5am, on Friday at 6am, and on Sunday buses depart at 6am, 9am and 10am ($1).

### Chugchilán–Sigchos ($1, one hour)

A daily milk truck leaves Chugchilán between 8am and 9am ($25), avoiding the 3am departure of the Chugchilán–Latacunga bus. Two other buses depart on Thursday and Saturday afternoon. Sunday departures are at 4am, 5am and noon.

### Sigchos–Chugchilán ($1, one hour)

Transportes Iliniza from Latacunga stops in Sigchos around 2pm, and the milk truck ($1) leaves Sigchos daily at 7am.

### Sigchos–Latacunga ($1.80, two hours)

Buses depart daily at 3am, 4am, 5am, 6am, 7am, 2:30pm and 4:30pm from beside the church. Additional buses leave on Wednesday, Friday, Saturday and Sunday afternoon. Buses stop in Saquisilí on the way.

### Latacunga–Sigchos ($1.80, two hours)

Transportes Nacional Saquisilí buses leave Latacunga's bus terminal at 9:30am, 10am, noon, 2pm, 4pm, 5pm and 6pm daily.

### Saquisilí–Latacunga ($0.35, 20 minutes)

Buses depart Plaza Concordia in Saquisilí every 10 minutes.

### Latacunga–Saquisilí ($0.35, 20 minutes)

Buses depart from Latacunga's bus terminal every 10 minutes.

## Getting There & Away

Vivero buses leave Latacunga's bus terminal for Isinliví ($3, three hours) at 1pm all days except Saturday, when it leaves at 11am, and Thursday, when it leaves from Saquisilí at 11am.

## SAQUISILÍ

POP 9296 / ELEV 2940M

The **Thursday morning market** is one of the best in the central highlands. It gets crowded with tour buses bringing gaggles of visitors each week. Still, it's a mostly authentic market and a fascinating place to observe an array of material goods that constitute life in the highlands. The market is composed of eight plazas, which are like a bustling outdoor department store with mostly indigenous shoppers; there's a department for *cuy*, *esteras* (straw mats), *angarillas* (donkey saddles), *sastrería* (tailoring services), *ollas* (pots) and hundreds, perhaps thousands, of other items.

Especially interesting is the **animal market**, a cacophonous affair with screaming pigs playing a major role. It starts before dawn and is on the edge of the market – just follow all the folks with animals.

No restaurants here cater to tourists, but there's never a shortage of food at the market and in the side streets. North of the cemetery, on Calle Chimborazo, the **Hostería Gilocarmelo** (272-1634; www.hosteriagilo carmelo.com; r per person $20; ) has nice rooms around a garden with hummingbird feeders, a common room with a fireplace, a sauna, and fresh-trout dinners. There's a large pool complex and a sad zoo with a pair of ostriches open to the public for $4. To take a ride on a remarkably unsafe-looking zip line, you'll need to shell out an extra $1.50.

Most travelers stay in Latacunga and jump on buses that start running at dawn ($0.35, 20 minutes).

## Ambato

📍03 / POP 217,075 / ELEV 2577M

While harried Ambato makes it onto few travelers' must-see lists, the town is not without its charms. The central plaza gives an authentic picture of big-city life in the Andes. Above town, there are fabulous views of the puffing Volcán Tungurahua (5016m), and Ambato's parks and quintas (historic country homes that have been converted into parks) offer some respite from the bustle of downtown.

The **Monday market** fills Ambato's central streets and plazas and, as a major hub in the flower trade, Ambato sometimes drips with roses, carnations and tropical varieties coming up from the coast.

The city is proud of its cultural heritage and nicknames itself 'Tierra de Los Tres Juanes' (Land of the Three Juans), after the writers Juan Montalvo and Juan León Mera, and lawyer/journalist Juan Benigno Malo. All three Juans are immortalized in Ambato's parks, museums and buildings.

In 1947, an earthquake destroyed Ambato, the capital of Tungurahua province, and a modern city was rebuilt.

## ◎ Sights & Activities

**La Quinta Atocha de Juan León Mera**　　GARDENS

(📞282-0419; Av Los Capulíes; admission $1; ⏰9am-4:30pm Wed-Sun) Several famous *ambateños* (people from Ambato) had quintas that survived the earthquake. They were probably once considered countryside homes, but today they are right on the edge of this growing city. **La Quinta de Juan León Mera** – set on the banks of the Río Ambato in the suburb of Atocha, about 2km northeast of downtown – is the best of the area's haciendas, and houses a museum and botanic garden. The estate, built in 1874, has period furnishing and is set in the **Jardín Botánico La Liria**, a lush garden with more than 200 plant species and a trail down to the river. Just on the north side of La Liria is the **Museo Histórico Martínez-Holguim**, another period quinta formerly owned by a famous mountain climber. To get to the complex by foot, walk northwest on Montalvo, cross the river and turn right on Capulíes. Buses for Atocha leave from 12 de Noviembre and Espejo. Taxis to the quintas from downtown cost $2.

## Ambato

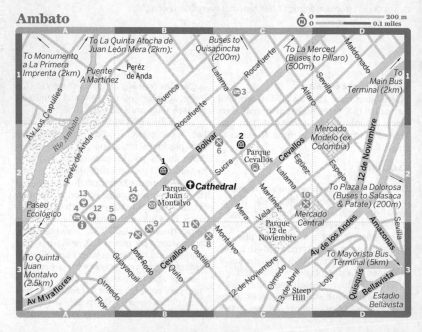

**La Quinta de Juan Montalvo** MUSEUM
(admission $1; ⊘9am-4:30pm Wed-Sun) This 200-year-old villa was home to Juan Montalvo, the 'Cervantes of America.' There's a tiny but well-done museum dedicated to the author – his house was really small – and the pretty gardens are worth a peek. To get here, cruise southwest up Avenida Miraflores. It's about a half-hour hike. You can also take the bus marked 'Ficoa' from Parque Cevallos. Taxis from downtown cost $2.

**Paseo Ecológico** PARK
For an afternoon by the Río Ambato, head down Flor to this nature trail that crisscrosses the river up to the Miraflores neighborhood. The trail continues for a good 2km

**Casa y Mausoleo de Montalvo** MUSEUM
(⊘282-4248; admission $0.50; ⊘9am-noon & 2-6pm Mon-Sat) The northwest side of the handsome **Parque Juan Montalvo** is taken up by this museum, Montalvo's pied-à-terre and where he is interred. It was closed at research time for renovation.

**Monumento a la
Primera Imprenta** VIEWPOINT
Ambato's best view of Volcán Tungurahua is found at this monument dedicated to

Ecuador's first printing press. It is located up the hill northwest of town. A taxi up to the top should cost no more than $2, and you can walk down to the bus stop to return downtown.

**Museo de Ciencias Naturales** MUSEUM
(⊘282-7395; Sucre & Lalama; admission $1; ⊘8:30am-12:30pm & 2:30-5:30pm Mon-Fri, 9am-5pm Sat) Although a bit dusty, this natural-history museum in the Colegio Bolívar houses Ecuador's most thorough collection of stuffed birds, mammals and reptiles. The historical photograph collage and a gruesome display of farm freaks, such as two-headed calves and six-legged lambs, make great fun for the whole family.

## 🎊 Festivals & Events

The annual **Fiesta de Frutas y Flores** (Festival of Fruit and Flowers), held during the last two weeks in February, has magnificent displays of, you guessed it, fruits and flowers. There are also bullfights, parades and the *Reina de Ambato* (Queen of Ambato) pageant.

## 🛏 Sleeping

Several cheap lodging options near Parque 12 de Noviembre cost around $5 per night, but there have been robberies reported inside these hotels so we have omitted them from this book.

**TOP CHOICE** **Hotel Roka Plaza** BOUTIQUE HOTEL $$
(⊘242 3845; www.hotelrokaplaza.com; Bolívar btwn Quito & Guayaquil; s/d/tr incl breakfast $47/74/94; P✶) Housed in an old *casona* (large, colonial-era house), this tasty boutique hotel has the nicest rooms in the city center. There's only seven of them, so call well ahead. Modern touches blend seamlessly with antiques and other colonial touches, and you'll find excellent art throughout.

**Hotel Ambato** BUSINESS HOTEL $$
(⊘242-1791/92; www.hotelambato.com; Guayaquil 01-08; s/d incl breakfast $52/74; ✶) Built into a hillside over the Río Ambato, this modern downtown business hotel has views of both the cathedral and the river and is your best bet after the Roka. The rooms are spacious and well lit, and the whole place is quiet.

**Gran Hotel** HOTEL $
(⊘282-4235; cnr Rocafuerte & Lalama; s/d $12/24; ✶) The Gran is definitely not so grand anymore, but the carpeted rooms have TVs and the staff is helpful and pleasant, making this

## PRAISING NATURE IN AMBATO'S MODERN CATHEDRAL

Ambato once had an old cathedral, but it was destroyed along with the rest of the city by the 1947 earthquake. Many people consider the replacement temple on Parque Juan Montalvo, with its minimalist vertical lines, boringly modern in comparison to Ecuador's antique, ornate churches, and it's never competed well with the glacier-topped peaks and active volcanoes in the background. The cathedral, however, has recently been attracting attention for what's inside: in 2007, the church got a makeover by a young *ambateño* landscape artist, David Moscoso, who steered clear of the usual religious motifs and instead expressed his devotion through daring representations of Ecuador's natural beauty: over 500m of murals depict the Avenue of the Volcanoes, a smoking Tungurahua, the cloud-enshrouded Llanganates and glaciered Chimborazo.

your best budget bet. We wish the pillows weren't so lumpy.

## Eating

### Restaurant Roka Plaza                  FUSION $$
(Bolívar btwn Quito & Guayaquil; mains $4-10) In the Roka Plaza's central courtyard, this wonderful restaurant serves grilled meats, amazing fresh juices, international favorites, and innovative items like a yummy vegetarian ceviche. The presentation is better than you'll find anywhere in the central highlands, and the ambience is exquisite.

### La Casa de Bottero                  ARGENTINE $$
(cnr Quito & Sucre; mains $6-18; ⊙noon-10pm Tue-Sat, noon-2pm Sunday) This authentic Argentinean restaurant specializes in *parrilladas* (grilled meats), but the pastas and pizzas are also quite good. While the pictures of Diego Maridona's 'hand of God' and the pulsating TV screens could go, the service is personable and the *chimichurri* is as good as it gets. The place ties with the Roka's restaurant as the best in town.

### Mercado Central                  MARKET $
(12 de Noviembre; mains $1.50; ⊙7am-7pm) The second floor of Ambato's indoor market has particularly good *llapingachos* (fried pancakes of mashed potatoes with cheese). Old ladies serve them with eggs, avocado slices and sausage (veggies can get it without the meat) for $1.50. The younger gals nearby blend super fresh juices made with bottled water ($1).

### Pizzería Fornace                  PIZZA $$
(Cevallos 17-28; pizzas $4-5, mains $8-10; ⊙noon-10pm) Cooked in a wood-fired brick oven, and with thin crusts and fresh ingredients, this is probably the best pizza in town. Locals enjoy the cuts of meat here as well.

### Delicias del Paso                  BAKERY $
(cnr Sucre & Quito; baked items $1-2; ⊙10am-6pm) This cafeteria has all its tasty quiches and cakes in the display out front, and you can order them to go right from the street.

### El Alamo Chalet                  ECUADORIAN $$
(Cevallos 17-19; mains $4-8; ⊙8am-10pm) Easily identified by its chalet-style wooden facade, El Alamo serves good, diner-style food: meat and chicken dishes, *llapingachos*, a hearty *desayuno montubiano* (a Manabi-province breakfast of fish, eggs, beans and fried plantains) and more basic morning dishes.

### Chifa Nueva Hong Kong                  CHINESE $
(Bolívar 768; mains $2-4; ⊙noon-11pm) Hong Kong comes to Ambato with fried rice, *tallarines* (noodles) and *agridulce* (sweet-and-sour) dishes. The little egg rolls are yummy.

## Drinking & Entertainment

### Los Vinitos                  PUB
(cnr Rocafuerte & Guayaquil; ⊙closed Sunday) This cozy two-story bar is perfect for quietly conspiring in a corner. It's one of our faves. Around the corner, Vinitos II has karaoke and caters to an older crowd.

### Link Club                  CLUB
(cnr Bolívar & Quito; ⊙till late Fri & Sat) Get your thump-thump on at this glitzy club catering to the area's youth in revolt.

## Information

Many robberies are reported on overnight buses here, and it's best to take a cab at night downtown. The areas – and hotels – around Parque 12 de Noviembre are especially sketchy at night.
**Banco de Guayaquil** (cnr Mera & Sucre) Bank with ATM.
**Banco del Pichincha** (Lalama near Sucre) Bank with ATM.

**Cabinas Telefónicas Internet** (cnr 12 de Noviembre & Quito; internet per hr $0.80) Internet and telephone booths.

**Lavandería Automatic** (cnr Colon & Vargas Torres) $4.70 per load; same-day service.

**Post office** (cnr Castillo & Bolívar)

**TAME** (☑282 6601/0322/2595; Bolívar 20-17) Airline office for flight reservations from other cities.

**Tourist office** (☑282-1800; www.turismo.gob.ec or www.ecuador.travel; Guayaquil & Rocafuerte; ☺8am-5pm Mon-Fri)

# ❶ Getting There & Away

QUITO Bus services to Quito ($2.50, 2½ hours), Riobamba ($1.25, one hour) and destinations beyond leave from Ambato's **main bus terminal** (☑282-1481; Avs de las Américas & Colombia), 2km from downtown. Head northeast on 12 de Noviembre, straight through the traffic circle and then left at the traffic light.

QUIAPINCHA Buses ($0.35, 25 minutes) to Quisapincha leave from the corner of Espejo and Moreno in Ambato. Taxis cost around $8.

SALASACA & PATATE Buses to Salasaca ($0.25, 25 minutes) and Patate ($0.70, one hour) leave every 20 minutes or so from Plaza La Dolorosa in the Ferroviaria neighborhood, a $1 cab ride from downtown. Any Baños-bound bus can drop you in these villages, too, but the direct buses depart from a stop closer to downtown.

BAÑOS Buses leave hourly for Baños ($1, one hour) from the **Mayorista Terminal**, about 5km south of the main bus terminal, near the roundabout at Amazonas and Julio Jaramillo. You can also catch passing buses, which are more frequent, at the roundabout itself.

PÍLLARO Buses to Pillaro leave frequently from Colón and Unidad Nacional near Parque La Merced ($0.48, 30 minutes). A taxi should run about $10.

# ❶ Getting Around

The most important local bus service for travelers is the route between Ambato's main bus terminal and downtown. From the terminal, climb the exit ramp to Avenida de las Américas, which crosses the train tracks on a bridge. On this bridge is a bus stop, where a westbound (to your right) bus, usually signed 'Centro,' will take you to Parque Cevallos for $0.25.

Buses marked 'Terminal' leave from the Martínez side of Parque Cevallos. A bus that goes to Miraflores and Ficoa runs along the Sucre side.

# Around Ambato
☑03

From handicraft shopping to indigenous villages, from haciendas to rugged wilderness, the area around Ambato has it all.

**SALASACA**

You'll know when you've reached the rather ugly town of Salasaca, about 14km south of Ambato, because of the abundance of men walking around in long, black ponchos over crisp white shirts and trousers. Along with a broad-brimmed white hat, men wear the distinctive black Salasaca poncho. Women

## BUSES FROM AMBATO'S MAIN TERMINAL

| DESTINATION | COST (US$) | DURATION (HR) |
| --- | --- | --- |
| Cuenca | 8 | 7 |
| Esmeraldas | 7.50 | 8 |
| Guayaquil | 7 | 6 |
| Ibarra | 5 | 5 |
| Lago Agrio | 10 | 11 |
| Latacunga | 1 | ¾ |
| Loja | 9–11 | 11 |
| Machala | 7 | 8 |
| Manta | 8 | 10 |
| Puyo | 2.50 | 3 |
| Quito | 2.50 | 2½ |
| Riobamba | 1.25 | 1 |
| Santo Domingo | 4 | 4 |
| Tena | 5 | 6 |

wear colorful shawls and long wool skirts with a woven belt called a *chumbi*.

There is a **craft market** held every Sunday morning near the church on the Ambato–Baños road, and nearby are several craft stores that are open daily. **Hostal Runa Huasi** (☑09-984-0125; www.hostalrunahuasi.com; r per person incl breakfast $14), 2km north of the Panamericana in Salasaca, is a comfortable and friendly place run by the indigenous Pilla family. Ask here for a weaving demonstration and tours of the surrounding area.

On the Sunday after Easter, a magnificent street dance takes place on the road (slowing traffic considerably), and on June 15 the Salasacas dress up in animal costumes for **Santo Vintio**. Both **Corpus Christi** (on a movable date in June) and the **feast of St Anthony** (end of November) are colorfully celebrated. Buses ($0.25) run regularly to Ambato.

### PATATE & AROUND

Along the banks of the Río Patate and with great views of Volcán Tungurahua, Patate has became a popular destination for volcano-watchers during recent eruptions (see p149). The village is known for its *chicha de uva* (a fermented grape beverage) and *arepas* (they add squash to the traditional corn pancakes), lovingly prepared in wood ovens around town. There's a fun hike up the remarkably steep stairway known as **La Escalinata**, just east of town off Soria, while strolling through the lush main square and taking in the air is a favorite pastime for locals and visitors alike. If they aren't selling *arepas* on the plaza, head over on Gonzalez Suarez.

Your best bet for sleeping near the town, **Casta Restaurant and Hotel** (☑287-0364; juank_tamayo87@yahoo.es; r per person incl breakfast $15, mains $2-5; ☎) is a cozy mountain retreat with an excellent family restaurant and rustic cabin-style rooms with great views. The hotel is just 500m east of town up a steep hill.

From Patate, a back road called the **Ruta Ecológica** heads south to Baños and could make for a great mountain bike route (you'll need a 4x4 to take on the route by car).

**Hacienda Manteles** (☑in Quito 02-223-3484; www.haciendamanteles.com; s/d/ste incl breakfast & dinner $95/135/160; @), about 12km down the Ruta Ecológica, is a beautiful upscale, rustically styled resort engaged in certified ecotourism practices. Among other things, it supports local communities in creating microbusinesses, has an organic garden and protects 200 hectares of cloud forest that you can explore. Rooms and suites (the new suites come with Jacuzzi tubs!) have broad views of the Río Patate valley and of Volcán Tungurahua in the distance. Horseback-riding, canyoneering, bird-watching and zip-lining over the cloud forest are possible.

Buses run regularly from Ambato to Patate ($0.70).

## Baños

☑03 / POP 14,700 / ELEV 1800M

Baños is a mixed bag. The setting is amazing. From town you can see waterfalls, hike through lush forests, rest your bones in steaming thermal springs, hike down impossibly steep gorges, bike or boat all the way to the Amazon Basin, and marvel at the occasional eruption of nearby Volcán Tungurahua. But the town itself, with its drab architecture, garish tours and over-

---

> **WORTH A TRIP**
>
> ## QUISAPINCHA, PARQUE NACIONAL LLANGANATES & PÍLLARO
>
> Quick day trips or longer excursions from Ambato can take you to a handful of exciting colonial villages and a seldom-visited national park.
>
> **Quisapincha** Just 10km outside of Ambato, this quaint little village is a great spot to pick up leather goods. The views from up here are amazing.
>
> **Parque Nacional Llanganates & Píllaro** They say there's lost Inca treasure buried somewhere in the remote and inaccessible wilderness of the 2197-sq-km Parque Nacional Llanganates (admission $2). The park encompasses broad swaths of *páramo*, cloud forest, tropical forest and high 4000m peaks, and is home to tapir, puma, jaguar, capybara and more. You can hire a guide for about $20 a day in the small village of Píllaro, 20km northeast of Ambato, and tour operators in Baños also arrange excursions. December to February is the best time to visit. The running of the bulls on August 10 and during the first week of January in Píllaro are definitely worth the side trip.

crowded backpacker-ghetto feel, leaves a lot to be desired. This said, this is the central highlands' premiere destination for mountain-biking, hiking, rafting and partying, and while many folks will have their reservations about the town's look and feel, almost everybody leaves with a big smile on their face and great stories from their adventures.

## Sights & Activities

Most visitors here brave the outdoors on a horse, bicycle or boat. Numerous tour operators in town can set you up. Baños also offers an innovation in freefall insanity called *puenting* (think bungee jumping without the bounce). It crudely translates as 'bridging,' but it's really swinging, in this case along a rope tethered to two bridges.

Baños is tiny and the mountains towering over town make everything easy to reference. Almost everything is within walking distance from the bus terminal. Few buildings in Baños have street numbers.

### Basílica de Nuestra Señora de Agua Santa
CHURCH

(Ambato at 12 de Noviembre; admission free; ☉7am-8pm) Within the town itself, this Basílica is dedicated to the Virgin of the Holy Water (the same one with a shrine over by the waterfall). This illustrious lady is credited with several local miracles. Inside the church, paintings depict her wonders, with explanations in Spanish along the lines of: 'On January 30, 1904, Señor X fell off his horse as he was crossing the Río Pastaza bridge. As he fell 70m to the torrents below, he yelled "Holy Mother of the Holy Water" and was miraculously saved!' Other paintings show people being spared from exploding volcanoes, burning hotels and other misfortunes. The Virgin is particularly good at warding off transit accidents, so you may catch the site of a priest blessing a taxi or truck with holy water.

### Baths

Most of the baths are fed by thermal springs burbling from the base of Volcán Tungurahua. The water in the pools is constantly being recycled and only looks murky because of its mineral content, including healthful chlorates, sulfates and magnesium.

All the pools have changing rooms and clothing storage. Towels are available for rent, but generally not until after 8am, and they can run out. Everyone is supposed to

shower and put on a bathing suit before entering the pools. Technically, you're supposed to have a bathing cap too, but it's okay if you don't – just pull back your hair.

### Las Piscinas de La Virgen
SWIMMING

(Montalvo; admission day/night $2/3; ☉5am-5pm & 6-10pm) These are the only hot pools in the town proper. Built as a community project in 1928, they are named for the Virgin Mary, who is said to have come here to dip her own feet. One bath is cold, another warm and a third reaches an intense 42°C (118°F). Check out the *ojo del agua,* where the water, heated by the volcano, gushes from the earth at a scorching 50°C (122°F).

### Piscinas Las Modernas/ Las Peñas
SWIMMING

(Martínez; admission $2; ☉9am-5pm Fri-Sun) With a waterslide, a swing set, water toys and cool pools, **Las Modernas** is packed with families on the weekends and holidays.

### Baños El Salado
SWIMMING

(admission $3; ☉5am-4:30pm) The best hot springs around, El Salado is 2.5km from town in a cozy canyon. It consists of hot, medium and cool pools with an icy river close by. To get here, head past the cemetery on Martínez, where you'll end up on a track that crosses a stream (Quebrada de Naguasco) on a small wooden footbridge. From there, the trail continues on the other side to a road, where you turn left to reach the springs. Buses come out here ($0.25, 10 minutes), departing from the stop on Rocafuerte.

### Massages & Spa Treatments

Baños has an endless supply of spas with such treatments as the *baños de cajón* (steam baths in a box), massage, medicinal mud baths and, yes, even intestinal drainage. The high-end hotels all have spas open to nonguests.

### Spa Garden El Refugio
SPA

(☏274-0482; www.spaecuador.info; Camino Real; treatments $2.50-25) Full-service day spa; by appointment or walk-in.

### Stay In Touch
SPA

(☏274-0973; Ibarra) For excellent massages ($20 to $55) and other spa treatments ($65 to $90), by appointment or walk-in.

### Chakra
MASSAGE

(☏274-2027, 09-355-6698; Alfaro & Martínez; ☉8am-7pm & by appointment) For one-hour

# Baños

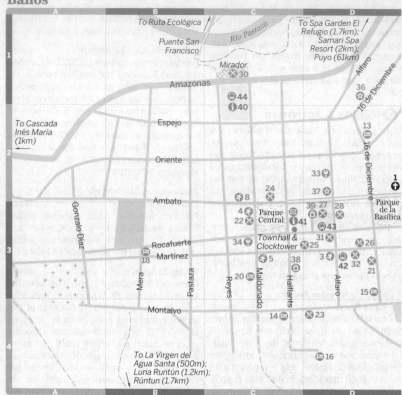

To Ruta Ecológica
Río Pastaza
To Spa Garden El Refugio (1.7km); Samari Spa Resort (2km); Puyo (61km)
Puente San Francisco
Mirador 30
Amazonas
44
40
36
To Cascada Inés María (1km)
Espejo
13
Oriente
33
24
37
Ambato
8
Parque de la Basílica
1
4
22
Parque Central
41
39 27 28
43
Rocafuerte
34
Townhall & Clocktower
31
25
26
18
Martínez
5
38
3
42 32
21
20
15
Montalvo
14
23
To La Virgen del Agua Santa (500m); Luna Runtún (1.2km); Rúntun (1.7km)
16

Swedish, hot-stone and reflexology massages ($20), visit Carmen Sánchez at Chakra.

## Mountain-Biking

Several companies rent mountain bikes starting at about $6 per day ($10 gets you disk brakes and suspension), but check that the bike, helmet and lock are adequately maintained or even ask to take a quick test ride before agreeing to rent. The most popular ride is the dramatic descent past a series of waterfalls on the road to Puyo, a jungle town 61km to the east. Various other mountain-biking options are available and the outfitters will be happy to tell you about them.

On the issue of safety, the Baños–Puyo road has several narrow, long and pitch-black tunnels. Bike riders should bypass the tunnels by veering down on the signed trails that swing around them.

## Hiking

The tourist office provides a crude but useful map showing some of the trails around town.

The walk down to Río Pastaza is easy and popular. Just behind the Sugarcane Stalls by the bus station, a short trail leads to the **Puente San Francisco**, the bridge that crosses the river. You can continue on trails up the other side as far as you want.

Going south on Maldonado takes you to a path that climbs to **Bellavista**, where a white cross stands high over Baños. The path then continues to the settlement of **Runtún**, some two hours away, where the views are outstanding. You can then loop around and back down to Baños, ending up at the southern end of Mera. This takes you past the statue of **La Virgen del Agua Santa**, about half an hour from town. The whole walk takes four to five hours.

detailed information about other climbing and hiking peaks in Parque Nacional Sangay, see p149.

The town's tour operators rent gear. Climbs, which generally involve an overnight stay in *refugios* (mountain refuges), run between $120 to $150 per person, not including park and *refugio* fees.

### Horseback-Riding

Horse rentals cost around $5 per hour or $35 per day. Many half- or full-day trips start with a long jeep ride out of town, and the actual riding time is short – inquire carefully to be sure to get what you want.

**José & Two Dogs**   HORSEBACK-RIDING
(☎274-0746; josobalu_99@yahoo.com; cnr Maldonado & Martínez) Recommended by locals.

### Rafting

The town's tour operators offer guided trips on the Río Patate and Pastaza. The trips bring you to Class III and IV water (Class IV is enough to really get your heart pumping). Trips cost $35 for a half day, and $90 for a full day.

## ☞ Tours

For jungle treks, trips to the neighboring national parks, rafting, volcano climbs, canyoneering and more, check out these recommended tour operators:

**Rainforest Tour**   ADVENTURE TOUR
(☎325-4046, 223-9822; www.rainforestur.com; Ambato 800) This is a long-standing operation.

**Expediciones Amazónicas**   ADVENTURE TOUR
(☎274-0506; Maldonado) Head here for your Amazon adventure.

## ☞ Courses

One-on-one or small-group Spanish classes start from around $6 per hour. **Fundación Arte del Mundo** (☎274-2244; www.artedelmundoecuador.com; Oriente & Cañar) Runs an afterschool arts and reading program, and also has a free language exchange Tuesdays at 7pm.

**Baños Spanish Center**   LANGUAGE COURSE
(☎274-0632; Oriente & Cañar) This well-established school is locally recommended.

**Raíces Spanish School**   LANGUAGE COURSE
(☎274-1921; www.spanishlessons.org; 16 de Diciembre & Pablo Suarez) Another good school in a funkier setting.

West of town on Amazonas, turn right by a religious shrine and walk down to Puente San Martín and visit the impressive falls of **Cascada Inés María**, a few hundred meters to the right of the bridge.

### Jungle Trips

Many Baños tour operators lead trips to the jungle, but they vary in quality and experience. For more information, see p205.

Three- to seven-day jungle tours cost about $50 to $75 per person per day, depending on the destination (usually with a three- or four-person minimum). Always full of travelers, Baños is a good place to organize a group if you are not already with one.

### Climbing

The climbing conditions on Tungurahua (5016m), an active volcano, are naturally in flux. At the time of research, the volcano was active, and closed to climbing. For

# Baños

## 🎊 Festivals & Events

Baños became the seat of its canton on December 16, 1944, and an annual fiesta is celebrated around this date. There are the usual processions, fireworks, music and a great deal of street dancing and drinking. These festivities rev up again in October as the various barrios of Baños take turns paying homage to the local icon, Nuestra Señora de Agua Santa.

## 🛏 Sleeping

Rates are highest on weekends and during vacations, when hotels can all fill up.

TOP CHOICE **Posada del Arte**    BOUTIQUE HOTEL **$$**
(☎274-0083; www.posadadelarte.com; Ibarra; s/d incl breakfast from $28/52; 🐾) They say that small is beautiful, and that is certainly the case at Posada del Arte, an exquisite little guesthouse with colorful, comfortable rooms, wood floors, gigantic breakfasts and art all around. The midrange rooms have views, as do the priciest rooms, which also have fireplaces.

**Hostal Chimenea**    HOSTEL **$**
(☎274-2725; www.hostalchimenea.com; Martínez & Vieira; dm/s/d from $6.50/$8.50/20; @🐾🌊) From the rather dark reception area, you wouldn't know that this reader-recommended hostel is the best budget offering in town. The bright and clean rooms and dorms come with rainbow-colored blankets, and the upstairs terrace has great views of the waterfall. A small dip pool, hot tub and sauna out back add to the mix. Dorm rooms

all have attached baths and sleep four to six people.

**Hostal Plantas y Blanco** HOSTEL $
(274-0044; option3@hotmail.com; Martínez & 12 de Noviembre; dm $6.50, r per person $11, with shared bathroom $9.50; @🛜) A bit disco in the common areas, the hyperclean and eternally popular 'Plants and White' (you figure it out) scores big points for its rooftop terrace, outstanding breakfasts, on-site steam bath and overall value. Some rooms have weird layouts (such as walking through the shower to the toilet), but no one seems to mind.

**La Floresta Hotel** HOTEL $$
(274-1824; wwwlaflorestahotel.com; Montalvo & Haflants; s/d/tr $33/55/66; @🛜) This comfortable inn situated around a pretty interior garden is located in a quiet part of town that is still close to the baths and everything else. The staff here are friendly, and the spacious, tile-floor rooms have big windows and comfortable beds.

**Luna Runtún** SPA & RESORT $$$
(274-0882; www.lunaruntun.com; r per person incl breakfast & dinner $77; @🛎) Perched at the top of a sheer cliff (2260m) looking high over Baños and up to the Tungurahua summit, Luna Runtún is all about location. Just laying eyes on the spa (open to nonguests for $30 per day) will relax you. The restaurant has the best scenery – and worst service – in town. Ultimately, it's about the view, one of the most stunning offered by any central sierra hotel. It's 6km beyond Baños via the road to Puyo – get the bus or a taxi ($6) up to the hotel, and walk down to town via a well-maintained trail.

**Samari Spa Resort** SPA & RESORT $$$
(274-1855; www.samarispa.com; Vía a Puyo Km 1; d/ste/tr incl breakfast from $186/253/292; @🛎) A five-star resort built on the site of an 18th-century Jesuit monastery, Samari's grounds make it the most luxurious hotel and spa in town. However, the rooms leave something to be desired and, for the money, you may be happier up the hill at the Runtún. The spa is situated around a heavenly indoor pool. It's located about 2km east of town on Amazonas.

**Hostal Transilvania** HOSTEL $
(274-2281; www.hostal-transilvania.com; 16 de Diciembre y Oriente; r per person incl breakfast $7.50; 🛜) There's nothing Transilvanian about the simple, clean rooms here, but there are some nice common areas and a pool table at this party-oriented hostel.

**La Petite Auberge** HOTEL $
(274-0936; www.lepetit.banios.com; 16 de Diciembre; s/d $18/27; 🛜🛁) This French-owned, hacienda-style hotel has big rooms with *chimeneas* (fireplaces) and lofts. A huge games room makes it popular with families. Other than the slightly out-of-date baths, this is a great option for the private-room budget set.

**Hostal Huillacuna** HOTEL $
(274-2909; 12 de Noviembre; r per person incl breakfast $15; 🛜) This art lover's paradise houses one of the town's best galleries and has a large open-air common room with art, antiques and a cozy fireplace. The rooms are a little dank but clean, and the friendly owners make you feel at home.

**Timara Hostal** HOSTEL $
(274-0599; Maldonado; r per person $9, with shared bathroom $5; 🛜) This long-running family business has recently added three stories of colorful new rooms with private bathrooms and cable TV. The older rooms with shared bathrooms are run-down but well lit and acceptable. There are guest kitchen facilities too.

**Sangay Spa Hotel** SPA & RESORT $$$
(274-0490; www.sangayspahotel.com; Montalvo; s/ste $91/164, cabins $134; @🛎🛁) A resort-style hotel complete with kids' club and pool, the Sangay comes up short on refinement in both its business-style modern rooms and overly priced colonial offerings in the old section. Nevertheless, the cabins sleep up to four people, making this a viable option for families.

**Residencia Princesa María** HOSTEL $
(274-1035; Mera & Rocafuerte; r per person $7; 🛁) This friendly, family-run hostel offers private baths, rock-hard beds, good security and a communal kitchen.

**Monte Selva Hotel Spa** SPA & RESORT $$
(274-0244; www.monteselvaecuador.com; Halflants; s/d/tr/q $38/63/82/97; 🛎) The lobby feels pretty swanked out, but the wooden cabins, funky dark rooms and sauna facilities leave a bit to be desired. You're better off at other midrange offerings, unless you absolutely must have a pool.

# ✗ Eating

Baños is famous for its *melcocha,* a chewy taffy that's softened and blended by swinging it onto wooden pegs, usually mounted in the doorways of shops. Pieces of chewable *caña de azúcar* (sugarcane) and *jugo de caña* (sugarcane juice) are sold at the **sugarcane stalls** across from the bus terminal.

**Casa Hood** INTERNATIONAL $
(Martínez at Halflants; mains $4-7; ☺8am-10:15pm) Named for owner Ray Hood, a long-standing gringo-in-residence, this excellent cafe has nourishing breakfasts, a cheap *almuerzo* and a menu of Thai, Mexican and Middle Eastern dishes. The Casa is a welcoming place to eat, exchange books, meet with friends, chill *solito* (alone), and even take yoga classes.

**Posada del Arte** INTERNATIONAL $
(Ibarra; mains $3-7; ☺8am-10pm) Like the hotel, this restaurant is a welcoming and cozy place with a warming fireplace. It serves excellent international dishes, wonderful breakfasts (including Tungurahua pancakes – they don't explode!) and lots of great, small plates for snacking (try the fried yuca).

**Café Mariane** FRENCH $$
(Montalvo; mains $6-9; ☺11am-11pm) Mariane's French-Mediterranean cuisine is a real standout in Baños. The cheese-and-meat fondues are a lot – even for two people, and the pasta and meat dishes are quite elegant. It's quite popular, so you'll need to be patient when it comes to service.

**Swiss Bistro** SWISS $$
(Martínez, near Alfaro; mains $7-9; ☺noon-11pm) This small bistro's cow fetish is evident in its decor and delicious Swiss and European specialties, which include fondue, steaks, big, fresh salads and a Swiss potato dish called *roesti.*

**Quilombo** ARGENTINE $$
(cnr Montalvo & 12 de Noviembre; mains $4-8; ☺noon-11pm Wed-Sun) Quilombo means 'mess' or 'insanity' in Argentine slang and is a perfect descriptor for this irreverent restaurant. A bizarre grab-bag menu, hodgepodge decor and kooky Argentine owner add to the insanity. But the steaks are pretty good and the wine flows freely.

**La Bella Italia** ITALIAN $
(Martínez; mains $5-6; ☺noon-11pm) This elegant little Italian bistro serves pasta and pizzas in a quiet atmosphere.

**Ponche Suizo** CAFE $
(Alfaro; snacks $1-3; ☺8am-6pm) Between Ambato and Rocafuerte, this little spot serves cakes and coffee, but everyone comes for the 'Ponche Suizo,' a trade-secret treat that's a cross between a shake and a mousse.

**Café Good** INTERNATIONAL $
(16 de Diciembre; mains $4-7; ☺8am-10pm) An imitator of the Hood joints, the Good also serves better-than-good veggie dishes with wholesome brown rice as well as some chicken and fish.

**Café Hood** INTERNATIONAL $
(Maldonado; mains $3-6; ☺10am-9pm Thu-Tue) Crunchier and stickier than the other 'goods' and 'hoods' in town, Café Hood has a groovy groupie feel, plenty of international dishes – from Mexican to Greek to Indian – and a cheap backpackers' lunch. The ingredients are less fresh than we would like.

**Café Rico Pan** BAKERY $
(Ambato; mains $2-5; ☺7am-7pm Mon-Sat, to 1pm Sun) *Panaderías* (bread shops) in Baños tend to have good coffee and breakfasts. Rico Pan, near Maldonado, has one of the earliest served.

**Super Bodega** SUPERMARKET $
(Alfaro & Rocafuerte; ☺8:30am-8pm) This centrally located market is the place to stock up.

**Mercado Central** MARKET $
(Alfaro & Rocafuerte; ☺7am-6pm) A reliable place to find fresh fruits and veggies.

# 🍷 Drinking & Entertainment

Nightlife in Baños means dancing in local *peñas* (bars or clubs featuring live folkloric music) or hanging out in one of many character-filled bars.

**Jack Rock** THEME BAR
(Alfaro 5-41; ☺8pm-2am) Jack Rock has a rock 'n' roll theme and the best pub atmosphere in town. It plays classic rock during the week and salsa, merengue and *reggaetón* (a blend of Puerto Rican *bomba*, dancehall and hip-hop) on weekends.

**Stray Dog Brew Pub** PUB
(cnr Rocafuerte & Maldonado; ☺closed Tue) The only brew pub in Baños features surprisingly good artisanal offerings like light Llamas' Breath Belgian and bold Stray Dog Stout.

**Peña Ananitay**     LIVE MUSIC
(16 de Diciembre; ☺9pm-3am Fri & Sat) Near Espejo, this is the best place in town to catch live *folklórica* (Andean folk music). It can get packed, but that's part of the fun.

**Peña Bar Mocambo**     LIVE MUSIC
(Alfaro; ☺10am-2am Mon-Sat) Always popular, thanks to its sidewalk bar with a funny Last Supper-inspired mural, party atmosphere and upstairs billiards room. Near Ambato.

**Fundación Arte del Mundo**     CINEMA
(☑274-2244; www.artedelmundoecuador.com; Oriente & Cañar) This kids' arts and reading program hosts movie night on Wednesday at 8pm.

## Shopping

**Pasaje Artesanal**     HANDICRAFTS
(☺8am-8pm) At this outdoors crafts market, between Ambato and Rocafuerte, you'll find endless quantities of locally made baubles and a regional craft called *tagua* carving – white, golfball-size nuts that resemble ivory and are dyed and transformed into figurines and jewelry.

**Galería de Arte Huillacuna**     GALLERY
(12 de Noviembre, near Montalvo; ☺8:30am-9pm) Exhibits and sells excellent Ecuadorian art. You're free to roam without buying.

**Guitarras Guevara**     MUSIC
(Halflants 2-84; ☺daily) For more than 50 years, Jacinto Guevara has been hand-making guitars. Pick one up for anywhere from $75 to $300.

## ℹ Information

Eruptions of Tungurahua forced locals to evacuate in 1999 and 2006. In 2011, the volcano was at it again, leading authorities to evacuate some nearby villages. This said, it's a well-monitored situation and shouldn't be a major concern. More worrying are the widespread reports of robberies on the trails outside Baños. When heading out for a hike, bring only a small amount of cash and leave your expensive cameras and mobile devices behind. Hiring a guide is a good way to contribute to the local economy and reduce your risk. Ask your hotel staff about evacuation procedures in the event of an eruption.

Internet cafes ($0.80 to $1 per hour) come and go but are always plentiful, as are laundry joints ($1 per kilo).

**Corporación Nacional de Telecomunicaciones** (cnr Rocafuerte & Halflants) Telephone center.

**Banco del Pacífico** (cnr Halflants & Rocafuerte)

**Banco del Pichincha** (cnr Ambato & Halflants)

**Hospital** (☑274-0443/0301; Montalvo) Near Pastaza; pharmacies are along Ambato.

**Ministerio del Ambiente Parque Nacional Llanganates** (☑274-1662; ☺hr vary Mon-Fri) Administration office for Llanganates; has small, photocopied topo maps and lots of information. At the bus terminal.

**Police station** (☑274-0251; Oriente near Mera)

**Post office** (☑274-0901; Halflants near Ambato)

**Tourist offices** (☑274-0483; mun_banos@andinanet.net; Halflants near Rocafuerte & in bus terminal; ☺8am-12:30pm & 2-5:30pm Mon-Fri) Lots of info, free maps and emergency-evacuation information.

## ℹ Getting There & Away

The Baños **bus terminal** (Amazonas) is within easy walking distance of most hotels. Transportes Baños offers frequent buses direct to Quito ($3.50, 3½ hours) that stop in Salasaca, Ambato ($1; one hour) and Latacunga as well. The first half of the Baños–Riobamba road (up to Penipe) remains closed – you will have to backtrack through Ambato. To the Oriente, buses depart regularly for Puyo ($2, two hours), Tena ($4, five hours) and Coca ($10, 10 hours). There are daily buses to Guayaquil ($8, seven hours).

## ℹ Getting Around

Westbound local buses leave from Rocafuerte, behind the Mercado Central. Marked 'El Salado,' they go to the Piscinas El Salado ($0.25, 10 minutes). Eastbound local buses go as far as the dam at Agoyán; they leave from Alfaro at Martínez.

Round-trip taxi tours for Pailón del Diablo ($20) leave from the bus terminal.

# From Baños to Puyo

☑03

Nicknamed 'La Ruta de las Cascadas' (Highway of the Waterfalls), the road from Baños to Puyo is one of the region's most dramatic routes. It hugs the Río Pastaza canyon as it drops steadily from Baños, at 1800m, to Puyo, at 950m and passes more than a dozen waterfalls on the way. The bus ride is great, but zipping down on a mountain bike is even better. The first third of the route is mostly downhill, but there are some definite climbs, so ready those legs (it's about 61km if you do the whole thing). Mountain bikes can be rented in Baños.

Most people go only as far as the spectacular Pailón del Diablo waterfalls, about 18km from Baños, but if you're up for a much bigger ride, making it to Río Negro allows you to see the change in ecology as you head into the lower elevations. Along the route, there are plenty of hidden waterfalls and family-run swimming holes not included in this guidebook. Leave an entire day to really explore the area.

Along the way, the road shoots through tunnels that seem to swallow you up like a black hole. Some are quite long and bikers or all-terrain vehicle riders should take the signed, dirt-trail detours that skirt around them. Watch your speed on curves and approaches to the tunnels and ride on the right side of the road. From Puyo (or any point on the way), you can simply take a bus back to Baños, putting your bike on the roof (the bus driver's assistant will help you load it).

Make sure that you rent a helmet and a bike lock (and use both!). Insects on the trails can be unrelenting, so bring repellent and don't forget your raincoat.

### BAÑOS TO RÍO VERDE

Before the first tunnel, you'll pass the Agoyán hydroelectric project. After the tunnel, you'll catch a little spray from the first waterfall, and about 45 minutes' riding time from Baños you'll pass the spectacular **Manto de La Novia** waterfalls. For a closer look at the falls, take one of the engine-powered *tarabitas* (cable cars, $1 to $2) around Km 10. They'll transport you 500m across the river gorge at hair-raising heights above 100m.

From Manto de La Novia, it's a good 30- to 45-minute ride to the village of **Río Verde** (between the fourth and fifth tunnels), the access point for the 15-minute downhill hike to the thundering **Pailón del Diablo** (Devil's Cauldron) waterfalls. One view of the falls is from the suspension bridge and the other is an up-close view from *behind* the falls (admission $1.50, at the Pailón del Diablo cafeteria). To get here, go through the crafts stalls just east of the town center and on down the trail.

Just east of Río Verde, you'll find the wonderful **Hostal Pequeño Paraíso** (www. pprioverde.com; dm/r per person incl breakfast & dinner $17/20). It offers lodging and camping amid lush and beautiful jungle, as well as excellent opportunities for hiking, rock climbing and canyoneering. Vegetarian meals available.

On the north side of the road at the Río Verde entrance, the **Miramelindo** (☎249-3004; hosteriamiramelindo@hotmail.com; Km 18 on the Baños–Puyo rd; r per person incl breakfast $30; 🖭🄼) has a pool, Jacuzzi, *baños de cajón* and wonderfully rustic rooms accented in wood and earthy colors.

### RÍO VERDE TO PUYO

Just beyond Río Verde, the road starts to climb. After about a half hour's riding, you come to **Machay**, a nice place to stop for a picnic lunch and a dip in the river. A 2.5km trail leads into the cloud forest and past eight **waterfalls**, which range from wee tumblers to the beautiful **Manantial del Dorado** 2.5km in. Several outfits now charge you to access the trails here. The **Asociación de Ecoturismo Comunitario** at Km 17 charges $1 to get in.

After Machay, you have two good climbs, then it's downhill nearly all the way to Río Negro, 15km from Río Verde. As the road drops, the vegetation rapidly becomes more tropical; the walls of the Río Pastaza canyon are covered with bromeliads, giant tree ferns and orchids. Before you hit Río Negro, you'll pass through the village of **San Francisco**, which has a dirt plaza, a few simple eateries and places to buy water or beer.

After San Francisco, it's only another 10 to 15 minutes to **Río Negro**, a funky little town built up along the main road. There are restaurants (some of which are surprisingly slick) and plenty of places to buy refreshments. There's even a hotel.

After Río Negro, you start really feeling tropical. After 17km you pass **Mera**, which might have a police checkpoint (have your passport ready), and is slowly developing as a tourism spot. For folks who have some time and a love of animals, the **Merazonia Foundation** (☎08-421-3789, 08-437-2555; www. merazonia.org; r per volunteer per week incl meals $100), a refuge for injured rainforest animals just outside of Mera, offers volunteer opportunities with its projects rescuing and protecting birds, mammals and other creatures. It has facilities with composting toilets and hot showers.

Some 7km further, you pass **Shell**, an important air-transport hub into the jungle, where there might be another police checkpoint. On the other side of the bridge, near the main square, **Alexander's** doubles as a small grocery store and serves good *almuerzos* ($1 to $2). Just east of the military base, **Aero Regional** (☎09-280-8080) is an air-taxi

## WHAT'S IN A GRAIN?

Ecuador is corn and potato country. The hills, with their patchwork of green and golden cultivation, show that. But for thousands of years, quinoa (*Chenopodium quinoa*) was also king. A critical protein source, this morsel, the size of a pin head, sustained the Inca, who called it 'Mother Grain' on their long marches, and to this day it is an important staple throughout the Andes.

In rural Ecuador you'll still find the tiny grain in *sopa de quinua* (quinoa soup) and other recipes, thanks in part to its cultural importance and to its UN designation as a 'supercrop' for its high nutritional value. With international prices on the rise, many rural communities are taking advantage of optimal market conditions to reclaim quinoa as a cash crop.

One such community is in, strangely enough, a community-based radio station called the Escuelas Radiofónicas Populares del Ecuador (referred to locally as ERPE or *Radiofónica*; tune in at AM 710 or FM 91.7 or check out www.erpe.org.ec). ERPE started in 1962 as an education program that broadcast to campesinos in surrounding provinces. In the 1980s it started an organic farm, something it already knew how to do well, to fund its activities, and it soon realized that it could target the international market with its organic produce. ERPE taught more than 3500 farming families in four provinces how to grow organic quinoa, and in 1997 it received its first order from the United States. Since then, it has produced more than 800 tons of quinoa for export, increased local consumption of the supercrop and nearly doubled the salaries of many quinoa-farming families.

In 2002, Slow Food International awarded ERPE the prestigious Slow Food Prize, putting these farmers in the ranks of the world's finest organic food producers.

company with chartered flights to lodges and villages in the jungle.

At the end of the descent, 61km from Baños, you arrive at the humid jungle town of Puyo (p225).

## Parque Nacional Sangay

This 2710-sq-km **national park** (admission $2) contains three of Ecuador's most magnificent volcanoes – the mightily active Sangay, the remittently active Tungurahua and the extinct El Altar – as well as flora, fauna and terrain of immense diversity. The Ecuadorian government established the park in 1979, and Unesco made it a World Heritage Site in 1983.

From the *páramo* in the park's western heights, which climb to over 5000m around each of the three volcanoes, the terrain plunges down the eastern slopes of the Andes to elevations barely above 1000m. In between is terrain so steep, rugged and wet (over 4m of rain is recorded annually in some areas) that it remains a wilderness in the truest sense. The whole park is home to some 500 bird species and 3000 plant species, and the thickly vegetated slopes east of the mountains are the haunts of very rarely seen mammals, such

as spectacled bears, mountain tapirs, pumas, ocelots and porcupines.

Only two roads of importance enter the park: One goes from Riobamba to **Alao** (the main access point to Volcán Sangay) and peters out in the *páramos* to the east. The second is the Guamote–Macas road, which despite the protected status of the park, runs right through it, inviting the negative environmental impact of colonization and hunting.

### VOLCÁN TUNGURAHUA

With a (pre-eruption) elevation of 5016m, Tungurahua (from the Kichwa for 'Throat of Fire') is Ecuador's 10th-highest peak. It *was* a beautiful, cone-shaped volcano with a glacier plopped on top of its lush, green slopes, but since 1999 many eruptions have melted the snow and changed the shape of the cone and crater. Lava and lahar flows from the August 2006 eruption covered about 2km of the Ambato–Baños road (now repaired), and a significant explosion in November 2011 triggered evacuations in the area.

Before 1999, travelers liked to walk part of the way up the volcano, perhaps as far as the village of Pondoa and the (now destroyed) refuge at 3800m. People have made it up to the refuge during periods of calm in recent years, but climbing beyond Pondoa is currently prohibited. It only takes about three months of relative silence, however, for the carefully monitored Tungurahua to get an all-clear for climbing from local authorities, so ask in Baños about the current situation.

## VOLCÁN EL ALTAR

At 5319m, this long-extinct volcano is the fifth-highest mountain in Ecuador and one of its most picturesque and fascinating peaks. Before the collapse of the western side of the crater in prehistoric times, the 'Altar' may have been one of the highest mountains in the world. The crater walls, which surround a gem-colored lake called Laguna Amarilla, actually form nine distinct peaks, most of which have religious-themed names like Obispo (Bishop; 5315m) and Monja Chica (Little Nun; 5080m). In 2000, part of a glacier fell into the lake, creating a massive wave of water that charged down the west slope and over the Collanes plane (3900m), leaving huge boulders strewn across the landscape.

To get to El Altar, take a bus from Riobamba to Penipe, a village halfway between Riobamba and Baños. A road between Ambato and Penipe via Baños exists, but recent Tungurahua eruptions have made the bridges between Baños and Penipe impassable; inquire locally about current conditions. From Penipe, take a bus or hire the occasional truck to the tiny village of Candelaria (3100m), 12km to the southeast. From Candelaria it's about 2km to Hacienda Releche (☎03-296-0848; r per person $6) and the nearby ranger station, where you pay the park fee ($2). The owners of Releche also own the thatch-roofed refugio (per person $6) on the Collanes plane, and they rent horses ($8 each way, plus $8 for a guide).

The hike to the Collanes plane, which is the best place to camp near the peak, is straightforward, but slick mud can make for a slow-going walk. Rangers and hacienda staff can indicate the beginning of the trail, and in dry weather a fit hiker could power from Candelaria to the Collanes plane in six to seven hours. Once up on the plane, you will encounter many bulls (keep your distance), and their poop is spread all over the place (watch your step). Flooding occurs, but rarely. The best times to go are December to March. The wettest months are April and May, and the foggiest are July and August.

## VOLCÁN SANGAY

Constantly spewing out rocks, smoke and ash, 5230m-high Sangay is one of the world's most active volcanoes and a highly dangerous ascent. For those who do try, some guides actually recommend carrying a metal shield as protection from rocks blown out of the crater (now *that'll* lighten your load). Hiking up to the base or perhaps just to La Playa (The Beach) is possible, especially from December to February, when the area is driest.

The Instituto Geográfico Militar (IGM) in Quito can provide topo maps. To get to Sangay, take a bus from Parque La Dolorosa in Riobamba to the village of Alao ($1.50; 1½ hours; 5:30am, 6:30am and hourly noon to 6pm). At the national-park entrance in Alao, you can pay the park fee and get information about a cooperative of local guides that works out of Alao and nearby Guarguallá.

## LAGUNAS DE ATILLO & OZOGOCHE

With the opening of the Guamote–Macas road, the spectacular *páramo* lakes region of Lagunas de Atillo became easily accessible, and the area is being slowly developed for horseback-riding, hiking, trout fishing and even mountain-biking. Still, Atillo gets very few visitors, and it's an amazing place to see remote landscape and rural life.

About 79km from Riobamba, the road passes through Atillo (population 300), which is really two villages, Atillo Grande and Atillo Chico, spaced about 1km apart. From this area, which is surrounded by the Atillo lakes, you can hike six to eight hours over a nearby ridge to the Lagunas de Ozogoche and another three to four hours to the village of Totoras, where you can camp or ask around in the village for a *choza* (thatch-roofed hut; approximately $1) to sleep in. In Atillo Chico, a woman named Dora Paña at Paradero Los Saskines (☎03-260-6000; Vía Cebadas-Macas Km 38; r per person $5) offers basic lodging and meals, and close to Atillo Grande, the Cabaña Atillo Grande (Vía Cebadas-Macas Km 41; r per person $8) offers similar facilities. If you are camping, get your supplies in Riobamba and pick up a topo map at the IGM in Quito.

From Atillo the road winds through the national park before ending in Macas in the southern Oriente (see p231 for details of park access from Macas). Pro Bici in Riobamba offers two- and three-day biking trips along the Guamote–Macas road, passing through the lakes area.

Cooperativa Unidos buses leave Riobamba for Atillo at 5:30am, noon and 3:20pm (2:30pm on Sundays; $2, 2½ hours) from Velasco and Olmedo. All buses to Macas also pass Atillo, leaving Riobamba's Terminal Oriental at 2:30am, 5:45am, 10am, 1pm, 4pm and 5pm.

# Guaranda

✆03 / POP 30,987 / ELEV 2650M

Half the fun of Guaranda is getting there. The 99km 'highway' from Ambato reaches altitudes over 4000m and passes within 5km of the glacier on Volcán Chimborazo (6310m). From here, the mountain almost looks easy to climb. The capital of Bolívar province, Guaranda is small and uneventful. It sits amid seven steep hills that have prompted the moniker, 'the Rome of the Andes.' It certainly didn't get this nickname for its cultural offerings. The Wednesday and Saturday markets in the **Plaza 15 de Mayo** are worth checking out, as are the **Carnaval** celebrations, with water fights, dances, parades and a little liquor with local herbs called 'Pájaro Azul' (Blue Bird).

## 🛏 Sleeping

**Hostal de las Flores**          HOTEL $
(✆298-6202; Pichincha 4-02; r per person $10; 🛈) This is Guaranda's most traveler-oriented hotel, a pretty place in a nicely refurbished old building. The cheerful rooms open onto a small interior courtyard and have cable TV, firm beds and telephones. It is two blocks southwest of Parque Simón Bolívar.

**Hotel Bolívar**          HOTEL $
(✆298-0547; Sucre 7-04; r per person $18; 🛈) Another good option for discerning travelers, the rooms here are welcoming and clean, and there's a pleasant courtyard. The attached restaurant has good *almuerzos* ($2 to $3). It's two blocks south of Parque Simón Bolívar.

## 🍴 Eating

**Los 7 Santos**          CAFE $
(Convención de 1884; mains $1-3; ⊙10am-11pm Mon-Sat) A half a block downhill from Parque Simón Bolívar, Los 7 Santos offers all that you would expect from an artsy cafe in Quito. There's breakfast in the morning and small sandwiches and *bocaditos* (snacks) all day.

**La Bohemia**          ECUADORIAN $
(Convención de 1884 & 10 de Agosto; mains $2-4; ⊙8am-9pm Mon-Sat) Close to Parque Bolívar, La Bohemia serves *almuerzos* ($2) in a laid-back but attentive atmosphere. Chase your meal down with one of the giant *batidos* (fruit shakes).

## ❶ Information

**Banco del Pichincha** (Azuay near 7 de Mayo)
**Clínica Bolívar** (✆298-1278; near Plaza Roja)
**Hospital** (Cisneros s/n)
**Post office** (Azuay near Pichincha)

## ❶ Getting There & Away

Guaranda's bus terminal is a solid 20-minute walk or a $1 cab ride from downtown. Afternoon buses can get booked up in advance, so plan ahead.

Bus services depart hourly for Ambato ($2.10, two hours) and Quito ($5, five hours). Almost as frequently, there are buses for Babahoyo ($2.50, 2½ hours) and Guayaquil ($4, four hours). There are numerous daily buses to Riobamba ($2.10, two hours) that take in outrageous views; this route passes the Chimborazo park entrance and access road to the mountain refuges, and the views of Volcán Chimborazo are amazing.

Buses for Salinas ($0.25, one hour) depart from the Plaza Roja at 6am, 7am and hourly from 10am to 4pm Monday through Friday and on weekends at 6am and 7am only. Cooperative-owned, white-pickup collective taxis also run frequently to Salinas ($1, 45 minutes) from Plaza Roja, waiting to fill up before they go.

# Salinas

✆03 / POP 1000 / ELEV 3550M

The remote village of Salinas, about 35km north of Guaranda, sits at the base of a dramatic and precipitous bluff surrounded by high *páramo*. Famous as a model of rural development, Salinas is a terrific place to see what successful community-based tourism is all about. Monday through Saturday you can visit cooperative-run factories that make cheese, chocolate, dried mushrooms, salami and *turrón* (a taffylike, honey-based candy). Local guides lead walks and horseback rides to the factories, nearby mushroom-picking areas and through the stunning countryside.

**Tienda El Salinerito** (Plaza Central; ⊙9am-5pm) is Salina's local outlet for all the products made by the communities, including fuzzy wool sweaters and a cool comic book about the village's history.

## 🛏 Sleeping & Eating

**El Refugio**          HOTEL $$
(✆221-0042; fugjs@andinanet.net; r per person $20) Two blocks above the plaza, El Refugio is a nice traveler's lodge with wood details, views of town and a roaring fireplace in the lobby. It is owned and operated by the community of Salinas.

## SUSTAINABLE DEVELOPMENT IN SALINAS: FROM CHOZAS TO CHEESES

When an Italian Salesian missionary named Antonio Polo rode into town one July day in 1971, Salinas was still a town of *chozas* (thatch-roofed huts). For generations, *salineritos* (people of Salinas) had lived in dire poverty, unable to demand a fair price for their production of milk, vegetables and wool; half of all Salinas children died before the age of five.

Polo saw a better future for local families making and selling dairy-based products. He helped the campesinos (peasants) set up a credit cooperative, buy equipment and bring in technical expertise. Emphasizing high standards of freshness and sanitation, the cooperative eventually opened more than 20 *queserías* (cheese factories) around Salinas and branched out into other provinces. It has also created new cooperatives that produce chocolate, dried mushrooms, wool clothing, salamis, candies and buttons, and it has even started a community tourism project. Visitors can tour the area's micro- and macro-enterprises for $3. Check in at the tourism office to learn more.

**La Minga Café**　　　　　CAFE $
(El Salinerito at Guayamas; mains $1.50-3; ⊙7:30am-10pm) Facing the main plaza, this cafe has good set meals and serves tourists and locals throughout the day.

###  Information

The **tourist office** (☑239-0022; www.salinerito.com; ⊙9am-5pm), on the main plaza next to the post office, can help you hire a guide and offers information on solo activities. If it's not open, head over to the El Refugio hotel for assistance. There are no banks or other tourist services in the village.

### ❶ Getting There & Away

Buses for Guaranda ($0.25, one hour) depart at 11am, 1pm and 3pm daily. Collective taxis also run frequently ($1, 45 minutes).

## Volcán Chimborazo

Called 'Taita' (Father) by indigenous people in the area, Volcán Chimborazo (6310m) is the country's tallest mountain, a hulking giant topped by a massive glacier. Along with its smaller, craggier companion **Volcán Cariuairazo** (5020m) to the northeast, and the Río Mocha valley that connects them, Chimborazo makes up a remote, even desolate, area populated by only a few indigenous communities. The western side of Chimborazo is called the *arenal* (arena means 'sand') and is so arid that some people compare it to the Altiplano of Bolivia.

Not only is the extinct Volcán Chimborazo the highest mountain in Ecuador, but its peak, due to the earth's equatorial bulge, is also the furthest terrestrial point from the center of the earth.

Chimborazo and Carihuairazo are both within the **Reserva de Producción Faunística Chimborazo** (admission $2). It is called a 'fauna-production reserve' because it is home to hundreds of vicuña (a wild relative of the llama). Once hunted to extinction, they were imported from Chile and Bolivia in the 1980s. Now prospering, it's easy to catch their elegant silhouettes in the mist on the bus ride between Guaranda and Riobamba, and you'll surely see them poking around if you explore the park.

Climbing Chimborazo or Carihuairazo is an adventure only for well-acclimatized, experienced mountaineers with snow- and ice-climbing gear (contact the guides in Riobamba (p155) or Quito (p62)). Reaching the refuge on Chimborazo or getting started with a multiday hike requires hiring a car from Riobamba and assembling some gear and maps.

Temperatures can drop well below freezing at night. July to September, as well as December, are the driest (but coldest) times in this region.

### ◉ Sights & Activities

Care should be taken to properly acclimatize if you plan to do physical activities around Chimborazo and Carihuairazo. All of the accommodations listed under Sleeping are good sites to do this, although you should also consult a qualified guide if you are planning hard hiking or climbs on either peak. You can arrange mountain-bike descents from the high-altitude refuges with the tour operators in Riobamba.

The small indigenous community of **Pulinguí San Pablo** (3900m) on the Riobamba–Guaranda road is well worth an afternoon visit, and climbers and hikers can stay overnight in the community lodge for a unique experience. The Puruhá people have lived on Chimborazo's flanks for centuries and are now working to bring tourism to the region through the **Proyecto El Cóndor** (Condor Project; www.interconnection.org/condor). Through the project, locals provide basic guiding services, rent mountain bikes, and will take you on the fascinating interpretation trails in the area. A women's weaving cooperative rounds out the activities. Information can be obtained from Riobamba resident **Tom Walsh** (☑03-294-1481; twalsh@ch.pro.ec), who has been instrumental in helping the villagers set up the project.

### Hiking

The walk from Urbina along the Río Mocha, reaching over the Abraspungo pass and emerging at the Ambato–Guaranda road, is particularly well trodden. Allow three days for this hike. Maps are available at the IGM in Quito.

### Climbing

Most climbers do multiple acclimatization ascents and spend the night at increasingly higher elevations before tackling Chimborazo, which is a notoriously laborious climb that also requires technical know-how. Most parties these days follow the **Normal Route**, which takes eight to 10 hours to the summit and two to four to return. The **Whymper Route** is currently unsafe.

There are no refuges on Carihuairazo, so guides usually set up a base camp on the south side of the mountain. The climb is relatively straightforward for experienced climbers, but ice-climbing gear is needed.

## 🛏 Sleeping

All of these places are bone-chilling from the late afternoon on, so bring appropriate clothing and sleeping bags.

### 🏠 La Casa del Cóndor   HOSTEL $
(☑357-1379; r per person $5) The cheapest place to stay in the area is in the small indigenous community of Pulinguí San Pablo. Families still live in the round *chozas* typical of the area, but La Casa del Cóndor is a stone building with a basic hostel featuring hot showers and a communal kitchen.

### Posada La Estación   HOSTEL $
(☑in Riobamba 295-1389; Urbina; dm $7) Just outside the Reserve's boundary, southeast of Chimborazo, is Urbina, which at 3618m was the highest point on the Trans-Andean Railway. The former train station, built in 1905, now functions as a simple but comfortable *hostal*. Popular for acclimatization and scenic hikes, the *hostal* has eight rooms, hot showers, a kitchen and meals. The only road access to Urbina is from the Panamericana. You'll need to arrange transport through a tour operator in Riobamba, or take a bus along the Panamericana and ask the driver for the Urbina road, almost 30km north of Riobamba. Urbina lies about 1km up that road.

### Refugio Carrel & Refugio Whymper   CABIN $
(dm $10) The lower Refugio Carrel is at 4800m, and the upper Refugio Whymper, Ecuador's highest-altitude lodging, is at 5000m and is named after Edward Whymper, the British climber who in 1880 made the first ascent of Chimborazo with the Swiss Carrel brothers as guides. Both refuges have caretakers, equipped kitchens, storage facilities and limited food supplies.

## ℹ Getting There & Away

Several buses go from Riobamba to Guaranda daily via a paved road. About 45 minutes from Riobamba, it passes Pulinguí San Pablo, and about 7km further it passes the signed turnoff (4370m) for the Chimborazo refuges. From the turnoff, it is 8km by road to the parking lot at Refugio Carrel and 1km farther to Refugio Whymper. If you're walking up this road, allow several hours to reach the *refugios*.

Most hotels in Riobamba can arrange a taxi service to Refugio Carrel via this route. It's about $50 to hire a taxi to drop you off and pick you up on a later day. One-way trips will cost around $30.

## Riobamba

📞 03 / POP 181,960 / ELEV 2750M

Riobamba takes its name from a combination of the Spanish word for 'river' and the Kichwa word for 'valley.' This bilingual moniker describes the topography of the area, as well as the rich mix of cultures that live here. Riobamba has a strong indigenous presence, which grows to wonderfully colorful proportions during the Saturday market, but the city's layout and architecture

# Riobamba

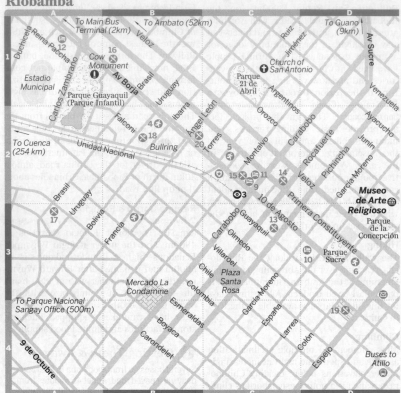

are imposing reminders of Spanish colonization.

The Puhurá Indians were the first people to live in the vicinity, followed by the Inca for a brief period. In 1534, the Spanish founded the city of Riobamba on the site of Cajabamba, 17km south on the Panamericana, but in 1797 a huge landslide destroyed the city and the people moved it to its present-day site. Spain's grip on Ecuador was officially broken in Riobamba with the signing of Ecuador's first constitution in 1830.

## ⊙ Sights & Activities

### Museo de Arte Religioso                    MUSEUM
(Argentinos; admission $2; ◷9am-noon & 3-6pm Tue-Sat) Inside the beautifully restored, 16th-century convent of the Conceptas nuns, Riobamba's only museum houses one of the country's finest collections of 17th- and 18th-century religious art. The museum's signature piece is a priceless, meter-tall monstrance inlaid with more than 1500 precious stones. Made of solid gold with a solid silver base, it weighs over 360kg (making it incredibly difficult to steal).

### Parks                                      PARK
The handsome, tree-filled **Parque Maldonado** (Primera Constituyente at Espejo) is flanked by Riobamba's **cathedral** on the northeastern side. A few blocks southeast, **Parque La Libertad** (Primera Constituyente at Alvarado) is anchored, near Alvarado, by its neoclassical **basilica** (Veloz), famous for being the only round church in Ecuador. It's often closed, but try Sundays and evenings after 6pm. Just north of downtown, the **Parque 21 de Abril** (Orozco at Ángel León) has an observation platform with views of the surrounding mountains.

### Saturday Market                            MARKET
The Saturday market transforms Riobamba into a hive of commercial activity, when

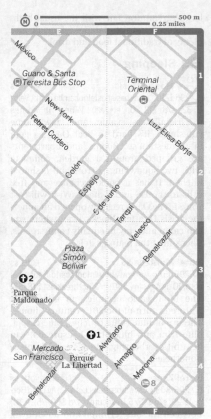

**CENTRAL HIGHLANDS** RIOBAMBA

thousands of people from surrounding villages come to barter, buy and sell, spreading out their wares along the streets northeast of Parque de la Concepción.

### Train Station
HISTORIC BUILDING

While rail service from Riobamba to Alausí was suspended as of press time, plans were in the works to get the line operational. Check out the historic **train station** (☑1-800-873-637; www.ferrocarrilesdelecuador.gov.ec; Av León Borja at Unidad Nacional) to see if the train is up and running. No matter what, it's worth a quick peek inside to check out the interesting rotating exhibits and crafts market.

### Rappeling
ADVENTURE SPORTS

Rappel down the highest building in Riobamba, the seven-story **Hotel Zeus** (☑296-8036; www.hotelzeus.com.ec; Av León Borja 41-29) for $15.

## 🞂 Tours

Thanks to Riobamba's proximity to Chimborazo, the country's highest peak, the city is home to some of the country's best climbing operators and mountain guides. Two-day summit trips start from around $260 per person for Chimborazo and include guides, gear, transportation and meals, but not park entrance fees ($2).

One-day mountain-biking trips start at $45 per person. Downhill descents from the refuge on Chimborazo – an exhilarating way to take in the views – are very popular.

Guided treks to the neighboring national parks will cost around $120 per day.

### Veloz Coronado Mountain Guides
ADVENTURE TOUR

(☑296-0916; www.velozexpediciones.com in German; Chile 33-21 & Francia) A pioneer in Ecuadorian mountaineering, and owner of this excellent guide shop, Enrique Veloz is practically a historical personage in Ecuador, having climbed Chimborazo more than 500 times. Guides have high standards for safety, climb most of the peaks in the central sierra, and also offer mountain-climbing courses.

**Julio Verne Tour Operator** ADVENTURE TOUR
(☑296-3436; www.julioverne-travel.com; Espectador 22-25) A respected Ecuadorian–Dutch-owned, full-service operator offering affordable, two-day summit trips to Chimborazo and other peaks, as well as to the Oriente and Galápagos. The company also offers downhill mountain-biking on Chimborazo.

**Pro Bici** ADVENTURE TOUR
(☑295-1759; Primera Constituyente & Larrea) This is one of the country's best mountain-bike operators, with many years of experience and excellent trip reports from clients. It offers mountain-bike rentals (per day $15 to $25, depending on the bike), excellent maps, good safety practices and fascinating day tours. The friendly owners speak English, and the store is located on the 2nd floor of a fabric factory.

**Andean Adventures** ADVENTURE TOUR
(☑295-1389; www.andeannadventures.com; Av León Borja & Uruguay) This respected shop specializes in Chimborazo climbs, but also arranges mountain bikes, treks and other custom adventures.

## ✱✰ Festivals & Events

Riobamba's annual fiesta celebrates the **Independence Battle of Tapi** of April 21, 1822. On and around April 21, there is a large agricultural fair with the usual highland events: street parades, dancing and plenty of traditional food and drink.

## 🛏 Sleeping

**TOP** 
**CHOICE** **Hostal Oasis** HOSTEL $
(☑296-1210; www.oasishostelriobamba.com; Veloz 15-32; s/d $12/20; ᴾ☻☜) When it comes to friendliness, value and down-home cutesiness, it's hard to beat Oasis, a gem of a guesthouse. Rooms and apartments are grouped around a garden, complete with two squawking parrots and a shared kitchen. It has a book exchange and free calls to the US and Canada. Wi-fi will cost you $1. The Oasis recently opened an annex, the Oasis II, a few blocks away, where you can camp and stay in equally comfy rooms. Check in at the main hostel.

**Hotel Montecarlo** HOTEL $$
(☑296-1577; www.hotelmontecarlo-riobamba.com; 10 de Agosto 25-41; s/d incl breakfast $18/32) The Montecarlo occupies an attractively restored, turn-of-the-20th-century house. The use of blue (blue couches, blue carpet, blue trim and blue-plaid bedspreads) can be a bit overbearing, but it's a lovely place nonetheless.

**Hotel Zeus** BUSINESS HOTEL $$
(☑296-8036; www.hotelzeus.com.ec; Av León Borja 41-29; s/d $37/53, executive s/d $60/75; ᴾ☜) Between the bus terminal and downtown, Hotel Zeus is a seven-story hotel with a range of room styles and amenities as well as gym access. The pricier rooms are excellent (some have five-star views of Chimborazo).

---

WORTH A TRIP

## GUANO & SANTA TERESITA

Besides serving as a playground for families from Riobamba on the weekends, the village of **Guano**, 8km north of Riobamba, is an important craft center that specializes in carpets and items made of leather and *totora*. Stores selling them are right around the main square (where the bus stops). Also near the main square is a **museum** (admission $1) holding the mummified remains of a Franciscan monk from the 16th century, and **ruins** of a convent dating to the 1660s. The **mirador** over town has excellent views (on a clear day) of El Altar.

From the main plaza, you can continue by bus or walk to the village of **Santa Teresita**, 2km away. At the end of the bus ride, turn right and head down the hill for about 20 minutes to **Parque Acuático Los Elenes** (admission $1; ⊙8am-6pm), where swimming pools are fed by natural mineral springs. The water is quite cool (22°C, or 72°F), but the views of Tungurahua and El Altar are marvelous.

Local buses to Guano and Santa Teresita leave Riobamba from the stop at Pichincha and New York and cost just $0.25.

### Hotel Tren Dorado
HOTEL **$**

(296-4890; www.hoteltrendorado.com; Carabobo 22-35; s/d $12/20; P) Not surprisingly, the 'Golden Train' is close to the train station. It has spotless, comfortable rooms, dated furniture, a cool terrace out back and sweet lion bed covers (grrrr). A self-serve breakfast will cost you $3 extra. The hot water seems infallible and the TVs are big.

### Hotel El Libertador
HOTEL **$**

(294-7393; www.hotelellibertador.com; Av León Borja & Carabobo; r per person $12.50-15;) This basic hotel in a renovated building with wood floors sits conveniently across the street from the train station. There's a busy restaurant-grill downstairs that opens early and closes late.

### Hostería La Andaluza
HOSTERÍA **$$**

(294-9370; www.hosteriaandaluza.com; s $40-60, d $50-70;) About 15km north of Riobamba on the Panamericana, this renovated, colonial hacienda has panoramic views and beautiful grounds. Two restaurants, a small exercise room and sauna, and a game room complete with foosball tables are among the amenities, but the best part is the isolated countryside setting. We only wish the modern room decor matched the splendid architecture.

### Albergue Abraspungo
HACIENDA **$$$**

(236 4031; www.abraspungo.com.ec; s/d/ste $78/109/193;) Situated 3.5km northeast of town on the road to Guano, Abraspungo is a first-class hotel built around a whitewashed, tile-roofed hacienda. Filled with antiques and rustic details, Abraspungo offers spacious themed rooms, a restaurant and bar, some spa services and horseback-riding. It is also a certified ecotourism project with excellent local hiring practices.

## Eating

### Mercado La Merced
MARKET **$**

(Mercado M Borja; Guayaquil btwn Espejo & Colón; mains $3; 7am-6pm) The ladies hawking *hornado* (whole roast pig) put on a pretty hard sell, yelling out for your attention and offering samples. If you can stand the pressure and you're up for dining with flayed Wilburs on every side, then the market is fun and interesting. The pork is superfresh. Saturdays are busiest.

### Pizzería D'Baggios
ITALIAN **$$**

(Av León Borja & Angel León; pizzas $3-8; noon-10pm Mon-Sat) Dozens of different kinds of medium-thick-crust pizzas are prepared before your eyes in Baggios' wood oven. The oven keeps the whole place nice and toasty.

### Café El Delirio
ECUADORIAN **$$**

(Primera Constituyente 28-16; mains $7-10; noon-10pm Tue-Sun) Named for a poem by the great liberator, Simón Bolívar, this historic-monument-turned-restaurant serves *comida típica* (traditional Ecuadorian food) in a dimly lit, antique atmosphere. Service is slow, but the patio is simply amazing.

### La Abuela Rosa
ECUADORIAN **$**

(Brasil & Esmeraldas; mains $0.80-1.50; 4-9pm Mon-Sat) Drop by Grandma Rosa's for *comida típica* and tasty snacks, including sandwiches, chocolate and cheese. Friendly, cozy and popular with locals.

### El Rey del Burrito
MEXICAN **$**

(Av León Borja 38-36; mains $4-6;) 'The King of the Burrito' serves large burritos, tacos and enchiladas with superspicy salsa (*ole!*). There must be a vegetarian in the house, because they have wonderful options for herbivores. Service is friendly and the atmosphere is enlivened by some cool murals.

### La Parrillada de Fausto
ARGENTINE **$**

(Uruguay 20-38; mains $5-7; noon-3pm & 6-10:30pm Mon-Sat) This fun, Argentine-style grill serves great barbecued steaks, trout and chicken in a ranch-style setting. Don't miss the cool, cavelike bar in back.

### Chifa Casa China
CHINESE **$**

(10 de Agosto; mains $4-5; 10am-10pm) Like most Chinese food in Ecuador, it's a little heavy on the grease, but the lovely Chinese family that runs this *chifa* (Chinese restaurant) serves large portions with plenty of fresh vegetables and seafood.

### Bom Café
CAFE **$**

(Pichincha 12-37; small plates $2-4) Serving absolutely perfect coffees, cappuccinos and other caffeinated beverages, this narrow cafe tucked into a side street also has pressed sandwiches and cheese plates.

## Shopping

You can buy handicrafts at Parque de la Concepción and in the train station. As you're walking around, keep your eyes peeled for locally made *shigras* (small string bags),

## THE PANAMERI-WHAT?

Right around Cajabamba, the Panamericana splits: the easternmost branch is the Ecuadorian Panamericana, which becomes a regular road when it hits the border with Peru, and the westernmost branch is the international Panamericana, still referred to as such once it hits the Peruvian border. Throughout the rest of this chapter, references to the Panamericana should be understood as the Ecuadorian, not international, Panamericana.

*tagua* nut carvings, and *totora* baskets and mats woven by the indigenous Colta from the reeds lining the shores of nearby Laguna de Colta.

## ☆ Entertainment

Nightlife, limited as it is, centers on the intersection of Avenida León Borja and Torres and northwest along León Borja toward Duchicela. Both areas have bars and discos.

## ℹ Information

**Corporación Nacional de Telecomunicaciones** (Tarqui at Veloz; ⊙8am-10pm) Telephone center.

**Banco de Guayaquil** (Primera Constituyente) Bank with ATM.

**Banco del Pichincha** (cnr García Moreno & Primera Constituyente) Bank with ATM.

**Clínica Metropolitana** (☏294-1930; Junín 25-28) Locally recommended clinic.

**Hospital Policlínico** (☏296-1705/5725/8232; Olmedo 11-01) Hospital, southeast of downtown.

**Parque Nacional Sangay Office** (☏295-3041; parquesangay@andinanet.net; Av 9 de Octubre; ⊙8am-1pm & 2-5pm Mon-Fri) West of downtown, near Duchicela; get information and pay entry fees to Parque Nacional Sangay here.

**Police station** (☏296-1913/9300; Av León Borja)

**Post office** (cnr Espejo & 10 de Agosto)

**Su Lavandería** (Veloz 14-53) Same-day laundry for $0.70 per kilo.

## ℹ Getting There & Away

### Bus

Riobamba has two bus terminals. The **main bus terminal** (Av León Borja at Av de la Prensa), about 2km northwest of downtown, has hourly buses for Quito ($3.85, four hours) and intermediate points, as well as buses for Guayaquil

($4.75, 4½ hours). Transportes Patria has a Machala bus at 9:45am ($6.35, six to seven hours), and there are several buses a day to Cuenca ($6, six hours). Buses for Alausí leave 20 times a day between 5am and 8pm with CTA ($1.90, two hours). Flota Bolívar has morning and afternoon buses to Guaranda ($2.10, two hours); some continue on to Babahoyo. Guaranda-bound buses pass the access road to Chimborazo and the mountain refuges.

For buses to the Oriente, you have to go to the **Terminal Oriental** (Espejo & Luz Elisa Borja), in the northeast of town, where you can catch buses to Coca ($20), Puyo ($6), Macas ($5) and Baños ($2). The direct road between Riobamba and Baños is now open, but you'll need to inquire locally about the road's condition. Bus service still passes through Ambato.

Buses to Atillo in Parque Nacional Sangay (p150) leave from the corner of Velazco and Olmedo.

Three long blocks south of the main bus terminal (turn left out of the front entrance), off Unidad Nacional, is a smaller terminal with frequent local buses for Cajabamba, Laguna de Colta and the chapel of La Balbanera. Buses for Guamote also leave from there.

To visit the villages of Guano and Santa Teresita, take the local bus ($0.25) from the stop at Pichincha and New York.

### Train

At press time, the Riobamba–Alausí run on the Ferrocarril Transandino (Trans-Andean Railway) was soon to resume. Check at the train station for more information.

## ℹ Getting Around

North of the main bus terminal, behind the Church of Santa Faz (the one with a blue dome), is a local stop for buses going downtown. These run along Avenida León Borja, which turns into 10 de Agosto near the train station. Going the other way, take any bus marked 'Terminal' on Primera Constituyente. The fare is $0.25.

You can taxi nearly anywhere in town for $1.

## South of Riobamba

📍03

About 17km south of Riobamba, the Panamericana speeds through the wee village of Cajabamba, the original site of Riobamba until an earthquake-induced landslide buried the city in 1797, killing thousands. You can still see a huge scar on the hillside as you arrive.

Further south and just off the Panamericana, you'll pass the unmistakable colonial-era chapel of La Balbanera. Although much of it crumbled in the 1797 earthquake, parts of the facade date from 1534.

About 4km south of Cajabamba, the waters of **Laguna de Colta** appear choked with a golden reed called *totora*. For anyone who has ever visited Lake Titicaca in Bolivia, this setting and the small *totora* rafts used to sail around Laguna Colta will look familiar. Ethnobiologists believe that *totora* seeds may have been brought here in prehistoric times, but whatever the case, the reeds form an important crop for the indigenous Colta, who use them to make their famous baskets and *esteras*. Indigenous Colta women dye the fringes of their hair a startling golden color.

A **trail** with broad views of Chimborazo will take you around the lake in a couple of hours, and on the weekends small lakeside eateries serve the local specialty, *cariucho*, a kind of tuna stew.

You can easily visit any or all of these sites on a day excursion from Riobamba by local buses or hired taxi. Buses from Riobamba heading south on the Panamericana will drop you at any of them. They're close enough to each other that you could walk between them too.

## Guamote

📞03 / POP 2788 / ELEV 3050M

A charming maze of brightly painted adobe buildings, Guamote is a proud indigenous community in little (immediate) danger of losing its identity. The village is famous for its unspoiled **Thursday market**, one of the largest in rural Ecuador. Although a bit sleepy, it's a place where Kichwa-speaking old-timers walk the streets in bare feet (as they have their whole lives) and people still gather in the main square to share tales and pass their Sunday afternoons.

You can stay at **Inti Sisa** (📞291-6529; www. intisisa.org; JM Plaza at Garcia Moreno; dm $7.50,

---

### THE DEVIL'S NOSE

Train buffs will be excited to learn that an illustrious rail system known as the Ferrocarril Transandino (Trans-Andean Railway), built around the turn of the 20th century, once ran between Quito and Guayaquil. It was an economic lifeline between the coast and highlands and was considered a technological marvel.

Sadly, however, the heyday of Ecuadorian rail transport has ended. Highway construction, along with constant avalanche damage from heavy rains, spelled its demise and by 2000 only a few short runs, mostly frequented by tourists, remained.

The best-known and most exciting of these is the section from Alausí to Sibambe down La Nariz del Diablo (the Devil's Nose), a 765m sheer cliff of solid rock. In 1902 track engineers devised a clever way up this monster by carving a zigzag route into the side of the mountain (many lives were lost in the process). The train tugs a bit north, switches track, tugs a bit south and again switches track, slowly making its way up and down the Devil's Nose.

Somewhere along the Nariz, the old choo choo (it's actually more like a retro-fitted bus) inevitably derails. Not to worry, though! The conductors ask everyone to get off and by using advanced technology – big rocks and sticks – they steer the iron horse back on track. The entire ride should take you about 2½ hours, with an hour stopover in Sibambe, where you are greeted by a local dance troupe and have the chance to buy some artisan goods and check out a small ethnographic museum. A guide accompanies every tour group. Adrenaline-seekers will be sad to hear that you can no longer ride on the train's roof.

While there are only a few sections of the old Trans-Andean line currently open, a massive restoration of the whole network (including the long detour to Cuenca – more than 400km in all) and many of the 45 old train stations is under way. Despite controversy about the costs and even the environmental impact of harvesting wood for the sleepers (the wood planks on which the tracks rest, *not* sleeping cars), the revival of the Ferrocarril Transandino seems inevitable.

For now, the **train** (📞1-800-873-637, 293-0126; www.ferrocarrilesdelecuador.gov.ec; round-trip adult/child $20/10) leaves Alausí's train station at the north end of 5 de Junio Tuesday through Sunday at 8am and 11am. It does a special afternoon run at 3pm if there are more than 15 people.

r per person $14.50), part of a community tourist project run by a Belgian-Ecuadorian. It's a cozy, well-run place with dorm rooms, clean and cheery private rooms, and meals for under $4. It also offers mountain-biking and horseback-riding trips, and can arrange local homestays. Inti Sisa also runs an early childhood education program in town. Check here about volunteer opportunities – it currently requires a one-year minimum commitment. Call ahead to book your room if you can, especially for Wednesday-night stays. The hostel is located near the top of the village, about 1km from the Panamericana (ask around, everybody knows about it).

Guamote is on the Riobamba–Cuenca bus route, which has several services per day. Unless your bus is actually going to Guamote (usually only on Thursdays), you will be dropped off on the Panamericana and have to walk about 1km up the hill to the main plaza.

At the time of research, there was no train service in Guamote.

# Alausí

03 / POP 8111 / ELEV 3323M

Set almost dizzyingly on the edge of the Río Chanchán gorge and presided over by a giant statue of St Peter, Alausí is the jumping-on point for the famous **Nariz del Diablo** train run. Alausí is wonderfully picturesque, especially near the train station and on the cobblestone streets, where old adobe buildings with wooden balconies take you back in time. Alausí is really just a whistle-stop these days, but it banks on train tourism and has renovated some of its old railroad infrastructure as well.

Alausí lies about 97km south of Riobamba and has a busy **Sunday market**. The train station is at the north end of 5 de Junio.

## 🛏 Sleeping & Eating

Most of Alausí's slim pickings are on Avenida 5 de Junio, the main street. Places fill up on Saturday nights with Sunday market-goers and weekend visitors.

### Hostería Pircapamba                   HOSTERÍA $$
(293-0180; www.pircapamba.com; r per person incl breakfast $20) Three kilometers outside of town, the Pircapamba has studiedly rustic rooms with fireplaces and whitewashed brick-and-wood walls, excellent views of the valley down below and plenty of com-

mon areas. It's a great choice – especially for families. But there's no restaurant on site, making it inconvenient without your own wheels. Horseback-riding and excursions to area sites are available.

### Hotel Europa                          HOTEL $
(293-0200; www.hoteleuropa.com.ec; 5 de Junio 175 at Orozco; r per person $12, with shared bathroom $8; P) With old wooden balconies and corridors, the renovated Europa is your best budget option in the town proper. The rooms don't quite live up to the promise, but they have cable TV. It's right across from the bus station.

### Hotel Gampala                         HOTEL $$
(293-0138; www.hotelgampala.com; 5 de Junio 122; s/d/tr/ste incl breakfast $26/44/60/60; ♠) Believe it or not, this small, 35-year-old hotel has hosted several famous Ecuadorian politicians and artists. The recently renovated rooms are a bit dark, but they have comfy beds, flatscreens and updated bathrooms. You can also hang out in a cute little sitting room or the downstairs cafe.

### Hotel Panamericano                    HOTEL $
(293-0278; 5 de Junio & 9 de Octubre; r per person $12, with shared bathroom $8) The rooms without bathrooms don't have windows, but the others are clean and comfortable. The hotel's restaurant also serves as its lobby, day-care and TV room.

### Punta Bucana Café                      MEXICAN $
(Plazaleta Guayaquil; mains $2-5) This small eatery on the north end of 5 de Junio serves up fresh Central American and Mexican food (with a small Ecuadorian twist). The service is a bit slow, but the food is worth it.

## ✦ Getting There & Away

The **bus station** is on Avenida 5 de Junio. Buses for Riobamba ($1.90, two hours) depart hourly; buses for Cuenca ($5, four hours) depart several times daily. Quito-bound travelers will need to change in Riobamba. Many buses between Riobamba and Cuenca enter town – if not, it's a 1.5km walk (all downhill) into town from the Panamericana.

Old buses (or pickup trucks acting as buses) leave from 5 de Junio for nearby destinations. Some of the bus rides can be quite spectacular, especially the one to Achupallas, the departure point for the Inca Trail hike (see boxed text 'Camino del Inca,' p164), about 23km by road to the southeast.

# Southern Highlands

## Best Places to Eat

» Café Eucalyptus (p172)

» Café Austria (p173)

» El Tamal Lojano (p185)

» Charlito's (p192)

## Best Places to Stay

» Hotel Victoria (p171)

» Hostal Achik Wasi (p181)

» Grand Victoria Boutique Hotel (p183)

» Copalinga (p189)

» Hostería y Restaurante Izhcayluma (p191)

## Why Go?

Emerging out of the shadows of glaciers and active volcanoes in the north, the passage down the southern spine of the Ecuadorian Andes brings intrepid travelers through a splendid patchwork of gently rolling mountains and valleys, colonial cities and remote indigenous villages.

From humid lowland forest to chilly elfin woodland, the region is home to hundreds of bird species, thousands upon thousands of plant species, and scores of mammals. These habitats provide unsurpassable outdoor experiences, and a trip to any of the region's large national parks should definitely be on the agenda.

Most adventures begin in the regional capital of Cuenca. The city has one of Latin America's best-preserved colonial centers and a thriving arts scene. From there, it's a choose-your-own-adventure romp southward to the new-age community of Vilcabamba, seldom-visited wild areas and bustling regional capitals.

## When to Go
### Cuenca

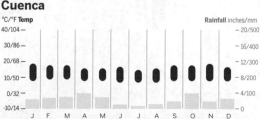

| Year-round | Oct–May | May & Aug |
|---|---|---|
| South of Cuenca, especially around Loja and Vilcabamba, it's spring year-round. | The rainy season is colder, wetter and greener; morning sun and showers later. | Festivals celebrating the Virgen del Cisne bring devotees from around Ecuador. |

# Southern Highlands Highlights

**1** Wander the cobblestone streets of colonial **Cuenca** (p165), a Unesco World Heritage Site

**2** Keep your eyes peeled for orchids, birds and rare mammals in the diverse habitats of **Parque Nacional Podocarpus** (p187)

**3** Perfect the art of relaxation in **Vilcabamba** (p189) with massages, horseback-riding and strolls in the clean country air

**4** Grab your boots for a hike in the eerie moors of **Parque Nacional Cajas** (p177)

**5** Ponder the engineering mysteries of the Incan ruins at **Ingapirca** (p164)

Río Cenepa

PERU

Río Marañón

Río Comaina

Río Numpatkaka

Cordillera del Cond

El Pangui

Vantzaza

Guadalupe

Zumbi

La Paz

28 de Mayo

Río Nangaritza

Nambija

Namirez

Saraguro **7**

Río Zamora

**Zamora** **1**

Bombuscaro
Ranger Station

Cajanuma
Ranger Station **1**

oja

Zamora-
Chinchipe

Romerillos **1**

Parque
Nacional
Podocarpus **2**

El Cisne

San Pedro de
la Bendita

Catamayo

Río Mayo

Zaruma

Piñas

Portovelo

Balsas

Malacatos

Gonzanamá

Vilcabamba **3**

Valladolid

Zumba

La Balsa

Loja

Chaguarpamba

Olmedo

Catacocha

Carranga

PERU

Torata

Saracay

Represa
de Tahuín

Río Puyango

To Huaquillas
(75km)

Celica

El Empalme

Sozoranga

Macará

106

N

0   25 miles

0   50 km

**6** Head out for a
day of crafts shopping
at the traditional
Sunday markets in the
villages of **Gualaceo,
Chordeleg and
Sigsig** (p179)

**7** Dive into
indigenous culture
in the proud and
resilient town of
**Saraguro** (p180)

**8** Leave the gringo
trail behind with a **DIY
adventure** through
the seldom-visited
indigenous villages of
the region

## National Parks

The southern highlands' two national parks – **Parque Nacional Cajas** near Cuenca and **Parque Nacional Podocarpus** near Loja – are easily accessible and offer wonderful hiking opportunities. Podocarpus itself has a startling range of terrains within its own borders, so it's worth visiting both of its sectors (highlands and lowlands) for the full effect. Part of **Parque Nacional Sangay** falls within this region, but its access points are further north (see p149).

### ℹ Getting There & Around

Daily direct flights from both Quito and Guayaquil go to Cuenca as well as Loja. Loja is a convenient departure point for Peru, via Macará, Zumba (passing through Vilcabamba), or even Huaquillas to the west. Guayaquil, on the coast, is only about 3½ hours by bus from Cuenca.

# Ingapirca

📷 07 / ELEV 3230M

Ecuador's best-preserved archaeological site, **Ingapirca** (admission $6 with guided tour; ⊙8am-6pm), 1km from the town of Ingapirca, pales in comparison to large archaeological sites in neighboring Peru. This said, the small site, with its semi-intact temple, grazing llamas and open fields, is definitely worth a stopover if you are headed this way. And hikers won't want to miss the three-day Camino del Inca trek.

The ruins were originally used by the Cañari people as an observatory. The strategic site was later taken over and developed by the Inca during the 15th century as a military stronghold. Unfortunately, the Spanish carted away much of Ingapirca's stone to build nearby cities.

What's left of the site is still important to the indigenous Cañari, and they now control the administration of the ruins and the **museum** (admission included with Ingapirca) displaying Inca and Cañari artifacts.

Without doubt, the centerpiece of the site is the **Temple of the Sun**, a large structure that was originally used for ceremonies and solar observation. Nearby, signs point to pits called *colcas* that were used to store food and to the *acllahuasi,* the place where the ceremonial, and ultimately sacrificial, virgins lived. The trapezoidal niches you see in the stone work are identical to those found in other ruins, such as Machu Picchu in Peru and San Agustín de Callo near Latacunga.

Agencies in Cuenca organize day trips to the site, starting at $40 per person.

---

## CAMINO DEL INCA

Though it sees only a fraction of the traffic of the Inca Trail to Machu Picchu, the three-day trek to Ingapirca is a popular hike. For approximately 40km, it follows the original Ingañan Incan royal road that linked Cuzco with Tomebamba (at present-day Cuenca) and Quito. In its heyday, this transportation and communication network rivaled that of the Roman Empire.

The starting point for the hike is the village of **Achupallas**, 23km southeast of Alausí (see p160). From there, the Trail climbs, passing rivers and lakes and eventually the ruins of an Incan town. The next day takes you past the ruins of an Incan bridge and a large structure at **Paredones**, where some walls are still standing. At times you'll be able to easily make out the Ingañan itself. On the third day the hike lets out at the magnificent ruins at **Ingapirca**.

You'll need a GPS and three 1:50,000 topographical maps (*Alausí, Juncal* and *Cañar*) available at the Instituto Geográfico Militar (IGM) in Quito. Also be prepared for extremely persistent begging from children; most travelers refuse to hand anything out in order to discourage begging.

To get to Achupallas, take one of the daily midday buses from Alausí or, more reliably, hire a taxi-pickup for about $10 to $15 one-way. Alternatively, south-bound Panamericana buses from Alausí can drop you at **La Moya** (also known as **Guasuntos**), where you can wait for passing trucks headed to Achupallas, 12km up a slim mountain road. You can hire guides in Achupallas for about $30 per day, or **Julio Verne Tour Operator** in Riobamba runs trips for about $250 per person. If you want to go on your own, check out a hiking guide, such as *Ecuador: Climbing and Hiking Guide* by Rob Rachowiecki and Mark Thurber.

## 🛏 Sleeping & Eating

There are toilet facilities and a simple cafe near the site entrance. Camping is free.

**Posada Ingapirca**                    HACIENDA $$$
(☑283-1120, in Cuenca 282-7401; www.posadain
gapirca.com; Larga 6-93 at Borrero; s/d $71/90; 🛜)
Just above the archaeological site, this converted hacienda offers the only lodgings in Ingapirca. The cozy rooms would be lovely even without amazing views of the ruins. Check online for discounts.

## ❶ Getting There & Away

Cooperativa Cañar buses ($2.50, two hours) go direct from Cuenca, leaving at 9am and 12:20pm and returning from Ingapirca to Cuenca at 1pm and 3:45pm. Buses also leave every half hour from Cuenca for El Tambo, 8km from Ingapirca. From El Tambo, buses leave about every half hour to Ingapirca, or take a taxi ($5).

## Cañar

☑07 / POP 16,470 / ELEV 3104M

Cañar, a dusty town with gently leaning adobe buildings and wooden balconies, has been the Cañari people's most important crossroads since the 16th century. Sunday is *the* day, when hundreds of Cañari in their colorful woolens gather in town for the **market**.

The men wear *chumbis*, distinctive belts made by a local weaving method and decorated with Catholic and indigenous motifs. These are available in the market, but down at the jail the prisoners make and sell them too (some with distinctive 'prison' motifs). You will be allowed in to make purchases.

**Hostal Cañar** (☑223-5996; cnr 24 de Mayo & Nieto; r per person with shared/private bathroom $10/15) has simple rooms and electricity-heated showers (zap!).

Cañar market stalls and simple restaurants serve *almuerzos* (set lunches; $1.50) and *meriendas* (set dinners; $1.50).

Buses frequently run to Cuenca's main bus terminal ($1.50, 1½ hours).

## Biblián

☑07 / POP 6480 / ELEV 2843M

As the Panamericana bends around the wee village of Biblián, about 26km south of Cañar, you'll notice one thing: the **Santuario de la Virgen del Rocío** (Sanctuary of the Virgin of the Dew), a castle-like church

built into the hill over town. Hoof it up (30 minutes from town) to see how the altar and neo-Gothic arches are carved right into the exposed rock face. There is a huge pilgrimage on September 8 and a smaller one on Good Friday. If you find yourself needing a bed, head 7km south to Azogues, which has more options.

## Azogues

☑07 / POP 41,300 / ELEV 2500M

The capital of Cañar province has a highly visible hillside church, **Iglesia de la Virgen de las Nubes** (Church of the Virgin of the Clouds). This stone and stained-glass structure offers broad views of the countryside. At the lively **Saturday market** at Rivera and Sucre, woven panama hats are sold and sent to Cuenca for finishing.

**Hostal Rivera** (☑224-8113; cnr Calles 24 de Mayo & 10 de Agosto; s/d $20/30; 🛜) has straightforward carpeted rooms with mod cons. On the north end of town, **Hotel Paraíso** (☑224-4729; cnr Váscones & Veintimilla; s/d inc breakfast from $22/32) is a glass and steel giant (by Azogues standards) with big, clean rooms and a business-hotel feel.

Several inexpensive restaurants around town serve *almuerzos* ($1.50) and *meriendas* ($1.50).

Buses to Cuenca ($0.70, 45 minutes) leave from the local bus terminal on Rivera, about three blocks south of the main market. There are daily departures to Quito ($8, eight hours) and Guayaquil ($6, four hours).

## Cuenca

☑07 / POP 417,000 / ELEV 2530M

After Quito, Cuenca is Ecuador's most important and beautiful colonial city. But don't tell that to the locals, who insist that their laid-back culture, cleaner streets, and more agreeable weather outclass the capital, hands down.

Dating from the 16th century, Cuenca's historic center, a Unesco World Heritage Site, is a place that time keeps forgetting; nuns march along cobblestone streets, kids in Catholic-school uniforms skip past historic churches, and old ladies spy on promenading lovers from their geranium-filled balconies.

In addition to its trademark skyline of massive rotundas and soaring steeples, Cuenca is also famous for its *barranco* (cliff)

# Cuenca

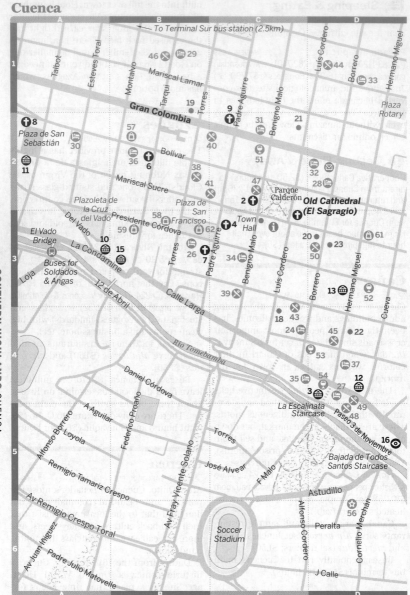

along Calle Larga, where the city's 18th- and 19th-century 'hanging houses' seem to hover over the rocky Río Tomebamba. The city is the center of many craft traditions, including ceramics, metalwork and the internationally famous panama hat.

At least three cultures have left their imprint on Cuenca. When the Spanish arrived in the 1540s, they encountered the ruins of a great but short-lived Incan city called Tomebamba (Valley of the Sun). The Spanish eagerly dismantled what was left of

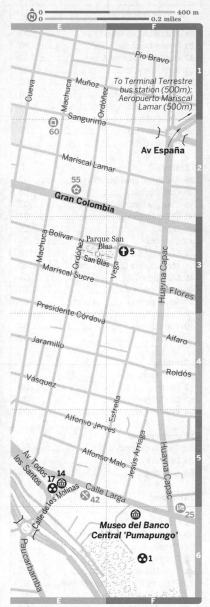

it, incorporating the elegantly carved Inca stones into their own structures. Before the Inca, the indigenous Cañari people had lived in the area for perhaps 3000 years. They, too, had a city here, called Quanpondelig (Plain as Big as the Sky). Except for a few limited but interesting sites, the physical remains of these pre-Columbian cultures have been erased.

## ⊙ Sights & Activities

It seems like a church, shrine or plaza graces every corner in Cuenca, and sometimes there are all three. Churches are generally open from 6:30am to 5pm Monday to Saturday, and until 8pm on Sunday.

### Plaza de San Sebastián                    PLAZA
(Parque Miguel León; cnr Mariscal Sucre & Talbot) Marking the western edge of the historical center, this quiet plaza is anchored by the 19th-century **Church of San Sebastián** (cnr Bolívar & Talbot). In 1739, when the plaza was still used for bullfights, it was a mob of *cuencanos* (folks from Cuenca) – not the bull – who mauled a member of explorer La Condamine's geodesic expedition here, apparently because of an affair with a local woman.

### Museo de Arte Moderno                    MUSEUM
(cnr Mariscal Sucre & Talbot; admission by donation; ◷9am-7pm Mon-Fri, 10am-5pm Sat, 10am-1pm Sun) On the south side of Plaza de San Sebastián, this fun museum was once a home for the insane. It now houses a highly regarded collection of Ecuadorian and Latin American art.

### Church of San Cenáculo                    CHURCH
(cnr Bolívar & Tarqui) Two blocks east of Plaza de San Sebastián, this bare 19th-century church is worth a quick look if you happen to be passing by.

### Church of Santo Domingo                    CHURCH
(cnr Gran Colombia & Padre Aguirre) This church has some fine carved wooden doors and colonial paintings inside. Although it looks older, the church was built in the early 20th century.

### Church of El Carmen de la
### Asunción                                   CHURCH
(Padre Aguirre, near Mariscal Sucre) The stark, white church was founded in 1682 and contrasts beautifully with the colorful **flower market** held on the small Plazoleta del Carmen out front.

### Church of San Francisco                    CHURCH
(Padre Aguirre & Presidente Córdova) The 19th-century Church of San Francisco features an important gold-leaf altar from the colonial period. It towers handsomely above the not-so-attractive (but still very interesting) **Plaza de San Francisco**, which is flanked by old arcaded buildings with wooden

# Cuenca

SOUTHERN HIGHLANDS CUENCA

balconies as well as a permanent ramshackle street market.

**Church of San Blas**　　　　　CHURCH
(Vega) On the east end of the historical center and occupying what was once known as the 'low neighborhood,' this church on the Parque San Blas is one of the city's largest, and the only one built in the form of a Latin cross.

**Parque Calderón**　　　　　PLAZA
The city's largest plaza, Parque Calderón, is dominated by **Catedral de la Inmaculada**

Concepción, also known as the 'new cathedral,' which began construction in 1885. Its giant domes of sky-blue Czech tile are visible from all over Cuenca, and if it looks like the bell towers are bit short, that's because they are – a design error made the intended height of the belfries impossible for the building to support.

On the other side of the park stands the whitewashed 'old cathedral,' also known as **El Sagrario**. Construction began in 1557, the year Cuenca was founded, and in 1739 La Condamine's expedition used its towers as a triangulation point to measure the shape of the earth. It is now deconsecrated and serves as a religious museum and recital hall.

FREE **Museo del Banco Central 'Pumapungo'** MUSEUM
(www.pumapungo.org, in Spanish; Calle Larga btwn Arriaga & Huayna Capac; ☺5am-5:30pm Mon-Fri, 9am-1pm Sat) Cuenca's most important museum has an entire floor of colorfully animated dioramas displaying traditional costumes of Ecuador's diverse indigenous cultures, including Afro-Ecuadorians from Esmeraldas province, the cowboy-like *montubios* (coastal farmers) of the western lowlands, several rainforest groups and all major highland groups. The finale features five rare and eerie *tzantzas* (shrunken heads) from the Shuar culture of the southern Oriente. Included in your visit is the **Archaeological Park** out back, where you can walk through the extensive ruins of buildings believed to be part the old Incan city of Tomebamba. Thanks to the Spanish conquistadors who carted off most of the stone to build Cuenca, there's not much left.

**Museo del Monasterio de las Conceptas** MUSEUM
(Miguel 6-33; admission $2.50; ☺9am-6:30pm Tue-Fri, 10am-1pm Sat) This religious museum in the Convent of the Immaculate Conception, founded in 1599, offers a glimpse into the centuries-old customs of the cloistered nuns who live here. You can't see the nuns (they're cloistered, after all) but you can see their primitive bread-making equipment and dioramas of their stark cells, as well as some religious art.

**Mirador de Turi** VIEWPOINT
For a lovely view of Cuenca, take a taxi ($4) 4km south of town along Avenida Solano to the stark, white Church of Turi. The views of Cuenca's famous, romantic skyline are especially pretty at sunset and on November and December evenings, when the city fires up the Christmas lights.

### RÍO TOMEBAMBA & CALLE LARGA
Majestic colonial buildings line the grassy shores of the Río Tomebamba, which effectively separates Cuenca's historic sector from the new neighborhoods to the south. The building facades actually open onto the street of Calle Larga, which runs parallel to and above the Tomebamba, while their back sides 'hang' over the river. This arrangement gives rise to the local name for the fashionable neighborhood, El Barranco (cliff). Steep stone stairways lead down to Avenida 3 de Noviembre, which follows the river's northern bank and is slated to become a pedestrian walk if the city planners get their way.

FREE **Museo Manuel Agustín Landivar** MUSEUM
(cnr Calle Larga 2 23 & Vega; ☺9am-1pm & 3-6pm Mon-Fri) At the east end of Calle Larga, this museum has archaeological exhibits and tours of the **Ruinas de Todos Santos**, which reveal Cañari, Inca and Spanish ruins, layered one over the other. If you don't want a guide, you can also look at them from below on Avenida de Todos Santos.

**Puente Roto** BRIDGE
(Broken Bridge; Av de Todos Santos & Machuca) Most of this bridge was washed away during a flood, but its stone arches make a nice venue for an open-air **art fair** (☺10am-5pm Sat) and cultural events every Saturday.

**Museo de las Culturas Aborígenes** MUSEUM
(Calle Larga 5-24; museoarq@etapaonline.net. ec; admission $2; ☺9am-6pm Mon-Fri, to 3pm Sat) This labyrinthine indigenous culture museum has more than 5000 archaeological pieces representing more than 20 pre-Hispanic Ecuadorian cultures going back some 15,000 years.

FREE **Centro Interamericano de Artes Populares** MUSEUM
(Cidap; www.cidap.org.ec; cnr 3 de Noviembre & La Escalinata; ☺9:30am-1pm & 2-6pm Mon-Fri, 10am-1pm Sat) Just down the stairs on the riverbank, the Inter-American Traditional Art Center exhibits indigenous costumes, handicrafts and artwork from around Latin America and has a classy, well-priced crafts store.

## UNRAVELING CUENCA FASHION

Most travelers will be struck by the vibrant and ornate traditional dress of indigenous women in and around Cuenca. While most men in the region have lost the custom of wearing a poncho, many women still wear their traditional garb with pride. The women's skirts, called *polleras*, fall just below the knee and have a distinctive embroidered hem that can identify which community a woman comes from. Although fine *polleras* can cost hundreds of dollars, no part of an indigenous woman's wardrobe is prized more than her *paño*, a beautiful fringed shawl made with a complicated pre-Columbian weaving technique known as *ikat*. Top that off with a straw hat, clunky metal earrings called *zarcillas*, and a pair of long braids, and you have a look that has withstood every fashion trend the past 100 years have had to offer, including jelly bracelets, acid-washed jeans and bell-bottoms… timeless!

### EL VADO
Clustered around the Plazoleta de la Cruz del Vado and Calle La Condamine are galleries, cafes, restaurants and *talleres* (artisanal studios) specializing in everything from traditional embroidery to copperware to saddles.

#### Prohibido Museo de Arte Extremo
GALLERY
(La Condamine 12-102; ⊙noon-late) El Vado, an up-and-coming area, has some unusual establishments, such as this Grim Reaper-themed gallery, bar and nightclub.

#### Laura's Antiguidades y Curiosidades
GALLERY
(La Condamine 12-112; ⊙daily) Laura's showcases a hodgepodge of curios and objets d'art in a 19th-century house. It's also where you'll find some of Cuenca's famous old-time hat makers.

###  Courses
Most language schools charge $5 to $7 per hour for one-to-one classes.

#### Centers for Interamerican Studies
LANGUAGE COURSE
(CEDEI; ☑283-4353; www.cedei.org; Luís Cordero 5-66) A nonprofit school offering drop-in and/or long-term courses in Spanish, Kichwa and Portuguese.

#### Sampere
LANGUAGE COURSE
(☑282-3960; www.sampere.es; Hermano Miguel 3-43) A highly recommended and busy Spanish-owned school.

#### Sí Centro de Español e Inglés
LANGUAGE COURSE
(☑282-0429; www.sicentrospanishschool.com; Borrero 7-67) Has a 20-hour/one-week ($140) minimum.

#### Simón Bolívar Spanish School
LANGUAGE COURSE
(☑283-9959; www.bolivar2.com; Luís Cordero 10-25) Offers homestays and excursions.

### Tours
Local operators arrange no-hassle day trips to Ingapirca, Parque Nacional Cajas, nearby villages and markets, and other local attractions. Most operators charge $35 to $40 per person (excluding park entrance fees) and will pick you up at your hotel.

#### Expediciones Apullacta
ADVENTURE TOUR
(☑283-7815; www.apullacta.com; Gran Colombia 11-02, 2nd fl) A big operation that organizes day tours to Ingapirca, Parque Nacional Cajas and the Chordeleg area, among other sites.

#### Mamá Kinua Cultural Center
CULTURAL TOUR
(☑284-0610; Casa de la Mujer, Torres) A community tourism project offering tours and homestays in nearby indigenous communities ($48 per person per night; two-person minimum). You can participate in all kinds of activities, including listening to folkloric music, cooking, farming, medicinal plant demonstrations and cheese-making. All revenue goes to a community health network. No English is spoken.

#### Terra Diversa Travel Center
TOUR
(☑282-3782; www.terradiversa.com; Hermano Miguel 5-42) Specializes in biking and horseback-riding day trips (per person $48) as well as overnight horseback-riding trips that include staying at haciendas or camping along the Inca Trail north of Ingapirca. Also Parque Nacional Cajas and Amazon tours. Three-hour Cuenca city tours cost about $15.

**Tinamu Tours**                    ADVENTURE TOUR
(📞09-780-9320; www.tinamutours.com; Borrero 7-68) A recommended agency that rents camping gear, conducts tours all over the region, and offers parapenting (tandem hanggliding) trips ($48).

## ✨ Festivals & Events

**Independence Day**                    CIVIC
Cuenca's Independence Day is November 3, which combines with November 1 and 2 (All Saints' Day and All Souls' Day) to form an important vacation period for the city and the whole country.

**12 de Abril**                    CIVIC
April 12, the anniversary of Cuenca's founding in 1557, often comes on the heels of Easter celebrations. It's a time when school kids take loyalty pledges to the city, and the Reina de Cuenca (Queen of Cuenca) is selected. *Cuencanos* display their abundant civic pride with elaborate fireworks-laced floats from different neighborhoods.

**Carnaval**                    FESTIVAL
As in other parts of Ecuador, Carnaval is celebrated with boisterous water and talcum powder fights in which *no one* is spared.

**Pase del Niño**                    RELIGIOUS
In keeping with Cuenca's strong Catholic identity, the Christmas Eve procession occupies participants with preparations throughout the whole year and culminates in one of Ecuador's most spectacular religious displays.

**Corpus Christi**                    RELIGIOUS
This Catholic celebration is usually held on the ninth Thursday after Easter and often coincides with the indigenous celebration called Inti Raymi on the June solstice. Carried out with the same fervor as other big Cuenca holidays, it spills over into a weekend full of processions and fireworks displays. Parque Calderón is transformed into a big outdoor candy festival, with vendors selling traditional sweets.

## 🛏 Sleeping

Cuenca has a great selection of hotels, many of which are located in old restored houses and mansions. They come in all price categories, but still run a tad higher than elsewhere. During vacation periods they fill up fast and go up in price.

**Hotel Victoria**                    HACIENDA $$
(📞282-7401; www.hotelvictoriaecuador.com; Calle Larga 6-93; s/d incl breakfast $52/73; @🛜) One of several grand 17th-century houses on the *barranco* over Río Tomebamba, the Victoria's 23 impeccable hacienda-style rooms have exposed wooden beams, comfy beds and modern bathrooms. Two suites have giant terraces over the river and many rooms have views, making this the best mid-range deal in town.

**Hostal Macondo**                    HOTEL $
(📞284-0697; www.hostalmacondo.com; Tarqui 11-64; s/d incl breakfast with shared bathroom $19/28, with private bathroom $25/35; 🛜) The colonial-style Hostal Macondo has spotless palatial rooms in the front, older section, and small but cozy rooms situated around a big, sunny garden out back, making this a top pick for the budget set. Longer-staying guests will enjoy access to the well-equipped and spotless kitchen, and everyone likes the continental breakfasts with bottomless cups of coffee.

**Hostal Posada del Angel**                    B&B $$
(📞284-0695; www.hostalposadadelangel.com; Bolívar 14-11; s/d/tr incl breakfast $45/60/87; 🅿@🛜) This yellow-and-blue B&B in a – you guessed it! – colonial-era house has comfortable rooms with cable TV and big beds. Those off the interior balconies have high ceilings, and several others reached by a narrow wooden staircase are tucked away in the quiet reaches. Breakfasts in the sunlit lobby are watched over by the eponymous angel.

**Mansión Alcázar**                    HISTORIC HOTEL $$$
(📞282-3889; www.mansionalcazar.com; Bolívar 12-55; s/d incl breakfast $122/201; 🅿@🛜) With unsurpassed service and rooms decorated with unique themes, the Alcázar is the best high-end offering in Cuenca. A water fountain spills over with fresh flowers in the interior courtyard, and the sumptuous garden, library and international restaurant all convey the management's tireless attention to detail.

**Posada del Río**                    HOSTEL $
(📞282-3111; posadadelriocuenca@yahoo.com; Hermano Miguel 4-18; dm/s/d $7/$15/22; @🛜) Run by the sweet and earnest Torres sisters, this simple and tasteful inn near the river has a rooftop terrace with views (where you can barbecue) and a communal kitchen. Bright colors and woodwork adorn the hostel throughout, and the

shared bathrooms are squeaky clean, making it one of our top budget picks.

### Hostal Alternative HOSTEL $
(408-4101; anhostels@gmail.com; cnr Huayna Capac & Cacique Duma; r per person with shared bathroom $13; 🛜) Although it's a bit removed from the action, this sparkly new hostel (with a scary logo, cleaner-than-Clorox rooms, shared kitchen, TV room and excellent terrace) has a ton of potential. The modern octagon-shaped building offers small- and medium-size dorm rooms with good mattresses and plenty of space.

### Hotel Los Balcones HISTORIC HOTEL $$
(284-2103; www.hotellosbalconescuenca.com; Borrero 12-08; s/d/tr/q $55/84/105/140; P🛜) This new kid on the block sits in a converted colonial-era home with a remarkable chandelier in the central courtyard, small but well-appointed rooms, hand-painted walls and a rooftop terrace with views fit for a queen. The modular Jacuzzi showers are a bit funky, but set it on pulse and feel the wonder of a thousand hands massaging you at once.

### Cabañas Yanuncay GUESTHOUSE $
(288-3716; yanuncay@etapaonline.net.com.ec; Gualaceo 2-149; r & cabins per person incl breakfast $20; 🛜) If you are looking for a place a bit outside of town, this quiet guesthouse on a working farm, 3km southwest of downtown (take a cab, you'll never find it by foot), has two rooms in the owner's house, and two cabins. The sauna and Jacuzzi are divine, the whole place is relaxing and quiet, and the organic dinners are tremendous ($7). You can also take advantage of the nice kitchen to whip up your own dishes. English and German spoken.

### El Cafecito HOSTEL $
(283-2337; www.cafecito.net; Vásquez 7-36; dm/r per person $7/8; 🛜) A longtime favorite of the *mochilero* (backpacker) and local hipster scenes, El Cafecito has seen better days. The dorm rooms right off the cafe are spacious but close to nightly festivities (maybe too close for some), and the beds have definitely lost most of their spring. This said, it's clean and remains ground zero for meeting other travelers in town.

### Hotel El Dorado BUSINESS HOTEL $$$
(283-1390; www.eldoradohotel.com.ec; Gran Colombia 7-87; s/d incl breakfast $110/122; 🛜📺) This large hotel serves the business set with bright, minimalist decor, all the usual free gels and liquids, and a fitness center. Rates include a huge buffet breakfast.

### Hostal La Orquídea HOTEL $$
(282-4511; alexandrasolis@etapanet.net; Borrero 9-31; s/d/tr/ste $25/35/45/100) Only a block from bustling Parque Calderón, the 'Orchid' has slightly rundown rooms (ask for a newer room upstairs) with hardwood floors, cable TV and mini-fridges. The common areas are lovely.

### Hotel Posada del Rey HOTEL $$
(284-3845; www.posadadelreyhotel.com; Benigno Malo; s/d/ste incl breakfast $35/60/90; 🛜) In a restored colonial-style house, 10 rooms with hand-painted murals surround a central courtyard full of wood and iron. It's not quite fit for a king, as the name implies, but all the relatively comfy rooms have balconies, cable TV and an odd disinfectant odor.

### Hostal Cofradía del Monje B&B $
(283-1251; www.hostalcofradiadelmonje.com; Presidente Córdova 10-33; s/d incl breakfast $26/42) In a refurbished century-old home practically on top of the Church of San Francisco, the 'Brotherhood of Monks' B&B has high timbered ceilings and expansive views of the plaza and market below. With the thick wooden shutters closed, the rooms become as serene as a monastery. The area can be a bit dodgy at night.

### Hotel Carvallo HISTORIC HOTEL $$$
(283-2063; www.hotelcarvalloecuador.com; Gran Colombia 9-52; r incl breakfast $134; P🛜) The Carvallo's 30 rooms are a bit stale and dark, but we love the tin-pressed ceilings found in some, as well as the religious antiques and big fluffy bedcovers you will find throughout. All things told, it's still a little overpriced.

### Hostal La Escalinata HOSTEL $
(284-5758; Calle Larga 5-83; r per person $8; 🛜) The foam mattresses are a little Jell-O-ish and the threadbare sheets and dirty bathrooms will leave you wishing for home, but the garret rooms have cool sloped ceilings, and the price is ridiculously low for the location.

##  Eating

### Café Eucalyptus INTERNATIONAL $
(Gran Colombia 9-41; small plates $3-6; 🕐5-11pm Mon-Tue, 5pm-midnight Wed & Thu, 5pm-1am Fri,

7pm-4am Sat) The irreverent Eucalyptus menu proudly declares that it doesn't serve 'customs officials, crazy bus drivers, or airline executives.' For the rest of us, dozens of Cuban, Vietnamese, Spanish and other reliably delicious international dishes are served at cozy tables near roaring fireplaces, and an extensive variety of wines and beers flows from the gorgeous bar. This wonderful restaurant should cure any gringo's hankering for home, and, thankfully, it still serves guidebook writers.

**Café Austria**                    AUSTRIAN **$$**
(Benigno Malo 5-95; mains $5-8; ☺9am-11pm; 🛜) Every caffeinated drink known to humankind, dainty Austrian cakes, pressed sandwiches and goulash make for a great menu at this relaxed Austrian-owned cafe. English-language newspapers are always available.

**Todosantos**                    ECUADORIAN **$$**
(Calle Larga 5-19; mains $7-13) Sprawling across several levels of a still-operational monastery with exposed wood beams and stone-masoned walls, this upscale eatery specializes in grilled meats but also offers up a smattering of yummy dishes from across the globe, including lasagna, Ecuadorian favorites like *seco de chivo* (goat stew), pork in grape sauce and coconut-crusted *corvina* (sea bass).

**Mamá Kinua Cultural Center**    ECUADORIAN **$**
(Casa de la Mujer, Torres; mains $2-3; ☺8am-5:30pm Mon-Fri) This cooperative restaurant run by Indigenous women has served tasty, traditional *almuerzos* ($2) for many years. They're wholesome, filling and help out a great cause.

**Moliendo Café**                    COLOMBIAN **$**
(Vásquez 6-24; light meals $2-4; ☺9am-9pm Mon-Sat) From Ecuador's neighbors to the north, the hearty *arepas* (maize pancakes) are a specialty here. Topped with anything from beans and cheese to slow-cooked pork, they go well with a cold beer or a strong Juan Valdez coffee. Whether you get a little or a lot, it's essentially old-fashioned comfort food, Colombian-style.

**Akelarre Tapas Españolas**        SPANISH **$$**
(Torres 8-40; tapas & mains $2-12; ☺11am-10pm Mon-Fri, 3-5pm Sat) Akelarre serves petite plates of Spanish classics like 'Papas Bravas' (spicy fried spuds) and Gallecian squid nightly.

**Guajibamba**                    ECUADORIAN **$$**
(Luís Cordero 12-32; mains from $4; ☺noon-3pm & 6-11pm Mon-Sat) This atmospheric restaurant has a small menu of traditional plates like *seco de chivo* and gourmet *fritada* (fried chunks of pork, served with hominy, avocado and other garnishes). It's also one of the best places to try *cuy* (guinea pig); if you're game, call an hour before you go for prep time ($17 for two).

**El Maíz**                    ECUADORIAN **$**
(Calle Larga 1-279 near de los Molinos; mains $4-7; ☺5-11pm Mon & Tue) Billing itself as purveyor of the 'new Ecuadorian cuisine,' El Maíz takes traditional ingredients like quinoa and *chochos* (marinated lupine beans) and turns them into modern and delicious fusion dishes. This restaurant feels more upmarket than its prices suggest.

**Sakura Sushi**                    SUSHI **$$**
(cnr Paseo 3 de Noviembre 2451 & Escalinata; rolls & mains $6-9; ☺noon-midnight) Cuenca's best sushi is fresh – the coast is only three hours away – and pretty authentic. The $3.50 lunch special includes soup, fish or chicken, teriyaki, rice, and a glass of wine.

**Raymipampa**                    ECUADORIAN **$**
(Benigno Malo 8-59; mains $4-6; ☺8:30am-11:30pm Mon-Sat) This Cuenca institution is popular with locals and travelers and stays open late. The food hangs somewhere between Ecuadorian comfort food and diner fare.

**Zoe**                    FUSION **$$**
(cnr Borrero 7-61 & Mariscal Sucre; mains $7-9; ☺5-11pm) This new, stylish restaurant, bar and gallery has laid modish decor over a colonial-style house. The food is also a hybrid:

traditional meat and seafood dishes cooked up with some newer, imported techniques. For all this hipness, the service is pleasantly down to earth.

### El Café Lojano y Tostador    CAFE $
(Mariscal Sucre 10-20; snacks $1) Sip southern Ecuador's famous coffee ($1), freshly roasted and ground before your eyes. You can also buy coffee by the pound ($2.60).

### Chicago Pizza Restaurant    PIZZA $
(Gran Colombia 10-43; mains $2-8; ⊙9:30am-11pm Mon-Sat, 11am-10pm Sun) Thick-crust slices are the preference here, along with pastas and sandwiches.

### New York Pizza    PIZZA $
(Tarqui; mains $2-4; ⊙9:30am-11pm Mon-Sat, 11am-10pm Sun) Pop in here for thin-crust pizza starting at $1.10 a slice.

### Govinda's    INTERNATIONAL $
(Jaramillo 7-27; set lunches $2, mains $2-4; ⊙8:30am-3pm Mon-Sat; ✐) Pizzas, lentil burgers and a little good karma to wash it down.

## 🍸 Drinking & Entertainment

Cuenca has a lot of nightlife offerings, from intimate taverns to smart cafes featuring live music to Hollywood-style clubs catering to the hook-up scene. Discos are open Thursday through Saturday nights from 10pm, but things don't really get moving until around midnight. Bars are generally open nightly, often as early as 5pm.

There are numerous cozy and welcoming little bars along Vásquez, near El Cafecito. East of Hermano Miguel along Presidente Córdova and along Calle Larga, there are several wildly popular (and equally loud) bars with dance floors.

Many of the town's museums offer theater and cultural performances, and the galleries in the El Vado neighborhood are also worth checking out. Movies cost about $4 per person and are listed in Cuenca's newspaper *El Mercurio*.

### La Compañía    PUB
(cnr Borrero & Vásquez) Cuenca's first – and only – microbrewery caters to a young rocker crowd and offers up decent hand-crafted stouts, Irish reds and golden brews.

### Dash    LOUNGE
(Presidente Córdova near Cueva) Of the bars along Presidente Córdova, this is the trendiest. It's nonstop dancing from about mid-

night to dawn Thursday to Saturday. There's a $2 drink minimum.

### WunderBar    BAR
(Escalinata 3-43; ⊙11am-1am Mon-Fri, 3pm-1am Sat) This Austrian-owned place is *voon*derful if you want a classic bar with big wooden tables to sit around with friends. Food is served, and there's a happy 'hour' from 11am to 6pm.

### Café Eucalyptus    BAR
(Colombia 9-41; ⊙5-11pm Mon & Tue, 5pm- midnight Wed & Thu, 5pm-1am Fri, 7pm-4am Sat) A bar on each of the two floors serves drinks to lively salsa and Cuban rhythms most evenings. Women drink free on Wednesdays from 6pm to 10pm (no kidding).

### La Mesa    CLUB
(Gran Colombia 3-55) This is where the locals go when they want to salsa, and boy, can they salsa. It's as fun to watch as it is to dance. The tiny sign out front is easy to miss.

### Multicines    CINEMA
(Milenium Plaza, Astudillo) Get your stadium seats, buckets of popcorn and blockbuster Hollywood flicks in English (with Spanish subtitles).

## 🛍 Shopping

Cuenca is the center of the *paja toquilla* (toquilla straw, or 'panama') hat trade. *Cuencano* nested baskets, gold- and silver-filigreed jewelry from the nearby village of Chordeleg, and ceramics of varying quality are typical finds.

### Casa del Sombrero Alberto Pulla    HATS
(Tarqui 6-91; ⊙6am-6pm) The hats of Cuenca's most famous hatter, the charming 81-year-old Alberto Pulla, have graced the noggins of presidents, celebrities and hundreds of local indigenous women.

### Markets    ARTS & CRAFTS
Both the **crafts market** (cnr Sangurima & Machuca; ⊙8am-5pm) near Plaza Rotary and the **Plaza de San Francisco Market** (cnr Padre Aguirre & Presidente Córdova; ⊙8am-5pm) have an interesting combination of basketry, ceramics, ironwork, wooden utensils, plastic trinkets, gaudy religious paraphernalia and guinea pig roasters (great gift for mom, but tough to get home). The San Francisco market also has a large contingent of *otavaleños* (people from Otavalo) selling sweaters and weavings on its north

side. On the west side of the plaza is the **Casa de la Mujer** (Torres; ☺9am-6:30 Mon-Fri, to 5pm Sat, to 1pm Sun), which houses over 100 craft stalls selling handmade musical instruments, embroidered clothing, baskets, jewelry and more.

**Eduardo Vega**                                    CERAMICS
(www.eduardovega.com; Vía a Turi 201; ☺9am-6pm Mon-Fri, 10am-1:30pm Sat) Just below the Mirador de Turi is the home, workshop and studio of Eduardo Vega, Ecuador's most important ceramic artist. His

colorful terracotta and enamel murals grace walls all over Cuenca and the rest of Ecuador. Sculpture, vases and plates are for sale, and the affable artist is often hanging around and ready to chat.

**Museo del Sombrero de Paja Toquilla**              HATS
(Calle Larga 10-41) This old hat factory has an interesting museum where you can see how panamas were made over the years and witness them being made in the present.

## IT'S NOT A PANAMA, IT'S A MONTECRISTI!

For well over a century, Ecuador has endured the world mistakenly crediting another country with its most famous export – the panama hat. To any Ecuadorian worth his or her salt, the panama hat is a *sombrero de paja toquilla* (toquilla-straw hat), and to the connoisseur it's a Montecristi, named after the most famous hat-making town of all. It's certainly not a paaa...

The origin of this misnomer – surely one of the world's greatest – dates to the 1800s, when Spanish entrepreneurs, quick to recognize the unrivaled quality of *sombreros de paja toquilla,* began exporting them via Panama. During the 19th century, workers on the Panama Canal used these light and extremely durable hats to protect themselves from the tropical sun, helping to solidify the association with Panama.

*Paja toquilla* hats are made from the fibrous fronds of the *toquilla* palm (*Carludovica palmata*), which grows in the arid inland regions of the central Ecuadorian coast, particularly around Montecristi and Jipijapa. A few Asian and several Latin American countries have tried to grow the palm to compete with the Ecuadorian hat trade, but none could duplicate the quality of the fronds grown here.

The work that goes into these hats is astonishing. First the palms are harvested for their shoots, which are ready just before they open into leaves. Bundles of shoots are then transported by donkey and truck to coastal villages where the fibers are prepared.

The preparation process begins with beating the shoots on the ground and then splitting them by hand to remove the long, thin, flat, cream-colored leaves. The leaves are tied into bundles and boiled in huge vats of water for about 20 minutes before being hung to dry for three days. Some are soaked in sulfur for bleaching. As the split leaves dry, they shrink and roll up into the round strands that are used for weaving.

Some of the finished straw stays on the coast, but most is purchased by buyers from Cuenca and surrounding areas, where the straw is woven into hats. Indeed, you'll see more panama hats in and around Cuenca than you'll see anywhere in Ecuador.

The weaving process itself is arduous, and the best weavers work only in the evening and early in the morning, before the heat causes their fingers to sweat. Some work only by moonlight. Weaves vary from a loose crochet (characteristic of the hats you see sold everywhere) to a tighter 'Brisa' weave, which is used for most quality panama hats.

Hats are then graded by the density of their weaves, which generally fall into four categories: standard, superior, *fino* (fine) and *superfino* (superfine). Most hats you see are standard or superior. If you hold a real *superfino* up to the light, you shouldn't see a single hole. The best of them will hold water and some are so finely woven and so pliable that they can supposedly be rolled up and pulled through a man's ring!

After the hats are woven, they still need to be trimmed, bleached (if they're to be white), blocked and banded. Then they're ready to sell. Although standard-grade hats start at around $15 in Ecuador, a *superfino* can cost anywhere between $100 and $500. While it may seem expensive, the same hat will easily fetch three times that amount on shelves in North America and Europe. And considering the work that goes into a *superfino,* it rightly should.

**Homero Ortega P & Hijos**                    HATS
(www.homeroortega.com; Gil Ramirez Davalos
386) More akin to a hat emporium, this is
Ecuador's best-known hat seller. The company exports around the world and has a
huge selection of high-quality men's and
women's straw hats. They are located a
couple blocks north of the bus station.

**Acción Sport**                              SPORTS
(Bolívar 12-70) Sells outdoor gear and rents
tents for $2 per day.

**Libri Mundi**                                BOOKS
(cnr Miguel & Sucre) This is a nice spot on a
rainy day.

# ℹ Information

## Dangers & Annoyances

Cuenca is pretty safe for a bigger city. This said,
at night it's best to walk on well-lit streets. The
area around Plaza San Francisco can get a big
gamey after dark.

## Emergency

**Police station** (☏286-4924; España near
Elialut in front of the airport)
**Police station** (☏284-0476; Plaza de San
Francisco; ◷8am-8pm)

## Internet Access

There are more internet cafes than you'll ever
need, and new ones open regularly. Most charge
$0.80 to $1 per hour and are open from 8am to
9pm daily.

## Internet Resources

**www.cuenca.com.ec** Cuenca's tourism
website.
**www.cuencanos.com** Loads of Cuenca
information, mostly in Spanish.

## Laundry

**La Química** (Borrero; per kg $0.90; ◷8am-
6:30pm Mon-Fri, 9am-1pm Sat)
**Lavanda** (Vásquez 6-76; per kg $0.70; ◷8am-
1pm & 3-6pm Mon-Fri, 8am-noon Sat)
**Lavandería Nieves** (Calle Larga 11-55; per kg
$0.80)

## Medical Services

The following medical clinics have some English-
speaking staff. Consultations cost about $20.
**Clínica Hospital Monte Sinaí** (☏288-5595;
Miguel Cordero 6-111)
**Clínica Santa Inés** (☏281-7888; Daniel Córdova 2-113) Can help with referrals to local
doctors.

## Money

It can be hard changing euros, Aussie dollars and
other currencies in Cuenca. Trust the greenback!
**Banco de Guayaquil** (Mariscal Sucre near Bor-
rero) Bank with ATM.
**Banco del Pichincha** (cnr Solano & 12 de Abril)
Bank with ATM.

## Post

**Post office** (cnr Gran Colombia & Borrero)

## Telephone

**Etapa** (Benigno Malo 726; ◷7am-10pm)
Telephone call center.

## Tourist Information

**Bus Terminal Information office** (☏282-4811)
In the bus terminal.
**Tourist office** (iTur; ☏282-1035; Mariscal
Sucre at Luís Cordero; ◷8am-8pm Mon-Fri,
8:30am-1:30pm Sat) Friendly and helpful;
English spoken.

## Travel Agencies

**Metropolitan Touring** (☏283-1185/1463;
www.metropolitan-touring.com; Mariscal Sucre
6-62) Good all-purpose travel agency.

# ℹ Getting There & Away

## Air

Cuenca's **Aeropuerto Mariscal Lamar** (Av
España) is 2km from the heart of town and just
500m from the Terminal Terrestre bus station.
**Aerogal** (☏410-3104; www.aerogal.com.
ec; Aguilar near Solano; ◷8:30am-1pm &
2-6:30pm Mon-Fri, 9:30am-12:30pm Sat) Flies
daily to Quito ($115) and Guayaquil ($110).
**TAME** (www.tame.com.ec) Airport (☏286-
2400); downtown (☏288-9097/9581; Astudillo
2-22; ◷8:30am-1pm & 2-6:30pm Mon-Fri,
9:30am-12:30pm Sat) Also flies daily to Quito
($115) and Guayaquil ($110).

## Bus

Cuenca has two major bus stations. Some
buses, including those to Parque Nacional Cajas,
Jima and Girón, leave from **Terminal Sur**, across
from the Feria Libre, west of the center.

The vast majority of buses (hundreds per day)
leave from Cuenca's **Terminal Terrestre** (Av
España), the main bus station about 1.5km from
downtown. Buses go daily from this station to
Ingapirca and Gualaceo, Chordeleg and Sigsig.

Two routes go to Guayaquil: the shorter via
Parque Nacional Cajas and Molleturo ($8, four
hours), and the longer via La Troncal and Cañar
($8, five hours).

## Car

The national chain **Localiza** (☏280-3198/93)
rents economy cars and 4WDs at the airport.

## BUSES FROM TERMINAL TERRESTRE

| DESTINATION | COST (US$) | DURATION (HR) |
| --- | --- | --- |
| Alausí | 5 | 4 |
| Ambato | 8 | 7 |
| Azogues | 0.70 | ¾ |
| Gualaquiza (via Sígsig) | 8 | 4–5 |
| Guayaquil | 8 | 4–5 |
| Huaquillas | 7 | 7 |
| Latacunga | 9 | 8.5 |
| Loja | 7.50 | 5 |
| Macas (via Guarumales) | 8 | 8 |
| Machala | 5.50 | 4 |
| Piura (Peru) | 15–17 | 14–16 |
| Quito | 10–12 | 10–12 |
| Riobamba | 7 | 6 |
| Saraguro | 5 | 3 |
| Sigsig | 1.25 | 1 |
| Zamora | 9.40 | 7-8 |

### ⓘ Getting Around

In front of the main bus terminal, regular buses head downtown ($0.25). From downtown to the terminal, take any bus marked 'Terminal' from stops on Padre Aguirre near the flower market. Taxis cost about $2 between downtown and the airport or bus terminal.

For Terminal Sur, take a cab ($2) or bus signed 'Feria Libre' from either Presidente Córdova or Mariscal Lamar.

Local buses for Turi ($0.25), 4km south of the center, go along Avenida Solano.

## Around Cuenca

🕗07

Cuenca is an easy base for day trips to indigenous villages in the surrounding area. Some of those listed here are invested in community-based tourism, so you can support local people by hiring local guides and buying traditional crafts. Gualaceo, Chordeleg and Sigsig can all be done together in one day, while Principal, Cajas and the ruins at Ingapirca (p164) are really separate day trips of their own.

### PARQUE NACIONAL CAJAS

**Cajas National Park** (admission $2), only 30km west of Cuenca, encompasses 2854 sq km of golden moorlike *páramo* (high-altitude Andean grasslands) dotted with hundreds of chilly lakes that shine like jewels against a bleak, rough countryside.

This extremely wet and foggy area feeds rivers that flow into Cuenca and is considered an important conservation area for birds, mammals and flora.

Especially important are small forests of *Polylepis* trees that are found in sheltered hollows and natural depressions. *Polylepis* trees have adapted to grow at higher elevations than almost any other tree in the world, making this one of the highest forests on earth. And wandering into one of these dense dwarf forests is like entering a Brothers Grimm fairy tale.

The park is named Cajas, according to some folks, because the lakes look (rather dubiously) like *cajas* (boxes). More likely, the name comes from *caxas*, the Kichwa word for cold. And cold it is...so cold that getting lost, which is easy to do, is a rather dangerous proposition. Night temperatures can drop below freezing, especially in the dry season. The driest months are August to January, but it can rain anytime.

Three main recreational areas, all at scenic lakes, lie along the Cuenca–Molleturo road: **Laguna Llaviucu**, which is closest to Cuenca and has a **control** where you can pay admission; **Laguna Cucheros**; and

# Parque Nacional Cajas

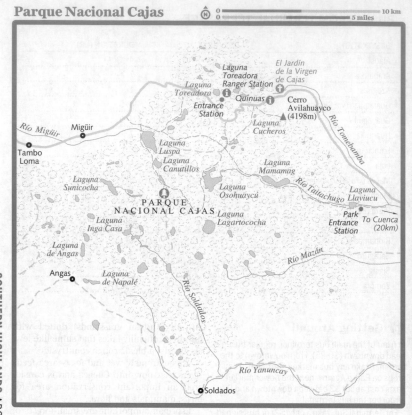

**Laguna Toreadora**, which has an information center. A second **control** appears at Quinuas, 3km west of Cucheros. The controls provide free, glossy topographical trail maps, which are also available at the tourist information office in Cuenca.

Outside the designated areas around Lagunas, Llaviacu, Cucheros and Toreadora, groups of eight or more are required to be accompanied by a guide, and all hikers outside these areas must register with the ranger stations (they must also carry a GPS or compass). Currently no overnight hiking trips may be conducted without an approved guide from Cuenca or the park itself. Most of the operators listed under 'Tours' in Cuenca can arrange a guide.

## Activities

The park has some rock-climbing spots, but for real thrill-seekers it offers bird-watching, llama-viewing, and even fishing! All of the recreation areas offer these activities and signed hikes of up to a few hours. Several multiday hikes across the park pass through sublime deserted landscapes and present more opportunities to see wild species, but make sure you know how to navigate through terrain that seems to defy its own topo maps – or hire a guide.

## Sleeping

Camping at any of the three recreational areas costs $4. *Refugios* (mountain refuges) and cabins are available, but they fill up fast and do not accept reservations.

## Getting There & Away

Cajas is accessible along two routes. The controls at Laguna Llaviucu and Laguna Cucheros are on the northern route, which is also the first leg of the highway journey to Guayaquil via Molleturo. A bumpy southern road passes the villages of Soldados, where there is a control, and Angas.

Transportes Occidental buses ($1.25, one hour) leave from Terminal Sur in Cuenca every day at 6:15am, 7am, 8am, 10am, noon, 1:30pm, 2:30pm, 4:10pm and 5:45pm. To return to Cuenca, flag any passing Cuenca-bound bus.

Buses for Soldados ($1.25, 1¼ hour) and Angas ($2, 1¾ hour) leave from the El Vado bridge in Cuenca at 6am and return in the afternoon.

You can also take a taxi (about $60 for the day) or go on a day trip with one of the tour agencies in Cuenca.

## GUALACEO, CHORDELEG & SIGSIG

If you start out early, you could easily visit the Sunday markets at all three of these towns and be back in Cuenca for happy hour. Between them all you'll find many traditional handicrafts: woven baskets, fine gold and silver filigreed jewelry, woodwork, pottery, guitars and ikat textiles – made using a pre-Columbian technique of weaving tie-dyed threads.

### GUALACEO

Along the banks of a small, swift-moving river lies the craft-shopper's paradise of Gualaceo (2591m). Over the bridge and a few blocks from the bus station, the **feria artesanal** sells excellent crafts from the region, and even more if you wander around town. Ikat weavings and *paños* (indigo-dyed cotton shawls with intricate macramé fringe) are especially sought after here.

En route to Gualaceo stop at the **Taller Artesanal de San Pedro** (San Pedro Crafts Workshop; 4km north of Gualaceo; admission free) to see how things are made. About 1km down the road, an **Orquideario** (orchid farm; 3km north of Gualaceo; admission $3) gives an in-

tro to flower farming in the region. At the entrance to town the **Museo López Abad** (admission $1.50), on the main road, is a private archaeological museum. On the main plaza, a **Tourist Information Office** (iTur; Gran Colombia near 3 de Noviembre; ⊙8am-5pm Mon-Fri) can give you good info on nearby hiking and adventure opportunities.

The family-run **Residencial Gualaceo** (✆225-5006; Gran Colombia 3-02; s/d $7/15) has spare, clean rooms one block north of the main plaza.

For lunch, try the **Mercado 25 de Junio** (cnr Cuenca & Vicente Peña Reyes), a couple of blocks uphill from the bus station.

### CHORDELEG

About 10km south of Gualaceo, Chordeleg has been an important jewelry-making center since before the arrival of the Inca. Its characteristic style is fine filigree. Fakery is common, however, so know how to discern high-quality gold before laying out the big bucks.

Chordeleg also produces woodcarvings, pottery, textiles and plenty of panama hats. On the central plaza, the small **Centro Agro Artesanal Chordeleg** (admission free; ⊙9am-1pm & 2-5pm Tue-Sun) details the history and techniques of many of these handicrafts and sells some locally made work.

### SIGSIG

About 26km south of Gualaceo lies Sigsig (2684m), a charming vestige of a colonial-era indigenous town, best known for its panama hats.

WORTH A TRIP

## DIY ADVENTURES OUTSIDE OF CUENCA

There are plenty of DIY adventures to be had from Cuenca in the nearby towns of Baños, Girón, Jima and Paute. Here are some hints to get you started.

**Baños** Just outside of Cuenca, this small village has thermal springs and a neat little church.

**Girón** Some 43km southwest of Cuenca on the road to Machala, Girón offers hiking to a 60m waterfall – nice! After busing it here from Cuenca, hire a truck for $5 to take you to the waterfall. Hire a guide from the first waterfall to take you to two hidden falls nearby.

**Jima** This peaceful agrarian village two hours south of Cuenca serves up easy access to a neighboring cloud forest in a community-run reserve. There's a *hostal* and information center in town where you can arrange a guide. Get here by bus from Cuenca.

**Paute** Good mountain-biking and hiking are to be had from this seldom-visited town just north of Gualaceo. It's an easy day trip from Cuenca, but staying the night will help out the community more.

There are a couple of restaurants and *residenciales* (cheap hotels) near the main market plaza.

### ℹ Getting There & Away

From Cuenca's Terminal Terrestre bus terminal, buses leave every half hour to Gualaceo ($0.80, one hour), Chordeleg ($1, one hour) and Sigsig ($1.25, 1½ hours). Buses run from town to town for $0.50 and can be flagged from the main street. Buses head from Sigsig to Cuenca about every hour ($1.25).

### PRINCIPAL

Just 37km beyond Sigsig, the small community of Principal (2791m) rests humbly in the shadow of **Volcán Fasayñan** (3907m), a huge pillar of rock from where, according to local legend, the Cañari people originated.

To promote sustainability in the community, Principal has a small association of certified guides who can lead hikes ($10 per person) up Fasayñan, to the **Infiernillo** (little hell) waterfall, and the **Three Lakes**, which dot the *páramo* with crystal waters. All destinations are within three to five hours' hiking, and *cabalgatas* (horseback-riding trips) to them are possible. Inquire about these activities and the local weaving cooperative that makes panama hats at **Hostal Anabel** (☏09-981-5821; r with shared bathroom per person $6), which is a modern guesthouse.

Buses to Principal ($0.50, 30 minutes) leave every 40 minutes from 6:30am to 6:30pm, from a stop four blocks from the main square in Chordeleg.

# Saraguro

☏07 / POP 4007 / ELEV 2520M

Surrounded by golden-green hills that have been sown with hearty tubers and grains for thousands of years, Saraguro, 165km south of Cuenca, is the center of indigenous Saraguro culture. This prosperous and proud indigenous group originally lived near Lake Titicaca in Peru but ended up here in the 1470s as a result of the Inca Empire's system of resettlement, or *mitimaes*.

During the last century, Saraguros have relocated (this time, of their own accord) to significantly lower altitudes to the southwest and often alongside Shuar communities in the Ecuadorian Amazon. In both the chilly mountains and humid lowlands, the Saraguro dress in traditional woolens. Women wear broad-brimmed white hats, long pleated skirts, ornate pins called *tupus* and elaborate beaded collars known as *chakiras*. Men wear fedora-like hats, black ponchos and knee-length black shorts, and they may also don small white aprons and woven, double-pouch shoulder bags called *alforjas*.

All the elements of Saraguro attire are important craft traditions maintained in nearby communities, which are fun to visit. The **Sunday market** draws Saraguros – dressed finely for the occasion – from the surrounding countryside.

An ATM and a call center are on the main square.

### ◉ Sights & Activities

The villages around Saraguro, most within a half-hour walk or 10-minute bus ride ($0.20), are full of outdoor and cultural activities. Buses to any of these places leave from the main square in front of the cathedral. Information and trail maps are available at iTur, also on the main plaza.

**Baños del Inka**                                    WATERFALL
(admission $2.50) Just north of town on the Panamericana, this nature area has impressive waterfalls and large rock formations.

**Bosque Protegido Washapamba**          FOREST
(admission $2.50) The Washapamba Forest Reserve, just south of town, is great for hiking.

**Lagunas Saraguro**                                    LAKE
Near the Lagunas Saraguro, women make *tupus* and textiles, making this an interesting cultural excursion.

**Tuncarta**                                              VILLAGE
The community of Tuncarta is known for its fine Saraguro hats.

### ☞ Tours

**Operadora de Turismo
Comunitario Saraurku**              CULTURAL TOUR
(☏220-0331; www.turismosaraguro.com; 18 de Noviembre & Loja) One block west of the main plaza, this community tour operator arranges tours to the neighboring sites. It also takes you to the Saraguro communities in the Amazon for $40 to $60 per person per day. Horseback-riding and mountain-bike trips are available.

## 🛏 Sleeping & Eating

**TOP CHOICE** **Hostal Achik Wasi** — HOTEL $$
(📞220-0058; www.saraguro.com; Intiñan in Barrio La Luz; r per person incl breakfast $15) A 10-minute walk up and out of town (taxi $1), this large adobe-and-wood *hostal* (small, reasonably priced hotel) has comfortable rooms with soft blankets and tall ceilings. The great views and immaculately landscaped grounds make this your best lodging option in town. It's part of a well-run tourism project that benefits the community.

**Operadora de Turismo
Comunitario Saraurku** — HOMESTAY $$
(📞220-0331; www.turismosaraguro.com; 18 de Noviembre & Loja; r incl meals $27.30) Check in at the Saraurku for homestay opportunities in nearby villages. You'll learn to work the family farm and get three square meals a day. More importantly, it's a chance to learn about – and be involved in – local life in the Andes.

**Residencial Saraguro** — HOTEL $
(📞220-0286; cnr Loja & Antonio Castro; r per person with shared/private bathroom $5/6) This small, rather unfriendly establishment just a block east of the main plaza is popular with travelers. Rooms and bathrooms are bare bones, but the sheets are clean.

**Mamá Cuchara** — ECUADORIAN $
(Parque Central; mains $1.50-2.50; ⊘7am-10pm Sun-Fri) 'Mother Spoon,' as the name aptly means, serves up hearty, tasty meals right on the main plaza. Money goes to the indigenous women's association that runs it.

**Central Market** — MARKET $
This market west of the main plaza has stalls selling traditional Ecuadorian dishes for $1 to $2.

## ℹ Getting There & Away

Any Loja-bound bus from Cuenca will drop you a block from Saraguro's main plaza ($5, 3½ hours, hourly). Buses to Loja ($2, 1½ hours, 62km) leave hourly during the day. The bus office is a block from the main plaza.

# Loja
📞07 / ELEV 2100M

The provincial capital of Loja makes a convenient base for visiting Parque Nacional Podocarpus, Vilcabamba and the southern Oriente, but it is also a special place in its own right and one that many Ecuadorians admire for its dignified culture. Despite the isolated location in the far south of Ecuador, Loja has an important conservatory and an internationally renowned university that attracts many international students. It is a music-loving town with a proud history of local virtuosos. The town itself is noisy and rather dirty, but a few colonial-era corridors may make a short stopover worth your time, especially for culture-lovers.

## ◉ Sights & Activities

Loja's historic center can be thoroughly covered in one full day. Living up to its ecologically friendly reputation, the parks are several and large and take more time to cover.

**Parque Central** — PLAZA
Loja's main square is always busy with shoeshine boys, newspaper vendors and local devotees stepping into the **cathedral** for their daily devotions to the Virgen del Cisne.

**Museo del Banco Central** — MUSEUM
(10 de Agosto; admission $1; ⊘9am-1pm & 2-5pm Mon-Fri) On the south side of Parque Central, a republican-era building houses this museum and its small exhibit of local archaeology, ethnography and art.

**Museo del Monasterio de Monjas
Concepcionistas** — MUSEUM
(10 de Agosto; admission $1; ⊘9am-1pm & 2-5pm Mon-Fri) One block east of Parque Central, this monastery has three public rooms housing religious treasures from the 16th to 18th centuries.

**FREE** **Casa de la Cultura
Ecuatoriana** — MUSEUM
(Valdivieso near Rocafuerte; ⊘8am-1pm & 2-6pm) Stop by this cultural center, which houses rotating art exhibitions.

**Museo de la Música** — MUSEUM
(Valdivieso 09-42; admission $0.25; ⊘9am-2pm & 3-6pm Mon-Fri) This fun museum located in an old school explores the lives of famous musicians who hailed from Loja. Many old instruments are on display.

**Parque Recreacional Jipiro** — PARK
(Santiago de las Montañas at Salvador Bustamante) North of town this kid-friendly park can induce the feeling that you've been shrunk down and tossed into a miniature-golf course. Kids scramble all over little bridges, a giant chess board, a skate park, a Chinese

# Loja

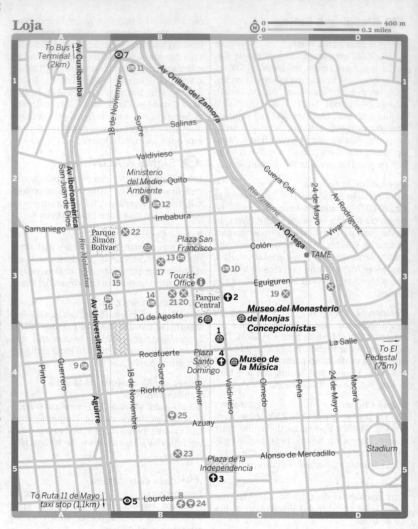

pagoda, a pint-size Kremlin, small animal enclosures, and a paddleboat pond. Green buses ($0.25) go there from the southeast corner of Eguiguren and Peña.

**Plaza San Francisco**                           PLAZA
(cnr Bolívar & Colón) Two blocks north of the Parque Central, this smallish plaza is crowned by a statue of the city's founder astride his horse.

**Church of Santo Domingo**               CHURCH
(cnr Valdivieso & Rocafuerte) Two blocks south of Parque Central, on the Plaza Santo Domingo, the interior of the Church of Santo Domingo is adorned with religious paintings.

**Plaza de la Independencia**                 PLAZA
(cnr Alonso de Mercadillo & Valdivieso) The Plaza of Independence is hemmed in by the **Church of San Sebastián** and colonial-era buildings with pillared overhangs and shuttered wooden balconies.

**Lourdes**                                    STREET
The narrow lane of Calle Lourdes is the oldest colonial street in Loja. There are some nice art galleries, but otherwise it hasn't changed much in the last half millennium.

# Loja

**FREE Puerta de la Ciudad**   MONUMENT
(Door to the City; ◔10am-10pm Mon-Fri, 11am-10pm Sat & Sun) North of downtown, the City Gate is a giant castle with an arched doorway spanning Sucre, a street entering downtown. Inside the castle are two floors of art galleries and several lookouts.

**El Pedestal**   LOOKOUT
For a pleasant walk, head east from the center on Rocafuerte and cross Río Zamora. From there, climb the small hill to El Pedestal, where the base of the bronze statue of La Virgen offers a broad vista.

**Parque Universitario La Argelia**   PARK
(admission $1; ◔9am-4pm) Almost 5km south of the center, the 90-hectare reserve has excellent trails. You'll need to cab it here ($1).

**Jardín Botánico Reynaldo Espinosa**   GARDENS
(admission $0.60; ◔9am-4pm Mon-Fri, 1-6pm Sat & Sun) Across the road from the Parque Universitario, this botanical garden has nearly 900 plant species.

**Parque La Banda/Orillas de Zamora**   ZOO
(8 de Diciembre; admission $0.50; ◔8am-6pm) From Parque Jipiro it is about a half-hour walk to this nice park, where a small outdoor zoo shelters monkeys, ostriches and a pair of spectacled bears. A beautifully designed **Orquideario** maintains over 200 species of orchids from southern Ecuador.

## ⊙ Tours

**Exploraves**   BIRD-WATCHING
(☏258-2434; www.exploraves.com; Lourdes 14-80; ◔closed for lunch) Offers bird-watching day tours in Podocarpus starting at $80 per day.

## ✳ Festivals & Events

**El Día de La Virgen del Cisne**   RELIGIOUS
Huge processions mark this Catholic festival, celebrated in Loja on August 20.

**Independence of Loja**   CIVIC
The celebrations on November 18 may go on for a week.

**San Sebastián**   RELIGIOUS
*Lojanos* celebrate the feast of Saint Sebastián annually on December 8.

## 🛏 Sleeping

**Grand Victoria Boutique Hotel**   HISTORIC HOTEL $$$
(☏258-3500; www.grandvictoriabh.com; cnr Valdivieso & Eguiguren; s/d incl breakfast $110/134; ℗@🛜🏊) Bringing the 'boutique hotel experience' to Loja, the Grand Victoria remembers all the little details, like bathrobes and rose petals, 800-thread-count cotton sheets and aromatherapy in the pool area. The rooms are supremely comfortable but lack the charm of the common areas, and service

## LA VIRGEN DEL CISNE

Throughout Ecuador, but especially in Loja province, you'll see figurines, shrines, pendants and all manner of trinkets dedicated to the Virgen del Cisne (Virgin of the Swan). According to legend, the Virgin Mary protected a medieval knight who appeared before his lover in a boat shaped like a swan. The knight's chivalric acts and the Virgin's kindly auspices inspired Franciscan monks so much that they erected statues of the 'Virgen del Cisne' throughout Europe. The Franciscans later hauled one of these statues to Ecuador, where she has been credited with miracles aplenty, mostly involving sickness and storms.

The Virgin you see today, installed by adoring *campesinos* (peasants) in 1594 in a little town also called El Cisne (70km west of Loja), wears gilded robes and a towering crown. This Virgin, the 'original,' lives in the town's Santuario, a Gothic-style cathedral, most of the year. Virgens del Cisne in other parts of Ecuador wear vestments inspired by local indigenous costumes, or even the Ecuadorian flag (especially when the national soccer team is playing a big game).

A huge festival is held in the Virgin's honor in El Cisne on August 15, after which thousands of pilgrims from Ecuador and northern Peru carry the statue on their shoulders to Loja, with many of the pilgrims walking the entire way. The Virgin finally arrives in Loja on August 20, where she is ceremoniously installed in the cathedral. On November 1, the process is repeated in reverse, and the Virgin rests in El Cisne until the following August. There is another major (if smaller) festival in El Cisne on May 30.

For most of the year, tours and buses make day trips to the village from Loja and Catamayo to see El Santuario and the statue. But on procession days, forget it! You walk like everybody else – the road is so full of pilgrims that vehicles can't get through. In recent years, cyclists have taken to riding this gorgeous route through the mountains alongside the pilgrims. No matter how you go, this display of devotion always amazes.

in the hotel and each of the three international restaurants is far above par.

### Grand Hotel Loja
BUSINESS HOTEL $$

(☑258-6600; www.grandhotelloja.com; cnr Aguirre & Rocafuerte; s/d incl breakfast $37/54; P ⓢ) Helpful and friendly, this large, modern hotel has comfortable rooms with 1970s-style golden bedspreads. It's also much quieter than most hotels and has a sauna and hot tub, making this the best midrange option in the city.

### Hotel Libertador
HOTEL $$

(☑257-8278; www.hotellibertador.com.ec; Colón 14-30; s/d incl breakfast $61/71; P @ ⓢ ⚊) This upmarket hotel is a good bet for the midrange set. Some rooms have dining areas and big bathtubs. It frequently offers a weekend special on double rooms.

### Hotel Podocarpus
HOTEL $$

(☑258-1428; www.hotelpodocarpus.com.ec; Eguiguren 16-50; s/d incl breakfast $30/45; P ⓢ) The Podocarpus' common areas exude a boutique chic not seen in other Loja offerings. The rooms aren't quite so modern, but are comfortable nonetheless, with recently renovated bathrooms and nice dark-wood furniture. The staff is eager to please.

### Hotel Metropolitan
HOTEL $

(☑257-0007; www.metropolitanohotel.com; 18 de Noviembre 6-41; r per person $12-15; ⓢ) The Metropolitan is a great budget hotel with friendly service, comfortable rooms with hardwood floors, decent beds and cable TV. It's dark, though, so try to score a window.

### Hostal Aguilera Internacional
HOTEL $$

(☑258-4660; ricar2aguilera@hotmail.com; Sucre 01-08 y Ortega; s/d incl breakfast $28/38; ⚊) If you want to stay closer to the bus terminal, try this spot next to the Puerta de la Ciudad. Family-owned and family-friendly, the Aguilar also offers nice, well-lit rooms and big, hot and dry sauna rooms.

### Hotel Londres
HOSTEL $

(☑256-1936; Sucre 07-51; r with shared bathroom per person $5) With creaky wooden floors, big white walls and saggy beds, Hotel Londres is as basic as they come, but it's a tried-and-true travelers' favorite, with spotless shared bathrooms and friendly young owners.

### Hostal San Luis
HOTEL $

(☑257-0370; Sucre 4-62; r per person $9) This cell-block of a hotel has 45 stark institutional-feeling rooms. It's little more than a place to bed down for the night, but the sheets are clean.

##  Eating

Loja's biggest specialty, *cuy*, is commonly served on Sundays, although it's sometimes available during the week. Other local delights include *cecina* (salty fried pork served with yuca) and some of the country's best *humitas*.

West of Bolívar, succulent grilled-chicken joints line Alonso de Mercadillo, where you can pick up a quarter-chicken with soup and fries for about $2.

**El Tamal Lojano**     ECUADORIAN $
(18 de Noviembre 05-12; light items $0.70-1; set lunches $2; ☺9am-2pm & 4-8pm Mon-Sat) The *almuerzos* are good, but the real reason to come is for the delicious *quimbolitos, humitas, empanadas de verde* and *tamales lojanos*. Try them all!

**El Fogón**     ARGENTINE $$
(cnr Eguiguren & Bolívar; mains $4-9; ☺noon-8pm) This family eatery serves large portions of grilled meats in the Argentine tradition.

**Salón Lolita**     ECUADORIAN $$
(Salvador Bustamante Celi at Guayaquil, El Valle; mains $4-12; ☺11am-10pm) About 1km north of downtown, this is *the* place for traditional food from Loja. The *cecina* is classic, and roasted *cuy* comes in $8, $10 or $12 portions.

**Cebichería 200 Millas**     CEVICHERÍA $
(Peña 07-41; mains $4-7; ☺9am-3pm) Ceviche is really a late-morning dish, and that's when everyone shows up for superfresh seafood at this local favorite.

**Casa Sol**     CAFE $
(24 de Mayo 07-04; snacks $0.80-1.50; ☺9am-11pm) The definition of a pleasant cafe, Casa Sol serves drinks and all the traditional snacks at balcony tables overlooking a little park and river. It's best in the evening, but if you go early, peek into the kitchen to see the whole family cooking up a storm.

**El Jugo Natural**     JUICE BAR $
(Eguiguren 14-20; light meals $1-3; ☺7am-8pm) Pure, all-natural juices, yogurt shakes, and fruit salads make up the menu at this small cafe. It's been in the juice business for 30 years.

**A lo Mero Mero**     MEXICAN $
(Sucre 06-22; mains $3-4, set lunches $2; ☺9:30am-9pm Mon-Sat; ) The Mexican menu here has bulging burritos (great for vegetarians) and hearty enchiladas served in a friendly and colorful dining room. The guacamole is good, but the salsa is 100% Ecuadorian (not spicy).

## 🍷 Drinking

Many cafes have unadvertised, low-key live music during the evenings, but otherwise Loja's nightlife is a pretty tame scene.

SOUTHERN HIGHLANDS LOJA

---

### SOUTHERN DELIGHTS

For many Ecuadorians living overseas, nothing beckons home more than the smell of corn- and plantain-based *delicias* (delights, or treats). They're common throughout the highlands, but everyone knows that they're better the closer you get to Loja. Many people wash them down with coffee or dress them with *ají* (hot sauce). Here's a primer:

**Humita** A corn dumpling steamed in a corn husk. The *sal* (salty) versions come with cheese; the *dulce* (sweet) versions are often flavored with anise.

**Quimbolito** A light corn-based cake steamed in *achira* leaves, usually topped with a raisin.

**Tamales de Loja** Close to a *humita*, but usually stuffed with shredded chicken.

**Empanada** A pocket of dough stuffed with sweet or savory fillings and fried to a golden, light crispiness. The *masa* (dough) in *empanadas de verde* is made with young plantain; *empanadas de maíz* are made of corn.

**Tortilla de choclo** A grilled pancake made with rough corn flour.

**Maduro con queso** A grilled, sweet plantain with cheese.

**Bolón de verde** A molded ball of young mashed plantain, fried with sausage.

**El Viejo Minero**                                   PUB
(Sucre 10-76) This rustic old watering hole
is the perfect place for a relaxed beer and
snacks in a friendly pub-like environment.

**Casa Tinku**                                        BAR
(Lourdes btwn Bolivar & Sucre) Casa Tinku is a
spirited little bar with a great vibe; there's
usually live music on weekends.

## ⓘ Information

### Emergency
**Police station** (☎257-5606; Valdivieso btwn
Imbabura & Quito)

### Internet Access
**Cyberpower** (Riofrío & Sucre; per hr $1;
☺8am-8pm)

### Internet Resources
**www.loja.gov.ec** Municipal website.
**www.lojanos.com** Loja's 'virtual community.'

### Laundry
**Lavandería Autoservicio** (cnr de Mayo &
Eguiguren; per kg $0.85; ☺8am-7pm Mon-Sat,
8:30am-1pm Sun)

### Medical Services
**Hospital** (☎257-0540; cnr & San Juan de Diós)

### Money
**Banco de Guayaquil** (Eguiguren near Valdivieso) Bank with ATM.

### Post
**Post office** (cnr Colón & Sucre)

### Telephone
**Corporación Nacional de Telecomunicaciones**
(Eguiguren near Olmedo) Telephone call center.

### Tourist Information
**Ministerio del Medio Ambiente** (☎258-5927;
Sucre 4-35, 3rd fl) Responsible for administer-
ing Parque Nacional Podocarpus; provides
information and simple maps.
**Tourist office** (iTur; ☎258-1251; cnr Bolívar &
Eguiguren; ☺8am-1pm & 3-6pm Mon-Fri, 9am-
1pm Sat) Helpful, with some maps available.
There is a second office at the bus station.

## ⓘ Getting There & Away

### Air
Loja is served by La Toma airport in Catamayo,
some 30km to the west. **TAME** (☎257-0248;
www.tame.com.ec; Av Ortega near 24 de Mayo;
☺8:30am-1pm & 2:30-6pm Mon-Fri, 9am-1pm
Sat) flies to/from Quito ($77) Monday to Sat-
urday and Guayaquil ($79) Tuesday through
Thursday.

### Bus & Taxi
Almost all buses leave from the **bus terminal**
(Av Cuxibamba), about 2km north of downtown.
There is an iTur office here to help you.

Vilcabambaturis has fast minibuses to Vilcabamba ($1.30, one hour, every 15 to 30 min-
utes from 6:15am to 9:15pm). Or a faster way is
on a *taxi colectivo* (shared taxi; $2, 45 minutes),
from Avenida Universitaria, about 10 blocks
south of Mercadillo in Loja; ask a local taxi driver
to take you to the Ruta 11 de Mayo taxi stop.

Huaquillas, on the main route to Peru, can
be reached by a bus leaving at 5pm ($10,
seven hours), so you can avoid backtracking to
Machala. Loja is also a departure point for buses

## DAILY BUSES FROM LOJA

| DESTINATION | COST (US$) | DURATION (HR) |
| --- | --- | --- |
| Ambato | 14 | 11 |
| Catamayo | 1 | ¾ |
| Cuenca | 7 | 5 |
| Gualaquiza | 6 | 6 |
| Guayaquil | 10 | 8–9 |
| Macará | 6 | 6 |
| Machala | 6 | 5 |
| Piura (Peru) | 10 | 9 |
| Quito | 14–17 | 14–15 |
| Riobamba | 13 | 10 |
| Zamora | 2.40 | 2 |
| Zumba | 7.50 | 6 |

to both southern border crossings into Peru via Macará and Zumba. There are no direct buses to Peru through Zumba; you will have to take a bus to Zumba, cross the border and transfer from there.

You can go directly to Piura (Peru) from Loja without stopping in Macará. The service ($10, nine hours) is offered at 7am, 1pm, 10:30pm and 11pm with Loja International. The bus stops at the border, waits for passengers to take care of exits and entries, and then continues to Piura. It's advisable to buy your tickets at least a day before you travel.

### Car

**Localiza** (☎258-1729; www.localiza.com; cnr Ayora & Nueva Loja; ☺8am-6pm Mon-Fri, 9am-1pm Sat & Sun) Rents economy cars and 4WDs, which can be returned in other major cities.

## ❶ Getting Around

Most taxi rides in town will cost about $1. For the airport, ask your hotel to call a taxi or shuttle service, which charges $5 per person for the 40-minute trip, or catch a bus to Catamayo ($1, 45 minutes) from the bus terminal.

## Parque Nacional Podocarpus

**Podocarpus National Park** (admission $2, camping free, refugios $3) fills in much of the triangle between Loja, Zamora and Vilcabamba as well as a huge swath to the southeast. Because altitude ranges so greatly within the park borders – from around 900m in the lowland sector to over 3600m in the highland sector – Podocarpus has some of the greatest plant and animal diversity in the world. Perhaps 40% of its estimated 3000 plant species occurs nowhere else in the world, and close to 600 bird species have been recorded. Rare mammals include foxes, deer, puma, mountain tapirs and bears.

Podocarpus' varied landscape is mesmerizing: high, windy *páramo* that looks vaguely like a coral-rich sea floor (especially when it's foggy); jewel-like lakes that sit in glacial depressions formed long ago; fairy tale elfin woodland buffeted by harsh weather; and lush, towering forests seething with the hum and whistle of insects and birdlife.

The park is named for the giant Podocarpus, Ecuador's only native conifer, but don't bank on seeing one, or any larger animals, for that matter. Loggers stole most of the Podocarpus years ago, and the mammals have been hunted down to small populations driven deep into the forest. On top of these threats, which continue despite the park's protected status, both legal and illegal mining and agriculture encroach on habitat throughout the park.

Birds, however, are abundant. In the highland sector, they include such exotic-sounding species as the lachrymose mountain-tanager, streaked tuftedcheek, superciliaried hemispingus and pearled treerunner; the lowland sector is home to coppery-chested jacamar, white-breasted parakeet and paradise tanager.

Rainfall in both sectors is heavy and frequent, so be prepared for it. October through December are the driest months.

### HIGHLANDS SECTOR

Access to the highland sector is through the **Cajanuma control**, which is about 10km south of Loja. From the Cajanuma control, where you pay admission, a dirt road leads 8.5km uphill to the **refugio** (cabañas per person $3), which has seven basic cabañas with mattresses, as well as a **camping area** (free).

From the *refugio*, some short, self-guided trails wend through the cloud forest. More strenuous and wide-ranging is the 5km **Los Miradores loop trail**, a four-hour hike up through the cloud forest and into the *páramo*. Another trail that branches off the Miradores leads 14.5km to the highland lakes of **Lagunas del Compadre** and requires a minimum of three days' round-trip for most hikers. There is no water between the trailhead and the lakes.

The Ministerio del Medio Ambiente (Ministry of Environment) in Loja can provide detailed information, and the control has simple maps.

### ❶ Getting There & Away

A taxi from Loja to the *refugio* will cost about $10. Set out early and you can hike for several hours before walking the 8.5km back to the Loja–Vilcabamba road, where you can flag a passing bus back to Loja. The two-hour walk from the Cajanuma Control station to the main road (all downhill) is itself rather enjoyable. There are rarely cars on the park road, especially during the week, so don't expect to be able to hitchhike.

### LOWLANDS SECTOR

The main access to the lowland sector is the **Bombuscaro control** (☺8am-5pm), 6km south of Zamora by a dirt road that follows

## CABAÑAS YANQUAM

East of Zamora, the Río Nangaritza flows past the vast Cordillera del Cóndor, a region of unparalleled biodiversity that is also home to indigenous Shuar communities. Traveling by boat along a blackwater tributary (it's actually a brown hue, caused by naturally occurring tannins), you'll see odd rock formations, waterfalls, rare birds and cliffs covered in orchids. **Cabañas Yanquam** (☑07-260-6147; www.lindoecuadortours. com; r per person incl breakfast $20, boat rides per person with 4-person minimum $30) outside Las Orquídeas can take you into this lost world, which is truly the end of the line for most travelers.

the Río Bombuscaro. This river is a popular playground for locals and great for a dip. From the parking area at the end of the road it's a half-hour walk on a wide, uphill trail to the control where you pay the entry fee. Two basic **cabañas** (per person $3) without mattresses are available, and you can camp for free.

From the Bombuscaro control, there are several short, maintained (but sometimes muddy) trails that meander into the forest, the most popular of which leads you to the **Cascada Poderosa** and **Chismosa Waterfalls**. The 6km **Los Huigerones** trail takes you into some primary forest, as does the five-hour **El Campesino** trail. Another trail leads to a deep (but very swift) swimming hole called the *área fotográfica* on the Río Bombuscaro.

Another infrequently used entrance is at the tiny village of **Romerillos**, about 25km south of Zamora by a different road.

The climate is hot and humid but beautiful, and the rainiest months are May through July. May and June are the best months for orchids.

### ❶ Getting There & Away

The easiest way to get to the Bombuscaro entrance is by taxi from Zamora ($4); find them behind the bus terminal. Taxis from Loja will cost you $10 one-way. You can have the driver from Zamora return to pick you up at the end of the day (additional $4), or you can walk back in about an hour on the flat road. Zamora also has buses to Romerillos ($1.50, two hours, 6am and 2pm).

## Zamora

☑07 / POP 15,112 / ELEV 970M

The hot, humid capital of the Zamora-Chinchipe province is part Oriente and part Sierra. Perched between these regions in the Andean foothills, it attracts settlers from the high-altitude communities of Saraguro and the Amazon Basin Shuar. The town bills itself as the 'City of Birds and Waterfalls' and is important for its proximity to Parque Nacional Podocarpus and huge mining concessions.

A century ago, Zamora was a village of wooden houses at the end of the old Loja–Zamora road. But decades of colonization by miners and growth into a provincial hub have created a town of mostly unremarkable, concrete structures. Zamora has, however, experienced a bit of a revival, with renovations to bridges, a spruced-up bus station, a brand new *malecón* (waterfront) along the Río Zamora and a relaxed little main plaza. If you need to know what time it is, just look up: the big hill to the top has a massive clock. The minute hand is exactly 11 meters and 34 centimeters long. This may very well be the largest timepiece in Ecuador and, according to some, the biggest in the world.

### ◉ Sights & Activities

It's all about the big clock across the street from the bus station and market. Central streets are signed, but few buildings use numbers. Zamora's main attraction is nearby Parque Nacional Podocarpus. There's also a good **swimming hole**, just east of town on your way to the Copalinga lodge.

**Refugio Ecológico Tzanka**   WILDLIFE RESERVE (☑260-5692; refugioecologicotzanka@yahoo.es; Mosquera at Tamayo; adult/child $2/1; ⊗9am-5pm) A block southwest of the main plaza up a steep hill, this wildlife rescue center has colorful parrots, coatis (big, acrobatic rodents), monkeys, sloths and a boa constrictor. It's probably your best bet for seeing wildlife in the area, and it has some short-term volunteer opportunities.

### ☞ Tours

**Bio Aventura Expeditions**   ADVENTURE TOUR (☑260-7063; j.soto75@hotmail.com; cnr Tamayo & Mosquera) Just around the corner from the Tzanka reserve, this tour operator has guided trips to Podocarpus ($20 to $30) and the Río Nangaritza ($40 to $50).

# 📖 Sleeping

### Copalinga
LODGE $$

(📞09-347-7013; www.copalinga.com; Vía al Podocarpus Km 3; cabins per person $24-42, breakfasts & dinners $12) Bird-watchers, ahem, flock to this Belgian-owned, private reserve for sure-thing sightings of exotic avian species, but even non-bird-watchers will love the orchid collection, hummingbird feeders and trails. Take your pick of a rustic or luxury cabin (both are lovely), and let the rushing river lull you to sleep. Hydropower runs the whole place, and meals are generous and tasty. Reservations are required, and you definitely want to book well in advance. It is 3km southeast of town. To get there, head east from the roundabout below the clock, following signs south after you cross the river.

### Hotel Samuria
HOTEL $$

(📞260-7801; hotelsamuria@hotmail.com; cnr 24 de Mayo & Diego de Vaca; s/d/tr/ste incl breakfast $20/32/48/50; 🅿❄🛜) Located half a block north of the main plaza, Zamora's newest hotel is also its finest, with firm beds, blowdryers, flatscreens and relatively quiet, modern rooms. The AC helps on hot nights.

### Hotel Betania
HOTEL $

(📞260-7030; Francisco de Orellana; r per person $12, 🅿🛜) Two blocks west of the bus station, the Betania is a comfortable and modern hotel with firm beds and an attached restaurant. It's one of the cleanest budget hotels in all of Ecuador, and we love the nudes in the showers (oh la la!).

### Hotel Chonta Dorada
HOTEL $

(📞260-6384; Jaramillo near Amazonas; r per person $9; 🅿🛜) While it's not as nice as the Betania, this is a decent budget option, three blocks west of the bus station. We only wish it would invest in toilet seats.

# 🍴 Eating

Unless you like *bagre* (catfish) and *ancas de rana* (frog's legs), eating in Zamora is a pretty humdrum affair. The nicer hotels serve better food, and the market has stalls selling soups and chicken plates.

### La Choza
ECUADORIAN $

(Sevilla de Oro; mains $2-3; 🕕6:30am-8pm) Serving fried fish, fried frog's legs and *churrasco* (served here as a simple slice of fried steak with eggs and rice), La Choza is a health foodie's nightmare, but it's good, and the fish

is local and fresh. To get here, head toward the clock from the main plaza.

### Agape Restaurant
ECUADORIAN $

(cnr Sevilla de Oro & 24 de Mayo; mains $3-5; 🕙10am-9pm Mon-Sat) Near the cathedral, Agape has a friendly and slightly fancier atmosphere. It serves fish, meat and sometimes frog's legs.

### King Ice
BURGERS $

(cnr de Vaca & Tamayo; mains $1.50-2.50; 🕗8am-midnight) This ice cream parlor on the main plaza serves burgers, hot dogs and frosty-cold beers.

# ℹ️ Information

**Banco de Loja** (cnr de Vaca & Héroes de Paquisha) ATM. Located opposite the market.

**Corporación Nacional de Telecomunicaciones** (cnr Amazonas & Tamayo) Telephone call-center a block northeast of the main plaza.

**Hospital** (Sevilla de Oro near Jaramillo) Opposite La Choza Restaurant.

**Ministerio del Ambiente** (📞260-6606; Vía Zamora-Loja s/n; 🕗8:30am-4:30pm Mon-Fri) Northwest of town; information on Parque Nacional Podocarpus.

**Post office** (cnr 24 de Mayo & Sevilla de Oro) Main plaza.

# ℹ️ Getting There & Away

The **bus terminal** (Av Héroes de Paquisha at Amazonas) is across the street from the big clock.

Buses leave almost hourly to Loja ($2.40, two hours) between 3am and 11pm. There are five daily buses heading north to Gualaquiza ($3.50, four hours) and a morning bus to Guayzimi ($2.25, three hours). For Cuenca (eight hours), Guayaquil (11 hours) or Quito (18 hours), head first to Loja and catch one of the frequent buses departing from there. See p188 for details about transport to Parque Nacional Podocarpus.

Buses to Las Orquídeas (for Cabañas Yanquam) leave from Zamora daily and pass through Guayzimi.

# Vilcabamba

📞07 / POP 4200 / ELEV 1500M

Vilcabamba is synonymous with longevity all throughout Ecuador. It became famous for a high number of centenarian residents after *Reader's Digest* did stories on them in 1955. Although residents readily concede that few *vilcabambenses* (people from Vilcabamba) celebrate a 100th birthday anymore, most agree that their simple,

# Vilcabamba

## Vilcabamba

### Activities, Courses & Tours

### Sleeping

### Eating

stress-free lives and fresh, Andean air are conducive to a long life.

The area's beautiful scenery, mild weather, and laid-back vibe attract waves of young backpackers and many American and European retirees – so many that Vilcabamba has experienced a sort of 'gringo boom.' The hills are dotted with big, new houses, and the gringo-ization has created some tension about the cost of land. The flip side is that jobs in tourism and construction are more plentiful than ever, and Vilcabamba is the rare Ecuadorian pueblo where young people have little ambition to leave for the big city.

Vilcabamba offers perfect weather for hiking and horseback-riding, as well as access to remote sections of Parque Nacional Podocarpus, but it's also an excellent place to chill out. Legions of specialists are ready to facilitate your relaxation with inexpensive massages and facials.

Most of the town surrounds the plaza, and addresses are rarely used.

## ◉ Sights & Activities

Most naturalists and horse guides charge about $15 for two hours, $20 for four and $30 for the whole day (not including park entrance fees).

**Hiking**     HIKING
Most hotels have trail maps, and some even have their own trail systems. Many area hikes are on private land, and you may need to pay a nominal fee ($1 to $2) to use the trail. The **Cerro Mandango** ($1.50) trail ascends the peak west of town and takes a couple of hours. Heading into Parque Nacional Podocarpus from the Río Yambala west of town, there's a long five- to eight-hour hike to a waterfall known as **Cascada el Palto** ($1). For an afternoon spin, consider a quick hike out of town to **Agua de Hierro** ($1), a small natural spring signs will take you there. The 30-hectare **Rumi-Wilco Ecolodge** ($2 for three-day pass) has an excellent signed trail system.

**Caballos Gavilán**     HORSEBACK-RIDING
(☑264-0209; gavilanhorse@yahoo.com; Sucre) This operation is run by the highly recommended Gavin, a New Zealander who has lived here for years. He guides two- to three-day horseback riding trips with overnight stays in his refuge near the park.

**Holgar's Horses**     HORSEBACK-RIDING
(☑08-296-1238; Cnr Valle Sagrado & Diego Vaca de la Vega) Easygoing horseback-riding trips.

**El Chino**     BICYCLE RENTAL
(cnr Sucre & Agua de Hierro) Rents bikes for $2 per hour or $10 per day.

## ☞ Courses

**Catalina Carrasco**     LANGUAGE COURSE
(☑08-267-8960; catycarrasco@yahoo.com) For private Spanish instruction, try Catalina Carrasco.

## ☞ Tours

**La Tasca Tours**     ADVENTURE TOUR
(☑08-556-1188; latascatours@yahoo.ec; Sucre) This well-known operator on the Central Plaza offers trekking, riding and adventure tours in the area.

**Monta Tours**     TOUR
(☑09-020-8824; Sucre) For one- and two-day treks in the park as well as horseback rides.

## 🛏 Sleeping

Vilcabamba has many inexpensive hotels, almost all with some version of a swimming pool. Those outside the village can be marvelously quiet and relaxing, while those in town are generally cheaper. Prices may fluctuate during high season and holidays.

### CENTRAL
**Rendez-Vous Hostal Guesthouse**   HOTEL $
(☑09-219-1180; www.rendezvousecuador.com; Diego Vaca de la Vega 06-43; dm/s/d/tr $12/18/28/36; @🛜) Call it adobe chic. Each of the meticulous rooms at French-owned Rendez-Vous has its own little terrace that looks out onto a calm interior garden, making this the best budget hostal in the city proper. Breakfast, served on the terraces, comes with homemade bread.

**Hostal Jardín Escondido**   HOSTEL $
(☑264-0281; www.jardinescondidovilcabamba.com; Sucre & Agua de Hierro; dm/r per person incl breakfast $10/15; 🛜🏊) Built around a tranquil interior garden filled with songbirds, this is a good budget bet. All rooms have high ceilings and big bathrooms, and breakfast comes with homemade bread and good coffee.

**El Descanso de Ramses Hostería**   HOSTERÍA $$
(☑264-0039; Agua de Hierro & Bolívar; s/d incl breakfast $20/36; 🏊🐾) This new, colonial-style *hostería* (small hotel) is popular with Ecuadorian families and groups. It lacks the funked-out feel of other spots in town, and some toilets lack seats. But the pool is lovely, and there are lots of games and diversions for kids.

### OUTSIDE OF TOWN
**Hostería y Restaurante Izhcayluma**   SPA & RESORT $$
(☑302-5162; www.izhcayluma.com; dm/s/d with shared bathroom $10/20/28, s/d/tr with private bathroom $25/35/45, cabins s/d $30/45, all incl breakfast; 🅿🛜🏊) Located 2km south of town, German-owned Izhcayluma packs excellent value into this casual but refined hilltop retreat. The outdoor dining area serves German and Ecuadorian cuisine and has sweeping panoramic views of the valley. A new 'holistic wellness room' offers massages and other treatments, and there is a bar and swimming pool. The cabins and rooms are quiet and spacious, and prices include use of a mountain bike to ride into town. This

place is always packed, so book your room at least a week in advance.

### Rumi-Wilco Ecolodge LODGE $

(rumiwilco@yahoo.com; dm $7, s/d with shared bathroom from $12/18) A 10-minute walk from the bus station, Rumi-Wilco has a series of remote cabins and dorm rooms set within the evergreen confines of the 30-hectare Rumi-Wilco Nature Reserve. The adobe houses have attractive rooms with hand-tiled floors, shared bathrooms and communal kitchens (great for small groups). The Pole House ($26 to $36) is a rustic cabin on stilts that overlooks the river and sleeps up to four people. The hot shower is fantastic, as is the location. Entrance to the reserve for nonguests is $2 per person (good for three visits).

### Madre Tierra Resort and Spa SPA & RESORT $$

(264-0269; www.madretierra.com.ec; s with shared bathroom $15; s incl breakfast $25-49, d incl breakfast $35-59; @奈鞈) On a hillside with waterfalls and gardens 2km north of town, Madre Tierra has a strong New Age vibe, replete with candles and healing ions. Rooms are meticulously decorated, and the newer suites have balconies and inset rock floors.

### Hostería Paraíso HOTEL $

(264-0266; r per person incl breakfast $15; @鞈) About 500m north of town, Hostería Paraíso has a great swimming pool, a flower-filled garden, a pyramid-shaped bioenergetic meditation room (really just a massage space), and slightly dank rooms that don't quite measure up to everything else. Rates include use of the pool and spa facilities.

## ✗ Eating

Several restaurants along Eterna Juventud (the part of the Panamericana that goes through town) serve cheap Ecuadorian-style *almuerzos*.

### Charlito's INTERNATIONAL $$

(Diego Vaca de la Vega; mains $3-7; ⊙11am-9pm Tue-Sun) The friendliest restaurant in town serves up simple food like burritos, pizza and pasta with a smile. The ingredients are the freshest around.

### Shanta's Bar PIZZA $$

(Diego Vaca de la Vega; mains $6-8; ⊙1:15-9pm) Shanta's serves pizza and big plates of frog's legs in an open-air, rustic setting with saddle seats at the bar and a bartender with a handlebar mustache.

### Terraza Center Restaurant INTERNATIONAL $$

(cnr Diego Vaca de la Vega & Bolívar; mains $4-8; ⊙9am-9:30pm) Grab a table outside for some serious people-watching at this laid-back eatery on the Central Plaza. It serves international favorites like burritos (with ruffles on the side), sandwiches and a few Asian noodle dishes.

### Jardín Escondido MEXICAN $$

(Sucre & Agua de Hierro; mains $5-7; ⊙8am-8:30pm) Not surprisingly, some of the best Mexican food in southern Ecuador comes from this little Mexican-owned cafe inside the eponymous hotel. Delicious dishes with *mole* (a chocolate-based spicy sauce), rich traditional soups and burritos are some of the specialties. You can get a big breakfast with homemade bread, too.

### Hostería y Restaurante Izhcayluma ECUADORIAN $$

(264-0095; www.izhcayluma.com; mains $4-7; ⊙8-11am & 12:30-6:30pm Tue-Sun, 8-11am Mon;鞈) Bavarian specialties and classic Ecuadorian dishes are the fare here. Izhcayluma also offers excellent vegetarian substitutions for the meat dishes. It's worth the trip up the hill.

### Restaurant Katerine ECUADORIAN $

(Sucre at Jaramillo; mains $2.50-4) Head here for cheap and wholesome Ecuadorian fare. The fixed lunch for $2.50 is a money saver. Opening hours are irregular.

## ❶ Information

There have been a few violent robberies on the trail up Cerro Mandango. The best way to avoid problems on any of the hikes in the area is to leave your camera, cash and MP3 player in your hotel.

**Banco de Guayaquil** (Cnr Bolívar & Diego de la Vaca) Bank with ATM.

**Craig's Book Exchange** (⊙1-5pm) Book exchange 1.5km east of town with an excellent community board listing new-age healers, tour operators, homestays, volunteer opportunities and more.

**Hospital** (267-3188; Av Eterna Juventud near Carpio)

**Internet** (Fernando de la Vega near Sucre; per hr $1.15; ⊙9am-9pm)

**Police station** (264-0896; Agua de Hierro near Bolívar) By the post office.

**Post office** (Bolívar)

## TAPICHALACA RESERVE

The small **Tapichalaca Reserve** (admission $20), 75km south of Vilcabamba, protects one of Ecuador's most rare and endangered birds, the Jocotoco Antpitta (*Grallaria ridgelyi*), which has under 20 known breeding pairs. Some of the birds have been habituated to eating grubs put out by the caretaker, however, so a sighting is more or less guaranteed. The rest of the reserve is an oasis of cloud forest in a region of heavy deforestation, and the hummingbird feeders are abuzz all day. To get there in time for the Antpittas' breakfast, catch the 5am bus from Loja or spend the night at the reserve's beautiful **lodge** (02-227-2013; www.fjocotoco.org; r per person incl meals $100).

**Rosita's Laundry** (Fernando de la Vega btwn Toledo & La Paz; laundry per kg $0.80; 8-11am & 1-4:30pm) Same-day laundry service.

**Tourist office** (iTur; 264-0090; cnr Bolívar & Diego Vaca de la Vega; 8am-1pm & 3-6pm Mon-Sat, 8am-1pm Sun) Good info and maps of area hikes.

### ❶ Getting There & Around

**Transportes Vilcamixtos** (364-0044) is a taxi-truck cooperative on the main plaza (you can't miss the green-and-white trucks). Most charge $1.50 to $4 for getting to nearby places.

Buses, minivans and taxis leave from the tiny **bus terminal** (Eterna Juventud & Jaramillo). Taxis colectivos ($2, 45 minutes) depart frequently to Loja after four people cram in; Vilcabambaturis minibuses ($1.30, one hour) leave on the hour.

Buses from Loja stop in Vilcabamba on their way south to Zumba ($6.50, five hours) and the Peruvian border.

## Zumba & the Peruvian Border

07

Vilcabamba is the end of the road for most travelers. Those heading to Peru, especially those eager to see the ruins at Chachapoyas, may continue on to Zumba on the border.

Zumba was an important military outpost during the wars with Peru between the 1940s and 1990s. The wars are over, but there's still an Ecuadorian military post here, and soldiers roam all over town, not doing much other than whistling at women. Basic *hostales* in Zumba have beds for about $5 per person, but there is little reason to stay. From Loja or Vilcabamba, it's an all-day journey to San Ignacio, Peru – the best place to spend the night.

**Transportes Nambija** ($7.50, six hours) buses leave from Loja for Zumba at noon

and midnight, and **Sur Oriente** (256 1649) services go at 5am, 8am, 5:30pm and 9:30pm. All stop in Vilcabamba after leaving Loja.

From Zumba, *rancheras* (open-sided trucks) leave at 8am, 10:30am and 5:30pm for the border at **La Balsa** ($2, 1½ to 2½ hours), where you get your exit stamp (or entry stamp if coming from Peru). The condition of the road between Zumba and La Balsa varies greatly, depending on recent weather. On the other side of the 'international bridge' in Peru there are *taxi colectivos* to **San Ignacio** ($3, 1½ hours), where you can spend the night.

From San Ignacio, there are regular minibuses to **Jaén** ($3.50, three hours) beginning at 4am. Once you're in Jaén, take a *mototaxi* (motorcycle taxi) to the *colectivo* stop and then get a *colectivo* to **Bagua Grande** (one hour). From Bagua Grande you then get a bus to **Chachapoyas** (three hours), the first town of any real size.

## Catamayo & Around

07

Loja was founded twice. The first time was in 1546, on what is now **Catamayo** (population 21,982); the second time was on its present site, two years later. Despite its long history, Catamayo is a totally unremarkable town except for its airport, La Toma, which serves Loja 30km away.

About 15km west of Catamayo, a well-paved road passes through the village of **San Pedro de la Bendita**, which is the turnoff to the village of **El Cisne**, 22km to the north and home to the famous Virgen del Cisne (see p184).

About 40km south of Catamayo, on the southernmost of two roads to Macará, **Gonzanamá** is noted for its weavers and for the production of *alforjas* (saddlebags); ask around if you want to buy. The route passes the villages of **Cariamanga** and **Sozoranga** before ending in Macará at the border. All three of these stops are little more than two- or three-horse towns and have only the simplest *residenciales* (cheap hotels).

All of these places are served regularly from Loja's bus terminal.

## Catacocha

🛏️ 07 / POP 5369 / ELEV 1886M

Declared a National Cultural Heritage Site in 1994, Catacocha takes pride in its places of worship, sun-baked adobe houses and wooden balconies, but has yet to capitalize on the tourism potential of its vaunted status. As such, strolling its streets is the best way to appreciate the timeless cycle of highland life.

The **Sunday market** is the most important event of the week in Catacocha, also known as Las Paltas. At dawn church bells call everyone to mass in the **Plaza Independencia**, and by 7am they are buying and selling homemade cheese, donkey saddles, farm-fresh eggs and mountains of veggies all over town. By dusk, the same plaza is a gathering spot for old-timers and bored teenagers.

The **Templo de Lourdes** is worth a peek inside for its replicas of famous European religious paintings. You won't mistake this church for the Louvre, but the canvases by a local monk give the surroundings an earnestly faithful, if slightly kitschy feel.

The infamous **Peña de Shiricalupo** is a shrine-cum-mirador (lookout) known for its vertigo-inducing views of the Casanga Valley.

**Hotel Tambococha** (cnr 25 de Junio & Lauro Gerrero; s/d $8/12) has clean, well-lit rooms, many of which look over the Plaza Independencia. All have cable TV and electricity-heated showers.

Dining options are spare, but you can get simple *menestras* (lentils and beans) with meat at **Casa Tradicional** off Plaza Independencia, or try the outdoor stalls next to the big 'Indio' statue.

The **municipio** (town hall; ☎268-3157; ☺Mon-Fri) on the Plaza Independencia can provide tourist information. Internet and ATMs have recently arrived in Catacocha, which in addition to telephones can be found on the Plaza.

Buses from Loja ($2.50, two hours) stop here en route to Macará and Piura (Peru).

## Macará & the Peruvian Border

🛏️ 07 / POP 14,727 / ELEV 470M

The descent from Catacocha toward the Peruvian border offers sweeping views of mountains and deep valleys that give way to hilly, dry tropical forest. Adobe ruins bake under the strong sun, and donkeys and cattle roam untethered along the road.

This arid forest's representative tree, the ceiba (kapok), with its green-tinted, swollen trunks and gnarly, usually leafless branches, stands out majestically – and sadly – on hillsides that have been logged and grazed. In these barren areas, the lonely giants have been spared the chainsaw because they are mostly hollow and of little utilitarian value.

To see this ecosystem in a healthier state, head to the **Jorupe Reserve** (www.fjocotoco.org; admission $20) run by Fundación Jocotoco outside of Macará. Primarily a bird-watching reserve, Jorupe is home to the white-tailed jay, blue-crowned motmot, and Ecuadorian trogan. Hire a taxi ($3) to take you to the reserve, about 5km down the road from Macará toward Sozorongo.

Most tourists heading south to the Peruvian border or north into Ecuador barely notice the sleepy border town of Macará. Surrounded by some fairly picturesque terraced rice cultivation, it's infested with crickets that jump about the streets and hotel rooms. If you're entering Ecuador through here, don't worry, it gets better as you head north.

### 🛏️ Sleeping

Accommodation is plentiful and cheap.

**Hostal Santigyn**  HOTEL $
(☎269-4539; cnr Bolívar & Rengel; r with/without air-con incl breakfast $12/9; ❄) Even though a painting of a joint-smoking Mona Lisa looms over the reception, this clean, smart hotel has well-lit rooms of various sizes. Some have air-conditioning, and all have cable TV.

**Hotel Karina**  HOTEL $
(☎269-4764; 10 de Agosto at Antonia Ante; r with/without air-con per person incl breakfast $12/8; ❄) Situated on a bustling street corner, Karina's small rooms have cable TV and include breakfast.

##  Eating

**El Buen Sabor Macareño** ECUADORIAN $
(Rengel near Bolívar; mains $2-3) Macará's dining options are slim and grim, but the friendly, service-oriented Buen Sabor is an exception, with its hit-the-spot *almuerzos* ($3).

**D'Marco's** ECUADORIAN $
(Jaime Roldos near Amazonas; mains $5-6) This nice option serves seafood.

## ℹ Information

**Banco de Loja** (cnr Ventimilla & Calderón) has an ATM ($200 limit) but no currency exchange. For Peruvian *soles,* exchange your money on the border.

## ℹ Getting There & Away

**Transportes Loja Internacional** (Lázaro Vaca at Juvenal Jaramilla) buses leave six times a day to Loja ($6, six hours) and take the Catacocha route. **Unión Cariamanga** (☎269-4047; www.unioncariamanga.com.ec; cnr Loja & Manuel E Rengel) has several buses a day to Loja ($6, six hours) via Cariamanga.

The crossing into Peru via Macará is much quieter than at Huaquillas and busier than at Zumba. Macará is 3km from the actual border crossing, or *puente internacional* (international bridge). Most people buy tickets direct to Piura (Peru) from Loja, but both companies listed above leave Macará for Piura (Peru) twice a day ($3, three hours). The bus stops at the border, waits for passengers to take care of exits and entries, and then continues to Piura.

# The Oriente

## Why Go?

This vast landmass holds more drama than a rip-roaring flood or crackling lightning storm. Rivers churn from the snowcapped Andes into the dense, sweltering rainforest on course to the Amazon basin and the distant Atlantic Ocean. Along the way, ancient indigenous tribes call the riverbanks home and, in many places, life goes on as it has for centuries.

Here, those lucky enough to get out to the more remote jungle lodges (often several hours downriver from the nearest town) will find an incredible array of wildlife and nature to enjoy: fish for piranhas on silent black-water lakes; spot the shining eyes of caiman at nighttime; hear the menacing screech of howler monkeys and see colorful parrots feeding at the famous clay licks (areas where nutrient-rich clay is abundant and birds gather to feed on it to supplement their diet). The rainforest is home to 50% of Ecuador's mammals, and exploring the Oriente gives you the unforgettable experience of seeing the natural world up close and personal.

## Best Places to Eat

» El Jardín (p227)
» El Vagabundo (p220)
» La Casa del Maito (p208)
» Guayusa Bar La Maravilla (p230)
» Marquis Grille (p220)

## Best Places to Stay

» Napo Wildlife Center (p211)
» Sacha Lodge (p210)
» Kapawi Ecolodge & Reserve (p231)
» Hamadryade Lodge (p222)

## When to Go
### The Oriente

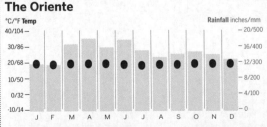

**Dec–Mar** The driest time of year when some rivers become impassable due to low water levels.

**Apr–Jul** The wettest time of year – more than ever make sure you've got a good raincoat!

**Oct–Nov** The best time of year – the rivers are all passable, it's not too wet and wildlife is easy to spot.

# THE NORTHERN ORIENTE

The Northern Oriente is the most accessible part of the Ecuadorian jungle, served as it is by good road and air connections to Quito, and with a developed tourism infrastructure. On the down side, this development and the omnipresence of the oil industry makes it somewhat harder to get into the remoter reaches of the rainforest, but making the effort to do so is definitely worthwhile. The biodiversity remains amazingly impressive, and while indigenous peoples are accustomed to outsiders jockeying for their land and resources, they still proudly share this unique region with the respectful visitor.

A paved road from Quito splits at Baeza; the northern fork makes it way to Lago Agrio, while the southern fork heads toward Tena. The other main road zips from highland Baños to Puyo in under two hours. In the rainiest months (June to August), roads can wash out and airports can close. If you have important air connections from Quito, allow an extra day or two in between.

# From Quito to Lago Agrio

## PAPALLACTA
ELEV 3300M

Slip into this tiny village's steamy, therapeutic waters to soothe sore muscles or combat the high-altitude chill. At Termas de Papallacta, more than three dozen sparkling pools offer the country's most luxurious thermal baths experience. The complex is about 3km outside the village of Papallacta and is a good day trip from Quito, 67km (two hours) away. Be prepared for cold nights and intense sun.

### ◉ Sights & Activities

**Termas de Papallacta**          THERMAL BATHS

About 1.5km before the village, on the left as you approach from Quito, a marked dirt road leads 2km uphill to Termas de Papallacta. The setting is grand: on a clear day you can see the snowcapped **Volcán Antisana** (5753m), 15km south, beyond the lush hillsides. Unfortunately the hot springs are a poorly kept secret; opt for a weekday visit if possible, or, for a truly wonderful experience, come after dark, when it's particularly magical and far less crowded.

There are two sets of pools: the **Balneario** (admission $7; ☉6am-11pm, last entry 9pm) and the **Spa** (admission $18; 9am-9pm). The Balneario boasts more than 25 blue pools of varying temperatures surrounded by plush grass and red-orange blossoms. Towels and lockers are available. There's little reason to visit the Spa pools, although they are less crowded, smaller and filled with jets. An indoor sauna can loosen you up for a spa treatment, which can range from $10 to $45. The sauna is free at the spa. The treatments include hydrothermal massages, reflexology, body wraps with Andean mud, Turkish baths, body lymphtic drainage and body exfoliation. Pool waters are changed daily.

### 🛏 Sleeping & Eating

**TOP CHOICE** **Hotel Termas de Papallacta**          LUXURY HOTEL $$$

(☏02-256-8989, 02-250-4787; www.termaspapallacta.com; r $135-155, 6-person cabin $192; P@🛜🏊) Most visitors to Papallacta come to stay at this supremely comfortable yet totally unpretentious resort, which is a great way to experience the thermal baths in style. Thatched adobe cabins with smart wood-paneled rooms surround private hot pools for guest use only, and there's a good restaurant, a sumptuous spa and even a set of spacious cabins across the way for groups of friends to share. All accommodations have private bathrooms, thermal heating, hot showers and tubs. Weekends and holidays reserved well in advance. The Sucus restaurant (mains $10 to $25) serves a wide range of international dishes including lamb chops, sea bass and filet mignon, and there are another two restaurants in the Spa and the Balneario.

**Hostería Pampallacta Termales**          GUESTHOUSE $$

(☏06-289-5014; www.pampallactatermales.com; s/d incl breakfast $36-55; P🛜🏊) This is the best midrange option in Papallacta. It's not quite as convenient for the Balneario as the Hostal Antisana, but it's warmer (all rooms have fireplaces) and more charming (all rooms have huge stone bathtubs you can fill with thermal spring water). Management is friendly, and if you don't fancy walking up the road to the Balneario, there's a number of small thermal pools in which to relax.

**Hostal Antisana**          GUESTHOUSE $$

(☏06-232-0626; s/d incl breakfast $25/40; 🏊) This echoey 10-room *hostal* (small, reasonably priced hotel) sits just meters from the Termas de Papallacta, but is a fraction of the price of its upscale neighbor, the Hotel

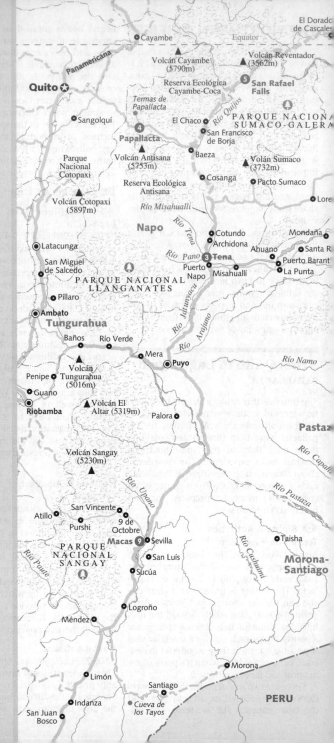

# The Oriente Highlights

**1** Immerse yourself in the wild rainforest and see an incredible array of wildlife at **lower Río Napo lodges** (p210)

**2** Stay inside fabulous **Parque Nacional Yasuní** (p214) and visit its exceptional Parrot Clay Lick

**3** Tame **white-water rapids** (p216) in a raft or kayak on the rivers outside of Tena

**4** Soak in pristine steaming waters at **Papallacta** (p197)

**5** Witness amazing **San Rafael Falls** (p201), Ecuador's highest waterfall

**6** Fish for piranhas and look out for pink dolphins in **Pañacocha** (p212)

**7** Spot an astonishing range of bird and animal life in the black-water paradise of **Reserva Producción Faunística Cuyabeno** (p204)

**8** Spend time with a **Huaorani tribe** (p206) with the help of a native guide

**9** Explore the pristine rainforest in the southern Oriente with a guided jungle tour from **Macas** (p229)

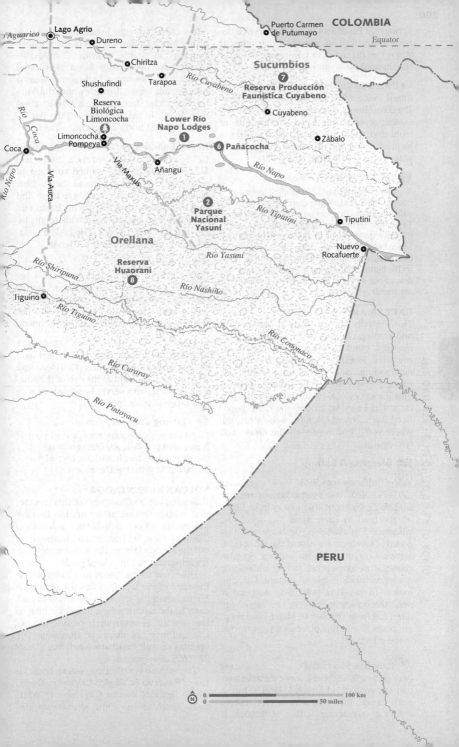

Termas De Papallacta. It's chilly (despite the friendly owner), so bring warm clothes if you spend the night, or take refuge in one of the thermal pools out back.

**La Choza de Don Wilson** SEAFOOD $
(mains $5-6; ⏲8:30am-8:30pm Mon-Wed, to 10pm Thu-Sun) Almost everyone comes to this unassuming restaurant for an excellent fillet of trout and shots of *aguardiente* (sugarcane alcohol). You'll find this place at the juncture with the road to Termas de Papallacta.

### ❶ Getting There & Away

Any of the buses from Quito heading toward Baeza, Tena or Lago Agrio can drop you off in Papallacta, as can the occasional Papallacta bus. To visit the Termas de Papallacta complex, ask the driver to let you off on the road to the baths, 1.5km before the village. Then catch a waiting *camioneta* (pickup or light truck) for the $2 ride up the bumpy road. To leave Papallacta, flag down a bus on the main road. Weekend buses are standing room only.

### BAEZA & AROUND

This friendly former Spanish missionary and trading outpost, first founded in 1548, makes a quiet base for walks in the surrounding foothills. Plants and birdlife are outstanding, and white-water culture is gaining momentum. The town is divided into Baeza Colonial (near the road to Papallacta and Lago Agrio) and the more populated Baeza Nueva (2km from the junction), where you'll find nearly all the hotels and restaurants.

### 🛏 Sleeping & Eating

**TOP CHOICE** **Cabañas Tres Ríos** CABINS $$
(☎09-792-0120; www.smallworldadventures.com; s/d $45/75; 🛜) About 10km away from Baeza on the road to Lago Agrio you reach the village of San Francisco de Borja and this group of lovely cabins east of the village and across Río Quijos. It can arrange Spanish classes, area tours, hikes, rafting and biking. A chef will cook meals on request. Catering mainly to kayakers (who may desperately need the on-site massages), the cabins are often full from October to March, and there are plans to run this place as a yoga retreat in the off season.

**Cabañas San Isidro** CABINS $$$
(Map p221; ☎02-290-6769; www.cabanasanisidro. com; Cosanga; s/d incl 3 meals $133/217) Once a cattle ranch, this 3700-acre nature reserve enjoys a spectacular setting at 2000m. It offers first-class bird-watching, and co-owner Mitch Lysinger is one of the top bird-watchers in South America. Comfortable cabins have decks with forest views, and rooms have hot-water bathrooms. Nearby hiking trails weave through wonderful, sub-tropical cloud forest. Advance reservation is required. To get here, turn off the Baeza–Tena road just north of Cosanga village.

**Hostal Bambu's** GUESTHOUSE $
(☎06-232-0003; Nueva Andalucía, Baeza; s/d $12/24) If you've ever wanted to sleep in a teenager's dream rec room, here's your chance. Rooms look out onto a large and well-kept indoor pool with diving board and inflatable toys, and there's a table-tennis table and billiards, to boot. The beds are unforgiving, but the welcome is friendly.

**Hostal Samay** GUESTHOUSE $
(☎06-232-0170; Nueva Andalucía, Baeza; r per person $10, without bathroom $6) Rooms in this friendly clapboard home come in all the colors of the rainbow. There's TV and hot water, and a pleasant chaletlike atmosphere.

**El Viejo** ECUADORIAN $
(Nueva Andalucía, Baeza; mains $5-10; ⏲7am-9pm) Baeza's main gathering place, this clean and welcoming restaurant at the end of the Nueva Andalucía strip serves breakfast, as well as a range of trout specialties.

### ❶ Getting There & Away

Flag down one of the many buses going to and from Lago Agrio, Tena and Quito and hope there's room. Coming from Quito, take a Tena-bound bus from the main terminal.

### VOLCÁN REVENTADOR

Following the 2002 eruption of this spectacular volcano, hiking to the summit became impossible. It's now possible to reach the top (3562m) again, but because lava flows wiped out the already faint trail, it's easy to get lost. It's important to hire a local guide.

Hike four to five hours to a campsite on the edge of the lava flow (it's usually possible to hire tents from guides), then depart early in the morning for a four-hour hike to the summit. Reventador is notoriously active and may not always be climbable. For updates consult **Instituto Geofisico** (☎02-222-5655; www.igepn.edu.ec).

The volcano is within the eastern boundaries of **Reserva Ecológica Cayambe-Coca**, which includes **Volcán Cayambe** (5790m; p92). There are no signs or entrance sta-

DON'T MISS

## SAN RAFAEL FALLS

Ecuador's highest waterfall is the spectacular 131m **San Rafael Falls** (admission $2; ☺7am-5pm) and it absolutely deserves a stop on the road between Baeza and Lago Agrio.

This may be your last chance to see this incredible waterfall at full strength, as a new hydroelectric dam, with a power plant built 20km (12 miles) upriver, is due to go online in 2016.

The power plant issue has polarized the country, which, since the election of President Rafael Correa in 2007, has actively sought to expand Ecuador's sustainable energy production.

Those who support the scheme say that the power plant will not affect the strength of the Coca River, which feeds the falls and, as such, this natural wonder is not in danger. Opponents disagree, stating that water flow to the falls has been dropping in recent years, and that the plant will not be able to operate for much of the year due to low water flow from the Coca River.

The plant is also being financed by a $1.7 billion loan from the Export Import Bank of China, and opponents of the scheme are alarmed at what they perceive to be the loan's very high interest rate (6.9%).

Those in the tourist industry worry that this stunning natural sight will lose its dramatic impact and that the area will no longer be a magnet for tourists.

Whatever the outcome, our advice is to come here and witness the falls at their full force before 2016.

A new access road has been built to ease your trip here, but at present it's not signed off the road. Look for a steeply descending road to the right if you're coming from Quito; there's a signpost for the nearby Hostelería Reventador here as your only indication – if you cross the Río Reventador, you've gone too far (you can ask your bus driver to stop at the appropriate spot). The road takes you down to a small visitor center where you'll pay the entrance fee and begin the easy 15- to 20-minute hike down to the viewpoint, which is breathtaking. Count on it taking around 30 minutes to get back, as it's all uphill – but it will have been worth the effort.

tions. The guard station is in the village of **El Chaco**, about 20km from Reventador on the road to Baeza.

The most obvious base for this trip is the very pleasant roadside **Hostería Reventador** (☎09-357-143; www.hosteriareventador.com; s/d $30/35; ℗☎☎), a friendly and recently totally renovated lodge by San Rafael Falls. Rooms are modern and include all creature comforts, although those on a budget may prefer the older and slightly cheaper rooms out the back. Guides for climbing Reventador can also be hired from the lodge, and there's an excellent restaurant here. Any bus from Quito or Baeza to Lago Agrio will pass right outside the hotel and can drop you off.

## Lago Agrio

☎06 / POP 48,500

This seedy, gray town pulses with the life of the oil industry, a chaotic market, dusty streets, thick traffic and gritty bars. The first oil workers nicknamed Lago Agrio 'bit-ter lake,' after Sour Lake, Texas, the former home of Texaco, which pioneered local drilling (see the boxed text, p203). The city's official name is Nueva Loja, although no one calls it that. Locals settle for 'Lago.'

Few tourists set foot here, and locals seem exasperated by the town's sad reputation. But certain realities exist, including a high amount of prostitution and crime related to the nearby Colombian border. Locals keep their heads down and mind their own business; visitors should do the same. Lago is the entry point to the spectacular Reserva Producción Faunística Cuyabeno (Cuyabeno Reserve), which draws some overnight travelers on their way to the jungle.

### Dangers & Annoyances

The ongoing conflict in neighboring Colombia has made border towns, such as Lago Agrio, havens for Colombian guerrillas, antirebel paramilitaries and drug smugglers. It is not recommended to cross into Colombia here. In town, bars can be risky and side streets

## BUSES FROM LAGO AGRIO

| DESTINATION | COST (US$) | DURATION (HR) |
| --- | --- | --- |
| Baeza | 5 | 5 |
| Coca | 3 | 3 |
| Guayaquil | 14 | 14 |
| Puyo | 9 | 8 |
| Quito | 8 | 8 |
| Tena | 7 | 7 |
| Tulcán | 10 | 10 |

unsafe, so stick to the main drag (especially at night) or take a taxi to the restaurants further out. Tourists rarely have problems.

### 🛏 Sleeping & Eating

Most decent hotels are spread out along the main street, Avenida Quito. Mosquitoes can be a problem, especially in the rainy months (June to August), making mosquito nets advisable. Lago has very few decent restaurants. Other than hotel restaurants, chicken rotisserie stalls and fast-food vendors along Avenida Quito are often your best bet.

**Araza Hotel**                     HOTEL $$
(☎283-1287/47; www.hotel-araza.com; cnr Av Quito 536 near Narvaez; s/d incl breakfast $44/56; P❄��🏊) This is the best place in town. It's popular with oil industry travelers and has a wide range of facilities and comforts. The rooms are anonymous and business-style, with desks, TV and bathroom. There's also a pleasant tropical courtyard, a restaurant, a bar with big-screen TV, a gym and swimming pool.

**Hotel D'Mario**           HOTEL, PIZZERIA $
(☎283-0456; www.hoteldmario.com; Av Quito 2-62; s/d incl breakfast $27/36; ❄�🏊) Tour groups favor this staple in the center of town, along a strip of midrange hotels on Avenida Quito. While service was somewhat indifferent on our visit, the bright rooms (though sometimes cramped) are perfectly comfortable. The downstairs restaurant serves a range of dishes, including breakfasts, but is known for its pizzas (mains $5 to $8) and is one of the best places in town.

**Hotel Selva Real**                  HOTEL $
(☎283-3867; Av Quito 261 near Colombia; s/d with fan $10/20, with air-con $15/40; ❄🦒)

Don't be put off by the driveway reception area. Rooms are neat and clean and have TVs. Bargain hunters should expect cold showers in the cheapest rooms.

**Gran Colombia Restaurant**     ECUADORIAN $
(Av Quito; mains $4-7; ⊙7am-10pm) Oil workers refuel here at the end of the day with set meals doused in lip-burning *ají* (hot sauce). The regular menu offers tasty plates such as *chuleta* (pork chops) and ceviche.

### ❶ Getting There & Away

#### Air

Flying prevents the need for a long bus trip on a corkscrew mountain road. Reservations fill up fast with jungle-lodge guests and oil workers traveling home for the weekend; book early. If you can't get a ticket, go to the airport and get on a waiting list in the hope of cancellations, which are frequent because tour companies book more seats than they can use.

**TAME** (☎283-0113; Orellana near 9 de Octubre) and **Aerogal** (www.aerogal.com.ec) both have several daily flights between Quito and Lago Agrio.

The airport is about 3km east of Lago Agrio (a 10-minute trip), and taxis (yellow or white pickup trucks) cost about $3.

#### Border Crossings

The Colombian border is less than 20km north of town but it's best to avoid it. The area is notorious for smugglers and guerilla activity. The most frequently used route from Lago Agrio is to La Punta (about 1½ hours) on Río San Miguel. Taxi-trucks leave Lago Agrio from the corner of Eloy Alfaro and Avenida Colombia and go to La Punta during the day.

#### Bus

The drive from the jungle into the Andes (and vice versa) is dramatic and beautiful, and worth doing in daylight. The bus terminal, about 2km northwest of the center of Lago Agrio, has a wide selection of routes and options. Buses depart regularly for certain destinations and you rarely have to book ahead. In addition, Transportes Putumayo buses go through the jungle towns of Dureno and Tarapoa for travelers wanting access to the Cuyabeno Reserve.

## Along Río Aguarico

☎06

This region of the Cuyabeno Reserve is home to the Cofán. The Cofán numbered in the tens of thousands before early contact with the conquistadors decimated them through disease. Today the Cofán people number less than 2000. Before the discovery of oil, most Cofáns' exposure to nonindigenous people was limited to the occasional missionary, and they still practice a traditional lifestyle. The Cofán are excellent wilderness guides with broad knowledge about the medicinal and practical uses of jungle plants.

The Cofán run well-organized **ecotourism trips** (www.cofan.org). Given the rapid environmental degradation of the area around Lago Agrio, multiday trips start at Chiritza but head to remote Zábalo.

### DURENO

Within an hour from Lago Agrio, Dureno has some primary rainforest and a Cofán settlement, which makes for a good day trip. Although you won't see much wildlife, a local guide can show and explain jungle plants.

Trips to Dureno cost $70 per person per day and can be organized through the **Fundación Sobrevivencia Cofán** (☎02-247-4763) in Lago Agrio. Both offices are Spanish-speaking. Visiting the village without advance notice is discouraged.

### ZÁBALO

This small Cofán community on Río Aguarico, near the confluence with the smaller Río Zábalo, is a seven-hour canoe ride from Lago Agrio. Across the river from the village is an interpretation center with a Cofán guide. Visiting the village without advance notice is discouraged and taking photographs is not allowed.

For more information and to make a tour reservation (from around $100 per day), contact **Randy Borman** (☎02-247-0946; randy@cofan.org), who is one of the few English-speaking guides in the area.

Randy is the son of American missionaries who came to the Oriente in the 1950s, and he was raised among the Cofán, before being formally educated in Quito. He subsequently founded the settlement of Zábalo, where he still has a house with his Cofán wife and family.

He is highly respected and is one of the leaders of the Cofán Federation. Randy guides occasionally, but spends much of his time in Quito working to preserve Cofán culture and the rainforest.

## A CRUDE LEGACY

Ecuador's president has described it as 'a crime against humanity,' and environmentalists argue that it's one of the greatest oil-related disasters of all time. Between 1964 and 1992 the Texaco oil corporation (now Chevron), in partnership with state-owned Petroecuador, extracted some 5.3 billion liters of oil from the northern Oriente, allegedly leaving behind hundreds of open pits full of toxic waste. In turn, Chevron argues that its behavior was entirely consistent with the environmental standards of the day and that it has already done its fair share of clear-ups.

In 2003, US attorneys filed a lawsuit in Lago Agrio (the case was moved from US courts after a decade of wrangling), on behalf of 30,000 Ecuadorians, against the then-named ChevronTexaco. They claimed that the company intentionally dumped 18 billion gallons of toxic wastewater into the rainforest, including 18 million gallons of crude oil – almost twice what was spilled by the *Exxon Valdez*. The plaintiffs say Texaco's practices helped decimate indigenous populations (especially the Cofán and Secoya), destroy ecosystems and create a toxic environment that's resulted in increased rates of cancer and aborted pregnancies.

In 1992, state-owned Petroecuador took over a majority of Texaco's operations, and Chevron says the Ecuadorian company is responsible for any existing pollution. Chevron says Texaco cleaned up its share of spills through a $40 million remediation program prescribed by the Ecuadorian government.

In the spring of 2008, a court-appointed expert recommended Chevron pay between $8 billion and $16 billion to clean up the rainforest. Following an appeal by Chevron, this was upheld in February 2011 and the company was ordered to pay a total of $18 billion in damages. At the time of press Chevron was appealing the ruling once again. In the meantime, the water and food supplies of local tribes are still badly polluted.

For more information on both sides of the case, see **Amazon Defense Coalition** (www.texacotoxico.org) and **Chevron** (www.chevron.com/ecuador).

# Reserva Producción Faunística Cuyabeno

This beautiful **reserve** (www.reservacuyabeno.org; admission $2) is a unique flooded rainforest covering 6034 sq km around Río Cuyabeno. Seasonally inundated with water, the flooded forest provides a home to diverse aquatic species and birdlife. Macrolobium and ceiba treetops thrust out from the underwater forest, creating a stunning visual effect. The black-water rivers, rich in tannins from decomposing foliage, form a maze of waterways that feed the lagoons.

The boundaries of the reserve shift with the political winds, but the area is substantially larger than it was originally. The reserve was created in 1979 to protect rainforest, conserve wildlife and provide a sanctuary in which the indigenous inhabitants – the Siona, Secoya, Cofán, Kichwa and Shuar – could lead customary ways of life. The numerous lakes and swamps are home to fascinating aquatic species, such as fresh water dolphins, manatees, caiman and anacondas. Monkeys abound, and tapirs, peccaries, agoutis and several cat species have been recorded. The birdlife is abundant.

Its protected status notwithstanding, Cuyabeno was opened to oil exploitation almost immediately after its creation. The oil towns of Tarapoa and Cuyabeno and parts of the trans-Ecuadorian oil pipeline were built within the reserve's boundaries. Roads and colonists followed, and tens of thousands of hectares of the reserve became logged or degraded by oil spills and toxic waste. At least six oil spills were recorded between 1984 and 1989 – many of the contaminants entered Río Cuyabeno itself.

Various international and local agencies set to work to try to protect the area – although legally protected, in reality it was open to development. Conservation International funded projects to establish more guard stations in Cuyabeno, to train local Siona and Secoya to work in wildlife management and to support Cordavi, an Ecuadorian environmental-law group that challenged the legality of allowing oil exploitation in protected areas.

Finally, in late 1991 the government shifted the borders of the reserve further east and south and enlarged the area it covered. The new reserve is more remote and better protected. Vocal local indigenous groups – which are supported by Ecuadorian and international nongovernmental organizations (NGOs), tourists, travel agencies and conservation groups – are proving to be its best stewards.

Due to its remoteness, and to protect the communities within it, travelers should only visit the reserve on a guided tour.

## Tours

Agencies in Quito offer Cuyabeno tours that are run by operators on location. Tour camps and lodges seem to open and close quickly here, but about 10 currently operate close to each other on the river; a few are close by on a lagoon. No location is significantly privileged; all have similar opportunities for spotting wildlife. Travel is mainly by canoe except between December and February, when low water levels limit canoe travel. Most visitors come during the wetter months of March to September.

The best rates, especially for solo travelers, are obtained by squeezing into an existing trip. When booking, check to see whether: transportation to and from Lago Agrio is included; the travel day is considered a tour day; water is boiled or purified (purified is preferred); and whether you can expect naturalist or native guides. A naturalist is preferred as they are able to tell you far more about plants scientifically, but native guides give the traditional uses and can show how indigenous people prepare various products. The better tours will have both a naturalist and a native guide. Moreover, a naturalist will nearly always speak English, whereas native-English-speaking guides are rare. The $2 entry fee to Cuyabeno reserve is paid at the guard post in Tarapoa. Transport from Quito to Lago Agrio is not included in packages.

## Sleeping

**Cuyabeno Lodge** JUNGLE LODGE $$$
(Map p211; ☎02-252-1212; www.cuyabenolodge.com; per person 3 nights $220-395, 4 nights $275-475) This highly recommended place is run by Quito-based **Neotropic Turis** (www.neotropicturis.com), in close cooperation with the local Siona people. Thatched huts spread out over a hillside offer a bit of privacy, most with private bathroom and hot water, although the cheapest rooms are four-berth dorms with shared facilities. The very best rooms are in the observation tower and are spacious and comfortable – perfect for those for whom no amount of nature-watching is enough. Solar power provides electricity.

## PREPARING FOR A JUNGLE TRIP

While it's possible to visit the jungle on your own, organized tours and jungle lodges get you into the wilderness quicker and without all the logistical challenges. Moreover, you'll avoid encountering indigenous peoples who prefer not to see tourists, or those who prefer to see tourists who are accompanied by guides.

First, figure out how much you can spend, what you want to see and how much time you have. The further you travel from roads and development, and the more time you spend in the jungle, the more wildlife you'll see. The same applies for cultural experiences – longer, more-remote trips result in more-exciting experiences and encounters.

### The Differences

Lodges and large hotel-style boats offer daily excursions from a comfortable base. Other tours may include camping or sleeping in communities.

Lower costs may translate to more basic accommodations, Spanish-speaking guides, non-naturalist guides, larger groups, boiled instead of purified water and visits to developed areas with less wildlife. In some cases, operators may cut corners with practices that are not ecologically sound, including hunting for food. The rainforest is over-hunted; a no-hunting policy is a must.

Different operators emphasize different aspects of the jungle, and can advise you on the probability of seeing specific wildlife. Observation towers enhance the chances of seeing birds and monkeys. High-end operators or community tourism make it possible to visit indigenous cultures. High-end programs offer translators and comfortable lodging and may run beneficial community programs. Community tourism usually offers a more authentic experience, and is better suited to Spanish speakers with a flexible itinerary.

Some unscrupulous outfitters will offer *ayahuasca* or other psychotropics used ritually in indigenous cultures. These illegal substances should be regarded with caution (see boxed text, p212).

Wherever you go, it's essential that you have a guide when outside towns and villages. Whatever choices you make, tread lightly and respect local communities.

### Tour Bookings

In Quito, there are numerous operators' offices (see p62), allowing for quick comparative shopping. Agencies can usually get you into the jungle with a few days' notice. Once booked on a tour, you usually have to travel to the town where it begins (most often Lago Agrio, Coca, Tena or Misahualli). Thoroughly discuss costs, food, equipment, itinerary and group size before booking. Booking a tour from Tena, Coca, Puyo or Macas is best if for shorter guided trips to nearby reserves or communities. The Cofán, Huaoranis, Kichwa, Shuar and other groups offer trips guided by their own community members.

### Guides

A good guide will show you things you would have missed on your own, whereas an inadequate guide may spoil the trip. Guides should be able to produce a license on request and explain their specialties. Recommended guides are always preferable, and many lodges are known for their quality guiding services. Make the most of guides – ask questions and let them know exactly what you're interested in seeing. Be prepared to tip your guide, and recommend their services to others if they prove to be good.

### What to Bring

Jungle towns have only basic equipment, including bottled water, tarps (for rain) and rubber boots in an array of sizes. Nearly all guided tours lend the essential boots and rain gear, but check beforehand. Mosquito nets are usually provided in places that need them. If you're serious about seeing wildlife, bring your own binoculars. Some guides will carry a pair, but will need them to make sightings. Besides general travel supplies, bring a flashlight (torch), sunblock, a sun hat and repellent with DEET. Depending on the time of year and your destination, you may need malaria pills (see p375).

Bilingual naturalist guides get top reviews from guests, and the food and attention are excellent. Prices include transfers from Lago Agrio, a guide, drinking water, coffee and tea. Canoes and kayaks are available to paddle around the lake; many guests jump in for a swim.

**Nicky Amazon Lodge**  JUNGLE LODGE **$$**
(Map p211; ☏02-254-6590; www.amazondracaena. com; per person 4/5 nights $200/240) Run by the Quito-based Dracaena Amazon Rainforest Explorations, Nicky Amazon Lodge offers seven stilted cabins with private bathrooms. Daily expeditions include piranha fishing, wildlife-spotting and a trip to a local community. A canopy tower enhances birdwatching opportunities. A new lodge being built in Laguna Grande means that on most tours you stay in both locations, allowing you to see far more of the reserve than if you just stay in one place.

# Coca

☏06 / POP 30,300

The unavoidable starting point for many of Ecuador's most fascinating jungle tours, Coca is the rather charmless public face of the Río Napo. In the 1990s the town was transformed by the oil industry from a tiny river settlement with dirt roads into a hot and busy collection of concrete. The capital of the Orellana province since 1999 (and officially known as Puerto Francisco de Orellana), Coca is the last act of 'civilization' before the Río Napo takes you deep into the rainforest to the Parque Nacional Yasuní and beyond, and where the controversial Vía Auca, a road that plunges south into Huaorani territory, begins.

There aren't really any sights in town, though the new Museo Arqueologico Centro Cultural de Orellana (or, mercifully, MACCO for short) was being built near the riverfront at the time of writing. A new suspension bridge across the Napo was also being built, allowing for the removal of the creaking oneway traffic bridge currently spanning the river.

What it may lack in sights and beauty, Coca compensates for with friendly locals, a lively market and safe streets. It's finally now got a park, after years without a single splash of green in its center, and the riverfront promenade is a pleasant place to wander at any time of the day.

## 👉 Tours

The number of local tour companies has decreased in Coca. It's best to book from Quito,

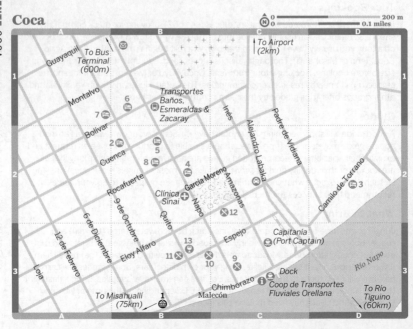

Coca

although a few independent guides operate in town.

**Amazon Wildlife Tours** WILDLIFE TOUR
(Map p206; ☎288-0802; robertvaca@amazonwildlife.ec; Hotel San Fermin, cnr Quito & Bolívar) This friendly agency offers an array of nature-watching tours, including a specialty jaguar expedition in Yasuní National Park, tours to see Amazon dolphins, and general wildlife-watching in the Limoncocha Reserve.

**Kem Pery Tours** JUNGLE TOURS
(☎ 02-250-5600; www.kempery.com; Ramíres Dávalos 117 near Amazonas, Quito) Leads tours to Bataburo Lodge, on the edge of Huaorani territory, about nine hours southeast from Coca by boat and bus. Canoes motor into the remote Ríos Tiguino and Cononaco and tours combine wildlife-viewing with cultural visits. Guides are bilingual and native.

**Jarol Fernando Vaca** NATURE GUIDE
(☎02-227-1094; shiripuno2004@yahoo.com) This Quito-based naturalist and butterfly specialist is a good independent guide. He can take visitors into the Shiripuno area and is authorized by the Huaorani to guide in their territory. He also runs Shiripuno Lodge (see p209), one of only two lodges inside Yasuní National Park.

**Luis Duarte** GUIDE
(☎288-2285; cocaselva@hotmail.com) Organizes customized tours, including river passage to Peru or stays with Huaorani families. Find him at La Casa del Maito, p208.

**Luis García** GUIDE
(☎09-959-4604; luisemerald@gmail.com) Luis is an experienced guide who speaks fluent English and works out of Sacha Lodge (p210) for much of the time. However, he is based in Coca, and can arrange bespoke tours for individuals and groups alike.

**Otobo's Amazon Safari** INDIGENOUS TOURS
(www.rainforestcamping.com) Operated by indigenous Huaorani Otobo and his family, this remote site on the Río Cononaco has platform tents and a thatched-roofed lodge. Visitors hike in the Parque Nacional Yasuní with a native English-speaking guide, visit lagoons and a local village.

## 🛏 Sleeping

**Hotel San Fermin** HOTEL $
(☎288-0802; robertvaca@amazonwildlife.ec; cnr Quito & Bolívar; s/d with shared bathroom $8/16, s/d/ste with private bathroom $15/25/32; 🅿🌀@🛜) This friendly and well-run place is an excellent deal: following a recent revamp, rooms are spacious, decked out in timbers and featuring TV, desks, and either fans or air-con. Grab a room on the highest floor if possible – these get the most light and are the most spacious.

**Hotel El Auca** HOTEL $$
(☎288-0166; tatiana.wall@yahoo.com; Napo; s/d/ste incl breakfast from $34/54/90; 🅿🌀🛜) This fancy establishment on one side of Coca's new city park is the smartest place in town. Choose from stylish polished-wood cabins out back in the garden, or equally civilized rooms in the detached building at the rear. There are also rooms in the main hotel – these get you more space but some street noise. El Auca is popular with tour groups, and the restaurant, Dayuma, can be overrun in the evenings, although it's a pleasant place for a meal.

**Hotel Río Napo** HOTEL $$
(☎288-0872; www.hotelrionapo.com; Bolívar 76-06; s/d $28/47; 🌀🛜) This smart, clean and bright midrange hotel in the center of town has 29 comfortable rooms. It's an orderly yet

slightly generic place, with good beds and friendly staff. All rooms have cable TV.

### Hostería La Misión
HOTEL $$

(☎288-0260/0544; hlamision@hotmail.com; Camilo de Torrano; s/d $28/41; P❄🐾🌊) This longtime Coca staple has clean and comfortable rooms overlooking the Río Napo. All come with cable TV, fridges, modern bathrooms and lampshades still covered in their factory plastic. Multiple swimming pools are usually teeming with children, while sneaky food-stealing monkeys live in the trees on-site, and the riverside La Misión restaurant and bar is the place to be on a warm evening.

### Hostal Omaguas
HOTEL $

(☎288-2436; cnr Quito & Cuenca; s/d $19/29; P❄🐾) Despite an uninspiring exterior, this hotel offers brightly tiled and gleaming, clean rooms with cable TV and hot water. The restaurant is a cool, quiet haven from the sweltering streets, and serves up decent Ecuadorian fare.

### Hotel Santa María
HOTEL $

(☎288-0097; Rocafuerte; r per person $8, s/d with air-con $15/20) Here you'll find the cheapest acceptable bed in town: don't expect much and don't hit your head on the low ceiling in the stairwell on the way to the cramped rooms.

### Hotel Lojanita
HOTEL $

(☎288-0032; hotelojanitacocaecuador@gmail.com; cnr Napo & Cuenca; s/d with fan $10/16, with air-con & hot water $15/24; P❄🐾) This hotel, which is convenient for catching early buses, needs a coat of paint in its rooms and an effort to rescue its musty bathrooms. However, it's quite cheap if you forego the air-con.

## ✗ Eating

For a cheap feast with plenty of local color, head to Calle Quito between Rocafuerte and Espejo after dark any night of the week. Cheerful street vendors serve up grilled meats that are barbecued right in front of you – it's a fantastic and very sociable place to eat.

### La Casa del Maito
SEAFOOD $

(Espejo; mains $4-6; ⊙7am-6pm) This unassuming little place sees locals crowding in for lunch of delicious fish (mostly tilapia and piranha) cooked in palm leaves on the grill outside. Other fillings such as chicken and heart of palm are also available, and

the friendly, English-speaking owner, Luis Duarte, also offers guiding services (p207).

### Matambre
STEAKHOUSE $$

(cnr Quito & Espejo; mains $6-10; ⊙noon-10pm) Fearsomely popular, this open-sided restaurant serves up melt-in-the-mouth cuts of beef in many different styles and is always full of family groups at lunch and dinner. Service can be hit and miss (the staff are always overworked, it seems), but the food is delicious, so persevere.

### Cevichería Colorado
SEAFOOD $

(Napo; mains $5-7; ⊙8am-8pm) This popular *cevichería* (ceviche restaurant) by the river is a great place for a bowl of frothy ceviche and a cold beer. The long room is usually busy from early in the day until closing time, and the wide menu is a real treat for anyone who likes seafood.

### La Misión
ECUADORIAN $$

(Hostería La Misión, Camilo de Torrano; mains $4-14; ⊙7am-10pm) For the best spot at this otherwise rather bland restaurant, eat on the concrete patio overlooking the river. The menu includes a selection of delicious grilled white river fish, grilled meat dishes and seafood.

### Restaurante Ocaso
ECUADORIAN $

(Eloy Alfaro btwn Quito & Napo; mains $3-6; ⊙6am-9pm) Locals recommend the saucy meat stews with fluffy rice and hot *patacones* (plantain fritters) served up at this fairly unexciting-looking family-run restaurant on the new park.

## ☕ Drinking & Entertainment

### Emerald Forest Blues
BAR

(Quito; ⊙9am-late) An '80s soundtrack fills the background of this rather sleazy-feeling little bar owned by Luís García, a popular local guide. It's not exactly a charming place, but it's one of the few dedicated bars in town.

### El Bunker
CLUB

(Hostería La Misión, Camilo de Torrano; ⊙9pm-midnight Mon-Fri, to 2am Sat & Sun) The name suits this windowless, downstairs location that gets steamy on weekends with a mixture of *reggaetón* (a blend of Puerto Rican *bomba,* dancehall and hip-hop), Latin pop and hip-hop.

## ℹ Information

There are several ATMs in town, but they nearly always have a queue waiting for them – it's best to bring your own cash from Quito.

**Clínica Sinai** (cnr Napo & Moreno) The best place for medical attention.

**Pancho.com** (Moreno; internet per hr $1; ⏱7am-noon) Internet cafe.

**Post office** (Napo near Montalvo)

**Tourist information office** (☎288-0532; Transportes Fluviales Orellana Bldg, Chimborazo; ⏱8am-noon & 2-6pm Mon-Sat) The new and helpful tourist office offers travelers free internet access, advice on transport to Río Napo lodges, and arranges lectures about the indigenous peoples and rare animals living in Yasuní National Park. No English is spoken, though staff are very friendly.

## ❶ Getting There & Away

### Air

The airport terminal is almost 2km north of town on the left-hand side of the road to Lago Agrio. The five-minute taxi ride there costs $1.

**TAME** (☎288-1078/3340; cnr Napo & Rocafuerte) Flies between Coca and Quito three times a day ($75 each way), with fewer flights at weekends.

**Aerogal** (☎288-1742; www.aerogal.com.ec; airport terminal) Flies the Coca-to-Quito route daily. The 30-minute flight also costs $75.

### Boat

**Coop de Transportes Fluviales Orellana** (☎288-0087/0231; Chimborazo at docks) Offers an upriver passenger service in a covered 60-passenger canoe. Buy your ticket early. It departs Sunday, Monday, Thursday and Friday at 7am for Nuevo Rocafuerte ($15, 10 hours) on the Peruvian border. It returns to Coca, departing Nuevo Rocafuerte on the same days at 5am (12 to 14 hours). Although there's usually a stop for lunch, bring food and water for the long trip.

**Venus Boats** (☎09-968-1354) If you want to charter your own canoe then ask around at the docks; however, readers have recommended Venus Boats, which rents out an 18-seat canoe for around $60 per hour.

For information on crossing to Peru by river, see p213.

### Bus

The main bus terminal is 600m north of the town center, and has good connections to towns around the country. However, many bus lines run services from near their offices in central Coca. Even so, ask where to board when you buy your ticket.

**Transportes Baños** (☎288-0182; cnr Napo & Bolívar) Has several buses daily to Lago Agrio ($3, two hours), Tena ($7, seven hours) and Quito ($10, 10 hours). The trip to Quito by Vía Loreto is fastest.

**Transportes Esmeraldas** (☎288-0272; cnr Napo & Bolívar) Has two night buses to Quito ($10, 10 hours).

**Transportes Zacaray** (☎288-0286; cnr Napo & Bolívar) Heads daily to Guayaquil ($16, 16 hours) and Ambato ($10, 10 hours).

*Rancheras* (open-sided buses, or trucks mounted with uncomfortably narrow bench seats – also known as *chivas*) leave from the terminal for various destinations between Coca and Lago Agrio, and to Río Tiputini to the south. Pickup trucks and taxis at **Cooperativa Camionetas Río Napo** (Alfaro) provide service around and outside of town.

## Vía Auca

☑06

This road from Coca crosses the Río Napo and continues south across Río Tiputini and Río Shiripuno, ending near the small community of **Tiguino** on Río Tiguino. Daily *rancheras* go as far as Tiguino. The area used to be Huaorani territory and virgin jungle, but when this oil-exploration road was built in the 1980s, the Huaorani were pushed eastward (some groups also went westward). The area is being colonized, and cattle ranches and oil rigs are replacing the jungle in spite of conservationist efforts.

The rivers crossed by the road provide access to remote parts of both the Huaorani reserve and Yasuní, but you should only enter with authorized guides. While some operators have long-standing relationships with the Huaorani, others do not, and the Huaorani insist on managing tourism on their own terms to protect their best interests.

Some 75km south of Coca you'll find **Shiripuno Lodge** (www.shiripunolodge.com), which was built and is run by the Huaorani people on their territory. It's a simple place with no electricity, deep in the forest and perfect for those seeking a real jungle experience. Contact Jarol Fernando Vaca (☎02-227-1094; shiripuno2004@yahoo.com) for more information.

Three to four hours downriver on Río Tiguino is the remote and simple **Bataburo Lodge**. Located in primary forest, the lodge has a canopy tower and rooms with shared and private bathrooms. Rates include meals, guiding and transportation from Coca. It's in a remote area, and upkeep of the trails is erratic. Safari Tours (p65) and Kem Pery Tours (p207) can book your trip.

## Lower Río Napo

*♫06*

The Río Napo flows east from Coca on a steady course toward the Amazon River in Peru. Just after Coca, the river widens into a powerful waterway that can flood villages and islands. This long, lonesome stretch of the Napo houses some of Ecuador's best jungle lodges and boasts some of the country's best wildlife-spotting possibilities.

### YARINA LODGE

The small tributary Río Manduro meets the Napo an hour downstream from Coca, and a further 10 minutes down this black-water stream you'll find **Yarina Lodge** *(♫02-250-4037/3225; www.yarinalodge.com; per person full board 2/3/4 nights $270/360/450)*, a hillside camp of 26 bamboo, thatched-roofed cabañas. Yarina is geared toward budget travelers and doesn't feel as remote as those camps further downstream, but it provides good services and has enthusiastic and professional guides. Meals, with vegetarian options, are well prepared in a communal lodge that features hammocks. Two- and three-bed cabins come equipped with mosquito nets, modern bathrooms, electricity and hot water 24 hours a day.

The lodge doesn't feel remote, but its pleasant surroundings offer river views, short trails, raised walkways and the opportunity to watch birds and paddle canoes. There's a tame parrot who will greet you in several different languages, a pet tapir who wanders around the property, and several other animals to see in the nearby 'rehabilitation area' (where animals rescued from traffickers in Coca spend time before being released into the wild). Rates include all meals and tours with Spanish- and English-speaking local guides. As well as all the normal jungle activities, Kichwa cookery classes are on offer.

### SACHA LODGE

Enjoying a truly spectacular setting on an inland lake a short hike and canoe ride from the Río Napo, **Sacha Lodge** *(♫02-256-6090; www.sachalodge.com; s/d full board 3 nights $1185/1580, 4 nights $1485/1980; @🤶)* is one of Ecuador's best jungle lodges. Opened in 1992, this Swiss-run place has never rested on its laurels and works tirelessly to meet the demands of even the most discerning travelers. The complex is built on the banks of Laguna El Pilche, a lake about 1km north of Río Napo.

As well as employing and training indigenous people to work in the tourism industry, Sacha has been steadily purchasing plots from Ecuadorian smallholders who are using it to farm, and allowing the rainforest to reclaim the land purchased. The lodge sits on 5000 acres of reclaimed land now fully protected for forestation, and is the largest private reserve in Ecuador.

The central lodge is a circular two-story thatched hut with a restaurant and bar, while nearby are huts housing a small library and an internet center. Its boardwalks tentacle out to 26 cabins, each with a modern bathroom, dry box for cameras, 24-hour hot water and electricity, and a hammock deck for shady siestas and wildlife-watching. Older units are built deeper into the jungle and are more rustic feeling, though rather dark. More recently constructed ones have far more light but also more modern interiors (despite being fashioned from bamboo) and present fewer opportunities to see animal life from the balcony than the older ones because they're not as deep in the jungle. All rooms have safes and are very well screened – mosquito nets aren't used because the threat is small. Food is superb, served in buffets and diners are seated in groups, and there's a pleasant upstairs bar that's popular in the evenings.

Small groups are the rule for excursions, and serious bird-watchers get top treatment. Hikes and canoe trips typically consist of about five tourists, with a bilingual naturalist and local guide. The terrain includes flat and hilly rainforest, various lakes, coiling rivers and swamps. The 2000 hectares are visited by six kinds of monkey, toucans, poison dart frogs, peccaries, sloths, anacondas, caiman and black agoutis.

The lodge's showpiece is a massive metal canopy that stretches between three platforms, 60m off the ground. Bird-watchers covet the early-morning experience of standing on the creaking giant to watch the fog lift on an array of monkeys and birds. A separate 45m-high wooden observation deck atop a huge ceiba tree is another way to get high. Sacha is an absolutely top choice for a luxurious jungle experience.

Getting here is an adventure in itself – a two-hour motorized canoe ride from Coca is followed by a leisurely walk through the forest on an elevated boardwalk. You're then taken on a 15-minute paddle up a backwater canal and across a lake in a dugout canoe.

## NAPO WILDLIFE CENTER

As the only lodge within the boundaries of Parque Nacional Yasuní, **Napo Wildlife Center** (NWC; ☏02-600-5893; www.napowildlifecenter.com; s/d full board 3 nights $1230/1640, 4 nights $1523/2030; @ 🛜) offers a pristine yet luxurious setting with unparalleled access to wildlife. This ecotourism project is 100% owned by Añangu's Kichwa community, which makes up almost the entire lodge staff.

One of the most enjoyable aspects of this place is simply arriving: you'll be paddled for around an hour from the Río Napo, down a thrillingly wild black-water creek packed full of wildlife. Eventually you'll arrive at Laguna Añangucocha, where NWC's 16 red-hued rooms enjoy a prime position on the far side. The rooms are luxurious, large and stylish with modern bathrooms and lake views from most. Four newly built suites are even bigger, with outdoor Jacuzzis on the terraces at the back. The fabulous communal areas are spacious and open, with a lovely wooden deck, small library and elevated viewing platform. Meals here are taken in groups with your guide and are delicious and varied.

Trips are guided by local Añangans trained as Yasuní park rangers and bilingual naturalist guides. Two parrot clay licks on the property are a major attraction for birdwatchers, who also come from surrounding lodges to see parrots, parakeets and macaws. Between late October and early April is the best time to see up to 10 species of parrot – sometimes numbering in the thousands. A short hike from the lodge, a 36m steel tower offers a spectacular canopy panorama and prolific birdlife. The rare zigzag heron has been spotted on the property.

The center has won numerous awards, not only for its connection to the local community, but for ecologically sound practices, including an environmentally sustainable sewage system, composting latrines, solar panels and quality guiding. It's generally held to be the most luxurious and most environmentally sensitive of the lower Río Napo lodges and is highly recommended.

## LA SELVA JUNGLE LODGE

The oldest lodge on the lower Napo, **La Selva Jungle Lodge** ☏02-254-5425, 255-0995; www.laselvajunglelodge.com; Sonelsa Bldg,

# Around Añangu

# Around Añangu

### 😴 Sleeping
| | | |
|---|---|---|
| 1 | Amazon Dolphin Lodge | B2 |
| 2 | Cuyabeno Lodge | B1 |
| 3 | La Selva Jungle Lodge | A2 |
| 4 | Napo Wildlife Center | A2 |
| 5 | Nicky Amazon Lodge | B1 |
| 6 | Sacha Lodge | A2 |
| 7 | Sani Lodge | B2 |
| 8 | Yarina Lodge | A2 |

6th fl, Mariscal Foch 265, Quito; per person full board 3/4 nights $948/729) has recently changed ownership and is now the property of a Norwegian-Ecuadorian family that is planning to make some much-needed changes to this rather faded but still spectacular place.

Set on the shores of Laguna Garzacocha, the 60-capacity lodge is being reduced to 40 by the new management. Some of the rather aged accommodation is being removed and replaced by new huts set right on the lake's edge, giving far more privacy and better views than were previously available. The huts that will remain are double cabins and one family cabin connected by raised walkways. All cabins and huts have a private bathroom with hot water, ceiling fan, mosquito nets and generator-powered electricity. Meals are delicious and presented in a spacious dining room overlooking the lake.

The upgrade to accommodation and services here is gradual, and is bringing them up to the high standards now commonly found in the area.

With more than 500 bird species, La Selva is a major attraction for bird-watching A 43m-high canopy platform, 20 minutes' walk from the lodge, affords even better viewing. Monkeys and other mammals are frequently seen and there are tens of thousands of plant and insect species, as well as giant anacondas. Brilliantly colored butterflies flit about in an enormous butterfly-breeding complex that's open to visitors. Swimming and canoeing are also both possible on the lake.

La Selva is about 2½ hours downriver from Coca in a motorized canoe. It's then reached by a gentle walk through the jungle, followed by a canoe trip across the lagoon.

### SANI LODGE

Owned by the local Sani community, **Sani Lodge** (Map p211; ☏02-323-7139; www.sanilodge.com; per person full board 3 nights s/d/tent $924/627/396, 4 nights $1166/814/506; ☜) is one of the lower-priced options available, but unlike other economy lodges it's located very deep in the rainforest and enjoys one of the most beautiful locations of any lodge in Ecuador.

The lodge came into being as part of a deal between the local community and the Occidental Oil Company. In exchange for allowing Occidental to explore for oil on its land, the Sani community asked them to build a tourist lodge they could run. Occidental did not find oil, but Sani Lodge was nevertheless built. All profits from tourism go back into the Kichwa community in the form of scholarships, a community store that eases the need for local hunting, emergency medical funds and other projects.

Employees are members of the community, which creates a family feel.

After traveling up a small tributary of the Río Napo, visitors encounter a group of thatched-hut buildings set on an enchanting backwater oxbow lake. Ten circular cabins each sleep two to three people and have private cold-water bathrooms, comfortable beds, mosquito screens and a small porch. There are also four family-sized cabins and a camping area in a separate part of the lodge, reachable by canoe. This can be a great way to save money – tents are provided and share modern bathrooms.

Monkeys, sloths and black caiman are regularly spotted, and the lodge's bird list records more than 570 species of birds in the area (the 30m-high tree tower will help you find them). Guides here are excellent for their knowledge of, and respect for, the jungle. Most enjoy showing visitors the Sani community to reinforce how the lodge has created an important, sustainable economy.

Tours include canoe transport to/from Coca (two to three hours upstream from the lodge) and daily excursions with both a native guide and an English-speaking naturalist guide. Highly recommended for travelers interested in wildlife and indigenous culture.

### LAGUNA PAÑACOCHA

This quiet, hidden backwater lagoon is a short boat ride off the Río Napo through a thrillingly wild network of creeks that are full of wildlife. Pañacocha, which means 'Lake of Piranhas' in Kichwa, is frequently visited by local lodge tour groups, who come up here on day trips to piranha-fish and spot

---

## WHAT KIND OF TRIP IS THIS?

Think twice if your jungle tour offers *ayahuasca*, a psychotropic plant used ritually in Amazon cultures, as part of the authentic experience. Only a professional shaman (who may not necessarily be 'dressed-up' for the occasion) has the trained ability to carry out 'readings' for patients as part of his diagnostic arts. The intake of this psychotropic plant should be considered only on rare occasions.

There are many factors that should be taken into account prior to taking *ayahuasca*, such as the need for dietary preparation and true professional supervision and guidance, and the timing of menstrual cycles – it's essential to be in the hands of a professional shaman. Dangerous side effects from *ayahuasca*, either due to medication you might be taking at the time or negligent preparation of the plant, could ruin your trip.

There are a number of books available on the subject. A good tour operator should be able to provide you with these for a deep-rooted, preliminary understanding of what a genuine *ayahuasca* ritual entails – if your operator can't supply these resources, find a new operator.

some of the pink freshwater dolphins that can often be seen in the lagoon.

There are several lodges up here now, but they're only sporadically used. The main one is **Amazon Dolphin Lodge** (www.amazondolphinlodge.com; per person 3/4 nights $600/750), which is set right on the lagoon and comprises 11 rustic cabins, each with two beds, mosquito nets, modern bathroom and electricity in the evenings. It's a relaxed place, with hammocks slung on each balcony, two good jungle hikes to do, and great lagoon swimming, fishing and kayaking to be had right on the doorstep.

To get here, hire a local canoe where the Río Pañayacu meets the Río Napo, which can be reached by a Nuevo Rocafuerte canoe from Coca (see p209).

Pañacocha is four to five hours downstream from Coca (depending on your motor), or about halfway to Nuevo Rocafuerte.

## NUEVO ROCAFUERTE
A distant dot on the map for many people, Nuevo Rocafuerte is certainly in no danger of losing its mystery. While backpackers may bubble with excitement at the idea of floating the Napo all the way to the Amazon River, only the most intrepid travelers should rise to the occasion. In this truly off-the-beaten-track adventure, aspiring 'survivors' may have to endure cramped and wet travel, the possibility of seeing their next meal slaughtered, and potential illness.

Nuevo Rocafuerte is on the Peruvian border, about eight to 10 hours from Coca along the Río Napo. This is a legal border crossing with Peru, albeit a highly independent one. Basic infrastructure, such as regular boats and simple hotels, are lacking.

If you are continuing to Peru, try to time your arrival with one of the five boats from Iquitos. Enquire at the Coop de Transportes Fluviales Orellana (p209) in Coca, when you buy your ticket downstream, for cargo-boat phone numbers and possible arrivals. But nothing guarantees timing; there's a good chance you'll get stuck here, so be prepared. Bring adequate supplies of water-purification tablets, insect repellent and food. Also, consider getting Peruvian currency in Quito before arriving.

There are a couple of hotels in town, but the best option is newly built **Hotel Chimborazo** (✆06-233-2109; r per person $5), where you'll find clean and comfortable wood-panelled rooms. The hotel can also arrange onward transportation.

Consider getting a boat downstream to Pantoja, Peru, which has a hotel, restaurant and disco. Or arrange for a tour in Parque Nacional Yasuní or Cuyabeno reserve while you wait.

For local information, tours or to hire a boat, contact local guide **Juan Carlos 'Chuso' Cuenca** (✆06-238-2182). His house is the second one after the marina.

## MANATEE RIVERBOAT
The **Manatee Amazon Explorer** (www.manateeamazonexplorer.com; s/d full board per person 3 nights $1084/715, 4 nights $1445/957) offers a different way to see the jungle. Guests stay aboard a three-story, flat-bottomed riverboat and make day trips to Parque Nacional Yasuní, Limoncocha, Tiputini and other tributaries off the Río Napo. It's an interesting idea that results in access to a wider range of habitats, thanks to efficient use of motor time (while guests are on excursions in motor canoes, the boat advances to its next destination). Cabins are basic but comfortable, and readers recommend the experience. Trips run for three, four or seven nights and can be booked through **Advantage Travel** (✆02-244-8985; www.advantagecuador.com; Av Gaspar de Villarroel 1100, Quito) or **Nuevo Mundo Expeditions** (✆02-250-9431; 18 de Septiembre E4-161 & Mera, Quito).

### ❶ Getting There & Away
Coop de Transportes Fluviales Orellana passenger canoes to Coca depart at 5am on Sunday, Tuesday, Thursday and Friday. The trip ($15) is approximately 12 hours, with a lunch stop in Pañacocha. The canoe is covered but you should still bring rain gear, food and water. Low-water conditions may prolong the trip. Even if you have a ticket, be sure to be at the departure point by 4.30am, as boats leave once they're full and readers have written to complain of being left behind.

#### TO/FROM PERU
Exit and entry formalities in Ecuador are handled in Nuevo Rocafuerte; in Peru, try your best to settle them in Pantoja, with Iquitos as backup. Boats from Nuevo Rocafuerte charge $40 per boat to Pantoja. Cargo boats travel from Pantoja to Iquitos (a four- to six-day trip) when they have enough cargo to justify the trip. A hammock and 19L of water, in addition to food, are recommended – food on the boats can be dodgy. Be warned that the experience can be rough: there may be only one bathroom, crowded conditions and lots of livestock on board. Boats vary in quality, but if you've been waiting a long time for one to arrive, you may not want to be picky.

# Parque Nacional Yasuní

With a massive 9620 sq km section of wetlands, marshes, swamps, lakes, rivers and tropical rainforest, **Yasuní National Park** (admission $2, parrot clay lick $20) is Ecuador's largest mainland park. Its staggering biodiversity led Unesco to declare it an international biosphere reserve and it was established as a national park shortly after, in 1979. Because this pocket of life was untouched by the last ice age, a diverse pool of species has thrived here throughout the ages, including more than 600 bird species, some previously unknown elsewhere. Resident animals include some hard-to-see jungle wildlife, such as jaguars, harpy eagles, pumas and tapirs.

Yasuní stands today as one of the last true wildernesses in Ecuador. Its inaccessibility has preserved it in ways that active protection cannot. Bordered by Río Napo to the north and Río Curaray to the southeast, the park encompasses most of the watersheds of Ríos Yasuní and Nashiño, as well as substantial parts of Río Tiputini. Its diverse habitats consist of 'terra firma' (forested hills), which are never inundated even by the highest floods; *varzea* (lowlands), which are periodically inundated by flooding rivers; and *igapó* (semipermanently inundated lowlands).

A small but not negligible number of Tagaeri, Taromenani and Oñamenane live within the park. Park territory was altered in 1990 and 1992 to protect these traditional populations of hunters and gatherers, who vehemently resist contact with the outside world. The nearby Reserva Huaorani contributes as an ecological buffer zone for the national park.

Oil discovery within the park has complicated this conservation success story. In 1991, despite Yasuní's protected status, the Ecuadorian government gave the US-based company Conoco the right to begin oil exploration. Since then the concession has changed hands several times. Conoco was soon replaced by the Maxus Oil Consortium, whose legacy is the Maxus road, which slices 150km into the park. While the road was designed to be lifted up and

## YASUNÍ ITT INITIATIVE

**Yasuní National Park** (www.mdtf.undp.org/yasuni) has more tree species within its borders than exists in the United States and Canada combined. It also has incredible biodiversity – if the previous tree fact wasn't enough for you, consider that the park boasts over 4000 plant species, 173 types of mammals and over 600 species of bird in an area half the size of Connecticut. This biodiversity is matched only by the park's stupendous mineral wealth, which means only one thing in Ecuador: oil.

In some parts of the park, oil extraction has been going on for over a decade. However, it's the fate of the enormous Ishpingo-Tambococha-Tiputini (ITT) oil field that is currently the hot topic in Ecuador's lively environmental protection-versus-development debate. In 2007 Ecuador's environmentally minded president, Rafael Correa, announced the Yasuní ITT Initiative to the world at the UN. Under the plan, Ecuador will leave the estimated 846 million barrels of oil here underground indefinitely in exchange for $3.6 billon (half of the projected revenue the oil would earn, were it to be exploited) being provided by the international community over 13 years.

In 2011 the fund received $116 million in donations and debt relief from countries around the world (most notably Italy, which forgave some $40 million of Ecuadorian debt), comfortably exceeding that year's goal of $100 million. However, the funding goal for 2012 and 2013 is significantly higher at $291 million per year, so the fundraising effort has its work cut out for it – if the fund ever fails to raise its annual minimum the entire initiative may be abandoned and the oil companies can move in.

Surely one of the largest attempts at crowd funding ever seen, this unique initiative has captured the attention of the international community. It's also attracted a bevy of celebrities such as Al Gore and Leonardo di Caprio, both of whom have given the project their vocal support. Detractors compare the program to blackmail, but the scheme has proved remarkably popular domestically, with locals who are unhappy with the experience around Lago Agrio (see boxed text, p203) wanting to put a halt to oil extraction in the rainforest.

## THE TAGAERI & TAROMENANI

The Tagaeri and Taromenani have a history of violent encounters with the outside world, which ultimately led to the withdrawal and self-imposed isolation of these subgroups of the Huaorani. In 1999 a presidential decree from the Ecuadorian government set up Intangible Zones to 'prevent more irreversible damage to indigenous communities and their environment.' It delineated an area of 7000 sq km (overlapping Parque Nacional Yasuní and Huaorani territory) where these groups could live as they have for centuries without threat of contact with outsiders.

Mining, logging and oil exploration are forbidden in these areas, which also protects an estimated 500 species of birds, jaguars, pumas, manatees and other wildlife. But with evidence of illegal logging, and still more violent encounters between outsiders and the tribes, the government has promised to staff outposts to keep smugglers, poachers and loggers out. However, the tribes roam to hunt and collect food, making boundaries and outposts ineffective barriers from the modern world.

removed, the forest cut in its wake is not as easily replaced, and the subsequent link to the interior for outsiders causes its own kind of degradation.

In 2007 the Ecuadorian government launched the Yasuní-ITT Initiative under which it effectively promises to leave the oil of the vast ITT oilfield underground in exchange for some $3.6 billion of foreign money and debt relief over 13 years.

You can stay within the park's boundaries at the Napo Wildlife Center (p211) and Bataburo Lodge (p209).

# Parque Nacional Sumaco-Galeras

A smooth, paved road connects Coca to Tena, passing by this large slice of cloud forest. Conveniently, this helps avoid the need for expensive boat travel. This is commonly called the 'Loreto road,' taking its name from the town of Loreto. As the road presses west into the Andean foothills, the little-explored Parque Nacional Sumaco-Galeras offers stunning, remote wilderness.

The park consists of 2052 sq km of thick rainforest, hidden caves and cliffs. Its centerpiece is the 3732m Volcán Sumaco, which is plagued by wet weather. The volcano is currently dormant, although vulcanologists believe it could become active. It lies about 27km north of the Loreto road.

Guides are essential for any summit attempts, which involve bushwhacking along poorly marked trails. The climb takes five to six days round-trip and includes overnight stays at one of the volcano's three new *refugios* (mountain refuges). Trails are

muddy year-round, but drier between October and December.

Hire experienced guides for the climb in the village of Pacto Sumaco, 8km north of the Loreto road, for $20 to $30 per day. The Sumaco Biosphere Reserve (www.sumaco. org) can also help arrange guide services. Facilities are minimal, so bring all food and equipment.

Located 1km south of Pacto Sumaco, Wildsumaco Lodge (Map p221; ☎06-301-8343; www.wildsumaco.com; s/d incl 3 meals $147/266) at the Wildsumaco Wildlife Sanctuary makes a good base for climbing the volcano, but the lodge insists on advance reservations – so be sure to book ahead. Set on a hilltop with panoramic mountain views, a wooden house with a deck serves as a gathering spot for guests. Most come for the superb birdwatching – a unique mixture of cloud forest, foothill and Amazonian species. Rooms are simple but tasteful with wooden floors, comfy beds, hot water and electricity. A web of trails starts at the lodge, providing access to the abundance of birds and wildlife. The price includes basic guide services; specialized bird guides can be requested in advance.

A short distance away in the same sanctuary, a second lodge, Wild Sumaco Biological Station (per person from $70), became operational in early 2012. While its primary use is to house visiting researchers, when not occupied it will be available for birders on a budget, with the price including all meals. Accommodation is in four rooms with bunk beds and shared bathrooms.

The Swedish and American owners are conservation-minded and started the Río Pucuno Foundation (www.riopucunofounda tion.org) to preserve forest in the area.

THE ORIENTE PARQUE NACIONAL SUMACO-GALERAS

## Archidona

♪06

The faded pastel facades and manicured palm plaza make the sleepy village of Archidona, 10km south of Tena, an agreeable stop. Originally a mission founded in 1560 (the same year as Tena), the town has maintained its smallness and tranquility. Sundays are choice for milling around, seeing the rural folk (including indigenous Kichwa) coming to the market, and checking out the zebra-striped concrete-block church near the plaza. A few small inexpensive hotels and restaurants line the square.

About 4km north of Archidona, you'll find **Cuevas de Jumandí** (admission $1, with guide $5; ⊙9am-5pm). Best known of many cave systems in the area, it has three main branches that remain partly unexplored. Forgo the sketchy waterslides that dump into a river-water pool, and tread slowly (with a flashlight/torch) to see stalactites, stalagmites and odd formations. Rubber boots and old clothes will serve you well. For thorough exploration, you'll need a guide from Tena or on-site – ask guide companies in Tena for a customized day trip to include a trip to the caves.

The best local accommodation is excellent **Orchids Paradise Lodge** (Map p221; ♪288-9232; www.elparaisodelasorquideas.com; r per person incl 3 meals $55; ⊡⊛⊜⊛), a friendly hotel set in its own sprawling grounds just off the main road. There's a huge pool, a spacious thatched-hut restaurant-bar, and cabins with screened windows and hot water. It's very popular with Ecuadorian families at weekends, so come midweek for peace and quiet. The lodge operates a monkey-rescue program – see the results swinging in the trees – and can arrange for day trips and multiday packages, including kayaking on the Río Misahuallí, which runs past the property.

## Tena

♪06 / POP 23,300 / ELEV 518M

Unusually for a jungle transport hub, Tena is a charming place where many travelers find themselves hanging around quite happily for days before or after a trip into the rainforest. While it won't win architectural prizes anytime soon, Tena has a friendly population, a gorgeous setting surrounded by jungle-covered hills and lots of infrastructure for backpackers. White-water fanatics from around the globe come to paddle and play on the high concentration of surrounding rivers, and the town is home to lots of experienced and highly recommended kayaking operators.

The capital of Napo province, Tena was founded in 1560 and plagued by early indigenous uprisings. Jumandy, chief of the Kichwa, led a fierce but unsuccessful revolt against the Spaniards in 1578. The anniversary of the town's foundation is celebrated on November 15 with live music and community events.

### ◉ Sights & Activities

On a clear day it's sometimes possible to see Volcán Sumaco (p215) looming from the jungle 50km away. Market days are Friday and Saturday.

**Parque Amazónico**                                    ZOO
(btwn Ríos Pano & Tena; admission $2; ⊙8am-5pm)
Take the ferry across the narrow river to this 27-hectare island. There's a self-guided trail that takes you past labeled local plants and animal enclosures, including those of tapirs and monkeys. It's no substitute for the real thing, though!

**River Rafting**

Tena is Ecuador's white-water rafting center. However, mining around the town is forcing operators to take groups further and further away to find pristine stretches of river. Trips range from gentle scenic floats to exhilarating rapids and first descents in gorgeous landscapes. Serious outfitters will have everything you would expect – decent life jackets, professional guides, first-aid supplies and throw bags. Many use safety kayakers who paddle alongside the boat in case of capsizings. It's worth signing up with one of these outfits. Kayakers can hire guides or arrange for transportation and put-ins through the recommended outfits in the following section.

One of the most popular local trips is to the upper Río Napo (called Jatunyacu locally, which means 'big water' in Kichwa), where rafters tackle a fun 25km stretch of Class III+ white water, suitable for all levels. For more excitement, the Río Misahuallí has wild Class IV+ rapids and includes a portage around a waterfall.

**TOP CHOICE River People**                            RAFTING
(♪288-8384/7887;  www.riverpeoplerafting.com; cnr Calles 15 de Noviembre & 9 de Octubre) Run

by the Dent family from England, River People is a top-notch outfitter that consistently gets rave reviews. River People has been pioneering rafting on previously untried rivers throughout the region, including the remote Río Hollín, where groups of experienced rafters camp overnight in pristine rainforest. One of the most popular tours on offer is a challenging two-day expedition to the nearby Río Quijos, site of the 2005 world rafting championships. Guides have a minimum of eight years' experience and speak English. Jungle camping, kayaking instruction and tailor-made trips are possible.

### Ríos Ecuador
RAFTING

(☎288-6727; www.riosecuador.com; Tarqui) This popular outfitter offers rafting trips for all tastes. Its most popular is a $59 day trip down a 25km stretch of the upper Napo (Class III), which runs daily. Another popular trip suitable for beginners is a one day excursion to the Ríos Toachi and Blanco, which between them boast some of the longest white-water runs in Ecuador. Ask about other rivers and multiday trips as there's a huge amount on offer. All guides speak English and safety is taken very seriously.

### AguaXtreme
RAFTING

(☎288-8746; www.axtours.com; Orellana) This operator, based on the riverfront in Tena, offers trips on the Jatunyacu for $50 per person and the Misahuallí for $70, and to plenty of other destinations, including the Río Hollín. The company also offers horseback-riding, caving, kayaking and biking trips. Guides speak English.

## ☞ Tours

### Ricancie
COMMUNITY TOURS

(Indigenous Network of Upper Napo Communities for Cultural Coexistence & Ecotourism; ☎288-8479, 02-290-1493; www.ricancie.nativeweb.org; Rueda; ☺8am-6pm) This excellent initiative unites 10 disparate Kichwa communities that use ecotourism to help support their 200-odd families. It offers adventure tours, bird- and animal-watching, demonstrations of healing plants, handicrafts and cooking classes – all for $40 per day, all inclusive. Guides speak Kichwa and Spanish, but normally no English. The staff can arrange stays in multiple local villages and can offer a huge number of activities from rafting and caving to hiking and remote community visits. Drop into the friendly Tena office and ask about what's on offer.

### Agency Limoncocha
JUNGLE TOURS

(☎284-6303; limoncocha.tripod.com; Sangay 533) Run from Hostal Limoncocha (p219), this agency offers tours to nearby jungle and indigenous villages for $40 to $55 per day, as well as rafting trips. German and English are spoken.

### Amarongachi Tours
JUNGLE TOURS

(☎288-6372; www.amarongachi.com; Calle 15 de Noviembre 438) Offers various jungle excursions. During its tours ($50 per person per day) you can stay with a family in the jungle, eat local food, go for hikes, climb up beside waterfalls, pan for gold and swim in the rivers. Amarongachi also operates the lovely Amarongachi and Shangrila cabins; the latter are on a bluff 100m above Río Anzu (a tributary of Río Napo) and feature great views of the river and more-mellow activities.

## 🛏 Sleeping

### Hostal Los Yutzos
HOTEL $$

(☎288-6717; www.uchutican.com/yutzos; Rueda 190; s/d incl breakfast $24/40, with air-con $37/50; P❄🐾🛜) The rooms at this riverside gem are spacious and tasteful. There's a tiled balcony with wooden loungers, overlooking the gurgling river and the city's northern bank. The garden is thick with green and hammocks. Book ahead at the weekend and during holidays as this place is very popular with out-of-towners.

### La Casa del Abuelo
GUESTHOUSE $

(☎288-8926; www.tomas-lodge.com; Calle Mera 628; s/d/tr $20/28/42; P❄@🛜) This attractively refurbished colonial-style home with large, wooden doors and comfortable, light rooms is tucked away on a quiet street. The corridors and public areas are stuffed full of local arts and crafts, and the friendly owners can make tour arrangements. Ask the owners about their rural guesthouse on the river, 5km away.

### Hostal La Posada
GUESTHOUSE $

(☎288-7897; Rueda 280; r per person $12, without bathroom $10; P🛜) This great value family-run place offers an array of spotless, simple fan-cooled rooms right on the riverside. Most rooms have desks, as well as hot running water. More rooms and a social area are in the pipeline.

### Welcome Break Hostal
HOSTEL $

(☎288-6301; Rueda 331; dm per person $8, d $30; P@🛜) This pleasant family-run hostel is

# Tena

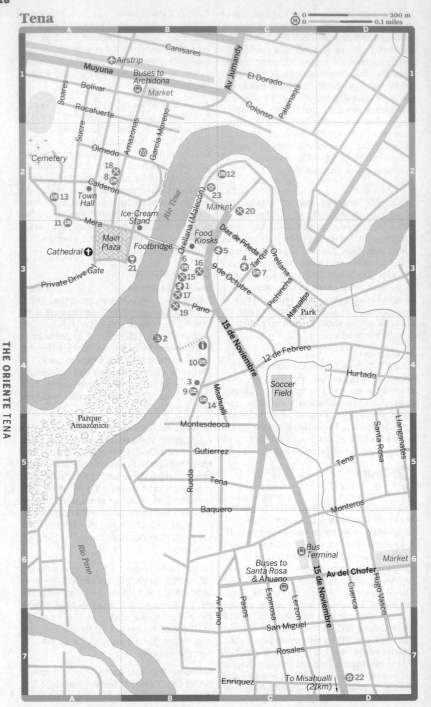

# Tena

spotless and is favored by local volunteers when they come to Tena to recharge their batteries. Most rooms are dorms, sleeping up to six people, though doubles and twins (both with and without private bathrooms) are available. There's a basic kitchen for guests to use, and the location is quiet, despite being in the center of town.

**Brisa del Río**  HOSTEL $$
(☎288-6444; Orellana; r per person $15, with shared bathroom $8; P❀🛜) Friendly owners, a great location on the river just moments to many backpacker haunts, and light, spacious rooms have made this riverfront place a popular choice. Shared bathrooms are very clean, while rooms with private bathrooms also have air-con.

**Hotel Pumarosa**  HOTEL $$
(☎287-0311; Orellana; s/d/tr $30/35/45; P❀🛜🏊) Inviting rooms have high wooden ceilings, large armoires and modern white-tiled bathrooms. There is reliable hot water, cable TV, lush gardens and billiards in the open-air lobby. The disco and roller-rink next door mean loud Friday and Saturday nights, but, on the plus side, guests enjoy free entry.

**Hostal Limoncocha**  HOSTEL $
(☎284-6303; limoncocha@andinanet.net; Av De Chofer; r per person $8, with shared bathroom $8; @🛜) Backpackers frequent this spot on the hill, 300m southeast from the bus station. Rooms are chipper, with hand-painted murals and clean private bathrooms. Breakfast

($2.50) is available, and there's a guest kitchen and on-site tour operator. Limoncocha also offers recommended kayaking tours.

**Hotel Cristian's Palace**  HOTEL $$
(☎288-6047; Mera; s/d incl breakfast $31/62; P❀🛜🏊) This place is on the large side by local standards, but it's friendly, family-run and perfectly welcoming. Rooms are spacious with good bathrooms, TV and writing tables in most, and surround a rather murky pool, a sauna and gym, which are all free for guests to use.

**Hostal Austria**  GUESTHOUSE $
(☎288-7205; Tarqui; r per person $12; P❀🛜) In the center of town, but on a quiet side street so you avoid the traffic noise, this large gated house has tiled, spotless rooms and Adirondack chairs. Some rooms have air-con, while others are fan cooled, and collections of coins and keys deck the communal areas.

**Hostal Canela**  HOTEL $
(☎288-6081; canelahostal@yahoo.com; cnr Amazonas & Calderón; r per person $12; P🛜) This very well maintained and spotlessly clean hotel has spacious, bright rooms with plaid bedspreads. Large windows overlook two busy streets and all rooms have TVs.

**Cotococha Lodge**  JUNGLE LODGE $$$
(Map p221; ☎02-223-4336; www.cotococha.com; per person all inclusive 3/4 nights $265/435) Located 17km from Tena along the southern shores of the Río Napo, a quiet collection of 22 thatched-roofed bungalows are connect-

ed by winding river-rock pathways in a lush setting. Oil lanterns create a romantic glow and cabins have fresh linens, hot water and private decks overlooking the river. Guests relax in wicker chairs around a fire pit after dinner. English-speaking guides lead walks and trips to waterfalls; tubing, rafting and visits to local communities can be arranged. It's a good way to get into the rainforest without having to take a long river trip.

## ✗ Eating

**TOP CHOICE El Vagabundo**                    MEXICAN $

(Orellana; mains $5-10; ⏰5pm-midnight Mon-Sat) This new and very welcome addition to Tena's dining scene is run by a friendly and multilingual German who keeps the locals happy at the bar. Meanwhile, his cook does an excellent job with modern Mexican (and the odd bit of German) cuisine. There's a garden to one side for alfresco dining, and there's a popular book exchange.

**Café Tortuga**                    INTERNATIONAL $

(Orellana; snacks $1.50-5; ⏰7:30am-9pm Tue-Sat, to 12.30pm Sun & Mon; 📶) Everyone in town seems to drop by this super-popular Swiss-run riverfront joint, whether it's for its wide choice of breakfasts, its cappuccino, its delicious *batidos* (fruit shakes) or its range of salads, sandwiches and cakes. Tortuga is especially popular with backpackers, and is a great place to meet other travelers or to catch up on the buzz in town after you've been in the jungle.

**Marquis Grille**          STEAKHOUSE, GRILL $$$

(📞288-6513; Amazonas 251; mains $9-22; ⏰noon-10pm Mon-Sat, to 6pm Sun) With a locked front door opened by formally attired staff, classical music and attentive service, this is the most formal restaurant for miles around. Browse the Chilean wine list, then choose from steamed tilapia, rich pastas and lobster. The whole feel may be rather faux-typical and aimed at tour groups, but the food is some of the best in town.

**Pizzería Hilton**                    PIZZERIA $$

(Calle 15 de Noviembre 195; pizzas $4-15; ⏰4-11pm) You'll find the best pizza in town at this friendly place on the main road. It's a family operation, and there's a huge choice of toppings and sizes. It's always bustling with locals and travelers alike, and you can also take away.

**Cositas Ricas**                    ECUADORIAN $

(Calle 15 de Noviembre; mains $4-8; ⏰7:30am-9:30pm) This rather unexciting-looking place nevertheless serves up a decent range of vegetarian and Ecuadorian plates, salads and fresh juices on the main drag.

**Pizzería Bella Selva**                    PIZZERIA $$

(Malecón; mains $2.50-18; ⏰5-10pm) This thatched-hut pizzeria on the Malecón serves heavily loaded cheesy pizzas and large piles of pasta. It's very popular with families, but it's not quite as good as Pizzería Hilton.

## 🍷 Drinking & Entertainment

The dance floors pulse on the weekends, so slip into the mix. Discos open from approximately 8pm to 2am Sunday to Wednesday, and to about 3am Thursday to Saturday.

**La Araña Bar Coctelería**                    BAR

(Main plaza; ⏰5pm-midnight Mon-Thu, to 2am Fri & Sat) The most popular place for drinking and carousing is the raucous 'spider,' across the river at the end of the footbridge. It's busy nightly, but is always packed with locals and travelers on the weekend. Expect a hangover.

**Discoteca La Galera**                    DISCO

(Orellana; admission $2) Found next to Hotel Pumarosa, La Galera has a fun but grown-up atmosphere, even though there's an attached roller-rink. Hotel guests enter for free.

**Discoteca Canambo**                    DISCO

(cnr Enriquez & Calle 15 de Noviembre; admission $2) At this student favorite, descend onto the mirrored dance floor for a bump-and-grind to Latin rhythms.

## ℹ Information

**Hospital** (📞288-6305) South of town on the road to Puerto Napo.

**Post office** (cnr Olmedo & Moreno) Northwest of the footbridge.

**Tourism office** (📞288-8046; Rueda; ⏰7am-5pm Mon-Fri) The friendly staff here will do their best to help you with whatever you need. Some staff members speak basic English.

## ℹ Getting There & Away

The **bus terminal** (15 de Noviembre) is at the southern end of town. Numerous daily departures go to Quito ($6, five hours) via Baeza, and to Coca ($7, six hours). Multiple daily departures go to Puyo ($2.50, three hours), Baños ($4, five hours) and Ambato ($5, six hours). Jumandy has a night bus to Lago Agrio ($7, eight hours). Café

Tortuga (p220) keeps a very useful complete list of current bus times.

### ℹ️ Getting Around

Local buses to Archidona ($0.25, 15 minutes) leave about every half-hour during the day from the west side of the market. Other local buses leave from 15 de Noviembre, near the terminal, to Ahuano ($1.20, one hour), Misahuallí ($0.75, 45 minutes) and Santa Rosa/San Pedro ($3, three hours).

## Misahuallí

♪ 06

Once an important transit point for travelers arriving by river from Coca, Misahuallí (mee-sah-wah-yee) sank into obscurity when the Loreto road connecting Coca to Tena was built. Positioned between two major rivers – at the literal end of the road – the town has a lovely sandy beach, a famous cadre of monkeys adept at swiping sunglasses from visitors, and little else. However, a new airport and a cacao processing plant are currently being built.

The surrounding area has been colonized for decades, which means wildlife has diminished greatly, although the town still makes a good alternative base to Tena for exploring the Río Napo.

### 👁️ Sights & Activities

**Cascada Las Latas**                                   WATERFALL

Misahuallí's most enjoyable sight is some way outside the town, but it's well worth spending a few hours to do the return riverside walk, which takes you through the rainforest. Take a Misahuallí–Puerto Napo bus and ask the driver to drop you at Río Latas, about 15 or 20 minutes from Misahuallí. All the drivers know *el camino a las cascadas* (the trail to the falls). Follow the river upstream to the falls, which takes an hour, passing several swimming holes en route. Be prepared to wade.

**Butterfly Farm**                                             ZOO

(Centro de Reproducción de Mariposas; admission $2.50; ⏰ 8:30am-5pm) Dazzling giant Morphos butterflies flutter about this fascinating place on the grounds of Hamadryade Lodge. It's run by Pepe and Margarita of Ecoselva (p222) and offers a close look at the developing stages of rainforest butterflies. The farm also takes volunteers, who pay $300 per month for food and board while working to maintain and run the farm.

## Around Tena 🧭

## Around Tena

**◎ Sights**

1 AmaZOOnico..................................... B2

**🛏️ Sleeping**

2 Arajuno Jungle Lodge....................... B2
3 Cabañas Aliñahui ............................... A2
4 Cabanas San Isidro............................. A1
5 Casa de Doña Maruja......................... B2
6 Cotacocha Lodge................................ A2
7 Hamadryade Lodge ........................... A2
8 La Casa del Suizo.............................. B2
Liana Lodge ................................(see 1)
9 Orchids Paradise Lodge..................... A1
10 Wildsumaco Lodge............................ A1
11 Yachana Lodge.................................. B2

**Chocolate Jungle**                   EDUCATIONAL CENTER

(♪ 08-079-1602; www.ecuadorjunglechocolate.com) Just downriver from Misahuallí you'll find Chocolate Jungle, a cacao plantation that's the personal project of Canadian expat Elizabeth Hendley (who now makes this slice of the rainforest home). The 20-hectare site on the Río Napo boasts three museums – one devoted to cacao, another to wild mushrooms and a third to snakes – and a full-day tour of the premises ($45 per person including transport and lunch) includes a demonstration of how to make chocolate, a visit to an indigenous village and a hike through the rainforest. There's also accommodation available – the center sleeps up to 20 people ($10 per person) in functional bunks. A tour of the plantation alone is $10. Call ahead to arrange a canoe transfer from Misahuallí.

THE ORIENTE M SAHUALLÍ

## ☞ Tours

Most travelers book tours in Quito, but it's possible to get good deals in Misahuallí: you'll find an accommodating guide (and price) far more quickly if you already have four or more people together when you arrive – however, stick to licensed guides and recommended outfits, as there are many amateurs who will approach you in the main plaza.

**Teorumi** ECOTOURS
(☏289-0313; tours per day $60; www.teorumi.com) Working with local indigenous communities, Teorumi is a good choice for anyone interested in native culture as well as wildlife. Tours can be tailored to fit your interests, though most feature bird-watching, fishing, medicinal plant demonstrations and jungle hikes. Other activities include panning for gold and horseback-riding. English and French are spoken.

**Douglas Clarke's Expeditions** JUNGLE TOURS
(☏289-0085; tours per day $35-50; douglasclarke expediciones@yahoo.com) This longtime operator offers one- to 10-day tours with native guides and boat trips for wildlife-watching that work out quite cheaply. Most overnight trips involve camping, and basic English is spoken.

**Ecoselva** ECOTOURS
(☏09-815-0532, 289-0019; tours per day from $45; ecoselva@yahoo.es) Pepe Tapia González takes visitors on fun one- to 10-day tours with overnight stays at his rustic lodge or jungle camps. He speaks fluent English, has a biology background and is knowledgeable about plants, birds and insects. Located on the Plaza.

**Selva Verde** ECOTOURS
(☏289-0165; www.selvaverde-misahualli.com; tours per day $40-60) Luís Zapata, an English-speaking guide with years of experience in the region, runs this recommended tour agency that has an office on the main square. He specializes in river trips and visits to indigenous villages.

**Runawa Tours** ECOTOURS
(☏289-0031; tours per day from $35; www.misa hualliamazon.com) This agency on the main square offers nocturnal jungle tours, tubing and rafting trips, bird-watching and river tours.

## ☰ Sleeping & Eating

You'll find plenty of cheap lodgings, especially on the main square, where a handful of restaurants serve Ecuadorian fare.

TOP CHOICE **Hamadryade Lodge** BOUTIQUE HOTEL $$$
(Map p221; ☏08-590-9992; www.hamadryade -lodge.com; s/d per person incl breakfast & dinner $230/275; P🌐🏊) Perched on a jungle hillside just outside Misahuallí, this ambitiously stylish yet ecofriendly French-owned lodge departs from the standard jungle lodge look with sleek, contemporary decor. Each private bungalow has its own balcony with gorgeous jungle views; there's a fantastic pool and lounging area perfectly perched over the rolling landscape; and traditional massage is also available. With just five bungalows, this a great place to chill out in style. The deluxe bungalow, which sleeps up to six people, is perfect for families.

**Hotel El Paisano** GUESTHOUSE $$
(☏289-0027; hotelelpaisano@yahoo.com; Riva deneyra; per person incl breakfast $18; P🌐🏊) This popular traveler haunt is one of the more charming places in town, with bright and spacious rooms, wooden floors, mosquito nets and a pool (which was under construction on our last visit). Other perks include laundry service, good coffee served at breakfast and a book exchange.

**France Amazonia** GUESTHOUSE $$
(☏289-0009; www.france-amazonia.com; Av Principal; s/d incl breakfast $24/36; P🌐🏊) Located just outside of town on the lip of the river, shady thatched huts surround a sparkling pool and sandy fire pit. Beds are small but rooms are pleasantly rustic. The garden offers plenty of nooks for enjoying the pleasant climate and sound of the river – the river itself can be accessed via a small trail.

**Hostería Misahuallí** HOTEL $$$
(☏289-0063; www.hosteriamisahualli.com; r per person without/with 3 meals $85/57; 🌐🏊) A fussy, manicured version of a jungle camp, this hotel has a resort feel and is popular with Ecuadorian families. It has a great position overlooking the river and Misahuallí (from which you have to take the complementary canoe to get here), but it's far more for relaxation and family fun than jungle tourism. New hotel-style rooms are sophisticated and cool, while the stilted cabins are rather aged.

### Hostal Shaw
HOSTEL **$**

(☎289-0019; r per person $8; ☎) Run by Ecoselva (p222), this friendly *hostal* on the plaza has simple rooms with fans, mosquito nets and private bathrooms with hot water. You'll find espresso and a good book exchange at the downstairs cafe, as well as morning pancakes and vegetarian dishes.

### Restaurant Doña Gloria
ECUADORIAN **$**

(Main square; mains $5-6; ☺7.30am-8pm Tue-Sun) The fanciest place to eat in town, Doña Gloria has white tablecloths, a wooden bar and bamboo walls. It serves a selection of breakfasts as well as *churrasco* (steak served with a fried egg) and fried tilapia.

### Restaurant Runawa
ECUADORIAN **$**

(Riverside; mains $5-6; ☺7am-9pm) Between the main square and the riverfront is this very pleasant place, housed in a makeshift treehouse-style structure. The menu includes shrimp, tilapia, chicken and beef dishes.

## ℹ Information

There is no bank or post office in Misahuallí. Carry your passport on buses, boats and tours in the region, and have a stash of small bills for boat travel.

## ℹ Getting There & Away

Buses leave from the plaza approximately every hour during daytime; the last bus is at 6pm. The main destination is Tena ($1, one hour). There's a daily 8.30am bus to Quito ($6, five hours) that leaves from the main square.

The need for passenger canoes has dried up thanks to the Tena–Coca (Loreto) road and others along the Río Napo. You can arrange trips with boat drivers on the beach for about $40 per hour, but nearby agencies offer better deals.

## Upper Río Napo
☑06

The Río Napo rushes northeast from Misahuallí toward Coca, gaining breadth as it passes nature reserves, small jungle communities, oil rigs and lodges. Unfortunately, road construction has altered wildlife habits for good, and visitors will see fewer animals and birds here now than in the past.

### RESERVA BIOLÓGICA JATUN SACHA & CABAÑAS ALIÑAHUI

This 2500-hectare biological station and rainforest reserve is located on the south side of Río Napo, 23km east of Puerto Napo. It is run by **Fundación Jatun Sacha** (☎02-243-2240; www.jatunsacha.org), an Ecuadorian nonprofit organization, which was formed to promote rainforest research, conservation and education.

With neighboring areas being rapidly cleared for logging and agriculture, the biodiversity of Jatun Sacha seems precious. Besides counting and tracking local species, the foundation develops reforestation initiatives and agro-forestry alternatives with local farming communities and indigenous groups.

Biostation workers and other guests stay in **Cabañas Aliñahui** (Map p221; ☎02-227-4947; www.ecuadoramazonlodge.com; r per person incl 3 meals $60) high up on a bluff inside the reserve with views of the twisting river basin. Situated amid a 2-hectare tropical garden, hammocks hang under eight stilted, rustic cabins with detached, shared bathrooms that have solar-heated water. The restaurant serves healthy Ecuadorian and international meals. Go bird-watching or meander through the surrounding forest, then check out the plant conservation center and botanical garden. There are discounts for groups and students.

To get to Jatun Sacha or Cabañas Aliñahui from Tena, take an Ahuano or Santa Rosa bus and ask the driver to drop you at either entrance. Aliñahui is about 3km east of the Jatun Sacha research station, or 27km east of Tena on the road to Santa Rosa.

### AHUANO

Uniformed schoolchildren skip through the puddles and dogs sleep in the road in this tiny village, a half-hour downriver from Misahuallí. Ahuano is the end of the road from Tena – buses arrive at La Punta on the other side of the river, and then you can cross by canoe to the village.

Friendly **Casa de Doña Maruja** (Map p221; ☎09-032-3182, 06-285-0094; r per person with/without 3 meals $10/5) offers bare-bones rooms with split-plank floors beside the swift river in Ahuano. Bathrooms are shared and meals are on the patio with the friendly family. A canoe can be rented for excursions. This is a great chance to really get to know locals, feel part of the community and explore the local rainforest in a low-key fashion, a world away from staying in a big rainforest lodge.

Most visitors come to stay at **La Casa del Suizo** (Map p221; ☎02-250-9504; www.lacasadelsuizo.com; s/d per person incl meals $99/115; ❅❄), a walled fortress from the outside, and a surprisingly typical-looking resort on the inside. A maze of covered boardwalks links thatched hotel-style rooms that have high-ceilings, pale adobe walls, electricity, fans, hot showers, and balconies with a hammock overlooking the river. More modern, far more comfortable but less charming new cabañas are nearing completion in late 2011, and plans are to modernize the entire place soon (including constructing a new pool and installing air-con throughout) – this is most likely to result in the loss of the last traces of the jungle experience. Buffet meals are seated in the barnlike restaurant and people with kids will feel very welcome here. However, it's about as far as you can get from your typical jungle experience, so don't come here with that as your goal.

Included in the daily rate are meals, and excursions with Spanish-speaking guides that include river trips, jungle hikes, community and mission visits, access to an on-site butterfly house, and wildlife walks.

Guests pay $60 per boatload for canoe transport from Misahuallí. For independent travelers, bus services from Tena run eight times a day to La Punta, about 28km east of Puerto Napo on the south side of Río Misahuallí. Although the bus doesn't actually go to Ahuano, it's called the Ahuano bus because most passengers transfer in dugout canoes across the river to Ahuano. Boats are frequent and cost $10 per boat to La Casa del Suizo.

## AMAZOONICO & LIANA LODGE

You're guaranteed to see all manner of jungle wildlife at excellent AmaZOOnico (Map p221; ☑288-7304; www.amazoonico.org; adult/child $3.50/2.50), a popular animal rehabilitation center. The center is located on the grounds of Selva Viva, a 1500-hectare reserve of primary forest on Río Arajuno, a narrow tributary of the Napo about 3km east of Ahuano. A Swiss/Kichwa couple founded the center in 1995 to care for confiscated or displaced rainforest animals, from toucans and capybaras to monkeys and boa constrictors.

While it's great to be able to see these animals close up, the circumstances belie an ugly reality. These animals have been displaced because illegal traffickers sold them for quick cash or their habitats were destroyed. Some of the stories you'll hear from the excellent tours are heartbreaking – animals abandoned in hotel rooms, rare birds whose irresponsible owners died, and severely traumatized 'pets' intercepted during trafficking attempts. Some healthy animals are released back into

the rainforest, but an unfortunate number of animals arrive here too domesticated to be re-released.

Bilingual volunteers, who know the animals intimately, lead all tours. The center is always looking for volunteers (who must pay $125 per month for living expenses), especially veterinarians, for a two-month-minimum stay.

At nearby Liana Lodge (Map p221; ☑09-980-0463; www.lianaolodge.ec; per person 2/3/4 nights $154/252/344), eight cabins are scattered throughout a forested hillside. Each has crafty touches, such as bamboo beds and hand-carved clothes hangers built with left-over wood from road building. Cabins have two double rooms, a hot shower and no electricity. The carefree riverside atmosphere revolves around bonfires, walks through the woods and a round bar overlooking the river with gorgeous views of the jungle. Packages include meals, tours (including lessons on making *chicha* – a fermented corn or yuca drink – and building a balsa raft) and canoe transport from Puerto Barantilla. Ask also about Runi Huasi, a nearby indigenous-run lodge that's managed by the Liana owners. Kichwa, English, Spanish, German and French are spoken at both lodges.

To reach AmaZOOnico, Liana Lodge or Runi Huasi, take a Tena bus to Santa Rosa ($2, one hour) and get off at Puerto Barantilla. Walk down the dirt road to the river, to a spot frequented by transport canoes – a trip to any of the three should cost you $2.

## ARAJUNO JUNGLE LODGE

If small and out of the way is your thing, check out former Peace Corps volunteer Thomas Larson's Arajuno Jungle Lodge (Map p221; ☑08-268-2287; www.arajuno.com; r per person 2 nights $200), slung in a bend of the Río Arajuno. A handful of hillside cabins are snug and screened and have solar-powered hot water. The thatched main lodge has a sprawling wooden deck and dining area perched over the river. Guests can roam the 80 hectares of forest, hike, canoe and visit the nearby AmaZOOnico.

The lodge works with local communities to develop new food sources and spread information about health and nutrition. Volunteers are accepted for stays of three to six months. The chef cooks up locally inspired gourmet food, such as smoked *cachama maitos* (fish grilled in palm leaves) and *tortilla de yuca* (cassava bread). Grown-up kids

## CHICHA, THE BREAKFAST OF CHAMPIONS

Before you could get a Coke and a smile in the Amazon Basin, there was *chicha* – not the boiled highland version, but a highly portable nutritional drink. Stored as a paste wrapped in leaves, *chicha* materializes when you add water.

The recipe is simple – *chicha* is yuca (cassava) or chonta palm masticated by women (yes, just women). For millennia, *chicha* has been a prime source of nutrition and vitamins for remote communities. It's an important staple in the jungle, where people eat very little and drink up to 6L a day. When fresh, *chicha* tastes mild and yogurtlike, but as time passes, it becomes more alcoholic as bacteria from the saliva turns carbohydrates into simple sugars. The older the *chicha*, the more potent it is. The flavor depends on who made the stuff; each woman's bacteria creates a distinctive taste.

Really terrible *chicha* is considered a portent of something bad – but will something bad happen to you, the visitor, if you try it? Contrary to what you might think, problems result not from the saliva, but from unfiltered river water that may have been mixed with the paste. However, very few people experience trouble after tasting just a sip. A highlight of many visits to local communities in Oriente is being able to see *chicha* being made and tasting it afterwards, too. Enjoy!

will love the rope swing that launches into the river. Services are bilingual.

### YACHANA LODGE

Set on a scenic bend in the Río Napo, **Yachana Lodge** (Map p221; ☎02-252-3777; www.yachana.com; bunkhouse/r per person incl all meals $195/120; ☎) offers guests a chance to experience 'geotourism' – tourism that sustains an environment, culture and its people – at its finest.

Located halfway between Misahuallí and Coca, a campus of stilted wooden buildings, groomed grounds and colorful gardens is upriver from the tiny community of Mondaña. The lodge has 18 rooms, which includes three cabins with a double and a triple room. Rooms have modern bathrooms with hot and potable tap water (the septic system can even accommodate toilet paper, a rarity in Ecuador), a balcony with hammock, and solar-powered electricity. The kitchen serves delicious, mostly vegetarian meals in an open, covered dining area overlooking the river. In addition, there's a conference center, library and internet access.

Guests visit the adjacent community, where fees from the lodge help fund a high school for rural, mestizo (mixed indigenous and Spanish descent) and indigenous kids, and a medical center. Other daytime activities include hiking, bird-watching, participating in a traditional healing ceremony, swimming and touring nearby protected forest in a *chiva*. Shuar and Kichwa indigenous guides speak English and provide treasure troves of information about the

forest. A new culinary program funded by the National Geographic Society lets visitors harvest and cook local, native foods. Costs include all meals and guide services, with optional additional airfare from Quito to Coca. From Coca, it's a 2½-hour motorized canoe ride upriver to the lodge.

## Puyo

☎03 / POP 35,000

A lazy river slinks through this concrete outpost, the informal dividing point between the northern and southern Oriente. Part mellow jungle town and part commercial, government hub, Puyo retains some vitality as the capital of the Pastaza province, but overall, it's just a built-up town with little to attract you. However, anyone traveling in southern Oriente is quite likely to pass through here. Dense green jungle flourishes close around the town's edges, and jagged snowcapped mountains rise in the distance. It is also a good starting point for reaching indigenous villages.

**Fiestas de Fundación de Puyo**, the weeklong celebration of Puyo's founding, take place in early May.

### ⊙ Sights & Activities

**Parque Omaere**                                    PARK
(www.fundacionomaere.org; admission $3, adult/student $3/1.50; ⊙9am-5pm Tue-Sun) Less than 1km north of the city center, this ethnobotanical park offers one- to two-hour guided tours (free with admission) of rainforest plants and

# Puyo

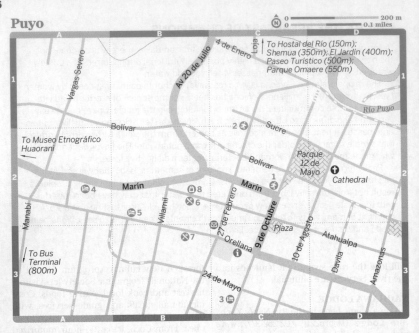

## Puyo

###  Activities, Courses & Tours

### 🛏 Sleeping

### ✗ Eating

### 🛍 Shopping

indigenous dwellings, by mostly indigenous guides. The park is run by Shuar plant expert Teresa Shiki and her husband, Chris Canaday. Chris is an American biologist, author of *Common Birds of Amazonian Ecuador* and a font of knowledge about everything from jungle plants to ecological dry toilets. Teresa helped found and plant the park and prepares natural medicine. Stomach troubles? Ask for a cure for parasites made from local fruits, seeds and sap.

Get here by following Loja north of town for about 500m until you reach the bridge over the river, then follow the sign. A pleasant trail (called the *paseo turístico*) continues past Omaere for 1.7km along the river to the Puyo–Tena road, where you can flag down a bus back to town every 20 minutes, or return along the trail.

**Volcán El Altar**　　　　　　　　　VOLCANO
Early risers may see the jagged white teeth of Volcán El Altar (5319m), the fifth-highest mountain in Ecuador, about 50km southwest. On clear days look southwest to see **Volcán Sangay** (5230m).

**Jardín Botáncio las
Orquídeas**　　　　　　　　　BOTANIC GARDEN
(☎288-4855; admission $5; ☺8am-6pm) Visitors rave about this privately run botanical garden, located 15 minutes south from Puyo on the road to Macas. Enthusiastic owner Omar Taeyu guides visitors through hills of lush foliage and fish ponds to see gorgeous plants and countless rare orchids. Call ahead to let them know you're coming.

**Museo Etnográfico Huaorani**　　　MUSEUM
(☎288-6148; Severo Vargas; admission $3; ☺10am-5pm) This recently built museum has a small exhibit and guided tour. Perhaps

more engaging than the artifacts themselves is the Huaorani's take on their culture and problems. Upstairs is Onhae, the political body of the Huaorani, which can help arrange visits to communities.

### ☞ Tours

**Madre Selva Tours** ECOTOURS
(☎289-9572; www.madreselvaecuador.com; cnr Marín & Calle 9 de Octubre; day trips per person from $40) Operates one- to five-day tours to visit local communities, raft, tube, hike and more. The tours get good reviews, guides speak English and overall good value for money is offered.

**Papangu-Atacapi Tours** COMMUNITY TOURS
(☎288-7684; papanguturismo@yahoo.es; cnr Calle 27 de Febrero & Sucre; tours per day from $40) An indigenous-run agency with a focus on community tourism. Trips go to Sarayaku and Mango Wasi (Kichwa communities) and Cueva de los Tuyos (Shuar). Guides are indigenous and speak Spanish and Kichwa, and some of the fees go to participating communities. Highly recommended by readers.

### 🛏 Sleeping

**TOP CHOICE** **El Jardín** GUESTHOUSE $$
(☎288-7770; Paseo Turístico, Barrio Obrero; r per person incl breakfast $38; P@🛰) This welcoming spot is Puyo's most charming hotel. It's just across the footbridge by the entrance to the Parque Omaere, some way from the center of town. It's a gorgeous place that feels more like a jungle lodge than a city hotel, with the 10 rooms housed in a wooden building on two floors and decorated with local arts and crafts. The namesake garden is as magnificent as you'd expect, and there's a superb restaurant. Luxuries, such as massage and a hot tub, are also available.

**Gran Hotel Amazónico** HOTEL $$
(☎288-3094; www.site.granhotelamazonico.com; Atahualpa; r per person incl breakfast $17; P@🛰) Right in the center of town, this smart, modern place caters to a business crowd with simple but comfortable rooms, wooden furniture and splashes of contemporary style. It's a good deal, though there can be some road noise in the rooms looking out front.

**Hostería Turingia** GUESTHOUSE $$
(☎288-6344; www.hosteriaturingia.com; Marín 294; s/d $25/40; P🛰🏊) This walled, Tyrolean outpost looks something like the set from *Heidi*, making for a weird but not unpleasant place to bed down in the center of Puyo. The somewhat overpriced rooms are on the dark side and bedding is rather ancient, but the cabins scattered around the manicured grounds are undeniably cute. There's also a full service restaurant here.

**Hostal del Río** GUESTHOUSE $
(☎288-6090; cnr Loja & Cañar; r per person incl breakfast $12) This rather classy place just on the way out of the town center has a wide range of rooms from twins to six-berth dorms surrounding an oversized indoor dining space. Upstairs rooms have balconies and access to a roof terrace.

**Hostal Mexico** HOTEL $
(☎288-5668; btwn Ortiz & Calle 24 de Mayo; r per person $12; 🛰) Parquetry floors and dark interior rooms are forgettable (although it's hard to forget some of the strange, carpeted walls), but overall the rooms are fine, with TV, hot water and fans. Only some rooms have private bathroom.

**Hotel Libertad** HOTEL $
(☎288-3282; cnr Orellana & Manzano; r per person $7) This tranquil spot offers cramped but spotless rooms, hot water and TV. There's no wi-fi and you'll have to go elsewhere to find food or charm, but, at this price, it's a great deal.

### 🍴 Eating

Try the riverside cafes for a typical dish of *ceviche boquetero*, which is literally 'dumptruck ceviche' - a combination of toasted corn kernels and banana chips with a can of tuna elegantly dumped on top.

**TOP CHOICE** **El Jardín** ECUADORIAN $$
(☎288-7770; Paseo Turístico, Barrio Obrero; mains $8-15; ⏰noon-4pm & 6-10pm Mon-Sat; 🛰) The best food in the Oriente may be at this ambient house by the river inside the charming hotel of the same name. The award-winning chef-owner Sofía prepares fragrant *pollo ishpingo* (cinnamon chicken – *ishpingo* is a type of cinnamon native to the Oriente); its decadent, delicate flavors awake the palate. Try the *lomo plancho* (grilled steak) for a tender, perfectly cooked slab among artfully arranged vegetables, or one of the vegetarian, fresh fish or seafood dishes.

## BUSES FROM PUYO

| DESTINATION | COST (US$) | DURATION (HR) |
|---|---|---|
| Ambato | 2.90 | 2½ |
| Baños | 1.90 | 1½ |
| Coca | 9 | 9 |
| Guayquil | 9 | 8 |
| Macas | 5.60 | 4 |
| Quito | 5.60 | 5½ |
| Tena | 2.90 | 2½ |

**Shemua**  FRENCH $$
(Barrio Obrero; mains $6-15; ☺10am-9.30pm Mon-Sat) This new place opposite El Jardín by the river serves up 'franco-amazonian' cuisine in a friendly, family-run environment. There's a full gastronomic menu for $25, or a cheaper *menú del día* (daily set menu) for $5.

**El Fariseo**  INTERNATIONAL $
(Atahualpa; mains $3-7; ☺7am-10pm Mon-Fri, 8am-10pm Sat; 🐾) It may not look like much, but this cafe has an espresso machine and serves up surprisingly delicious fare, including a very tasty *churrasco* (steak served with a fried egg). Burritos, burgers and steaks round out the menu.

**Pizzeria Buon Giorno**  PIZZERIA $
(☎288-3841; Orellana; mains $5-10; ☺3-11pm) One of the few decent restaurants in the town center, this simple place offers freshly made pizzas, lasagna and salads. It also delivers.

### 🔒 Shopping

**Waorani**  CRAFT
(Asociacion De Mujeres Waorani De La Amazonia Ecuatoriana; Atahualpa; ☺7:30am-1pm & 2-7:30pm Mon-Sat, 7:30am-2pm Sun) Sells artisanal crafts made by Waorani women, including jewelly, spears, hammocks, blowguns and palm string bags. Artisans receive a portion of every sale.

### ℹ Information

**iTur** (☎288-5937; Orellana; ☺8:30am-12:30pm & 3-6pm Mon-Fri) Inside the town hall, the tourist office provides regional maps and information about jungle tours.

**Post office** (Calle 27 de Febrero) Northwest of the market.

**Voz Andes Mission Hospital** (☎279-5172; Shell) American-owned and staffed. The best medical services in the area.

### ℹ Getting There & Away

The bus terminal is about 1km southwest of town. See the boxed text for journey details to various destinations.

### ℹ Getting Around

A taxi ride from downtown to the bus terminal costs $1, as should all rides within the city. Small local buses go to Shell ($0.25) every 30 minutes or so from south of the market along Calle 27 de Febrero.

# THE SOUTHERN ORIENTE

The southern Oriente may be the envy of its northern sister, with the southern area being wilder and more pristine. Rivers snake through vast jungle dotted with tiny indigenous settlements and no roads. Inaccessibility remains, for the most part, because of a lack of industry, although mining and oil exploration may change all that in the future. Most visitors come to see indigenous tribes, an adventurous pursuit that usually involves few creature comforts – the tourism industry has yet to bloom.

## Macas

☎07 / POP 14,000

The provincial capital of Morona-Santiago, Macas is the bustling crossroads of the southern Oriente, serving as a jumping-off point for tours into the least-explored corners of the Ecuadorian rainforest. Here you'll see men from nearby Shuar and Achuar territories wearing traditional beads over Nike T-shirts, while glass-and-concrete hotels rise above colonial-era homes.

### ⊙ Sights & Activities

**Our Lady of Macas Cathedral**  CHURCH
The town's most obvious sight is its cathedral, where a Technicolor virgin looms over the manicured plaza. Inside, a tranquil, column-free space draws attention to the tiled altar depicting a peaceful Macas in front of a bellowing volcano. Miracles are attributed to the painting of the Virgin of Macas (c 1592) on the altar.

# Macas

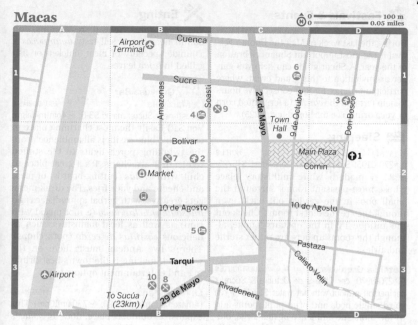

## Volcán Sangay
VOLCANO

The perfect snow-covered cone of Volcán Sangay (5230m), some 40km to the north-west, can be glimpsed on a clear day. It's Ecuador's seventh-highest mountain and one of the world's most active volcanoes; early missionaries construed it as hell.

## Tours

Macas is the place to book trips into the southern Oriente, but services are not as comprehensive here as those in the north. Be aware that the Shuar do not want unguided visitors in their villages; certain villages refuse visitors entirely. It's therefore essential to travel with a professional guide who can arrange access and is sensitive to the Shuar's stance on tourism.

### Tsuirim Viajes
JUNGLE TOURS

(270-1681; leosalgado18@hotmail.com; cnr Don Bosco & Sucre; tours per person per day $30-60) Offering a range of jungle tours, including community visits to the Shuar, shamanic rituals, canyoning, tubing and jungle-trekking.

### Yacu Amu Rafting
RAFTING

(02-290-4054; www.yacuamu.com; tours per person per day $40-80) Runs five-day trips through Río Upano's wild Namangosa Gorge, whose magnificent scenery comes from high waterfalls. The Class III/IV white water is suitable for kayakers.

### Planeta Tours
JUNGLE TOURS

(270-1328; www.planetaselva.travel; cnr Comín & Soasti; multiday trips per day $45-75) Offers cultural tours in Shuar territory, waterfall hikes, fishing, white-water rafting on the Río Upano, and canoeing. Some English is spoken.

## ✦ Festivals & Events

**Chonta Festival**  INDIGENOUS CELEBRATION
During the last week of May, the Chonta Festival is the most important Shuar celebration of the year. A Shuar guide can help you garner an invitation to this grand event, where participants dance for four consecutive hours to help ferment the *chicha* (a fermented corn or yuca drink; see the boxed text, p225).

## 🛏 Sleeping

**Hostal Casa Blanca**  HOTEL $
(✆270-0195; Soasti; s/d incl breakfast $15/25; 📶🗷) A modern white multistory place whose most-pleasant rooms surround the small pool in the garden out back, even though they're the oldest rooms. Check out the antique TV in the upstairs lounge, although the rooms up here are rather sterile and airless.

**Hotel La Orquidea**  GUESTHOUSE $
(✆270-0970; cnr Calle 9 de Octubre & Sucre; r per person without/with hot water $10/11; 🅿📶) Hard single beds and prim pink rooms add to the monastic ambience of this large, old-fashioned boarding house. Run by a friendly family, it's well situated away from the noise. Wi-fi costs $1 per day.

**Hotel Heliconia**  HOTEL $
(✆270-1956; Soasti; s/d $15/25; 🅿📶) This high-rise, 40-room place has parquetry floors and glass-walled panoramic views, but it's seen better days. Rooms have cable TV, phones and decent furnishings, while bathrooms are modern. Those overlooking the street have balconies.

### BUSES FROM MACAS

| DESTINATION | COST (US$) | DURATION (HR) |
|---|---|---|
| Cuenca | 8.50 | 8 |
| Gualaquiza | 8 | 8 |
| Guayaquil | 10 | 10 |
| Puyo | 7 | 5 |
| Quito | 8 | 8 |
| Riobamba | 5 | 5 |
| Sucúa | 1 | 45min |

## ✕ Eating

The *comedores* (cheap restaurants) on Comín near Soasti sell tasty *ayampacos* – a jungle specialty of meat, chicken or fish grilled in *bijao* leaves.

**Guayusa Bar**
**La Maravilla**  ECUADORIAN $
(Soasti near Sucre; mains $3-6; ⊘4pm-midnight Mon-Sat) Easily the most charming place in town, this blue casita is all ambience, from the twinkling porch lights to the stuffed red-leather armchairs. It's a great place to chill, with *tablas* (cutting-boards) of meat and cheese and yuca fries. The drink menu gets creative, with herbal aphrodisiacs and *hueso de chuchuguazo* (a root mixed with rum) as well as local mainstays, such as delicious *costillas de cerdo* (pork chops). There's live Andean music here on the weekend, making it the town's best drinking and entertainment option, too.

**La Napolitana**  PIZZERIA $$
(Amazonas; mains $6-20; ⊘7.30am-10pm) This expansive outdoor place does breakfasts ($2.50 to $5) and is open all day long, serving up a huge range of dishes ranging from tasty pizzas to salad and meat grills.

**El Jalepeño**  MEXICAN $
(Amazonas & Calle 29 de Mayo; mains $2.50-3.50; ⊘7am-11.30pm) This friendly hole-in-the-wall place serves up decent and supercheap Mexican fare, which makes a change if you've been on the road for a while.

**Chifa Pagoda**  CHINESE $
(cnr Amazonas & Comín; mains $4-8; ⊘11am-11pm) The decor is part wedding cake and part diner at the best *chifa* (Chinese restaurant) in town. It serves tasty wonton soup, sweet-and-sour shrimp and fried noodles.

## ❶ Getting There & Away

### Air
Daily flights connect the small Edmundo Carvajal Airport (Amazonas) with Quito, operated by both **TAME** (✆270-1162) and **Saereo** (✆270-2764; www.saereo.com). On the flight to Quito, the left side of the plane offers the best mountain views, including those of Sangay and Cotopaxi on clear days.

### Bus
The bus station is on Amazonas, right in the center of town. See the boxed text for information on daily trips to various destinations.

## Parque Nacional Sangay

For more on this **national park** (admission $2), see p149. Most access to the park is from the north and west; access from the south and east is difficult. If starting from Macas, make your goal the alpine lakes, including the scenic Lagunas de Tinguichaca or the popular Lagunas de Sardinayacu, which are teeming with wildlife. The volcano itself is inaccessible from here.

Buses from Macas go to the nearby villages of 9 de Octubre and San Vicente, both good starting points for hikes. The small settlement of Purshi is the official entrance. It's best to enter with a guide as trails are faint and require acute navigation and machete skills. Trips here are not for those unused to hiking in rough terrain.

At one point, the park was put on the List of World Heritage in Danger, largely due to construction of a road between Macas and Guamote. The road, which was finally finished in 2006, offers greater access to the park but also caused irreversible damage.

## Kapawi Ecolodge & Reserve

Located in the heart of Achuar wilderness, in one of the most remote parts of the Ecuadorian Amazon, **Kapawi** (☎02-600-9333; www.kapawi.com; s 3/4/7 nights $1119/1399/2379, d $1598/1998/3398) offers a pristine, ecologically and culturally sound experience. Many outfits claim similar practices, but few execute like this. The lodge has received many accolades for its approach.

Ecuadorian tour operator Canodros opened the lodge in 1996, but rented the land from the Achuar and trained locals in guiding and tourism. Management has slowly been transferred to the Achuar over the years, and in 2008 the tribe became the lodge's sole owners and operators.

Visitors arrive by air from the Oriente town of Shell only – the nearest town is a 10-day walk away. The lodge is made up of 18 thatched cabins built on stilts over a lagoon, each with private bathroom and a balcony. Low-impact technology such as solar power, trash management, recycling, sound water treatment and biodegradable soaps are used in daily operations.

Instead of just photographing the Achuar, guests are invited to their homes and offered cassava beer, which begins a unique cultural exchange. Small groups are accompanied by an Achuar guide and a bilingual naturalist, who work in tandem to explain the intricacies of the rainforest, both from an ecological and a cultural perspective.

The lodge is just off Río Pastaza, on an ox-bow lake on Río Capahuari, and is reached by canoe from the nearby landing strip. Make reservations at the main office in Quito. Transportation from Quito costs $274, round trip. Packages include all meals and guided tours.

## The Jungle from Macas

Maps show tracks or trails leading from Macas into the interior, most of which lead to Shuar indigenous villages and missions deep in the Oriente. Going to these areas on your own is not recommended, as most communities insist tourists come with a guide.

Frequent buses from Macas go to the mission (church and school) of **Sevilla** (Don Bosco) on the other side of Río Upano. This is a good place to buy Shuar crafts from local artisans. From here a broad track leads south to the village of **San Luís**, a good day trip from Macas that offers a glimpse of indigenous life.

To satisfy your craving for **caving**, or to see the rare oil bird (a nocturnal, fruit-eating bird that's prized by the Shuar for its medicinal oils), grab a guide and head to **Cueva de los Tayos** between Méndez and Morona. A five-hour trail leads to the extensive Coangos cave system, where you could easily spend a week exploring the caverns spiked with stalactites and stalagmites. One route requires technical equipment, as the journey starts with a 70m straight descent underground, while another follows a slippery underground trail to an underground river. Even for routes that don't require technical equipment, you'll need gloves, rubber boots and a flashlight (or two).

A river trip down Río Santiago toward Peru (not an authorized crossing), which often includes some good white water, will get you way off the beaten path. Arrange this kind of trip with an experienced guide in Macas (see p229).

## Sucúa

📍07 / POP 7900

This tiny town is the transition from the bustle of Macas to serene jungle. Old men slowly pedal bicycles as a vendor grills meats under the town's singular stoplight, across from a small plaza with ficus trees and chirping cicadas. Market day is Sunday.

**Hotel Romanza** (📞274-0943; r per person incl breakfast $12) is a bright spot with minty-green bedspreads and wood furniture. A block off the main plaza, **Tisho's Pizzeria** (cnr Pástor Bernal & Sangurima; mains $3-7; ⊗11am-11pm) offers American dishes inspired by the owner's years in the States, including Philly cheese–steak sandwiches and a 'Texas' pizza.

Frequent buses or pickups leave for Macas ($1, one hour) from dawn until dusk at the corner of the main plaza. Others head south to Gualaquiza ($7, seven hours).

## Gualaquiza

📍07 / POP 7945 / ELEV 950M

Spread against a gently sloping hillside surrounded by dense jungle, this friendly and rather charming colonial town is perhaps the most appealing settlement in the southern Oriente. Families meander through the town square at the base of a hillside church that has a fan of turquoise-painted steps, while, in the market, women tend to piles of citrus, yuca and chamomile. Lodging is limited, but ask around locally for information on the excellent **caving** 15km west of town near the village of Nueva Tarquí (spare flashlights and batteries are essential), as well as **waterfalls** and sandy river **beaches**. An excellent **bike ride** swoops through the hills to La Florida (2½ hours). You'll need to bring your own bike, however.

If you plan to stay here, your best bet is **Hotel Internacional** (📞278-0637; cnr Cuenca & Moreno; r per person incl breakfast $13), a functional if rather charmless multistory place with smallish rooms and varnished plywood floors. There are several places to eat around the main square, but don't count on much beyond takeaway fare.

The bus terminal is downhill from the center. Multiple daily buses go to Loja ($6, six hours) via Zamora ($4, four hours). There are two routes to Cuenca – the Sigsig route ($7, six hours) saves two hours. Buses heading north go to Sucúa ($7, seven hours) and Macas ($8, eight hours).

# North Coast & Lowlands

## Best Places to Eat

» Seaflower Lateneus
(p246)

» Amalur (p249)

» Puerto Amistad (p252)

» La Facha (p247)

## Best Places to Stay

» CasaGrande Oceanfront
Boutique Hotel (p252)

» Casa Ceibo (p252)

» Playa Escondida (p245)

» Iruña (p247)

## Why Go?

Ecuador's north coast may not feature the outstanding natural attractions found in much of the rest of the country, but its empty beaches, little-explored mangrove forests, indigenous settlements and delectable African-Ecuadorian cuisine are just a few of the reasons why many still come here. Although noticeably poorer than Ecuador's other regions, the north coast makes up for this with a fascinating warmth and cultural mix – visit the remote northern town of San Lorenzo to see Ecuador at its most vibrantly Afro-Ecuadorian, or head into the jungle in Esmeraldas to explore the magnificent reserve of Playa de Oro, a community-run project that's home to a superb array of wildlife (including big cats).

Those looking for a beach getaway have many options, from laid-back Same, with its wide stretch of empty sands that are perfect for strolling at sunset, to surfer paradise Canoa, to the laid-back fishing village of Mompiche.

## When to Go
### Manta

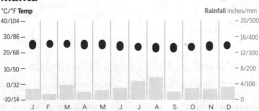

**Dec–May** The rainy season brings downpours, but also plenty of heat and sun between showers.

**Jul–Aug** Beach resorts heave with Ecuadorian tourists and the coast is alive with holiday fun.

**Sep–Nov** Come and enjoy the coast at its quietest while the weather is still great.

COLOMBIA

Palmareal
San Pedro
Reserva Ecológica de
Manglares Cayapas Mataje
**7** San Lorenzo
Olmedo
Limones
Manglares
de Majagual
La Tola
San Javier
de Cochaví
Río Verde
Lagarto
Borbón
Rocafuerte
Selva
Alegre
Esmeraldas
San
Miguel
**2** Playa de
Oro Reserva
de Tigrillos

Súa
Atacames
Punta Galera
**5**
Tonchigüe
Same

Río Muisne
Muisne
San Gregorio
**Mompiche** **1**
Daule
Reserva
Ecológica
Mache
Chindul

PACIFIC
OCEAN

Cojimíes
San José de
Chamanga

Pedernales

Montañas
de Mache

Río Esmeraldas
Río Verde
Río Onzole
Río Santiago

**Esmeraldas**

Cristóbal
Colón

Reserva
Ecológica
Cotacachi-
Cayapas

**Imbabura**

Quinindé

**6** Reserva
Biológica
Bilsa

Puerto
Quito
Reserva Biológica
Maquipucuna
Reserva Geobotánica
Pululahua

Equator

Punta Ballena
Jama

Cabo Pasado

**3** Canoa
San Vicente

**Bahía de Caráquez 4**
San Clemente
San Jacinto
Crucita
Manta
Jaramijó
Montecristi

Cabo San
Lorenzo

Chirije
Archeological
Site

Río Jama

Bosque
Protectora
La Perla
El Carmen

Santo Domingo
de los Colorados

Chone
Flavio Alfaro

**Manabí**

Embalse
Daule-
Peripa

Calceta

**Rocafuerte**

Portoviejo

Río Portoviejo

Pichincha

Río Blanco
Mindo
Chiriboga
**Pichincha** **Quito**

Volcán
Atacazo
(4463m)
Alóag
Volcán
Corazón
(4788m)

Reserva Río
Palenque
Patricia
Pilar

Río Toachi

Buena Fe

Empalme
Quevedo

**Cotopaxi**

Panamericana

Latacunga

Pujilí
San Miguel
de Salcedo

**Manabí**

Puerto
Cayo
Jipijapa
Machalilla
Agua Blanca

Parque
Nacional
Machalilla

Puerto López
Salango
Ayampe
Parque
Nacional
Machalilla

Río
Paján

Balzar

Río Daule

Palestina
Vinces
San Juan

**Los Ríos**

Río Quevedo

Ambato

Reserva
Faunística
Chimborazo
Penipe

**Bolívar**
Guaranda

Cajabamba
Riobamba

# North Coast & Lowlands Highlights

**1** Get out to the gorgeous sandy beach at still-off-the-radar **Mompiche** (p247) before the developers arrive

**2** Hike beneath the jungle canopy in the lush **Playa de Oro Reserva de Tigrillos** (p239)

**3** Take in the laid-back beach and surfer scene at hard-to-leave **Canoa** (p248)

**4** Take in charming **Bahía de Caráquez** (p250) and the nearby **Chirije archaeological site** (p253)

**5** Frolic in the waves in the idyllic beachside setting of **Same** (p244)

**6** Marvel at the verdant scenery of wildlife-rich **Reserva Biológica Bilsa** (p239)

**7** Take a trip to Ecuador's steamy northern border and enjoy the Afro-Ecuadorian rhythms of **San Lorenzo** (p236)

# WESTERN LOWLANDS

Fertile farmland and rolling hills stretch off toward the coast, with a swath of rivers traversing the region on their journey from Andean heights to the ocean. Between mountain and sea, big plantations now crisscross the land. They bear the fruits that help power the agricultural economy: cacao, African palm oil and bananas spread across the green horizon, where primeval forest once grew, while in between lie grimy and fast-growing cities.

## Quito to Santo Domingo de los Colorados

◢02

Dramatic scenery is a big part of the journey west from Quito, with steep pitches plunging toward the misty void as lush hills appear around sharp curves. It's best to travel this stretch in the morning, when skies are more likely to be clear.

Outside of Quito the road climbs into the *páramo* (high-altitude Andean grasslands), with views of the extinct **Volcanes Atacazo** (4463m) and **Corazón** (4788m) to the north and south, respectively. The tortuous descent leads into the Río Toachi valley, where the air thickens and tropical plants begin sprouting up.

About 16km outside of Santo Domingo, **Tinalandia** (◢02-244-9028; www.tinalandia. com; s/d $86/118) is acclaimed for its top-notch bird-watching. This rustic resort sits at 600m in a wet premontane forest. Guests stay in weathered bungalows with private bathrooms and hot showers. The driest months (May and June) are particularly popular with bird-watchers, who can come for day visits (day pass $10). Delicious meals with fresh veggies from the hydroponics farm cost extra.

Tinalandia is about 86km after the turnoff from the Panamericana in Alóag. Ask your driver to drop you off at Tinalandia, or watch out for the small stone sign on the right-hand side of the road as you drive from Quito. The hotel is 500m away on the left.

## Santo Domingo de los Colorados

◢02 / POP 368,000 / ELEV 500M

This bustling and very uninspiring town is an important commercial center and transport hub. However, there are few attractions to encourage you to do anything other than pass through. The chief reason to stop here is to arrange a visit to the fascinating Tsáchila community. Santo Domingo has a seedy side and visitors should be somewhat wary and avoid the market area and Calle 3 de Julio after dark.

### ◉ Sights & Activities

**Tsáchila & Chihuilpe**   INDIGENOUS COMMUNITY
The most interesting excursion is visiting the Tsáchila people, who number about 3000, spread across eight communities in a 10,500-hectare reserve (p237) around Santo Domingo. They offer a community tour that includes a demonstration of plants used for medicinal purposes, an explanation of customs and traditions, and even dancing. They produce lovely hand-woven goods in their signature wild rainbow colors, as well as jewelry.

Contact **José Aguabil** (◢09-770-8703), leader of the El Poste community, to arrange a visit. You can also visit Chihuilpe, located 17km from Santo Domingo on the road to Quevedo. Contact **Tsapini Calasacón** (◢09-750-3320), the leader of the community there. Visitors are charged about $5. Tour agencies in Santo Domingo can also book a tour; ask around in the city center.

### 🛏 Sleeping & Eating

**Hotel Del Pacifico**   HOTEL $$
(◢275-2806; Av 29 de Mayo 510; s/d $20/35; ❄🐾🛜) There's not really any reason to stay in Santo Domingo, but if you get caught overnight, try this hotel, the town's best option. It has clean and spacious rooms with tile floors and glazed windows; you'll find it in the center of town between the main square and the market.

**Restaurante Timoneiro**   ECUADORIAN $
(Av Quito 115; mains $3-7; ⊙7am-9pm) There are several eating options around the main square, including this friendly and pleasantly lit restaurant, which serves up traditional Ecuadorian fare.

### ❶ Getting There & Away

Santo Domingo is an important transportation hub, with connections all over Ecuador. The bus terminal, almost 2km north of downtown, has frequent buses to many major towns, as well as internet access, an ATM and left luggage.

## BUSES FROM SANTO DOMINGO

| DESTINATION | COST (US$) | DURATION (HR) |
| --- | --- | --- |
| Ambato | 4 | 4 |
| Atacames | 4 | 4 |
| Bahía de Caráquez | 5 | 5 |
| Baños | 5 | 5 |
| Coca | 13 | 14 |
| Esmeraldas | 4 | 3½ |
| Guayaquil | 5 | 5 |
| Loja | 11 | 12 |
| Manta | 6 | 6 |
| Mindo | 2.50 | 2 |
| Muisne | 6 | 5 |
| Quito | 3 | 3 |

# THE NORTH COAST

The north coast is a lush green swath of tropical rainforests and tangled mangroves, with a sprinkling of inviting beaches, dirt-poor backwater villages and laid-back surf towns. This is home to the country's largest Afro-Ecuadorian population, which gives the area its marimba music and lively festivals as well as outstanding seafood dishes.

Good sense and a taste for adventure are essential tools for travelers to this region, although some visitors are turned off by the obvious poverty and lack of creature comforts in some parts.

## San Lorenzo

☑ 06 / POP 15,000

Encircled by verdant jungle, at the edge of a dank, still river, San Lorenzo is a decrepit, lively hodgepodge of blaring heat, tropical beats and crumbling storefronts. Hollow marimba notes and salsa is what flavors this mostly Afro-Ecuadorian outpost, which goes all out in August with an annual music festival.

With road access only completed in the mid-1990s, the area still has the air of a forgotten outpost. It is extremely poor, tourism is barely developed and getting around isn't easy. Its treasure is its people, the most spirited you'll encounter, and they're real reason to come all this way. With little in common with the Ecuador that most visitors know, San Lorenzo makes a challenging but nonetheless fascinating destination. It's also a great base for visiting the nearby Reserva Ecológica de Manglares Cayapas Mataje.

## 🛏 Sleeping & Eating

Pickings are slim, but consider mosquito nets and fans as essentials, especially in the rainy season. The following places all have mosquito nets.

**Gran Hotel San Carlos**          HOTEL $
(☑278-0284, 278-1189; cnr Imbabura & José Garcés; s/d with shared bathroom $10/15, s/d with air-con $17/22; ▣❄) The Gran Hotel San Carlos No 1 has clean, bright rooms with large windows, while kitschy, rainbow-hued decor prevails in the common areas. The newer San Carlos No 2, a block down the same street, is even more comfortable with state-of-the-art air-con, cable TV and spotless floors.

**Hotel Pampa de Oro**          HOTEL $
(☑278-0214; Tácito Ortíz; s/d $9/18) This faded place is the cheapest option in town, with fan-cooled rooms and lots of plastic flowers in evidence.

**Doña Luca**          ECUADORIAN $
(Eloy Alfaro; mains $2.50-5; ⊙7:30am-8pm) Probably the best place in town, this smartish joint serves breakfasts and a wide variety of food, running from meat and fish to delicious local seafood. It's in the center of town between the main drag and Parque Central.

## El Chocó ECUADORIAN $

(Imbabura near Tácito Ortiz; mains $2-6; ☺6am-10pm Mon-Sat) On the main street, this clean and well-liked spot serves all the local seafood favorites including ceviche and *encocado de camarones* (shrimp and coconut stew).

### ⓘ Information

The **police station** (☐278-0672) faces Parque Central, and the **capitanía** (port captain) is at the main pier. If you're traveling into or out of Colombia (which is not recommended), take care of passport formalities at either of these places.

San Lorenzo's Catholic hospital, a short taxi ride from downtown, is reputedly the best in the area north of Esmeraldas. **Cyber San Lorenzo** (Calle 26 de Agosto; ☺8am-8pm) offers reliable web access.

### ⓘ Getting There & Away

#### Boat

**Ecuador Pacífico** (☐278-0161; andrescarvache@yahoo.es) services depart to Limones ($3, 1½ hours) at 7:30am, 10:30am and 1pm, and continue to La Tola ($5, 45 minutes). At La Tola, you can connect with a bus to Esmeraldas. Trips to nearby beaches leave at 7:30am and 2pm ($3). Tour guide Andres Carvache arranges

these and other trips. He can be found on the pier in a stilted storefront to the right of the pier.

To cross the Colombian border there are departures at 7:30am, 2pm and 4pm ($3), which also require bus connections to Tumaco in Colombia. Given nearby guerilla activity that occasionally sends refugees spilling over, it is not recommended to cross the border here.

Touring the mangroves isn't really possible via public transportation. To arrange a trip contact **Cooperativa San Lorenzo del Pailón** (☐278-0039), an authorized service offering private tours in boats for $20 to $30 per hour. You can also arrange tours through Andres Carvache for $60 and $80 for a two- to three-hour trip.

#### Bus

La Costeñita departures for Esmeraldas ($4.50, five hours) leave the Parque Central hourly from 5am to 4pm. Trans Esmeraldas buses leave regularly from their depot on 10 de Agosto to Quito ($7) via Ibarra ($4) and to Manta ($7).

# Reserva Ecológica de Manglares Cayapas Mataje

Millions of migratory birds pass through this coastal reserve in June and July, creating a cacophonous and memorable spectacle. This

---

## LOS TSÁCHILAS

The Tsáchilas, dubbed 'the Colorados' by colonists, are well known for their *curanderos* (medicine men) as well as for their beautiful woven crafts in shocks of rainbow colors. The group's signature dress is easy to recognize: they paint their faces with black stripes, and men dye their bowl-shaped haircuts red.

Nowadays it is much more probable to see Westernized Tsáchilas. With curio shops selling their postcard images, gawkers in Santo Domingo calling them 'painted tigers', and bus drivers protesting that the hair dye stains the backs of their seats, it's no wonder that the Tsáchilas have closeted their customs. Nevertheless, there have been some important victories for the Tsáchilas in recent years, most notably the creation of their own province in 2007, granting the group a much more prominent role in the nation's political system.

Kasama, the New Year (coinciding with Easter Saturday), is a time for the Tsáchila to reaffirm their roots. It unites all of the villagers, who gather to wish one another prosperity in the coming year. Cane sugar *chicha* (a fermented corn or yuca drink traditionally drunk by many indigenous cultures in Ecuador) is served and the festive atmosphere ignites with music, dance and theater. Despite being the most important Tsáchila celebration, it was shelved for 30 years and only began to be celebrated again in 1998. With the return of this celebration springs the small hope that other important features of the landscape – such as the *guatusa* (agouti, a type of rodent) and the armadillo – will eventually return as well.

While most Tsáchilas are reticent to receive visitors (or have their photograph taken), travelers are welcome in the towns of Chihuilpe and El Poste, both south of Santo Domingo on the road to Quevedo. As well as going to the tourist center in Chihuilpe, you can also visit one of the *curanderos,* who sell curative herbs or offer treatments. El Poste welcomes visitors to the above-mentioned annual Kasama festival.

51,300-hectare reserve supports five species of mangrove, and includes the tallest mangrove forest in the world – Manglares de Majagual – near the villages of La Tola and Olmedo. San Lorenzo lies in the middle of the reserve and makes a good base. Most of the reserve is at sea level and none of it is above 35m. A highlight of the reserve is the pristine 11km island beach of **San Pedro** near the Colombian border, but visitors should inquire about safety before venturing into this area.

There are basic, community-run cabañas (cabins) nearby at the settlement of **Palmareal**. If you stay, bring a mosquito net and water (or purification tablets). The reserve is accessible almost only by boat.

## San Miguel

San Miguel is a modest and friendly Afro-Ecuadorian community of stilted thatched huts set in the forest, with Chachi homes scattered nearby along the shores of the river. The village is the main base from which to visit the lowland sections of the Reserva Ecológica Cotacachi-Cayapas.

Accommodation is available in a simple guesthouse, run communally by the women's association. Prices are around $5 per person, and you can arrange for home-cooked meals for an extra $7 per day.

The **ranger station** (per person $5), perched on a small hill with spectacular views of the rainforest and river, has basic accommodation. Ask the *guardaparque* (park ranger) for permission to stay here. The station has a cold-water shower, a toilet and kitchen facilities. A shop in the village sells basic provisions or travelers can ask around, as sympathetic locals are eager to cook up simple meals of soup, rice and plantain for about $5.

The driver of the daily passenger canoe from Borbón (a down-on-its-luck lumber port 30km downriver) spends the night about 15 minutes downriver from San Miguel. He will not return to San Miguel unless passengers have made previous arrangements, so book ahead. The canoe leaves San Miguel around 4am.

### ❶ Getting There & Away

La Costeñita and Transportes del Pacífico run buses to Esmeraldas ($3, four hours) or San Lorenzo ($1.50, one hour) about every hour from 7am to 6pm.

---

**JOURNEY INTO THE JUNGLE**

Playa de Oro's end-of-the-earth location is the defining point of its existence. The huffing of margays can be heard at night outside a cabin window. The village is populated with the Afro-Ecuadorian descendants of slaves brought here to pan for gold 500 years ago. Located hours inland from the coast in a remote, roadless wilderness, Playa de Oro's near-inaccessibility has kept it a natural paradise.

To ensure that it would stay that way, the community designated 10,000 of its hectares as Playa de Oro Reserva de Tigrillos, a wildlife area protecting all species of indigenous wildcats: jaguars, cougars, ocelots, margays, oncillas and jaguarundi. They decided against registering the reserve with the national government, given its history of favoring big industry over sustainable development. Instead, locals decided to manage it as a community.

In Playa de Oro, every villager over the age of 14 gets to vote on important issues. Some villagers have long argued that ecotourism is the sensible, nondestructive way forward. But their insistence on maintaining control of their own ecotourism, and not allowing it to fall into the hands of large tour agencies who take a big cut, forces them to rely on independent travelers and small groups.

Much of the area around the reserve has changed dramatically in the last 15 years, owing to gold-mining activity. Small villages have disappeared and in their place lie heaps of gravel piled up by machinery sluicing for gold; the river water has become contaminated by cyanide and arsenic used in the mining process. So far the villagers have resisted overtures from gold-mining and lumber companies to receive goods and services (a generator, a new road, jobs to log their own forest) in exchange for their land. The question remains whether the income that trickles in will sustain the reserve for the years to come.

## RESERVA BIOLÓGICA BILSA

Rugged adventurers looking to get truly off the beaten path and into nature should head to **Reserva Biológica Bilsa**, 30km west of Quinindé. Crashing waterfalls and spectacular wildlife adorn this 30-sq-km reserve in the Montañas de Mache, and it's administered by **Fundación Jatun Sacha** (☏02-243-2240; www.jatunsacha.org; r per person incl 3 meals $40). Biodiversity is exceptionally high in these last vestiges of premontane tropical wet forest, with howler monkeys, endangered birds, jaguar and puma all present. This trip is for the hardy: rainy season access (January to June) requires hiking or mule-riding a mud-splattered 25km trail. Contact Jatun Sacha for reservations (there are discounts for groups and students) and volunteer or research information.

A daily passenger boat leaves at 11am for San Miguel ($8, five hours). This boat can drop you at any location on Río Cayapas or at San Miguel. Various boats run irregularly to other destinations – ask around at the docks. *Fletes* (private boats) can usually be hired; expect to pay at least $100 per day per group.

## Playa de Oro

Río Santiago leads inland from Borbón, and the furthest community up the river is the settlement of **Playa de Oro**, near Reserva Ecológica Cotacachi-Cayapas. Playa de Oro means 'Beach of Gold.'

Half an hour upstream from Playa de Oro is **Playa de Oro Reserva de Tigrillos**, a 10,000-hectare reserve owned and operated by the community of Playa de Oro. The reserve, which borders Cotacachi-Cayapas, protects native jungle cats, which are more plentiful here than elsewhere, but are nonetheless elusive. The best way to experience the reserve is by staying at the community-operated riverside **jungle lodge** (r per person per day $50). Prices include three meals and local guides. When you arrive, be sure to insist on staying in the rainforest lodge, not in the village. (Both accommodations cost the same, but offer a significantly different experience; your hosts may try to steer you toward the village digs.)

Playa de Oro's charm is its authenticity. Locals do what they and their ancestors have always done, whether that be roaming the forest, riding the river current, panning for gold, making drums or encouraging their children in traditional dances. When visitors show interest in their way of life, locals are quietly proud.

The village of Playa de Oro is about five hours upstream from Borbón, but there are no regular boats. You have to take the 7:30am bus from Borbón to Selva Alegre ($3, two hours). From Selva Alegre, if you made a reservation, a boat from Playa de Oro will motor you up to the village or the reserve (each way per boatload $50). If you didn't make a reservation, your best bet is to time your visit with the once-a-week market boat that goes out on Saturdays (leaving around noon and costing $10 per person). The river trip from Selva Alegre takes two hours (2½ hours if you're going to the reserve).

Another option for getting here is hiring Playa de Oro's point of contact, **Ramiro Buitron** (☏09-960-6918), who can drive travelers to the boat launch site from Otavalo, a four-hour trip.

## Reserva Ecológica Cotacachi-Cayapas

This 204,420-hectare **reserve** (admission $2) is by far the largest protected area of Ecuador's western Andean habitats. Altitude ranges from about 200m above sea level around San Miguel to 4939m at the summit of Cotacachi. Habitats change quickly from lowland, tropical, wet forest to premontane and montane cloud forest to *páramo,* with many intermediate habitat types. This rapid change of habitat produces the so-called 'edge effect' that gives rise to an incredible diversity of flora and fauna.

These hills are the haunts of such rarely seen mammals as giant anteaters, Baird's tapirs, jaguars and, in the upper reaches of the reserve, spectacled bears. However, the chances of seeing these animals are very remote. You are far more likely to see monkeys, squirrels, sloths, nine-banded armadillos, bats and a huge variety of bird species.

To visit the reserve you can approach from the highlands or San Miguel. Hiking between the two regions may well be impossible; the steep and thickly vegetated western Andean slopes are almost impenetrable. This is good news for the species existing there – they will probably be left alone for a little while longer.

The lower reaches of the reserve and rivers are the home of the indigenous Chachi. About 5000 remain, mostly fishers and subsistence farmers, living in open-sided, thatched river houses built on stilts. The Chachi are famous for their basketwork; try buying their crafts directly from the river folk (although many speak only Chachi). Over the last few decades, the Chachi have been swept by an epidemic of river blindness that's carried by black flies, which are particularly prevalent in April and May. About 80% of the population has the disease, to some extent. To protect yourself while traveling, use insect repellent and take malaria pills.

### When to Go

River levels are high during the rainy season (December to May), making for swifter travel. At this time mosquitoes, black flies and other insects are at their highest concentrations; definitely cover up at dawn and dusk when they come out in full force.

Even during the rainy months, mornings are often clear. Up to 5000mm of rain has been reported in some of the more inland areas, although San Miguel is somewhat drier. The drier months of September to the start of December are usually less buggy, and you have a better chance of seeing wildlife, although river navigation may be limited.

### ❶ Getting There & Around

Entrance into the reserve is payable at the ranger station in San Miguel (p238). The rangers can serve as guides, and charge about $10 per day, plus food. Two guides are needed for trips, with one for each end of the dugout canoe (these canoes require paddle and pole; engines are scarce). Alternatively, you can visit on a guided tour with one of the lodges. The lodge in Playa de Oro (p239) is also an access point for the reserve.

It is about two or three hours by canoe from San Miguel to the park boundaries. Another one or two hours brings you to a gorgeous little waterfall in the jungle. A guide is essential as the few trails are poorly marked. There are places to camp if you have tents and the necessary gear.

# Esmeraldas

🕗06 / POP 154,000

The Spanish conquistadors made their first Ecuadorian landfall on this broad, sandy bank flanked by a sparkling river and surrounded by low green hills. Esmeraldas has been an influential port town throughout history, though its modern incarnation is not a pleasant one, and visitors tend to pass through as quickly as possible. Many of its cement structures are either half-finished or half-fallen, the frenzied streets harbor drugs and petty crime, and the forests have been overtaken by scrub brush.

These days fishing and shipping take a backseat to the oil refinery that processes the contents of the trans-Ecuadorian oil pipeline – unfortunately, the refinery adds its share of noise and pollution to the city. This, combined with the fact that Esmeraldas is considered one of Ecuador's most dangerous major cities, makes it an unappealing destination. Most tourists just spend the night (if they have to) and continue southwest to the popular beach destinations of Atacames, Súa and Mompiche.

### Dangers & Annoyances

Esmeraldas is striving to beat its notorious reputation. In the meantime, avoid arriving after dark, or, if you do, take a taxi.

### ◉ Sights

**Centro Cultural Esmeraldas** CULTURAL CENTER
(Bolívar 427; admission $1; ⊗9am-5pm Tue-Fri, 10am-4pm Sat & Sun) This combined museum, library and bookstore contains materials ranging from recent local history to fine ceramics and gold work from the ancient Tolita culture. Some of the exhibit signs and documentary videos are in English, and the staff is very obliging.

### ☞ Tours

**Javier Valenciana** TOURS
(🕗09-139-1649; pandafinu@hotmail.com) Javier runs tours to far-flung destination in Esmeraldas.

### ⌷ Sleeping

Hotels are plentiful, but the cheapest ones are just about intolerable. During the wet months you should have a mosquito net in your room. The resort-suburb of Las Palmas, 3km north of downtown, offers better accommodation if being central isn't important to you.

# Esmeraldas

ing oversized rooms with a crisp finish and cable TV, but no hot water.

## 🍽 Eating

The food in the many cheap sidewalk cafes and *comedores* (cheap restaurants) is often good – try along Olmedo between Mejía and Piedrahíta.

**Restaurante Perla Verde**     ECUADORIAN **$$**
(cnr Piedrahíta & Olmedo; mains $6-10; ⊙7am-9pm) Located in the best hotel in town, this pleasant, classy space has a good selection of ceviches, grills and other seafood.

**Parrilladas El Toro**     STEAKHOUSE **$$**
(Calle 9 de Octubre 4-23; mains $7-10; ⊙5pm-midnight) Beyond the uninviting decor you'll find a decent steakhouse specializing in beef and chops. The thatched courtyard seating is preferable to sitting inside.

**AKI Supermercado**     SUPERMARKET **$**
(cnr Malecón Maldonado & Montalvo) This is a good supermarket for stocking up on provisions.

## 🛍 Shopping

**Centro Artesenal**     CRAFT
(cnr Malecón Maldonado & Plaza Cívica) This is where to come to browse for tapestries, baskets, tagua carvings and other Chachi pieces. The first shop, **Mandagua**, is also a good place to get info about visiting off-the-beaten-track locations in the province. Ask for **Javier Valenciana** (☎09-139-1649; pandafinu@hotmail.com).

**Hotel Perla Verde**     BUSINESS HOTEL **$$**
(☎272-3820; www.hotelperlaverde.com.es; cnr Piedrahíta & Olmedo; s/d incl breakfast $45/55; P❄🛜) This is the best hotel in town, boasting spacious rooms with lots of creature comforts (as long as you don't mind some truly awful art on the walls). Staff is friendly and you're in a central location. The downstairs restaurant is also one of the best in town.

**Hotel Central**     HOTEL **$**
(☎272-2502; Sucre 9-03; r per person $17; ❄) Right on the main plaza, this modern if slightly cramped place had rather unresponsive staff on our last visit, but it has perfectly good (if small) newish rooms with cable TV.

**El Trébol**     HOTEL **$**
(☎272-8031; Cañizares 1-18; r per person $16; ❄🛜) An immaculate fern-lined hotel offer-

## ❶ Information

**Immigration office** (☏271-0156, 272-4624) At the Policía Civil Nacional, 3km out of town (take a taxi). Have your passport stamped here for entry or exit via the rarely used – and not recommended – coastal route to Colombia.

**Police station** (cnr Bolívar & Cañizares) Two blocks south of the plaza.

**Tourist office** (☏272-7340; Bolívar; ⊙9am-noon, 2-6pm Mon-Sat) Located between Calle 9 de Octubre and Piedrahíta.

## ❶ Getting There & Away

### Air

The **TAME office** (☏272-6863; Bolívar near Calle 9 de Octubre; ⊙8am-12:45pm & 3-5:30pm Mon-Fri) is just off the central plaza. TAME has daily flights to Quito (one way $65), and less-frequent service to Guayaquil (one way $105) and Cali, Colombia (one way $115).

### Bus

The new bus terminal is 4km from the city center on the road to Atacames.

## ❶ Getting Around

The airport is 25km from town, across the Río Esmeraldas. Passengers and taxi drivers gather in front of the TAME office in town a couple of hours before flights, and four or five passengers cram into a taxi to the airport for $3 per person (15 minutes). Incoming passengers get together to do the same thing at the airport. A taxi charges about $25 to go directly from the airport to Atacames, thus avoiding Esmeraldas completely.

A taxi to the beach costs $1, or you can take a Selectivo bus signed 'Las Palmas No 1' northbound along Bolívar.

Taxis charge a $1 minimum, which doubles after 11pm.

### BUSES FROM ESMERALDAS

| DESTINATION | COST (US$) | DURATION (HR) |
|---|---|---|
| Atacames | 1 | 1 |
| Guayaquil | 9.20 | 9 |
| Manta | 9.35 | 10 |
| Mompiche | 3.15 | 2½ |
| Muisne | 2.15 | 2 |
| Quito | 7.25 | 6 |
| San Lorenzo | 4.65 | 5 |

# Atacames

☏06 / POP 15,460

This seething beach town is a source of endless entertainment at any time of the day or night for *serranos* (highlanders). There's an OK beach here, backed by massive overdevelopment and thatch-roofed bars that competitively blare *reggaetón* (a blend of Puerto Rican *bomba,* dancehall and hip-hop) the entire length of the strip. The whole place heaves with Ecuadorian tourists year round and can be unpleasantly dirty, loud and crowded – but if you want to party, then look no further. This place moves more than anywhere else on the coast.

### Dangers & Annoyances

The beach has a strong undertow and lifeguards work only midweek to weekends. People drown here every year, so stay within your limits.

The beach is considered unsafe at night, when assaults and rapes have been reported. Stay near the well-lit areas in front of the hotels, and avoid the isolated stretch between Atacames and Súa, as knifepoint robberies have been reported. Needless to say, the beach is not a place to bring your valuables at any time of the day.

## ☞ Tours

**Boat Tours** BOAT TOURS
Fishers on the beach can take you on a boat tour around the area, passing by Isla de Pajaros just off shore. Plan on about $20 per person for a 75-minute tour, and $40 per person for a fishing trip. Ask around or contact **Fidian Franco** (☏09-055-6409) to arrange an excursion.

## 🛏 Sleeping

Atacames is packed with hotels, but it can get awfully crowded on holiday weekends. Reserve in advance if arriving during the peak season.

**Arco Iris Resort** SPA & RESORT $$
(☏273-1654; www.arcoirisatacames.com; Malecón; d from $35; P❀❄☎❄) In a high-rise toward the eastern end of the beach, Arco Iris offers sleek modern rooms that are excellent value for the money. Some rooms have balconies with views.

**Hotel Jennifer** HOTEL $
(☏273-1055; near Malecón; s/d without hot water $10/18, with hot water $12/25) This simple,

# Atacames

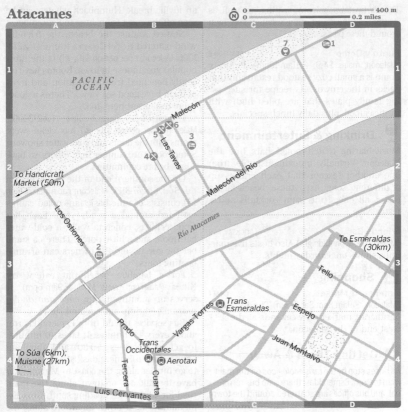

straightforward place has clean, spartan rooms that get a decent amount of light (windows in every room). Kind staff.

**Cabañas Los Bohíos**     CABINS **$**
(☑272-7478; Los Ostiones; s/d $10/20; ℗) Near the dark, fetid Río Atacames, Los Bohíos offers clean, inexpensive rooms with tile floors and wood and bamboo details. Cabins are slightly smaller and are made entirely of bamboo. It's surrounded by a concrete parking area with a few flowers and palms.

## ✗ Eating

Adventurous eaters should head to a row of open-air seafood stalls on a lane just off the Malecón. A bowl of *ceviche de concha* (shellfish ceviche) or *ceviche de pescado* (fish ceviche) starts at around $4, and the shrimp is precooked. *Cocada* (a chewy coconut sweet) and *batidos* (fruit shakes) are two local specialties sold everywhere.

| Atacames | |
|---|---|
| 🛏 **Sleeping** | |
| 1 Arco Iris Resort | D1 |
| 2 Cabañas Los Bohíos | A3 |
| 3 Hotel Jennifer | B2 |
| | |
| 🍽 **Eating** | |
| 4 Ceviche Restaurants | B2 |
| 5 Pizzería da Giulio | B2 |
| 6 Punto y Como | B2 |
| | |
| 🍷 **Drinking** | |
| 7 Friends Bar | C1 |

**Pizzería da Giulio**     PIZZERIA **$$**
(Malecón; mains $7-10; ◷5:30pm-midnight Tue-Fri, 10:30am-midnight Sat & Sun) Run by a Sardinian, this friendly restaurant serves up excellent thin-crust pizzas with fresh ingredients and old-world flavors (including real prosciutto).

There's upstairs balcony seating, as well as grappa, sambuca and other spirits rarely seen around these parts.

**Punto y Como** SEAFOOD **$**
(Malecón; mains $4-9; ⊗11am-10pm) Punto y Como is a small cozy seafood restaurant that packs in the crowds. Its recipe for success? Big family plates that are piled high with fresh seafood, plus daily lunch specials.

 **Drinking & Entertainment**

Music-blaring thatch-roofed bars line the Malecón. Virtually indistinguishable from one another (except that each cranks up a different song list), these beach-facing places all offer fruity rum cocktails and a festive vibe.

**Friends Bar** COCKTAIL BAR
(Malecón; ⊗noon-midnight) Also hosts live marimba shows on Saturday nights.

 **Shopping**

**Handicraft Market** CRAFT
(Malecón; ⊗9am-8pm Sat & Sun) There's a tiny handicraft market on weekends at the west end of the Malecón.

**❶ Getting There & Away**

All buses stop by the *taxis ecológicos* on the main road to/from Esmeraldas; there is no bus terminal, and bus offices are scattered around the town center. Buses for Esmeraldas ($1, one hour) normally begin from Súa. Most buses from Esmeraldas to Atacames continue on to Súa (10 minutes), Same (20 minutes) and Tonchigüe (25 minutes) for about $0.30. There are also regular buses to Muisne ($1.50, 1½ hours). *Ecovías* (motorcycle taxis) charge $2 to Súa and $7 to Same.

The following bus companies operate a daily service to Quito ($8, seven hours) as well as to Guayaquil ($9, eight hours): **Transportes Occidentales** (cnr Prado & Cuarta), **Trans Esmeraldas** (cnr Vargas Torres & Juan Montalvo) and **Aerotaxi** (Cuarta). If you're returning to Quito on a Sunday in the high season, be sure to buy your ticket in advance.

## Súa

❏02

Súa is more family-oriented, quieter and less popular than neighboring Atacames, with more-reasonable weekend hotel prices. That said, the cocktail bars along the beach still screech out music, so it's hardly the spot for an idyllic break. Humpback whales can be seen off the coast from June to September.

Nestled against the beach, the friendly, wind-battered **Hotel Chagra Ramos** (❏273-1006; Malecón; r per person $10; ᴘ) is the most popular guesthouse in town. Rooms have recently benefited from renovation and most of them have good sea views. There's a good-value restaurant here, too.

**Hostal Las Buganvillas** (❏273-1008; Malecón; r per person $10; ❄) has clean-swept rooms with tile floors and cold-water showers. Some rooms are sunnier than others, so have a look before committing.

On the southern end of the Malecón, **Sol de Súa** (❏247-3121; Malecón; cabin per person $5) consists of nine basic fan-cooled cabins scattered around a sandy yard. Each has wood ceilings, concrete walls, a cold-water bathroom and a little porch. There's a small bar for guests, and the owners can arrange boating tours.

For a bamboo beachfront eatery, try **Kikes** (Malecón; mains $5-8; ⊗9am-6pm). It serves up mouthwatering *encocado de camarones* (shrimp and coconut stew).

Bus services to and from Esmeraldas run about every 45 minutes. It takes 10 minutes to get to Atacames ($0.30) and about an hour to get to Esmeraldas ($1). If you want to go further along the coast to Muisne, you have to wait out of town along the main road for a bus that's heading south from Esmeraldas (flag it down anywhere along the road).

## Same & Tonchigüe

❏06

Same (pronounced *sah*-may) is a real mixed bag of a resort town, boasting a wonderful beach and a genial atmosphere, while also being dominated by a vast resort and condo complex (Casablanca). The latter takes up the entire northern end of the beach, and the town also features a half-finished highrise hulk of an apartment building that sits in the middle of the beach. The beach itself, while certainly beautiful, is far from pristine and would benefit from a community-wide effort to keep it clean, such as that seen in Mompiche. That said, Same is an unbridled delight compared to Atacames.

Tonchigüe is a tiny fishing village about 3km west of Same, along the same stretch of beach. Go early in the morning to see the fishers unloading their catch.

## 🛏 Sleeping & Eating

There is a handful of simple *comedores* right on the beach in Same who offer plates of *encocado* or *pescado* (fish) for around $5.

**Playa Escondida**                              BEACH CABINS $
(☑273-3122, 09-973-3368; www.playaescondida. com.ec; per person low season $10-15, r high season $20-36) Look no further for seclusion: the lovely and remote Playa Escondida offers accommodation in rustic cabins surrounding a beautiful beach cove, set amid 100 hectares of protected land. There's a restaurant serving seafood, meat and vegetarian dishes, and tours and other activities are offered. It's located 3km west of Tonchigüe and 10km down the road to Punta Galera. If you just want to get away from the crowds in Same, day entry to the private beach costs $5 per person for nonguests.

**El Acantilado**                              BEACH CABINS $$
(☑273-3466; www.hosteriaelacantilado.com; s/d/q $25/50/75; ▣☒) Perched on a cliff above the crashing waves, El Acantilado offers unobstructed sea views from its rooms, which make it great for whale-watching from June

to September. Rustic suites are open to the elements, with just bug screens separating the rooms from individual private gardens and views down to the sea and beach below. Larger cabins have three rooms and sleep up to eight people. The resort is run by a hospitable young family who speak English. It's located 1km south of Same.

**Casa de Amigos**                              GUESTHOUSE $$
(☑247-0102; www.casadeamigosecuador.com; Same; r per person $25-30; mains $5-7; ☒@) This superfriendly adobe-style guesthouse is right on the beach and has a great, relaxed vibe. It feels as though it's the beating heart of Same, with locals dropping in to the beach bar all day. Rooms are a little faded these days and are due for a spruce up, but are nicely designed and clean, with bright local artwork throughout. English, German and Spanish are spoken and there's also a good beachfront restaurant here serving up home-cooked Ecuadorian and European cuisine.

**Isla del Sol**                              HOTEL $$
(☑247-0470; www.cabanasisladelsol.com; Same; d/q/ste $40/72/80; ▣☒🛜☒) The somewhat

---

## NORTH COAST DELICACIES

Traveling along the north coast, keep an eye out for some of the scrumptious local dishes. Fresh seafood, plantains and coconut milk are combined to great success. Many Ecuadorians rate *cocina esmeraldeña* (dishes from the Esmeraldas province) as the country's best. Here are a few reasons why:

» **Bolas de platano** A soup with shrimp, coconut milk and a cheese-and-plantain mixture shaped into balls.

» **Cazabe** A type of sweet made from cooked corn, coconut juice, cinnamon, cloves and other spices.

» **Cazuela** A mixed seafood (or fish) stew made with peanut sauce and plantains, served in a clay pot.

» **Ceviche** A classic seafood dish of shrimp, squid, mussels or raw fish 'cooked' in lemon juice and served with banana chips (and preferably a cold beer). Prepared with panache in Esmeraldas.

» **Cocada** A round sweet made of brown sugar, coconut, milk and peanuts.

» **Encocado** A dish made from fresh mixed seafood or fish cooked with coconut milk and spices, often served with rice. Simply outstanding.

» **Frutipan** A dessert made by indigenous Chachis, made of bread-tree fruit that is mixed with sweet spices, butter and cheese, then baked.

» **Mazato** A dish made of boiled ripe banana mashed with coconut milk, cheese and egg, then baked in a *bijao* leaf.

» **Pusandao** A hearty dish of fish or pork prepared with coconut milk, plantain and yuca.

» **Tapao** An elegant dish of fish and plantain, seasoned with coconut and *chillangua* (a type of wild cilantro) and steamed beneath banana leaves.

rickety-looking beachfront cabins here are actually decent value and pretty comfortable. The best rooms have wooden floors, beamed ceilings and small verandas, and all have hot water and cable TV. There are also three brand-new suites of a more modern style, and these are definitely a step up in comfort. English is spoken and the friendly management arranges kayaking and tours to nearby beaches and ecological reserves.

### Azuca
HOTEL $

(☎08-882-9581; azuca2@hotmail.com; Same; r per person $5; mains $4-6) This incredibly cheap place is just a short walk from the beach (at the junction turn-off where Same's main 'street' leaves the coastal road). For this price it has pretty comfortable and spacious wooden rooms, all with balconies and mosquito nets. There's also a decent in-house restaurant serving up simple Ecuadorian meals.

### Seaflower Lateneus
SEAFOOD $$

(☎247-0369; Same; mains $10-25; ⊗8am-midnight) Boasting one of the best chefs along the north coast, Seaflower Lateneus serves delicious plates of grilled seafood and is by far the best place to eat in town. It's worth reserving a table on the weekend, when it's often packed with a smart crowd of cocktail-sipping weekenders – it also doubles as Same's best bar. You'll find it behind La Terraza.

### La Terraza
PIZZERIA $

(Same; pizza $6-10) Spanish-owned La Terraza has a great beach setting, rambling wooden premises, and popular pizzas that keep it packed with locals throughout the week.

## ❶ Getting There & Away

Buses heading northeast to Esmeraldas and south to Muisne pick up and drop off passengers at both Same and Tonchigüe. *Rancheras* (open-sided buses, or trucks mounted with uncomfortably narrow bench seats – also known as *chivas*) head to Tonchigüe from Esmeraldas.

## Muisne & Around

☎06

Muisne is a tumbledown, working-class island surrounded by river and sea. Its little ramshackle port bustles with a minor banana-shipping industry. Being relatively remote, Muisne attracts far fewer visitors than the more popular beaches, but it makes

an interesting foray off the beaten track. The long and lonely palm-lined beach at its back is its best feature.

The few remaining mangroves in the area are protected and worth a visit (see boxed text, p248).

### Dangers & Annoyances

Some beach cabins have had thefts, so check that your room is secure before you head out. Single travelers (especially women) should stick to the area of hotels and restaurants on the beach.

## ☞ Tours

### Fundecol
ECOTOURS

(☎248-0519; tours per day $25-50; www.fundecol.org) Community and mangrove tours are organized by the locally based Foundation for Ecological Defense. Costs vary depending on the tour and the group size, and include boat trips up Río Muisne to see the remaining mangroves and the impact of commercial shrimping (see boxed text, p248).

### Congal Bio-Station
ECOTOURS

Only 2km from Muisne is this 650-hectare marine reserve working with mangrove conservation and organic aquaculture. Volunteers are needed, but visitors are also welcome. There are great opportunities for snorkeling and scuba diving, plus comfortable private cabins with seafood on the menu. Room and full board costs $40 per person.

## 🛌 Sleeping & Eating

There are only budget options in Muisne and most owners were selling up when we last visited, so it's an idea to call ahead. Avoid the bleak hotels across the river and head to the island – here, you'll find beachfront cabañas on the far side. During the rainy months mosquitoes can be bad, so be sure to get a room with a net.

### Hostal Las Olas
HOTEL $

(☎248-0782; s/d $10/20) Facing the sea, Las Olas is a large, well-maintained guesthouse with nice woodwork throughout. Try to score room 11 up top, with a big sitting area adjoining the room: the rest of the accommodations are pretty basic and rather dark. There's also a popular open-sided restaurant on the ground floor.

### Calade Spondylus
GUESTHOUSE $

(☎248-0279; r/cabin per person $8/10) This basic place facing the beach has simple but clean rooms and wooden cabins. The best rooms have private bathrooms and open onto a shared balcony with ocean views. There's a sandy palm-filled yard surrounding the place.

**Viejo Willy** ECUADORIAN $
(main plaza; set lunch $2.25; ⏲8am-4pm) It seems like most of Muisne packs into this friendly place to enjoy the excellent set meals. You'll find it on the town square between the dock and the beach.

**Las Palmeiras** SEAFOOD $
(beach; mains $6; ⏲7am-7pm) This simple beach restaurant serves up shrimp or freshly caught fish with a sea view.

## Information

There is no bank in Muisne, and the post office (near the telephone office) is only open sporadically. An Andinatel office is located just off the main plaza.

## Getting There & Away

Buses from Esmeraldas go as far as the cement launch of El Relleno. From here take a motorized canoe across the mottled blue Río Muisne to the island ($0.20).

Buses depart from El Relleno about every 30 minutes to Esmeraldas ($2, 2½ hours) passing Same, Súa and Atacames en route. There are five buses a day to Santo Domingo de los Colorados ($6, five hours), where connections to Quito or Guayaquil are made. **Transportes Occidentales** (cnr Calle Principal & El Relleno) has a nightly bus to/from Quito ($9, 8½ hours). To go further south, take a bus to El Salto and then a bus to Pedernales ($3, three hours), from where you can connect to other towns down the coast.

## Getting Around

Muisne's main road leads directly away from the pier, crossing the center to the beach. It's 2km from end to end. Ecotaxis vie for passengers at the pier. It's $1 well spent for the wild ride at top rickshaw speed over potholes and sharp, rolling rubble.

# Mompiche

☎05

Famed for its world-class waves and gorgeous 7km-long strip of pristine (if grayish) sand, this little fishing village has finally been noticed by developers. Long popular with backpackers and surfers, Mompiche had barely been touched by the modern world until the creation of a good new road leading here. Even now, you still only see a few cars on the main road, and everyone in town still knows everyone else. Besides its fabulous stretch of palm-fringed sands, Mompiche has little else, and that's its beauty. But that may all change soon – a large hotel was under construction in 2012 and there are signs of more development to come. Hurry here to soak up the laid-back vibe, while you can.

## Sleeping & Eating

There is a growing number of hotels in town, including a large midrange hotel right on the beach that was under construction in 2012.

**Iruña** CABINS $$
(☎09-947-2458; teremompiche@yahoo.com; d $40, f from $50) A 45-minute walk down the beach from Mompiche's center takes you to this wonderfully isolated spot. Six spacious cabañas surround a pleasant restaurant and social area right on the beach, lurking among the palms. The wooden cabins come with mosquito nets, fridges, bathrooms and fans and good meals can be provided by arrangement. The hotel can arrange to pick you up in Mompiche, or organize a boat transfer from Muisne.

**Hostería Gabeal** HOTEL $
(☎09-969-6543; mompiche_gabeal@hotmail.com; per person without/with sea view $10/15; @) Housed in two large yet pleasingly rustic wooden blocks right on the beach, this long-standing favorite has simple, clean rooms with mosquito nets and decent bathrooms. It's worth spending more on a sea-view room. There's a restaurant on-site here, which serves breakfast. Other meals can be served by arrangement.

**Casa Yarumo** CABINS $
(☎08-867-2924; www.casayarumomompiche.com; per person $15) The home of a German family who have settled in Mompiche, this charming getaway has a cabin for two people and a far larger apartment in the main house. Both are comfortable and the location, a 10-minute walk down the beach from Mompiche, is just perfect – however, you'll have to ford the little stream as it runs into the sea. In case you aren't relaxed enough, professional massage is also available.

**La Facha** INTERNATIONAL $
(mains $5-8; ⏲noon-10pm) This excellent little restaurant is the best place to eat in town. A charming team of young locals (who also

## MANGROVES UNDER THREAT

Ecuador's coastal mangroves are an important habitat. In addition to helping to control the erosion of the coast, they provide homes, protection and nutrients for numerous species of birds, fish, mollusks and crustaceans. Unfortunately, mangroves have been in no-man's land, and it has been difficult to say who owns these coastal tropical forests, which are semipermanently inundated. Squatters took over areas of mangroves as their own, but this was not really a problem because their livelihood was based on low-impact fishing and gathering crabs and shellfish, allowing them to peacefully coexist.

This all changed in the 1980s with the arrival of shrimp farms, which produced shrimp in artificial conditions in numbers many times greater than could be caught by traditional shrimping methods. To build the farms, it was necessary to cut down the mangroves. The prospective owner of a shrimp farm purchased the land from the government, cut down the mangroves and began the shrimp-farming process. The net profits of the shrimp farms were very high, and the idea soon caught on and spread rapidly along the coast, resulting in the removal of 80% to 90% of Ecuador's mangroves during the 1980s and early 1990s. Although there are now laws controlling this destruction, these are difficult to enforce in the remote coastal areas.

The shrimp farms have had many negative short- and long-term effects. Previously, many families could find a sustainable livelihood in the mangroves, whereas shrimp farms employ only a handful of seasonal workers. Where before there were mangroves protecting a large diversity of species, now there's just commercial shrimp. Coastal erosion and pollution from the wastes of the shrimp farms have become serious problems. A combination of disease and economic decline means that today many farms lie abandoned. Meanwhile, efforts are being made in Muisne, Bahía de Caráquez and a few other coastal towns to start replanting mangroves. Fascinating boat tours of the remaining mangrove forests support the conservation efforts of Fundecol (p246).

run the hostel in the same building, and are all keen surfers) serve up mouthwatering burgers, salads and sandwiches. It's on the street behind the Malecón.

**Milicho's**                                         SEAFOOD $
(Malecón; mains $4-8; ☺8am-10pm) This popular local spot near Hostería Gabeal is your best bet for beachside breakfast. It serves up pancakes, eggs and fresh juices each morning, and there's also a good selection of fresh fish and seafood.

### ❶ Getting There & Away

Buses go to and from Esmeraldas a few times per day ($4, 3½ hours), passing Same and Atacames on the way.

## Canoa

05 / POP 6100

A sleepy village with a heart of gold, Canoa has a lovely stretch of beach framed by picturesque cliffs to the north and a disappearing horizon to the south. Despite its growing popularity with sunseekers and surfers, the village remains a low-key place, where kids frolic on the sandy lanes at dusk

and fishers head out to sea in the early hours before dawn. In the evenings the beachfront bars and guesthouses come to life as backpackers swap travel tales over rum cocktails.

International surf competitions come in the high season (December to February), when waves reach over 2m and accommodation becomes hard to find. Swimming is better after the surf season. At low tide you can reach caves at the north end of the beach, which house hundreds of roosting bats. Canoa is also a good place to make arrangements to visit the lush Río Muchacho Organic Farm.

### ⊙ Activities

Ask around about horseback-riding, kayaking, and rafting trips: you'll see all three being offered along the beach by various outfits.

**Surfing**                                          SURFING
(rental per half-day $5, per day $10) Surfboard rental is available at many guesthouses, as well as along the beach, where you'll be approached by many locals offering surfboard rental.

## 🛏 Sleeping

**Coco Loco** GUESTHOUSE $
(☎09-243-6508; hotalcocoloco@yahoo.com; dm $8, with shared bathroom $6, d incl breakfast $30, with shared bathroom $20; ☎) This backpacker favorite right on the beach has clean rooms with decent mattresses and bamboo furnishings, and a sand- and palm-filled yard in the front. People tend to stick around longer than planned: there's a laid-back happy hour, barbecue nights (Thursday to Sunday), and lots of activities on offer.

**Casa Shangri-La** GUESTHOUSE $
(☎258-8076, 09-146-8470; per person $8; ☎☎) This fantastic new place is just a few hundred meters north of town on the road to Pedernales. It's owned by a friendly Dutch guy who has created a chilled-out surfer spot with a big garden, very nice rooms and a super-relaxed vibe. It's a short walk to a secluded spot of beach away from the crowds in town.

**Posada Olmito** GUESTHOUSE $
(☎258-8174, 09-553-3341; Malecón; d $18, with shared bathroom $15; ☎) Right on the beach you'll find this decidedly rustic and rather higgledy-piggledy structure that's perfect for beach bums. The fan-cooled bamboo rooms have small bathrooms but come with hot water. The vibe is beyond relaxed.

**Amalur** GUESTHOUSE $
(☎08-303-5039, 08-812-9486; www.amalurcanoa.com; s/d/tr $10/20/30, ☎) The town's best restaurant also has a range of rooms tucked away out the back overlooking a sandy garden. Rooms are clean; all have hot water and mosquito nets; and it's a short stroll across the football field to the beach.

**Hotel País Libre** GUESTHOUSE $
(☎261-6536; r per person $15, with shared bathroom $10; ☎☎) Owned by an Ecuadorian surf pro, País Libre is a colorful multistory wood-framed building with hewn-log banisters and bamboo-crafted rooms. It has its own disco and swimming pool, and hammocks on the upper decks. The rooms come equipped with fans as well as hot water.

**La Posada de Daniel** GUESTHOUSE $
(☎09-750-8825; posadadaniel83@hotmail.com; r per person incl breakfast $17, camping per tent incl breakfast $8; ☎☎☎) One of Canoa's first guesthouses, La Posada de Daniel has smartened itself up with a full renovation recently and it's looking much better for it. Even if you choose not to stay in the comfortable rooms, the camping area provides good tents and thick air mattresses. There's also a small pool and a casual thatch-roofed bar. It's located a few blocks inland.

**La Vista** GUESTHOUSE $
(☎09-228-8995; Malecón; s/d/tr $16/24/30; ☎☎) La Vista is a slightly more upscale four-story guesthouse. Its spacious, nicely designed rooms have beamed ceilings and glass (rather than bamboo) windows, and it's right on the beach.

## ✗ Eating & Drinking

**TOP CHOICE Amalur** SPANISH $
(mains $4-8; ☎noon-9pm) Owned by a talented Spanish couple ('Amalur' means 'Mother Earth' in Basque), this trim, minimalist restaurant is a great place to dine and is a major step up from your average Ecuadorian small-town restaurant. A chalkboard lists the day's delicacies – a few recent favorites include fresh calamari in ink, gazpacho, grilled pork with red peppers, nicely seasoned eggplant in salsa and a marvelously tender sea bass. It's two blocks back from the beach overlooking the soccer field.

**Café Flor** INTERNATIONAL $
(mains $4-9; ☎4-10pm Mon-Sat) This sweet, family-run cafe serves a range of delicious, carefully prepared dishes, including pizzas, burritos, hamburgers, veggie burgers, steaks, American-style breakfasts and more. Inquire here about inexpensive surfing or Spanish lessons. There's also a popular daily happy hour (7pm to 9pm). It sits two blocks from the beach near the ballfields.

**Surf Shack** INTERNATIONAL $
(Malecón; mains $5-10; ☎8am-midnight) Another popular beachfront bar-restaurant, Surf Shack serves up pizzas, burgers, filling breakfasts and plenty of rum cocktails to a fun-seeking foreign crowd. There's also plenty of gear for hire here: kayaks, rafts, motorbikes, surfboards and more.

## 🛍 Shopping

**Organic Market** MARKET
On Saturday mornings, Río Muchacho (p250) sponsors an organic market on the main street, where local farmers bring their fresh produce and other homemade goodies for sale.

## ⓘ Information

There are no banks in Canoa (San Vicente has the nearest ATMs), but there are several public phone centers on the main street, and (slow) internet access at several places around the main street.

Because of unreliable phone service in town, most local businesses use mobile (cell) phones.

## ⓘ Getting There & Around

Buses between Bahía de Caráquez and Pedernales or Esmeraldas will all stop in Canoa. The bus lets passengers off on the Calle Principal (main street) in town. From here it's just a few short blocks to the beach, where many of the accommodation options are located.

## Around Canoa

At **Río Muchacho Organic Farm** (✆05-258-8184; www.riomuchacho.com), guests and locals get their hands dirty engaging in and learning about sustainable farming practices.

Lying along the river of the same name, this tropical organic farm is reached by a rough 8km track branching inland from the road north of Canoa. Transportation to the farm is normally on horseback, which is how the local *montubios* (coastal farmers) get around.

The farm is proactive in the community and has built a primary school that teaches children about reforestation and waste management (as well as their ABCs).

After touring the farm, inspecting the crops and learning about permaculture and organic farming, visitors are free to choose from a variety of activities including fishing for river shrimp or making ornaments from tagua nuts. Those who want unadulterated nature can take guided hikes, or go horseback-riding or bird-watching.

On the accommodation front, cabins are Thoreau-approved rustic, with shared showers and composting toilets. The coveted spot is a tree-house bunk. Guest groups are kept small and reservations are a must. Most people come here on a three-day, two-night tour costing $120 per person, with a minimum of two people.

Volunteers are welcome to stay longer and work in the school or on the farm, and are charged $150 for one week (or $400 a month) for food and lodging. Spanish courses are available, and the farm offers a month-long apprenticeship in organic agriculture (billed as a course).

For more information, contact the farm directly, or you can also arrange tours through Guacamayo Tours (p250) in Bahía de Caráquez.

# Bahía de Caráquez

✆05 / POP 19,700

Chalk-colored high-rises and red-tile roofs fill this bustling peninsula, which enjoys what must surely be the best location of any town in Ecuador. With the Río Chone on one side flowing into the Pacific on the other, this tidy former port city basks in the sun and enjoys a wonderfully laid-back feel. In the first half of the 20th century the city was Ecuador's principal port, but eroding sandbanks let the honor drift to Guayaquil and Manta, and Bahía was left to its housekeeping.

Despite a string of natural disasters (including the landslides induced by the 1998 El Niño and a bad earthquake that same year), Bahía has done a remarkable job of picking itself up and starting anew – at times reinventing itself, most recently as the vanguard of Ecuador's fledgling green movement. The market recycles its waste, organic farms surround the town, and reforestation projects target hillsides damaged after the 1998 El Niño and also focus on mangrove forests decimated by shrimp farming.

The town is also the base for the Chirije archaeological site (p253).

## ⊙ Sights & Activities

FREE **Museo Bahía de Caráquez**    MUSEUM
(cnr Malecón Santos & Peña; ☺8:30am-4:30pm Tue-Fri, 9am-2:30pm Sat) You'll find a good introduction to the area's indigenous history at this well-curated modern museum. The collection includes hundreds of pieces of pre-Columbian pottery, as well as local crafts for sale.

**Mirador La Cruz**    VIEWPOINT
High above the peninsula and boasting great views of the city, sea and river, this viewpoint at the south end of town can be reached on foot or by a short taxi ride.

## ☞ Tours

**Guacamayo Tours**    ECOTOURS
(✆269-1412; www.guacamayotours.com; cnr Bolívar & Arenas) is owned by an Ecuadorian–New Zealand couple. The company arranges tours to Río Muchacho Organic

# Bahía de Caráquez

N 0 ⸺ 200 m
0 ⸺ 0.1 miles

## Bahía de Caráquez

**◎ Sights**
1 Mirador La Cruz ........................... A5
2 Museo Bahía de Caráquez .................. B5

**🚴 Activities, Courses & Tours**
  Bahía Dolphin Tours ................... (see 4)
3 Guacamayo Tours ........................ A4

**🛏 Sleeping**
4 CasaGrande Oceanfront
    Boutique Hotel ....................... B1
5 Centro Vacacional Life ................... B2
6 Hotel Italia ............................ A3
7 Hotel La Herradura ..................... A2
8 Hotel La Piedra ........................ A2

**🍴 Eating**
9 Arena Bar .............................. A3
10 D'Camaron ............................ A2
  Hotel La Herradura .................. (see 7)
11 Puerto Amistad ........................ B5
12 Riverside Restaurants ................. B5
13 Vereda ............................... A2

Guacamayo also organizes a number of other tours, including canoe tours with a local fishers through mangrove forests that feature abundant birdlife. Learn about the problems facing the mangrove habitat by taking trips to local islands that have sea-bird colonies (including one of the coast's largest frigate-bird colonies), and visit a private zoo. There are also whale-watching trips that run from late September to early October. Río Muchacho goods, and products from the recycling center, are on sale at the Guacamayo office.

**Bahía Dolphin Tours**      TOURS
(☑269-0257; www.bahiadolphintours.com; Casa-Grande Oceanfront Boutique Hotel, Virgílio Ratti 606) This company owns the Chirije archaeological site (p253), and offers day visits or overnight tours to the site. The staff can arrange packages with overnight stays at Chirije and in Bahía, combined with visits to panama-hat workshops, an organic shrimp farm, frigate-bird islands and other local points of interest. Guides speak English, French and German.

## 🛏 Sleeping

Some of the cheap places have water-supply problems.

Farm (p250) and offers fascinating eco-city tours, where travelers can learn about the grassroots community projects that have made Bahía a model for sustainable development – projects such as organic shrimp farming, environmental education in schools, mangrove replanting and more.

Three-hour tours take in a reforestation project, followed by a visit to the waterfront via ecotaxi (bicycle taxi) and a stop at Ecopapel, a paper-recycling center where discarded paper is combined with fruit and vegetable fibers to make lovely hand-crafted paper products.

### CasaGrande Oceanfront Boutique Hotel
BOUTIQUE HOTEL **$$$**

(269-0257; www.casagrandebahia.com; Virgílio Ratti 606; r incl breakfast $104-147; P❄🖥🌊) With views toward the ocean, the lovely CasaGrande offers six handsomely furnished, spacious rooms with polished wood floors and modern bathrooms. The best rooms have balconies strung with hammocks. There's a comfy lounge, stylish public areas and a refreshing pool.

### Hotel La Herradura
HOTEL **$$**

(269-0446; Bolívar 202; s/d/ste from $50/60/100, s/d without air-con or hot water $25/40; P❄🖥) This old Spanish home brims with antiques and artwork and has been lovingly furnished – it looks almost like a New York or London interiors store. The cheaper rooms are pretty basic, while those upstairs are much better, with sea views, splashes of style and hot water.

### Casa Ceibo
LUXURY HOTEL **$$$**

(239-9399; www.casaceibo.com; Av Sixto Durán Ballén; r incl breakfast $366; P❄🖥🌊) If you're looking for pampering and seclusion, then this new gated luxury hotel 4km from the center of Bahía is the place for you (it's on the road out of town, just beyond the bus station). With plush rooms that have all creature comforts, minimalist public areas and huge manicured gardens that lead down to the river, this is definitely the smartest place in town. Kayaking, biking, use of the gym, sauna and pool are all included and there's a full service restaurant here as well.

### Hotel La Piedra
BEACH HOTEL **$$$**

(269-0780; www.hotellapiedra.com; Virgílio Ratti; s/d $91/112; P❄🖥🌊) This big full-service hotel offers large, clean rooms with great ocean views. There's also a sumptuous palm-shaded pool, ringed with lounge chairs, that's just steps from the crashing waves. It has the advantage of allowing for full resort-style relaxation, while just being moments from the bars and restaurants in town.

### Centro Vacacional Life
CABINS **$**

(269-0496; cnr Octavio Vitteri & Muñoz Dávila; r per person $15; ❄🖥) Ideal for families. Six small cabins with kitchens sit on this gated grassy lot, which features a playground. Each cabin has cable TV and hot water, and, to please animal lovers, there are lots of pets on the property.

### Hotel Italia
HOTEL **$$**

(269-1137; cnr Bolívar & Checa; per person s/d $18/37; P❄) An old-fashioned four-story hotel right in the heart of town, with simple high-ceilinged rooms, fans, hot water and cable TV. Rooms with air-con cost extra and on our visit the staff were on the frosty side.

##  Eating

You'll find a slew of weathered restaurants on the river pier, with perfect sunset ambience. They're popular for seafood (especially ceviche) and open from morning until midnight.

### TOP CHOICE Puerto Amistad
INTERNATIONAL **$$**

(Malecón Santos; mains $6-12; ⏰noon-11pm Mon-Sat) Puerto Amistad is an expat favorite for its delicious fare, strong cocktails and the attractive and airy deck over the water. Salads, savory crepes, quesadillas, seafood dishes and steaks are all excellent and service is friendly and professional. This slightly upscale restaurant also functions as Bahía's yacht club and is the place to bump into other visiting yachties.

### Hotel La Herradura
ECUADORIAN **$$**

(Bolívar 202; mains $5-10; ⏰7am-10pm) With its high ceilings and wrought-iron chandeliers, this attractive seafront place feels nothing like a hotel restaurant. The original menu offers delicious green-plantain bread and tart ceviches sprinkled with cilantro, although service is not always particularly warm.

### Arena Bar
PIZZERIA **$**

(Marañón; mains $3-8; ⏰5pm-midnight) Chow down to international rhythms and casual surf decor at this friendly place. The pizzas are good, but there is plenty of other choice, including excellent salads and tasty sandwiches.

### D'Camaron
SEAFOOD **$**

(Bolívar; mains $3-7; ⏰9am-6pm) As the name implies, shrimp is the specialty at this casual open-air spot near the water. Order them grilled, with a cocktail, and enjoy the ocean breezes.

### Vereda
SEAFOOD **$**

(Muñoz Dávila; mains $3-7; ⏰7am-7pm) This popular yet tiny family-run restaurant is winningly simple and serves up a range of regional favorites including crab, ceviche, grilled river fish and seafood platters.

## ℹ Information

**Banco de Guayaquil** (cnr Bolívar & Riofrío) Cashes travelers checks and has an ATM.

**Genesis Net** (Malecón Santos 1302; per hr $1; ⊙9am-9:30pm Mon-Sat, 10am-8pm Sun) Internet and cheap international calls.

## ℹ Getting There & Away

A new bridge now connects Bahía to San Vicente (and the rest of the north coast) over the Río Chone. This eliminates the need for long drives around the bay or a ferry ride across the river.

The bus terminal is 4km from the center of town on the Malecón as you head towards Chone. From there you'll find buses that offer regular or *ejecutivo* (first-class) services – they head to Quito (regular/*ejecutivo* $7.50/10, eight hours, four daily) via Santo Domingo (regular/ *ejecutivo* $5/6), and there are services to Guayaquil ($7, six hours, 7 daily), Manta ($2.50, three hours, three daily) and Canoa ($1, 45 minutes, every half-hour).

## Around Bahía de Caráquez

Located 15km south of Bahía, **Chirije archaeological site** (www.chirije.com) is riddled with ancient ceramics, burials, cooking areas, garbage dumps and jewelry, dating mainly from the Bahía culture (500 BC to AD 500).

The site is owned by Bahía Dolphin Tours (p251), and to visit you must arrange a guided trip through the agency. The sheer number of remains leads archaeologists to think that this was once an important port. Only small sections of the site have been professionally excavated, and some pieces are exhibited in the tiny on-site museum – but visitors will find shards of pottery all over the place.

Chirije is cut off by high tides, so visits have to be planned with this in mind (Bahía Dolphin Tours has this information). Visitors can spend the night and take advantage of trails into the coastal tropical dry forest. Four large solar cabins sleep up to eight people (although it's a squeeze) and have a porch, a private bathroom and a kitchen. Rates are $75 per cabin, and meals are available on request. A day tour of Chirije, including lunch, costs $45 per person.

## Manta

🗗05 / POP 217,500

The largest city in the province (and the fifth-largest in Ecuador), Manta is a bustling and prosperous port town, graced with high-rises, and a few urban beaches that draw mostly national tourists. As an important center for the fishing and tuna processing industries, it's the kind of place you smell before you arrive, and its quirkiest sight is a huge statue of a tuna. Indeed, there's not a lot of reason to come here – the beaches are far better elsewhere on the coast – but it's an important transportation hub, has a lively nightlife scene and you may pass through if you're visiting the handicraft town of Montecristi.

## ◉ Sights & Activities

**Museo del Banco Central**                    MUSEUM
(Malecón near Calle 20; admission $1; ⊙9am-5pm Tue-Sat, 11am 3pm Sun) The fully modernized city museum reopened in its new location in 2009, and showcases valuable artifacts from pre-Columbian Manta culture, a selection of Ecuadorian paintings and quirky fishing paraphernalia.

**Playa Murciélago**                                BEACH
This beach is less protected than Tarqui Beach, and it has bigger waves (although they're not very big, there's a powerful undertow). It's a couple of kilometers northwest of downtown and is the town's most popular beach, backed by snack bars, restaurants and umbrella rental spots.

**Tarqui Beach**                                     BEACH
The east end of this stretch of sand is a hive of activity early in the mornings, as vendors sell row upon row of shark, tuna, swordfish, dorado and other fish (whose size decrease with each passing year). You'll also find the so-called Parque del Marisco here: lots of stalls serving up fresh fish and seafood in a variety of different styles right on the beach, including what locals will swear to you is the best ceviche in the country. The beach is suitable for swimming.

## 🛏 Sleeping

Prices rise on vacation weekends and during the high seasons (December to March and June to August).

**Hotel Balandra**                          HOTEL $$$
(🗗262-0545; www.hotelbalandramanta.com; Av 7 near Calle 20; s/d/cabin $86/100/120; ❄@🛜🏊) This small but upscale hillside hotel offers pleasantly furnished rooms and swish two-bedroom cabins, some with balconies looking out to sea. Outside you'll find sculpted

# Manta

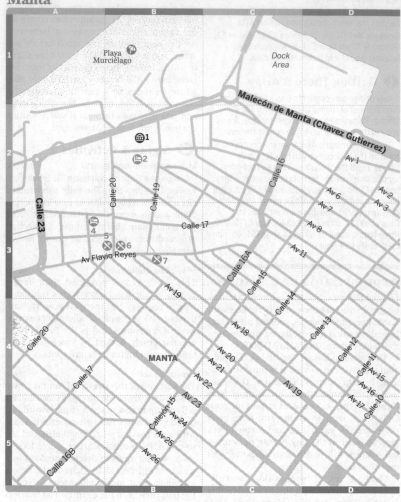

## Manta

shrubbery, a small gym and sauna, a pool and a playground.

**Manakin**      GUESTHOUSE **$$**
(☎262-0413; Calle 17 & Av 21; s/d/tr incl breakfast $40/50/65; ❄️@🛜) Near the heart of all the nightlife, Manakin is a converted one-story house with a pleasant laid-back vibe. Narrow, well-ordered rooms are nicely furnished, and the house offers fine places to unwind – including the front patio.

**Leo Hotel**      HOTEL **$**
(☎262-3159; Av 24 de Mayo; s/d $15/25; ❄️) Across from the bus station, Leo offers small,

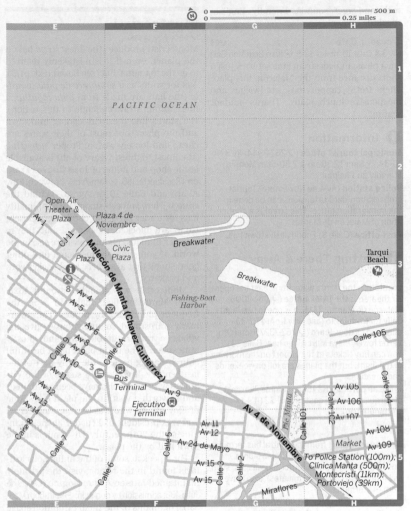

clean rooms, some of which lack windows. Convenient if you're just passing through.

## ✗ Eating

Seafood *comedores* line the east end of the beach on Malecón de Tarqui. Playa Murciélago has cafes front and center for enjoying beach action.

**Parrillada Oh Mar**  GRILL $$
(cnr Av 20 & Flavio Reyes; mains $7-12; ⊗noon-11pm Mon-Sat) This amenable glass-walled grill in the center of Manta's nightlife area is a great place for a filling steak and a glass of good Argentinian red wine.

**Beachcomber**  GRILL $
(cnr Calle 20 & Flavio Reyes; mains $4-10; ⊗6pm-midnight) Near the heart of the nightlife, the popular Beachcomber is a favorite for its grilled meats. Dine in the lush backyard garden or on the open-sided front porch.

**Trosky Burguer**  BURGERS $
(cnr Av 18 & Flavio Reyes; mains $3-7; ⊗6pm-3am Tue-Sun) This popular surfer-run snack spot serves juicy burgers grilled to order amid

rock and reef sounds. Friendly English-speaking owner.

**Trovador Café** CAFE $
(Av 3 & Calle 10; mains $2-5; ☺8am-8pm Mon-Sat)
On a pleasant pedestrian lane set back just a short distance from the Malecón, this place offers frothy cappuccinos, sandwiches and inexpensive lunch plates. There's outdoor seating.

## ❶ Information

**Municipal tourist office** (☎262-2944; Av 3 No 10-34; ☺8am-12:30pm & 2:30-5pm Mon-Fri) Friendly and helpful.

**Police station** (Av 4 de Noviembre) Tourist embarkation-card extensions can be done in the immigration office. This street is a continuation of Malecón de Manta.

**Post office** (Calle 8) Found at the town hall.

## ❶ Getting There & Away

### Air

Located on the Manta waterfront, past the open-air theater, is the **TAME office** (☎262-2006; Malecón de Manta). TAME has one to two flights daily to/from Quito (one-way from $70, 30 minutes) as does **Icaro** (☎262-7327; Hotel Oro Verde tower, Playa Murciélago near Calle 23). You can buy tickets at the airport on the morning of the flight, but the planes are full on weekends and vacations.

The **airport** (☎262-1580) is some 3km east of Tarqui, and a taxi costs about $2 (it's a 10-minute trip).

### Bus

Most buses depart from the central bus terminal in front of the fishing-boat harbor in Manta. Buses to nearby Manabí towns and villages, such as Montecristi ($0.50, 15 minutes), also leave from the terminal.

Buses serve Jipijapa ($0.90, one hour), Canoa ($4, 3½ to four hours), Bahía de Caráquez ($2.50, three hours), Guayaquil ($5, four hours), Esmeraldas ($7, six hours) and Ambato ($8, 10 hours).

*Ejecutivo* buses to Quito ($10, nine hours) and Guayaquil ($7.50, four hours) leave from a smaller nearby terminal on the Malecón throughout the day.

# Montecristi

📋 05 / POP 14,500

Montecristi produces the finest straw hat on the planet, even if it is mistakenly referred to as the 'panama' hat (see boxed text, p175). Ask for yours as a *sombrero de paja toquilla* (the hats are made from *paja toquilla*, a fine, fibrous straw endemic to this region). Hat stores line the road leading into town and the plaza, but most of their wares are cheap and loosely woven. Proper *superfino* (the finest, tightest weave of all) is available at the shop and home of **José Chávez Franco** (Rocafuerte 386; ☺7am-7pm), between Eloy Alfaro and Calle 10 de Agosto, behind the church. Here you can snatch up high-quality hats for under $100, but check them closely. None are blocked or banded but they're cheaper than just about anywhere else in the world. If you shop around you'll find other good shops that also carry local wickerwork and basketry.

Montecristi was founded around 1628, when Manteños fled inland to avoid the frequent plundering by pirates. The town's many unrestored colonial houses give the village a rather tumbledown and ghostly atmosphere. The main plaza has a beautiful church dating back to the early part of the last century. It contains a statue of the Virgin (to which miracles have been attributed) and is worth a visit. In the plaza is a statue of Eloy Alfaro, who was born in Montecristi and was president of Ecuador at the beginning of the 20th century. His tomb is in the town hall by the plaza.

For a peek at some of the indigenous artifacts found in the region, visit the privately maintained **Museo Arqueológico** (Calle 9 de Julio 436; admission by donation; ☺9am-6pm Mon-Sat). Highlights of the small exhibition space include a primitive percussion instrument, giant funereal urns and elaborate carvings in stone.

Montecristi can be reached during the day by frequent buses ($0.50, 30 minutes) from the bus terminal in Manta.

# South Coast

## Best Places to Eat

» Lo Nuestro (p285)
» Marea (p268)
» Beachfront Shacks (p263)
» Hostería Farallón Dillon (p268)
» Cevichelandía (p270)

## Best Places to Stay

» Hostería Mandála (p262)
» Balsa Surf Camp (p267)
» Samaí Lodge (p265)
» Mansion del Rio (p282)
» Camping in Parque Nacional Machalilla (p261)

## Why Go?

Stretching all the way from Puerto López in the north to the Peruvian border in the south, this region features a long, sandy coastline. A motley crew of international travelers heads to seriously mellow hangouts to surf and chill while *guayaquileños* (people from Guayaquil) and people sport-fishing and yachting fill the hotels and condominiums of resort towns. Trails through the coastal mountain cloud forests lead past small villages, rushing brooks and all manner of birdlife.

Guayaquil, Ecuador's largest city and commercial and business capital, includes the Disneyfied *malecón* (waterfront), museums and nightlife rivaling any in the country. All flights to the Galápagos Islands leave from here.

South of Guayaquil is mostly banana country, featuring miles and miles of the unripe green fruit, also known as *oro verde* (green gold). The regional capital of Machala makes a good base for exploring nearby mountain towns, and it's a convenient stopover for those heading to Peru.

## When to Go
### Guayaquil

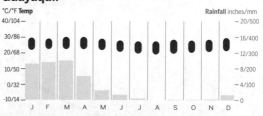

**Jan–May** The rainy season when the coast is hot, humid and sunny, with occasional heavy rains.

**Jun–Dec** The dry season is cooler and more overcast. Humpback whales visit June to September.

**End Dec–Apr** This is generally when Ecuadorians visit coastal resorts.

# South Coast Highlights

**1** Get up close and personal with nesting boobies and other birdlife on **Isla de la Plata** (p263)

**2** Slow down and do some serious chilling at surf mecca **Montañita** (p265)

**3** Hike one of the trails snaking their way through the coastal mountain **cloud forests** (p266)

**4** Take a Sunday stroll along the **Malecón 2000** (El Malecón; p273), Guayaquil's amusement-park-like riverfront promenade

**5** Breathe in the cool air and spectacular views around **Zaruma** (p294)

**6** Spot massive **humpback whales** breaching only meters away from your boat on their annual mating sojourn (p261)

**7** Chow down on piles of shellfish and freshly caught seafood at a beachfront restaurant in **Playas** (p268)

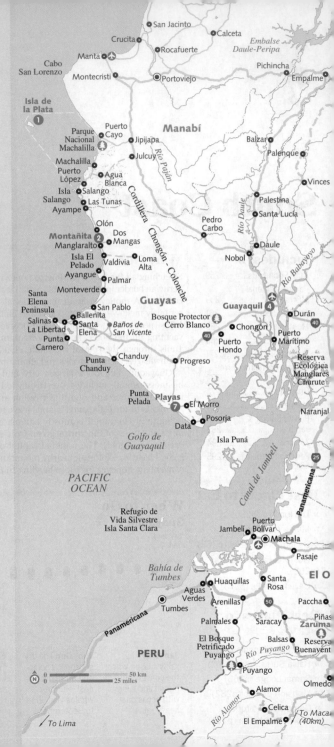

## Getting There & Away

Guayaquil is serviced by many direct international flights, as well as by frequent connections to Quito. All flights to the Galápagos Islands also leave from here. By road from Quito, most travelers head first to Manta (about nine hours from Quito) or Puerto López (nearly 10 hours from Quito) and work slowly down the coast from there, although there are also plenty of direct buses to Guayaquil. Guayaquil is about five spectacular hours from Guaranda (in the central highlands) and less than four hours from Cuenca via the road through Parque Nacional Cajas.

## Getting Around

You can get to most destinations around the south coast direct from Guayaquil. For spots along the Ruta Spondylus, it's usually one easy bus transfer in Santa Elena or La Libertad. Direct minivan services also link Guayaquil with several of these towns. For smaller towns south of Guayaquil, Machala is the secondary transport hub. Roads almost everywhere are paved; however, many are narrow two-lane highways crammed with heavily laden trucks, speeding buses, pickups that should have been decommissioned decades ago, and a general lack of concern for road-safety rules.

# RUTA SPONDYLUS

The coastline stretching from the Parque Nacional Machalilla south to the Santa Elena Peninsula is no longer known as the Ruta del Sol, in part to emphasize that there's much more than sun and sand here. Also, because a thick foggy mist blankets the landscape during the *garúa* (drizzly) months, the moniker Ruta del Sol was only periodically accurate. The area's geography runs the gamut from an uninspiring and lifeless mix of dry scrub and cactus to lush mountain-covered cloud forests and offshore islands teeming with unique flora and fauna.

## Parque Nacional Machalilla

♫05

Ecuador's only coastal national park is a reminder of what much of the Central and South American Pacific coast once looked like. Now, having almost entirely disappeared, it's one of the most threatened tropical forests in the world. The park, created in 1979, preserves a small part of the country's rapidly vanishing coastal habitats, protecting about 50km of beach (less than 2% of Ecuador's coastline), some 40,000 hectares of tropical dry forest and cloud forest, and about 20,000 hectares of ocean (including offshore islands, of which Isla de la Plata is the most important).

The tropical dry forest found in much of the inland sectors of the park forms a strange and wonderful landscape of characteristically bottle-shaped trees with small crowns and heavy spines (a protection against herbivores). In the upper reaches of the park, humid cloud forest is encountered. Some of the most common species include the leguminous *algarrobo*, which has green bark and is able to photosynthesize even when it loses its leaves. The fruits of the ceiba (kapok) tree yield a fiber that floats and doesn't get waterlogged. Before the advent of modern synthetics it was used in life jackets. Fig, laurel and palo santo trees are also commonly seen. Tall, spindly candelabra cacti are abundant on the hillsides, as is prickly pear.

Within this strange-looking forest is a variety of bird and animal life. Well over 200 species of bird have been recorded, including a range of coastal parrots and parakeets, as well seabirds such as frigate birds, pelicans and boobies – some of which nest on the offshore islands. Other animals include deer, squirrels, howler monkeys, anteaters and a variety of lizards, snakes and iguanas.

Most of the park's archaeological sites date from the Manta period, which began around AD 500 and lasted until the Spanish conquest. There are also remains of the much older Machalilla and Chorrera cultures, dating from about 800 BC to 500 BC, and the Salango culture (from 3000 BC). While important, none of the sites are particularly striking for the casual visitor.

The northern border of the park is marked by the somewhat desolate fishing village of Puerto Cayo. From the highway above town, it looks substantial enough, strung along the length of the shoreline. Upon closer inspection, especially at noon, it seems like a ghost town. If stopping for a break, head to one of the basic open-air seafood eateries located between the beach and town square.

From December to May, it is sunny and uncomfortably hot, with frequent short rainstorms. From June to November, it is cooler and often overcast.

# Parque Nacional Machalilla

N ☉

| 0 | 10 km |
| 0 | 5 miles |

Parque Nacional
Machalilla

Bahía Drake
Isla de    ℹ Ranger Station
la Plata      Sendero
              Punta
Punta         Escaleras
Machete  Sendero
         Punta    Punta
         Machete  Escalera

Inset

| 0 | 4 km |
| 0 | 2 miles |

To Isla de
La Plata (25km)
(see Inset)

Puerto
Cayo

Salaite

Julcuy

4WD Only

Machalilla

Los Frailes
Beach      ℹ Ranger
             Station
Park
Entrance
           Agua
           Blanca

La Playita       ● Puerto López   El Pital
Beach    Los Piqueros
         Overlook
Isla                Río          San
Salango  ● Salango  Blanco       Sebastián

                                  Río Piñas

PACIFIC
OCEAN    ● Puerto Rico   4WD      Manabí
                         Only
         ● Las Tunas              Casa Viejas
Ayampe                            Río Ayampe

Guayas

## ⊙ Sights & Activities

**Los Frailes Beach**                        BEACH
Marked by dramatic headlands on ei-
ther side, this truly breathtaking stretch
of beach is worth the price of admission.
Look for the turn-off about 10km north
of Puerto López, just before the town of
Machalilla. After purchasing or showing
your ticket at the ranger station, it's another 3km along a dirt road to the beach
(swimmers take caution; there are strong
undertows). There's also a 4km nature trail
that runs through the dry forest to two se-
cluded beaches and lookouts – keep your
eye out for blue-footed boobies.

**Agua Blanca**                    VILLAGE, HIKING
A visit to this small indigenous community
and its surrounding territory is a chance to
escape tar-and-concrete modern Ecuador.
Though the village of Agua Blanca itself is
nothing more than a scattering of simple

wood-and-bamboo dwellings, it's note-
worthy for what's missing: there's no noise
and no pollution – it's just fresh air and
strong breezes. You'll find the turn-off,
where you pay a $5 charge (which also cov-
ers museum admission and a guide) about
5.5km north of Puerto López on the right
side of the road. From here it's another 6km
down a dusty, bumpy road to the village. The
**archaeological museum** (⊙8am-6pm) is
well worth a visit; Spanish-speaking guides
explain the significance of the artifacts, including well-preserved ceramics and funeral
urns. The tour continues a short walk away
at the **Manta site**, believed to have been
an important political capital of the Manta
people. Only the bases of the buildings can
be seen, but there are thought to be approximately 400 buildings, some waiting for
more complete excavation.

Then it's a fairly delightful hour-plus
walk, across a bone-dry riverbed and

through an equally arid tropical forest. You can stop along the way to soak in the **sulfur pool**, where the combination of hot water and therapeutic mud are the equal of any spa treatment. Close to the end of the walk there's a raised platform with outstanding views and plenty of interesting **birdlife** and **plant life**, which knowledgeable guides will point out. Because of the merciless sun it's easy to succumb to heat exhaustion while walking in the area, so bring a hat, sunscreen and water.

### San Sebastián & Julcuy
CYCLING, HORSEBACK-RIDING
This excellent four-hour hike or horseback ride is to the southeast of Agua Blanca. The trail ascends a transition zone to humid remnant cloud forest at San Sebastián, about 600m above sea level. Horses (per person $10 to $15) can be hired if you don't want to hike the 20km round trip, and guides ($20) are mandatory. Contract one in Puerto López, Agua Blanca or San Sebastián (tour companies in Puerto López charge around $40 per person). It's best to stay overnight, but camping or staying with local people are the only accommodations.

Another option is to continue through Agua Blanca up the Río Julcuy valley to the northeast. From Agua Blanca, it's a six- to seven-hour hike through the park, coming out at the village of Julcuy, just beyond the park boundary. From Julcuy, it's about another three hours to the main Jipijapa-Guayaquil road. Four-wheel drives may be able to pass this road in good weather, but it's mainly a horse trail. Some tour agencies in Puerto López and guides in Agua Blanca (the latter don't provide bicycles) can arrange full-day mountain-biking trips (per person $35) from Jipijapa to Julcuy to Agua Blanca; only the aerobically fit should consider this option.

## Tours

### TOP CHOICE Humpback Whales
BOAT TOURS
Only the muscular ballet of mating humpbacks that abound in these waters between mid-June and early October (especially July and August) can compete with Isla de la Plata's natural wonders. Whale-watching is a booming business here, and despite the strict guidelines and legally enforced rules and etiquette, scientists are concerned about tourism's impact on the mating habits of these gentle beasts.

## Sleeping

Camping is allowed in much of the park, and is most often done as part of an overnight tour booked through an agency in Puerto López. There's also a designated **campsite** (per person $5), which is nothing more than a fenced-off patch of land with bathroom facilities in the forest – it's a few kilometers from Agua Blanca, a short walk from the sulfur pool. For camping and possible homestay opportunities in San Sebastián and Agua Blanca, inquire at the museum in Agua Blanca; tents and sleeping bags are provided. Check with park authorities about the availability of water, particularly during the dry season (June to December).

## Information

The **park headquarters** (230-0170; 8am-5pm) and a regional tourism office share a building in Puerto López on the opposite side of the market and plaza area from the bus terminals. The park entrance fee (adult/under 16yr $2/0.50) covers any or all sectors of the park (including the islands) and is valid for a single day.

## Getting There & Away

At least every hour, buses run up and down the coast between Puerto López and Jipijapa (hee-pee-*hah*-pah). You should have no difficulty getting a bus to drop you off at the park entrance or finding one to pick you up when you're ready to leave. However, while there is the occasional truck from the main road to Agua Blanca, it can be a long, hot wait; walking the 5km is an option if you're fit (bring water). However, the most sensible plan is to hire a taxi in Puerto López (round trip $10; includes a stop at Los Frailes).

Boat trips to Isla de la Plata are arranged through tour agencies in Puerto López and at accommodations along the coast.

## Puerto López
05 / POP 14,000
There's little to distinguish this ramshackle town, apart from a handful of hotels and tour agencies catering to foreigners. However, what it lacks in physical charm it more than makes up for with its long, wide beach and proximity to the wonders of the Parque Nacional Machalilla. During whale-watching season especially, tourists wander the *malecón* and the dusty streets, transforming this otherwise quiet fishing village into a bustling and amiable base camp. In the wee morning hours – before tour groups escape for the day and the handful of sunbathers take up

positions on the sand – fishermen gut their catch on the beach, and the air teems with frigate birds and vultures diving for scraps.

## Tours

Numerous agencies offer tours to Isla de la Plata or the mainland part of the park. Hiking, horseback-riding, mountain-biking and fishing trips are also offered. Some companies have English-, German- and French-speaking guides.

From June through September, whale-watching tours combined with visits to Isla de la Plata are popular (whale-watching only $25; including park entry fee $45). During July and August, good whale sightings are pretty much guaranteed, and in June and September sightings may be brief, distant or just of single animals. On Isla de la Plata groups have lunch, a guided hike and a brief opportunity to snorkel. The trip to the island takes well over an hour and can be rough; bring a rain jacket for the wind and spray.

Licensed companies are found along Córdova and Malecón Julio Izurieta. We don't recommend bargain-hunting for cheaper whale-watching trips on the street, because fishing boats on those trips tend to be slower and smaller and lack officially mandated equipment.

Outside of the whale-watching season, similar tours to the island ($40) are offered to see birds and sea lions, and you may well see dolphins, too. Most of the operators will also arrange a variety of other local trips, such as fishing (June to January), visits to local beaches, and camping and/or horseback-riding in the Agua Blanca and San Sebastián areas. It is usually cheaper to make your own way to Agua Blanca.

### Bosque Marino                    FISHING

(☏230-0004; www.bosquemarino.com; Malecón Julio Izurieta) Half-day fishing trips $300 for up to six people.

### Exploramar Diving                DIVING

(☏230-0123; www.exploradiving.com; Malecón Julio Izurieta) Expect to pay $95 for two dives.

### Machalilla Tours           ADVENTURE TOURS

(☏230-0234; www.machalillatours.org; Malecón Julio Izurieta) Runs standard tours, plus hang-gliding ($40) and kayaking trips to Isla Salango ($25), and rents out motorbikes (per day $40).

## Sleeping

Reserve ahead during the busy whale-watching season, and during the coastal high season (end of December to April).

### TOP CHOICE Hostería Mandála        CABINS $$

(☏230-0181; www.hosteriamandala.info; s/d/tr cabin $30/44/57; @🛜) Easily the nicest place to stay in town, Mandála boasts a beachfront location north of the *malecón,* its entrance is marked by the massive well-preserved skeleton of a humpback whale. The cabins are scattered throughout a thick and lush flower garden, and the rooms are subdued, rustic and sophisticated: wood, bamboo and colorful textiles combine to make charming, cozy hideaways. Out the front, you'll find a large, attractive lodge with a bar, and a restaurant serving delectable breakfasts as well as Italian and seafood entrees ($7). Cash only throughout.

### Hosteria Mantaraya               HOTEL $$$

(☏244-8985; www.mantarayalodge.com; r from $80; @🛜💦) A Mediterranean villa transported to a hillside with views of Puerto López below, the Mantaraya is a surprising splash of pastel colors. It's popular with groups or those with their own vehicles – the only downside is the noise from downshifting trucks on the passing roadway. Vaulted archways and Spanish-style stucco are signatures of the property, and the light-filled rooms are charming. A nice restaurant, a trellis-covered outdoor sitting area and a pool offer alternative lounging areas for a day off. It's a few kilometers south of town.

### Nantu Hostería                   HOTEL $

(☏230-0040; www.hosteriananantu.com; s/d incl breakfast $22/33; ❄🛜💦) Only a little further north of Hostería Mandála, this is the next best option for beachfront accommodations. While it's certainly a step down in terms of atmosphere, the Nantu nevertheless offers spotless and modern rooms with cable TV and a small pool. The two-story lounge and bar has a billiard table and full food menu.

### Sol Inn Hostería               HOSTERÍA $

(☏230-0248; hostal_solinn@hotmail.com; Juan Montalvo near Eloy Alfaro; r per person with shared/private bathroom $7/12) What the compact wood-and-bamboo rooms lack in size, they make up for in funky character at this mellow backpacker retreat. There's just enough space for front-porch hammocks, but there's more elbow room in the outdoor kitchen and living area. English and French are spoken.

### Hostería Itapoá

HOSTERÍA $

(☏255-1569; itapoa _25@hotmail.com; Malecón Julio Izurieta; cabins incl breakfast per person $10) A handful of thatch-roofed cabins tucked back in a lush courtyard, Itapoá is a friendly, family-run operation. Rooms are tidy and efficient, and an above-average breakfast is served in the raised wooden platform cafe out front along the *malecón*. There are mountain bikes for hire, and an English-speaking biologist runs tours out of here.

### Hotel Pacífico

HOTEL $$

(☏230-0147; www.hotelpacificoecuador.com; cnr Lascano & Malecón Julio Izurieta; s/d with fan $25/40, with air-con $35/60; ❄☎☐) Maybe the largest, most modern hotel on the *malecón*, the Pacífico offers ordinary but uninspiring rooms; to feel as though you're at the beach, ask for one of the sea-facing rooms with a balcony (although street noise can then be an issue). Its *raison d'être*, however, is a pool set in a lovely and lush backyard garden. Breakfast included.

### Hostería Playa Sur

HOSTERÍA $

(☏09-004-8967; playasurpuertolopez@hotmail. com; Malecón Julio Izurieta; s/d $10/16) If you're not claustrophobic, these stand-alone cabañas (cabins) at the northern end of the beach are worth considering. There is barely enough room to slide past the bed but each of these tidy wooden structures does have its own private bathroom with hot water, and there's little noise to disturb your sleep.

### Hostal Yemayá

HOSTERÍA $

(☏08-864-6118; Gral Córdova; per person $10; ☎) Although it lacks the atmosphere of the other cheapies, there's no questioning the value of this somewhat unfinished place a few doors down from Patacon Pisa'o. The handful of fan-cooled rooms have hot water, small TVs and few flourishes, though some come with interior brick walls. There's a postage-stamp-sized interior courtyard for drinking coffee.

### Piedra del Mar Hotel Boutique

HOTEL $$

(☏230-0011; www.piedradelmarhotel.com; Gral Córdova; s/d incl breakfast $25/50; ☎) Although certainly not a boutique hotel, this is nevertheless an entirely pleasant option with clean modern rooms and a pool in the concrete courtyard. During the low season, rates are half-price (no breakfast).

## 🍴 Eating & Drinking

There's no better place to start or end the day (or, for that matter, while the day away) than at one of the nearly dozen **beachfront shacks** serving up juices, cocktails, basic breakfasts, seafood meals and snacks. All

**DON'T MISS**

## ISLA DE LA PLATA

Isla de la Plata (Silver Island) is a reasonably accurate facsimile of an island in the Galápagos – and it's only an hour or so by boat from Puerto López. If you're traveling in the area, it's an island not to be missed. After passing through various private hands, including a businessman from Guayaquil who built a hotel (which is now the park office and the only facility on the island) and an airstrip, the island was later incorporated into the national park. This was a good thing, too, for the survival of the birdlife – fishermen used to club albatross until they dropped their day's catch.

The origin of the island's name has a couple of explanations – one alludes to claims that Sir Francis Drake buried treasure here, and the other points to the color of the guano-covered cliffs in the moonlight. The island is home to nesting colonies of **seabirds**: large numbers of blue-footed boobies reside here, and frigate birds, red-footed boobies and pelicans are frequently recorded, as is a variety of gulls, terns and petrels. Albatross can be seen from April to October, dolphins pass by, and there's year-round **snorkeling** in the coral reefs around the island.

It's a steep climb from the boat landing to two loop hikes, one to the east and one to the west: the 3.5km **Sendero Punta Machete** and the 5km **Sendero Punta Escaleras**. Either way, the trail is rough and exposed, so good footwear and plenty of water are essential.

The only way to enjoy this 'poor person's Galápagos' is by taking a guided boat tour from Puerto López.

offer lounge chairs on the sand and some show sports on TV at nighttime. The only downsides are instant coffee, and, unfortunately for those seeking peace and quiet, many pump out loud music.

The majority of travelers end up having dinner at one of the handful of seafood restaurants lining the *malecón* south of the intersection with Córdova. **Carmita's**, **La Caída del Sol** and **Restaurante Sol, Mar y Arena** serve up comparable fresh fare (fish $7, lobster $14). Next to the central market and around the corner from the bus terminals is a collection of informal and cheap **comedores** (cheap restaurants) where locals lunch. There are two good **panaderías** (bakeries) near here.

**Patacon Pisa'o**                    COLUMBIAN $
(Gral Córdova; mains $4; 🛜) This friendly eatery, nothing more than a few outdoor tables, serves delicious Colombian specialties such as *hoga'o* (tomato and onion sauce), *arepas* (maize pancakes) and its namesake dish: large, thin, crisply fried plantains with your choice of meat topping. Good for breakfast, brewed coffee and an afternoon hangout.

**Etnias Café**                           CAFE $
(Gral Córdova; mains $3; ⊙8am-3pm; 🛜) Another cozy place just down the block from Patacon Pisa'o, this French-owned spot does good crepes, waffles, desserts and frozen coffee drinks.

## ❶ Information

**Banco del Pichincha** (Malecón) has a reliable ATM. Several internet cafes charge $1.25 per hour and also operate as call centers. Several drop-off machine-wash laundries (around $4 per load) catering to foreign travelers are along the *malecón*.

## ❶ Getting There & Away

**To Quito**
**Reina de Camino** (Gral Córdova) Has the fastest, most secure service to Quito, with 1st-class buses at 8am and 10pm ($12, 10 hours). Passengers can get off at Santo Domingo de los Colorados, but new passengers cannot board there. The buses don't stop for dinner.
**Carlos Aray Ejecutivo** (cnr Gral Córdova & Machalilla) Also has buses to Quito ($11, 10 hours) at 5am, 9am and 7pm via Jipijapa, Portoviejo, Chone and Santo Domingo. Alternatively, you can catch the bus to Portoviejo or Manta to make connections.

**To South Coast & Guayaquil**
**Transportes Manglaralto** (cnr Gral Córdova & Machalilla) buses leave frequently for Montañita ($2.50, 1¼ hours) and La Libertad ($4, 2¾ hours). Several other companies between Jipijapa and La Libertad stop at the corner of Gral Córdova and Machalilla at least every hour during daylight hours; you can get off at any point along the coast.

The rickety, dilapidated-looking buses of **Cooperativa Transportes Jipijapa** have eight departures daily to Guayaquil ($4, 4½ hours) via Jipijapa. Another option is the crowded Jipijapa-bound **Trans Turismo Manta** service. Buses leave from the corner of Gral Córdova behind the market; from here you can transfer to services for Guayaquil or other northbound destinations.

## ❶ Getting Around

The whole town is walkable, but if you're feeling sluggish look for *tricimotos* (motorized tricycles) on the *malecón* or near the buses. The Asociación de Camioneros has cars and pickups in front of the church. The 24-hour service goes to Agua Blanca for $10 round trip and to Los Frailes and Agua Blanca for $15.

# South of Puerto López

Only 6km south of Puerto López is the sleepy little fishing town of **Salango**. You can hire fishing boats ($10 per person) to buzz the 2km out to **Isla Salango**, a haven for birdlife including blue-footed boobies, pelicans and frigate birds, and good snorkeling. There are two good seafood restaurants in town within a block of one another near the central church.

About 8km south of Salango, on the very southern edge of the village of Puerto Rico and the northern tip of the beachside village of Las Tunas is **Hostería Alandaluz** (☏04-278-0686; www.alandaluzhosteria.com; camping per person $7, s/d/tr $24/55/85; ☒), a sprawling, low-key eco-conscious resort featuring a variety of accommodations scattered on both sides of the highway. The seaside cabins (especially the charming wood cabins), found at the end of paths snaking through the forest, are recommended. The restaurant serves superb seafood, cooked with locally grown fruits and veggies. Tours to Parque Nacional Machalilla can be arranged here, as can walking and cycling trips to **Cantalapiedra**, a property deep in the lush mountains of the Cordillera Chongón-Colonche east of Ayampe. There's also a zip-line and an organic farm on the property.

Only a little further south of Hostería Alandaluz, perched on a hill on the inland side of the road, are the thatch-roofed bungalows of **Azuluna Eco-Lodge** (☑04-278-0693; www.azuluna-ecuador.com; r from $20; ❋❞). The buildings, including an attractive restaurant (mains $8) and lounge area are made with wooden floors and stone walls.

Along the beach in Las Tunas is **Hostería La Barquita** (☑04-278-0051; www.labarquita-ec.com; r per person from $24), immediately recognizable for its whimsically designed restaurant-bar resembling a large wooden boat, complete with portholes and thatch-roofed sails. The surrounding cabins, charming and cozy, are set amid a beautifully landscaped garden on the beach-front. Only a few meters away is **La Perla Hostería** (☑04-278-0701; www.hosterialaperla.net; s/d incl breakfast $25/40), a haphazardly decorated, weathered beach house with several clean wood-floored cabañas; yoga classes sometimes offered.

At **Ayampe**, where the Río Ayampe empties into the ocean (the strong undertow here makes swimming difficult), the luxuriant green hills close in on the beach. Tucked back into one of these hills, surrounded by dense woods, is the highly recommended **Finca Punta Ayampe** (☑09-488-8615; www.fincapuntaayampe.com; r per person $15, cabañas $36), which feels like an end-of-the-road hideout (no internet or wi-fi). The high-ceilinged bamboo bedrooms are filled with light. Surfing, scuba diving, kayaking and bird-watching tours can be arranged here. With bags, it is a bit of a slog from the highway. **Cabañas La Tortuga** (☑09-383-4825; www.latortuga.com.ec; per person from $15; ❞), the only beachfront accommodations in Ayampe, has a collection of well-maintained thatch-roofed cabins. Kayaks and bikes can be rented here, and there's a restaurant, a bar and satellite TV. Its camping annex, **Tortuga Tent Camp** (per person $6), a row of fairly developed blue-canvas shelters with private bathrooms, is a short walk away.

## Olón

A few kilometers north of Montañita is the coastal village of **Olón**. It has a long beach with waves that are good for beginner surfers, and an inland landscape that marks the beginning of a dramatic departure from the dry scrubland further south. This lush cloud forest is part of the **Cordillera Chongón-**

**WORTH A TRIP**

### EL PITAL

Another option for reaching the high forest in and around San Sebastián is to go via **El Pital** (☑08-526-9042; www.elpital.org), a community ecotourism project 9km (35 minutes by 4WD) east of Puerto López. Guides are available here to take you on foot or horseback along trails that crisscross several streams, including the seven-hour *sendero* (track) La Bola de Oro. There's a small 'community lodge,' a brick and thatch-roofed hut with four double rooms, and meals are available; camping is also possible.

Colonche, climbing over a low coastal mountain range. It's one of the few places in the world with a cloud forest and a beach in such close proximity; jaguars, howler monkeys and the endangered great green macaw all reside here.

Taking advantage of this truly unique setting, with walking paths deep into the forest, is magical **Samaí Lodge** (☑03-288-7979; www.redmangrove.com; s/d/tr incl breakfast $75/95/115; @❋). It's an idyllic oasis, combining a sophisticated aesthetic sensibility with rustic charm. A few cabins are scattered throughout the property; most have floor-to-ceiling windows with views all the way to the coast. There's a Jacuzzi, a pool and tasty food.

## Montañita

☑04 / POP 1000

An omnipresent laid-back atmosphere and good year-round surf draw a steady stream of cosmopolitan backpackers – as many South Americans as gringos – to the beachfront village of Montañita. The cheap digs and Rasta vibe mean some travelers put down temporary roots and take up hair braiding and jewelry making or the staffing of their guesthouse's front desk. No *localismo* here: it's an easygoing surfing community willing to share its waves. Montañita is ideal for the kind of person who, regardless of age, balks at the typical restaurant dress code: bare feet and no shirt is practically *de rigueur*.

The beach break is rideable most of the year (though it's best from December to

**WORTH A TRIP**

## DETOUR FROM THE SUN

Most often visited as a side trip from Montañita a few kilometers away, the inland village of **Dos Mangas** is a starting point for walks or horseback rides further into the tropical humid forest of the Cordillera Chongón-Colonche. Tagua carvings and *paja toquilla* (toquilla straw) crafts can be purchased in the village.

Travelers have the chance to visit remote coastal villages and stay overnight with local families for a nominal fee that includes meals, guides and mules. The villages are usually an easy day's walk or horse ride from Manglaralto and each other. Overnight tours can be arranged for bird-watching and visiting remote waterfalls and other natural attractions.

Guides and horses can be hired at the Centro de Información Sendero Las Cascadas, a small kiosk in Dos Mangas. The friendly guides speak Spanish only, and will take you on a four- to five-hour hike through the forest to an elevation of 60m and to the 80m **waterfalls** (these dry up in the dry season). They charge $10 for up to three people and an extra $3 per person for horses, and lunch can be arranged in local homes. The park entrance fee is $1.

Trucks to Dos Mangas ($0.25, 15 minutes) leave the highway from Manglaralto every hour or so. Taxis from Montañita are more convenient and are only about $2.

A 40-minute, 17km bus ride from the coastal village of Valdivia will bring you to **Loma Alta** (🖉in the USA 212-279-7813; www.pansite.org; admission $10), a community-protected, 2428-hectare cloud forest (for overnight visits, call several days in advance). The ride passes through the villages of Sinchal and Barcelona before a final 10km stretch over a rough road leading to the forest. This watershed eco-preserve has howler monkeys and more than 200 species of bird (including 20 species of hummingbirds). It's ideal for hiking, or taking horses or mules the four to six hours to its simple cabins and campsites. With a guide, you can also hike from Loma Alta to the village of El Suspiro.

May) but beginners should keep in mind that waves can be big, and riptides are common. Real surfers ride the wave at the northern end of the beach at la punta (the point), a right that can reach 2m to 3m on good swells. An international surf competition is usually held around Carnaval. Most accommodations can arrange surfboard rentals (per full day $10) and lessons (per two hours $15). Wet suits and bodyboards are also available.

Women should be cautious about walking alone along the beach at night as there have been reports of assaults.

### ☞ Tours

On Calle Principal, at the second intersection in from the highway, is **Montañita Tours** (🖉206-0043; www.montanitatours.com), a one-stop shop for all your transportation and travel needs. Just a few of the trips offered are paragliding ($45), horseback-riding ($45), sport fishing ($60), walking tours of the rainforest around Dos Mangas ($25) and surfing lessons and board rental ($10).

**Otro Mundo Montañita Dive Center** (🖉206-0059; www.montanitadiving.com), on the

main street next to the Banco Bolivariano ATM, runs trips out near Punta Ayangue and Islote El Pelado (two dives $75).

### 🛏 Sleeping

Noise is an issue and earplugs are recommended at many of the hotels in town, especially on weekends and during the high season. But if you're interested in peace and quiet, as well as beachfront accommodations, check out the places just outside of town.

The prices quoted here are for the high season (end of December through April). Almost all hotels cut their rates for the rest of the year, and discounts are almost always available for extended stays.

Calle Principal is the main drag down to the beach. Most hotels have mosquito nets, and sea breezes for ventilation; some places only have cold water.

#### IN TOWN

**Hotel Hurvínek**                                      HOSTERÍA $
(🖉206-0068; www.actiweb.es/hurvinek; Calle 10 de Agosto; r per person incl breakfast $11; 🖘) The fan-cooled, spacious rooms at this bright and sunny guesthouse are beautifully craft-

ed, from the polished-wood floors to the charmingly tiled bathrooms. Groups can occupy the top floor open-air balcony, which has bunk beds. A buffet breakfast is served in the ground floor lounge area. To find the Hurvínek, make your first left after turning into town from the highway; it's located halfway down on the right.

### Tiki Limbo Surf Hostel
HOSTEL $

(☏254-0607; www.tikilimbo.com; r per person from $10; 🛜) Especially good for groups of three or four, Tiki Limbo outdoes its cheapie competitors in terms of style: the pastel-colored rooms have four-poster beds made of bamboo. The 2nd floor lounge area is a good place to crash, write or play guitar. Surf lessons are offered ($20 for two hours plus use of board for additional two hours).

### Hostal Las Palmeras
HOTEL $

(☏08-541-9938; dlgpalmeras@yahoo.com; r per person from $12) Las Palmeras offers basic modern rooms – many with bunk beds (good for groups) – if with some loss of character. The newer whitewashed adobe addition is a better choice (rooms per person $20) and there are hammocks in the courtyard. Coming from the highway, make the second and final left; the hotel is located halfway down this beachfront road on the right.

### Casa Blanca
HOSTERÍA $

(☏218-2501; r per person $8) One of the anchors of the busiest intersection in town. Unlike some of the budget places, Casa Blanca is a good deal. The small bamboo rooms here come with private bathrooms that supply hot water, and balconies with hammocks. Queen-sized beds (which can be hard to find elsewhere) are available.

### Hostal Mohica Sumpa
HOSTERÍA $

(☏09-938-7483; hostalmohicasumpa@hotmail.com; r per person $15) The two two-story thatch-roofed buildings here occupy prime real estate overlooking the ocean at the end of Calle Principal. All rooms are small, basic wood and bamboo affairs, but those with views are worth the extra bucks.

### Montezuma
HOSTERÍA $

(☏09-718-2965; www.montezumahostal.com; r with shared/private bathroom incl breakfast $8/15) Centrally located and friendly but rooms, some with bunk beds, are generally small.

### OUT OF TOWN
All of these places are either on or near the beach on the other side of the creek that marks the northern border of town.

### 🔲 TOP CHOICE Balsa Surf Camp
BUNGALOWS $$

(☏09-757-2450; www.balsasurfcamp.com; s/d from $55/75; 🛜) This lovely hideaway of hand-crafted two-story thatch-roofed bungalows is set in a lush garden across a sandy pathway to the beach. The vibe is laid-back surfer, and the design aesthetic is Balinese retreat. Named after the type of wood the owner uses to make surfboards, this is a gem catering to beginners as well as the experienced.

### Hostal Kundalini
HOSTERÍA $

(☏09-954-1745; www.hostalkundalini.com.ec; s/d $20/30; 🛜) Sitting directly in front of a surf break (which, unfortunately, along with the beach, is obscured by a row of bushes), Kundalini is nothing more than a thatch-roofed building set out on a lawn with beachfront access. There are four small rooms here, each with bamboo walls and furniture, and private hammocks.

### Hanga Roa Hostal
HOSTERÍA $$

(☏09-942-0752; www.hangaroamontanita.com; s/d $20/35; 🛜) A pleasant concrete patio – which is great for sunset drinks – hangs over the sand here. However, four of the hostel's rooms are in a low-slung building extending out to the road. They're good-sized and colorful, with bamboo walls and modern bathrooms. The wood-and-bamboo house next door with a 2nd-floor balcony also has rooms.

### Paradise South
HOSTERÍA $

(☏09-787-8925; r $12-30; ❄) Just north of the bridge, Paradise has a large, well-kept central lawn surrounded by several low-slung buildings. The thatch-roofed stone cottages sporting adobe walls and ceramic-tiled floors are worth the extra bucks; more-ordinary rooms meant for groups feature several bunk beds.

### 🌿 Hostal Esperanto
HOSTERÍA $

(☏09-970-4569; www.esperantohostal.com; dm $14, r per person $17; 🌐) You can't miss this four-story silo-shaped building, immediately on the far side of the creek. Besides the cozy wood-accented rooms, there's a small TV lounge and rooftop deck with panoramic views.

## Eating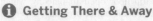

Almost every street-side space has been converted into an informal restaurant including **street carts** selling *encebollado* (soup with fish, yuca and onion; $1.75), ceviche ($5) and burgers ($1). Spanish and English menus cater to foreigners' taste buds, serving everything from pizzas to empanadas and bubbling *cazuelas* (seafood stews). Those catering to Ecuadorians are more likely to offer economical *almuerzos* (set lunches; from $1.50 to $4) and *meriendas* (set dinners).

**Tiki Limbo**                    INTERNATIONAL **$$**
(mains $9; 🛜) The eclectic menu with specialties from Mexico to Thailand; the lounge beds–cum–tables; and the well-polished wooden floor make this centrally located restaurant, while pricier than most, one of Montañita's best.

**Marea**                              PIZZERIA **$**
(mains $7; ⊘7-11pm) Down a side street toward the beach, Marea is the place for thin-crust brick-oven pizza. Family-style seating means it's good for groups, making it easy to sample different varieties.

**Papillon**                              FRENCH **$**
(mains $4; 🛜) You'll find an excellent variety of sweet and savory crepes at this place, which is next door to Tiki Limbo.

**Donde Garci**                        BAKERY **$**
(cakes $0.75) Delicious Columbian-style cookies and pastries, found right on the intersection of the highway and Calle Principal.

## Drinking

The side street that ends at the beach is lined with **carts** doling out inexpensive mixed drinks ($2), beers and shakes until late most nights. Anchoring the end of this street is the massive two-story disco **Nativa Bambu** with live music and DJs most weekend nights. **Hola Ola** is another big bar with live music and dancing. **Zoe** is a more laid-back place that's good for cocktails and beers, a block before the end of Calle Principal.

Otherwise, you can get drinks at any of the restaurants.

## Information

Banco de Guayaquil and Banco Bolivariano have ATMs in town. There's a handful of internet cafes charging $1.50 per hour. Most hotels provide laundry services, and there are several stand-alone *lavanderías* (laundries).

## Getting There & Away

CLP buses leave from Olón just to the north of Montañita (15 minutes prior to the following departure times) and stop in Montañita on their way south to Guayaquil ($5.50, 2½ to 3 hours, 4:45am, 5:45am, 10am, 1pm, 3pm and 4:45pm). These are much more comfortable than other buses that stop on their way to Santa Elena ($1.50, two hours), La Libertad or north to Puerto López ($2.50, 1¼ hours). However, these pass by every 20 minutes or so.

**Montañisol S.A.** (📞08-378-2643; montanisol@gmail.com) is one of two taxi companies just in from the highway that offers service to destinations from Puerto López ($25) to as far away as Guayaquil ($80).

# SANTA ELENA PENINSULA TO GUAYAQUIL

The area around La Libertad (the largest town on the peninsula) and Santa Elena (toward the end of the peninsula) is a dusty urban zone. East of Santa Elena Peninsula, the landscape seems fit for a cowboy. It becomes increasingly dry and scrubby, and the ceiba trees give way to 5m-high candelabra cacti. To the south along the coast, the resorts draw *guayaquileños* but fewer foreigners, because the beachfronts – primarily Salinas and to a lesser extent Playas – are backed by concrete and buildings, and outside of the water itself the towns hold little appeal. Santa Elena has an oil refinery, a radio station and a small archaeological museum.

On the outskirts of Ballenita just north of Santa Elena is the charmingly idiosyncratic **Hostería Farallón Dillon** (📞04-295-3611; www.farallondillon.com; s/d/tr $48/60/80; 🖨🖼). A whitewashed complex perched on a cliff with views to the horizon (and migrating whales from June to September), this place is a more interesting and even convenient alternative to the conventional hotels in Salinas, if you're passing through. From the trippy restaurant to the all-wood rooms, the ruling aesthetic is eclectic nautical, appropriately enough for a hotel with its own extensive maritime museum. At the very least it's worth stopping here for a meal (mains $9) or a drink.

# Salinas

📞04 / POP 31,000

From afar Salinas looks like Miami Beach, a row of tall white condominiums fronting a pale sandy expanse filled with sun worshippers. Up close, especially only a block behind the beach, the streets look more 'down-and-out' than playground for wealthy Ecuadorians. Nevertheless, Salinas is the biggest resort town on the south coast, and is the most westerly town on the Ecuadorian mainland.

Salinas is overpriced and crowded during the high season (mid-December through April), when international yachts dock at the yacht club on the west end of the waterfront. The water is warmest for swimming from January to March. In July and August, Salinas is overcast and dreary, although the whale- and bird-watching is fairly good. During Carnaval (in February), the place is completely full.

The resort itself stretches for several kilometers along the beachfront and *malecón* with restaurants and bars. On one side it ends at the large Barcelo Colón hotel; on the other is the yacht club, town plaza and church. West of here is a long sandy stretch, though the apartment buildings are directly on the beach. Most locals go by landmarks rather than street names.

## 👁 Sights & Activities

**Whale-watching** trips are the major draw from June through October. Beginning about 13km offshore from Salinas, the continental shelf drops from 400m to over 3000m (about 40km offshore), so a short, one-hour sail can take you into really deep water for excellent **sport fishing** for the likes of swordfish, sailfish, tuna, dorado and black marlin (the best season is September to December). **Bird-watchers** can tour the private Ecuasal lakes by the Salinas salt factory, where 120 species of bird have been recorded.

Zona de Mar bravo is a beach south of Punta Carnero (one-way taxi $2) that has good breaks for **surfing**. Sea lions and blue-footed boobies congregate on the rocks around the air-force base.

**Oystercatcher Bar**                    BIRD-WATCHING
(Bar de Ostras; 📞277-8329; bhaase@ecua.net.ec; Enrique Gallo 1109 btwn Calles 47 & 50) Run by Ben Hasse, who is a pioneer of whale-watching in the area (he has a small whale museum and a 10m humpback-whale skeleton out

the back). Hasse knows more about coastal birds than anyone in the area and leads tours (group of eight $30) to Ecuasal.

**Pesca Tours**                               FISHING
(📞277-2391; www.pescatours.com.ec; Malecón 577) This outfit charters boats for up to six anglers, for about $350 per day (6am to 4:30pm). The trip includes a captain, two crew members and all the fishing gear, but you have to provide your own lunch and drinks.

**Avista Travel**          FISHING, WHALE-WATCHING
(📞277-0331) Located on the *malecón,* Avista books sport-fishing and whale-watching tours.

## 🛏 Sleeping

Accommodations aren't geared toward foreign travelers looking for a laid-back beach getaway. Prices quoted here are for the high season – they often drop 20% to 30% from May to mid-December and are higher during Easter week, Christmas, New Year and Carnaval.

**Hotel Francisco III**                    HOTEL $$
(📞277-4883; cnr Malecón & Calle 27; www.ho telesfrancisco.com; s/d incl breakfast $30/35; ✹@🛜⊠) The largest, newest and nicest of the Salinas Franciscos is well located in the middle of the *malecón*. A nice touch is the sunny outdoor hallways though, unfortunately, the rooms themselves could use more natural light. **Francisco I** (📞277-4106; Enríquez Gallo btwn Calle 19 & 20; s/d $25/35; ✹⊠), a block off the *malecón* across from the Mi Comiserato supermarket, has aging but clean rooms.

**Hotel Marvento I**                       HOTEL $$
(📞277-0975; cnr Guayas & Enríquez Gallo; www. hotelmarvento.com, in Spanish; r per person incl breakfast $25; ✹@🛜⊠) If sea views aren't a priority, the Marvento, only a block from the *malecón,* is excellent value. Everything from the polished marbled floors to the rustic wooden furniture is in mint condition. The rooftop has a small pool. Several blocks away is the newer **Marvento II** (📞277-0827; cnr Enríquez Gallo & Digno Nuñez; r incl breakfast $40; ✹@🛜⊠), a step up in terms of furnishings, TV quality and the indoor pool and courtyard.

**Hotel El Delfin**                         HOTEL $$
(📞277-0601; www.hoteleldelfin.com.ec; s/d incl breakfast $20/40; ✹@🛜⊠) Directly behind

the defunct water park is this well-kept hotel with small modern rooms and a compact courtyard featuring a pool.

**Barcelo Colon Miramar**  HOTEL **$$$**
(📞252-2790; www.barcelo.com; r with three meals $230; ✳@🛜🌊) The largest hotel in town has seen better days, but it does have the facilities of a resort complex: a pool, gym, three restaurants and several bars and lounges. Still, it's of questionable value.

## 🍴 Eating & Drinking

Most of the restaurants are located either on the *malecón* or a block or two away. However, some may be closed or have limited hours during the low season. **Cevichelandía**, the nickname for a highly recommended collection of inexpensive seafood stalls at the corner of Calles 17 and Enríquez, are mainly open for lunch. A handful of bars and discos on or near the *malecón* come alive during high-season weekends. The salsateca **Gringos Bar** is near the Banco de Guayaquil and **Nassau** and **La Casa de Roy** have music, sometimes live, out near the Barcelo Colon.

**Amazon Restaurant**  ECUADORIAN, PIZZERIA **$$**
(Malecón; mains $9) The Spanish hacienda decor and excellent brick-oven pizza make this restaurant one of Salinas' best. It also has wide-ranging menu with *churrasco* (a popular local plate of a slice of fried beef, rice, fried eggs, avocado, cold vegetable salad, and french fries), seafood and hearty soups, plus a selection of South American wines. You'll find it next to the Banco de Guayaquil.

**Restaurant Oh Mar**  SEAFOOD **$$**
(Malecón; mains $7; ⊙8am-10pm) This seafood eatery is toward the western end of the *malecón* near a couple of shwarma joints, and it features a wide-ranging menu including stewed crab ($9) and a variety of *cazuelas* ($7).

**Cafeteria del Sol**  ECUADORIAN **$**
(Malecón; mains $5; ⊙7am-midnight) Between the Banco del Pichincha and Calypso Hotel is the trellis-covered restaurant, with everything from burritos ($4) to seafood paella ($13).

**Mar y Tierra**  ECUADORIAN **$$**
(Malecón; mains $10) This nautically themed restaurant (look out for the boatlike facade) is a relatively formal affair with the usual meat and seafood selections.

**Cevicheria Lojanita**  SEAFOOD **$**
(cnr Enriquez Gallo & Aviles; mains $5; ⊙9am-9pm) A large, yellow complex a block from Cevichelandía; portions are large and come with popcorn.

**Cranberry Coffee Bar**  CAFE **$**
(mains $3; ⊙9am-8:30pm; 🛜) A family-run spot a block from the *malecón* with an outdoor patio and hammocks for lounging. Crepes, sandwiches, cocktails and good brewed coffee.

## ℹ Information

Banco de Guayaquil, Banco Bolivariano and Banco Pinchincha all have ATMs and are located along the *malecón*. The **Camara de Turismo** (📞277-2079; www.salinas.gob.ec) can help with hotel information, though staff speak only Spanish. It's past the defunct waterpark and a block inland.

## ℹ Getting There & Away

La Libertad is the center of bus services on the peninsula, but if you're not headed to Salinas it's easier to be let off in Santa Elena, bypassing La Libertad, and make the transfer to another bus heading either north along the coast or east to Guayaquil.

Buses to Salinas run all day from Calle 8 and Avenida 2 in La Libertad. A taxi between the two towns costs about $2. To get to Santa Elena from La Libertad, flag down one of the minibuses that run frequently along Calle 9 de Octubre.

### To Guayaquil

To get to Guayaquil ($3.50, 2½ hours, every 15 minutes) from Salinas, you can take **Cooperativa Libertad Peninsular (CLP)**, **Cooperativa Intercantonal Costa Azu (CICA)** or **Liberpresa** buses from the bus terminal at Calle 7, behind the defunct water park a block inland at the western end of the *malecón*; keep in mind that it will make a stop in La Libertad for more passengers.

### To the North

To continue further north to destinations such as Montañita ($1.50, two hours) and Puerto López ($4, three hours), catch a CITUP, Cooperativa Manglaralto or CITM bus in La Libertad at a terminal near the market. Note that buses may be booked out in advance during weekends in the high season. These buses also service other coastal villages to the north, including Ballenita, Valdivia, Ayangue and Palmar.

Trans Esmeraldas has three daily evening buses from La Libertad to Quito ($8, 10 to 12 hours).

# Playas

☑04 / POP 27,000

It's something of a relief to come upon Playas (called General Villamil on some maps), even when it reveals itself to be crumbling and dusty – like the absolutely parched landscape you pass through upon approach. But weekending *guayaquileños* don't come here looking for urban sophistication; they come for the long, broad and relatively close expanse of beach and delicious fresh seafood. There's also some good **surfing** in the area; stop by **Jalisco** (Av Paquisha), a restaurant a block from the beach, and ask Juan Gutiérrez for information.

Playas is still an active fishing village: a handful of the old balsa rafts used a generation ago, which are nothing more than three logs tied together with a sail attached (similar to those used before the Spanish conquest) can be seen having their catches unloaded at the western end of the beach. Several impressive-looking condominiums tower above; however, up close they appear to be empty shells.

The town is busy from December to April but quiet at other times. On an overcast midweek day in the low season it can feel downright gloomy.

## 🛏 Sleeping

En route to Data, southeast of the center, and further afield to Posorja 16km away, are several quiet places near the beach that tend to fill up and charge much higher rates on high-season weekends. A handful of new hotels, though none with ocean views, have been built or rather semi-built (often, 2nd floor and above are stalled construction sites) in recent years.

**Hotel Arena Caliente**  HOTEL $
(☑276-1580; www.hotelarenacaliente.com; cnr Guayaquil & Paquisha; s/d $25/35; ❋ 🛜 🌊) Across the street from Nevada (see the following review), Arena Caliente is a small step up in quality. The tiled rooms are larger, as are the TVs, and the linens are certainly better, but the real added value is the nice courtyard swimming pool and lounge area. The ground-floor restaurant is good for breakfast and the standard *almuerzo*.

**Hotel Nevada Playas**  HOTEL $
(☑276-0759; www.hotelnevadaplayas.com; cnr Guayaquil & Paquisha; s/d $25/35; ❋ 🌊) Only two blocks from the beach, the Nevada

has comfortable rooms with chintzy decor, and bath towels the size and thickness of a dishrag. Spacious family rooms, good for up to six, are in the new building attached. The little rooftop pool, no larger than a compact car, is sometimes filled with water; at least there is a hammock and good views of the city.

**Hotel Ana**  HOTEL $$
(☑276-1770; www.hotelanaplayas.com; r $30; ❋ 🌊) One of the last hotels you come to on the way to Data, this is probably also the most pleasant. Look for the faux-red-brick building along the beachfront. There's a small plunge pool in the front, although it's good enough for not much more than a toe in the water. The tile-floored rooms are simply furnished.

**La Posada del Sueco**  HOTEL $
(☑09-372-2888; www.laposadadelsueco.com; Km 2; dm $15, r from $40; 🛜 🌊) Owned by a friendly Guayaquil lady and her Swiss husband, this lovely beachfront complex surrounds a lush garden.

## 🍴 Eating & Drinking

It's **cevichería** (ceviche restaurant) central around the intersection of Roldos Aguilera and Paquisha (next to and across the street from Hotel Arena Caliente and Hotel Nevada Playas). They have piles of oysters and crabs on display and do a variety of ceviche ($6), grilled fish and lobster ($7), as well as meat and rice dishes ($4.50); a few serve thick and sizzling shrimp, calamari or *cazuela*. For a slightly more upscale version (as far as seating and decor go), try **Restaurant El Pescaito** (mains $6), just a few blocks away toward the central plaza.

**Empanadas de Playas** (Roldos Aguilera) is a no-frills restaurants with plastic tables, serving cheap chicken and meat empanadas (each $0.70). **Restaurant Jalisco** (cnr Paquisha & Av 7; mains $3; ⊙8am-5pm), a long-running local institution serves cheap *almuerzos* and seafood plates.

There are more than a half-dozen **comedores** along the beach, where staff compete for your patronage by waving menus and shouting seafood specials upon your approach.

On Avenida Aguilera, near the paved town soccer field, are two informal *parrillas* (steak houses) serving inexpensive chicken and meat dishes.

In the high season, *discotecas* (night-clubs) are open nightly, but only on weekends during the low season. Most are fairly ad-hoc affairs near the central plaza.

## ℹ Information

Banco de Guayaquil, Banco Bolivariano and Banco Pichincha have ATMs on the central plaza; Banco de Guayaquil has a larger branch at Avenida Guayaquil at Paquisha. A few internet cafes and call centers are only a few blocks from the plaza.

## ℹ Getting There & Away

**Transportes Villamil** (Mendez Gilbert) and **Transportes Posorja** have buses to Guayaquil ($2.75, 1¾ hours, 97km); buses leave every 10 minutes with either company from 4am until 8pm. **Transportes 9 de Marzo** (Guayaquil at Paquisha) has frequent buses to Posorja ($0.50, 30 minutes) during the day.

To get to Santa Elena or further north along the coast, get off at the highway junction at Progreso ($0.75, 25 minutes) and wait for any northern-bound bus. However, the buses that you may catch here are often full upon leaving Guayaquil.

On Sunday afternoons in the high season (end of December to April), everybody is returning to Guayaquil. The road becomes a one-way bus-fest and few (if any) vehicles can travel south into Playas.

# Bosque Protector Cerro Blanco

Located about 15km west of Guayaquil, this is one of the few areas of tropical dry forests left in the country, and counts jaguars, pumas, monkeys, deer and raccoons among its wildlife. More than 200 bird species call the 6078-hectare Cerro Blanco home – including the rare great green macaw (the reserve's symbol), which is considered critically endangered. There are stands of dry forest with huge ceiba trees and more than 100 other tree species, as well as views of coastal mangrove forests in the distance. Several trails take you into this area of rolling coastal hills.

This is a private **reserve** (adult/child $4/3; ☺9am-4pm Sat & Sun, weekdays by reservation) administered by **Fundación Pro-Bosque** (☎04-287-4947; www.bosquecerroblanco.org). There's an organic farm, an education center with exhibits on the local ecology and birdlife in Spanish, and a **wildlife rescue center** where endangered species are cared for, including a large aviary for several Guayaquil macaws. Spanish-speaking guides for one of the nature-trail hikes (two to four hours) are available for $10 to $15 per group (up to eight people).

From January to May there's plenty of water and the plants are green, but there are lots of mosquitoes (no malaria) so bring repellent. From June to December (the dry season) the trees flower and it's easier to see wildlife because the animals concentrate in the remaining wet areas. Early morning and late afternoon are, as always, the best times to see wildlife. The visitors center sells a bird list and booklets, and dispenses information and trail maps.

Just west of Cerro Blanco, on the southern side of the Guayaquil–Salinas highway near the small community of Puerto Hondo, are the **Puerto Hondo Mangroves**. Charged with the protection of this threatened environment is **Club Ecológico Puerto Hondo** (☺9am-4pm Sat & Sun, weekdays by reservation), which arranges pleasant canoe rides (per canoe $15) through the area; dozens of bird species can be seen. Contact Fundación Pro-Bosque for more information.

## 🛏 Sleeping

Cerro Blanco has a visitors center and **campground** (3-person tent rental $8), with the charge for camping included in the reserve admission price. The campground features barbecues, bathrooms and running water (even showers), while one cabin, called the **ecolodge** (s/d/tr $12/20/30) – basically a large thatch-roofed hut with a cold-water shower and bathroom – is also available, as is spotty, solar-powered electricity. Backcountry camping may be permitted. Fundación Pro-Bosque has a reservation form on its website.

## ℹ Getting There & Away

To get to Cerro Blanco and Puerto Hondo, take a Cooperativa de Transportes Chongón bus from the corner of Calle 10 de Agosto and García Moreno in downtown Guayaquil, or hop on any Playas- or Salinas-bound bus from the central bus terminal in the northern suburbs. Ask to be dropped off at the park entrance at Km 16. Get off before the cement factory; you'll see a sign. A one-way taxi costs about $20.

From the reserve entrance, it's about a 10-minute walk to the visitors center and camping area.

# GUAYAQUIL

☑04 / POP 2.16 MILLION

Guayaquil is not only the beating commercial heart of the country but is a vibrant sprawling city growing ever more confident. A half-dozen or more high-rises give it a big-city profile and several hillsides are engulfed by shantytowns, but it's the Río Guayas' *malecón* (the city's riverfront town square–cum-eatery-cum-playground) that defines the city's identity.

The picturesque barrio of Las Peñas, which perches over the river, anchors the city both geographically and historically, while the principal downtown thoroughfare Avenida 9 de Octubre funnels office workers, residents and shoppers into one hybrid stream. Amid revitalized squares, parks and massive urban-renewal projects, the city has a growing theater, film and arts scene and lively bars, fuelled in part by several large universities.

Note that all flights to the Galápagos Islands either stop at or originate in Guayaquil, so the city is the next best place after Quito to set up a trip.

## History

Popular legend has it that Guayaquil's name comes from Guayas, the great Puna chief who fought bravely against the Incas and later the Spanish, and his wife, Quill. Guayas is said to have killed Quill, rather than allow her to be captured by the conquistadors, before drowning himself. Several historians claim the city's name actually comes from the words *hua* (land), *illa* (beautiful prairie) and Quilca, one of Río Guayas' tributaries, where the Quilca tribe lived until being wiped out in the 17th century. Under this theory, Guayaquil is literally 'the land like a beautiful prairie on the land of the Quilcas.'

A settlement was first established in the area around 1534, and it moved to its permanent home of the Santa Ana Hill in 1547. The city was an important port and ship-building center for the Spanish, but it was plagued by pirate attacks and several devastating fires, including one in 1896 – known as the Great Fire – in which huge parts of the city were simply burned to the ground. Guayaquil achieved its independence from the Spaniards on October 9, 1820, and was an independent province until Simón Bolívar annexed it as part of Gran Colombia in 1822. When Bolívar's experiment failed in 1830, Guayaquil became part of the newly formed republic of Ecuador.

## Dangers & Annoyances

The city has its fair share of poverty and urban woes, but nothing to justify paranoia. Post-ATM-withdrawal robberies are a problem; however, the main tourist areas of Avenida 9 de Octubre, the Malecón 2000, Las Peñas and the restaurant strip in Urdesa are perfectly safe. The area directly north and south of the Parque del Centenario can feel dodgy at night, but simply use common sense and take the normal precautions for visiting any large city. Avoid outlying neighborhoods called *los suburbios*, which aren't to be mistaken for prosperous suburbs in other parts of the world.

## ⊙ Sights & Activities

While the majority of visitors breeze in and out on their way to the Galápagos, the city has a fair share of sights, most within walking distance of one another. If your time is limited be sure to walk the Malecón 2000 (also called Malecón Simón Bolívar or simply *el malecón*) and visit the northern neighborhood of Las Peñas – an especially pleasant destination at night, when cool breezes waft from Río Guayas and the bright lights of the city sparkle below. Sunday is a good day to go by foot because traffic is limited.

The center of town, which is organized in a gridlike fashion, is on the west bank of the river. Most of the streets are known interchangeably by a number or proper name – the latter often changes depending on how far north or south one goes. The city sprawls in other directions including across the river, but most of these areas are residential or industrial and of little interest to the traveler.

### EL MALECÓN

One of the most extensive urban-renewal projects in South America, the **waterfront** (☉7am-midnight) is a gated, policed public space stretching 2.5km along the wide Río Guayas with ponds, playgrounds, gardens, restaurants, a museum, a performance space, an IMAX movie theater and a shopping mall. At the far northern end are good views of the colonial district of Las Peñas and Cerro Santa Ana and, far beyond, the impressive Puente Rafael Mendoza Aviles Bridge – the biggest in the country.

# Guayaquil – City Center

To Puente Rafael
Mendoza Aviles
Bridge (4.5km)

See Guayaquil - Northern Suburbs Map (pp278-9)

SOUTH COAST GUAYAQUIL

Av Kennedy
Bombona
Ricaurte
Libertador
Manuela Sáenz
Giradot
O'Leary
Saeadi
27
Carabobo
Alameda Ráez
Rodriguez
Bello
Coronel
Pedro Menéndez
Coronel

Piedrahita (Calle 8 NO)

Galecio (Calle 7 NO)
(Calle 6 NO) Lascano
TARQUI
39
(Calle 5A NO) Vernaza
(Calle 5 NO) Padre Solano
(Calle 4 NO) Urdaneta
García Moreno (Av 3 NO)
Ejército (Av 4 NO)
ROCA
Moncayo (Av 1 NE)
Rumichaca (Av 4 NE)

Tunguíahua
Los Ríos
(Calle 3 NO) Quísquis
(Calle 2 NO) 1 de Mayo
Padre Solano (Calle 5 NE)
Urdaneta
Junín (Calle 3 NE)

11
40
30
9 de Octubre (Eje E)
42
Machala (Av 1 NO)
Quito (Eje N'S)
Rendón (Calle 2 NE)
17
55

Carchi (Av 9 NO)
Tulcán
Hurtado
58
21
59
Garaycoa (Av 3 NE)

Vélez
Parque del Centenario
41

Luque (Calle 3 SO)

Aguirre (Calle 4 SO)
José de Antepara (Av 2 NO)
Vélez (Calle 2 SE)
ROCAFUERTE
Luque (Calle 3 SE)

Esmeraldas
Ballén (Calle 5 SO)
Aguirre (Calle 4 SE)

10 de Agosto (Calle 6 SO)
Sucre (Calle 7 SO)
Parque Victoria
Ballén (Calle 5 SE)

Colón (Calle 8 SO)
Buses to Terminal Terrestre
Market
10 de Agosto (Calle 6 SE)

Sucre (Calle 7 SE)

SUCRE
Alcedo
Colón (Calle 8 SE)

Ejército
Gómez
Machala
Quito (Eje N'S)
Moncayo
Montúfar (Av 1 A SE)
6 de Marzo (Av 2 SE)

Ayachuco
Garayoca (Av 3 SE)
Rumichaca (Av 4 SE)
Romero (Cjón 9 SE)

Manabí
BOLÍVAR
Ayachuco (Calle 11 SE)
Franco Dávila (Calle 11A SE)
Avilés (Av 5 SE)

Huancavilca

Nájera

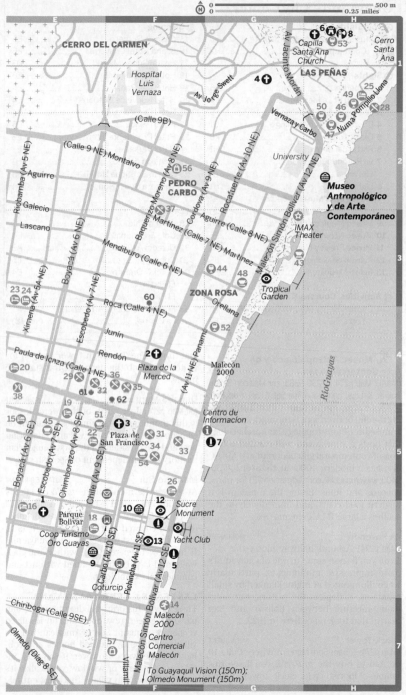

CERRO DEL CARMEN

Cerro
Santa
Ana

Capilla
Santa Ana
Church

LAS PEÑAS

Hospital
Luis
Vernaza

Av Jorge Swett

Av Jacinto Morán

Numa Pompilio Llona

Vernaza y Carbo

(Calle 9B)

(Calle 9 NE) Montalvo

Riobamba (Av 5 NE)

Aguirre

Galecio

Lascano

Baquerizo Moreno (Av 8 NE)

Cordova (Av 9 NE)

Rocafuerte (Av 10 NE)

PEDRO
CARBO

University

Malecón Simón Bolívar (Av 12 NE)

Museo
Antropológico
y de Arte
Contemporáneo

Martínez (Calle 7 NE) Martínez

Aguirre (Calle 8 NE)

Mendiburo (Calle 6 NE)

IMAX
Theater

Boyacá (Av 6 NE)

Escobedo (Av 7 NE)

Roca (Calle 4 NE)

ZONA ROSA

Tropical
Garden

Junín

Orellana

Ximena (Av 5 NE)

Rendón

Plaza de la
Merced

(Av 11 NE) Panamá

Malecón
2000

Paula de Icaza (Calle 1 NE)

Boyacá (Av 6 SE)

Escobedo (Av 7 SE)

Chimborazo (Av 8 SE)

Chile (Av 9 NE)

Plaza de
San Francisco

Centro de
Informacíon

Parque
Bolívar

Coop Turismo
Oro Guayas

Sucre
Monument

Yacht Club

Carbo (Av 10 SE)

Pichincha (Av 11 SE)

Malecón Simón Bolívar (Av 12 SE)

Coturcip

Chiriboga (Calle 9SE)

Malecón
2000

Olmedo (Diag 8 SE)

Villamil

Centro
Comercial
Malecón

To Guayaquil Vision (150m);
Olmedo Monument (150m)

RíoGuayas

# Guayaquil – City Center

TOP CHOICE **Museo Antropológico y de Arte Contemporáneo** MUSEUM
(MAAC; Map p274; ☎230-9383; cnr Malecón Simón Bolívar & Loja; admission Tue-Sat $1.50, Sun free; ☺10am-5:30pm Tue-Sat, 11am-3:30pm Sun) Marking the end of riverfront is the modern MAAC, a museum of anthropology and archaeology that hosts a superb and well-curated collection of contemporary Ecuadorian art. MAAC also has a modern 400-seat **theater** (☎230-9400; www.maaccine.com; admission $2) for plays, concerts and films. Beside the museum is a modern food court, and immediately to the south is a large IMAX cinema ($4).

**La Rotonda** MONUMENT
(Map p274) Around halfway along the *malecón* you'll soon come to one of Guayaquil's more impressive monuments, particularly when illuminated at night. Flanked by small fountains, it depicts the historic but enigmatic meeting between Bolívar and San Martín that took place here in 1822.

**Clock Tower** MONUMENT
(Map p274; ☺9am-6pm Mon-Fri) Where Calle 10 de Agosto hits the *malecón* you'll see this famous Moorish-style clock tower, which dates from 1770 but has been replaced several times. The 23m-high tower is open for visitors to climb the narrow spiral staircase inside.

**Olmedo Monument** MONUMENT
(off Map p274) Just north of the Mercado Sur is this monument honoring José Joaquín de Olmedo (1780–1847), who was an Ecuadorian poet and the president of the first Ecuadorian territory to be independent of Spanish rule.

**Mercado Sur** NOTABLE BUILDING
At the southern end of the *malecón* stands a handsome steel structure, sometimes called the Crystal Palace. When this Belgian-designed covered market was built in 1907, it was the biggest marketplace in Guayaquil. It has now been restored, with giant glass walls, and is periodically filled with art and commercial exhibitions.

**LAS PEÑAS & CERRO SANTA ANA**
These two historic neighborhoods (Map p274) have been revamped into an idealized version of a quaint South American hillside village, all brightly painted homes and cobblestone alleyways. However, if you peek inside an open door or window, you realize it's a bit of a Potemkin village that's not entirely

sanitized, as residents still live their everyday lives as they would elsewhere in the city. The views from the top are spectacular, especially at night. Small, informal, family-run restaurants and neighborhood bars line the steps and it's completely safe, patrolled by friendly security officers making sure foot traffic up the steep stairway flows unimpeded.

**Numa Pompilio Llona** STREET
(Map p274) This historic street, named after the well-known *guayaquileño* poet (1832–1907), begins at the northern end of the *malecón,* to the right of the stairs that head up the hill called Cerro Santa Ana. This narrow, winding street has several unobtrusive plaques set into the walls of some of its houses, indicating simple residences of past presidents. The colonial wooden architecture has been allowed to age elegantly, albeit with a gloss of paint. Several artists live in the area, and there are a few good art galleries.

**Cerro Santa Ana** NEIGHBORHOOD
(Map p274) Retrace your footsteps back along Numa Pompilio Llona and instead of continuing south along the *malecón,* hang a sharp right and head up the 444 steps of Cerro Santa Ana. The stairs lead past dozens

of refurbished, brightly painted homes, cafes, bars and souvenir shops, and up to the hilltop **Fortín del Cerro** (Fort of the Hill; Map p274). Cannons, which were once used to protect Guayaquil from pirates, aim over the parapet toward the river and are still fired today during celebrations. You can climb the **lighthouse** (Map p274; admission free; ☉10am-10pm) for spectacular 360-degree views of the city and its rivers.

**Puerto Santa Ana** NEIGHBORHOOD
(Map p274) Numa Pompilio Llona dead-ends at steps leading into Guayaquil's stalled redevelopment project, a high-end condominium and office complex with a few ice-cream and fast-food kiosks. Much of the area is unoccupied but the paved walkway along the river makes for a nice stroll. **Museo de la Musica Popular Guayaquileña Julio Jaramillo** (Edificio 3, 2nd fl; admission free; ☉10am-5pm Wed-Sat) is a small museum dedicated to traditional Ecuadorian music.

**Church of Santo Domingo** CHURCH
(Map p274) Behind the open-air Teatro Bogotá is the oldest church in Guayaquil. Founded in 1548 and restored in 1938, it's worth a look.

# Guayaquil – Northern Suburbs

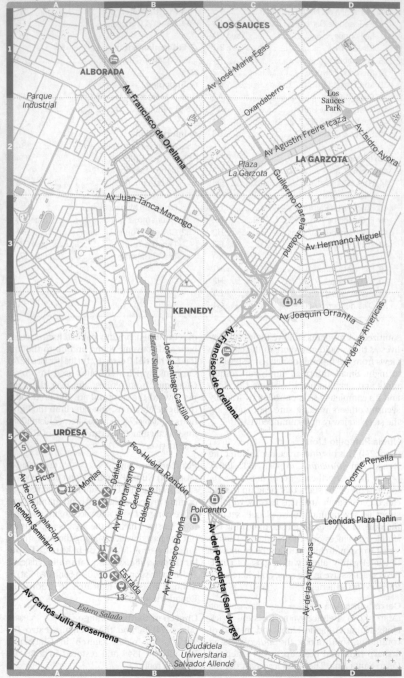

LOS SAUCES

ALBORADA

Parque
Industrial

Av José María Egas

Oxandaberro

Los
Sauces
Park

Av Francisco de Orellana

Av Agustín Freire Icaza

Av Isidro Ayora

Plaza
La Garzota

LA GARZOTA

Av Juan Tanca Marengo

Guillermo Pareja Rolando

Av Hermano Miguel

KENNEDY

Av Joaquín Orrantia

14

Av Francisco de Orellana

Estero Salado

José Santiago Castillo

Av de las Américas

2

URDESA

5

6

9

Ficus

Fco Huérta Rendón

Cosme Renella

12

Monjas

Dátiles

7

15

Policentro

Leonidas Plaza Dañín

Av de Circunvalación

Rendón Seminario

3

8

Cedros

Bálsamos

Av del Rotarismo

Av Francisco Boloña

Av del Periodista (San Jorge)

11

4

10

Estrada

13

Av de las Américas

Av Carlos Julio Arosemena

Estero Salado

Ciudadela
Universitaria
Salvador Allende

## DOWNTOWN AREA

There are several ordinary colonial-era buildings in the streets immediately south of Las Peñas, but soon all the architecture turns mostly modern and dull. **Avenida 9 de Octubre**, downtown Guayaquil's main commercial street, is lined with shoe stores, high-end electronics shops, department stores and fast-food restaurants.

### Church of San Francisco                CHURCH
(Map p274; Av 9 de Octubre near Chile) This church, originally built in the early 18th century, was burned down in the devastating fire of 1896 that destroyed huge swaths of the city. It was then reconstructed in 1902 and beautifully restored in the late 1990s. The plaza in front contains Guayaquil's first public monument, a statue of Vicente Rocafuerte, Ecuador's first native president, who held office between 1835 and 1839. (Ecuador's first president, Juan Flores, was a Venezuelan.)

### FREE Museo Nahim Isaias              MUSEUM
(Map p274; ☎232-4182; www.museonahimisaias. com; cnr Pichincha & Ballén; ☺10am-6pm Tue-Sat, 11am-3pm Sun & holidays) Nahim Isaias is a few blocks away from the Church of San Francisco, in the Plaza de Administración building. It exhibits an excellent collection of sculptures, paintings and artifacts from the colonial period.

### Palacio Municipal & Palacio de Gobierno          HISTORIC BUILDINGS
(Map p274) Across the street from the *malecón* is the ornate, gray building of the Palacio Municipal, separated from the simple and solid Palacio de Gobierno by a small but pleasant pedestrian mall. Both buildings date from the 1920s. The Palacio de Gobierno replaced the original wooden structure, which was destroyed in the great fire of 1917.

### Church of La Merced                CHURCH
(Map p274; cnr Rendón & Rocafuerte) Like most of Guayaquil's colonial buildings, the original wooden church built in 1787 was destroyed by fire. The current incarnation dates from 1938 and has a richly decorated golden altar.

## PARQUE BOLÍVAR AREA

Guayaquil may be the only city in the world that has **land iguanas**, some over a meter in length, living downtown. These prehistoric-looking animals (a different species from

SOUTH COAST GUAYAQUIL

## Guayaquil – Northern Suburbs

### Sleeping
1 Dreamkapture Hostal..........................B1
2 Hilton Colón Guayaquil .....................C4

### Eating
3 Cevicheria Lojanita.............................A6
4 El Café Espanol....................................B6
5 Lo Nuestro ..........................................A5
6 Malek El Shawarma............................A5
7 News Café Restaurant .......................B6
8 Pique & Pase.......................................A6
9 Riviera..................................................A5
10 Sushi Isao...........................................B6
11 Sweet & Coffee..................................A6

### Drinking
12 Frutabar..............................................A6
13 Rollings Tone.....................................B7

### Shopping
14 Mall del Sol........................................C4
15 San Marino Mall.................................C6

### Information
Dreamkapture Travel.....................(see 1)
Metropolitan Touring....................(see 2)

those found in the Galápagos) are a startling sight in one of Guayaquil's most famous plazas, **Parque Bolívar** (Map p274), which is also known as Parque Seminario. Around its small ornamental gardens are several of Guayaquil's top-end hotels.

FREE **Museo Municipal**                    MUSEUM
(Map p274; ☎252-4100; Sucre; ⊙8:30am-4:30pm Tue-Fri, 10am-2pm Sat & Sun) A block south of Parque Bolívar, you'll find this museum and the municipal **library**. The archaeology room on the ground floor has mainly Inca and pre-Inca ceramics, and several figurines from the oldest culture in Ecuador, the Valdivia (c 3200 BC). Also on the ground floor is a colonial room with mainly religious paintings and a few period household items. Upstairs, there's a jumble of modern art and ethnography rooms.

**Cathedral**                                    CHURCH
(Map p274) On the west side of Parque Bolívar is this cathedral whose original wooden building was built in 1547 – however, like much of Guayaquil, it was destroyed by fire. The present structure, completed in 1948 and renovated in 1978, is simple and modern, despite an extremely ornate front entrance.

### DOWNTOWN NORTH
**Malecón El Salado**                          PLAZA
Like its more famous sister development on the Río Guayas to the east, the Malecón El Salado is an attempt to reclaim the city's waterfront for the everyday use of its residents. There are several eateries and cafes in a streamlined modern mall-like building along the estuary. The large square just south of the *malecón* called the **Plaza**

**Rodolfo Baquerizo Moreno** is dominated by a large modernist structure. Expositions and events are held here periodically. Locals with kids in tow head to Malecón El Salado on weekend nights to see the 'dancing fountains', a choreographed waterworks display at 7pm, 7:30pm and 8pm.

FREE **Museo Presley Norton**              MUSEUM
(☎229-3423; Av 9 de Octubre; ⊙9am-5pm Mon-Sat) A few blocks southeast of Malecón El Salado is this museum, featuring an impressive collection of archaeological artifacts. These include pottery and figurines made by the original settlers of Ecuador, housed in a beautifully restored mansion. It occasionally hosts film screenings and live music.

**Parque del Centenario**                      PARK
This plaza, found along Avenida 9 de Octubre (Map p274), is the largest in Guayaquil and marks the midway point between the Río Guayas and the Estero Salado. It's four square city blocks of manicured gardens, benches and monuments, the most important of which is the central **Liberty column** surrounded by the founding fathers of the country.

**City Cemetery**                              CEMETERY
(Map p274; Pedro Menéndez) Incorporated into the city landscape a short ride from the city center is this landmark cemetery, founded in 1823. It contains hundreds of above-ground tombs (and 700,000 graves in total) stacked atop one another so that it resembles a crowded apartment complex. A walkway leads to several monuments and huge mausoleums, including the impressive grave of President Vicente Rocafuerte.

**OUTSIDE GUAYAQUIL**

**Parque Histórico Guayaquil**  ZOO, MUSEUM
(Map p278; ☑283-2958; www.parquehistorico
guayaquil.com; Av Esmeraldas; adult/child Wed-Sat
$3/1.50, Sun $4.50/3; ☺9am-4:30pm Wed-Sun)
Historic Williamsburg meets the zoo at this
large sight across the Puente Rafael Mendoza
Aviles Bridge, on the east side of Río Daule.
The park is divided into three 'zones': the Endangered Wildlife Zone, which has 45 species
of bird, animal and reptile in a seminatural
habitat; the Urban Architecture Zone, which
has a restaurant and showcases the development of early-20th-century architecture in
Guayaquil; and the Traditions Zone, which
focuses on local traditions, with an emphasis
on rural customs, crafts and agriculture.

A taxi from the city costs up to $4, or you
can take the red-and-white Duran 4/30 bus.
It's easier to catch the bus back to the city
from in front of the large mall on the main
road about a 200m walk from the park.

**Zoologico el Patanal**  ZOO
(☑226-7047; Km 23; adult/child $4/2; ☺9am-5pm)
Located north of the city on the way to Daule,
this is a rescue and rehabilitation center for
injured and abandoned wildlife, as well as
being a zoo with monkeys, crocodiles and
some large cats. If you want to visit at 4am,
the best time for bird-watchers, you need to
call in advance. A guide costs around $15.

A taxi from downtown is $15; otherwise,
get on a Nobol-bound bus ($1, 40 minutes)
from the Terminal Terrestre in Guayaquil.

**Jardín Botánico de Guayaquil**  GARDENS
(☑241-7004; Francisco de Orellana; adult/child
$3/1.50; ☺8am-4pm) About a half-hour drive
north of town near Cerro Colorado, this
botanical garden has more than 80 orchid
varieties and nearly 700 plant species. Paths
and trails lead you past the plant exhibits,
and tropical birds flutter overhead. There is
a gift shop, a nice cafe and a butterfly garden. Insect repellent is recommended in the
rainy months. With a few days' advance notice, a guided tour can be arranged.

The most efficient way of getting here is
to take a taxi (one way $12) and ask for Ur-
banización de Los Orquídeas. It's also possible to catch a bus from anywhere along Av
Quito (one hour).

## ☞ Tours

**Captain Henry Morgan**  BOAT TOUR
(Map p274; ☑230-4824; cnr Malecón Simón Bolívar & Colón) Named for the infamous pirate
(who never made it to Guayaquil), this rep-
lica sailboat makes hour-long river trips ($6)
from Tuesday to Sunday at 4pm, 6pm and
7:30pm, with later departures on weekends.
There's booze and dancing, but the tour itself is child-friendly.

**Ferrocarriles del Ecuador**  TRAIN TOUR
(☑280-8064; www.ferrocarrilesdelecuador.gov.ec;
adult/under 18yr round trip $10/5; ☺tours 8am
& 1pm Sat & Sun) This short train trip (1¼
hours) takes you from Durán to Yaguachi,
east of Guayaquil. You'll learn some historical facts, though only in Spanish. A taxi to
the start in Durán should cost no more than
$7 from anywhere in the city center.

**Guayaquil Vision**  BUS TOUR
(Map p274; ☑288-5800; www.guayaquilvision.
com; adult/child $6/3) Runs double-decker
bus tours of the downtown and surrounding
suburbs (1½ hours). There are five tours a
day starting from the Plaza Olmedo on the
*malecón;* the first is at 10:40am. There are
four other hop-on and hop-off points.

## ✦ Festivals & Events

**Carnaval**  CULTURAL, RELIGIOUS
A movable feast, held on the days immediately preceding Ash Wednesday and Lent. In
addition to the traditional throwing of water,
Carnaval is 'celebrated' by dousing passersby
with all manner of unpleasant liquids.

**Simón Bolívar's Birthday &**
**Founding of Guayaquil**  CULTURAL, HISTORICAL
Falling on July 24 and 25 respectively. The
city goes wild with parades, art shows, beauty pageants, fireworks and plenty of drinking and dancing. Hotels are booked well in
advance, and banking and other services are
usually disrupted.

**Independence Day &**
**Día de la Raza**  CULTURAL, HISTORICAL
These two events combine to create another
long holiday full of cultural events, parades
and bigger-than-usual crowds on the *malecón*. Independence Day is October 9 (1820)
and Día de la Raza is October 12.

**New Year's Eve**  CULTURAL
Celebrated with bonfires and life-sized puppets called *viejos* (literally 'the old ones'),
which are made by stuffing old clothes –
these represent the old year. The *viejos* are
displayed on the main streets of the city,
especially the *malecón,* and then burned at
midnight in bonfires.

SOUTH COAST GUAYAQUIL

## 🛏 Sleeping

Some visitors choose to stay in the northern suburbs, but these are really no more convenient to the airport or bus terminal than staying downtown, and you'll be forced to take taxis wherever you go. It's also no safer than downtown, so if you do choose to stay here, be sure to base your decision on each accommodation's merits.

You may be charged up to 22% tax on the listed price – beware, as this is usually the case when booking online – but most of the cheaper hotels don't bother.

During holiday periods, finding a room can be problematic, especially in the better hotels, and prices are usually higher than the listed price. Outside the holiday season, some of the budget and midrange places are willing to negotiate.

### DOWNTOWN

Cheap hotels here aren't built with budget-minded foreign travelers in mind. Street noise can be an annoyance regardless of the category of hotel.

### TOP CHOICE Mansion del Rio                      HOTEL $$$

(Map p274; ☑256-5827; www.mansiondelrio-ec.com; Numa Pompilio Llona 120, Las Peñas; r incl breakfast from $135; ✳@🖥) Housed in a lovingly restored home from the 1920s and hidden down a riverside cobblestone street in the Las Peñas neighborhood, this is the only hotel to take advantage of Guayaquil's history and location. Maria, the owner, makes a charming host and the 11 rooms are comfortably designed with well-curated antique furnishings. The rooftop terrace offers great views. Opposite Artur's Café.

### Hostal Suites Madrid                      HOTEL $

(Map p274; ☑230-7804; www.hostalsuitesmadrid.com; Quísquis 305 near Rumichaca; r from $20; P✳@🖥) One of the few hotels in the city geared toward foreign travelers, Madrid offers a superclean and secure refuge only a block north of the Parque del Centenario. It has hot water, high ceilings, a bright and cheerful color scheme and a rooftop terrace with computers for guests' use. Staff are extremely helpful and friendly; the manager Christopher Jimenez speaks English, French and Italian and runs the affiliated travel agency. Plans are afoot for a next-door addition, including a pool and bar.

### Hotel Oro Verde                      LUXURY HOTEL $$$

(Map p274; ☑232-7999; www.oroverdehotels.com; Av 9 de Octubre & García Moreno; r $152-317; P✳@🖥🏊) About four blocks west of Parque del Centenario, the Oro Verde is still the classiest hotel in town – not so much for superior-quality rooms as for its high-end facilities, casino and several excellent restaurants.

### Hotel Palace                      HOTEL $$$

(Map p274; ☑232-1080; www.hotelpalaceguayaquil.com.ec; Chile 214; r incl breakfast from $110; P✳@🖥) Only steps from Avenida 9 de Octubre and a few blocks from *malecón,* the professionally run Palace is the best-located business-class hotel. It's also one of the city's oldest, though you'd never know it from the up-to-date, compact, but tastefully done rooms, which pack in boutique-style touches with high-end TVs.

### Casa de Romero                      B&B $$

(Map p274; ☑488-6116; www.casaderomero.es.tl; cnr Vélez 501 & Boyacá, 7th fl; s/d incl breakfast $25/40; ✳@🖥) For a taste of downtown *guayaquileño* living, try this friendly place, located in a high-rise apartment building. Five good-sized rooms – all but one with private bathroom – are down the hall from a TV lounge area. Ask for the room with a small balcony.

### Manso Boutique Hotel                      HOTEL $$

(Map p274; ☑252-6644; www.manso.ec; cnr Malecón 1408 & Aguirre; dm $12, r $43-115; ✳@🖥) The unrivalled location aside –boasting a *malecón* address – Manso is at least as much hostel as boutique hotel. Check out several rooms before committing since there's a range in terms of comfort – street noise may be a problem in the airy, more spacious rooms in front while the smaller, darker rooms in back may be undermined by noise from the bar. Friendly and helpful staff are always on hand, and there's a restaurant and spa attached.

### Grand Hotel Guayaquil                      HOTEL $$$

(Map p274; ☑232-9690; www.grandhotelguayaquil.com; cnr Boyacá & Calle 10 de Agosto; r incl breakfast from $85; P✳@🖥🏊) Only a block from Parque Bolívar, this large complex does live up to its name, at least in terms of size. One entire side of the sunny inner courtyard is backstopped by the cathedral next door. This magnificence aside, the carpeted rooms aren't as modern or well maintained as the lobby. There's a pool, a rooftop gym and saunas, as well as two restaurants and a bar.

### Hotel Las Peñas
HOTEL **$$**

(Map p274; ☎232 3355; www.hlpgye.ec, in Spanish; Escobedo 1215 & Vélez; s/d incl breakfast $45/55; ✴🖥) Good-value Las Peñas has extremely spacious rooms with cable TV and mini-fridges, a short walk from the *malecón* and Avenida 9 de Octubre. Breakfast is at the attached California cafe.

### Hotel Presidente Internacional
HOTEL **$$**

(Map p274; ☎230-6779; www.presidenteinternacional.com, in Spanish; Quísquis 112 near Riobamba; s/d $40/50; ✴@) A traditionally outfitted doorman is a bit of an anomaly in this rather worn-down part of the city; however, the nine-story Presidente is real value considering the polished-wood floors, quality bathrooms and low-key artwork – there's even a small gym for the fitness obsessed.

### Hotel Continental
HOTEL **$$$**

(Map p274; ☎232-9270; www.hotelcontinental.com.ec; Chile 510; r $100-175; P✴@🖥) One of the oldest of the city's luxury hotels, the fortress-like Hotel Continental has comfortable, though not especially large, rooms. It's right across from Parque Bolívar and has several good restaurants.

### Hotel Versailles
HOTEL **$$**

(Map p274; ☎230-8773; infohotelversailles@yahoo.es; cnr Quísquis 100 & Ximena; s/d $30/35; ✴@🖥) While it inevitably falls short of its namesake, the Versailles is a good deal only a few blocks from Avenida 9 de Octubre. The large marble-floored rooms are spotless and they even sport high-end shower fixtures and flat-screen TVs.

### Hotel Nueve de Octubre
HOTEL **$**

(Map p274; ☎256-4222; Av 9 de Octubre 736; r with air-con $15; ✴) This behemoth occupies prime real estate in the heart of the downtown shopping strip. The Soviet era–style hallways and basic rooms are paragons of cleanliness to make up for their lack of character. Important: there's no hot water or internet.

#### NORTHERN SUBURBS
Several standard-issue, business-class hotel chains like Sheraton and Howard Johnson are out near the Mall de Sol.

### Iguanazú Hostal
HOSTEL **$$**

(☎220-1143; www.iguanazuhostel.com; Ciudadela La Cogra manzana 1 villa 2, Km 3.5, Avenida Carlos Julio Arosemena; dm $12, r per person $40; ✴@🖥) An oasis of tranquility perched on a hill a few blocks from a busy roadway, the Iguanazú is an ideal base to explore the area. The only downside is that it's hard to find on your own. The owner (a former backpacker) and her friendly bulldog will make you feel at home. Besides charming wood-floored rooms, there's a terrace with hammocks and wonderful views of the city below, a lush and well-tended lawn, a pool and a living room–restaurant area. Breakfast is included in all rates.

### Dreamkapture Hostal
HOSTEL **$**

(Map p278; ☎224-2909; www.dreamkapture.com; Alborada 12A etapa, Manzana 2, Villa 21, Juan Sixto Bernal; dm $10, s/d from $17/22; ✴@🖥) A small, friendly Canadian-Ecuadorian-owned *hostal* (a reasonably priced hotel) on a side street in the suburb of Alborada with a garden courtyard and a tiny pool for cooling off. There are several rooms including one good for groups of four or five, and tasty breakfast is included. Also operates a highly recommended travel agency. The *hostal* is hard to find – look for the fantasy paintings on the compound walls.

### Hilton Colón Guayaquil
LUXURY HOTEL **$$$**

(Map p278; ☎268-9000; www.hiltoncolon.com; Francisco de Orellana; r from $185; ✴@🖥) This massive complex, including several restaurants, shops, a pool, a gym and a casino, is the most luxurious choice. Pony up for a suite and you get a balcony with spectacular views.

### Tangara Guest House
GUESTHOUSE **$$**

(Map p274; ☎228-2828; www.tangara-ecuador.com; Ciudadela Bolivariana, cnr Manuela Sáenz & O'Leary, Block F, Casa 1; s/d incl breakfast $45/56; ✴🖥) Even though there's an inviting small outdoor patio with hammock, and a friendly English-speaking owner, the price tag seems high for these basic rooms. Located a few blocks from the University of Guayaquil.

## ✖ Eating

*Guayaquileños* love their *encebollado,* a tasty soup made with fish, yuca and onion and garnished with popcorn and *chifles* (crispy fried banana slices). The best *encebollados* are sold in cheap mom-and-pop restaurants. They usually sell out by lunchtime. *Cangrejo* (crab) is another local favorite. The majority of the best restaurants are in the northwestern suburb of Urdesa.

## DOWNTOWN

There are bunches of little inexpensive eateries catering to working folk, but there are few standout restaurants. Informal *parrillas* are everywhere and there are several concentrations of bright, clean fast-food restaurants serving seafood and Ecuadorian rice, beans and meat dishes along the Malecón 2000 and the Malecón El Salado. American chains can be found on Avenida 9 de Octubre.

There are a handful of mostly indistinguishable *chifas* (Chinese restaurants) scattered throughout the city.

All of the top-end and a few of the midrange hotels have at least one restaurant. Most are dressed to impress but the value and quality of the food isn't necessarily what you'd expect.

For fresh fruits, vegetables and meat, try the outdoor Mercado El Norte, a block south of El Mercado Artesenal Loja between Aguirre and Martínez.

**Pique & Pase**          ECUADORIAN $$
(Map p274; Lascano btwn Tulcán & Carchi; mains $7) The best restaurant for traditional Ecuadorian specialties also has traditionally clad waiters. It's worth sharing several small dishes, possibly the *bolon verde* (fried plantain with mashed cheese) or *humitas* (corn dumpling steamed in a corn husk) or *guatita con moro de lentejas* (beef tripe stew with mixed rice and lentils) before enjoying one of the meat or seafood mains. Another branch (Map p278) is on Dátiles just off Ave Kennedy in Urdesa.

**La Canoa**          EUCADORIAN $
(Map p274; ☑232-9270; Chile 510; mains $3-7; ☺24hr) One of the more recommended places for a taste of Ecuadorian-style diner food is here, in the Hotel Continental. Instead of hamburgers, the quick dish of choice is ceviche or fried rice with crab. Also in the hotel is the chichi and more-expensive **El Fortín** (mains $17).

**Cocolon**          ECUADORIAN $$
(Map p274; Av Pedro Carbo; mains $9) Directly across from the plaza for the Church of San Francisco, Cocolon has a T.G.I. Friday's aesthetic with a menu of Ecuadorian dishes (although fewer than that of Pique & Pase), as well as burgers and sandwiches.

**Restaurant Ali Baba**          MIDDLE EASTERN $$
(Map p274; Av 9 de Octubre; mains $2) A downtown eatery serving hummus, falafel, juicy shawarmas and filling empanadas ($0.80). Service may not come with a smile but it's still a good place for a quick eat or a lazy drink at one of the street-side tables.

**Caracol Azul**          INTERNATIONAL $$$
(Map p274; ☑228-0461; cnr Av 9 de Octubre 1918 & Los Ríos; mains $20; ☺noon-3:30pm & 7pm-midnight Mon-Sat) Even with its affectations of old-school gourmet fine dining – tuxedoed waiters pushing around silver carts – this downtown institution is more welcoming than stuffy. Granted, some of the fish and meat dishes are plain and dry, but the lobster and shellfish can be recommended.

**Artur's Café**          INTERNATIONAL $$
(Map p274; ☑231-2230; Numa Pompilio Llona 127, Las Peñas; mains $7; ☺6:30pm-2am) A longstanding hideaway perched over the Río Guayas, Artur's serves ordinary Ecuadorian and international standards such as pasta. It's a pleasant spot despite the chintzy decor and dark lighting; there's live music on many weekends.

**La Tasca de Carlos**          SPANISH $$
(Map p274; cnr Cordova & Paula de Icaza; mains $12) Of the several Spanish-style restaurants downtown – all focused on getting things accurate aesthetically, from the waiters' uniforms to the wall hangings – this is the best of the bunch. Serves passable paellas, tortillas and other traditional dishes.

**La Parrilla del Nato**          ECUADORIAN $$
(Map p274; cnr Luque & Pichincha; mains $10) This Guayaquil institution (there's another branch in Urdesa) is usually bustling at lunchtime. Specializing in personalized grills – meat or seafood – fired up at your table, almost everything is available on the menu, from pastas to pizzas. However, the formally dressed waitstaff don't justify the somewhat inflated prices.

**Le Gourmet**          FRENCH $$$
(Map p274; ☺232-7999; cnr Av 9 de Octubre & García Moreno; mains $20; ☺7pm-1am) Your best bet for a splurge is this top-flight French restaurant in the Hotel Oro Verde. El Patio (serving Ecuadorian standards at upscale prices) and Swiss restaurant Le Fondue are also found at this hotel.

**Restaurante 8-28**          CHINESE $
(Map p274; Av 9 de Octubre btwn Rumichaca & Avilés; mains $4.50; ☺11am-11pm Sun-Thu, to midnight Fri & Sat) Large portions and a clean

modern atmosphere make this *chifa* a good choice.

### Delicias Orientales
CHINESE $
(Map p274; Baquerizo Moreno near Paula de Icaza; mains $4; ⊙11am-midnight) A good option.

### Lorenabo
VEGETARIAN $
(Map p274; Paula de Icaza, btwn Moreno & Cordova; mains $3; ⊙11am-5pm, ⏸) One of the few options for meat-free Italian and Ecuadorian dishes.

### Café & Bananas
ECUADORIAN $
(Map p274; Paula de Icaza btwn Baquerizo Moreno & Escobedo; mains $2) Above-average *almuerzos* ($2.30) and an espresso machine; try the *empanadas de verde* (empanadas made with plantain dough) for breakfast.

### Fragela Heladería Artesenal
ICE CREAM $
(Map p274; Av 9 de Octubre btwn Malecón & Pichincha; ice-cream cone $1.75) A pleasant downtown ice-cream shop.

### Mi Comisariato
SUPERMARKET $
(Av 9 de Octubre btwn Avilés & Boyacá) This cavernous grocery is the most convenient downtown place for self-catering.

### NORTHERN SUBURBS
Avenida Estrada, the main drag in the suburb of Urdesa 4km northwest of downtown, is lined with cafes, fast-food joints and restaurants – some slick and upscale. Other good eateries are scattered throughout the suburbs of Alborada, La Garzota and Los Sauces. There are large food courts and other restaurants in the Mall del Sol and San Marino Mall.

### TOP CHOICE Lo Nuestro
ECUADORIAN $$$
(Map p278; ☑238-6398; Estrada 903; mains $8-25) Housed in a century-old mansion complete with wooden shutters and period furniture, Lo Nuestro is one of the most atmospheric places in Guayaquil to eat seafood dishes that are typical of the region. Musicians play on Friday and Saturday evenings, when reservations are recommended. At lunchtime the place fills up with local bigwigs.

### Sushi Isao
JAPANESE $$
(Map p278; Balsamos 102 near Estrada; mains $10-15; ⊙noon-11pm Tue-Sat, to 10pm Sun) This is one of the better of the more than half-dozen Japanese restaurants along Estrada. Popular with Japanese expats (a good sign of authenticity), the ingredients are fresh and preparation is highly skilled. Unpretentious Sushi Isao is open Sunday, when much of the area shuts down.

### Riviera
ITALIAN $$$
(Map p278; ☑288-3790; cnr Estrada 707 & Ficus; mains $20; ⊙12:30pm-11:30pm Mon-Sun) Every night looks like Christmas Eve at this festively lit Italian restaurant. Serving conventional Italian fare, it also offers an extensive wine selection.

### Red Crab
SEAFOOD $$
(Estrada 1205 near Laurales; mains $12; ⊙9am-11pm) Crab done over a dozen ways is served up at this popular and festive restaurant, as is a wide range of traditional Ecuadorian dishes.

### News Café Restaurant
SOUTH AMERICAN $$$
(Map p278; Dátiles 211; mains $15) Peruvian specialties and traditional Ecuadorian and Western sandwiches, served in a stylish and modern setting.

### Malek El Shawarma
MIDDLE EASTERN $
(Map p278; cnr Estrada & Guayacanes; mains $4) More than five Middle Eastern shawarma and kebab joints are congregated near this intersection. All of them are open-air informal spots.

### El Café Espanol
CAFE, SPANISH $
(Map p278; cnr Estrada 302 & Cedros; mains $4; ⊙8am-11pm Mon-Thu & Sun, to 1am Fri & Sat; ⏸) Two-story upscale combination cafe and Spanish-style delicatessen (ham is the specialty) with indoor and outdoor seating.

### Brasa Brazil
BARBECUE $$$
(Centro Comercial Albán Borja, Carlos Julio Arosemena; mains $22) An excellent all-you-can-buffet in a chic and stylish dining room.

### Cevicheria Lojanita
SEAFOOD $
(Map p278; Estrada; mains $5) A no-frills eatery serving ceviche and other seafood dishes.

## 🍷 Drinking & Entertainment

The *farra* (nightlife) in Guayaquil is spread around town. Though particular places tend to come and go, there are specific areas to check out: the former red-light district (still called the **Zona Rosa**) behind the *malecón* between Aguirre and Orellana has more than 20 bars and clubs, many more trendy than seedy (average cover is $10 on weekends), as well as a few gay and lesbian clubs with drag shows on weekend nights. **Las Peñas**, the hillside to the north of downtown, has more-modest hangouts, while the northern suburb of **Urdesa** and the Samborondón area, across Río Daule near the Parque Histórico, are where the beautiful and chic mix. Places in Alborada and Kennedy Norte are less class-conscious. The city's luxury hotels all have casinos and sedate bars. Names, locations and hotspots change with frequency. Check out www.farras.com for up-to-date information.

## Cafes

### Dulceria La Palma                                    CAFE
(Map p274; Escobedo btwn Vélez & Luque; ⊙7:30am-7:30pm) Perhaps the most atmospheric place downtown is this old-school cafe with swirling overhead fans and black and white photos of the city. Try the *cachitos* (crispy mini-croissants; $0.11) and ice-cream cake. Service can be slow during the morning rush.

### Aroma Cafe                                          CAFE
(Map p274; Malecón) A lovely shaded location alongside an artificial waterway. Great for breaking up your waterfront wanderings. Mains $6.

### Sweet & Coffee                                      CAFE
(Map p274; cnr Carbo & Luque; 🛜) A popular Starbucks imitator with excellent cakes; there's another branch near Oro de Verde on Avenida 9 de Octubre, and on Estrada in the northern suburb of Urdesa.

### Frutabar                                         JUICE BAR
(Map p274; Malecón; drinks from $3; ⊙8am-midnight) This surfer-themed fruit shake and juice place also has sandwiches ($4.50), snacks and light meals; another branch is on Avenida Estrada in Urdesa (Map p278).

### Las 3 Canastas                                   JUICE BAR
(Map p274; cnr Vélez & Chile; drinks from $2) A busy daytime spot with street-side tables, bar stools and a large variety of fruit drinks.

### Fruttila                                         JUICE BAR
(cnr Malecón & Aguirre) Another recommended *jugería* (juice bar).

## Bars & Nightclubs

### La Paleta                                            BAR
(Map p274; Numa Pompilio Llona; ⊙8pm-2am Tue-Sat) One of the more sophisticated and interesting bars with cave-like nooks, comfy benches and an eclectic crowd. Serves beers and high-end cocktails such as martinis ($8), as well as tapas.

### Puerto Pirata                                        BAR
(Map p274; Escalón 384; ⊙noon-midnight) After summiting Cerro Santa Ana, stop in for a breather at this faux pirate ship below the lighthouse. It has drinks and food (mains $5), and live music on weekends.

### Bar El Colonial                                      BAR
(Map p274; Rocafuerte 623; ⊙4pm-midnight Mon-Thu, to 2am Fri & Sat) One of the Zona Rosa's long-surviving hotspots with live music on weekend nights.

### La Carlos Alberto Salsateca                        DANCE
(Alborada 12A etapa, Manzana 26, Villa 15, Av Benjamin Carrion; ⊙9pm-4am Wed-Sat) Professional-level salsa dancers.

### El Rincon de las Peñas                               BAR
(Map p274; Escalón 27, Cerro Santa Ana; ⊙5pm-1am Wed & Sun, to 3am Thu-Sat) Formerly Café Gelería Quimbita, this is still one of the more popular late-night spots in the neighborhood.

### La Taberna                                           BAR
(Map p274; Cerro Santa Ana) Just to the left at the bottom of the steps in Las Peñas is this grunge drinking bar with Latin rock and pop in the background.

### Diva Nicotina                                        BAR
(Map p274; Cerro Santa Ana; ⊙7pm-midnight Mon-Thu, to 2am Fri & Sat) At the foot of the hill, this place draws a young crowd and is one of the more happening spots when there's live music.

### Shanny                                             DANCE
(Map p274; Rumichaca; ⊙8pm-3am Mon-Sat) A small, narrow *salsateca* (a nightclub where dancing to salsa music is the main attraction) with strobe lights and cheap beer, around the corner from Hostal Suites Madrid.

### Rollings Tone                                        BAR
(Map p278; Jorge Perez Concha) An upscale sports bar near the start of the commercial strip on Estrada in Urdesa. Billiards, foosball and cover bands on weekend nights.

### Ojos del Perro Azul                                 CLUB
(Map p274; cnr Panama 213 & Roca; ⊙8pm-midnight Wed & Thu, to 2am Fri & Sat) One of the Zona Rosa clubs with live cover bands; also has billiards and a voluminous whiskey selection.

## Cinemas

*El Telégrafo* and *El Universo* publish show times for all cinemas in the city. Filmgoers in the northern suburbs have their choice of several multiscreen cinemas in large malls; English-language movies with Spanish subtitles are usually shown. There are two cinemas, an IMAX and an arthouse theater on the *malecón*.

## Sports

*Guayaquileños* bleed yellow and black, the colors of their beloved soccer team, **Barceloña Sporting Club** (BSC; www.bsc.ec). On game days much of the city looks like it's gone into hiding, since those not at the 90,000-seat Estadio Monumental Banco del Pichincha in the northern suburb of El Paraíso are glued to their TVs at home or in bars. However, the city's other team, **Emelec** (www.emelec.com.ec), whose stadium is in Centenario just south of downtown, has been the better side in recent years. When Barceloña and Emelec meet it's best to avoid wearing either team's colors, especially if attending the game in person (tickets from $5), so as not to provoke the ire of partisan fans. For game schedules check out the sports link on www.eluniverso.com.

##  Shopping

If you prefer a more sedate shopping atmosphere, try one of the indoor shopping malls along the *malecón* or the department stores along Avenida 9 de Octubre. One of the largest malls in all of South America is **Mall de Sol** near the airport. **San Marino**, in the suburb of Kennedy, is a large, equally high-end mall.

**El Mercado Artesanal Loja**  MARKET
(Map p274; Baquerizo Moreno; ⊙9am-7pm Mon-Sat, 10am-5pm Sun) A large artisans' market taking up an entire block downtown. It has a huge variety of crafts from all over Ecuador, including Otavalo-style sweaters, panama hats, carved chessboards, mass-produced paintings and just about every knickknack imaginable. Bargaining is expected.

**La Bahía**  MARKET
(Map p274; btwn Carbo & Villamil) Just outside the *malecón's* blue fence between Olmedo and Colon is this sprawling street market, a crowded maze of vendors selling everything from knock-off name-brand watches to brassieres and bootleg CDs.

##  Information

### Bookstores

The best selection of books, both in Spanish and English, are in the Mr Books shops in the Mall del Sol and San Marino mall in the northern suburbs.

### Cultural Centers

**Alliance Française** (Map p274; ☑253-2009; www.alianzafrancesaguayaquil.com; cnr Hurtado 436 & Mascote) This French cultural center located near the American embassy holds exhibitions, concerts and various courses and lectures.

**Casa de Cultura** (Map p274; ☑230-0500; cnr Av 9 de Octubre & Moncayo; ⊙10am-6pm Tue-Fri, 9am-3pm Sat) Holds art exhibitions, lectures and poetry readings. It also has a bookstore and small cinema.

**Centro Ecuatoriano Norteamericano** (Map p274; ☑256-4536; www.cenecuador.org; cnr Roca & Córdova) Also known as the Ecuador–United States Cultural Center; periodically hosts concerts, exhibitions and other performances.

### Emergency

**Cruz Roja** (Red Cross; ☑131)
**Police** (☑101)

### Internet Access

Many of the midrange and top-end hotels offer free wi-fi, and at the very least have their own terminals for internet access. The stand-alone internet cafes scattered throughout downtown all charge about $1 per hour.

### Laundry

Most laundries in downtown Guayaquil specialize in dry cleaning. Midrange and top-end hotels offer laundry at often exorbitant prices. The best bet for reasonable rates is to inquire at one of the budget hotels. There are machine wash *lavanderías* (laundries) scattered about the northern suburbs.

### Media

*El Universo* and *El Telégrafo* are Guayaquil's two main local papers, which list all the cultural goings-on about town.

### Medical Services

A number of 24-hour pharmacies can be found on Avenida 9 de Octubre.

**Clínica Kennedy** (☑238-9666; Av del Periodista) One of the better hospitals in Guayaquil, by the Policentro shopping center in the suburb of Kennedy. Avenida del Periodista is also known as San Jorge.

### Money

All of Ecuador's major banks are represented in Guayaquil, with several branches of each scattered around the downtown area. There are stand-alone ATMs all over downtown, especially around Plaza de la Merced.

### Post

**Post office** (Map p274; cnr Carbo & Ballén; ◷8am-7pm Mon-Fri, to noon Sat) Part of a huge building.

### Telephone

Most of the internet cafes also double as call centers. Pacifictel and other phone companies also have offices all over the city.

### Tourist Information

**Dirección Municipal de Turismo** (Map p274; ☎232-4182; www.visitaguayaquil.com; at Museo Nahim Isaias; ◷9am-5pm Tue-Sat) At least one English-speaking staff member is usually on hand. It's a center for city (and soon regional) tourism information.

### Travel Agencies

Although Guayaquil is the last stop for the Galápagos, prices are no lower here than they are in Quito. However, you do save about $45 on the flight to the islands (and over an hour's flying time). More details are given in the Planning Your Galápagos Adventure chapter (p35).

**Centro Viajero** (Map p274; ☎230-1283; centrovi@telconet.net; Baquerizo Moreno 1119 near Av 9 de Octubre, Office 805, 8th fl) Organizes Galápagos packages. Spanish, English and French is spoken; ask for the manager, Douglas Chang.

**Dreamkapture Travel** (Map p278; ☎224-2909; www.dreamkapture.com; Alborada 12A etapa, Manzana 2, Villa 21, Juan Sixto Bernal) Good deals on Galápagos cruises and other trips. French, Spanish and English are spoken.

**Galasam Tours** (Map p274; ☎230-4488; www.grupogalasam.com; Av 9 de Octubre 424, Grand Pasaje Bldg, ground fl, Office 9A) Known for economical Galápagos cruises; however, go in with your eyes open.

**Metropolitan Touring** (Map p278; ☎233-0300; www.metropolitantouring.com; Hilton Colón, Francisco de Orellana) Can arrange luxury trips to the Galápagos and also books tours throughout the country.

**Tangara Tours** (Map p274; ☎228-2828; www.tangara-ecuador.com; Ciudadela Bolivariana, cnr Manuela Sáenz & O'Leary, Block F, Casa 1) Run out of the guesthouse of the same name, and highly recommended for local day tours including trips to the Reserva Ecológica Manglares Churute (p290).

**Travel Galapagos** (Map p274; ☎233-1335; www.travelgalapagos.ec; Quísquis 305 near Rumichaca) This especially recommended agency shares space and management with Hostal Suites Madrid. Ask for Christopher Jimenez, the extremely knowledgeable and

affable manager. Can arrange all manner of trips, especially to the Galápagos.

**Tropiceo** (☎02-222-5907; www.tropiceco.com; Quito) An experienced and well-respected company specializing in ecotours; runs group trips to Reserva Ecológica Manglares Churute (p290).

 **Getting There & Away**

### Air

Guayaquil's sleek and modern **José Joaquín de Olmedo International Airport** Map p278; ☎216-9209) is one of Ecuador's two major international airports and is about as busy as Quito's. It's located on the east side of Avenida de las Américas, about 5km north of downtown (however, plans are in the works to relocate the airport 20km from the city center, in Daular). Anyone flying to the Galápagos Islands either leaves from here or stops here on their way from Quito; those flying from Quito rarely have to change planes. Free wi-fi access is available throughout. A desk with accommodations and transport information is immediately outside the arrivals hall.

#### DOMESTIC

There are many internal flights to all parts of the country, but times, days and fares change constantly, so check the following information. The most frequent flights are to Quito with Icaro, LanChile or TAME, which charge about $70 one way (one hour). For the best views, sit on the right side when flying to Quito.

TAME also flies to Cuenca ($80, 30 minutes) and Loja ($87, 45 minutes) daily. There are usually flights to Tulcán and Esmeraldas as well.

AeroGal, TAME and LanChile fly to Baltra (two hours) and San Cristóbal (two hours) in the Galápagos. There are two morning flights every day, costing $480 per round trip ($440 in the low season – mid-January to mid-June and September to November).

Domestic airline offices in Guayaquil:

**AeroGal** (☎268-7566; www.aerogal.com.ec; Junín 440)

**Icaro** (☎229-4265; www.icaro.aero; main airport)

**LanChile** (☎269-2850; www.lan.com; 1042 Córdova)

**TAME** Gran Pasaje (☎256-0728; www.tame.com.ec; Av 9 de Octubre 424); Main Airport (☎216-9150)

#### INTERNATIONAL

International airlines serving Guayaquil:

**Aerogal** (☎268-7566; www.aerogal.com.ec; Junín 440) Direct flights to New York City.

**Avianca** (☎216-9130; www.avianca.com)

**Copa** (☎230-3211; www.copaair.com)

**KLM** (216-9070; www.klm.com)
**LanChile** (269-2850; www.lan.com; 1042 Córdova) Direct flights to New York City.
**TACA** (288-9789; www.taca.com; Luque btwn Carbo & Pichincha)

### Bus & Minivan

The enormous **Terminal Terrestre** (Bus Terminal; Map p278; www.terminalguayauil. com), just north of the airport, is as much a high-end mall (shops, restaurants, internet cafes etc) as it is a transportation facility. There are more than 100 bus companies with small offices lined up along one side of the bottom floor of the building. The kiosks are grouped by region, and most of the destinations and departure times are clearly marked. Buses depart from the 2nd and 3rd floor.

Check the website for a listing of departures. Most bus companies sell tickets in advance, which will guarantee you a seat. Otherwise, just show up at the terminal and you'll usually find a bus to your destination leaving shortly. Friday nights and holidays can become booked up.

#### DOMESTIC

The best services to Quito are with **Transportes Ecuador** and **Panamericana**. They have several direct evening departures, which cost around $10 and take eight hours. Non-direct buses leave every half-hour.

**Super Semeria** is the most highly recommended bus for Cuenca ($9, four hours, 9:50am, 12:45pm and 8pm). Other companies go frequently along the more indirect route via La Troncal ($8, five-plus hours), which drops passengers off along the way.

For Baños ($10, five hours, 4pm), **Riobamba** has one daily direct departure.

For Machala, **Coop Turismo Oro Guayas** (Map p274; 232-0934; cnr Carbo & Ballén) has very comfortable five-passenger SUVs ($11, 2½ hours), and **Coturcip** (Map p274; 251-8895; Sucre 202 near Pichincha) has minivans leaving from downtown ($11, 2½ hours). **Transfrosur** (232-6387; www.transfrosur.com; Chile 416) has a similar service to Huaquillas ($12).

#### INTERNATIONAL

Ecuadorian bus companies such as CIFA, Transportes Rutas Orenses and Ecuatoriana Pullman go to Huaquillas on the Peruvian border (and to Machala). Transportes Loja has one bus in the evening to the border at Macará.

However, the easiest way to Peru is with one of the international lines. Most highly recommended is **Cruz del Sur** (www.cruzdelsur.com. pe), which has newer buses than those of the domestic lines; with wi-fi; larger, more comfortable seats; and better-quality lunches. It charges $75 to Lima (26 hours, 2pm Sunday, Tuesday and Friday). Next, we recommend **Expreso**

**Internacional Ormeño** (214-0847; www. grupo-ormeno.com.pe), **Rutas de America** (223-8673; www.rutasenbus.com; Los Rios 3012 near Letamendi) and **CIFA Internacional**. **Ormeño** (213-0379; www.cifainternacional. com) has daily departures for Lima ($80, 26 hours, 11:30am). Its office and terminal is on Avenida de las Americas, just north of the main bus terminal.

These services are very convenient because you do not have to get off the bus to take care of border formalities.

## ❶ Getting Around

Walking is the easiest and most convenient way of getting around downtown. Yellow taxis – which are a quick and relatively inexpensive way of covering long distances – are everywhere. Buses, both the older blue-and-white Selectivos and the newer Metrovia system, are convenient for travel between downtown and the suburbs.

### To/From the Airport

The **airport** (Av de las Américas) is about 5km north of downtown. A taxi in either direction should cost $4 to $5. The majority of taxis at the airport are yellow and labeled **Cooperativa de Transportes Aeropuerto Guayaquil** (216-9141); these will take you into the city or, for that matter, anywhere else in the country. Rates are posted in the back seats.

Cross the street in front of the airport to take a bus downtown. From the center, the best bus to take to the airport is bus 2 Especial, which only costs $0.25 and takes under an hour. It runs along the *malecón* but is sometimes full, so you should leave yourself plenty of time.

### To/From the Bus Terminal

The bus terminal is about 2km away from the airport. You can walk the distance if you want to, although it means crossing a busy highway and is not recommended if you're carrying heavy bags. Turn right out of the airport and head for the obvious huge terminal. A taxi between the two is $1.

Buses from the city center to the bus terminal leave from Parque Victoria near Calles 10 de Agosto and Quito.

Several buses leave from the terminal for downtown, including bus 71.

A taxi to or from downtown is about $3.50.

### Bus

City buses are cheap (about $0.25) but the routes are complicated and are not much use for getting around downtown. With all the waiting and traffic, you're better off walking. However, buses are efficient for returning from the northern 'burbs to downtown.

The **Metrovia** ($0.25), an expanding rapid transit system, has articulated double-sized buses running along designated lanes from downtown to northern suburbs. Terminal Río Daule, opposite the Terminal Terrestre, is the end of one of the lines.

### Car

There are several international car-rental agencies at the airport including **Budget** (☎216-9026; www.budget-ec.com) and **Hertz** (☎216-9035; www.hertz.com.ec). Ask about the condition of the roads where you intend driving; a 4WD vehicle might be worth the extra cost. Driving in the city is not for the faint of heart – rules, regulations, safety...everything is out the window.

### Taxi

You should be able to get between any two points downtown for about $1.50 and to the northern suburb of Urdesa for between $3 to $4. Agree on fares before you get into cabs, otherwise you may be overcharged. Another strategy is simply to hand drivers what you suspect is the lower end of the proper price, and if they accept it without comment, great. If they ask for more, you know you've probably low-balled them.

If you can't find a taxi on the street, try **Cooperativa de Taxis Paraíso** (☎220-1877).

# SOUTH OF GUAYAQUIL

Though it's usually seen by travelers as a place to pass through on their way south to Peru, this agriculturally important part of the country boasts several nature reserves and a charming mountain town.

## Reserva Ecológica Manglares Churute

☎04

This 50,000-hectare **national reserve** (admission $10) protects an area of mangroves southeast of Guayaquil. Much of the coast used to be mangrove forest – an important and unique habitat (see p367). This is one of Ecuador's few remaining mangrove coastlands; the rest have been destroyed by the shrimp industry. Inland is some tropical dry forest, on hills reaching 700m above sea level.

Studies of the area within the reserve indicate that the changing habitat from coastal mangroves to hilly forest supports a wide biodiversity with a high proportion of endemic species. Dolphins have frequently been reported along the coast, and many other animal and bird species are seen by wildlife-watchers, who are the main visitors.

The reserve entrance is on the left side of the main Guayaquil–Machala highway, about 50km southeast of Guayaquil. Here you'll find an **information center** (☎09-276-3653), where you pay the admission. Park rangers can arrange boats for you to visit the mangroves (about $60 for the whole day for four or five people), and there are also several kilometers of hiking trails. The best season for boats is January to May, when water levels are high (but there are also more insects then).

Several tour companies in Guayaquil run day trips here.

A few basic **cabañas** ($5) near the information center – little more than concrete shelters – are available. **Camping** ($3) can be arranged if coordinated in advance with the reserve office.

Any bus between Guayaquil and Naranjal or Machala can drop you off at the information center. When you're ready to leave, flag down a bus at the sign on the road (drivers know the sign). A taxi from Guayaquil is around $40, round trip.

## Machala

☎07 / POP 228,000

Surrounded by banana plantations – the *oro verde* (green gold), which is the province's moniker – Machala is the commercial and administrative capital of El Oro province. The city is a convenient stop south from Guayaquil on the way to the Peruvian border or for journeys further into the mountains directly to the east. Puerto Bolívar, only 7km away, is the local international port and seafood centre.

The **Feria Mundial del Banano**, held the third week in September, is when Machala celebrates all things banana. An international contest is held to elect La Reina del Banano (The Banana Queen).

### 🛌 Sleeping

**Hostal Saloah**                                    HOTEL **$**
(☎293-4344; Colón 1818; s/d incl breakfast $22/30; ✷@☞) Steps away from several bus companies, the good-value rooms at the Saloah are surprisingly quiet, all things considered – tiny windows help. Each of the four floors has a larger, brighter street-

facing suite that's worth the few extra dollars. There's also a rooftop patio where breakfast is served with panoramic views of the city.

**Grand Hotel Americano**　　　HOTEL **$$**
(☑296-6400; www.hotelesmachala.com; cnr Tarqui & Av 25th de Junio; r incl breakfast from $30; ✳@☎) A step up from the Saloah is

# Machala

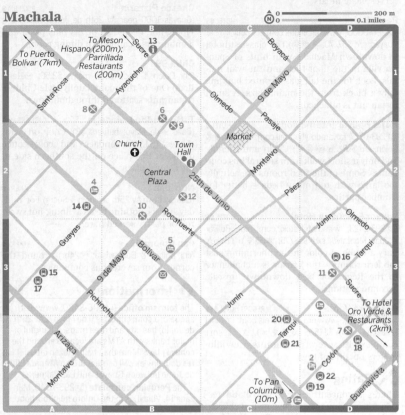

# Machala

this business-class hotel with clean, modern rooms, professional staff and a central location. All rooms have air-conditioning and cable TV and the attached restaurant serves basic meals.

### Regal Hotel HOTEL $$
(✆296-0000; www.regalhotel.com.ec; Bolívar near Guayas; s/d $57/70; ❄@🛜) The classiest hotel in downtown Machala, with hints of Spanish villa in the floor tiles and the wall murals. Look for the tall glass-fronted building only a block from the main plaza. A small restaurant is attached.

### Hotel Bolívar Internacional HOTEL $
(✆293-0727; falvarado@hotmail.com; cnr Bolívar & Colón; s/d $18/26; ❄@🛜) Clean and friendly and only a short walk from several bus companies. Some of the tiled rooms are actually too large with too many beds – better for slumber parties.

### Veuxor Executive Hotel HOTEL $$
(✆293-2423; www.hotelveuxor.com; cnr Bolívar & Juan Montalvo; s/d $58/75; ❄@🛜) There's nary a touch of color in the uberminimalist modern rooms – the Veuxor is a challenger to the Regal for best downtown upscale accommodations.

### Hotel Oro Verde RESORT HOTEL $$$
(✆298-5444; www.oroverdehotels.com; r incl breakfast from $150; ❄@🛜⊛) A resort complex with several restaurants, a few kilometers outside of town.

## ✖️ Eating

There's a concentration of **parrillada** restaurants serving inexpensive grilled chicken and steaks on Sucre near Tarqui and on Las Palmeras in front of the stadium – an especially good choice on Sunday and holidays, when much of the city shuts down. A number of hotels have restaurants. Consider heading over to Puerto Bolívar for a fresh seafood lunch.

El Paseo, a modern shopping mall 3.5km south of town, has an enormous department store with a grocery section, a food court and a cinema.

### Meson Hispano INTERNATIONAL $$
(cnr Las Palmeras & Sucre; mains $5-12; ⊙11am-midnight Mon-Thu, to 1am Fri & Sat) Qualifying as swank for Machala, this restaurant has uniformed waiters, tablecloths and a large sophisticated menu – from Caesar salad ($5) to chateaubriand ($9).

### El Paraiso de la Vida VEGETARIAN $
(Ayacucho near Av 25th de Junio; mains $4) Sandwiches and breakfasts in a narrow dining room with indoor and outdoor space.

### Chesco Pizzeria PIZZERIA $
(Guayas 1050 near Av 25th de Junio; mains $4) Piping-hot, deep-dish pizzas plus pasta and hamburgers in a modern dining room.

### Chifa 99 CHINESE $
(cnr Colón & Rocafuerte; mains $2.50; ⊙11am-11pm) One of the many family-style Chinese restaurants scattered throughout town.

### Tutto Freddo Heladeria ICE CREAM $
(Calle 9 de Mayo; burgers $3) Cool off with shakes ($1.75), sundaes and cold coffee drinks at this place on the southern side of the central plaza.

### Nutripan BAKERY $
(Guayas btwn Av 25th de Junio & Sucre) For midday snacks, nothing beats a piping-hot sweet roll or pastry served here.

### Pan Columbia BAKERY $
(cnr Bolívar & Buenavista; ⊙24hr) Around the corner from several bus companies.

## ℹ️ Information

The **tourism office** (✆296-8480; www.visitandoeloro.com; cnr Calle 9 de Mayo & Av 25th de Junio) has city and area maps. A handful of major banks with ATMs are located around the central plaza. More than half a dozen internet cafes doubling as call centers are on Avenida 25th de Junio between Guayas and Las Palmeras.

The **Peruvian consulate** (✆293-7040; Manzana 14, Villa II) is in the Unioro neighborhood.

## ℹ️ Getting There & Away

### Air
Weekday morning flights to Quito ($125) are available with **TAME** (✆296-4865; Montalvo near Pichincha). The airport is 1km from downtown and a taxi ride there will cost about $1.

### Bus
Machala has no central bus terminal. There are **CIFA** (cnr Guayas & Bolívar) buses that go to the Peruvian border at Huaquillas ($1.50, 1½ hours), leaving every 30 minutes during daylight hours, and buses also go hourly to Guayaquil ($4.50, three hours). **Rutas Orenses** (Rocafuerte near Tarqui) and **Ecuatoriana Pullman** (Av 25th de Junio near Colón) have slightly more comfortable air-conditioned buses and frequent services to Guayaquil and Huaquillas.

## EL BOSQUE PETRIFICADO PUYANGO

The largest petrified forest, at 2659 hectares, in Ecuador and probably the whole continent of South America. Fossilized araucaria tree trunks (many of them millions of years old) up to 11m long and 1.6m in diameter have been found at **El Bosque Petrificado Puyango**. The reserve is also home to more than 130 bird species.

Puyango is in a valley at about 360m above sea level, some 55km inland from the coast. The entrance fee is $5 and camping is allowed for a small fee; ask at the **information center** (⊙8am-4:30pm; www.bosquepuyango.ec). A lookout point and trails have been constructed.

In the small nearby village of **Puyango** there is no hotel as such, although the villagers will find you a bed or floor space. Locals know the reserve and some will act as guides.

Transportes Cooperativa Loja buses from Machala and Loja will drop you in Puyango. Alternatively, take a CIFA bus to the town of Arenillas, from where you can catch an infrequent local bus for the further 55km to Puyango. You may be stopped for a passport check, since the park is close to the border.

**Piñas Interprovincial** (cnr Colón & Rocafuerte) and **Transportes T.A.C.** (Colón) both service Piñas ($2.75, 2½ hours) and Zaruma ($3.25, three hours). The latter goes hourly and also has evening departures to Quito ($8, 10 hours).

**Panamericana** (Colón near Bolívar) has buses to Quito ($10, 10 hours) every two hours from 7:45am to 9:30pm. It also has buses to Santo Domingo ($6, eight hours) and an evening bus to Tulcán.

**Cooperative Pullman Azuay** (Sucre near Tarqui) has frequent departures for Cuenca ($5.50, four hours) from 4:30am to 11:15pm.

**Transportes Cooperativa Loja** (Tarqui near Bolívar) goes to Loja ($4.50, five hours).

### Minivan

A handful of minivan companies lines Guayas between Pichincha and Serrano, including **Coturcip SA** (☑296 0849) and **Coop Turismo Oro Guayas** (☑293-4382). These have hourly departures to Guayaquil ($10, 2½ hours).

**Oro y Plata** (☑06-972-7364; cnr Sucre & Vela) has hourly vans to Zaruma ($5, 2½ hours) and Piñas ($4, 2 hours).

## Puerto Bolívar & Jambelí

☑07

An otherwise banal stretch of concrete, the port of Puerto Bolívar, only 7km from Machala, is of interest to seafood connoisseurs and those who want to glimpse the southern coast's bananas and shrimp before they're shipped overseas. The port itself is really nothing more than a concrete *malecón* with around 20 *cevicherías* and a slightly dodgy feel at night.

Motorized dugouts can be hired for cruising the mangroves ($25 and can include snorkeling), for **bird-watching** or to visit the nearby island beach at **Jambelí** (mosquito-ridden during the wet season). While it's understandably popular for Machala residents seeking a quick escape from the city, it's not an especially attractive destination in and of itself. Jambelí can be busy on weekends and completely overcrowded during Carnaval and Semana Santa. There's some good snorkeling around the nearby mangrove island of **Isla de Amor**, part of a community ecoproject to preserve the marine environment.

**El Faro Playa Spa** (☑292-0414; www.elfaro. com.ec; r per person with three meals $45; ☀) on the northwestern tip of Jambelí has nice A-frame, thatch-roofed cottages, and **Toa Toa** (☑291-5864; s/d $25/30) has small basic bamboo cabañas, both on the beach. A number of beachside shacks serve seafood on weekends, but many are closed midweek.

Take bus 1 or bus 13 from Machala's central plaza, or take a taxi (about $2). To Jambelí you can either charter a boat from Puerto Bolívar or take one of the passenger shuttle boats (round trip $2.40, 25 minutes, every two hours or so from 7:30am to 6pm). The boats drop you off on a canal on the mainland side of the island and you have to walk the few hundred meters to the beach.

# Zaruma

📞07 / POP 12.500 / ELEV 1150M

After winding your way up and over lushly covered mountains with gushing streams pouring through the foliage, the final climb up to Zaruma (southeast of Machala) feels like the end of a pilgrimage. And for those traveling along the washboard-flat coastal roadway, this old gold-mining town (c 1549) is a revelation, with its narrow, hilly streets and wooden balustrades decorated with potted plants. While its mines are mostly exhausted or closed to the public, you can arrange a visit to the 500m-long tunnel of nearby **La Mina el Sexmo** (which refers to the tribute paid to the Spanish crown) with Tito Castillo at **Oroadventure** (📞297-2761; Plaza de Independencia); Tito charges around $20 for small groups. An interesting **museum** with historical and archeological artifacts shares space with the town's tourism office.

Architecturally more modern and less charming, **Piñas** is probably best visited as a side trip while based in Zaruma. In 1980 a new bird species, the El Oro parakeet, was discovered near here. The best place to see the bird is Fundación Jocotoco's **Reserva Buenaventura** (admission $15), a 1500-hectare cloud-forest reserve about 9km from Piñas. Oroadventure offers day tours ($40) here.

## MONEY MATTERS

It's best to avoid the informal money-changers on either side of the border. On the Ecuadorian side they're the guys with the briefcases, sitting on plastic chairs. Problems with fake currency are common and money-changers will tell patent lies like 'the machines don't work.' Banks in Huaquillas or Aguas Verdes don't normally do exchange transactions, but it's worth trying. There are a number of ATMs on the Ecuadorian side.

If you're leaving Peru, it's best to get rid of as much Peruvian currency as possible before arriving at the border. If you're leaving Ecuador, your US currency is easily exchanged in Peru, but it's best to wait to do the bulk of your transactions further south of the border.

## 🛏 Sleeping

**Roland Hotel** HOTEL $$

(📞297-2800; rolandhotel@hotmail.com; s/d from $22/40; 🅿🏊) The first place you come to on the main road from Piñas up to town, Roland truly takes advantage of the scenery. The main building has small modern rooms with hot-water bathrooms and TVs – be sure to ask for one with windows opening onto the valley below. There are slightly more expensive, small, pastel-colored chalets surrounding the pool in the concrete courtyard. The only downside is the short uphill slog to eat, since the hotel's restaurant only opens for groups.

**Hotel Blacio** HOTEL $

(📞297-2045; www.hotelblacio.com; cnr Sexmo 015 & Sucre; r per person $10) Closer to the central plaza and only a block or so above the bus stop is this small, friendly place with hot water and well-cared-for rooms.

**Hostería El Jardín** HOSTERÍA $

(📞297-2706; Barrio Limoncito; per person incl breakfast $17; @) A family-run lodge a 10-minute walk from the central plaza, with a courtyard garden and comfortable rooms.

## 🍴 Eating

**200 Miles** ECUADORIAN $

(mains $4; ⏰8am-10pm; 🅿) Just down the road from the bus company offices, with views of the valley below, is Zaruma's nicest restaurant. A good breakfast and a wide variety of specialties are served up by the friendly husband-and-wife owners.

**Rincon Zarumen** ECUADORIAN $

(mains $2.50) Just below Plaza Independencia, this casual eatery serves basic chicken and rice dishes as well as *tigrillo,* an area specialty made from green bananas, eggs and cheese.

**Imperdible Coffee Shop** ECUADORIAN $

(mains $2.50; 🅿) This small, modern place at the entrance to the plaza has brewed coffee drinks and a variety of deli-style sandwiches.

**Cafetería Uno** ECUADORIAN $

(mains $2.50; ⏰6:30am-8pm Mon-Sat, to 1pm Sun) A tiny spot with three tables, good light and *almuerzos.*

**Tangobar Restaurant** ECUADORIAN $

(mains $3) On the plaza itself, this place has charming wooden floors and good, cheap *almuerzos.*

## ℹ️ Information

The friendly **tourism office** (📞297-3101; www.vivezaruma.com.ec; ⊙8am-noon & 2-6pm Mon-Fri, 9am-4pm Sat, 8:30am-12:30pm Sun) is on the plaza. In town there's a Banco de Guayaquil and a Banco de Machala (both with ATMs), several internet cafes with call centers, and a wash-and-dry laundry.

## ℹ️ Getting There & Away

Piñas has departures every hour on the half-hour from 7am to 7:15pm and TAC has four daily departures to Machala ($3.25, three hours) via Piñas ($1, 45 minutes). The former also has a 2pm departure to Cuenca, a 6pm trip to Quito and three trips to Loja. TAC offers a few daily direct departures to Guayaquil ($6, six hours, 9:15am, 2:15pm and 7pm); Piñas buses to Guayaquil leave at 1pm and 2pm.

**Oro y Plata** (📞297-2173) runs minivans with direct connections to Machala ($5, 2½ hours) and less frequently to Guayaquil ($11, 5 hours); the office is near the central plaza.

In your own vehicle it's no more than a two-hour drive to/from Machala.

---

# Peru via Huaquillas

On the route taken by most overland travelers, it's about 80km from Machala to the Peruvian border town of Huaquillas. The highway passes through banana and palm plantations, as well as the dusty market towns of **Santa Rosa** and **Arenillas**. The border itself is at **Río Zarumilla** (⊙24hr), a mostly dry riverbed that's crossed by an international bridge linking Huaquillas to **Aguas Verdes** in Peru (bridge guards won't bother you with formalities; you can walk back and forth as you please).

If you're stuck in Huaquillas for the night, **Hotel Vanessa** (📞299-6263; www.hotelvanessa-ec.com; Calle 1 de Mayo & Hualtaco; s/d $18/24; ❄️🛜) and next door **Hotel Hernancor** (📞299-5467; grandhotelhernancor@gmail.com; Calle 1 de Mayo; s/d $20/35; ❄️@🛜) are good choices. The latter is the grand dame of town with wide hallways, high ceilings and large but impersonal rooms.

There are several informal eateries and *juguerías* (juice shacks) just behind the municipal government building; look for the clock tower in the parque central.

The **Ecuadorian Immigrations Office** (⊙24hr) is inconveniently located about 4km north of the bridge; all entrance and exit formalities are carried out here. If

you're traveling by bus from Machala, the driver does not wait for you. You must save your ticket and board the next Machala–Huaquillas bus (they pass every 20 minutes or so) or continue on to the border by taxi.

In Aguas Verdes, there are buses and *colectivos* (shared station wagon taxis; about $3.50 per person) running to Tumbes in Peru, which has plenty of hotels, as well as transportation to take you further south. **Transportes Flores** (www.floreshnos.net) has four daily departures from the Peruvian side of the border south to Lima ($18, 20 hours) and points in between. The 6pm trip has more comfortable double-decker buses with reclining seats, bathrooms, TVs and dinner ($25).

Coming from Guayaquil, the most convenient options (which allow you to avoid changing buses at the border) are the Cruz del Sur and Expreso Internacional Ormeño buses direct to Lima (see p289).

If you're leaving Peru and entering Ecuador, first obtain an exit stamp in your passport from the Peruvian immigration office about 2km south of the border. After walking across the international bridge you'll find yourself on the main road, which is crowded with market stalls and stretches out through Huaquillas. Take a taxi (about $1.50) or a Machala-bound bus to the Ecuadorian immigration office; you'll probably then have to return to Huaquillas to catch an onward northbound transport.

To make your way further into Ecuador, head to one of the bus companies scattered within half-a-dozen blocks of one another and the border. **CIFA** (cnr Santa Rosa & Machala) has five daily departures for Guayaquil ($5, four hours, 9:15am, 11:15am, 1pm, 3:15pm and 5pm) and three for Machala ($1.50, 1½ hours, 8am, 10am and noon). You can also board any Guayaquil-bound bus and get off in Machala. **Transfrosur** (Santa Rosa) runs frequent minivans to Guayaquil ($12, four hours).

**Panamericana** (cnr Teniente Cordovez & 10 de Agosto) has seven buses a day to Quito ($9, 11 hours) via Ambato and some via Santo Domingo. If you're in a headlong rush to make it to Colombia, there's a daily 4pm trip to Tulcan ($18, 19 hours) near the Colombian border. **Pullman Sucre** and **Azuay Internacional**, both on Teniente Cordovez, have four departures daily to Cuenca ($7, five hours, 10:45am, 2pm, 4:15pm, 6pm).

# The Galápagos Islands

## Includes »

## Why Go?

The Galápagos Islands may just inspire you to think differently about the world. The creatures that call the islands home, many found nowhere else in the world, act as if humans are nothing more than slightly annoying paparazzi.

This is not the Bahamas and these aren't typical tropical paradises; in fact, most of the islands are devoid of vegetation and some look more like the moon than Hawaii. More humans live here than is commonly assumed, and there's a surprising level of development in the islands' towns, mostly geared toward the thriving tourism industry.

This isolated group of volcanic islands and its fragile ecosystem has taken on almost mythological status as a showcase of biodiversity. Yet you don't have to be an evolutionary biologist or an ornithologist to appreciate one of the few places left on the planet where the human footprint is kept to a minimum.

## Best Places to Eat

» Angermeyer Point Restaurant (p306)

» Iguana Crossing Boutique Hotel (p320)

» Parrillada San José (p314)

## Best Places to Stay

» Finch Bay Hotel (p304)

» La Casa Marita (p320)

» Casa Blanca (p313)

## When to Go

### Galápagos Islands

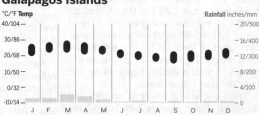

**Jan–May** Sunny, warm, occasional short downpours. Water is less rough and winds slacken.

**Jun–Dec** The cool and dry season. Seas tend to be choppier due to the Humboldt current.

**Jun–Dec** Sea mammals and land birds tend to be at their most active during this time.

# Connections

Isla Baltra hosts one of the islands' two major airports. A public bus or ferry connects the Isla Baltra airport with Puerto Ayora.

The other major airport is at Puerto Baquerizo Moreno on Isla San Cristóbal.

Regular public ferries or private boats provide interisland transportation, although some of the uninhabited islands can only be visited on tours.

## ISLAND BASICS

The islands lie in the Pacific Ocean on the equator, about 90 degrees west of Greenwich. There are 13 major islands (ranging in area from 14 sq km to 4588 sq km), six small islands (1 sq km to 5 sq km) and scores of islets, of which only some are named.

Five of the islands are inhabited. About half the residents live in Puerto Ayora, on Isla Santa Cruz in the middle of the archipelago. Puerto Baquerizo Moreno on Isla San Cristóbal (the easternmost island) is second in importance to Puerto Ayora when it comes to tourism.

The other inhabited islands are Isla Isabela (the largest island, accounting for half the archipelago's land mass), with the small, increasingly popular town of Puerto Villamil, Isla Baltra and Isla Santa María, with Puerto Velasco Ibarra. The remaining islands are not inhabited but are visited on tours.

Most of the islands have two, or sometimes three, names. The earliest charts gave the islands both Spanish and English names (many of these refer to pirates or English noblemen), and the Ecuadorian government assigned official names in 1892. The official names are used in this guide in most cases.

## Fees & Taxes

The Galápagos national park fee is $100. It must be paid in cash at one of the airports after you arrive, or in advance through a prebooked tour, and you will not be allowed to leave the airport until you pay. Make sure you have your passport available when you pay, and hang onto your ticket until you leave. A transit control fee of $10 must be paid at the Instituto Nacional Galápagos (INGALA) window next to the ticket counter in either the Quito or Guayaquil airports; the charge is already included in the price of many prearranged boat tours.

## AT A GLANCE

» **Money** ATMs in Puerto Ayora and Baquerizo Moreno only

» **Cell Phones** Only GSM phones work; reception spotty

» **Time Zone** One hour behind mainland Ecuador time

## Fast Facts

» **Area** 7880 sq km of land over 50,000 sq km of ocean

» **Distance from the Mainland** 1000km

» **Number of Islands** 125

» **Highest Point** Volcán Wolf, 1646m

» **Population** 30,000

» **Capital** Puerto Baquerizo Moreno

## Set Your Budget

» **Midrange hotel room** $55

» **Two-course evening meal** $15

» **All-inclusive boat tours** $200 to $400+ per day

» **Two-boat-dive day trip** $200

» **Bottle of beer** $1.50

## Resources

» **Galapagos National Park** www.galapagospark.org

» **Discover Galapagos** www.discovergalapagos.com

» **Lonely Planet Thorn Tree** www.lonelyplanet.com/thorntree

THE GALÁPAGOS ISLANDS

# ISLA SANTA CRUZ (INDEFATIGABLE)

The island of Santa Cruz has the largest and most developed town in the Galápagos; almost every visitor to the islands spends at least some time here, even if it's simply commuting from the airport on nearby Isla Baltra to a cruise ship in the harbor of Puerto Ayora. However, to anyone who stays for longer, the island of Santa Cruz is more than just a way station or place to feel connected

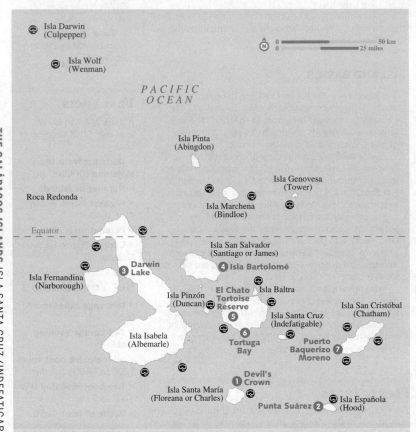

## The Galápagos Islands Highlights

**1** Relax and let the current zip you past rays, turtles and sharks while snorkeling around **Devil's Crown** (p324), just off Isla Santa María

**2** Witness the pageantry of birdlife around the dramatic cliffs at **Punta Suárez** (p325), on Isla Española

**3** Huff it up to the trail above **Darwin Lake** (p318)

on northern Isla Isabela, for inspired views

**4** Take in spectacular views at **Isla Bartolomé** (p323), where you may feel like one of the last people on earth

**5** Engage in a staring contest with the slumbering beasts in the **El Chato Tortoise Reserve** (p299), in the highlands of Santa Cruz

**6** Sunbathe alongside marine iguanas on the beautiful white sand of **Tortuga Bay** (p301)

**7** Pick your outdoor adventure – surf, snorkel, kayak, bike or dive – within minutes of the sleepy town of **Puerto Baquerizo Moreno** (p312) on Isla San Cristóbal to the modern, man-made world; it's a destination in itself, full of visitor sites, easily accessible beaches and remote highlands in the interior, and a base for adventurous activities far from the tourism trail.

If Puerto Ayora is too 'bright lights, big city' for you, book in at **Royal Palm Hotel** (📞252-7408; www.royalpalmgalapagos.com; r from $375; ✳@🛜🏊), a beautifully designed luxury hotel in the highlands around Santa Rosa.

## ◉ Sights & Activities

Several sites of interest in the highlands of Santa Cruz can be reached from the trans-island road and are part of the itineraries of many cruises. Access to some sites is through colonized areas, so respect private property.

**El Chato Tortoise Reserve**  WILDLIFE RESERVE
(admission $3; ⊘8am-5pm) South of Santa Rosa is El Chato Tortoise Reserve, where you can observe giant tortoises in the wild. When these virtually catatonic, prehistoric-looking beasts extend their accordionlike necks to feed, it's an impressive sight. The reserve is also a good place to look for short-eared owls, Darwin's finches, yellow warblers, Galápagos rails and paint-billed crakes (these last two are difficult to see in the long grass).

A downhill and often muddy trail from Santa Rosa leads through private property to parkland about 3km away. Horses can be hired in Santa Rosa – ask at the store/bar on the main road for directions to the outfitter's house. The trail forks at the park boundary, with the right fork going up to the small hill of **Cerro Chato** (3km further) and the left fork going to **La Caseta** (2km). The trails can be hard to follow, and you should carry water. The reserve is part of the national park and a guide is required.

**Rancho Primicias**  WILDLIFE RESERVE
(admission $4; ⊘8am-5pm) Next to El Chato is this private ranch, owned by the Devine family. There are dozens of giant tortoises, and you can wander around at will. The entrance is beyond Santa Rosa, off the main road – ask locals for directions. Remember to close any gates that you go through. There is a cafe selling cold drinks and hot tea, which is welcome if the highland mist has soaked you.

**Lava Tunnels**  UNDERGROUND TUNNELS
(admission $3; ⊘8am-5pm) These impressive underground tunnels southeast of the village of Santa Rosa are more than a kilometer in length and were formed when the outside skin of a molten-lava flow solidified. When the lava flow ceased, the molten lava inside

THE GALÁPAGOS ISLANDS ISLA SANTA CRUZ (INDEFATIGABLE)

## Isla Santa Cruz

0 — 10 km
0 — 5 miles

the flow kept going, emptying out of the solidified skin and thus leaving tunnels. Because they are on private property, the tunnels can be visited without an official guide. The owners of the land provide information and guides, as well as all-important electrical lighting (you can also hire flashlights/torches). Tours to the lava tunnels are offered in Puerto Ayora.

### Los Gemelos                           LOOKOUT
Part of the highlands that can be visited from the road are these twin sinkholes (not volcanic craters), surrounded by scalesia forest. Vermilion flycatchers are often seen here, as are short-eared owls, on occasion. Los Gemelos are about 2km beyond Santa Rosa on the trans-island road. Although the craters lie only 25m and 125m from either side of the road, they are hidden by vegetation, so ask your driver to stop at the short trailhead.

### Cerro Crocker                          HIKING
A path north from Bellavista leads toward Cerro Crocker (864m) and other hills and extinct volcanoes. This is a good chance to see the vegetation of the scalesia, miconia and fern-sedge zones and to look for birds such as the vermilion flycatcher, the elusive Galápagos rail and the paint-billed crake. It's around 5km from Bellavista to the crescent-shaped hill of **Media Luna**, and 3km further to the base of Cerro Crocker. This is national park, so a guide is required.

### El Garrapatero Beach                    BEACH
A 30-minute taxi ride from Puerto Ayora through the highlands, plus a 15-minute walk, brings you to this beautiful beach. It has tidal pools that are good for exploring and snorkeling on calm days, and a lagoon with flamingos, white-cheeked ducks and black-necked stilts.

### Punta Estrada Beach                     BEACH
The small beach in front of the Finch Bay Hotel is a good place to while away a few hours. The water here is pristine and sharks have been known to pass through the cove. The remaining Santa Cruz visitor sites are reached by boat and with guides. On the west coast are **Whale Bay** and **Conway Bay**, and on the north coast are **Black Turtle Cove** (Caleta Tortuga Negra) and **Las Bachas**. Conway Bay has a 1.5km trail passing a lagoon with flamingos; north of here is **Cerro Dragón**, which has two small lagoons that may have flamingos. It also has

a 1.75km trail that leads through a forest of palo santo (holy wood) trees and opuntia cacti to a small hill with good views. There are some large repatriated land iguanas here.

There is no landing site in Black Turtle Cove, which is normally visited by *panga* (small boats used to ferry passengers from a larger boat to shore). The cove has many little inlets and is surrounded by mangroves, where you can see lava herons and pelicans. The main attraction is in the water: marine turtles are sometimes seen mating, schools of golden mustard rays are often present and white-tipped sharks may be seen basking in the shallows. The nearby Las Bachas beach, although popular for sunbathing and swimming, is often deserted.

# Puerto Ayora
☑05 / POP 18,000
This town, the largest in terms of population and size in the Galápagos, is a surprise to most visitors, who don't expect to find anything but plants and animals on the islands. Puerto Ayora looks and feels like a fairly prosperous mainland Ecuadorian coastal town, despite the sea lions and pelicans hanging around the waterfront. Most of the hotels, restaurants and tourist facilities line Avenida Charles Darwin, and the airport is on Isla Baltra, around an hour away to the north. Several blocks inland, travel agencies give way to ordinary, humble dwellings and shops. Some of the descendants of the handful of Norwegian, Swiss and German families that originally settled here four generations ago maintain a presence in the tourism industry.

## ◉ Sights & Activities

### Charles Darwin Research Station              WILDLIFE RESERVE
(☑252-6146; www.darwinfoundation.org; ◷6am-6pm) Just northeast of town, this site can also be reached by dry landing (you won't get wet) from Academy Bay. More than 200 scientists and volunteers are involved with research and conservation efforts, the most well-known of which involves a captive breeding program for giant tortoises. The station features a national-park information center; a small, aging museum where a video in English or Spanish is presented several times a day; a **baby-tortoise house** with incubators (when the tortoises weigh about

THE GALÁPAGOS ISLANDS PUERTO AYORA

1.5kg or are about four years old, they're repatriated to their home islands); and a walk-in adult tortoise enclosure, where you can meet the Galápagos giants face to face. Several of the 11 remaining subspecies of tortoise can be seen here. **Lonesome George**, the only surviving member of the Isla Pinta subspecies, has been living here since 1972.

Other attractions include a small enclosure containing several **land iguanas**, with explanations in Spanish and English concerning efforts to restore their populations on islands where they've been pushed to the brink of extinction. Several paths lead through arid-zone vegetation such as salt bush, mangroves and prickly pear and other cacti. A variety of land birds, including Darwin's finches, can be seen. Outside of the islands, the research station is supported by contributions to the **Galápagos Conservancy** (www.galapagos.org).

Just after the entrance to the site is a sign for **Playa Estación**, a small patch of sand fronted by large rocks and a nice little swimming area that's good for children.

### TOP CHOICE Tortuga Bay  BEACH
In terms of sheer white-sand beauty, this beach is the rival of any in South America. You'll find it at the end of a 2.5km paved trail southwest of Puerto Ayora. But in addition to swimming (a spit of land provides protection from the strong and dangerous currents on the exposed side), surfing or just sunbathing you can see sharks, marine iguanas, pelicans and the occasional flamingo. There's no drinking water or other facilities. It's about a half-hour walk from the start of the path – often used by local runners – where you must sign in between 6am and 6pm. At the foot of the hill before the start of the path is the **Centro Comunitaria de Educación Ambiental Miguel Cifuente Arias** (7:30am-12:30pm & 2-5pm Mon-Fri, 8am-noon Sat), a good place to learn about conservation efforts and issues in the waters around the archipelago.

### Laguna Las Ninfas  SWIMMING
Just behind Lodging House Casa del Lago and Hotel Fiesta is this emerald-green watering hole that's popular with cannon-balling children.

### Diving
Because live-aboards are costly and space is limited, most divers experience the underwater wonders of the Galápagos on day trips

booked from Puerto Ayora. Suitable for intermediate to advanced divers, currents can be strong and most are drift dives.

Gordon Rocks, Caamaño Islet, La Lobería, Punta Estrada and Punta Carrión are popular dives sites, as is North Seymour Island, a short boat trip from Isla Baltra. Devil's Crown, Enderby or Champion off the northern tip of Isla Santa María are good for barracudas, rays and sharks. One of the recommended sites for those with a few dives under their belt is Academy Bay off the Puerto Ayora harbor.

The standard rate for two boat dives is $200 ($165 if booked 'last minute'); all offer PADI certification courses to newcomers and have English-speaking dive masters.

Recommended dive shops:

### Academy Bay Diving  DIVING
(252-4164; www.academybaydiving.com; cnr Av Charles Darwin & Islas Plaza)

### Galápagos Sub-Aqua  DIVING
(230-5514; www.galapagos-sub-aqua.com; Av Charles Darwin) This is the longest-running full-service dive center in the Galápagos.

### Scuba Iguana  DIVING
(252-6497; www.scubaiguana.com; Av Charles Darwin) Run by two of the most experienced divers in the Galápagos.

### Surfing
There are several good surf breaks near Puerto Ayora itself, including **La Ratonera** and **Bazán** near the Charles Darwin Research

WORTH A TRIP

## LAS GRIETAS

For nice swimming and snorkeling, head to this water-filled crevice in the rocks. Talented and fearless locals climb the nearly vertical walls to plunge gracefully (and sometimes clumsily) into the water below. Take a water taxi (per person $0.60 from 6am to 7pm) to the dock for the Angermeyer Point restaurant, then walk past the Finch Bay Hotel, then past an interesting salt mine, and finally scramble up and around a lava-rock-strewn path to the water. Good shoes are recommended for the walk from the dock, which takes about 30 minutes (662m, in total). Keep an eye on any valuables that you leave on the rocks.

# Puerto Ayora

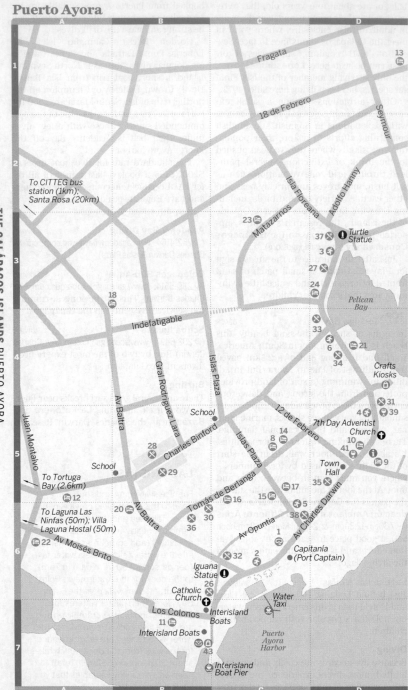

THE GALÁPAGOS ISLANDS PUERTO AYORA

To CITTEG bus
station (1km);
Santa Rosa (20km)

Fragata

18 de Febrero

Seymour

Adolfo Hanny

Matazarnos

Isla Floreana

Turtle
Statue

Pelican
Bay

Indefatigable

Crafts
Kiosks

Islas Plaza

Gral Rodriguez Lara

Av Baltra

Charles Binford

School

12 de Febrero

7th Day Adventist
Church

School

Juan Montalvo

To Tortuga
Bay (2.6km)

Islas Plaza

Tomás de Berlanga

Town
Hall

To Laguna Las
Ninfas (50m);
Villa
Laguna Hostal (50m)

Av Baltra

Av Opuntia

Av Charles Darwin

Av Moisés Brito

Capitanía
(Port Captain)

Iguana
Statue

Catholic
Church

Water
Taxi

Los Colonos

Interisland
Boats

Interisland Boats

Puerto
Ayora
Harbor

Interisland
Boat Pier

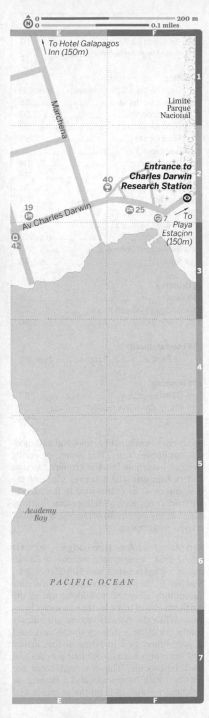

Station beach. If hauling your board a few kilometers is no problem, Tortuga Bay has several good breaks.

An hour or so by boat takes you to **Punta Blanca** and further north to **Cerro Gallina**, **Las Palmas Chica** and **Las Palmas Grande**, considered to be three of the best breaks in the Galápagos. There are also several breaks off the west side of Isla Baltra.

## ☞ Tours

Daily trips to Islas Santa María, Isabela, Bartolomé and North Seymour, as well as nearby Santa Cruz sites, are offered by almost every travel agency in town. Some include snorkeling as well as visits to land-based sites for wildlife.

**Albatross Tours**       TOUR
(☎252-6948; albatrosstours@gpsinter.net; Av Charles Darwin) Santa Cruz day tours, equipment rental and diving.

**Iguana Travel**       TOUR
(Av Charles Darwin) Rents out bicycles (per day $15), arranges day tours and books last-minute overnight yachts on the lower end of the price scale.

**Joybe Tours**       TOUR
(☎252-4385; Islas Plaza & Opuntia) Last-minute overnight boat deals and day tours.

**Metropolitan Touring**       TOUR
(☎252-6297; www.metropolitan-touring.com) Located at the Finch Bay Hotel, it books the *M/V Santa Cruz*, yachts *Isabela II* and *La Pinta* and any land- or water-based tours in the islands.

**Moonrise Travel**       TOUR
(☎252-6348; Av Charles Darwin) Run by a family of Galápagos experts and guides, who can arrange camping at their private highlands ranch, plus boat- and hotel-based tours and diving trips.

**Red Mangrove Inn**       TOUR
(☎252-6564; www.redmangrove.com; Av Charles Darwin) Located at Red Mangrove Aventura Lodge (p304), this company offers day tours, diving and hotel-based tours of the islands, and camping. It also rents out sea kayaks, surfboards, mountain bikes and snorkeling equipment.

**We Are The Champions**       TOUR
(☎252-6951; www.wearethechampionstours.com; Av Charles Darwin) Offers all manner of land and boat-based tours.

# Puerto Ayora

## 🛌 Sleeping

You get much less bang for your buck compared to the mainland. Most of the hotels are within a few blocks of Avenida Charles Darwin, and prices tend to rise during the heaviest tourism seasons (December to January and June to August), but are negotiable during the remainder of the year. Family-run accommodations pop up all the time; look for flyers posted around town.

### WATERFRONT

**TOP CHOICE Finch Bay Hotel** RESORT $$$
(☎252-6297; www.finchbayhotel.com; r from $275; ✳@🛜🏊) Power down and disconnect at this ecologically minded retreat across the bay from Puerto Ayora. It's in a class by itself, in part because it's the only hotel with a beach on its doorstep. Lava gulls and herons hang out by the pool and every facet of the property's design and service is dedicated to encouraging a sense of place. The rooms themselves, a mix of tasteful wood and modern appliances (no TVs), aren't especially large or luxurious but the grounds, Jacuzzi and restaurant, which serves some of the best and most inventive food in the islands, are worth coming for. Metropolitan Touring, based in the hotel, can arrange any outdoor activity imaginable.

**Red Mangrove Aventura Lodge** HOTEL $$$
(☎252-6564; www.redmangrove.com; Av Charles Darwin; s/d incl breakfast from $118/260; ✳@🛜) Nestled in a shady mangrove cove, this charmingly designed red-adobe inn at the northern end of town feels like a secret hideaway. While the standard rooms are suitably comfy, it's quite a step up to the next level of accommodation in terms of size, luxury and sunniness with its outdoor porches and tiled bathrooms. The common areas are outfitted with hammocks and a Jacuzzi, an excellent restaurant is on the premises and

all manner of day and overnight trips can be arranged.

**Angermeyer Waterfront Inn**    HOTEL $$$
(☎252-6561; www.angermeyer-waterfront-inn.com; r $150; ❋@🤝) Across the harbor (accessible by water taxi) is this sun-splashed complex that has simple rooms and outstanding views from the garden patio as well as from the rooms with balconies in the newer multi-story annex. The management and staff are exceptionally welcoming and personable. **La Cueva de Gus Red** (mains $12), built on a deck overlooking the twinkling lights of town, serves burgers, pizza, fish and lobster.

**Hotel Sol y Mar**    HOTEL $$$
(☎252-6281; www.hotelsolymar.com.ec; Av Charles Darwin; r incl breakfast from $225; ❋@🤝⊠) Occupying a sought-after waterfront location with pelicans, sea lions and marine iguanas for neighbors, this hotel (for better or worse) resembles a Florida condo complex. The rooms are no-nonsense, efficient and comfortable, each with a small private balcony; however, it is the seaside Jacuzzi, pool, bar and restaurant area that justify consideration.

**Grand Hotel Lobo de Mar**    HOTEL $$$
(☎252-6188; www.lobodemar.com.ec; Av 12 de Febrero; s/d incl breakfast from $75/100; ❋@⊠) Although noteworthy for its waterfront location and indoor pools, the rooms are less than grand.

### NEAR SOUTHERN END OF AVENIDA CHARLES DARWIN

🖋 **Lodging House Casa del Lago**    APARTMENTS $$$
(☎252-4116; www.casadellagogalapagos.com; cnr Moisés Brito & Juan Montalvo; d/tr/q incl breakfast $115/125/140; ❋@🤝) Ideal for laid-back families or small groups. Choose from several suites with fully stocked kitchens and charming private patios or porches: everything is made from recycled materials and decorated with colorful tiles and textiles. A short walk from the harbor and next to Laguna Las Ninfas, it's owned and operated by a friendly culturally and environmentally conscious couple who also run the charming attached cafe.

**Hotel Sir Francis Drake**    HOTEL $$
(☎252-6221; www.sirfrancisdrakegalapagos.com, in Spanish; Av Baltra; s/d $20/40; ❋🤝) Hidden behind a small department store with nothing more than a dark hallway marking its entrance, you wouldn't think this friendly hotel, only a short walk from the pier, is one of the better values in town. Ask the owner, Fanny, for one of the ground-floor rooms all the way in the back – these have large windows that let in lots of natural light. Common space is limited to an inner patio with no seating and a single balcony.

**Hotel Crossman**    HOTEL $$
(☎252-4359; www.crossmanhotel.com.ec, in Spanish; cnr Juan Montalvo & Charles Binford; s/d incl breakfast $30/65; ❋🤝) A promisingly appealing exterior with a red-tiled roof and arched windows reveals a solid, if unspectacular, midrange choice of rooms inside. Though unadorned, they're good-sized with cable TV, and some have balconies.

**Hotel Castro**    HOTEL $$
(☎252-6113; hotel_castro@hotmail.com; Los Colonos; s/d $45/78; ❋🤝) The Castro looks like a charming Mexican villa. However, warmth and atmosphere are thinly applied inside. Although the rooms are clean and well maintained, beds are unusually low to the ground and the rooms tucked away in the back are dark.

**Villa Laguna Hostal**    HOTEL $$$
(☎252-4819; www.villalaguna.com.ec; near cnr Moisés Brito & Juan Montalvo; s/d incl breakfast $110/140; ❋❋⊠) A whitewashed three-story building noteworthy for its resort-style front courtyard pool area and location on a quiet street across from Laguna Las Ninfas. The spacious rooms are immaculate and have up-to-date furnishings.

**España Hotel**    HOTEL $$
(☎252-6108; www.hotelespanagalapagos.com, in Spanish; Tomás de Berlanga; r incl breakfast with fan/air-con from $25/30; ❋🤝) This traveler-oriented place next to the Gardner, another hotel of similar value, has ordinary rooms, including a room on the ground floor with four beds (per person $10) for the budget-conscious.

**Hotel Gardner**    HOTEL $$
(☎252-6979; Tomás de Berlanga; s/d $30/45; ❋🤝) The Gardner has a covered rooftop patio with lounge chairs and hammocks to distinguish it from the España next door.

**Hotel Palmeras**    HOTEL $$$
(☎252-6139; www.hotelpalmeras.com.ec; Tomás de Berlanga; s/d $65/95; ❋@⊠) Institutional-looking and large, this complex is worth considering for its 2nd-floor outdoor pool area.

### Hotel Salinas
HOTEL $$

(☎252-6072; Islas Plaza; s/d incl breakfast from $31/38; ✳🖧) The small, dark ground-floor rooms with fans are OK (the much higher-priced air-con rooms are not worth paying the extra). A small, central courtyard has a few plastic tables, chairs and wi-fi reception.

### Hotel Lirio del Mar
HOTEL $

(☎252-6212; Islas Plaza; r per person $17; ✳) Nothing but the basics here, with unadorned concrete rooms and cold-water bathrooms, but many of the 2nd-floor rooms catch breezes. More expensive rooms with air-con aren't good value.

### Hotel Santa Cruz
HOTEL $

(Av Baltra near Indefatigable; r per person $10-15; 🖧) This basic utilitarian crash pad is located far enough up Baltra to feel as though you're in any ol' ordinary town. Window-free rooms are dark.

### NEAR NORTHERN END OF AVENIDA CHARLES DARWIN

### Hotel Galápagos Inn
HOTEL $$

(☎09-200-2065; www.hotelgalapagosinn.com; cnr Fragata & Scalecia; s/d from $35/55; ✳🖧🖧) Million-dollar rooftop ocean views and sun-splashed top floor rooms with balconies make this hotel, previously known as La Casa de Judy, exceptionally good value. Some of the smaller standard rooms open up onto a lovely courtyard pool. It's on an extremely quiet block, almost on the outskirts of town, although still only a short walk to the *malecón* (waterfront).

### Peregrina B&B
HOSTERÍA $$

(☎252-6323; peregrinagalapagos@yahoo.com; cnr Av Charles Darwin & Indefatigable; s/d incl breakfast $32/52; ✳🖧) Not exactly a typical B&B, this collection of snug and comfortable rooms, some larger and more nicely decorated than others, occupies prime real estate. A few hammocks in the small cacti garden contribute to the impression of a relaxing hideaway.

### Mainao Inn
HOTEL $$$

(☎252-4128; www.hotelmainao.com; Matazarnos; s/d incl breakfast $98/142; ✳@🖧) A mix of Greek island with Moroccan casbah, this white stucco complex features a beautifully landscaped flowering courtyard. Rooms are clean and spacious, if unexceptional for the price. However, a handful of spots (including the rooftop) are great for reading, coffee or simply catching some rays.

### Hotel Fernandina
HOTEL $$$

(☎252-6499; cnr Av 18 de Febrero & Los Piqueros; s/d $120/155; ✳🖧) Only a short walk from Avenida Charles Darwin, this family-run, friendly hotel nevertheless feels pleasantly secluded. Rooms are surrounded by a nicely landscaped garden, and there is a pool and Jacuzzi on the premises.

### Hostal Los Amigos
HOSTERÍA $

(Av Charles Darwin; r with shared bathroom per person $10; 🖧) Possibly the best-value cheapie in town. The lack of hot water in the hallway bathroom is excused by the absolutely central location and gleaming wood-floored, though admittedly small, rooms. A kitchen and lounge with TV is available for guests.

### Hotel Silberstein
HOTEL $$$

(☎252-6277; www.hotelsilberstein.com; Av Charles Darwin; s/d $140/210; ✳@🖧✳) A Mexican-style villa with rooms surrounding an attractive inner courtyard with a pool and garden.

## 🍴 Eating

Often it's only higher prices that distinguish restaurants catering to locals from those catering to tourists, although almost all the latter are found along Avenida Charles Darwin from the harbor to the Charles Darwin Research Station. Many of the hotels have restaurants.

There's more than a half dozen popular **food kiosks** selling inexpensive and hearty meals – mainly meat and fish dishes, with a pizza thrown into the mix – along Charles Binford, just east of Avenida Baltra. The best time to go is a weekend night, when there's a festive atmosphere with tables set out on the street and couples and families chowing down at their favorites.

### 🅃🄾🄿 Angermeyer Point
### Restaurant
INTERNATIONAL $$$

(☎252-7007; mains from $11; ⏱5-10pm) Rustic and romantic. A candlelit dinner is highly recommended at this picturesque spot, which is perched over the water (grab a water taxi at the pier). With above-average seafood and a few international dishes, as well as sushi on Friday nights and tapas in the early evenings, it's often booked by large groups, so reservations are a good idea.

### Restaurant Tintorera
ECUADORIAN $$

(Av Charles Darwin; mains $9; closed Mon; 🖧) This spot at the northern end of town has an outdoor patio and becomes atmospheric at night. There's a wide selection of fare, from burgers and lasagna to Cajun blackened fish and lobster. Homemade ice cream and a good selection of cakes are available for dessert. It's open for breakfast, too.

### La Dolce Italia
ITALIAN, PIZZERIA $$
(☏09-455-4668; Av Charles Darwin; mains $12; ⊙11am-3pm & 6-10pm) With its warm, nautically inspired decor and gregarious Sicilian owner, this upscale Italian bistro is popular with groups on a break from boat buffets. A number of excellent pizzas and pastas are served and if you just can't be bothered to go ashore, it does deliver to boats.

### Red Sushi
JAPANESE $$
(Red Mangrove Aventura Lodge, Av Charles Darwin; mains from $10; 🐟) Thanks to this upscale hotel restaurant, sushi lovers don't have to go hungry. It has a rustically elegant dining room and a large menu with Japanese specials, from sashimi to teppanyaki.

### Rock
ECUADORIAN, INTERNATIONAL $$
(cnr Av Charles Darwin & Islas Plaza; mains $10; 🐟) Something of a TGI Friday's with an Ecuadorian twist, this restaurant-bar is popular with students, volunteers and tour groups out for the night. The menu is more varied than at most places, and the linguini with coconut sauce and lobster ($12) is especially recommended.

### Garrapata
ECUADORIAN $$
(Av Charles Darwin; mains $9) More sophisticated than other tourist haunts, this popular outdoor restaurant serves substantial meat, seafood and chicken dishes with Italian and Ecuadorian flavors. Good wine, nice shore breezes and a pebble floor make it an attractive place for the night.

### Il Giardino
INTERNATIONAL, ICE CREAM $$
(cnr Av Charles Darwin & Charles Binford; mains $10) This polished version of an Italian trattoria boasts a lovely patio dining area, sophisticated meat and seafood specials, and some of the best desserts. A heladería (ice-cream shop) is attached. Note: a 22% charge for service and tax is added to the bill.

### Galápagos Deli
DELI, PIZZERIA $
(Tomás de Berlanga; mains $4; ⊙10:30am-10:30pm Tue-Sun; 🐟) Tired of standard almuerzos (set lunches)? Head to this sleek and modern place for brick-oven pizza (small $5) and high-quality deli sandwiches, as well as brewed coffee and delicious gelato ($2).

Because it's on a block with few pedestrians, it feels like a secret.

### Hernan Café
ECUADORIAN, INTERNATIONAL $$
(Av Baltra; mains $6-12) A standout, not because of its near-standard menu of pasta, pizza, fish and meat dishes, but because of its location at the busiest intersection in town. There's even a bit of a nighttime buzz when groups pack the outdoor dining room till late.

### Casa de Lago Café Cultural
CAFE $
(cnr Moisés Brito & Juan Montalvo; mains $5; 🐟) This boho cafe with a few indoor and outdoor patio tables serves excellent breakfasts, empanadas and salads, as well as homemade ice cream, fruit drinks and brewed coffee.

### Isla Grill
BARBECUE, INTERNATIONAL $$
(Av Charles Darwin; mains $8; ⊙closed Mon) It's not a knock to say that this restaurant is geared toward tourists looking for familiarity, both in ambience and menu. It's better to go for the seafood cooked on the open grill than the pizza.

### El Chocolate
ECUADORIAN $
(Av Charles Darwin; mains $3-6; ⊙7:30am-10pm Mon-Sat) A long-running malecón eatery, El Chocolate has outdoor patio tables and serves seafood, sandwiches and burgers besides tasty chocolate cake.

### Descanso del Guia
ECUADORIAN $
(Av Charles Darwin near Los Colonos; mains $4) Because of its proximity to the passenger pier, this cafeteria is always bustling at lunchtime.

### Lo & Lo
ECUADORIAN $
(Tomás de Berlanga; mains $6; ⊙closed Mon; 🐟) A little open-air place that does balones (balls of unripe plantains mashed with cheese) and empanadas.

## 🍷 Drinking & Entertainment
Most of the restaurants are also good places for a relaxing drink, and several double as happening bars.

### Bongo Bar
BAR
(Av Charles Darwin; ⊙7pm-2am; 🐟) What nightlife there is in Puerto Ayora centers mainly on this bar, a trendy 2nd-floor spot replete with flat-screen TVs, music and a lubricated mix of hip locals, guides and tourists.

### La Panga
CLUB
(Av Charles Darwin; ⊙8:30pm-2am) Downstairs from Bongo Bar, this disco is where to

go to grind the night away ($10 cover on weekends).

### Limón y Café
BAR

(Av Charles Darwin) A more local and younger crowd head here. It's a modest outdoor bar with a gravel floor and pool tables.

### Galapagos Break Point
BAR, CAFE

(Av Charles Darwin) Located at the far northern end of town, this outdoor lounge features recessed alcoves with couches – good for small groups. It also has a menu with ceviche and the other light fare.

##  Shopping

Every imaginable item has been covered with a Galápagos logo and is on sale in Puerto Ayora. T-shirts with booby *double entendres* are plentiful. The profits from gifts and clothes sold at the Charles Darwin Research Station go to support the institution. Avoid buying objects made from black coral, turtle and tortoiseshell – these threatened species are protected and it is illegal to use these animal products for the manufacture of novelties.

### Galería Aymara
GALLERY, JEWELLRY

(www.galeria-aymara.com; cnr Av Charles Darwin & Seymour) A high-end artists' boutique selling uniquely designed handicrafts, jewelry and ceramics.

### Proinsular Supermarket
SUPERMARKET

(Av Charles Darwin) Food, beer, wine, toiletries, sunblock and other necessities are available at this store near the water-taxi pier.

##  Information

### Internet Access

The majority of midrange and top-end hotels offer wi-fi in public spaces; in rooms, less often. Several restaurants and cafes also provide wi-fi. Internet cafes are scattered throughout town and along Av Charles Darwin – most charge around $2.50 per hour and some have headsets for Skype users.

### Laundry

Convenient mom-and-pop shops have popped up all over to meet the dirty traveler's needs, including **Laundry Lava Flash** (Islas Plaza; per kg $1.50; ☺8am-1pm & 2-7pm).

### Money

**Banco del Pacífico** (Av Charles Darwin; ☺8am-3:30pm Mon-Fri, 9:30am-12:30pm Sat) Has an ATM and changes traveler's checks. Other ATMs for this bank, Banco Bolivariano and BAN RED

can be found steps from the water-taxi pier in front of Proinsular Supermarket.

### Post

There's a post office near the harbor.

### Telephone

There are *multicabinas* (telephone cabins) on Avenidas Charles Darwin and Baltra. Most internet cafes are also calling centers.

### Tourist Information

**Cámara de Turismo** (Tourist Information Office; ☎252-6614; www.galapagostour.org, www.santacruz.gob.ec; Av Charles Darwin) Has hotel information and maps; some staff speak English. Report any complaints here about boats, tours, guides or crew.

##  Getting There & Away

### Air

For more information on flights to and from Santa Cruz, see p332. Reconfirming your flight departures with **Aerogal** (☎252-6798; cnr Av San Cristóbal & Lara), **LanChile** (☎269-2850; Av Charles Darwin; ☺8am-6pm Mon-Sat & 10am-1pm Sun) or **TAME** (☎252-6527; cnr Av Charles Darwin & Av 12 de Febrero; ☺8am-noon & 2-5pm Mon-Fri, 9am-noon Sat) offices is recommended. Flights are often full, and you may have difficulty changing your reservation or buying a ticket.

**EMETEBE** (☎252-6177; Av Charles Darwin, Proinsular Supermarket, 2nd fl) has small aircraft that fly between Islas Baltra, San Cristóbal and Isabela. See p332 for more information.

### Boat

Private speedboats head daily to Islas Isabela ($25, two to 2¼ hours) and San Cristóbal ($25, two hours) at 2pm. There are no toilets on these boats and the ride can be rough and unpleasant for some. Advance reservations aren't required; however, during the high season especially, you should purchase tickets a day in advance. Stop by the offices near the water-taxi pier to book with whatever companies are operating at the time.

##  Getting Around

Hotels, travel agencies, tour agencies and some cafes rent out bicycles (per hour $2). To reach boats docked in the harbor, or one of the several hotels or sites southwest of town, take a water taxi (per person from 6am to 7pm $0.60, from 7pm to 6am $1).

### To/From Airport

The airport is on Isla Baltra, a small island practically touching the far northern edge of Isla Santa Cruz. If you're booked on a prearranged tour, you will be met by a boat representative upon arrival, and ushered onto a bus for the 10-minute drive to the channel (separating Baltra from Santa Cruz) and the boat dock.

If you're traveling independently, take the public bus signed 'Muelle' to the dock (a free 10-minute ride) for the ferry to Isla Santa Cruz. A 10-minute ferry ride ($0.80) will take you across to Santa Cruz, where you will be met by a CIT-TEG bus to take you to Puerto Ayora, about 45 minutes to an hour away ($1.80). This drive (on a paved road) provides a good look at the interior and the highlands of Santa Cruz.

You can buy your ticket on the bus or at one of the ticket booths near the airport exit. The ride is always crowded.

Buses from Puerto Ayora to Isla Baltra (via the ferry) leave every morning at 7am, 7:30am and 8:30am (schedules change, so definitely verify before showing up) from the CITTEG **bus station** (Av Baltra) around 2km north of the harbor; a taxi to the station costs $1. If you're going to the airport to make a flight, it's a good idea to allow 1½ hours or more for the entire journey from town.

Taxis between town and the Santa Cruz side of the channel are $15 (35 to 40 minutes).

### Buses & Taxis

Buses from the CITTEG bus station in Puerto Ayora leave for Santa Rosa (about $1) four or five times a day from Monday to Saturday, and less often on Sunday.

The most convenient way of seeing the interior, and ensuring that you don't get stuck, is to hire a bus or taxi for the day with a group of other travelers.

All taxis are pickups, so you can toss your bike in the back if you want to return to Puerto Ayora by pedal power. To Bellavista by taxi is around $2 and to Santa Rosa is around $7 – both one way.

## AROUND ISLA SANTA CRUZ

The one sizable island in the central part of the archipelago that has no visitor sites is Isla Pinzón (Duncan). It is a cliff-bound island, which makes landing difficult, and a permit is required to visit it (permits are usually reserved for scientists and researchers).

## Islas Seymour & Mosquera

Separated from Isla Baltra by a channel, Isla Seymour is a 1.9-sq-km uplifted island with a dry landing. There is a rocky, circular trail (about 2.5km) leading through some of the largest and most active seabird-breeding colonies in the islands. Magnificent frigate birds and blue-footed boobies are the main attractions. Whatever time of year, there is always some kind of courtship, mating, nesting or chick-rearing to observe. You can get close to the nests, as there is always at least one pair of silly boobies that chooses the middle of the trail as the best place to build their nest. Swallow-tailed gulls also nest here, and other birds are often seen as well. Sea lions and land and marine iguanas are common, while occasional fur seals, lava lizards and Galápagos snakes are seen, too. It's well worth visiting for the wildlife.

Isla Mosquera is a tiny sandy island (about 120m by 600m) that lies in the channel between Islas Baltra and Seymour. There isn't a trail, but visitors land on the sandy beach to see (or swim with) the sea lion colony. Make sure you protect yourself since males are territorial and if you swim too close to females or young they could in theory charge or swim into you to scare you away.

## Islas Plazas

These two small islands, just off the east coast of Santa Cruz, can be visited on a day trip from Puerto Ayora. They were formed by uplift due to faulting. Boats anchor between them, and visitors can land on **South Plaza** (the larger of the islands), which is only about 13 hectares in area. A dry landing on a jetty brings you to an opuntia cacti forest, where there are many land iguanas. A 1km trail circuit leads visitors through sea-lion colonies and along a cliff-top walk where swallow-tailed gulls and other species nest. The 25m-high cliffs offer a superb vantage point from which to watch various seabirds such as red-billed tropicbirds, frigate birds, pelicans and Audubon's shearwaters. Snorkeling with the sea lions is a possibility.

## Islas Daphne

These two islands of volcanic origin are roughly 10km west of Seymour. **Daphne Minor** is much eroded, while **Daphne Major** retains most of its typically volcanic shape (called a tuff cone). A short but steep trail leads to the 120m-high summit of this tiny island.

There are two small craters at the top of the cone, and they contain hundreds of blue-footed booby nests. Nazca boobies nest on the crater rims, and a few red-billed tropicbirds nest in rocky crevices in the steep sides of the islands.

The island is difficult to visit because of the acrobatic landing – visitors have to jump from a moving *panga* on to a vertical cliff and scramble their way up the rocks. The steep slopes are fragile and susceptible to erosion, which has led the national park authorities to limit visits to the island. You must arrange special permission in advance, and groups must be no larger than 12 people.

## Isla Santa Fé (Barrington)

This 24-sq-km island, about 20km southeast of Santa Cruz, is a popular destination for day trips. There is a good anchorage in an attractive bay on the northeast coast, and a wet landing (a beach landing where you step from the boat into the water) gives the visitor a choice of two trails. A 300m trail takes you to one of the tallest stands of opuntia cacti on the islands, some over 10m high. A somewhat more strenuous 1.5km rough trail goes into the highlands, where the **Santa Fé land iguana** (found nowhere else in the world) may be seen, if you're lucky. Other attractions include a sea-lion colony, excellent snorkeling, marine iguanas and, of course, birds.

# ISLA SAN CRISTÓBAL (CHATHAM)

Some local boosters say that San Cristóbal is the capital of paradise – and technically, it is, because its port town of Puerto Baquerizo Moreno is the political seat of the Galápagos. It's the only island with fresh water and an airport in town, and it has several easily accessible visitor sites, all of which means that its tourism profile is second only to Santa Cruz. San Cristóbal is the fifth-largest island in the archipelago and has the second-largest population. The Chatham mockingbird, common throughout the island, is found nowhere else.

Though first settled in 1880, it was the establishment of a sugar factory by Manuel J Cobos in 1891 that signaled the start of any significant human presence on the island. Cobos recruited jailed mainlanders to work in his factory at El Progreso; imported train cars; and minted his own money, called the cobo. The experimental utopian project lasted for 13 years until the workers revolted and killed him in 1904; his son took over

but was not very successful. The site is now a small village, where you can see the factory ruins and the site where Cobos is buried.

## ◉ Sights & Activities

About an hour's boat ride northeast of Puerto Baquerizo Moreno is **León Dormido (Kicker Rock)**, so named because of its resemblance to a sleeping lion. The island is an imposing, vertical, sheer-walled tuff cone that has been eroded in half; smaller boats can sail between the two rocks. Because there's no place to land, this site is usually seen by snorkelers, passing boats or from the top of Cerro de las Tijeretas outside of Puerto Baquerizo Moreno, often to dramatic effect when the sun is setting.

A half-hour northeast of Puerto Baquerizo Moreno by boat is the tiny, rocky **Isla Lobos**, the main sea-lion and blue-footed booby colonies for visitors to San Cristóbal, with a 300m-long trail where lava lizards are often seen. Both the boat crossing and the trail tend to be rough, and there are better wildlife colonies elsewhere.

### SOUTHERN SAN CRISTOBAL

**El Junco Lagoon**           LAKE

From the highland village of El Progreso you can rent a 4WD or walk east along a dirt road about 10km to El Junco Lagoon – a freshwater lake at about 700m above sea level. It's one of the few permanent freshwater bodies in the Galápagos. Here you can see frigate birds shower in the fresh water to remove salt from their feathers; white-cheeked pintails and common gallinules; and the typical highland miconia vegetation and endemic tree ferns. The weather is often misty or rainy.

**Cerro Brujo**           BEACH

Possibly one of the nicest beaches in the Galápagos, Cerro Brujo is a huge, white, expanse found on the west side of the island. The sand here feels like sifted powdered sugar. A colony of sea lions and blue-footed boobies call Cerro Brujo home, and behind the beach is a lagoon where you'll find great egrets and great blue herons. There's also good snorkeling in the turquoise waters.

**Ochoa Beach**           BEACH

On the western side of the island you'll find this horseshoe-shaped cove with a white sandy beach and shallow water that's good for snorkeling. Sea lions, frigate birds, pelicans and blue-footed boobies can be found frolicking here; however, it's only accessible

# Isla San Cristóbal

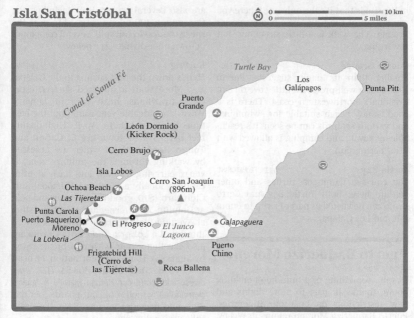

by boat and usually with a guide. Kayaks are a possibility.

## Galapaguera
WILDLIFE RESERVE

Galapaguera is part of the national park on the southeastern part of San Cristóbal, where giant tortoises live in semi-natural conditions. A taxi can take you there and back from Puerto Baquerizo Moreno for around $30.

## El Progreso
VILLAGE

A potholed paved road leads from the capital to the village of El Progreso, about 8km to the east and at the base of the 896m-high Cerro San Joaquín, the highest point on San Cristóbal. It's a sleepy, ramshackle village with nothing much to see. Buses go here several times a day from Puerto Baquerizo Moreno or you can hop in a taxi for $2.

For an ordinary meal in a less than ordinary setting, head to **La Casa del Ceibo** (301-0160; mains $4; ⊙8am-noon & 2-6pm Sat & Sun), a small shed built halfway up an enormous ceiba tree. It's possible to spend a night in the treehouse (per person $20) or camp out on the small grounds.

## Puerto Chino
BEACH

The road to El Junco continues across the island to the isolated beach of Puerto Chino (now accessible by an improved paved

trail), one of two places where camping is a possibility with permission from the Galápagos National Park office in Puerto Baquerizo Moreno. This is one of the better places for beginner surfers since this is a beach break. A taxi from Puerto Baquerizo Moreno is $35.

## NORTHERN SAN CRISTÓBAL

### Los Galápagos
WILDLIFE RESERVE

At the northern end of San Cristóbal is Los Galápagos, where you can often see giant **Galápagos tortoises** in the wild, although it does takes some effort to reach the highland area where they live.

One way to reach Los Galápagos is to land in a bay at the north end of the island and then hike up – it takes about two hours to get to the tortoise area following the trail. Some visitors report seeing many tortoises, while others see none.

It's also possible to get to Los Galápagos by taking the road from Puerto Baquerizo Moreno through El Progreso and on to El Junco Lagoon from where you can hike in.

### Punta Pitt
BIRD-WATCHING, SNORKELING

The northeasternmost point of the island is Punta Pitt, where volcanic tuff formations are of interest to geologists (and attractive in their own right), but the unique feature

THE GALÁPAGOS ISLANDS ISLA SAN CRISTÓBAL (CHATHAM)

of the site is that it's the only one where you can see all of the Galápagos booby species nesting. The walk is a little strenuous, but rewarding.

### Puerto Grande                    BEACH
Smaller than its name suggests, Puerto Grande is a well-protected little cove on San Cristóbal's northwestern coast. There is a good, sandy beach suitable for swimming, and various seabirds can be seen. It's reachable by kayak, and camping is allowed with prior permission.

### Turtle Bay              WILDLIFE-WATCHING
You can see flamingos, turtles and other wildlife here; both Turtle Bay and Cerro Brujo can be visited as part of a trip to Punta Pitt and Los Galápagos.

# Puerto Baquerizo Moreno

⌀05 / POP 10,000

Despite something of a mini hotel-building boom, thanks in part to more flights and new restrictions on boat-tour itineraries, Puerto Baquerizo Moreno retains its sleepy, time-stands-still fishing village feel. And though an increasing number of trips begin or end here, it remains under the shadow of Puerto Ayora, its larger and more high-profile sister city in the Galápagos. The surfing is world-class, and you can explore many places on the island from here on your own.

## ◉ Sights & Activities

### La Lobería                       BEACH
Just after the school, and before the airport, a road leads several kilometers (about a 30-minute walk) to La Lobería, a rocky beach with a lazy sea-lion colony. It's good for year-round surfing, and there are lots of land iguanas along the trail leading past the beach. Bring water and protection from the sun. Taxis charge about $2 to take you out here and you can walk back (or pay an extra $4 for the driver to wait).

### Diving                          DIVING
There are several good spots for diving nearby. Eagle rays, sea turtles, sea lions, and hammerhead and white-tip sharks can be found at León Dormido (Kicker Rock). Schools of jacks, eagle rays, stingrays and sea horses are seen around Stephanie's Rock. Roca Ballena is a cave at about 23m to 24m down with corals, parrotfish, and rays; strong currents mean it's for experienced divers only. There

are also several wreck dives including the *Caragua*, a 100m-long cargo ship near the site of the *Jessica* oil spill. Several companies in town offer diving – see below.

### Surfing                        SURFING
Hands down the best surfing in the Galápagos. More than a hundred surfers, especially Brazilians, head here in January. Waves are rideable year round but the best time is December to April. High-quality reef breaks near town are **El Cañon** and **Tongo Reef**, both of which are accessed by walking through the military zone. If you're carrying a board and flash identification – ideally a local San Cristóbal Surf Club card ($10, good for one year and sold at Dolphin, an internet and telephone shop at Avenida 12 de Febrero) – you'll be waved through. **La Lobería** and **Punta Carola** are also excellent spots with reef breaks. Stop by Sharksky Tours for information, or head to **Dive & Surf Club** (⌀08-587-7122; www. divesurfclub.com; cnr Hernán Melville & Ignacio Hernández), which rents out boards (per day $20) and provides lessons ($35). It's also a full-service dive shop.

### Malecón                          PLAZA
The restored *malecón* is Baquerizo Moreno's de facto town plaza. Built of high-quality, all-natural materials, it has benches, a small plaza for nighttime concerts and a water slide where local kids play.

## ☞ Tours

**TOP CHOICE** **Sharksky Tours**    SNORKELING, DIVING
(⌀252-1188; www.sharksky.com; Av Charles Darwin) This company has snorkeling day trips ($50), overnight hotel-based tours, and scuba diving (two boat dives $145) and is probably the best resource for surfing information and board and bike rentals ($15).

### Chalo Tours                      DIVING
(⌀252-0953; chalotours@hotmail.com; Av Charles Darwin) Offers day and overnight scuba trips, and day trips on San Cristóbal and to nearby islands; it also rents out snorkeling, kayaking and biking equipment.

### Galakiwi                     GROUP TOURS
(www.galakiwi.com; Av Charles Darwin) Run by a New Zealand–Galápagoan couple, offering land tours and snorkeling around San Cristóbal (per person $30); full-day tours to Isla Española ($85); overnight boat tours; snorkeling gear for hire; and daily

dive tours (per two dives $100). Located next to the Miconia hotel.

**Tranquilo Divers** DIVING
(📞301-0271; www.tranquilodivers.com; Av Charles Darwin) Another recommended operation running a variety of San Cristóbal tours.

## 🛏 Sleeping

### WATERFRONT

TOP CHOICE **Casa Blanca** HOTEL $$
(📞252-0392; www.casablancagalapagos.com; Av Charles Darwin; s/d/tr/q $45/50/70/80; ❄) There's no better place to base yourself in town: not only does this whitewashed adobe building have charmingly decorated rooms and tile floors, but it sits on the *malecón* directly across from the passenger pier, meaning rooms with sea-facing balconies have great views. Reception is on the 3rd floor, where there's also a little breakfast nook. Especially recommended is the circular top-floor room that has tons of sunlight, pastel-painted walls and rooftop lounge chairs.

**Casa Opuntia** HOTEL $$$
(📞02-604-6800; www.opuntiahotels.com; s/d incl breakfast from $100/130; ❄🛜🏊) This white-washed villa anchoring one end of the *malecón* has airy and sparsely decorated rooms, some with wicker and island knickknacks. Some rooms open onto balconies facing the pool and Jacuzzi (which may or may not be filled with water) in back, while others have views of the sea overlooking the pleasant front courtyard, which has hammocks.

**Miconia** HOTEL $$$
(📞252-0608; www.miconia.com; Av Charles Darwin; per person incl breakfast from $87; ❄@🛜🏊) Just steps from Casa Opuntia on the waterfront, this is the most full-scale operation on the island. The seven attractive suites in the original low-slung building have separate living-room areas with wicker furniture and earthy pastel colors, and there's a tiny pool and Jacuzzi back here as well. Less spacious but equally finished are four floors of rooms next door. There's a full-service gym and a restaurant overlooking the harbor.

**Suites Bellavista** HOTEL $$$
(📞252-0352; Av Charles Darwin; per person $50; ❄) On the *malecón* across the street from Casa Blanca, this is a good option. The 2nd and 3rd floor of this utilitarian building have a handful of nice, warm rooms with gleaming wooden floors, minifridges, cable

TV and modern bathrooms. The office is in the street-level store.

**Albatross Hostal** HOTEL $
(Av Charles Darwin; s/d $15/25) It's never a good sign when a place gives off a prison vibe. Nevertheless, this is one of the cheapest options in town, especially for large groups, who choose the cement dorm room. It offers only cold water and little light.

### ELSEWHERE

TOP CHOICE **Casa Iguana Mar y Sol** HOTEL $$$
(📞252-1788; r from $100; ❄) Everything in this hotel, only minutes from the *malecón* toward Playa Mann, is lovingly and painstakingly handcrafted – from the railings to the iguana carved into the front door. Each room is a large boutique-quality suite with surprising flourishes; the ground-floor lounge/bar/breakfast area is as stylish as a Soho hotel; and the rooftop deck/bar is ideal for a sundowner.

**Casa de Laura Hostal** HOSTERÍA $
(📞252-0173; hostalcasadelaura@hotmail. com; Av de la Armada; per person $15; ❄) This friendly, family-owned hideaway is one of the best-value places in town. Located in a two-story adobe building with modern hot-water rooms, there's a nicely landscaped courtyard, and hammocks in the tiny cacti garden in front. You'll find it at the end of a short driveway across from the basketball court at the western end of Av Charles Darwin.

**Hostería Pimampiro** HOSTERÍA $$
(📞252-0323; www.hosteriapimampiro.com; Av Quito & Tulcan; s/d incl breakfast $50/70; ❄🛜🏊) It's a bit of an uphill trudge to this small walled-off complex overlooking town. If that isn't a problem, Pimampiro's villa-style buildings and stone and concrete rooms are an excellent choice. There's an especially cozy breakfast dining room.

**Cabañas Don Jorge** BUNGALOW $$
(📞252-0208; www.cabanasdonjorge.com; Av Alsacio Northia; s/d $25/40; 🛜) Looking very much like a wilderness ranger station, this is a hodgepodge of rustic aging cabañas (cabins). Kitchens are fully stocked and good for self-catering. Look for Don Jorge on your right on the way to Playa Mann.

**Hostal León Dormido** HOTEL $
(📞252-0169; hostaleondormido@hotmail.com; Av José de Villamil; s/d $25/40; ❄🛜) Somewhat

warmer rooms and a more central location only a half-block off the *malecón* gives León Dormido the edge over its closest competitor, the Gran Hotel.

### Gran Hotel Paraiso Insular HOTEL $$
(☎252-0901; www.grandhotelparaisoinsular.com; Av Alsacio Northia; r per person $25; ✻🖥) A strictly functional, officelike building with well-kept rooms featuring small, wall-mounted cable TVs and plastic tables and chairs. Located out toward the airport.

## ✕ Eating

For better or worse, there aren't many restaurants catering to tourists in Puerto Baquerizo Moreno – most are informal spots with a few tables on the street and they close early on Sundays. Several humble eateries serving inexpensive *almuerzos* can be found in the side streets a block or more inland from the *malecón*.

### La Playa ECUADORIAN, INTERNATIONAL $$
(Av de la Armada; mains $10) Foreign groups are the name of the game at this waterfront restaurant to the west of town, just in front of the entrance to the naval zone. It has outdoor seating, and, more importantly, excellent grilled seafood and ceviche; pasta, pizza and sandwiches are also on the menu. Unlike many other places, it's open on Sundays.

### Parrillada San José BARBECUE $$
(cnr José de Villamil & García Moreno; mains $10; ⊙6-10pm) Crackling sounds and smoky smells of juicy BBQ waft through the air at this festive outdoor eatery. Choose your protein – shrimp, lobster, beef, chicken, lamb, pork – and grab a seat at one of the picnic tables.

### Sheanovi Restaurant & Bar ECUADORIAN, ITALIAN $$
(cnr José de Villamil & Ignacio Hernández; mains $8; ⊙5-10pm) A pleasant 2nd-floor dining room with a few upscale pretensions. Sometimes reserved by boat groups who use the projec-

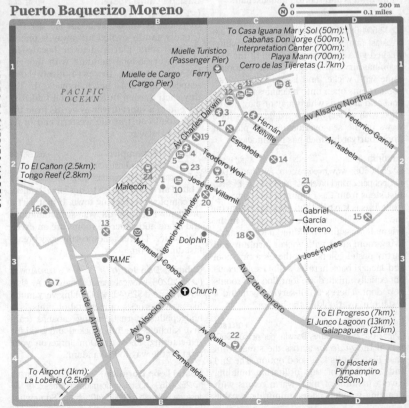

Puerto Baquerizo Moreno

tor to screen Galápagos-related videos. Pasta, fajitas, fish and crepes are on the menu.

### Calypso Restaurant
ECUADORIAN, INTERNATIONAL $$

(Av Charles Darwin; mains $11) The Calypso does good seafood dishes as well as burgers, pizzas and salads. It's an informal place right on the patio at the western end of the *malecón,* and it's equally good for a coffee, juice or delicious slice of chocolate cake.

### Miconia
ECUADORIAN, INTERNATIONAL $$$

(Av Charles Darwin; mains $15) Occupying the 2nd floor of the hotel of the same name, this restaurant offers a wide range of international standards such as pizza and pasta, as well as local meat and seafood dishes.

### Mockingbird Café
INTERNATIONAL $

(cnr Española & Ignacio Hernández; mains $5.50; ◷8am-11pm Mon-Sat, 11am-9pm Sun; @🛜) This travelers' hangout serves salads, burgers and good breakfasts. It's one of the few places open on Sundays.

### El Descanso Marinero
SEAFOOD $

(Av Alsacio Northia; mains $6) Ceviche and other fresh-caught seafood is served up in a lovely outdoor garden with picnic tables. Opening days and times are unreliable, and the menu is dependent on the day's catch.

### Patagonia Café & Bar
ECUADORIAN $

(Av Charles Darwin; mains $3.50) One or two tables on the *malecón* and a large, homey dining room serving snacks like empanadas, as well as burgers and simple seafood and meat dishes.

### Galamarket
SUPERMARKET $

(J José Flores) The largest, best-stocked grocery is at the top of a hill southeast of the town center.

## 🍷 Drinking & Entertainment

Every Friday night on the *malecón,* between Wolf and Villamil, locals put on a show of *folklórica* (folk music) and modern music, including performances by schoolchildren with Shakira-like ambition.

### Cabaña Mi Grande
JUICE BAR

(José de Villamil; drinks $1.50) This 2nd-floor perch is known for its array of *batidos* (fruit shakes) and juices. It also does burgers, snacks and good breakfasts including granola with fruit and yogurt ($3). Open on Sundays.

### Muana Café
CAFE

(cnr Av Charles Darwin & Hernán Melville) Arriving and departing boat passengers congregate at this attractive spot below the Casa Blanca Hotel. Good for a coffee, beer or dessert.

### Bar Arrecife
BAR

(García Moreno) The place for karaoke-filled evenings. Downstairs, Bar Arrecife is a typical bar, while the open-air, upstairs patio is less claustrophobic.

### Rosita
BAR

(cnr Ignacio Hernández & Teodoro Wolf) An outdoor bar with a vaguely nautical theme. It serves food but is best visited for drinks at night.

## Café del Mar                                   BAR

(Malecón) At this somewhat incongruous structure directly on the *malecón*, there's live music on the weekends or whenever the owner (who plays in a band) is in town.

## Bar Iguana Rock                               BAR

(cnr J José Flores & Quito) A good hangout for the college-age crowd. It has a pool table and even gets an off-island band or two.

## ℹ Information

### Internet Access

There are several internet cafes in town, including Mockingbird Café (p316), a popular hangout with good coffee and snacks.

### Laundry

**Laundry** (Av Alsacio Northia; per kg $1) This efficient machine-wash and dry laundry is next to the church.

**Lavandería Sebastion** (Av 12 de Febrero; per kg $1) A few blocks away from the Av Alsacio Northia laundry.

### Money

**Banco del Pacifico** (Av Charles Darwin) Has an ATM and changes traveler's checks.

**Banco Nacional de Fomento** (BNF; cnr Av 12 de Febrero & Hernández) There's an ATM here.

### Telephone

**Dolphin** (Av 12 de Febrero) Has a long row of *multicabinas*, as well as internet service.

There are also a few other *multicabinas* (telephone cabins) scattered around town.

### Tourist Information

**Municipal tourism office** (☎252-0119; www. turismosancristobal.com; Avs Charles Darwin & 12 de Febrero; ◷8am-12:30pm & 2-5pm Mon-Fri) Maps, accommodation and transportation information.

## ℹ Getting There & Away

### Air

The airport is half a kilometer from town – a five-minute walk or a $1 taxi ride (taxis are white pickup cabs). For information on flights to Guayaquil and Quito, see p332. Regardless of the airline, you should check your luggage at least two hours in advance; you can always return to town to spend your final hours in the islands more comfortably.

**Aerogal** (☎252-1118) At the airport.

**EMETEBE** (☎252-0036) At the airport; flies between the islands.

**LanChile** At the airport.

**TAME** (☎252-1089; cnr Avs Charles Darwin & Quito; ◷8am-noon & 2-5pm Mon, Tue & Thu,

9am-noon Sat) Has an office in town and at the airport.

### Boat

Small speedboats head daily to Puerto Ayora ($25, 2¼ hours, 7am), on Isla Santa Cruz, and very rarely direct to Islas Santa María and Isabela. If your destination is Isabela it makes sense to buy the ticket for the second leg of your journey from Puerto Ayora to Isabela (Puerto Villamil) with the same boat company for only $45 in total. Several places around Puerto Baquerizo Moreno book these boats, including **Via Mar** (☎09-428-0687; cnr Hernán Melville & Av Charles Darwin), across the street from Casa Blanca, and **Galapagos Dava Tours SA** (Arrecife Boats; ☎252-0494; Av Charles Darwin).

## ℹ Getting Around

In Puerto Baquerizo Moreno, **Cooperativa de Transporte Terrestre** (☎252-0477) pickup truck taxis hang out along the *malecón* and have fixed round-trip rates to destinations on San Cristóbal, but they don't always stick to them. They'll take you to La Lobería ($2), El Progreso ($2), El Junco Lagoon ($10) and Puerto Chino ($30). You can also negotiate for day trips where the driver will take you to multiple sites. A half-day tour to El Junco, Galapaguera and El Chino is $65.

# ISLA ISABELA (ALBEMARLE)

Isabela is the largest island in the archipelago at 4588 sq km, but despite its size and imposing skyline of mostly-still-active volcanoes, it's the delicate sights like frigates flying as high as the clouds or penguins making their way tentatively along the cliffs that reward visitors.

It's a relatively young island and consists of a chain of five intermittently active volcanoes, including Volcán Sierra Negra, which erupted in late 2005 and sent up a 20km-high smoke column – fortunately, Puerto Villamil (22km to the south) and nearby wildlife were not in danger. One of the island's volcanoes, Volcán Wolf, is the highest point in the Galápagos at 1707m (some sources claim 1646m). There is also a small, older volcano, Volcán Ecuador (610m).

In response to an ecosystem-wide threat and dwindling tortoise population on Isabela and especially around Volcán Alcedo (1097m), the Charles Darwin Research Station and Galápagos National Park Service successfully completed a project to eradicate

## CERRO DE LAS TIJERETAS

The modern and easy to digest **Interpretation Center** (☑252-0358, ext 102; admission free; ⊗8am-5pm) on the north side of the bay explains the history and significance of the Galápagos better than anywhere else in the islands. Exhibits deal with the biology, ecology, geology and human history of the islands, and it definitely deserves a visit even if you've already been inundated with facts from boat guides.

From the center, there are various well-marked and paved trails that wind around the scrub-covered Cerro de las Tijeretas (Frigate Bird Hill). One trail leads over the hill to the small Las Tijeretas bay, which has excellent **snorkeling**; there's no beach here – just step in from the rocks. Other paths lead to **viewing points** with breathtaking panoramas.

Directly in front of the Interpretation Center is **Playa Mann**, a small beach popular with locals and tourists alike, especially for lovely sunsets and on weekends. The large building across the street houses the **Galápagos Academic Institute for the Arts & Sciences** (GAIAS; ☑02-297-1845; www.usfq.edu.ec/galapagos), which hosts semester-abroad international students and special marine-ecology and volunteer programs.

From the end of the dirt road that passes in front of the Interpretation Center, there's a short trail to **Playa Punta Carola**, a narrow beach nicknamed 'Playa del Amor' (Beach of Love) because the sheltering mangrove trees are favorite make-out spots (the sea lions here show little interest in the goings on). Surfing off the nearby point is excellent.

tens of thousands of feral goats through ground and aerial hunting.

Although Isabela's volcanoes dominate the westward view during passages to the western part of Isla Santa Cruz, the island itself is not frequently visited by smaller boats. This is because most of the best visitor sites are on the west side of the island, reached only after a long passage (over 200km) from Santa Cruz.

### ◉ Sights & Activities

**Volcán Sierra Negra**                    VOLCANO
Northwest of the tiny settlement of Santo Tomás lies the massive Volcán Sierra Negra (1490m), which last erupted in late 2005. An 8km trail leads around the east side of the volcano to some active fumaroles. It's possible to walk all the way around the caldera, but the trail peters out. You should carry all your food and water or hire horses.

Galápagos hawks, short-eared owls, finches and flycatchers are among the birds commonly seen on this trip. The summit is often foggy (especially during the June-to-December *garúa* season) and it is easy to get lost. There are spectacular views from nearby Volcán Chico, a subcrater where you can see more fumaroles. Trucks or 4WDs can be rented for the 18km ride from Puerto Villamil to the village of Santo Tomás ($40 round trip); from here it's a further 9km up

a steep trail to the rim of the volcano – horses can be hired in the village ($10, one hour).

Halfway up the slope is **Campo Duro** (☑252-9358, 05-545-3045; www.redmangrove. com; per person incl breakfast $60), a full-service campsite with exceptionally good food run by Red Mangrove Inn in Puerto Ayora. Rates include transport to and from Puerto Villamil. Otherwise, a taxi from Puerto Villamil should cost no more than $10. Another very comfortable, developed camping option in the highlands is **Rancho Valle Negro** (☑08-831-8842; www.volcanohotel.com.ec; per person $35; ☒).

**Volcán Alcedo**                    VOLCANO
The summit of this volcano is famous for its 7km-wide caldera and steaming fumaroles. Hundreds of **giant tortoises** can be seen here, especially from June to December, and juvenile hawks soar on thermal updrafts. The view is fantastic. Permits are required to hike this long, steep and waterless trail and to camp near the summit (two days required).

**Darwin Lake**                    LAKE
A dry landing deposits you at the beginning of a 2km-long trail that brings you past this postcard-perfect saltwater lagoon. It has twice the salinity of the ocean, and is a tuff cone, like a chimney from the main volcano.

# Isla Isabela & Isla San Salvador

The trail leads to the lower lava slopes of Volcán Darwin (1280m), where various volcanic formations and stunning views of surrounding slopes can be observed. There are some steep sections on this trail. A *panga* ride along the cliffs will enable you to see the historical graffiti and various seabirds, usually including Galápagos penguins and flightless cormorants. There are snorkeling opportunities in the cove.

**TOP CHOICE** **Los Túnneles**     SNORKELING
Around a 30- to 40-minute boat ride from Puerto Villamil is this wonderful spot for snorkeling, formed by convoluted lava formations standing between mangroves and the open sea. Look out for white-tipped sharks, manta rays, eagle rays, sea lions, turtles and even sea horses in the shallows.

**Punta García**     BIRD-WATCHING
A few kilometers north of the landing for Alcedo is Punta García, which consists mainly

of very rough *aa* lava (a sharp, jagged lava); there are no proper trails, but you can land. This is one of the few places where you can see the endemic flightless cormorant without having to take the long passage around to the west side (sightings are not guaranteed).

**Punta Albemarle**     BIRD-WATCHING
At Isabela's northern tip is Punta Albemarle, which was a US radar base during WWII. There are no trails, and the site is known for the flightless cormorants. Further west are several points where flightless cormorants, Galápagos penguins and other seabirds can be seen, but there are no visitor sites. You must view the birds from your boat.

**Punta Vicente Roca**     SNORKELING
At the west end of the northern arm of Isabela is the small, old Volcán Ecuador, which comes down almost to the sea. Punta Vicente Roca, at the volcano's base, is a rocky point with a good snorkeling

and diving area, but there is no official landing site.

## Punta Tortuga
BIRD-WATCHING

The first official visitor-landing site on the western side of Isabela is this mangrove-surrounded beach at the base of Volcán Darwin. Although there is no trail, you can land on the beach and explore the mangroves for the mangrove finch – it's present here but not always easy to see. This finch is found only on Islas Isabela and Fernandina.

## Tagus Cove
HISTORIC SITE

Just south of Punta Tortuga is this cove where early sailors frequently anchored and scratched the names of their vessels into the cliffs. It's a strange sight to behold graffiti, the oldest from 1836, in an otherwise pristine environment next to where sea lions lazily roam.

## Urbina Bay
BIRD-WATCHING, WALKING

This bay lies around the middle of the western shore of Isabela and is a flat area formed by an uplift from the sea in 1954. Evidence of the uplift includes a coral reef on the land. Flightless cormorants, pelicans, giant tortoises and land and marine iguanas can be observed on land, and rays and turtles can be seen in the bay. A wet landing onto a beach brings you to a 1km trail that leads to the corals. There is a good view of Volcán Alcedo.

## Elizabeth Bay
WILDLIFE-WATCHING

Near where the western shoreline of Isabela bends sharply toward the lower arm of the island, there's a visitor site that's known for its marine life. Elizabeth Bay is best visited by a *panga* ride, as there are no landing sites. Marine turtles and rays can usually be seen in the water, and various seabirds and shorebirds are often present. Islas Mariela, at the entrance of the bay, is frequented by penguins.

## Punta Moreno
BIRD-WATCHING

West of Elizabeth Bay is Punta Moreno, where you can make a dry landing on to a lava flow and some brackish pools. Flamingos, white-cheeked pintails and common gallinules are sometimes seen, and various pioneer plants and insects are found in the area.

# Puerto Villamil

⏱05 / POP 2000

More than any other settlement in the Galápagos, Puerto Villamil (on the southeastern corner of Isla Isabela) embodies the archetypal end of the road – in a good way, the kind that lures weary city folks to pick up and move halfway around the world. Backed by a lagoon where flamingos and marine iguanas live, and situated on a beautiful white-sand beach, it's a sleepy little village of sandy roads and small homes. However, overdevelopment threatens and there's been something of a mini building boom in the past several years. All of the islands' fresh water is shipped by boat from Isla Santa Cruz.

Undoubtedly, when General José Villamil moved here in 1832 with hopes of organizing a model community made up mostly of whalers, he found the location as beguiling as do today's visitors. Unfortunately, the draftees' peaceful inclinations proved to be more utopian than real and they ended up destroying the colony. Villamil later introduced cows, horses and donkeys, which quickly reproduced, threatening the island's delicate ecosystem.

## ◉ Sights & Activities

### TOP CHOICE Los Tintoreras
SNORKELING

Only a five-minute boat ride or so from town is this wonderful snorkeling spot, a small volcanic island with marine iguanas, boobies and other birdlife. Rays, marine turtles, the occasional white-tip reef shark and penguins can be seen, and it's especially fun to swim through the narrow fissures in the rocks, like underwater hallways decorated with plant and coral life.

### Villamil Lagoon
LAGOON, WILDLIFE RESERVE

Behind and to the west of the village is this lagoon, known for its marine iguanas and migrant birds, especially waders – more than 20 species have been reported here. A trail (◷6am-6pm) a little over a kilometer long begins just past the Iguana Crossing Hotel. The wooden boardwalk takes you over the lagoon, passing through mangroves and dense vegetation, eventually ending in the Centro de Crianza de Tortugas (Giant Tortoise Breeding Center). Volunteers here can explain the work being done to help restore the population of this species on Isabela. Pickups from town ($1) can drop you at the entrance on the road to the highlands; finding one back is difficult.

### Muro de las Lágrimas
HISTORIC SITE

West of Puerto Villamil is the Muro de las Lágrimas (Wall of Tears), a 100m-long wall of lava rocks built by convicts under harsh and abusive conditions. The penal colony closed in 1959 but the wall stands as a monument to an infamous chapter in the island's history. Most tours of the highlands stop here; otherwise, it's a $5 taxi from town.

You can also snorkel in the small bay around **Concha de Perla**, accessible by a boardwalk through the mangroves near the port. Isla Tortuga and Roca Cuatro Hermanos are **dive sites** within range of Puerto Villamil. The only full-service operation in town is **Galápagos Dive Center** (www.buceogdc.com).

There are a handful of good **surf breaks** for experienced surfers near town, some only reached by boat; stop by Caleta Iguana Hotel & Surf Camp for board rentals (per half-day $15) and lessons ($35).

## ☞ Tours

Most of the accommodations we recommend offer tours, as do a few agencies including **Sharksky Tours** (☑252-9395). Some standard trips are half-day Sierra Negra tours (walking $35, by horse $60), Los Túnneles snorkeling ($60) and Los Tintoreras snorkeling ($25).

## 🛏 Sleeping

### BEACHFRONT

**La Casa Marita**                 INN **$$**
(☑252-9301; www.casamaritagalapagos.com; r incl breakfast from $68; ✳@🛜) This beautiful property, the last to occupy beachfront space on the way to the harbor, has uniquely decorated rooms with their own color schemes as well as kitchenettes. It also has a Jacuzzi, bar, library, hammocks in the garden and a lovely patio with lounge chairs out over the sand. Rooms in the small annex across the street are cheaper.

**Iguana Crossing Boutique Hotel**          LUXURY HOTEL **$$$**
(☑252-9484; www.iguanacrossing.com.ec; r $225; ✳@🛜🏊) It's something of a revelation to find such a swanky place in such a low-key Galápagos village. That's not to say there's anything ostentatious about Iguana Crossing; in fact, it fairly blends into its location across the sandy street from the beach at the edge of town, just before the road turns north. Think glossy design magazine furnishings and taste throughout; there's a pool, a jacuzzi and a **restaurant** that serves the best food on the island.

**Caleta Iguana Hotel & Surf Camp**      HOSTERÍA **$**
(Casa Rosada; ☑301-6612; www.caletaiguana.com; r per person with shared bathroom $15, s/d with private bathroom from $30/40) With its beachfront bar, hammocks, bonfires, live music and sea-facing deck, this is the place to go for a lively, laid-back social scene. It's especially good for small groups (one or two rooms have bunk beds) and surfers and decidedly not for those looking for privacy. There's a large kitchen for guests, and all manner of tours are on offer. It's on the beach at the western edge of town.

**Hotel Albemarle**             HOTEL **$$$**
(☑252-9489; www.hotelalbemarle.com; r incl breakfast from $125; ✳@🛜🏊) Occupying a prime stretch of beachfront property in the center of town, this two-story Mediterranean-style villa has stylish, stone, boutique-style bathrooms and high ceilings, with modern conveniences like in-room water coolers, mini-fridges and cable TV. Glass-paneled doors lead to balconies with ocean views.

**Sierra Negra**              HOTEL **$**
(☑252-9046; www.sierra-negra-galapagos.com; per person from $25; ✳🛜) Directly on the beach only a few blocks from the central square, this unadorned and modern building's lack of character is more than compensated for by the large windows in the oceanfront rooms. Pop them open for front row sunset seats. Large, comfortable beds and quality showers.

**La Casita de la Playa**            HOTEL **$**
(Casa Isabela; ☑252-9103; casitadelplaya@hotmail.com; per person $25) Next door to Sierra Negra and somewhat more charmingly designed, this white adobe building with orange accents is a solid option. The red, tile-floored rooms are simple and there are hammocks and lounge chairs in a small lawn facing the sea.

**Cormorant Beach House**        BUNGALOWS **$$**
(☑252-9192; www.galapagosislandshotel.com; r $65; ✳) This place features two beachfront bungalows with five comfortable (if ordinary) rooms, connected by a 2nd-floor deck. It's on the beach, just before Caleta Iguana.

### ELSEWHERE IN TOWN

**Wooden House**              HOTEL **$$$**
(☑252-9235; www.thewoodenhousehotel.com; s/d incl breakfast $105/135; ✳@🛜🏊) Located off the dusty road between the pier and town,

this meticulously upgraded and renovated all-wood (almost Balinese-like) home is an excellent choice if beachfront location isn't a priority. Besides the tastefully decorated, cozy rooms with rainwater showerheads it has an outdoor lounge/restaurant/bar and a little pool in the front-yard garden.

**La Posada del Caminante** HOSTERÍA $
(☎252-9348; www.posadadelcaminante.com; per person $10; ☎) One of the best-value budget options is this friendly family-run place, a few blocks behind Poza Salinas and west of the intersection of Avenidas 16 de Marzo and Cormorant. A handful of rooms surround a narrow courtyard with several hammocks; there are bananas and other fruit for the picking and guests have use of the kitchen.

**Jungle** HOSTERÍA $
(☎301-6690; www.thejungleisabelagalapagos.com; per person incl breakfast $20; ☎) Ignore the chintzy decor and go for one of the top-floor rooms with almost floor-to-ceiling windows displaying sea views; it's good for groups because some rooms have up to five beds. You'll find it near the intersection of Avenida Antonio Gil and the road heading north to the Centro de Crianza de Tortugas, and close to the beach.

**Hotel San Vicente** HOTEL $
(☎252-9140; www.gruposanvicentegalapagos.com; cnr Escalecias & Cormoran; per person incl breakfast $28; ✴☎) Often occupied by groups on hotel-based tours, this efficiently run hotel is found several blocks north of the central plaza (far from the beach). There are white stucco rooms and an attractive front yard with a Jacuzzi; the latter is filled with rain water, so you'll be out of luck in the dry season.

**Coral Blanco Lodging** HOSTERÍA $
(☎252-9125; hotelcoralblanco@gmail.com; Av Antonio Gil; per person incl breakfast $15; ✴☎) Features small, basic rooms a few blocks from central plaza and across the road from the beach. All manner of tours offered.

**Hotel Plaucio** HOSTERÍA $
(r per person incl breakfast $12) The lodging option closest to the dock is this small hand-made encampment built by the friendly owner, a mixed-media artist. There's one building with a couple of basic rooms and hot-water showers.

**La Gran Tortuga** HOSTERÍA $
(☎252-9198; www.viajaragalapagos.com; cnr Las Fragatas & Av 16 de Marzo; r per person incl breakfast

from $20; ☎) Clean and simple rooms with hot showers surround a small courtyard.

## 🍴 Eating & Drinking

There are a half-dozen restaurants located on the central square on Av Antonio Gill, between Las Fragatas and Avenida 16 de Marzo. Boat tour groups usually head to either **Pizzeria Cafeteria Los Delfines** or **El Encanto de la Pepa**, where seafood mains run from $10 to $20. Locals tend to eat at **Restaurante Tres Hermanas** at the corner of Avenida 16 de Marzo for inexpensive *almuerzos* and *meriendas* (inexpensive set-dinner menus). The restaurant at the Iguana Crossing Boutique Hotel offers creative interpretations of traditional seafood dishes.

**El Cafetal Café Cultural** ECUADORIAN, INTERNATIONAL $
(Las Fragatas; mains $5; ☉8am-noon & 4:30-10pm) This contemporary little spot on the central plaza has brewed coffee and tasty desserts as well as burgers, vegetarian sandwiches and *cazuelas* (seafood stews).

**Sea Lion Bar** BAR
Behind the square, at the end of a pier running out from the town beach, this is an atmospheric and fun place for sunset drinks.

## ℹ️ Information

There is no ATM that accepts foreign cards, so bring all the cash you'll need. You can change traveler's checks at Gram Money. There are several places in town to access the internet, all charging around $2 per hour. A few *lavanderías* (laundries) do wash and dry.

## ℹ️ Getting There & Away

### Air

**EMETEBE** (cnr Antonio Gil & Las Fragatas) connects Isabela to San Cristóbal and Baltra. See p332 for more information. Stop by **Blue Concept** (☎252-9144; Av Antonio Gil) for help with Aerogal, LanChile and TAME tickets.

### Boat

There are daily 6am boats to Santa Cruz ($25, 2¼ hours) from Puerto Villamil. From Santa Cruz, boats leave at 2pm. Tickets can be purchased at the dock or from **Transmartisa** (☎252-9053; cnr Av Antonio Gil & Las Fragatas), attached to the EMETEBE office. An alternative is the *L/P Splendor*, which has a 3:30pm departure to Santa Cruz on Monday, Thursday and Saturday; stop by Blue Concept for tickets ($30, 2¼ hours). When arriving at the passenger pier east of town you have to pay a $5 fee.

Group charters are always a possibility, but they're a more expensive option.

### ℹ️ Getting Around

Buses to/from Villamil to Santo Tomás and further into the highlands leave at 7am and noon, returning two hours later. Twin-cab trucks can be rented at other times – call **Cooperativa Sierra Negra** (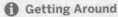252-9147); the taxi fare for the airport is $2 and the harbor is $1.

# ISLA FERNANDINA (NARBOROUGH)

Even by the Galápagos' standards, Fernandina is unique. It's home to thousands of lethargic marine iguanas, and for the volcanically minded, it's the island on which you'll most likely witness an eruption – the most recent was in February 2009. At 642 sq km, Fernandina is the third-largest, as well as the westernmost and youngest, of the main islands. Unlike other parts of the Galápagos, no introduced species have taken root here.

The one visitor site at **Punta Espinoza**, just across from Tagus Cove on Isabela, is a memorable one. Marine iguanas, too many to count, can be seen sunning themselves on the black-lava formations, a dramatic sight that looks like a museum diorama on dinosaurs come to life. **Flightless cormorants** nest nearby, **hawks** soar overhead and Galápagos penguins, turtles and sea lions sometimes frolic in an admirable display of multispecies tolerance in the lagoon near the landing.

A dry landing brings you to two trails: a 250m trail to the point and a 750m trail to recently formed lava fields. Here you can see various pioneer plants, such as the *Brachycereus* cactus as well as *pahoehoe* and *aa* lava formations. Several movies, most famously *Master and Commander,* filmed scenes here in front of a now-iconic white-mangrove tree.

# ISLA SAN SALVADOR (SANTIAGO OR JAMES)

Once a hideout for British buccaneers and one of the stops on Darwin's itinerary, Isla San Salvador (also commonly known as Isla Santiago) is the fourth-largest of the islands. It's a frequent stop on boat tours because there are several interesting visitor sites and its terrain of rough lava fields is an example of the island's challenging beauty.

One of the most popular sites in all the islands is **Puerto Egas**, on James Bay on the west side of Isla San Salvador. It was named after Dario Egas, the owner of a salt mine on the island that was once, as a result of presidential patronage, the only producer of salt in all the country. Here, there is a long, flat, black-lava shoreline where eroded shapes form lava pools, caves and inlets that house a great variety of wildlife. This is a fabulous place to see colonies of marine iguanas basking in the sun. The tide pools contain hundreds of red Sally Lightfoot crabs, which attract hunting herons of all the commonly found species.

The inlets are favorite haunts of the Galápagos **fur seals**, and this is a great opportunity to snorkel with the surprisingly agile animals as well as with many species of tropical fish, moray eels, sharks and octopuses.

Just behind the black-lava shoreline is **Sugarloaf Volcano**, which can be reached via a 2km path. Lava lizards, Darwin's finches and Galápagos doves are often seen on this path. It peters out near the top of the 395m summit, but from here the views are stupendous. There is an extinct crater in which feral goats are often seen (wild goats are a major problem on San Salvador), and Galápagos hawks often hover a few meters above the top of the volcano. North of the volcano is a crater where the salt mine used to be; its remains can be visited by walking along a 3km trail from the coast.

At the north end of James Bay, about 5km from Puerto Egas, is the brown-sand **Espumilla Beach**, which can be reached with a wet landing. The swimming is good here, and by the small lagoon behind the beach you can see various wading birds including, at times, flamingos. A 2km trail leads inland through transitional vegetation where there are various finches and the Galápagos flycatcher.

At the northwestern end of San Salvador, another site that is normally visited by boat is **Buccaneer Cove**, so called because it was a popular place for 17th- and 18th-century buccaneers to careen their vessels. The cliffs and pinnacles, which are used as nesting areas by several species of seabirds, are the main attraction these days.

**Sullivan Bay** is on San Salvador's east coast. Here, a huge, black, century-old lava flow has solidified into a sheet that reaches to the edge of the sea. A dry landing enables visitors to step onto the flow and follow a trail of white posts in a 2km circuit on the lava. You can see uneroded volcanic formations such as *pahoehoe* lava, lava bubbles and tree-trunk molds in the surface. This site is of particular interest to those interested in volcanology or geology.

# AROUND ISLA SAN SALVADOR

## Isla Bartolomé

Panoramic views and frisky penguins make this tiny island, just off Sullivan Bay, a common stop for boat tours. A path from a jetty (for a dry landing) leads up to the wind-whipped 114m summit of the island, where the dramatic views make it *de rigueur* for group photos. This trail leads through a wild and unearthly looking lava landscape, where a wooden boardwalk and stairs have been built to aid visitors and to protect the trail from erosion.

The other visitor site is a small, sandy beach in a cove (wet landing), from where you can don your snorkeling gear and swim with the speedy Galápagos penguins that frequent this cove. Marine turtles and a gaudy variety of tropical fish are also frequently seen.

The best way to photograph the penguins is by taking a *panga* ride close to the rocks on either side of the cove, particularly around the aptly named Pinnacle Rock, which is to the right of the cove from the seaward side. You can often get within a few meters of these fascinating birds – this is the closest point to Puerto Ayora where you can do so. Other penguin colonies are on the western side of Isabela.

From the beach, a 100m trail leads across the narrowest part of Bartolomé to another sandy beach on the opposite side of the island. Marine turtles may nest here between January and March.

## Sombrero Chino

This tiny island, just off the southeastern tip of Isla San Salvador, is less than a quarter of 1 sq km in size and is a fairly recent volcanic cone. The accuracy of its descriptive name, translated as 'Chinese Hat,' is best appreciated from the north. There is a small sea-lion cove on the northern shore, where you can anchor and land at the visitor site. Opposite Sombrero Chino, on the rocky shoreline of nearby Isla San Salvador, penguins are often seen.

A 400m trail goes around the cove, where there are snorkeling and swimming opportunities, and through a sea-lion colony. Marine iguanas scurry everywhere.

### CSI: FLOREANA

After the departure of Patrick Watkins, the first known resident in all of the archipelago, Isla Santa María (Floreana) was turned into an Ecuadorian penal colony. Then, in the 1930s, three groups of German settlers arrived and strange stories have been told about them ever since.

The most colorful of the settlers was a baroness who arrived with three lovers. Another settler, Dr Friedrich Ritter, an eccentric who had all of his teeth removed before arriving to avoid having dental problems, was accompanied by his mistress. The third arrivals were the Wittmers, a young couple from Cologne.

Despite their common nationality, there was a great deal of friction among the groups, and one by one the settlers died under mysterious circumstances. The baroness and one of her lovers simply disappeared, while another lover died in a boating accident. The vegetarian Dr Ritter died of food poisoning after eating chicken. The only ones to survive were the Wittmers, with Margret Wittmer the last to die, in 2000 at the age of 95. Her children and grandchildren run a small hotel and restaurant in Puerto Velasco Ibarra.

Although several books and articles have been written about the strange happenings on Isla Santa María (including one by Margret Wittmer herself), no one is really sure of the truth.

## Isla Rábida (Jervis)

This approximately 5-sq-km island, also known as Jervis, lies 5km south of Isla San Salvador. There is a wet landing onto a comparatively dark red beach, where sea lions haul out and pelicans nest – it's one of the best places to see such nesting.

Behind the beach there's a saltwater lagoon where flamingos and white-cheeked pintails are sometimes seen. This lagoon is also the site of a **sea-lion colony**, where the *solteros* (lone males), deposed by the dominant bull, while away their days in bachelor ignominy.

There is a 750m trail with good views of the island's 367m volcanic peak, which is covered with palo santo trees. At the end of the trail there's a great snorkeling spot.

# SOUTHERN ISLANDS

## Isla Santa María (Floreana or Charles)

This, the sixth-largest of the islands, is known as much for the tragic history of its first residents (see boxed text, p323) as for its intensely pink flamingos and top-flight snorkeling sites.

### ⊙ Sights & Activities

**Devil's Crown**   SNORKELING

TOP CHOICE

This ragged semicircle of rocks, poking up out of the ocean a few hundred meters from Punta Cormorant, is one of the most outstanding marine sites in all of the Galápagos. A strong current sweeps snorkelers briskly past thousands of bright tropical fish, a small coral formation, sea lions, marine turtles and the occasional shark. A *panga* ride around the semisubmerged volcanic cone will give views of red-billed tropicbirds, pelicans, herons and lava gulls nesting on the rocks.

**Post Office Bay**   HISTORIC SITE

There are three visitor sites on the north coast of Isla Santa María. Most groups spend several perfunctory minutes at Post Office Bay, where there are a few gone-to-seed barrels surrounded by scraps of wood covered in graffiti. Although a functioning mailbox for American and British whalers from the late 18th century, these days it's tourists who leave postcards, hoping they will find their way, like a message in a bottle. Actually, it's more prosaic than that; visitors are asked to grab a few to post when they return to their home countries. About 300m behind the barrels is a **lava cave** that can be descended with the aid of a short rope and flashlight. The path is slippery and involves sloshing through some chilly water. Nearby is a pleasant swimming **beach** and the remains of a canning factory; a wet landing is necessary.

**Punta Cormorant**   BEACH

Also reached with a wet landing is Punta Cormorant, a greenish beach (green because it contains crystals of the mineral olivine) where sea lions play and the swimming and snorkeling are good. A 400m trail leads up and over an isthmus to a white-sand beach where turtles sometimes lay their eggs. The beach is also good for swimming, but beware of stingrays and procreating turtles.

**Lagoon**   BIRD-WATCHING

Between the two beaches you'll find a lagoon where several dozen **flamingos** are normally seen. This is also a good place to watch for other wading birds such as black-necked stilts, oystercatchers, willets and whimbrels. You must stop at the wooden rail on the edge of the lagoon – be sure to bring binoculars and your longest zoom lens, otherwise the flamingos will just be indistinct blurs on the horizon. White-cheeked pintail ducks are often seen in the lagoon and Galápagos hawks wheel overhead. It's an especially dramatic tableau when the dark shadows, cast from the setting sun, suggest a stillness that has lasted for eons.

**Asilo de la Paz**   BIRD-WATCHING

From the village of Puerto Velasco Ibarra, a road runs inland for a few kilometers to this official visitor site. It's an all-day hike there and back – you can hire a guide. There are no taxis. Here you can see the endemic medium tree finch, which exists only on Isla Santa María. Early settlers once lived in the nearby caves.

### PUERTO VELASCO IBARRA

This tiny port, the only settlement on Isla Santa María, is set on a black-sand beach on a sheltered bay. Sea lions and flamingos almost outnumber the 150 or so human residents. The highlands are accessed by a road, though it sees little traffic other than that of the foot variety.

The descendants of the Wittmers run **Hostal Wittmer** (📞05-252-9506; s/d/tr $30/50/70), which also doubles as the best eatery and information and guide center. Around half of the beachfront rooms with private balconies are in a small, white two-story building and the other half are in a newer, modernist-looking addition.

Another option, **Red Mangrove Floreana Lodge** (📞05-552-6564; www.redmangrove.com; r $120), is a collection of tidy little cabins set out on black-lava rock a few minutes from town. It makes for a peaceful refuge from civilization, and is often occupied by tour groups organized through Red Mangrove Inn in Puerto Ayora.

Boats between Islas Santa María and Santa Cruz can be arranged at travel agencies in Puerto Ayora.

## Isla Española (Hood)

Certainly one of the more dramatically beautiful of the islands in the Galápagos, the 61-sq-km Española is also the most southerly. Because it's about 90km southeast of Santa Cruz, captains of some of the smaller boats may be reluctant to go this far.

Española is especially worth visiting from late March to December, because it has the only colony of the waved albatross, one of the Galápagos' most spectacular seabirds. The opuntia cactus and giant tortoise population, virtually extinct in the 1960s due to introduced goats and hunting, has rebounded thanks to an aggressive restoration program – tortoises rely on the cacti for food, water and protection.

A wet landing at **Punta Suárez**, on the western end of the island, leads to a rocky 2km-long trail that takes visitors through masked and blue-footed booby colonies, a beach full of marine iguanas and, maybe most uniquely, a **waved albatross** colony (late March to early December, when much of the world's albatross population comes here to breed). Even at a few months old, these enormous birds are spectacular to behold, their long, curved yellow beak, fluffy molting hair and aware eyes make them seem more vulnerable than they are. Equally breathtaking are the views from the wave-battered cliffs to the south – **blow holes** in the rocky shore below shoot water high into the air and seabirds, especially the red-billed tropicbirds, perform their aerial acrobatics and their clumsy take offs and landings.

Other birds to look out for are the Hood mockingbird (found nowhere else), swallow-tailed gulls and oystercatchers. There are three species of finches: large cactus, small ground, and warbler – all part of the Darwin's finch family that may hop along after you hoping to get at some of your fresh water. The large cactus finch is found on few other islands.

Reached with a wet landing at the northeast end of Isla Española is **Gardner Bay**, a beautiful white-sand beach with good swimming and a large sea-lion colony. It's a little like walking through a minefield (albeit one that moves occasionally), and it's a good idea to give the large male bulls a wide berth lest they interpret your curiosity as a challenge to their dominance. Marine iguanas and Sally Lightfoot crabs can be found on the rocks at the eastern end of the beach. An island a short distance offshore provides good, but sometimes rough, snorkeling and scuba diving – there's one rock that often has white-tipped reef sharks basking under it, and hammerheads, marine turtles, rays, sea stars and red-lip bat fish are often seen.

# NORTHERN ISLANDS

## Isla Genovesa (Tower)

Whatever you call it – Isla Genovesa, Tower Island or even Booby Island – lovers of the sometimes goofy- and cuddly-looking booby won't want to miss this. Watch your feet, since it's quite easy to miss a fluffy little baby booby or a camouflaged iguana while you're scanning the horizon for distant sperm whales or the hard-to-sight Galápagos owl.

The most northeastern of the Galápagos Islands, Isla Genovesa covers only 14 sq km and is the only regularly visited island that lies entirely north of the equator (the northernmost part of Isabela pokes above the line). Therefore, this often creates an opportunity for a little shipboard humorous advice to 'hold tight as we pass over the bump.'

Because it's an outlying island, Isla Genovesa is infrequently included on shorter itineraries. It's the best place to see a **red-footed booby** colony, and it provides visitors with the opportunity to visit colonies of great frigate birds, red-billed tropicbirds, swallow-tailed gulls, Nazca boobies and many thousands of storm petrels. Other bird attractions include Galápagos doves and short-eared owls. Sea lions and fur seals are present, and there's the chance to snorkel with groups of hammerhead sharks. The island is fairly flat and round, with a large, almost landlocked cove named Darwin Bay on the south side.

There are two visitor sites, both on Darwin Bay. **Prince Philip's Steps** (also called El Barranco) is on the eastern arm of the bay and can be reached with a dry landing. A steep and rocky path leads to the top of 25m-high cliffs, and nesting red-footed and masked boobies are sometimes found right on the narrow path.

At the top of the cliffs, the 1km-long trail leads inland, past dry-forest vegetation and various seabird colonies to a cracked expanse of lava, where thousands of storm petrels make their nests and wheel overhead. **Short-eared owls** are sometimes seen here.

The second visitor site, **Darwin Bay Beach**, is a coral beach reached by a wet landing. There is a 750m trail along the beach that passes through red-footed booby colonies and several tide pools, and ends at a viewpoint over the cliffs. A pleasant *panga* ride along here, often followed by playful sea lions, gives a good view of birds nesting above.

## Islas Marchena (Bindloe) & Pinta (Abington)

Isla Marchena, at 130 sq km, is the seventh-largest island in the archipelago and the largest to have no official visitor sites. There are some good scuba-diving sites, however, so you may get to see the island up close if on a dive trip. The 343m-high volcano in the middle of the island was very active during 1991 – ask your guide about its current degree of activity.

Isla Pinta is the original home of the tortoise Lonesome George, the sole surviving member of a subspecies decimated by whalers and pirates. Just two centuries ago, the tortoises numbered an estimated 5000 to 10,000. In 2010, 39 tortoises of a hybrid species (they were sterilized, as repopulation is not the goal) raised in captivity were released into the wild on Pinta.

It's also the ninth-largest of the Galápagos Islands, and is further north than any of the bigger islands. There are landing sites, but the island has no visitor sites, and researchers require a permit to visit.

## Isla Wolf (Wenman) & Isla Darwin (Culpepper)

The northernmost islands are the twin islands of Isla Wolf and Isla Darwin, about 100km northwest of the rest of the archipelago. They are seldom visited except on **scuba-diving trips** (no snorkeling at either). Both have nearly vertical cliffs that make landing difficult. Frigates, boobies, tropicbirds and gulls nest on these islands by the thousands. Isla Darwin was first visited in 1964, when a helicopter expedition landed on the summit.

# UNDERSTAND THE GALÁPAGOS ISLANDS

## History

The Galápagos archipelago was discovered by accident in 1535, when Tomás de Berlanga, the first Bishop of Panama, drifted off course while sailing from Panama to Peru. The bishop reported his discovery to King Charles V of Spain and included in his report a description of the giant Galápagos tortoises, from which the islands received their name, and an amusing note about the islands' birds that any visitor today can appreciate: '...so silly that they didn't know how to flee and many were caught by hand.'

It is possible that the indigenous inhabitants of South America were aware of the islands' existence before 1535, but there are no definite records of this and the islands don't appear on a world map until 1570, when they are identified as the 'island of the tortoises.' In 1953, Norwegian explorer Thor Heyerdahl discovered pottery shards that he thought to be pre-Columbian, but the evidence seems inconclusive. The first rough charts of the archipelago were made by buccaneers in the late 17th century, and scientific exploration began in the late 18th century.

For more than three centuries after their discovery, the Galápagos were used as a base by a succession of buccaneers, sealers and whalers. The islands provided sheltered anchorage, firewood, water and an abundance of fresh food in the form of the giant Galápagos tortoises, which were caught by the thousands and stacked, alive, in the ships' holds. More than 100,000 are estimated to have been taken between 1811 and 1844. The tortoises could survive for a year or more

## THE MAN BEHIND THE MYTH

In the general public's mind, the life and work of Charles Darwin is so closely connected with the Galápagos Islands that many people assume he spent a significant amount of time here. They also assume that the inspiration for ideas he sketches out in the *Origin of Species* came to him in a 'Eureka!' moment while touring the islands. Neither assumption is true.

Darwin spent only five weeks in the Galápagos, at first primarily interested in geology rather than biology, and his later observations of pigeons and the methods of dog breeders in England were both much more influential than the finches that have become poster children for the shorthand of evolutionary theory.

Darwin lived in London for five years after he returned from the Galápagos, and then retreated to an estate in the countryside. From then on he hardly traveled and was confined to a sedentary lifestyle, in part because of chronic health concerns.

From an early age, he was inspired more by free-thinking religious figures than secular atheists and was never motivated to disprove the role of a divine figure. After he spent 22 years trying to prove his theory, he renounced Christianity in his middle age and described himself as an agnostic.

Originally sent to Cambridge to be a clergyman, Darwin instead became inspired by the botany lessons of his mentor, JS Henslow. He collected beetles as a hobby and formed a club organized around the eating of animals that were unknown to the European kitchen. It was only after his uncle Josiah Wedgwood intervened that Darwin's father allowed him to go on a voyage at the age of 22. Darwin slept in a hammock on the *Beagle,* rode on top of Galápagos turtles and, in what is a violation of modern-day park rules, dined on their meat.

From 1831 to 1836, the *Beagle*'s task was to survey the South American coastline and chart harbors for the British navy, stopping in Brazil, the Falklands, Argentina and Chile before the Galápagos. Darwin returned with more than 1500 specimens, though for many of those from the Galápagos he neglected to label where each was found.

By the time the boat reached Bahía, Brazil, in 1836, Darwin was ready to return, writing in his journal, 'I loathe, I abhor the sea and all ships which sail on it.' In 1859, the *Origin of Species* sold out on its first day in print. Only 1% of the book refers to the Galápagos Islands.

and thus provided fresh meat for the sailors long after they had left the islands. The fur seal population was also decimated, with thousands killed for their valuable pelts.

The first resident of the islands was Patrick Watkins, an Irishman who was marooned on Isla Santa María in 1807 and spent two years living there, growing vegetables and trading his produce for rum with passing boats. The story goes that he managed to remain drunk for most of his stay, then stole a ship's boat and set out for Guayaquil accompanied by five slaves. No one knows what happened to the slaves – only Watkins reached the mainland.

Ecuador officially claimed the Galápagos Archipelago in 1832 and General Villamil was named the first governor – basically in charge of a single colony of ex-rebel soldiers on Floreana. For roughly one century thereafter, the islands were inhabited by only a few settlers

and were used as penal colonies, the last of which, on Isla Isabela, was closed in 1959.

The Galápagos' most famous visitor was Charles Darwin, who arrived in 1835 aboard the British naval vessel the *Beagle*. Darwin stayed for five weeks, 19 days of which were spent on four of the larger islands, making notes and collecting specimens that provided important evidence for his theory of evolution. It was not until decades later that he formulated and published his evidence. He spent the most time on Isla San Salvador observing and, for that matter, eating tortoises. Darwin devoted as much of his attention to geology and botany as he did to the animals and marine life of the Galápagos.

Some islands were declared wildlife sanctuaries in 1934, and 97% of the archipelago officially became a national park in 1959. Organized tourism began in the late 1960s and in 1986 the government formed the Marine Resources Reserve.

# Geology

The oldest of the islands visible today were formed roughly four to five million years ago by underwater volcanoes erupting and rising above the ocean's surface (the islands were never connected to the mainland). The Galápagos region is volcanically very active – more than 50 eruptions have been recorded since their discovery in 1535. The most recent was the February, 2009 Volcán La Cumbre eruption on Fernandina, overall probably the most active island. Thus, the formation of the islands is an ongoing process; the archipelago is relatively young compared with the age of the earth (which is about 1000 times older).

Geologists generally agree that two relatively new geological theories explain the islands' formation. The theory of plate tectonics holds that the earth's crust consists of several rigid plates that, over geological time, move relative to one another over the surface of the earth. The Galápagos lie on the northern edge of the Nazca Plate, close to its junction with the Cocos Plate. These two plates are spreading apart at a rate of about 1km every 14,000 years, which is pretty fast by plate-tectonic standards.

The hotspot theory states that deep within the earth (below the moving tectonic plates) are certain superheated areas that remain stationary. At frequent intervals (measured in geological time), the heat from these hotspots increases enough to melt the earth's crust and produce a volcanic eruption of sufficient magnitude to cause molten lava to rise above the ocean floor and, eventually, above the ocean's surface.

The Galápagos are moving slowly to the southeast over a stationary hotspot, so it makes sense that the southeastern islands were formed first and the northwestern islands were formed most recently. The most ancient rocks yet discovered on the islands are about 3.25 million years old and come from Isla Española in the southeast. In comparison, the oldest rocks on the islands of Isla Fernandina and Isla Isabela are less than 750,000 years old. The northwestern islands are still in the process of formation and contain active volcanoes, particularly Isabela and Fernandina. In addition to the gradual southeastern drift of the Nazca Plate, the northern drift of the Cocos Plate complicates the matter, so that the islands do not get uniformly older from northwest to southeast.

Most of the Galápagos are surrounded by very deep ocean. Less than 20km off the coasts of the western islands, the ocean is over 3000m deep. When visitors cruise around the islands, they can see only about the top third of the volcanoes – the rest is underwater. Some of the oldest volcanoes in the area are, in fact, completely underwater. The Carnegie Ridge, a submerged mountain range stretching to the east of the Galápagos, includes the remnants of previous volcanic islands, some of which were as much as nine million years old. These have been completely eroded away; they now lie 2000m beneath the ocean surface and stretch about half the distance between the Galápagos and the mainland.

Most of the volcanic rock forming the Galápagos Islands is basalt. Molten basalt is more fluid than other types of volcanic rock, so when an eruption occurs, basalt tends to erupt in the form of lava flows rather than in the form of explosions. Hence, the Galápagos Islands have gently rounded shield volcanoes rather than the cone-shaped variety that most people associate with volcanic formations.

# Ecology & Environment

Every plant and animal species in the Galápagos arrived from somewhere else after journeying hundreds to thousands of kilometers on fortuitous wind, air and sea currents, mostly from South America and the Caribbean. Some flora and fauna arrived later less naturally, brought by settlers and others visiting the islands by ships and planes. There are no large terrestrial mammals. For more on the fascinating wildlife of the Galápagos, see the Galápagos Wildlife Guide (p333).

Concern about the islands' environment is not new. Even as early as the beginning of the 1900s, several scientific organizations were already alarmed. In 1934, the Ecuadorian government set aside some of the islands as wildlife sanctuaries, but it was not until 1959, the centenary of the publication of *The Origin of Species,* that the Galápagos were officially declared a national park (Unesco declared it a World Heritage Site in 1978). The construction of the Charles Darwin Research Station on Isla Santa Cruz began soon after, and the station began operating in 1964 as an international nongovernmental organization (NGO) dedicated to conservation. The Galápagos National Park Service (GNPS) began operating in 1968 and is the key institution of the Ecuadorian government responsible for the park. Both entities work together to manage the islands. In 1986, the Ecuadorian government granted more protection to the islands by creating the 133,000 sq km Galápagos Marine Resources Reserve. A law that was passed in 1998 enables the park and reserve to protect and conserve the islands and surrounding ocean; it also encourages educational and scientific research while allowing sustainable development of the islands as an Ecuadorian province.

## Invasive Species

The introduction of domestic animals on every one of the main islands, except Fernandina, is one of the major challenges the archipelago faces. Feral goats and pigs and introduced rats decimated (or caused the extinction of) native species in just a few years – the goats themselves are thought to be responsible for the extinction of four to five species. It took more than 127 years to eliminate the feral pig population on the island of San Salvador.

Cattle, cats, dogs, donkeys, frogs and rats are other threats to the survival of endemic flora and fauna; hundreds of insect species have been introduced, including a wasp species feared to be the cause of a declining number of caterpillar larvae, an important food for finches. Nearly 800 plant species have been introduced to the islands; blackberry is considered one of the worst because it reduces biodiversity by as much as 50%.

## Overfishing

A major problem in all the world's seas, overfishing is a continuing source of tension in the islands. There have been periodic protests, and several quite serious incidents, organized by fishermen unhappy with the restrictions on various fisheries – the protests are primarily over the fishing of sea cucumbers and lobster, two of the more lucrative catches. Coastal no-take zones have been established and large-scale commercial fishing has been banned since 1998; however, laws are regularly flaunted by both Ecuadorian and foreign-flagged ships. Most damaging are the longliners (hundreds or thousands of baited hooks hanging from a single line that's often miles long).

Although sea-cucumber fishing became illegal back in 1994, hundreds of thousands are exported illegally every year, chiefly for their purported aphrodisiac properties. Other illegal fishing activities include taking shark fins for shark-fin soup, killing sea lions for bait, and overfishing lobster to feed tourists and locals.

Only 'artisanal' fishing in small boats is permitted. However, this regulation has been controversially interpreted to allow sport fishing for tourists. Encouraged for a short time, then banned in 2005, it is once again permitted – although the handful of licensed operators are highly regulated.

## Other Issues

Some islanders see the national park as a barrier to making a living in agriculture. They argue that if more food is cultivated locally, less food will need to be imported, resulting in a cheaper cost of living for residents (with fewer concomitant environmental costs). Thus, there's an effort to promote the production of high-quality, organic foodstuffs in the islands. Of course, agriculture leads to habitat loss and the alteration of landscapes. An added complication is scarce water resources – springs have mostly run dry, coastal groundwater can be polluted and the little water there is to be found in the highlands is difficult to direct efficiently.

After an Ecuadorian oil tanker ran aground near Puerto Baquerizo Moreno on San Cristóbal in 2001, the government, along with the World Wildlife Fund (WWF), worked to modernize and rebuild the main

THE GALÁPAGOS ISLANDS ECOLOGY & ENVIRONMENT

## READING LIST

» *Floreana* by Margret Wittmer

» *Galápagos* by Kurt Vonnegut

» *Galápagos: World's End* by William Beebe

» *My Father's Island* by Johanna Angermeyer

» *The Beak of the Finch: A Story of Evolution in Our Time* by Jonathan Weiner

» *The Galapagos Affair* by John Treherne

» *The Origin of Species* by Charles Darwin

» *Voyage of the Beagle* by Charles Darwin

## EVOLUTION IN ACTION

When the Galápagos Islands were formed, they were barren volcanic islands, devoid of all life. Because the islands were never connected to the mainland, it's most likely that all species now present must have somehow crossed 1000km of open ocean. Those that could fly or swim long distances had the best chance of reaching the islands, but other methods of colonization were also possible.

Small mammals, land birds and reptiles, as well as plants and insects, may have been ferried across on floating vegetation. For those animals that survived the trip, plant seeds or insect eggs and larvae may have been brought over in their stomachs, or attached to the feathers or feet of birds.

When the first migrating species arrived millions of years ago, they found there were few other species to compete with. Some animals were able to survive, breed and produce offspring. The young were the same species as their parents, but some had subtle differences.

A classic Galápagos example of this is a bird that produces a chick with a bill that is slightly different from those of its parents or siblings. In the different environment of the islands, some chicks with slightly different bills are more able to take advantage of the surroundings. These birds are said to be better adapted and are more likely to survive and raise a brood of their own.

These better-adapted survivors may pass on favorable genetic traits (in this case, a slightly better-adapted bill) to their offspring, and thus, over many generations, certain favorable traits are selected 'for' and other less favorable traits are selected 'against'. Eventually, the difference between the original colonizers and their distant descendants is so great that the descendants can be considered a different species altogether. This is the essence of Darwin's theory of evolution by natural selection.

With a variety of islands and habitats, various types of bills could confer adaptive advantages to birds in different ecological niches. One ancestral species could therefore give rise to several modern species, which is called adaptive radiation. This explains the presence in the Galápagos of 13 similar, endemic species of finches called 'Darwin's finches.'

For many years, evolutionary biologists puzzled over how so many unique species could have evolved in the Galápagos over the relatively short period of about four million years (the age of the oldest islands). The answer was provided by geologists and oceanographers who found nine-million-year-old remnants of islands under the ocean to the east of the existing islands. Presumably, the ancestors of the present wildlife once lived on these lost islands, and therefore had at least nine million years to evolve – a span of time that evolutionary biologists find acceptable.

fuel depot facility on Baltra so that it meets the highest environmental standards. More recently, in partnership with the UN and some of the world's largest utilities, the Ecuadorian government has pledged to wean the islands off fossil fuels completely by 2015 through the use of solar and wind power; a large-scale wind-turbine project already exists on San Cristóbal.

Certain species, most notably Galápagos penguins, green sea turtles and marine iguanas (the only sea-going lizard in the world), are vulnerable to the rising sea temperatures and sea levels associated with global warming. Increasingly protracted and severe El Niño years – 1998 was the worst in a half-century – have disrupted various Galápagos ecosystems.

## Conservation Efforts

In 2001 the Galápagos Marine Resources Reserve was added to the list of Unesco World Heritage Sites; only six years later the UN declared the Galápagos environment in its entirety to be 'in danger'. In response, the Correa government and the national park cracked down on violators and made progress in terms of some areas of sustainability and conservation. However, in 2010, in response to the Ecuadorian government's lobbying efforts, Unesco made the controversial decision to remove the islands from the endangered list.

More than 50% of flora and fauna species are threatened or endangered (no Galápagos bird species has been declared extinct), including the Floreana mockingbird and the Galápagos petrel. Despite these alarming numbers, more than 95% of the species inhabiting the islands before human contact still exist and the only wild extinct species are the giant land tortoise of Pinta and San Salvador land iguanas. Large-scale culling of nonnative and invasive species through hunting, breeding and repatriation programs, nest protection, protective fencing and reforestation are some of the primary strategies of conservationists working in the islands.

Metropolitan Touring's **Fundacion Galápagos** (www.fundaciongalapagos.org) partnered with various corporations and travel companies to build a recycling plant in Puerto Ayora, and now every home in the islands is supposed to have three color-coded bins for recycling. The foundation also runs volunteer coastal clean up programs and pays local fishermen to collect trash at sea.

There are various solutions to the problems facing the Galápagos Islands. These include an emphasis on sustainable tourism over the extraction of limited underwater and underground resources, because the extractions could alter the environment irreparably. One extreme view is to prohibit all colonization and tourism – an option that appeals to few. Many colonists – there are around 30,000 full-time residents – act responsibly and actively oppose the disruptive and threatening behavior of some. They also provide the labor for the booming tourism industry.

That being said, the government periodically expels Ecuadorian nationals living in the islands who don't have residency or work permits. There are only three ways Ecuadorians are able to establish permanent residency in the Galápagos: they lived there for five years prior to 1998 or, from that point on, they were born there or married another permanent resident. Many find this strategy discriminatory, asking, 'why not reduce the number of relatively wealthy tourists allowed, instead?' However, the tourism industry is important for Ecuador's economy, accounting for nearly $200 million a year – a quarter of which ends up in local coffers. The majority of stakeholders believe the best solution to be a combination of environmental education for residents and visitors and a program of responsible and sustainable tourism, which may necessarily involve measures to reduce or cap tourist visits. Realistically, the islands can't be restored to their pre-human-contact pristine condition.

## Park Rules

Regulations regarding cruising itineraries were overhauled in early 2012. This was done in an attempt to reduce the number of stops at the most-visited sites; to reduce the total number of visitors; and to relieve pressure on the Baltra airport. Shorter trips are now discouraged, and boats can no longer visit the same site twice (except the Darwin Research Station in Puerto Ayora) within a two-week period.

By law, tour boats must be accompanied by certified naturalist guides that have been trained by the National Park Service. However, in reality, guides on less-expensive boats may lack any kind of certification and there is only a limited number of Naturalist III Guides (the most qualified, usually multilingual, university-educated biologists intent on preserving and explaining wildlife) – in early 2012 only 77 were working in the islands.

Visitors to the islands are restricted to the official visitor sites (70 land and 79 marine sites). Important park rules protect wildlife and the environment, and they're mostly a matter of courtesy and common sense: don't feed or touch the animals; don't litter; don't remove any natural object (living or not); don't bring pets; and don't buy objects made from plants or animals. You are not allowed to enter the visitor sites after dark or without a qualified guide, and a guide will accompany every boat. On all shore trips, the guide will be there to answer your questions and also to ensure that you follow park rules.

## BACK FROM THE BRINK

In January 2012 a team of Yale University biologists discovered a species of giant tortoise that was thought to have been extinct for over 150 years. After extensive genetic testing, they concluded that at least 38 of 84 tortoises examined from Isla Isabela are, in fact, pure-bred members of a species originally endemic only to Isla Santa María, 320km away. In an interesting bit of sleuthing, they used DNA samples from 19th-century specimens in American museums as a base for reference.

# Tourism

Until the mid-1960s, few tourists visited the islands, other than tycoons and princes on their private yachts or the extremely intrepid who were willing to bed down with livestock on a cargo ship. After the research station opened and charter flights began operating, organized tourism was inaugurated with a trickle of a little over 1000 visitors a year. This figure soon increased dramatically. By 1971, there were six small boats and one large cruise ship operating in the islands. In less than two decades, the number of visitors had increased tenfold; in the early 1990s, an estimated 60,000 visited annually. Current figures indicate that around 140,000 tourists visited the islands in 2011, including Ecuadorian residents as well as foreign visitors. There are around 85 boats (with sleeping accommodations) carrying four to 96 passengers; the majority carry fewer than 20.

While this is good for the economy of Ecuador, environmental problems have resulted. The Ecuadorian government and environmental organizations are aware of these issues and are working to reverse, or at the very least halt, the direction of development (including stopping the building of high rises and reducing cruise-ship demand) to protect the flora, fauna and people of the Galápagos.

# SURVIVAL GUIDE

## Getting There & Away

### Air

Flights from the mainland arrive at two airports: Isla Baltra just north of Santa Cruz, and Isla San Cristóbal. There are almost an equal number of flights to Baltra and San Cristóbal.

The three airlines flying to the Galápagos Islands are **Aerogal** (www.aerogal.com.ec), **LanChile** (lan.com) and **TAME** (www.tame.com. ec). All operate two morning flights daily from Quito via Guayaquil to the Isla Baltra airport (two hours), which is just over an hour away from Puerto Ayora by public transportation. They also provide one or two daily morning flights to the San Cristóbal airport (1½ hours). Return flights are in the early afternoons of the same days.

Round-trip flights from Guayaquil cost around $480/440 in the high/low season, and round trips from Quito are around $530/480 in the high/low season (there are periodic promotional discounts with the various airlines); the latter trips include a layover in Guayaquil, although you don't have to get off the plane. It's also possible to fly from Quito and return to Guayaquil or vice versa; it's often more convenient to fly into Baltra and out of San Cristóbal (or vice versa). If you're booked on a boat through an agency, it will likely make the arrangements for you. There is a limit of 20kg for checked luggage (per person) on the flight to the Galápagos.

Flights are sometimes booked solid well in advance, but often there are many no-shows. Travel agencies book blocks of seats for their all-inclusive Galápagos Islands tours, releasing the seats on the day of the flight when there is no longer any hope of selling their tour.

## Getting Around

Most people get around the islands by organized boat tour, but it's very easy to visit some of the islands independently. Islas Santa Cruz, San Cristóbal, Isabela and Santa María all have accommodations and all but the latter are reachable by mid-priced inter-island boat rides or more expensive flights.

### Air

**EMETEBE** (☎Puerto Ayora 05-252-6177, San Cristóbal 05-252-0615, Puerto Villamil 05-252-9255, Guayaquil 04-229-2492; www.emetebe. com) offers daily flights on five- and nine-passenger aircraft between Baltra (Santa Cruz) and Isla Isabela (35 minutes), between Baltra and San Cristóbal (35 minutes), and between San Cristóbal and Isla Isabela (45 minutes). On average, fares are $184/296 one way/round trip and there is a 9kg baggage limit per person (although this is flexible if the plane isn't full).

Domestic airline **AERO** (☎in Guayaquil 04-216-9147; www.saero.com) will begin operating inter-island flights sometime in 2012.

### Boat

Private speedboats known as *lanchas* or *fibras* (short for fiberglass boats) offer daily passenger ferry services between Santa Cruz and San Cristóbal, and Santa Cruz and Isabela (there are no direct trips between San Cristóbal and Isabela). Fares are $25 on any passage and are purchased either the day before departure, or the day of. Ask around in Puerto Ayora, Puerto Baquerizo Moreno and Puerto Villamil; see the Getting There & Away sections of these towns for more information.

# Galápagos Wildlife Guide

Ecuador's famed archipelago was known to early explorers as Las Islas Encantadas (The Enchanted Isles). Although the name has changed, the Galápagos Islands have lost none of their power to captivate. This remote, seemingly barren chain of volcanic islands is home to an astounding variety of wildlife – including many species found nowhere else on earth. It remains one of the world's best places for interacting with animals in the wild at close range, both above and below the sea.

Giant tortoise

# Mammals

**The rich plankton-filled waters of the Galápagos attract some of the largest animals on earth, including 25 species of cetaceans. Close-up interactions with extroverted sea lions, dolphins riding your boat's bow wave or breaching whales could occur in any stretch of ocean here.**

## Killer Whale

**1** Truly spectacular to see in the wild, the killer whale is actually a species of dolphin. It is a ferocious hunter (but no threat to humans), traveling at up to 55km per hour, while preying on fish or other whales. **Where to see:** Canal Bolívar.

## Galápagos Sea Lion

**2** Nearly everyone's favorite island mammal is the widespread Galápagos sea lion, which numbers about 50,000 and is found on every island. These delightful animals often lounge about on sandy beaches and will often swim with snorkelers and bathers. **Where to see:** Everywhere.

## Galápagos Fur Seal

**3** More introverted than its sea lion cousin, the endemic Galápagos fur seal has a dense, luxuriant, insulating layer of fur. Although it was nearly hunted to extinction in the 19th century, it has made a remarkable comeback and numbers some 30,000 animals. **Where to see:** Santiago (Puerto Egas, p322), Genovesa (p325).

## Bottlenose Dolphin

**4** The most commonly sighted cetacean in Galápagos waters is the bottlenose dolphin, which has a playful and inquisitive nature. They typically feed cooperatively in pods of 20 to 30 individuals and have a varied diet, diving up to 500m offshore. **Where to see:** Everywhere.

---

**Clockwise from top left**
**1** Killer whale **2** Galápagos sea lion **3** Galápagos fur seal
**4** Pod of bottlenose dolphins

# Land Birds

From powerful predators to flittering songsters, you don't have to be an ornithologist to enjoy bird-watching in the Galápagos. Look for yellow warblers, mockingbirds and Darwin's finches – made famous by the great naturalist himself.

## Galápagos Hawk

**1** A generalist hunter, the endemic Galápagos hawk preys on creatures as small as insects and as large as small goats. **Where to see:** Española (p325), Santa Fé (p310), Fernandina (Punta Espinoza, p322).

## Darwin's Finches

**2** All of the islands' finches are believed to be descendants of a common ancestor, and evolved into 13 unusual species, including the blood-sucking vampire finch. **Where to see:** Santa Cruz (Los Gemelos, p300; Media Luna, p300), Española (Punta Suárez, p325), Genovesa (p325).

## Galápagos Flamingo

**3** These striking birds are one of the largest of the world's five species of flamingo. They're spread in small groups among the islands' shallow, brackish lagoons and number no more than 500. **Where to see:** Floreana (Punta Cormorant, p324), Rábida (p324), Isabela (Puerto Villamil, p319).

## Short-Eared Owl

**4** Unlike most, this subspecies of owl hunts during the day as well as night. You can spot these regal-looking birds quartering their prey with slow, deep wing beats. **Where to see:** Genovesa (p325), Santa Cruz (Media Luna, p300).

## Mockingbirds

**5** These thrush-sized birds are actually fine songsters and are often the first birds to investigate visitors at beach landings, poking around in bags and perching on hats. **Where to see:** Santa Cruz (p298), Santa Fé (p310), Genovesa (p325).

**Clockwise from top left**
1 Galápagos hawk 2 Male ground finch 3 Galápagos flamingo 4 Short-eared owl

# Sea Birds

Oceanic wanderers, such as the waved albatross and the flightless cormorant call the islands home. The surprisingly agile Galápagos penguin, the comical blue-footed booby and the supremely maneuverable frigate birds join the amazing array of species.

## Blue-Footed Booby

**1** These boobies, one of four booby species on the islands, perform an enchanting, if rather clownish display during courtship. **Where to see:** Española (Punta Suárez, p325), Genovesa (p325), San Cristóbal (Punta Pitt, p311).

## Waved Albatross

**2** The waved albatross is helpless in calm weather, relying utterly on southeast trade winds to transport it to feeding areas. The archipelago's largest bird (weighing 5kg with a 2.4m wingspan) is the only albatross species that breeds at the equator. **Where to see:** Española (Punta Suárez, p325).

## Frigate Birds

**3** Dazzling fliers, frigates ride high on thermals above coastal cliffs, sometimes harassing smaller seabirds into dropping their catch and then swooping to snag the booty in midair. **Where to see:** North Seymour (p309), Genovesa (p325), San Cristóbal (Punta Pitt, p311).

## Galápagos Penguin

**4** Today the Galápagos penguin is the most northerly penguin in the world and the only species that lives in the tropics. **Where to see:** Isabela (p316), Fernandina (p322), Bartolomé (p323).

## Flightless Cormorant

**5** Apart from penguins, the flightless cormorant is the only flightless seabird in the world, and it is endemic to the Galápagos. About 700 pairs remain. **Where to see:** Fernandina (Punta Espinoza, p322), Isabela (Tagus Cove, p319; Urbina Bay, p319).

**Clockwise from top left**
**1** Blue-footed boobies **2** Waved albatrosses **3** Male frigate birds **4** Galápagos penguins

RICHARD I'ANSON/LONELY PLANET IMAGES ©

# Reptiles

**Giant, prehistoric-looking tortoises and fearsome-looking land iguanas can be observed and photographed on land, while snorkelers can glimpse the bizarre seagoing iguana and graceful sea turtles in the water.**

## Giant Tortoise

**1** The archipelago's most famous reptile is the giant tortoise, or Galápagos ('saddle' in Spanish), after which the islands are named. They can live for several hundred years. **Where to see:** Santa Cruz (highlands, p298), Isabela (Urbina Bay, p319), San Cristóbal (Galapaguera, p311)

## Galápagos Land Iguana

**2** Despite their large size and fearsome appearance, land iguanas are harmless vegetarians. Mature males are territorial, engaging in head-butting contests to defend their terrain. **Where to see:** South Plaza (p309), Isabela (p316), Santa Cruz (Cerro Dragón, p300), Fernandina (p322), Baltra and North Seymour (p309).

## Lava Lizards

**3** The most commonly seen reptiles on the islands are the various species of lava lizard, which are frequently seen scurrying across rocks or even perched on the backs of iguanas. **Where to see:** Everywhere.

## Marine Iguana

**4** The remarkable marine iguana is the world's only seagoing lizard. Its size and coloration vary between islands, with the largest specimens growing up to 1.5m. **Where to see:** Everywhere.

## Green Sea Turtle

**5** Adult green sea turtles can reach 150kg in weight and 1m in length. They can be seen readily surfacing for air at many anchorages in calm water and are often encountered by snorkelers. **Where to see:** Santa Cruz (Black Turtle Cove, p300), Fernandina (Punta Espinoza, p322), Santiago (Espumilla Beach, p322), abundant elsewhere.

RALPH HOPKINS/LONELY PLANET IMAGES ©

**Clockwise from top left**
**1** Giant tortoise **2** Galápagos land iguana **3** Lava lizard
**4** Marine iguana

# Sea Life

The archipelago is home to a startling array of marine life. There are many thousands of aquatic species in all shapes and sizes, including 25 species of dolphin and whale, and 400 species of fish. Most famous of all are the Galápagos sea lion and the Galápagos fur seal.

## Tropical Fish

**1** More than 400 fish species have been recorded in Galápagos waters, including some 50 endemic species. Some commonly sighted species while snorkeling are blue-eyed damselfish, white-banded angelfish, yellow-tailed surgeonfish, Moorish idols, blue parrotfish and concentric puffers. **Where to see:** Everywhere.

## Hammerhead Sharks

**2** You don't need to scuba dive to spot schools of this intimidating and bizarre-looking species of shark (though of course it heightens the experience). **Where to see:** North Seymour (p309), Santa Cruz (Gordon's Rocks, p301), Floreana (Devil's Crown, p324), Santa Fé (p310), Genovesa (p325), Wolf (p326), Darwin (p326).

## Sally Lightfoot Crab

**3** This abundant marine animal is blessed with spectacular coloration. Sally Lightfoot crabs (named by English seafarers) adorn the rocks on every island and are extremely agile. They can jump from rock to rock and even appear to walk on water. **Where to see:** Everywhere.

## Manta Ray

**4** Of the 15 species of ray inhabiting Galápagos waters, the magnificent manta ray is the largest of the bunch – and one of the world's largest fish. Some giants reportedly stretch 9m across the 'wings', although 4m adults are more common. **Where to see:** Canal Bolívar, deep channels elsewhere

---

**Clockwise from top left**
**1** Moorish idols **2** Scalloped hammerhead shark **3** Sally Lightfoot crab **4** Manta ray

# Habitats

The entire archipelago is volcanic in origin, with the main islands just the tips of vast submarine volcanoes. In the relatively short span of geological time since the islands were formed, they have been transformed from sterile lava flows into complex vegetation communities with many unique species.

## Coastline

**1** Ever-eroding lava flows make up the rocky shoreline, providing habitat for sea lions, marine iguanas and Sally Lightfoot crabs. Mangroves provide breeding and nesting sites, as well as protective and shaded refuges for birds, sea lions and turtles.

## Highlands Zone

**2** The high peaks of several islands have eroded into rich volcanic soil, which along with occasional rainfall, support dense tropical vegetation. Fascinating species flourish here, such as the 15m-high scalesia (tree daisy), whose trunk and branches are covered in epiphytes: dripping mosses, ferns, orchids and bromeliads.

## Arid Zone

**3** Poor volcanic soils cover much of the islands, with bristling cacti towering above the surrounding vegetation. Despite the challenging environment, diverse species thrive here, including the endemic lava cactus, which takes root in the cracks in barren lava flows.

## Ocean

**4** Highly productive currents bathe the islands in a year-round supply of nutrients. Plankton drift on the sunlit surface, sustaining fish, their predators further up the food chain and some of the world's largest animals – the great whales.

**Right**
**1** Rocky cliffs of Isla Wolf **2** Highlands of Isla Santa Cruz

# Understand
# Ecuador

**population per sq km**

ECUADOR    USA    UK

≈ 58 people

# Ecuador Today

## A New Development Paradigm

» Population: 15 million

» GDP per capita: $7800

» GDP growth rate: 6%

» Unemployment rate: 6.1%

» Poverty rate: 28.6%

» Adult literacy rate: 91%

Until recently, Ecuador was an economic basket case, plagued by widespread poverty, economic inequality and political turmoil – with more than 80 changes of government since the republic's founding in 1830. In the past decade, Ecuador has seen momentous development, with investment in education, health care and infrastructure. For many Ecuadorians, it's one of the most hopeful and empowering times in the nation's history.

Much of the credit for these events is given to Rafael Correa, Ecuador's popular president, who ushered in a series of changes following his election. A new constitution in 2008, approved by referendum, laid the groundwork for a new social archetype that increased spending on health care and the poor, gave more rights to indigenous groups, accorded new protections to the environment and even allowed civil unions for gay couples.

Ecuador has doubled social spending since 2006, investing $8.5 billion in education and $5 billion-plus in health care. More than 5500km of roads and highways have been built or repaired. A new disability program has helped 300,000 people, while the poorest now receive a monthly stipend. The poverty rate has fallen, declining by 9% between 2006 and 2011. Middle-class Ecuadorians have also benefited under programs such as a $5000 grant for first-time homebuyers.

## A Crude Legacy

What's fueling this growth in public spending? It's the worldwide thirst for oil and high crude prices on the world market. Ecuador is particularly well endowed when it comes to petroleum; it's home to the third-largest oil reserves in South America after Venezuela and Brazil, accounting for more than 30% of government revenues and half of all export earnings.

## Top Books

**The Farm on the River of Emeralds** (1978) Moritz Thomsen's compelling memoir about living on the Ecuadorian coast.
**Floreana** (1961) Recount of eccentrics and colorful episodes on the Galápagos by Margret Wittmer.

**The Villagers** (1934) Jorge Icaza's portrait of the hardships of Andean indigenous life.
**Savages** (1995) Hilarious, eye-opening account of the Huaorani vs the oil industry by Joe Kane.

## Top Films

**Qué tan lejos** (2006) Road movie about two young women on a journey of self-discovery in the Andean highlands.
**Entre Marx y una Mujer Desnuda** (1996) Portrays a group of young intellectuals in Quito.

## belief systems
(% of population)

Roman Catholics    Protestants

95    4 1

0.6    0.2    0.1

Atheists and others    Indigenous Religions    Buddhists

## if Ecuador were 100 people

65 would be mestizo (Amerindian and white)
25 would be Amerindian
7 would be white (European descent)
3 would be black

Until Correa, much of the wealth from Ecuador's reserves flowed out of the country. A new law in 2010 changed the terms of contracts with multinational corporations and increased the government's share of gross oil revenues from 13% to 87%, boosting state revenues by $870 million in 2011.

Oil is a hot topic in Ecuador – particularly following the landmark $18 billion judgment by an Ecuadorian court in 2011 against Chevron. Texaco, which is now owned by Chevron, allegedly dumped billions of gallons of toxic wastes in the Ecuadorian jungle when it operated in the country from 1972 to 1992. Chevron is appealing the decision. Parque Nacional Yasuní, a pristine area of the Amazon, holds huge oil reserves that the government has offered to leave untapped if money can be raised on the world market. President Correa proposed that foreign investors raise approximately half the estimated value of the reserves – roughly $3.6 billion – during a 13-year period. The funds will be earmarked towards investment in alternative energy, social programs and key infrastructure, such as hospitals and schools.

> Highest point: Volcán Chimborazo (6310m)
> Bird species: more than 1600
> Plant species: 25,000
> Protected areas: 18% of country
> Number of languages spoken: 23

## Continuing Challenges

Despite his popularity, Correa is not without critics. His often combative approach has earned him enemies, particularly among those who feel targeted by the reformist agenda. In 2010, political unrest continued, when Correa was taken hostage by a group of mutinous police. It ended following a shoot-out with loyal military troops who rescued him.

Some also worry about Correa's relations with Venezuelan president Hugo Chávez, and his periodic anti-American rhetoric. Expelling the US ambassador in 2010 and then welcoming Iran's Ahmadinejad in 2012 didn't help, although the US remains Ecuador's largest trading partner. More worrying is Ecuador's poorly diversified economy: if oil prices fall significantly the effect on Ecuador's ambitious social programs could be devastating.

## Dos & Don'ts

**Hellos** Do greet people ('buenos dias', 'buenas tardes' or 'buenas noches') when entering a shop or restaurant.
**Invitations** If you invite someone out (to eat or drink), it's polite to pay for your guest.

**Greeting People** A handshake between gents, a brushing kiss on the cheek for gals.
**Walking** Vehicles have the right of way over pedestrians, so take care crossing the street.

# History

The land of fire and ice certainly has a tumultuous history. Since becoming an independent nation in 1830, Ecuador has gone through nearly 100 changes in government and 20 constitutions – the most recent drafted in 2008. Fueling the Andean nation's volatility are rivalries both internal (conservative, church-backed Quito versus liberal, secular Guayaquil) and external (border disputes with Peru).

Ecuador's varied peoples have seen the rise and fall of leaders great and small, who have left a mixed legacy in this Andean nation. For scholars, the unsung heroes of Ecuadorian history are its resilient indigenous groups, descendents of some of the great cultures that once flourished in the Americas.

## Early Cultures

Although the majority of indigenous people today live in the highlands and the Oriente, in pre-Spanish (and pre-Inca) times the coastline supported the densest concentration of peoples. The coastal cultures of La Tolita, Bahía, Manta, Valdivia and Machalilla are paramount to Ecuadorian identity, their importance in many ways even eclipsing the Inca, who didn't arrive in present-day Ecuador until a half century before the Spanish.

It's now generally accepted that Ecuador was populated by people migrating west from Brazil, who were drawn to the habitable landscapes along the shore. Ecuador's first permanent sedentary culture was the Valdivia, which developed along the Santa Elena Peninsula more than 5500 years ago. One of the oldest settled cultures in the Americas, the Valdivia are famous for their finely wrought pottery, particularly the 'Venus of Valdivia.' These were feminine ceramic figurines with exaggerated breasts and genitalia, depicted in various stages of pregnancy and childbirth. They were likely used in fertility rituals.

While the Valdivia was the first of Ecuador's settled cultures, the Chorrera was the most widespread and influential of the groups that

| **TIMELINE** | **3500 BC** | **600 BC** | **AD 800** |
| --- | --- | --- | --- |
| | Ecuador's first sedentary culture develops around Santa Elena Peninsula. Fishers and farmers, the Valdivia cultivate maize, yuca, beans, squash and cotton (for clothing), and are famed for their earthenware pottery. | Indigenous societies become more stratified. Tribes are headed by an elite caste of shamans and merchants who conduct long-distance maritime trade – reaching as far north as Central America. | Different cultures begin to merge, creating more hierarchical societies. Emergent powers include Manteños, Huancavilcas and Caras on the coast; and Quitus, Puruhá and Cañari of the Sierra. |

appeared during this so-called Formative Period (4000 BC to 300 BC). Both the Chorrera and the Machalilla culture (which inhabited southern Manabí and the Santa Elena Peninsula from 1500 BC to 800 BC) are known for the practice of skull deformation. As a form of status, they used stones to slowly elongate and flatten their craniums, and they often removed two front teeth to further enhance their appearance.

Beginning sometime around 600 BC, societies became more stratified: they were ruled by an elite caste of shamans and merchants who conducted highly valued long-distance trade. These included the Bahía, Jama-Coaque, Guangala and La Tolita cultures on the coast and the Panzaleo in the highlands. It is likely the Panzaleo was the first culture to practice the technique of *tzantza* (shrinking heads) for which the Shuar of the southern Oriente are much more famous (they practiced it until the mid-20th century).

Slowly, beginning probably around AD 800, cultures became integrated into larger, more hierarchical societies. These included the Manteños, the Huancavilcas and the Caras on the coast; the Quitus (from which the city of Quito takes its name) of the northern highlands; the Puruhá of the central highlands; and the Cañari of the area around present-day Cuenca. Around the end of the 1st century AD, the expansionist Caras of the coast conquered the peaceful Quitus of the highlands and the combined cultures became collectively known as the Quitu-Caras, or the Shyris. They were the dominant force in the Ecuadorian highlands until about the 1300s, when the Puruhá of the central highlands became increasingly powerful. The third important culture was the Cañari, further south. These were the cultures the Inca encountered when it began its expansion into the north.

## The Inca Empire

Until the early 15th century, the Inca Empire was concentrated around Cuzco in Peru. That changed dramatically during the rule of Pachacuti Inca Yupanqui, whose expansionist policies set into motion the creation of the vast Inca Empire, Tahuantinsuyo, meaning 'Land of the Four Quarters' in Quechua. By the time the Inca reached Ecuador they were under the rule of Tupac Yupanqui, Pachacuti's successor, and were met with fierce resistance.

The Cañari put up a resolute defense against the Inca, and it took some years for Tupac Yupanqui to subdue them and turn his attention to the north, where he was met with even greater resistance. At one point, the Cañari drove the invading army all the way back to Saraguro. When they were finally overcome, the Inca massacred thousands of Caras and dumped them into a lake near Otavalo, which supposedly turned the waters red and gave the lake its name, Laguna Yaguarcocha (Lake of Blood).

Pre-Columbian Wonders
» Ingapirca (p164), southern highlands
» Museo Nacional (p61), Quito
» Museo Guayasamín (p57), Quito
» Museo del Banco Central 'Pumapungo' (p169), Cuenca

HISTORY THE INCA EMPIRE

At the height of its empire, the Inca ruled more than 12 million people across some 1 million sq km.

| 1463 | 1500 | 1526 | 1532 |
|---|---|---|---|
| The Inca, under the leadership of Pachacuti Inca Yupanqui, begin the conquest of Ecuador. His son Tupac leads the attack, facing down surprising resistance along the way. | Tupac's son Huayna Capac conquers the Cañari (around modern-day Cuenca); the Cara (in the north); and the Quitu (around modern-day Quito). Ecuador becomes part of the vast Inca Empire. | Inca ruler Huayna Capac dies suddenly (probably from smallpox or measles) and leaves the Inca Empire to his two sons, Atahualpa and Huáscar. A bitter power struggle ensues. | Spanish conquistador Francisco Pizarro arrives with 180 men in present-day Ecuador. Hearing of fabled Inca riches, he plans to conquer the country for the Spanish crown. |

Inca ruler Huayna Capac had a third son, Manco Capac. He was the last Inca ruler and staged one of the greatest revolts against the Spanish. He was killed by a Spaniard whose life he had saved.

The subjugation of the north took many years, during which the Inca Tupac fathered a son with a Cañari princess. The son, Huayna Capac, grew up in Ecuador and succeeded his father to the Inca throne. He spent years traveling throughout his empire, from Bolivia to Ecuador, constantly suppressing uprisings from all sides. Wherever possible, he strengthened his position by marriage and in the process produced two sons: Atahualpa, who grew up in Quito, and Huáscar, who was raised in Cuzco.

When Huayna Capac died in 1526 he left his empire not to one son, as was traditional, but to two. Thus the Inca Empire was divided for the first time – an event that fatefully coincided with the mystifying appearance of a group of bearded men on horseback in present-day Esmeraldas province. They were the first Spaniards in Ecuador, led south by the pilot Bartolomé Ruiz de Andrade on an exploratory mission for Francisco Pizarro, who remained, for the time being, further north.

Meanwhile, the rivalry between Huayna Capac's two sons worsened, and the Inca nation broke into civil war. After several years of fighting,

## LIFE UNDER THE INCA

The Inca arrived in Ecuador a short time before the Spanish conquistadors overthrew them, but they had a lasting effect on the indigenous peoples of the area. Agriculture, social organization and land ownership saw pronounced changes. The Inca introduced new crops, including cocoa, sweet potatoes and peanuts, and new farming methods using llamas and irrigation. Private land ownership was abolished, with land collectively held by the *ayllu*, newly established agrarian communities. Each family was allotted a small plot of arable land within the *ayllu*. The state and high priests also held sizeable plots of land, upon which the emperor's subjects labored as part of their required public service.

The Inca state was highly organized. It introduced the Quechua language, levied taxes and built an extensive network of roads (later used with disastrous success by the horse-riding conquistadors). A system of runners relayed messages, allowing important news to travel hundreds of miles a day. The Incas spread their religion, whose pantheon of gods included Inti (the sun god) and Viracocha (the creator god). Local populations were required to worship the sun god, but their native beliefs were tolerated.

The economy was entirely based on farming, with maize and potatoes chief among the crops. They also raised *cuy* (guinea pigs), ducks, dogs, and llamas and alpacas, whose wool was spun for clothes. Cotton was also grown.

The Inca for their part grew quite fond of Ecuador. Emperor Huayna Capac made Quito a secondary capital of the Inca Empire and lived there until his death in 1526. Locals were largely left alone as long they paid tribute and acknowledged his divinity. Those who opposed him were exiled to far reaches of the kingdom, with other colonists brought in to take their place. This forced migration of peoples also helped to spread Quechua, the language of the empire.

| 1533 | 1563 | 1600s | 1600 |
|---|---|---|---|
| The Inca ruler Atahualpa is killed by the Spanish, effectively decapitating the Inca Empire. Pizarro heads south to Cuzco (in present-day Peru) and plunders the once great capital of Tahuantinsuyo. | The Spanish crown declares Ecuador the Audiencia de Quito, shifting political administration away from Lima, Peru. The territory extends far beyond today's borders from Cali (Colombia) to Paita (Peru). | The use of the *encomienda* is widespread throughout the Spanish colonies: settlers are granted land, along with its inhabitants and resources – a system of virtual slavery of the indigenous. | The Quito School of Art (Escuela Quiteña) emerges, with indigenous artists and artisans producing some of the finest religious art in the Americas. Masterful, syncretic works appear over the next 150 years. |

Atahualpa finally defeated Huáscar near Ambato and was thus the sole ruler of the weakened and still-divided Inca Empire when Pizarro arrived in 1532 with plans to conquer the Incas.

## The Spanish Conquest

Pizarro's advance was rapid and dramatic. His horseback-riding, armor-wearing, cannon-firing conquistadors were believed to be godlike, and although they were few in number, they spread terror among the local people. In late 1532, a summit meeting was arranged between Pizarro and Atahualpa. Although Atahualpa was prepared to negotiate with the Spaniards, Pizarro had other ideas. When the Inca arrived at the prearranged meeting place (Cajamarca, in Peru) on November 16, the conquistadors captured him and massacred most of his poorly armed guards.

Atahualpa was held for ransom, and incalculable quantities of gold, silver and other valuables poured into Cajamarca. Instead of being released when the ransom was paid, however, the Inca was put through a sham trial and sentenced to death. Atahualpa was charged with incest (marrying one's sister was traditional in the Inca culture), polygamy, worship of false gods and crimes against the king, and he was executed on August 29, 1533. His death effectively brought the Inca Empire to an end.

When Atahualpa was executed, his war-general Rumiñahui was supposedly on his way to Cajamarca with large quantities of gold and treasure as ransom for the Inca. Legend has it that, upon hearing of Atahualpa's death, Rumiñahui stashed the treasure in the impenetrable mountains of present-day Parque Nacional Llanganates (p140); it has never been found.

Rumiñahui then continued to fight against the Spaniards for two more years. The general was so fierce that according to legend he dealt with a Spanish collaborator (and possible heir to Atahualpa's throne) by murdering him, breaking all the bones in his body to bits, extracting them through a hole, and stretching the body – with head and appendages intact – into a drum. By the time Pizarro's lieutenant, Sebastián de Benalcázar, had finally battled his way to Quito in late 1534, he found the city razed to the ground by Rumiñahui, who preferred to destroy the city rather than leave it in the hands of the conquistadors. Quito was refounded on December 6, 1534, and Rumiñahui was finally captured, tortured and executed in January 1535.

Despite the Inca's short presence in Ecuador (just over 100 years), they left a indelible mark on the country. Quechua (now Quichua in Ecuador) was imposed on the population and is still spoken today by a quarter of all Ecuadorians. The Inca built a vast system of roads that connected Cuzco in the south with Quito in the north, and part of the 'royal highway' – the Inca trail to Ingapirca – can still be hiked today. Ingapirca

HISTORY THE SPANISH CONQUEST

**Incas & Conquistadors – Top Reads**

» *The Conquest of the Incas* (1973), John Hemming

» *River of Darkness: Francisco Orellana's Legendary Voyage of Death and Discovery Down the Amazon* (2011), Buddy Levy

» *The Last Days of the Incas* (2007), Kim MacQuarrie

Written in the 16th century, Bartolomé de las Casas' *A Short Account of the Destruction of the Indies* is a searing, and readable account of the Spaniards' abuse of the native population during colonization.

### 1690

An epidemic of smallpox and diphtheria rages throughout Ecuador, killing one-third of the population. The native population (estimated at one million at the time of conquest) declines dramatically.

### 1736

A French scientific mission arrives in Ecuador. They carry out research and share Enlightenment ideals (nationalism, individualism and self-destiny), which will figure critically in the early independence drive.

» The colonial legacy can be seen in Quito's buildings

itself (p164) is Ecuador's most important Inca archaeological site and has splendid examples of the Inca's mortarless stonework.

# The Colonial Era

From 1535, the colonial era proceeded with no major uprisings by indigenous Ecuadorians. Francisco Pizarro made his brother Gonzalo the governor of Quito in 1540.

During the first centuries of colonial rule, Lima, Peru, was the seat of Ecuador's political administration. Originally a *gobernación* (province), in 1563 Ecuador became the Audiencia de Quito (a more important political division), which in 1739 was transferred from the viceroyalty of Peru to the viceroyalty of Colombia (then known as Nueva Grenada).

Ecuador remained a peaceful colony throughout this period, and agriculture and the arts flourished. New products such as cattle and bananas were introduced from Europe, which remain important in Ecuador today. Churches and monasteries were constructed atop every sacred indigenous site and were decorated with unique carvings and paintings that blended Spanish and indigenous artistic influences. This so-called Escuela Quiteña (Quito School of Art), still admired by visitors today, left an indelible stamp on the colonial buildings of the time and Ecuador's unique art history.

Life was comfortable for the ruling colonialists, but the indigenous people (and later the mestizos, people of mixed Spanish and indigenous descent) were treated abysmally under their rule. A system of forced labor was not only tolerated but encouraged, and by the 18th century there were several indigenous uprisings against the Spanish ruling classes. Social unrest, as well as the introduction of cocoa and sugar plantations in the northwest, prompted landowners to import African slave laborers. Much of the rich Afro-Ecuadorian culture found in Esmeraldas province today is a legacy of this period.

# Independence

The first serious attempt to liberate Ecuador from Spanish rule was by a partisan group led by Juan Pío Montúfar on August 10, 1809. The group managed to take Quito and install a government, which lasted only 24 days before royalist troops (loyal to Spain) regained control.

Independence was finally achieved by Simón Bolívar, the Venezuelan liberator who marched southward from Caracas, freed Colombia in 1819 and supported the people of Guayaquil when they claimed independence on October 9, 1820. It took almost two years before Ecuador was entirely liberated from Spanish rule. The decisive battle was fought on May 24, 1822, when one of Bolívar's finest officers, Mariscal (Field

| 1767 | 1790 | 1791 | 1809 |
|---|---|---|---|
| King Charles III expels the Jesuits from the Spanish Empire. Missions in the Oriente are abandoned, while some of colonial Ecuador's best schools and haciendas fall into decline. | Following a century of economic mismanagement by Spain, the Ecuadorian economy suffers a severe depression. Its cities are in ruins, with the elite reduced to poverty. | Early independence advocate Eugenio de Santa Cruz y Espejo becomes director of the 'patriotic society,' aimed at civic improvement. His writings land him in prison, where he dies in 1795. | A partisan group attempts to liberate Ecuador from Spanish rule. They take Quito and install a government, which lasts only 24 days before Spanish loyalist troops regain control. |

## THE MYTHICAL AMAZON

One of the most significant events of the early colonial period was the epic journey of Francisco de Orellana along the Río Napo. Orellana set off in December 1541 to search for food to bring relief to a hungry contingent of Gonzalo Pizarro's men following a rigorous crossing of the Cordillera Oriental. Once Orellana caught sight of the lush promise of dense jungle lining the riverbanks, however, he quickly abandoned his original mission and set off in search of gold. These were the days when Spanish conquistadors spoke of legendary lost cities of gold, and Orellana was obsessed with finding El Dorado. 'Having eaten our shoes and saddles boiled with a few herbs,' Orellana wrote, 'we set out to reach the Kingdom of Gold.' It was a grueling journey that would leave half of his comrades dead.

On June 5, 1542, some five months after setting sail, Orellana's boats reached a large village decorated with carvings of 'fierce lions' (probably jaguars). One of the villagers said that the carvings represented the tribe's mistress and their ruler. When his boat later came under ferocious attack (following several raids by his own men on other riverside settlements), Orellana was convinced that female warriors were leading the onslaught. He later named the river after the Amazons, the mythical all-female warriors of ancient Greece. By the time he reached the Atlantic Ocean – some eight months after he began – he had given up his quest for gold. He became the first European to travel the length of the Amazon River, a feat not to be repeated for another 100 years. The event is still commemorated in Ecuador during the annual Aniversario del Descubrimiento del Río Amazonas (Discovery of the Amazon River), celebrated on February 12.

Marshal) Antonio José de Sucre, defeated the royalists at the Battle of Pichincha and took Quito. This battle is commemorated at a stunningly situated monument (p55) on the flanks of Volcán Pichincha, overlooking the capital.

Bolívar's idealistic dream was to form a united South America, and he began by amalgamating Venezuela, Colombia and Ecuador into the independent nation of Gran Colombia. This lasted only eight years, with Ecuador becoming fully independent in 1830. In the same year, a treaty was signed with Peru, drawing up a boundary between the two nations; this boundary is the one shown on all Ecuadorian maps prior to 1999. The border had been redrawn in 1942 after a war between Ecuador and Peru, but was not officially acknowledged by Ecuadorian authorities until a peace treaty was signed with Peru in late 1998.

## Political Development

Following independence from Spain, Ecuador's history unfolded with unbridled political warfare between liberals and conservatives. The

| 1822 | 1830 | 1851 | 1859 |
|---|---|---|---|
| Two years after Guayaquil declares independence from Spain, António Jose de Sucre defeats Spanish royalists at the Battle of Pichincha. Ecuador becomes part of Gran Colombia. | Ecuador leaves Gran Colombia and becomes an independent nation. A group of Quito notables draws up a constitution, placing General Flores in charge of military and political matters. | General José Maria Urbina frees the nation's slaves. His successor, General Francisco Robles, puts an end to 300 years of required annual payments by the indigenous. | García Moreno comes to power. Decried by opponents as a dictator, he nevertheless makes vital contributions in education, public welfare and economic development. He is assassinated in 1875. |

Science and history buffs and those after a good (real-life) adventure story should check out Larrie D Ferreiro's *Measure of the Earth: The Enlightenment Expedition That Reshaped Our World* (2011). It describes the fascinating 18th-century European scientific expedition to Quito to determine the true shape of our planet.

turmoil frequently escalated to violence. In 1875, the church-backed, conservative dictator President García Moreno (who attempted to make Catholicism a requisite for citizenship) was hacked to death with a machete outside Quito's presidential palace. In 1912 liberal President Eloy Alfaro, who attempted to undo much of García Moreno's legacy, was murdered and burned by a conservative mob in Quito. Rivalries between these factions continue to this day, albeit less violently. Quito remains the main center for the church-backed conservatives, while Guayaquil stands, as it has for centuries, on the side of more liberal and sometimes socialist beliefs.

Throughout much of the 20th century, Ecuador's political sphere remained volatile, though the country never experienced the bloodshed or brutal military dictatorships suffered by other Latin American countries. That's not to say the military never took the reins of power, with the 20th century seeing almost as many periods of military rule as civilian rule. One president, José María Velasco Ibarra, was elected five times between 1934 and 1972 and was ousted by the military before he could complete any one of his terms. Ibarra wasn't alone: in the 10 years between 1930 and 1940, 17 different presidents took a shot at leading Ecuador, not one of whom completed a term.

## Yellow Gold to Black Gold

Until the 1970s, Ecuador was the archetypal 'banana republic,' and the fruit was the country's single most important export. In fact, Ecuador exported more bananas than any country in the world. Although bananas are a staple of the country's economy today, they ceased being Ecuador's sole export after the discovery of oil in the Oriente in 1967. By 1973, oil exports had risen to first place, and by the early 1980s they accounted for well over half of total export earnings. Oil undoubtedly boosted the economy, though politicians from the left, allied with indigenous-rights groups, say much of the largesse remained in the hands of a few controlling interests with little benefit to the many. The statistics support this claim, with the majority of the rural population at an equal – or lower – living standard than they experienced in the 1970s.

After oil was discovered, Ecuador began to borrow money, with the belief that profits from oil exports would enable the country to repay its foreign debts. But this proved impossible in the mid-1980s due to the sharp decline in Ecuador's oil exports; world oil prices slumped in 1986, and in 1987 a disastrous earthquake wiped out about 40km of oil pipeline, severely damaging both the environment and the economy. The discovery of oil also opened up vast tracts of Ecuador's Amazon Basin to exploration, affecting both the rainforest and the local indigenous tribes – some of whom had never before encountered outsiders.

| 1890 | 1895 | 1920 | 1930s |
|---|---|---|---|
| Cacao drives the economy, with production up from 6.5 million kilograms in 1852 to 18 million in 1890. Ecuador's exports grow from $1 million to $10 million over the same period. | José Eloy Alfaro Delgado takes power. A champion of liberalism, he strips the Church of power, legalizes civil marriage and divorce, and establishes freedom of speech and religion. | Economic problems cripple Ecuador. A fungal disease and declining demand destroy the cacao industry. The working class protest rocketing inflation and deteriorating living standards. Strikes are brutally suppressed. | Following a period of reform in the late 1920s (including pensions for state workers), the Ecuadorian economy crashes. Unemployment soars and political instability rocks the government. |

Ecuador continues to rely on oil as its economic mainstay, but reserves are not as large as had been anticipated. Overreliance on oil revenues has also wreaked havoc on the economy when the world price of oil collapses (as it did most recently in 2008).

## Return to Democracy

The 1980s and early '90s were a continuing struggle between conservatives and liberals, with a few corruption scandals that weakened public confidence in the ruling elites. The contenders in the 1996 election were two firebrand politicians from Guayaquil, both known for their brashness. The candidate who won, Abdala Bucaram, was nicknamed 'El Loco'

### THE QUITO SCHOOL OF ART

As the Spanish colonized present-day Ecuador, religious conversion became the key to subduing the indigenous population and remaking the New World in a likeness of the Old. The most successful tool for conversion was art, whose story-telling power and visual representations had long served the Catholic Church for gaining believers. At first, sculptures and paintings were imported from Spain, but from the mid-16th century the Church set up guilds and workshops to train a local base of indigenous artisans. From these workshops blossomed one of the most important artistic genres in Latin America: the Escuela Quiteña (Quito School of Art).

The beauty of the Escuela Quiteña lies in its fascinating blend of indigenous concepts and styles and European art forms. The beliefs and artistic heritages of the artisans crept into their work. If you look closely at paintings in Quito's many religious museums and churches, you'll see many non-European themes: Christ eating a plate of *cuy* (roast guinea pig), or the 12 apostles dining on *humitas* (a type of corn dumpling). Religious figures are often depicted with darker skin or stouter builds that reflect indigenous Ecuadorian body types. Inside churches, sun motifs and planetary symbols appear on ceilings that are decorated in what appear to be Moorish patterns.

The Escuela Quiteña became renowned for its mastery of the realistic. By the 18th century, artisans were using glass eyes and real hair and eyelashes in their sculptures. They added moving joints, inserted tiny mirrors into mouths to mimic saliva, and their accomplished polychrome painting (the use of multiple colors) became famous. Some sculptures, particularly those of the 18th-century carver Manuel Chili (nicknamed 'Caspicara'), are so realistic they almost seem to be alive. Notable painters of the Escuela Quiteña include Miguel de Santiago (whose huge canvases grace the walls of Quito's Monastery of San Agustín), Manuel Samaniego, Nicolás Goríbar and Bernardo Rodríguez.

After Quito gained independence from Spain in 1822, the religious art of the Escuela Quiteña lost both its potency and necessity. Today, Caspicara's work can be seen in Quito's Monastery of San Francisco (p51) and the Museo Nacional (p61).

| 1941 | 1948 | | 1948–52 |
|---|---|---|---|
| Tensions rise over disputed Amazon territories, and Peru invades Ecuador with 13,000 troops. Following peace accords, Ecuador cedes over half its territories, but doesn't acknowledge its new borders. | Galo Plaza is elected president, marking an era of progress and prosperity. He slows inflation, balances the budget and invests in schools, roads and other infrastructure. |  | As disease plagues plantations in Central America, Ecuador becomes one of the world's top banana producers, with exports growing from $2 million to $20 million between 1948 and 1952. |

» Galo Plaza

(The Madman) for his fiery, curse-laden style of oration and his penchant for performing at rock concerts as part of his campaign. Bucaram promised cheap public housing, lower prices for food staples and free medicine; but instead he promptly devalued Ecuador's currency, the sucre, and increased living costs, and was often spotted carousing in nightclubs by Quito residents.

Within a few months, massive strikes led by trade unions and the Confederation of Indigenous Nationalities of Ecuador (Conaie) paralyzed the country. Congress declared Bucaram 'mentally unfit' and terminated his presidency, and Bucaram fled to Panama.

After Bucaram was ousted, his vice president, Rosalía Arteaga, became Ecuador's first female president, albeit for fewer than two days. Congress voted overwhelmingly to replace her with Fabián Alarcón, the head of congress. He led the government until 1998, when *quiteño* Jamil Mahuad of the Popular Democracy party was elected president.

Mahuad had his political savvy put to the test. The effects of a nasty El Niño weather pattern and the sagging oil market of 1997–98 sent the economy into a tailspin in 1999, the same year that shrimp exports dropped by 80% following devastating shrimp diseases. When inflation topped 60% – making Ecuador's the worst in Latin America – the embattled president took drastic measures: he pinned Ecuador's economic survival on dollarization, a process whereby Ecuador's unstable national currency would be replaced by the US dollar.

> Former president Abdala Bucaram (aka The Madman) recorded a CD titled *El Loco Que Ama (Madman in Love)*. The 18-track album featured a photo of him on the cover in presidential sash, with his signature Chaplin-esque moustache.

## Dollarization

Dollarization has been used successfully in a few other struggling countries, including nearby Panama (where the US dollar is called a balboa), but when President Mahuad declared his plan to dump the national currency, the country erupted in strikes, protests and road closures. On January 21, 2000, marches shut down the capital, and protesters took over the legislative palace, forcing Mahuad to resign.

The protesters were lead by Antonio Vargas, Colonel Lucio Gutiérrez and former supreme court president Carlos Solorzano, who then formed a brief ruling triumvirate. Two days later – and largely due to the international pressure that followed Latin America's first military coup in two decades – the triumvirate turned the presidency over to Vice President Gustavo Noboa.

Noboa went ahead with dollarization, and in September 2000 the US dollar became the official currency. Although only one year earlier 6000 sucres bought one dollar, people were forced to exchange their sucres at the dramatically inflated year 2000 rate of 25,000 to $1. Their losses were severe.

> John Perkin's *Confessions of an Economic Hitman* is an insider's exposé in which the author claims the US government played a key role in Ecuador's acceptance of huge development loans, as well as in ensuring the lucrative projects were contracted to US corporations.

| 1955 | 1970s | 1992 | 1995 |
|---|---|---|---|
| Ecuadorian officials seize two US fishing boats, charging them with fishing inside Ecuador's 200-nautical-mile territory. It was the opening salvo in what was later known as 'the tuna wars.' | Following the discovery of oil in the Oriente, Ecuador undergoes profound changes. The government budget, exports and per-capita income increase 500%, and a small middle class begins to emerge. | Thousands of indigenous protesters seeking land reform march in Quito on the 500th anniversary of Columbus' arrival. In ensuing negotiations they are granted title to 2.5 million acres in Amazonia. | Ecuador and Peru have another short but intense border dispute that leaves 400 dead. A 1998 peace treaty resolves hostilities, with both sides dedicated to removing thousands of land mines. |

# The 21st Century

Along with dollarizing the economy, Noboa also implemented austerity measures to obtain $2 billion in aid from the International Monetary Fund (IMF) and other international lenders. At the end of 2000, gas and cooking-fuel prices sky-rocketed (largely because of dollarization) and the new year saw frequent strikes and protests by unions and indigenous groups. The economy finally stabilized, and Noboa left office on somewhat favorable terms.

After Noboa, former coup leader Lucio Gutiérrez, elected president in 2002, promised a populist agenda but instead implemented IMF austerity measures to finance the country's massive debt. Protests erupted in the capital, and in 2005 congress voted overwhelmingly to remove Gutiérrez (the third Ecuadorian president ousted in eight years), replacing him with Vice President Alfredo Palacio.

A political newcomer who referred to himself as a 'simple doctor,' Palacio soon turned his attention to the social problems his predecessor had abandoned. In order to fund health and education programs and kick start the economy, Palacio announced he would redirect oil profits earmarked for paying the foreign debt. An essential partner in this endeavor was Rafael Correa, a US-educated economist, whom Palacio appointed as his finance minister and who later carried out even more aggressive social reforms – while also consolidating power – after becoming president in 2006.

O Hugo Benavides' Making Ecuadorian Histories: Four Centuries of Defining Power is an excellent if scholarly exploration of nation-building, gender, race and sexuality as it relates to the corridors of power inside Ecuador.

HISTORY THE 21ST CENTURY

| 2000 | 2008 | 2010 | 2011 |
|---|---|---|---|
| Facing spiraling inflation and contracting GDP, Ecuador dumps the sucre (the national currency) for the US dollar. The economy makes a modest recovery, although many Ecuadorians slip into poverty. | In a nationwide referendum, Ecuadorians approve a new constitution, which expands the president's powers while increasing spending on social welfare and enshrining rights for indigenous people and the environment. | A new law gives further government control over Ecuador's oil industry. It stipulates that Ecuador will own 100% of all oil and gas produced in the country. | Following an 18-year court case, the US oil giant Chevron is ordered to pay $18 billion to clean up decades of petro-contamination in the northeast Oriente. |

# Indigenous Ecuador

Ecuador's diverse indigenous population is made up of nearly 4 million people, roughly 25% of Ecuadorians (another 65% of the population are mestizos, with mixed indigenous and European ancestry). There are more than a dozen distinct groups in Ecuador, speaking some 20 different languages.

Ecuador's indigenous people have suffered from centuries of discrimination and remain at the bottom of the heap in the country's highly stratified social class structure. It's a well-known truth that if you're indigenous in Ecuador, you're more likely to be poor, have fewer years of education and have less access to basic healthcare. According to a report by the World Bank, poverty among Ecuadorian indigenous people is about 87% and reaches 96% in the rural highlands. To make matters worse, oil drilling, mining and logging has led to the widespread displacement of indigenous groups or to the polluting of their natural environment – the $18 billion lawsuit against Texaco (which is now owned by Chevron) for the heavy petro-contamination of the Amazon is but one high-profile example.

Despite the enormous hardships the indigenous face, they have made some strides on the political front. Through marches and popular uprisings, the Confederation of Indigenous Nationalities of Ecuador (CONAIE) has lobbied for greater autonomy and land reform – protesting, in particular, the expropriation of indigenous lands to multinational companies. Since their founding in the 1980s, CONAIE's political power has grown, and the government has made a few concessions – granting 16,000 sq km of land to indigenous groups in 1992 and giving them greater autonomy and recognition in the new constitution, drafted in 2008.

## Kichwa

The country's largest indigenous ethnic group, the Kichwa number well over 2 million. They live in both the Sierra and the Amazon, and vary considerably in customs and lifestyles. Those in the mountains subsist on small plots of farmland, raising sheep and cattle, and their fine textiles and weavings are an essential source of income.

One of the best-known groups within the Kichwa community are the *otavaleños*. Like other indigenous groups, they have a unique dress that sets them apart from other groups. For men, this consists of a blue poncho, a fedora, white calf-length socks, and a *shimba* (a long braid that hangs down nearly to the waist). Wearing the hair in this fashion probably dates back to pre-Inca times, and is an established and deeply rooted tradition. The women's dress may be the closest to Inca costume worn anywhere in the Andes. White blouses, blue skirts, shawls and jewelry are all part of the way of outwardly expressing their ethnicity.

For insights into the customs and cosmology of the Shuar, read *Spirit of the Shuar* (2001) by John Perkins and Shakaim Chumpi. Through interviews with members of the Amazonian tribe, Perkins explores Shuar warrior culture, healing and sexual practices, spiritual beliefs and challenges in the face of ever-encroaching development.

## LOVE & WAR AMONG THE SHUAR

One of the most studied Amazonian groups, the Shuar were once feared as 'headhunters' and had a reputation for being fierce warriors – in fact, they were never conquered by the Spanish. Up until the mid-20th century they were famous for the elaborate process of *tzantza,* shrinking the heads of slain opponents. Shuar believed the *muisak* (soul) of the victim remained inside the head and that keeping the *tzantza* would bring the warrior good fortune and please the spirits of his ancestors.

Shuar men take one or two wives, and girls are often married between the ages of 12 and 14. Unlike some other societies, women are given autonomy in the marriage; those that are dissatisfied with their husbands can leave and return to their families. The men, however, cannot abandon their wives (those that run off will be fetched back by the wife's family!). Outside of marriage, some Shuar take lovers, which may or may not be tolerated by the spouse. Older wives sometimes take it upon themselves to teach young unmarried men the arts of lovemaking, and having multiple partners is not necessarily frowned upon. Nevertheless, misunderstandings are not uncommon, and bloody, longstanding family feuds have sometimes resulted from such infidelities.

## Huaorani

Short in stature (men average 1.5m or about 5ft tall), the Huaorani are an Amazonian tribe living between the Río Napo and the Río Curaray in the Oriente. They number no more than 4000 and remain one of Ecuador's most isolated indigenous groups. They have a reputation for being warriors, defending their territory against outsiders – whether rival tribes or oil developers. They have a complex cosmology – making no distinction between the physical and spiritual worlds – and an intimate understanding of the rainforest in cultivating medicine, poisons for defense and hallucinogens for spiritual rites. Some still refer to them as the Auca, meaning 'savage' in Kichwa, which the Huaorani find extremely offensive.

## Shuar

Until the 1950s the Shuar, from the Amazonian lowlands, were a society of male hunters and female gardeners. To preserve their culture and lands, the Shuar (which today number 40,000), formed the first ethnic federation in Ecuadorian Amazonia in 1964. Traditionally, they were seminomadic, practising small-scale slash-and-burn agriculture, planting crops (such as *yuca* and sweet potato), moving on before the soil was depleted. Like other Amazonian groups, Shuar shaman administer *ayahuasca,* a psychoactive infusion, to reach higher planes of consciousness in spiritual practises.

## Chachi

The Chachi originally lived in Ecuador's highlands, but fled to the Pacific coast (in present-day Esmeraldas province) in the wake of Inca and Spanish conquests. With a population of around 4000, they live in homes made of palm fronds, travel by canoe through a watery landscape and cultivate cocoa and tropical fruits. They are highly skilled artisans, particularly known for their hammocks.

## Cofán

Straddling the Ecuador-Colombia border in the northeast, the Cofán number about 1500, half of whom live in Ecuador. Like other Amazonian groups they have seen a significant loss and degradation of their environment, largely due to oil drilling. However, in recent years they have waged a successful campaign for land rights, and are presently in control of 4000 sq km of rainforest (a seemingly large number, but only a fraction of the 30,000 sq km originally belonging to the group).

One of the more unusual Amazonian leaders is the 50-something 'Gringo Chief' Randy Borman. Born to American missionaries living in the Amazon, he has become one of the Cofán's most influential chiefs. He speaks flawless Cofán and has helped the tribe win major land concessions.

# The Sounds of Ecuador

Poncho-wearing, flute-playing Andean groups are a staple in nearly every large city across the globe. The musical traditions of this culturally rich nation, however, are far more complex than simple Andean versions of well-known Beatles hits one might hear in Times Square, for instance. In fact, early indigenous music dates back to pre-Columbian times, with the melancholic and haunting sounds of panpipes a mainstay of Incan culture. Since the Spanish conquest, indigenous elements have mixed with European styles to produce a range of unique genres in both music and dance. African heritage has also played a role in shaping the national soundtrack.

## Música Folklórica

One of the most recognizable tunes of traditional Andean *música folklórica* (folk music) is Simon and Garfunkel's version of 'El Cóndor Pasa (If I Could)'. This was already a classic Andean tune (written by Peruvian composer Daniel Alomía Robles in 1913) before the popular duo got their hands on it.

Andean songs like this one typically have a breathy, mournful quality courtesy of the panpipes – which in Ecuador is known as the *rondador*, a single row of bamboo pipes in a pentatonic (five-note) scale. It's considered Ecuador's national instrument and varies from other Andean instruments such as the *zampoña* (two rows of cane pipes, originating in the highlands area around Lake Titicaca) and the *quena* and *pingullo* (large and small bamboo flutes). Other traditional instruments include the *charango,* a mandolin-like instrument with ten strings and a sounding box that was originally made with an armadillo shell.

## Pasillo

Although most people associate Ecuador with *folklórica*, the country's most popular national music is the *pasillo,* which is rooted in the waltz. *Pasillo's* origins date back to the 19th century when Ecuador (along with Colombia, Venezuela and Panama) was part of Gran Colombia. These poignant songs with their melancholic melodies often touch on themes of disillusionment, lost love and unquenchable longing for the past. Less commonly, the lyrics celebrate the beauty of the Ecuadorian landscape (or its women), the valor of its men (indeed, the *pasillo* was popular during the Ecuadorian War of Independence) or the charm of its towns and cities.

*Pasillo's* most famous voice was that of Julio Jaramillo, known affectionately as 'JJ' (pronounced 'jota jota' in Spanish). Born in 1935, this handsome singer from Guayaquil popularized the genre throughout Latin America with his lyrical songs. Unfortunately, hard living led to

The biopic *Julio Jaramillo: Ruisenor de America* (1996) does an excellent job capturing the brilliance and decadence of the Latin American music legend. Throughout a 20-plus-year career, he recorded over 4000 songs, living an alcohol-fueled bohemian life and leaving behind a string of lovers (and dozens of illegitimate children).

## TOP SONGS

'A Mi Lindo Ecuador' – Pueblo Nuevo
'Algo Así' – Fausto Miño
'Andarele' – Grupo Bambuco
'Ayayay!' – Tomback
'Caderona' – Papá Rincón
'Codominio de Cartón' – Rocola Bacalao
'De Mis Manos' – Manolo Criollo
'Homenaje a Mis Viejos' – Raíces Negras
'Inti Raymi' – Faccha Huayras
'Light It Up' – Esto Es Eso
'Luz de Mi Vida' – Jayac
'Ñuca Llacta' – Ñanda Mañanchi
'Soy El Hombre' – Azúcar
'Super Girla' – Sudakaya
'Te Odio y Te Quiero' – Julio Jaramillo

his early death (from cirrhosis of the liver) at the age of 42. At the time of his death, he had become a legend, and some 250,000 mourners came out for his funeral. Jaramillo's version of 'Guayaquil de Mis Amores' is a well-known paean to the city that's sure to induce nostalgia in any Ecuadorian expat.

## Afro-Ecuadorian Music

Northwest Ecuador, particularly Esmeraldas province, is the heart of the country's Afro-Ecuadorian population. Here – and in Afro-Colombian communities of neighboring Colombia – you can find musical traditions quite distinct from other parts of Ecuador.

The iconic instrument here is the *marimba* (a percussion instrument laid out like a xylophone but with wooden bars), which produces a range of bright but mellow sounds. It's accompanied by the congadrum-like *cunuco*, the bigger *bomba* (large sheepskin drum) and the maraca-like *guasá*. Big West African–style beats back the simple choral arrangements; traditional dances like the stylized *bambuco* sometimes accompany the music.

In addition to the north coast, in the Chota Valley, there's also an Afro-Ecuadorian community, the only population of its kind found anywhere in the highlands. The music there blends more indigenous elements (including pan flutes) to African rhythms and is called *bomba,* named after the large drum that lays down the heavy beats.

Among the more popular Afro-Ecuadorian music and dance groups is Azúcar, which is named in honor of the group's early ancestors, who labored on sugar-cane plantations. The outstanding Esmeraldas-based Grupo Bambuco add a horn section to the driving, highly danceable beats.

## Other Styles

Musical hybrids have flourished in Ecuador over the last 200 years, creating new genres from traditional Spanish styles shaped by indigenous influences.

The *sanjuanito* (which means 'little St John') is a joyful dance and music style (though it too has melancholic undertones) with traditional Andean rhythms and instrumentation. Its origin dates back to religious celebrations held on June 24 – an important day to both Catholics (St

For profiles of Ecuador's music scene, including folk and rock bands, visit www.goecuador. com/magazine/ ecuador-mp3-music.html. You can even listen to MP3s of featured groups.

John's Day) and the indigenous (Inti Raymi or the Incan Festival of the Sun).

Born in the early 20th century, the *pasacalle* is a distant relative of the Spanish *pasodoble*, the march-like music typically played at bullfights. The Ecuadorian variant is equally fast-paced with dramatic elements and a clean 2/4 beat.

If there's one inescapable music in this Andean country, it's *cumbia*, whose rhythm resembles that of a trotting three-legged horse. Originally from Colombia, Ecuadorian *cumbia* has a rawer (almost amateur), melancholic sound, and is dominated by the electronic keyboard. Bus drivers love the stuff, perhaps because it so strangely complements those backroad journeys through the Andes (and hopefully it keeps them awake at the wheel).

A nightclub favorite is Caribbean-born *reggaetón* (a blend of Puerto Rican *bomba*, dancehall and hip-hop) with its grinding melodies and racy lyrics. Salsa, merengue and *rock en español* (Latin rock) also get plenty of airtime on radio stations and in nightclubs around the country.

# The Natural World

## The Land

Ecuador straddles the equator on the Pacific coast of South America, and is bordered by Colombia to the north and Peru to the south and east. Despite its small size Ecuador is one of the world's most varied countries, making it possible to experience astonishingly different landscapes in a single day.

At 283,560 sq km, Ecuador is about the size of New Zealand or the US state of Nevada, and it's somewhat larger than the UK. The country is divided into three regions. The dramatic Andean mountain range runs roughly north to south and splits the country into the western coastal lowlands and the eastern jungles of the upper Amazon Basin, known as the Oriente. The Andes (known in Ecuador as the highlands) stretch high above the landscape, with Volcán Chimborazo, Ecuador's highest peak, topping out at 6310m.

The central highlands contain two parallel volcanic mountain ranges, each about 400km long. The valley nestled between them was appropriately dubbed 'the Avenue of the Volcanoes' by the German explorer Alexander von Humboldt, who visited the country in 1802. Quito lies within this valley and, at 2850m, is the world's second-highest national capital, second only to La Paz in Bolivia. The central highlands are also home to countless towns and tiny villages well known for their indigenous markets and fiestas. This region has the highest population density in the country.

The western coastal lowlands were once heavily forested, but encroaching agriculture has meant the replacement of forest with fruit plantations and the clear-cutting of mangroves for shrimp farming. The beaches are blessed with warm water year-round and provide decent surfing, but are not as pretty as the beaches of the Caribbean.

The eastern lowlands of the Oriente still retain much of their virgin rainforest, but colonization and oil drilling have damaged this delicate habitat. The population of the Oriente has more than tripled since the late 1970s.

Ecuador's territory also includes the Galápagos Islands, which are on the equator about 1000km west of the mainland.

## Wildlife

Ecologists have labeled Ecuador one of the world's 'megadiversity hotspots.' The tiny nation is one of the most species-rich countries on the planet. Ecuador's astounding biodiversity is due to the great number of habitats within its borders, with dramatically different fauna in the Andes, the tropical rainforests, the coastal regions and the numerous

The Doldrums was the name sailors gave to the windless belt around the equator. It is caused by intense heating along the equator, causing air to rise rather than blow, spelling disaster for sailing ships. The word later entered common usage to mean a period of boredom, inactivity or despondency.

transitional zones. The result is a wealth of habitats, ecosystems and wildlife.

## Birds

Bird-watchers from all over the world flock to Ecuador for one simple reason: the country is home to nearly 1600 bird species – twice the number found in the continents of Europe and North America combined. It's impossible to give a precise number because formerly unobserved species are often reported, and very occasionally a new species is discovered – an incredibly rare event in the world of birds. Bird-watching is outstanding year-round and every part of the country offers unique habitats. For more information, see p31.

For many visitors, the diminutive hummingbirds found throughout Ecuador are the most delightful birds to observe. About 120 species have been recorded in Ecuador, and their exquisite beauty is matched by extravagant names such as green-tailed goldenthroat, spangled coquette, fawn-breasted brilliant and amethyst-throated sunangel.

In two outstanding (if rather cumbersome) volumes, *The Birds of Ecuador* (by Robert Ridgeley and Paul Greenfield) covers the entire country, the only bird-watching guide to do so. The first has more details for the serious bird-watcher, while the second has great pictures and descriptions.

## Mammals

Some 300 species of mammals have been recorded in Ecuador. These range from monkeys in the Amazonian lowlands to the rare Andean spectacled bear in the highlands.

For many, the most amusing mammals to spy upon are monkeys. Ecuadorian species include howler monkeys, spider monkeys, woolly monkeys, titi monkeys, capuchin monkeys, squirrel monkeys, tamarins and marmosets. The best places to see them in their natural habitat include Reserva de Producción Faunística Cuyabeno (p204), Parque Nacional Yasuní (p214) in the Amazonian lowlands, and the rarely visited lowlands sector of Reserva Ecológica Cotacachi-Cayapas (p103), near the coast. A group of marvelously mischievous capuchin monkeys has taken over the central plaza in the Oriente town of Misahuallí (p221), where you're guaranteed an up-close (and sometimes too personal) experience.

---

## FINE & FEATHERED: ECUADOR'S GREATEST HITS

Ecuador's unique and diverse habitats are home to a wondrous array of bird species both great and small. A few perennial favorites include the following (for Galápagos wildlife, see p333):

» **Andean Condor** Ecuador's emblematic bird with its 3m wingspan is one of the largest flying birds in the world. In 1880, the British mountaineer Edward Whymper noted that he commonly saw a dozen condors on the wing at the same time. Today there are only a few hundred pairs left in the Ecuadorian highlands, so sighting one is a thrilling experience.

» **Scarlet Macaws** These brilliantly colored birds, with blue, red and yellow feathers, are a magnificent sight and one of more than 40 parrot species found in Ecuador. They often travel in pairs and have lifespans of 40-plus years.

» **Harpy Eagle** One of the world's largest birds of prey, with a wingspan of up to 2m and weighing up to 10kg, this apex predator has powerful claws capable of carrying off coatis, sloths, monkeys and other tree-dwelling mammals.

» **Plate-Billed Mountain Toucans** Among the best known Latin American birds, toucans have huge (but mostly hollow) beaks perfectly suited for nibbling ripe fruit off the ends of branches. This particular species, with its black and ivory bill, is found on the west Andean slopes and makes quite a racket with loud vocalizations heard up to 1km away.

» **American Pygmy Kingfisher** Weighing just 18 grams and topping out around 12cm, this diminutive bird has a classic kingfisher appearance (long bill and short tail) but is often mistaken for a hummingbird as it flits past.

In the Oriente you may hear howler monkeys well before you see them; the males' eerie roars carry great distances and can sound like anything from a baby crying to wind moaning through the trees.

Other tropical specialties include two species of sloth: the diurnal three-toed sloth and the nocturnal two-toed sloth. It's very possible to spot the former while hiking in the Amazon. They are usually found hanging motionless from tree limbs or progressing at a painfully slow speed along a branch toward a particularly succulent bunch of leaves, which are their primary food source.

There are far fewer species of mammal in the highlands than in the lowlands, but include commonly seen deer and rabbits and the more rarely sighted Andean fox. One of the icons of the Andes is the llama, which is domesticated and used primarily as a pack animal. Its wild relative, the lovely vicuña, has been reintroduced to the Chimborazo area (p152) – you're almost guaranteed to see them as you drive, bus or walk through the park.

Other possible mammal sightings include anteaters, armadillos, agoutis (large rodents), capybaras (even larger rodents, some weighing up to 65kg), peccaries (wild pigs) and otters. River dolphins are occasionally sighted in Amazonian tributaries. Other exotic mammals, such as ocelots, jaguars, tapirs, pumas and the Andean spectacled bear, are very rarely seen.

## Amphibians & Reptiles

The majority of Ecuador's approximately 460 species of amphibian are frogs. There are tree frogs that spend their entire lives in trees and lay their eggs in water trapped inside bromeliads (a type of epiphytic plant). The ominously named poison-dart frog is among the most brightly colored species of frog anywhere. Its colors run the spectrum from bright red-orange with jet-black spots to neon green with black wavy lines. Some poison-dart frogs have skin glands exuding toxins that can cause paralysis and death in animals and humans.

Of Ecuador's reptiles, four really make an impression on visitors. Three of them – the land tortoise, the land iguana and the marine iguana – live in the Galápagos and are easy to see. The fourth is the caiman, which inhabits lagoons in the Oriente. With a little patience and a good canoe guide, you'll spot these spooky creatures as well.

Snakes, which are much talked about but seldom seen, make up a large portion of Ecuador's reptiles. They usually slither away into the undergrowth at the sound of approaching humans, so only a few fortunate visitors get to see them. Perhaps Ecuador's most feared snake is the fer-de-lance, which is extremely poisonous. Visitors are rarely bitten, but it is wise to take precautions. If you do see a snake, keep a respectful distance and avoid provoking it.

## Habitats

Some 25,000 species of vascular plants reside in Ecuador's diverse habitats (compared to 17,000 species in North America), and new species are being discovered every year. Cloud forests, rainforests, *páramo* (high-altitude Andean grasslands) and mangrove swamps all set the stage for discovering Ecuador's photogenic natural wonders.

For info on the surreal volcanic landscapes of the Galápagos see p328.

## Rainforests

The Oriente is Ecuador's slice of the Amazon, the greatest rainforest habitat in the world. It is home to an astounding variety of plants and animals, located in much denser concentrations than in temperate forests.

Lianas (thick dangling vines) hang from high in the canopy, and the massive roots of strangler figs engulf other trees, slowly choking them

**THE NATURAL WORLD HABITATS**

Hummingbirds beat their wings up to 80 times per second in a figure-eight pattern that allows them to hover in place or even to fly backward.

No one knows for sure why the sloth engages in its fastidious toilet habits: climbing down its tree once a week, digging a hole into which it will defecate and then covering it afterwards. This exposes the sloth to predators, though the tree surely appreciates the nutrient-rich deposit!

The largest ant in the South American rainforest is the Conga or 'bullet' ant, so nicknamed because its extremely painful sting is likened to being shot. The paralyzing neurotoxic venom produces severe pain that can last up to 24 hours.

of light and life. Spread across the forest floor are the buttressed roots of tropical hardwoods, which are sometimes so massive you can just about disappear inside their weblike supports. Equally impressive are the forest's giant leaves, which are thick and waxy and have pointed 'drip tips,' which facilitate water runoff during downpours.

Much of the rainforest's plant and animal life is up in the canopy rather than on the forest floor, which can appear surprisingly empty to the first-time visitor. If you're staying in a jungle lodge, find out if it has a canopy tower; climbing into the canopy provides spectacular views.

## Tropical Cloud Forests

One of Ecuador's most enchanting habitats is the tropical cloud forest. These moist environments are found at higher elevations and earn their name from the clouds they trap (and help create), which drench the forest in a fine mist. This continual moisture allows particularly delicate forms of plant life to survive. Dense, small-leaved canopies and moss-covered branches set the scene for a host of plant life within, including orchids, ferns and bromeliads. The dense vegetation at all levels of this forest gives it a mysterious and delicate fairy tale appearance. Some people find it even more beautiful than the rainforest since many of the plants grow closer to the forest floor. This creates a far more luxuriant environment where the diverse fauna thrives – and remains easier to spot.

## Páramo

Above the cloud forests lie the Andes' high-altitude grasslands and scrublands, known as the *páramo*. The *páramo* is characterized by a harsh climate, high levels of ultraviolet light and wet, peaty soils. It is an extremely specialized habitat unique to the neotropics (tropical America) and is found only in the area between the highlands of Costa Rica and northern Peru.

The *páramo* is dominated by cushion plants, hard grasses and small herbaceous plants that have adapted well to the harsh highland environment. Most plants up here are small and compact and grow close to the ground. An exception is the giant *Espeletia*, one of the *páramo*'s strangest sights. These bizarre-looking plants stand as high as a person, and have earned the local nickname *frailejones* (gray friars). They are an

Caterpillars are masters of disguise, some mimicking twigs, others the head of a viper, even a pile of bird droppings – all in the name of defense.

Regardless of your science background (or lack of it), the entertaining and highly readable classic *Tropical Nature*, by Adrian Forsyth and Kenneth Miyata, is an excellent read before or during any trip to the rainforest.

## UNSEEN BOUNTY OF THE RAINFOREST

Home to poisonous snakes, toxic plants and flesh-eating fish (not to mention predatorial caiman and jaguars), the Amazon rainforest may not seem like the world's most inviting habitat. But for the indigenous people who have always lived there, the rainforest has everything needed for survival; it functions as their supermarket, pharmacy, hardware store and cathedral.

For those of us that couldn't imagine living without Western medicine, it's perhaps most fascinating to read about life in the Oriente, where village shamans still serve as healers, harnessing the powerful extractions of the rainforest for all manner of ailments. There are remedies for headaches, fevers, insect bites, constipation, muscular aches, nervous disorders, diarrhea, asthma, epilepsy, ulcers and intestinal parasites – and plants are even used as contraceptives. In addition to medicinal use, rainforest plants and animals serve many other purposes. The tiny but extremely lethal poison-dart frogs – one of which has enough toxicity to kill about a dozen humans – play a key role in hunting; while the psychotropic plant *ayahuasca* is a powerful hallucinogen used in spiritual ceremonies.

unmistakable feature of the northern Ecuadorian *páramo,* particularly in the El Ángel region (p109).

The *páramo* is also characterized by dense thickets of small trees, often of the *Polylepis* species that, along with Himalayan pines, are the tallest-growing trees in the world. They were once extensive, but fire and grazing have pushed them back into small pockets.

## Mangrove Swamps

Mangroves are trees that have evolved with the remarkable ability to grow in salt water. The red mangrove is the most common in Ecuador and, like other mangroves, it has a broadly spreading system of intertwining stilt roots to support the tree in the unstable soils of the shoreline. These roots trap sediments and build up rich organic soil, which creates a protected habitat for many plants and fish, as well as mollusks, crustaceans and other invertebrates. The branches provide nesting areas for seabirds, such as pelicans and frigate birds. Extensive mangrove areas on Ecuador's coastline have been cleared for shrimp farms, and most are now found in the far northern and southern coastal regions. For more information, see p248. The tallest mangroves in the world are inside the Reserva Ecológica de Manglares Cayapas Mataje (p237).

## Tropical Dry Forests

This fascinating habitat is fast disappearing and is found primarily in the hot coastal areas near Parque Nacional Machalilla (p259) and in southwest Loja Province en route to Macará (p194). Its definitive plant species is the majestic bottle-trunk ceiba (also known as kapok), a glorious tree with a massively bulging trunk and seasonal white flowers that dangle like lightbulbs from the bare branches.

## National Parks & Reserves

Ecuador has more than 30 government-protected parks and reserves (of which nine carry the title of 'national park') as well as numerous privately administered nature reserves. A total of 18% of the country lies within protected areas. Yet despite their protected status, many of these areas continue to be susceptible to oil drilling, logging, mining, ranching and colonization.

Many parks are inhabited by indigenous groups, whose connection to the area long precedes modern park or reserve status. In the case of the Oriente parks, the indigenous people maintain traditional hunting rights, which also affect the ecology. The question of how to protect the national parks from damage by heavy industry (oil, timber and mining) while recognizing the rights of indigenous peoples – all in the context of keeping the nation financially solvent – remains a hot-button topic in Ecuador.

## Environmental Issues

According to the US Agency for International Development (USAID), Ecuador has one of the highest deforestation rates in South America. The country also has a very poor environmental record. Deforestation is Ecuador's most severe environmental problem. In the highlands, almost all of the natural forest cover has disappeared and only a few pockets remain, mainly in private nature reserves. Along the coast, once-plentiful mangrove forests have all but vanished, too. These forests harbor a great diversity of marine and shore life, but they have been removed to make artificial ponds in which shrimp are grown for export (see p248).

About 95% of the forests of the western slopes and lowlands have become agricultural land, mostly banana plantations. These forests were

For a deeper understanding of the plants, animals and unique ecosystems of South America, pick up John Kricher's *A Neotropical Companion.* Illustrations and color photographs supplement the detailed overview covering ecology, evolutionary theory, ornithology, pharmacology and conservation.

Thanks to the earth's equatorial bulge, the summit of Volcán Cotopaxi is the furthest point from the center of the earth and the closest to the sun.

THE NATURAL WORLD NATIONAL PARKS & RESERVES

ECOSYSTEM

host to more species than almost anywhere on the planet, many of them endemic. Scientists suggest that countless species have likely become extinct even before they were identified, and in recent years a small preservation movement has taken root.

Although much of the rainforest in the Ecuadorian Amazon still stands, it is seriously threatened by fragmentation. The main threats to the rainforest are logging, cattle ranching and oil extraction. The discovery of oil has brought with it roads and new settlements, and rainforest clearing has increased exponentially.

Equally destructive to the environment is mining, which has the potential to wreak as much havoc on the southern Amazon as oil has on the north. Among the most serious concerns is contamination of groundwater and nearby rivers with chemicals used for processing minerals and ore.

Clearly, these issues are tightly linked with Ecuador's economy. Oil, minerals, bananas and shrimp are some of the nation's top exports. Industry advocates claim the cost of abandoning these revenue sources is too high for a small, developing country to shoulder. Environmentalists, on the other hand, claim the government has given free rein to big industry, which has resulted in at times catastrophic damage to the local ecology. An infamous 18-year-long environmental class-action

## NATIONAL PARKS

| NAME OF PARK | FEATURES | ACTIVITIES | BEST TIME TO VISIT |
| --- | --- | --- | --- |
| Cajas (p177) | *páramo*, lakes, small *Polylepis*, forests | hiking, fishing, bird-watching | year-round |
| Cotopaxi (p124) | *páramo*, Volcán Cotopaxi: Andean condor, deer, rabbits | hiking, climbing | year-round |
| Galápagos (p296) | volcanically formed islands: seabirds, iguanas, turtles, rich underwater life | wildlife-watching, snorkeling, diving | Nov–Jun |
| Llanganates (p140) | *páramo*, cloud forest, lowland forest: deer, tapirs, jaguars, spectacled bears | hiking | year-round (access difficult) |
| Machalilla (p259) | coastal dry forest, beaches, islands: whales, seabirds, monkeys, reptiles | hiking, wildlife-watching | year-round |
| Podocarpus (p187) | *páramo*, cloud forest, tropical humid forest: spectacled bears, tapirs, deer, birds | hiking, bird-watching | year-round |
| Sumaco-Galeras (p215) | Volcán Sumaco, subtropical and cloud forest | off-trail hiking | year-round (access difficult) |
| Sangay (p149 and p231) | volcanoes, *páramo*, cloud forest, lowland forest: spectacled bears, tapirs, pumas, ocelots | hiking, climbing | year-round |
| Yasuní (p214) | rainforest, rivers, lagoons: monkeys, birds, sloths, jaguars, pumas, tapirs | hiking, wildlife-watching | year-round |

## DRILLING IN YASUNÍ?

The Yasuní reserve is considered one of the world's most biodiverse regions, full of rare animal species, isolated tribes and an enormous variety of plant life (with more hardwoods in one hectare than found in the entire North American continent, for instance). Yet it's also home to one of Ecuador's largest known oil reserves – an estimated 900 million barrels. Oil companies have long lobbied the government to open up the area to drilling, which could bring in billions of dollars. President Correa, under increasing pressure, has offered one last-ditch effort to preserve the park before giving the green light to oil companies.

Correa first floated this controversial idea before the world community in 2008: pay us not to tap the reserves in this environmentally sensitive area. He proposed that foreign investors put up some $3.6 billion in donations over 13 years, which would be equal to about half the market value of the reserve's deposits. In 2010, Ecuador signed an agreement with the UN Development Group, establishing the Yasuní ITT Trust Fund, which would prohibit any future drilling, provided the country received compensation for at least half of the lost revenue.

If the scheme is successful, it will enhance the protection of some 5 million hectares of Ecuadorian nature reserves, promote environmentally friendly rural development and protect indigenous tribes.

Critics say that the scheme will create a dangerous precedent in a world dependent on such reserves. Advocates of the controversial plan say it will keep half a billion tons of carbon dioxide sequestered in the earth – no small matter to a world increasingly concerned with global warming.

As of 2011, Ecuador had raised the first $100 million. Over the next 12 years, it hopes to raise some $350 million per year. The funds, incidentally, will be earmarked for investment in renewable-energy projects in Ecuador as well as spending on social welfare for the indigenous communities of Yasuní.

lawsuit was finally decided in 2011, when Chevron (which now owns Texaco) was ordered to pay $18 billion in damages for dumping billions of gallons of toxic waste in the Amazon and abandoning 900 waste pits (see p203). However, Chevron considers the ruling illegitimate and plans to appeal, so the issue is unlikely to be settled any time soon.

The rainforest's indigenous inhabitants – who depend on the rivers for drinking water and food – are also dramatically affected. Oil residues, oil treatment chemicals, erosion and fertilizers all contaminate the rivers, killing fish and rendering formerly potable water undrinkable. Past Ecuadorian governments have actively supported oil exploration. The current administration, however, has tried to find a balance between development and preservation, even floating some radical ideas before the world community (see above).

# Survival Guide

# Directory A–Z

## Accommodations

Ecuador has a wide range of accommodations, from wooden shacks in the mangroves to high-end jungle lodges in the Amazon, lovely haciendas in the Andes to traveler-friendly hostels and pleasant family-run guesthouses crisscrossing the country.

Nearly every town of any size has a hotel, but unless you stick to the most touristy destinations, you'll have to tolerate the occasional saggy bed, lousy shower or noisy neighbor – all part of the equatorial experience.

Most hotel rooms have a private bathroom, and reviews throughout this book assume so unless shared bathrooms are specified. Hot water is hardest to come by along the coast and in the Oriente, where most locals might call you crazy for want-ing it in the first place. In the highlands, you can assume that water is hot unless noted otherwise in our review.

It's fairly easy to rock into town and find a bed for the night. The rare exception is during major fiestas or on the night before market day.

### B&Bs

Bed-and-breakfasts are a tried-and-true concept in Ecuador and are especially popular in tourist destinations such as Quito, Baños, Cuenca and Otavalo. Once you're out in the countryside, there's a fine line between B&Bs and *hosterías* (small hotels).

### Camping

Camping is allowed on the grounds of a few rural hotels, in the countryside and most national parks. There are no campgrounds in towns. There are climbers' *refugios* (mountain refuges) on some of the major mountains, in some national parks, but you need to bring a sleeping bag.

## Haciendas & Hosterías

The Ecuadorian highlands have some fabulous haciendas (historic family ranches that have been refurbished to accept tourists). They usually fall into the top-end price bracket, but the price may include home-cooked meals and activities such as horseback-riding or fishing. The best-known haciendas are in the northern and central highlands.

*Hosterías* are similar but often smaller, and more intimate. *Hosterías* regularly have rates that include full board and/or activities.

## Homestays

Spanish-language schools can often arrange homestays, allowing travelers to stay overnight, eat meals and interact with a local family. Homestays are mostly available in Quito and Cuenca and are difficult to find elsewhere.

In some rural communities, where there are no hotels, you can ask around and often find a local family willing to let you spend the night. This happens only in the most off-the-beaten-track places, and you should always offer payment (though it may not be accepted).

## Hostels

Ecuador has a limited hostel system, though Quito is packed with hostels. The cheapest hostels start at around $6 per person in dorms. They run the range from saggy, dark and decrepit to cheery, traveler enclaves.

## Hotels

Budget hotels range from $10 to $15 per person, and may be basic, with just a bed and four walls, they can nevertheless be well looked after, very clean and excellent value. The cheapest hotels

## PRACTICALITIES

» Ecuador uses the US dollar ($) for currency.

» Ecuador uses the metric system for weights and measures.

» In Ecuadorian addresses, the term 's/n' refers to *'sin numero'* (without number), meaning the address has no street number.

» Quito's two biggest newspapers are *El Comercio* (www.elcomercio.com) and the more liberal *Hoy* (www.hoy.com.ec). Guayaquil's papers are *El Telégrafo* (www.telegrafo.com.ec) and *El Universo* (www.eluni verso.com). Ecuador's best-known news magazine is *Vistazo* (www.vistazo.com). International newspapers, including a locally published edition of the *Miami Herald,* can be found in Quito.

» For DVDs, Ecuador uses region 4, common through-out Latin America as well as Australia and Oceania.

have communal bathrooms, but you can often find rooms with a private bathroom for not much more.

Midrange hotels, run about $30 to $80 for a double and usually offer a bit more charm and more amenities – cable TV, reliably hot water and a better location – than their budget cousins.

Top-end hotels are found in only the larger cities. They generally offer a bit more luxury – spacious or heritage rooms, great views, top-notch service and the like.

No matter where you stay, make sure to always peek at a room before committing.

### Lodges

Ecolodges and jungle lodges provide a fantastic way to experience Ecuador's wildlife. Lodges are most popular in the Oriente and in the cloud forests of the western Andean slopes. The lodges in the Oriente are generally only available as part of a three- to five-day package, but this usually includes meals and activities. The lodge will arrange any river or jungle transportation, but you may have to get to the nearest departure town on your own.

### Prices

Room rates are highest throughout Ecuador around Christmas and New Year's Eve, around Semana Santa (Easter week) and during July and August. They also peak during local fiestas. Hotels along the coast, sometimes charge higher rates (and certainly draw bigger crowds) on weekends. Hotels are required to charge 12% sales tax (called IVA), though it's often already included in the hotel's quoted rate; prices quoted in this book include this tax where possible. Better hotels often tack on an additional 10% service charge, so be sure to check whether the rate you're quoted includes this.

Most hotels charge per person.

### Reservations

Most hotels accept reservations without a credit-card number. If you haven't prepaid, however, always confirm your reservation if you're arriving late in the day, to avoid it being given to someone else. Pricier hotels may request prepayment.

## Business Hours

Reviews found throughout this book provide opening hours when they differ from the following standard hours.

| BUSINESS | OPENING HOURS |
|---|---|
| Restaurants | 10:30am-11pm Mon-Sat |
| Bars | 6pm-midnight Sun-Thu, to 2am Fri & Sat |
| Shops | 9am-7pm Mon-Fri, 9am-noon Sat |
| Banks | 8am-2pm or 8am-4pm Mon-Fri |
| Post offices | 8am-6pm Mon-Fri, 8am-1pm Sat |
| Telephone call centers | 8am-10pm daily |

## Children

Foreigners traveling with children are still a curiosity in Ecuador (especially if they are gringos), and a crying or laughing child at your side can quickly break down barriers between you and locals. Parents will likely be met with extra-friendly, attention. As throughout most of the

---

### SLEEPING PRICE RANGES

The following price ranges refer to a double room in high season. Room prices include bathroom. Exceptions are noted in specific listings.

| $ | less than $30 |
|---|---|
| $$ | $30–80 |
| $$$ | more than $80 |

world, people in Ecuador love children. Lonely Planet's *Travel with Children* is an excellent resource.

### Practicalities

Children pay full fare on buses if they occupy a seat, but they often ride for free if they sit on a parent's lap. The fare for children under 12 years is halved for domestic flights (and they get a seat), while infants under two cost 10% of the fare (but they don't get a seat). In hotels, the general rule is simply to bargain.

While kids' meals are not normally offered in restaurants, it is perfectly acceptable to order a meal to split between two children or an adult and a child.

Changing facilities are rarities in all but the best restaurants. Breast-feeding is acceptable in public. Formula foods can be difficult to come by outside the large big-city supermarkets, but disposable diapers are sold at most markets throughout the country.

Safety seats are generally hard to come by in rental cars (be sure to arrange one ahead of time), and in taxis they're unheard of. This is, after all, a country where a family of four can blaze across town on a motorcycle.

### Sights & Activities

Ecuador is not a country that's big on fun parks, children's rides and organized spectacles for kids. That said, there's plenty of real-world excitement here, whether it's tramping through rainforest, canoeing down a river or playing in the waves.

Whale-watching is a must while in Puerto López (p261). Older children are likely to enjoy the snorkeling and animal-watching in the Galápagos (p296). Quito (p66) has a healthy number of activities that the young ones will enjoy, including a reptile zoo, a theme park and good museums.

## Customs Regulations

Each traveler is able to import 1L of spirits and 300 cigarettes duty-free. There is no problem in bringing in the usual types of personal belongings.

Pre-Columbian artifacts and endangered-animal products, which includes mounted butterflies and beetles, are not allowed to be taken out of Ecuador or imported into most other countries.

## Discount Cards

Aside from reduced museum entrance fees (which can add up), the only substantial discount is 15% off high-season flights to the Galápagos. The **International Student Identity Card** (ISIC; www.isic.org) is generally accepted only when issued from the traveler's home country and presented in combination with a valid student ID card.

## Electricity

120V/127V/60Hz

120V/127V/60Hz

## Embassies & Consulates

Hours are short and change regularly, so it's a good idea to call ahead. New Zealand does not have an embassy or consulate in Ecuador.

**Australia** (☎04-601-7529; ausconsulate@unidas.com. ec; Rocafuerte 520, 2nd fl, Guayaquil)

**Canada** Guayaquil (☎04-215-8333; cnr Avs Joaquin Orranita & Juan Tanca Marengo); Quito (☎02-245-5499; www.canada international.gc.ca/ecuador -equateur; cnr Av Amazonas 4153 & Unión Nacional de Periodistas)

**Colombia** Guayaquil (☎04-263-0674/5; www.ccolombia guayaquil.com; Francisco de Orellana, World Trade Center, Tower B, 11th fl); Lago Agrio (☎06-283-0084; Av Quito 1-52); Quito (☎02-222-2486; Av Colón 1133 & Amazonas, 7th fl); Tulcán (☎06-298-0559; Av Manabi 58-087)

**France** Guayaquil (☎04-232-8442; cnr José Mascote 909 & Hurtado); Quito (☎02-294-3800; cnr Leonidas Plaza 127 & Av Patria)

**Germany** Guayaquil (☎04-220-6867/8; cnr Avs Las Monjas 10 & CJ Arosemena, Km 2.5, Edificio Berlín); Quito (☎02-297-0820; Naciones Unidas E10-44 at República de El Salvador, Edificio Citiplaza, 12th fl)

**Ireland** (☎2-357-0156; cnr Yanacocha N72-64 & Juan Procel, Quito)

**Netherlands** (☎02-222-9229; www.embajadade holanda.com; cnr Av 12 de Octubre 1942 & Cordero, World Trade Center, Tower 1, 1st fl, Quito)

**Peru** Guayaquil (☎04-228-0114; www.consuladoperu guayaquil.com; Av Francisco de Orellana 501); Loja (☎07-257-9068; Sucre 10-56); Machala (☎07-293-0680; cnr Bolívar & Colón); Quito (☎02-246-8410; www.embajadadelperu.org.ec; cnr República de El Salvador N34-361 & Irlanda)

**UK** Guayaquil (☎04-256-0400; cnr Córdova 623 & Padre Solano); Quito (☎02-297-0800; http://ukinecuador.fco. gov.uk/en; cnr Naciones Unidas & República de El Salvador, Edificio Citiplaza, 14th fl)

**USA** Guayaquil (☎04-232-3570; http://guayaquil.uscon sulate.gov; cnr 9 de Octubre & García Moreno); Quito (☎02-398-5000; http://ecuador. usembassy.gov; cnr Av Avigiras E12-170 & Eloy Alfaro)

# Food

Throughout this book we've used the following price ranges, based on the cost of a standard main course. Unless otherwise stated, the tax (12%) and service charge (10%) is not included in the price.

| PRICE RANGE | SYMBOL | BUDGET |
| --- | --- | --- |
| Budget | $ | < $7 |
| Mid-range | $$ | $7–14 |
| Top End | $$$ | > $14 |

# Gay & Lesbian Travelers

Same-sex couples traveling in Ecuador should be wary of showing affection when in public. All same-sex civil unions were recently enshrined in the new 2008 constitution, and for most Ecuadorians gay rights remains a non-issue in a political context. But homosexuality was technically illegal until 1998, and antigay bias still exists.

Several fiestas in Ecuador have parades with men cross-dressing as women. This is all meant in fun, rather than as an open acceptance of sexual alternatives, but it does provide the public at large (both gay and straight) a popular cultural situation in which to enjoy themselves in an accepting environment.

## Useful Websites and Organizations

**Gay Ecuador** (www.gayecua dor.com)

**Gay Guide to Quito** (http://quito.queercity.info)

**FEDAEPS** (☎02-290-4242; www.fedaeps.org; Av La Coruñ N28 near Bello Horizonte, Quito) A community center for lesbian, gay, bisexual and transsexual people, as well as an AIDS-activist organization.

**Zenith Travel** (☎02-252-9993; www.galapagosgay.com; cnr Juan Leon Mera N24-264 & Luis Cordero, Quito) Specializes in gay and lesbian tours.

# Health

Medical care is usually available in major cities, but may be quite difficult to find in rural areas. Most doctors and hospitals will expect payment in cash, regardless of whether you have travel health insurance. Pharmacies in Ecuador are known as *farmacias*.

# Environmental Hazards

## ALTITUDE SICKNESS

Altitude sickness may develop in travelers who ascend rapidly to altitudes greater than 2500m, including those flying directly to Quito. Symptoms may include headaches, nausea, vomiting, dizziness, malaise, insomnia and loss of appetite. Severe cases may be complicated by fluid in the lungs (high-altitude pulmonary edema) or swelling of the brain (high-altitude cerebral edema). Most deaths are caused by high-altitude pulmonary edema.

To lessen the chance of getting altitude sickness, ascend gradually to higher altitudes, avoid overexertion, eat light meals and avoid alcohol.

## Infectious Diseases

### CHOLERA

This is the worst of the watery diarrheas, and medical help should be sought. Outbreaks of cholera are generally widely reported, so you can avoid problem areas. Fluid replacement is the most vital treatment – the risk of dehydration is severe, as you may lose up to 20L a day. If there is a delay in getting to a hospital, then begin taking tetracycline. The adult dose is 250mg four times daily.

### DENGUE FEVER

Unlike the malaria mosquito, the *Aedes aegypti* mosquito, which transmits the dengue virus, is most active during the day and is found mainly in urban areas, in and around human dwellings.

Signs and symptoms of dengue fever include a sudden onset of high fever, headache, joint and muscle pains (hence its old name, 'breakbone fever'), and nausea and vomiting. Seek medical attention as soon as possible.

## HEALTH ADVICE

It's usually a good idea to consult your government's travel health website before departure (if one is available):

» **Australia** (www.smarttraveller.gov.au)
» **Canada** (www.travelhealth.gc.ca)
» **UK** (www.nhs.uk/LiveWell/TravelHealth)
» **USA** (www.nc.cdc.gov/travel)

### MALARIA

Malaria is transmitted by mosquito bites, usually between dusk and dawn. The main symptom is high-spiking fevers, often accompanied by chills, sweats, headache, body aches, weakness, vomiting or diarrhea. Severe cases may involve the central nervous system and lead to seizures, confusion, coma and death.

Taking malaria pills is recommended for all rural areas below 1500m. Risk is highest along the northernmost coast and in the northern Oriente. There is no malaria risk in the highlands.

### TYPHOID

A dangerous gut infection, typhoid fever is caused by contaminated water and food. Medical help must be sought.

In its early stages, sufferers may feel they have a bad cold or flu on the way, as initial symptoms are a headache, body aches and a fever that rises a little each day until it is around 40°C (104°F) or more. The victim's pulse is often slow relative to the degree of fever present – unlike a normal fever, during which the pulse increases. There may also be vomiting, abdominal pain, diarrhea or constipation.

### YELLOW FEVER

This viral disease is endemic in South America and is transmitted by mosquitoes. The initial symptoms are fever, headache, abdominal pain and vomiting. Seek medical care urgently and drink lots of fluids. If you're traveling into the Amazon, you should definitely get a vaccine (highly effective and good for 10 years) prior to departure.

## Insurance

In addition to health insurance and car insurance (see p385), a policy that protects baggage and valuables, such as cameras and camcorders, is a good idea. Keep your insurance records separate from other possessions in case you have to make a claim.

Worldwide travel insurance is available at www.lonelyplanet.com/travel_services. You can buy, extend and claim online anytime – even if you're already on the road.

## Internet Access

Internet cafes are widespread in Ecuador, with reasonably fast connections that cost around $1 an hour. Many hotels have a computer or two for guest use, with prices varying wildly. Accommodations options in this book that have a computer for internet access are labeled with the @ symbol.

Wi-fi is slowly becoming more common, with guesthouses in Quito, Guayaquil and Cuenca leading the way. The symbol 🛜 indicates where wi-fi is available.

For useful websites, see p17.

## Language Courses

Ecuador is one of the best places to study Spanish in South America. Ecuadorian Spanish is clear and precise, and similar to Mexican and Central American Spanish, and rates are cheap. Quito (p62) and Cuenca (p170) are the best places to study, and both have a plethora of language schools. Expect to pay between $6 and $10 per hour for private lessons. Accommodations with local families can be arranged. There are also schools in Baños (p143) and Otavalo (p94) if you want a more small-town experience.

## Legal Matters

Drug penalties in Ecuador for possession of even small amounts of illegal drugs are much stricter than those in the USA or Europe. Defendants often spend many months in jail before they are brought to trial, and if convicted (as is usually the case), they can expect several years in jail.

Drivers should carry their passport, as well as their driver's license. In the event of an accident, unless it's extremely minor, the vehicles should stay where they are until the police arrive and make a report. This is essential for all insurance claims. If the accident results in injury and you are unhurt, you should take the victim to obtain medical help, particularly in the case of a pedestrian accident. You are legally responsible for a pedestrian's injuries and will be jailed unless you pay, even if the accident was not your fault. Drive defensively.

### Coming of Age

Voting: 16
Drinking: 18
Driving: 18

## Money

Ecuador's official currency is the US dollar. Aside from Euros, Peruvian *soles* and Colombian *nuevos soles*, it's very difficult to change foreign currencies in Ecuador. Western Union offices are in most big cities.

For exchange rates, see p17.

### ATMs

ATMs are the easiest way of getting cash. They're found in most cities and even in smaller towns, though they are occasionally out of order. Make sure you have a four-digit Personal Identification Number (PIN); many Ecuadorian ATMs don't recognize longer ones. Bancos del Pacífico and Bancos del Pichincha have MasterCard/Cirrus ATMs. Bancos de Guayaquil and Bancos La Provisora have Visa/Plus ATMs.

### Cash

US dollars are the official currency; they are identical to those issued in the USA. Coins of one, five, 10, 25 and 50 cents are identical in shape, size and color as their US equivalents, but bear images of famous Ecuadorians. Both US and Ecuadorian coins are used in Ecuador. The $1 'Sacajawea' coin is widely used.

The biggest problem when it comes to cash is finding change. It can be hard to cash a $20 bill even in big cities. No one ever has *sueltos* (literally 'loose ones,' meaning 'change'), so change your bills when you can. Try to avoid bringing bills higher than $20.

### Credit Cards

Credit cards are great as backup. Visa, MasterCard and Diners Club are the most widely accepted cards. First-class restaurants, hotels, souvenir shops and travel agencies usually accept MasterCard or Visa. Small hotels, restaurants and stores don't. Even if an establishment has a credit-card sticker in the window, don't assume that credit cards are accepted. In Ecuador, merchants accepting credit cards will often add between 4% and 10% to the bill. Paying cash is often better value.

### Moneychangers

It is best to change money in the major cities of Quito, Guayaquil and Cuenca, where rates are best. Because banks have limited hours (see p372), *casas de cambio* (currency-exchange bureaus) are sometimes the only option for changing money. They are usually open 9am to 6pm Monday to Friday and until at least noon on Saturday.

### Tipping

Better restaurants add a 12% tax and a 10% service charge to the bill. If the service has been satisfactory, add another 5% for the waiter. Cheaper places don't include a tax or service charge.

To tip your server, do so directly – don't just leave the money on the table.

Taxi drivers are not normally tipped, but you can leave them the small change from a metered ride.

Guides are usually paid low wages, and tips are greatly appreciated. If you go on a guided tour, a tip is expected. If you are in a group, tip a top-notch guide about $5 per person per day. Tip the driver about half that. If you hire a private guide, tip about $10 per day.

If you are going on a long tour that involves guides, cooks and crew (eg the Galápagos Islands), tip about $25 to $50 per client per week, and distribute among all the personnel.

## Post

Ecuador's postal service is reliable. Allow one to two weeks for a letter or package to reach its destination. Courier services including FedEx, DHL and UPS are readily available in sizable towns, but the service is costly.

## Public Holidays

On major holidays, banks, offices and other services close. Transportation gets crowded, so buy bus tickets in advance. Major holidays are sometimes celebrated for several days around the actual date. If an official public holiday falls on a weekend, offices may be closed on the nearest Friday or Monday.

**New Year's Day** January 1.

**Epiphany** January 6.

**Semana Santa** (Easter Week) March/April.

**Labor Day** May 1.

**Battle of Pichincha** May 24. This honors the decisive battle of independence from Spain in 1822.

**Simón Bolívar's Birthday** July 24.

**Quito Independence Day** August 10.

**Guayaquil Independence Day** October 9. This combines with the October 12 national holiday and is an important festival in Guayaquil.

**Columbus Day/Día de la Raza** October 12.

**All Saints' Day** November 1.

**Day of the Dead** (All Souls' Day) November 2. Celebrated by flower-laying ceremonies in cemeteries.

**Cuenca Independence Day** November 3. Combines with the national holidays of November 1 and 2 to give Cuenca its most important fiesta of the year.

**Christmas Eve** December 24.

**Christmas Day** December 25.

See p21 for details of festivals and events around the country.

# Safe Travel

Don't be overly paranoid; most unpleasant incidents can be avoided by using common sense. No matter where you travel, it's wise to get some travel insurance; see p375 for more information.

## Drugs

Imbibing illegal drugs such as marijuana and cocaine can either land you in jail, land your money in the hands of a thief, or worse. Unless you are willing to take these risks, avoid illegal drugs.

Lonely Planet has received a couple of letters from travelers who were unwittingly drugged and robbed after accepting food from a stranger.

## Robbery

Long-distance, nighttime bus robberies occasionally occur, and have been reported in the province of Guayas, in the area surrounding Guayaquil; and on buses between Quito and Riobamba. If you can take a day bus to avoid the risk.

If it can be avoided, do not carry valuables on day hikes, especially in areas commonly visited by tourists. Armed attacks have been reported on the hikes near Baños (central highlands). Robberies have also occurred on the trails near Vilcabamba (southern highlands).

Hotel rooms near bus stations will often save you a couple bucks, but can be dangerous and often double as brothels.

If you are driving a car in Ecuador, never park it unattended. Never leave valuables in sight in the car – even attended cars will have their windows smashed by hit-and-run merchants.

On the off chance you are robbed, you should file a police report as soon as possible. This is a requirement for any insurance claim, although it is unlikely that the police will be able to recover the property.

## Scams

Be wary of false or crooked police. Plainclothes 'policemen' may produce official-looking documents, but always treat these with suspicion, or simply walk away with a smile and a shrug. On the other hand, a uniformed official who asks to see your passport in broad daylight in the middle of a busy street is probably just doing their job.

## Theft

Armed robbery is rare in Ecuador, although parts of Quito and some coastal areas are dangerous. Specific information is given in the appropriate regional chapters of this book.

Sneak theft is more common, and you should always watch your back (and back pockets) in busy bus stations, on crowded city buses and in bustling markets. Theft on buses is common, especially on nighttime trips and journeys between Quito, Latacunga, Baños and Riobamba in the central highlands. All of these places are worked by bag-slashers and pickpockets. But you can avoid playing victim to them by being smart.

It's wise to carry a wallet with a small amount of spending money in your front pocket and keep the important stuff hidden in your money pouch beneath your clothes.

Leaving money in the hotel safe deposit boxes is usually reliable, but make sure that it is in a sealed, taped envelope. A few readers have reported a loss of money from deposit boxes in the cheaper hotels.

## Trouble Spots

Due to the armed conflict in neighboring Colombia, areas along the Colombian border (particularly in the northern Oriente) can be dangerous. Tours into the Oriente are generally safe, but there have been a few isolated incidents of armed robbery.

# Telephone

For important nationwide numbers see p17. Travelers who aren't sporting mobile phones can find a *centro de llamada* (telephone call center) in larger towns, though it's often cheaper to make international calls through internet cafes, most of which have terminals equipped with Skype; many also have separate phone booths with net-to-phone service (international per-minute rates starting around 10 cents).

Public street phones are also common. Some use phonecards, which are sold in convenient places such as newsagents. Others accept only coins. All but the most basic hotels will allow you to make local city calls.

Hotels that provide international phone connections very often surcharge extremely heavily.

All telephone numbers in Ecuador have seven digits, and the first digit – except for cellular phone numbers – is always a '2.' If someone gives you a six-digit number (which sometimes happens), simply put a '2' in front of it.

## Cell Phones & Ecuadorian Networks

Cellular telephone numbers in Ecuador are always preceded by ☑09 or 08. As far as bringing your own phone, GSM cell phones operating at 850MHz (GSM 850) will work on Claro and Movistar networks. Alegro uses 1900MHz (GSM 1900). The cheapest way of staying connected is to purchase a SIM card (called a 'chip', and costing around $5 to $7) from one of the above networks. Add credit by purchasing a phone card (*tarjeta prepago*) with your chosen carrier; these are available at convenience stores, supermarkets and pharmacies.

## Phone Codes

Two-digit area codes beginning with '0' are used throughout Ecuador; these are provided beneath each destination heading in this book. Area codes are not dialed if calling from within that area code, unless dialing from a cellular phone.

Ecuador's country code is ☎593. To call a number in Ecuador from abroad, call your international access code, Ecuador's country code, the area code *without* the 0, and the seven-digit local telephone number.

## Time

The Ecuadorian mainland is five hours behind Greenwich Mean Time, and the Galápagos are six hours behind. Mainland time here is equivalent to Eastern Standard Time in North America. When it's noon in Quito, it's noon in New York, 5pm in London and 4am (daylight-saving time) in Melbourne. Because of Ecuador's location on the equator, days and nights are of equal length year-round, and there is no daylight-saving time.

## Toilets

As throughout South America, Ecuadorian plumbing has very low pressure, and putting toilet paper into the bowl is a serious no-no anywhere except in the fanciest hotels. Always put your used toilet paper in the basket (it's better than a clogged and overflowing toilet!). A well-run cheap hotel will ensure that the receptacle is emptied and the toilet cleaned daily.

Public toilets are limited mainly to bus terminals, airports and restaurants. Lavatories are called *servicios higiénicos* and are usually marked 'SS.HH.' You can simply ask to use the *baño* (bathroom) in a restaurant. Toilet paper is rarely available, so the experienced traveler always carries a personal supply. Remember 'M' on the door means *mujeres* (women) not 'men.' Men's toilets are signed with an 'H' for *hombres* (men) or a 'C' for *caballeros* (gentlemen).

## Tourist Information

Ecuador's system of government-run tourist offices is hit or miss, but is getting better. Tourist information in Quito and Cuenca is excellent.

The government-run **Ministerio de Turismo** (http://ecuador.travel) is responsible for tourist information at the national level. Many towns have some form of municipal or provincial tourist office. The quality of information you'll get depends entirely on the enthusiasm of the person behind the desk. Most of the time, the staff is good at answering the majority of questions.

An excellent resource, especially once you've arrived in Ecuador, is **South American Explorers** (SAE; ☎02-222-5228; www.saexplorers.org; cnr Jorge Washington 311 & Leonidas Plaza Gutiérrez, Quito; ⏰9:30am-5pm Mon-Fri, to noon Sat; @🛜), a member-supported nonprofit organization with clubhouses in Quito; Lima and Cuzco in Peru; Buenos Aires; and a head office in Ithaca, New York. The clubhouses function as information centers for travelers, adventurers, researchers etc, and provide a wealth of advice about traveling in Latin America.

Annual SAE membership is $60/90 per individual/couple. Membership includes the use of all clubhouses, plus quarterly issues of the informative *South American Explorer* magazine. The Quito clubhouse has a lending library; maps; trip reports left by other travelers; luggage storage; reading and TV rooms; current advice about travel conditions; volunteer information; a notice board; regularly scheduled presentations and excursions; and other services.

## Travelers with Disabilities

Unfortunately, Ecuador's infrastructure for disabled travelers is virtually nonexistent. Wheelchair ramps are few and far between, and sidewalks are often badly potholed and cracked. Bathrooms and toilets are often too small for wheelchairs. Signs in Braille or telephones for the hearing impaired are practically unheard of.

Nevertheless, Ecuadorians with disabilities get around, mainly through the help of others. It's not particularly unusual to see travelers with disabilities being carried onto a bus, for example. Buses are (legally) supposed to carry travelers with disabilities for free. Local city buses, which are already overcrowded, won't do that, but long-distance city buses sometimes do. Travelers with disabilities are also eligible for 50% discounts on domestic airfares.

When it comes to hotels, the only truly accessible rooms are found at the international chain hotels in Quito and Guayaquil.

## Visas

Most travelers entering Ecuador as tourists, including citizens of Australia, New Zealand, Japan, the EU, Canada and the USA, do not require visas. Upon entry, they will be issued a T-3 embarkation card valid for 90 days. Residents from a handful of African and Asian countries (including China) require visas.

All travelers entering as diplomats, students, laborers, religious workers, businesspeople, volunteers and cultural-exchange visitors require nonimmigrant visas.

Various immigrant visas are also available.

All (nontourist) visa holders must register at the **Dirección General de Extranjería** (☎02-225-3082; Av Gaspar de Villaroel E10-288 nr 6 de Diciembre, edificio Karina; ◷8:30am-4:30pm Mon-Fri) in Quito within 30 days of arrival in Ecuador. If visa holders wish to leave the country and return, they need a *salida* (exit) form from the Jefatura Provincial de Migración, which can be used for multiple exits and re-entries. Visa holders who apply for residency need to get an exit permit from the immigration authorities in Quito before they leave the country.

### Stay Extensions

New regulations mean it's a real headache getting visa extensions. Unless you're from an Andean Pact country, tourist visas are not extendable. If you wish to stay longer than 90 days, you'll need to apply for a 12-IX Visa; you can also do this while in Ecuador, though it's more time-consuming than doing it in advance through an Ecuadorian consulate in your home country. Pick up the necessary paperwork for the 12-IX Visa, and pay the $230 fee at the **Ministerio de Relaciones Exteriores** (☎02-299-3200; www.mmrree. gob.ec; Carrión E1-76 & Av 10 de Agosto, Quito).

No matter what, don't wait until your visa has expired to sort out your paperwork, as the fine for overstaying can be hefty – $200 to $2000.

# Volunteering

Numerous organizations look for the services of volunteers, however the vast majority require at least a minimal grasp of Spanish, a minimum commitment of several weeks or months, as well as fees (anywhere from $10 per day to $700 per month) to cover the costs of room and board. Volunteers can work

in conservation programs, help street kids, teach, build nature trails, construct websites, do medical or agricultural work – the possibilities are endless. Many jungle lodges also accept volunteers for long-term stays. To keep your volunteer costs down, your best bet is to look when you get to Ecuador.

South American Explorers (see p378) in Quito has a volunteer section where current offerings are posted. The clubhouse itself often needs volunteers. The classifieds section on **Ecuador Explorer** (www.ecuadorexplorer.com) has a long list of organizations seeking volunteers.

Volunteer organizations in Ecuador:

**AmaZOOnico** (www. amazoonico.org) Accepts volunteers for the animal rehabilitation sector.

**Andean Bear Conservation Project** (www.andean bear.org) Trains volunteers as bear trackers.

**Bosque Nublado Santa Lucia** (www.santaluciaecua dor.com) Community-based ecotourism project in the cloud forests of northwest Ecuador. It regularly contracts volunteers to work in reforestation, trail maintenance, construction, teaching English and more.

**FEVI** (Fund for Intercultural Education & Community Volunteer Service; www.fevi.org) FEVI works with children, the elderly, women's groups and indigenous communities throughout Ecuador.

**Fundación Arte del Mundo** (www.artedelmun doecuador.com) Baños afterschool arts and reading program with volunteer opportunities. Volunteers are required to pay a $170 per month fee, which includes a place to stay. There is a one-month minimum.

**Fundación Natura** (www. fnatura.org) Ecuadorian nongovernment organization (NGO) that regularly hires Spanish-speaking volunteers

to work in research, reforestation and more.

**Galápagos Organic Rescue** (www.galapagosor ganicrescue.org) Planting crops, removing invasive species and reforestation.

**Inti Sisa** (www.intisisa.org) In Guamote, this hostel has info on volunteer opportunities in early childhood education.

**Junto con los Niños** (www. juconi.org.ec) Organization that works with street kids in the slum areas of Guayaquil. One-month minimum preferred.

**Merazonia** (www.merazonia. org) A central highlands refuge for injured animals. See p148 for more information.

**Mindo Animal Rescue** (www.mindoanimalrescue. com) Accepts volunteers to help look after the animals, as well as help out with farming.

**New Era Galápagos Foundation** (www.neweragalapa gos.org) Nonprofit offering volunteerships focused on community empowerment and sustainable tourism in the Galápagos. Volunteers live and work on Isla San Cristóbal.

**Rainforest Concern** (www. rainforestconcern.org; www. aventure.co.uk) British nonprofit organization offering volunteer positions in forest environments in Ecuador.

**Reserva Biológica Los Cedros** (www.reservaloscedros. org) This biological reserve in the cloud forests of the western Andean slopes often needs volunteers. Also see p105.

**Río Muchacho Organic Farm** (www.riomuchacho. com) Coastal ecotourism project offering one-month apprenticeships in organic agriculture with volunteer opportunities. Also see p250.

**Yanapuma Foundation** (☎02-290-7643; www.yana puma.org; 2nd fl, Veintimilla E8-125 near Av 6 de Diciembre, Quito) Offers a number of ways for volunteers to get involved: teaching English, building houses in remote communities, helping with reforestation projects or taking part in coastal clean-ups. Stop by its Quito headquarters and language school (p62) for more information.

## Women Travelers

Generally, women travelers will find Ecuador safe and pleasant, despite the fact that machismo is alive and well. Ecuadorian men often make flirtatious comments and whistle at single women, both Ecuadorian and foreigners. Really, it's just sport – a sort of hormonal babbling among groups of guys – and the best strategy is to ignore them.

On the coast, come-ons are more predatory, and solo female travelers should take precautions such as staying away from bars and discos where they'll obviously get hit on, opting for taxis over walking etc.

Lonely Planet has received warnings in the past from women who were molested while on organized tours. If you're traveling solo, it's essential to do some research before committing to a tour: find out who's leading the tour, what other tourists will be on the outing and so on. Women-only travel groups or guides are available in a few situations.

## Work

Ecuador has 10% unemployment and 43% underemployment, so finding work isn't easy. Officially, you need a worker's visa to be allowed to work in Ecuador. Aside from the occasional position at a tourist lodge or expat bar, there is little opportunity for paid work. The one exception is teaching English.

Most paid English-teaching job openings are in Quito and Guayaquil. Schools sometimes advertise for teachers on the bulletin boards of hotels and restaurants. Pay is just enough to live on unless you've acquired a full-time position from home. If you have a bona-fide teaching credential, so much the better. Schools such as the American School in Quito will often hire teachers of mathematics, biology and other subjects, and may help you get a work visa. They also pay much better than the language schools. Check ads in local hotels and newspapers. One of the best online English-teaching resources, complete with job boards, is **Dave's ESL Café** (www.eslcafé.com).

# Transportation

## GETTING THERE & AWAY

### Entering the Country

Entering the country is straightforward, and border officials, especially at the airports, efficiently whisk you through. At land borders, officers may take a little more time examining your passport, if only to kill time. Officially, you need proof of onward travel and evidence of sufficient funds for your stay, but this is rarely requested. Proof of $20 per day or a credit card is usually evidence of sufficient funds. However, international airlines flying to Quito may require a round-trip or onward ticket or a residence visa before they let you on the plane; you should be prepared for this possibility, though it's unlikely. Though not law, you may be required to show proof of vaccination against yellow fever if you are entering Ecuador from an infected area.

Flights, tours and rail tickets can all be booked online at www.lonelyplanet.com/bookings.

### Passport

All nationals entering as tourists need a passport that is valid for at least six months after arrival. You are legally required to have your passport on you at all times. Many people carry only a copy when they're hanging around a town, though this is not an officially acceptable form of ID. For visa requirements, see p378.

## Air

### Airports & Airlines

About 20km east of Quito, a new international airport is scheduled to open in late 2013. Check www.quiport.com for the latest details.

Currently, two international airports serve Ecuador: Quito's **Aeropuerto Mariscal Sucre** (UIO, ☎02-294-4900; www.quitoairport.com; Av Amazonas at Av de la Prensa) and Guayaquil's **Aeropuerto José Joaquín de Olmedo** (GYE; ☎04-216-9000; www.tagsa.aero; Av de las Américas s/n).

**TAME** (www.tame.com.ec) and **Aerogal** (www.aerogal.com.ec) are Ecuador's main airlines, but offer limited international flights. Aerogal has an impressive safety record; TAME less-so, though it's been in the process of upgrading its fleet in recent years.

See p383 for more details on domestic flights.

The following international airlines serve Ecuador. Unless otherwise noted, the telephone numbers given are for Quito offices.

**Aeropostal Alas de Venezuela** (airline code VH; ☎02-226-4392; www.aeropostal.com; hub Caracas, Venezuela)

**Air Europa** (airline code UX; ☎02-256-7646; www.aireuropa.com; hub Madrid, Spain)

## CLIMATE CHANGE & TRAVEL

Every form of transport that relies on carbon-based fuel generates $CO_2$, the main cause of human-induced climate change. Modern travel is dependent on airplanes, which might use less fuel per kilometer per person than most cars but travel much greater distances. The altitude at which aircraft emit gases (including $CO_2$) and particles also contributes to their climate change impact. Many websites offer 'carbon calculators' that allow people to estimate the carbon emissions generated by their journey and, for those who wish to do so, to offset the impact of the greenhouse gases emitted with contributions to portfolios of climate-friendly initiatives throughout the world. Lonely Planet offsets the carbon footprint of all staff and author travel.

**Air France** (airline code AF; 02-222-4818; www.airfrance.com; hub Paris, France)

**American Airlines** (airline code AA; 02-299-5000; www.aa.com; hubs Dallas, TX & Chicago, IL, USA)

**Avianca** (airline code AV; 02-330-1379; www.avianca.com; hub Bogotá, Colombia)

**Continental Airlines** (airline code CO; 02-225-0905; www.continental.com; hub Houston, TX & Newark, NJ, USA)

**Copa** (airline code CM; 02-227-3082; www.copaair.com; hub Panama City, Panama)

**Iberia** (airline code IB; 02-256 6009; www.iberia.com; hub Madrid, Spain)

**KLM** (airline code KL; 02-396-6728; www.klm.com; hub Amsterdam, Holland)

**LAN Airlines** (airline code LA; 1800-10-1075; www.lanchile.com; hub Santiago, Chile)

**Lufthansa** (airline code LH; 02-254-1300, 250-8396; www.lufthansa.com; hub Cologne, Germany)

**Santa Bárbara Airlines** (airline code S3; 380-0082; www.sbairlines.com; hub Caracas, Venezuela)

**TACA** (airline code TA; 1800-00-8222; www.taca.com; hub San Salvador, El Salvador)

## Tickets

Ticket prices are highest during tourist high seasons: mid-June through early September, and December through mid-January. Working with a travel agent that deals specifically in Latin American travel is always an advantage.

Departure tax is now included in ticket prices rather than payable at the airport.

## Land

### Border Crossings

Peru and Colombia are the only countries sharing borders with Ecuador. If you are entering or leaving Ecuador, border formalities are straightforward if your documents are in order. No taxes are levied on tourists when entering or exiting overland.

If you're leaving the country and have lost your embarkation card (see p378), you should be able to get a free replacement at the border, assuming the stamp in your passport has not expired. If your documents aren't in order, one of two things might happen. If you've overstayed the allowed time, you'll have to pay a hefty fine or you will be sent back to Quito. If you don't have an *entrada* (entrance) stamp, you will also be sent back.

### COLOMBIA

The main border crossing to Colombia is via Tulcán (p111) in the northern highlands, currently the only safe place to cross into Colombia. The border crossing north of Lago Agrio (p202) in the Oriente is unsafe due to smuggling and conflict in Colombia.

### PERU

There are three important border posts connecting Ecuador and Peru.

**Huaquillas** (p295) This crossing, south of Machala, gets most of the international traffic between the two countries. It's very busy, and you'll need to be on guard as some travelers have been robbed by taxi drivers.

**Macará** (p195) Increasingly popular because it's more relaxed than the Huaquillas crossing, and the journey from Loja (p181) in the southern highlands is beautiful. Direct buses run between Loja and Piura, Peru (eight hours) via Macará, and wait for you at the border while you take care of formalities; it's easy.

**La Balsa at Zumba** (p193) South of Vilcabamba (p189), this little-used crossing is remote and interest-ing and gets little traffic. People often hang out in Vilcabamba for a few days before heading to Zumba and Peru.

### Bus

Bussing into Ecuador from Colombia or Peru is straightforward and usually requires walking across one of the earlier mentioned international borders and catching another bus once you're across. Some international bus companies offer direct, long-haul services from major cities such as Lima and Bogotá.

### Car & Motorcycle

Driving a private vehicle into Ecuador can be a huge hassle, depending largely upon the mood of the official who stops you at the border. To bring your car into Ecuador, you are officially required to have a Carnet de Passage en Douane (CPD), an internationally recognized customs document that allows you to temporarily 'import' a vehicle into Ecuador without paying an import tax. The document is issued through an automobile club in the country where the car is registered, and you are strongly advised to obtain one well in advance. Motorcycles seem to present fewer hassles at the border.

## River

Since the 1998 peace treaty was signed with Peru, it has been possible to travel down the Río Napo from Ecuador to Peru, joining the Amazon near Iquitos. The border facilities are minimal, and the boats doing the journey are infrequent, but it is possible to do the trip – see p213. It is also geographically possible to travel down Río Putumayo into Colombia and Peru, but this is a dangerous region because of drug smuggling and terrorism, and is not recommended.

# GETTING AROUND

Ecuador has an efficient transportation system, and because of its small size you can usually get most places fairly easily.

## Air

### Airlines in Ecuador

Ecuador's most important domestic airline is TAME, followed by Aerogal and a few small regional lines. In addition to domestic flights, TAME flies twice weekly between Guayaquil and Manaos (Manaus), Brazil and operates daily flights from Tulcán to Cali, Colombia. TAME also had plans to operate daily flights between Lima, Peru and Guayaquil. Aerogal flies to Bogotá, Colombia, from both Quito and Guayaquil. It also flies Quito to Medellín, and Quito to Miami. All of the Ecuadorian airlines enjoy safety records on par with most world airlines, although TAME has had more incidents than Aerogal.

With the exception of flying to the Galápagos Islands, internal flights are generally fairly cheap, rarely exceeding $90 for a one-way ticket. All mainland flights are under an hour and often provide you with incredible views over the Andes.

Flights to most destinations originate in Quito or Guayaquil only. Detailed flight information is given under the appropriate cities throughout this book. The following are Ecuador's passenger airlines with their reservation numbers in Quito:

**Aerogal** (☎1800-237-6425; www.aerogal.com.ec) Serves Quito, Guayaquil, Cuenca, Isla Baltra (Galápagos), Isla San Cristóbal (Galápagos), Manta, plus Bogotá (Colombia), Medellín (Colombia), and Miami (USA).

**Emetebe** (☎09-932-2907; www.emetebe.com) Galápagos-based airline that flies between Isla Baltra, Isla San Cristóbal and Isla Isabela. Also flies from Quito via Guayaquil to Baltra and San Cristóbal.

**LAN** (☎02-330-1484; www.lan.com) Flies from Quito to Cuenca, Guayaquil and the Galápagos (San Cristóbal and Isla Baltra, both via Guayaquil).

**Saero** (☎02-330-1152; www.saereo.com) Serves south-

## Internal Air Services

ern destinations (including Macas and Santa Rosa, near Machala) from Quito and/or Guayaquil.

**TAME** (☏02-396-6300; www. tame.com.ec) Serves Coca, Cuenca, Esmeraldas, Isla Baltra (Galápagos), Isla San Cristóbal (Galápagos), Guayaquil, Lago Agrio, Loja, Macas, Manta, Portoviejo, Quito, Tulcán, plus Cali (Colombia) and Manaos (Brazil).

## Bicycle

Cycling in the Andes is strenuous, not only because of hill climbs but because of the altitudes. Other challenges: road rules are few, bike lanes are nonexistent and some roads are in poor shape (though infrastructure countrywide is dramatically improving). Mountain bikes are recommended, as road bikes don't stand up to the poor road quality.

Bike shops are scarce outside of Quito, and those that do exist usually have a very limited selection of parts. Bring all important spare parts and tools from home. For mountain-biking destinations in Ecuador, see p33. The country's best mountain-bike tour operators are in Quito (p61) and Riobamba (p155).

### Hire

Renting bikes is mainly for short tours, mostly from Quito, Riobamba, Cuenca and Baños.

## Boat

Boat transportation is common in Ecuador and can be divided into several types.

### Canoe

The most common boat is the motorized canoe, which acts as a water taxi or bus along the major rivers of the Oriente (especially on the Río Napo) and parts of the northern coast. Most people

experience this novel form of transport during a tour in the Amazon, as motorized canoes are often the only way to a rainforest lodge.

These canoes often carry as many as three-dozen passengers. Generally, they're long in shape and short on comfort. Seating is normally on hard, low wooden benches which accommodate two people each. The most important piece of advice: *bring seat padding.* A folded sweater or towel will make a world of difference on the trip.

### Other Boats

In the Galápagos, you have a choice of traveling in anything from a small sailboat to a cruise ship complete with air-conditioned cabins and private bathrooms. Passenger ferries run infrequently between the islands, offering the cheapest means of inter-island transport. Only folks traveling around the islands independently (ie not on a cruise) need consider these (see p332).

In addition to the dugout canoes of the Oriente, one cruise ship, *Amazon Manatee Explorer,* makes relatively luxurious passages down Río Napo (see p65).

## Bus

In terms of scope and affordability, Ecuador's bus system is impressive to say the least. Buses are the primary means of transport for most Ecuadorians, guaranteed to go just about anywhere. They can be exciting, cramped, comfy, smelly, fun, scary, sociable and grueling, depending on your state of mind, where you're going and who's driving.

To be blunt: many Ecuadorian bus drivers are maniacs – they pass on blind turns, they ride the air brakes till they smoke, they hit the gas going downhill and they race other buses for fun.

Most major cities have a main *terminal terrestre* (bus terminal), although some towns have a host of private terminals – and you'll have to go to the right one to catch the bus going where you need to go. Most stations are within walking distance or a short cab ride from the town's center. Smaller towns are occasionally served by passing buses, in which case you have to walk from the highway into town, usually only a short walk since only the smallest towns lack terminals.

If traveling lightly, take your luggage inside the bus with you. The luggage compartment is sometimes filthy or leaky, so using a protective sack is a good idea (though not crucial if rain is out of the question). Many locals use grain sacks as luggage; you can buy them for a few cents in general stores or markets and toss your bag inside it.

On average, bus journeys cost about $1 per hour of travel. Remember to always have your passport handy when you're going anywhere by bus, as they are sometimes stopped for checks. This is especially true in the Oriente.

### Classes

There are rarely classes to choose from – whatever's available is the class you ride. Most *autobuses* (buses) are nondescript passenger buses (as opposed to school-type buses), and they rarely have a bathroom on board unless they're traveling over about four hours. Some of the long-haul rides between large cities have air-conditioned buses with on-board toilets, but they are few and far between.

### Long-Distance Buses

These usually stop for a 20-minute meal break at the appropriate times. The food in terminal restaurants may be somewhat basic, so if you're a picky eater you should bring food with you.

On remote routes, full buses allow passengers to travel on the roof. This can be fun, with great views but minimal comfort and a certain amount of danger involved – watch out for oncoming obstacles!

## Reservations & Schedules

Most bus companies have scheduled departure times, but these change often and may not always be adhered to. If a bus is full, it might leave early. Conversely, an almost empty bus may spend half an hour *dando vueltas* (driving around), with the driver's assistant yelling out of the door in the hope of attracting more passengers.

The larger terminals often have information booths that can advise you about routes, fares and times.

For rides over four hours, you can usually purchase a ticket a few days in advance at the bus terminal. Except on weekends and during vacations, you'll rarely have trouble getting a ticket but it never hurts to buy one a day in advance or arrive an hour or two early.

## Car & Motorcycle

Driving a car or motorcycle in Ecuador presents its challenges, with potholes, blind turns, and insanely fast bus and truck drivers. The good news is that infrastructure is dramatically improving, with new roads and bridges making road travel much smoother.

## Automobile Associations

Ecuador's automobile association is **Aneta** (☏1800-556-677; www.aneta.org.ec), which offers a few member services to members of foreign automobile clubs including Canadian and US AAA members. It provides 24-hour roadside assistance to Aneta members.

## Driver's License

You are required to have a driver's license from your home country and a passport whenever you're driving. The international driver's license can also come in handy when renting a car (though it's not officially required).

## Fuel

There are two octane ratings for gasoline in Ecuador: 'Extra' (82 octane) and 'Super' (92 octane). Gasoline is sold by the gallon and costs about $1.50 per gallon for Extra and about $2 per gallon for Super; note that the latter is not always available in rural areas. Dirty diesel is available throughout the country.

## Hire

Few people rent cars in Ecuador, mainly because public transport makes getting around so easy. Most of the international car rental companies, including **Avis** (www.avis.com), **Budget** (www.budget.com), **Hertz** (www.hertz.com) and **Localiza** (www.localiza.com.ec), have outlets in Ecuador, but it is difficult to find any agency outside of Quito, Guayaquil or Cuenca.

To rent a car you must be at least 25 years old and have a credit card, a valid driver's license and a passport. Occasionally a company will rent to someone between 21 and 25 years old, though it may require a higher deposit. Typical rates start at around $40 per day for a compact car, but can go over $100 for a 4WD vehicle (high clearance can be a life saver during ventures off the beaten track). Be sure to ask if the quoted rate includes *seguro* (insurance), *kilometraje libre* (unlimited kilometers) and IVA (tax) – most likely it won't.

The best place to hire a motorcycle is in Quito. In the Mariscal, **Freedom** (☏250-4339; www.freedombikerental.com; Mera N22-37; motorbike per day from $39) rents touring and off-road bikes with gear as well as scooters and bicycles.

You can also hire motorbikes in Baños (p140) where 250cc Enduro-type motorcycles are available for about $10 per hour or $40 per day. Riders with their own machines will find helpful information at www.horizonsunlimited.com.

## Insurance

Car-rental companies offer insurance policies on their vehicles but they can carry a hefty deductible – anywhere between $1000 and $3500, depending on the company – so be sure you read the fine print. Even if an accident is not your fault, you will likely be responsible for the deductible in the event of a collision.

## Road Hazards

Hazards in Ecuador include potholes, blind turns and, most obvious of all, bus and truck drivers who pass other buses and trucks at seemingly impossible moments. Always be alert for stopped vehicles, sudden road blocks and occasional livestock on the road. Signage in Ecuador is poor.

## Hitchhiking

Hitchhiking is never entirely safe in any country, and we don't recommend it. Travelers who decide to hitchhike should understand that they are taking a small but potentially serious risk. People who do choose to hitchhike will be safer if they travel in pairs and let someone know where they are planning to go.

Hitching is not very practical in Ecuador for three reasons: there are few private cars, public transportation is relatively cheap and trucks are used as public transportation in remote areas, so trying to hitch a free ride on one is the same as trying to hitch a free ride on a bus. Many drivers of *any* vehicle will pick you up but will also expect payment, usually minimal.

## Local Transportation

### Bus

Local buses are usually slow and crowded, but they are also very cheap. You can get around most towns for $0.20 to $0.25. Local buses often travel to nearby villages, and riding along is a good, inexpensive way to see the area.

Outside of Quito, the concept of a fixed bus stop is pretty much nonexistent. Buses stop (or at least come to a slow roll) when people flag them down. When you want to get off a local bus, yell '*¡Baja!,*' which means 'Down!' (as in 'the passenger is getting down'). Another favorite way of getting the driver to stop is by yelling '*¡Gracias!*' ('Thank you!'), which is unmistakably polite.

### Taxi

Ecuadorian taxis come in a variety of shapes and sizes, but they are all yellow. Most taxis have a lit 'taxi' sign on top or a 'taxi' sticker on the windshield.

Always ask the fare beforehand, or you may be overcharged. Meters are rarely seen, except in Quito where they are obligatory. A long ride in a large city such as Quito or Guayaquil shouldn't go over $5. The minimum fare nearly everywhere is $1, and you'll be required to pay $1 in Quito even if the meter only says $0.80. On weekends and at night, fares are always about 25% to 50% higher.

You can hire a taxi for a day for about $40 to $60. Hiring a taxi for a few days is comparable to renting a car, except that you don't have to drive. But you will have to pay for the driver's food and room. Some tour companies in Quito rent 4WD vehicles with experienced drivers.

In less urban areas, you're also likely to see *ecotaxis* (a three-wheeled bicycle with a small covered carriage in back that fits two people) as well as *taxis ecológicos* (motorcycle taxis with a two-seater carriage in back).

### Truck

In certain towns, especially in rural areas where there are many dirt roads, pickup trucks act as taxis. If you need to get to a national park, a climbers' refuge or a trailhead from a town, often the best way to do so is hiring a pickup, which is usually as easy as asking around.

## Tours

If you're short on time, the best place to organize a tour is Quito. A plethora of operators for every budget offer trips including Galápagos cruises, climbing and hiking tours, horseback-riding, jungle tours, mountain-biking tours, hacienda tours and more.

Tour costs vary tremendously depending on what your requirements are. The cheapest camping jungle tour can be as low as $40 per person per day, while the most expensive lodges can crest $200 per person per night including all meals and tours. Climbs of the volcanoes average about $160 per person for a two-day climb. Galápagos boat cruises range from $800 to over $3000 per week excluding air fare, taxes and entrance fees. Day tours out of Quito range from $25 to $80 per person per day.

## Train

Ecuador's rail system is finally being restored – although travel for the moment remains limited. The most famous line is the dramatic descent from Alausí along La Nariz del Diablo (The Devil's Nose; see the boxed text, p159) a spectacular section of train track that was one of the world's greatest feats of railroad engineering. The second is the weekend train excursion between Quito and the Área Nacional de Recreación El Boliche, near Cotopaxi (see p86). You can also continue all the way down to Latacunga on this line. Trains typically run in the morning from Thursday to Saturday only and are mostly for tourists.

Plans are underway to continue restoring the tracks, and it may someday be possible to travel between Quito and Guayaquil or Cuenca by rail (as it once was in the last century). For the latest info, visit www.trenecuador.com.

## Truck (Ranchera & Chiva)

In remote areas, trucks often double as buses. Sometimes these are large, flatbed trucks with a tin roof, open wooden sides and uncomfortable wooden-plank seats. These curious-looking 'buses' are called *rancheras* or *chivas*, and are seen on the coast and in the Oriente.

In the remote parts of the highlands, *camionetas* (ordinary trucks or pickups) are used to carry passengers; you just climb in the back. If the weather is good, you get fabulous views and the refreshing sensation of Andean wind in your face. If the weather is bad, you hunker down beneath a tarpaulin with the other passengers.

Payment is usually determined by the driver and is a standard fare depending on the distance. You can ask other passengers how much they are paying; trucks typically charge about the same as buses.

# Language

## WANT MORE?

For in-depth language information and handy phrases, check out Lonely Planet's *Latin American Spanish Phrasebook*. You'll find it at **shop.lonelyplanet.com**, or you can buy Lonely Planet's iPhone phrasebooks at the Apple App Store.

Latin American Spanish pronunciation is easy, as most sounds have equivalents in English. Also, Spanish spelling is phonetically consistent, meaning that there's a clear and consistent relationship between what you see in writing and how it's pronounced. Read our coloured pronunciation guides as if they were English, and you'll be understood. Note that kh is a throaty sound (like the 'ch' in the Scottish *loch*), v and b are like a soft English 'v' (between a 'v' and a 'b'), and r is strongly rolled.

There are some variations in spoken Spanish across Latin America, the most notable being the pronunciation of the letters *ll* and *y* – depending on where you are on the continent, you'll hear them pronounced like the 'y' in 'yes', 'lli' in 'million', the 's' in 'measure', the 'sh' in 'shut' or the 'dg' in 'judge'. In our pronunciation guides in this chapter they are represented with y because they are pronounced as the 'y' in 'yes' in Ecuador (as in many other parts of Latin America).

The stressed syllables are indicated with an acute accent in written Spanish (eg *días*) and with italics in our pronunciation guides.

The polite form is used in this chapter; where both polite and informal options are given, they are indicated by the abbreviations 'pol' and 'inf'. Where necessary, both masculine and feminine forms of words are included, separated by a slash and with the masculine form first, eg *perdido/a* (m/f).

## BASICS

| | | |
|---|---|---|
| Hello. | Hola. | o·la |
| Goodbye. | Adiós. | a·dyos |
| How are you? | ¿Qué tal? | ke tal |
| Fine, thanks. | Bien, gracias. | byen gra·syas |
| Excuse me. | Perdón. | per·don |
| Sorry. | Lo siento. | lo syen·to |
| Please. | Por favor. | por fa·vor |
| Thank you. | Gracias. | gra·syas |
| You're welcome. | De nada. | de na·da |
| Yes. | Sí. | see |
| No. | No. | no |

**My name is ...**
Me llamo ...                     me ya·mo ...

**What's your name?**
¿Cómo se llama Usted?   ko·mo se ya·ma oo·ste (pol)
¿Cómo te llamas?           ko·mo te ya·mas (inf)

**Do you speak English?**
¿Habla inglés?               a·bla een·gles (pol)
¿Hablas inglés?             a·blas een·gles (inf)

**I don't understand.**
Yo no entiendo.             yo no en·tyen·do

## ACCOMMODATIONS

| | | |
|---|---|---|
| I'd like a ... room. | Quisiera una habitación ... | kee·sye·ra oo·na a·bee·ta·syon ... |
| single | individual | een·dee·vee·dwal |
| double | doble | do·ble |

**How much is it per night/person?**
¿Cuánto cuesta por       kwan·to kwes·ta por
noche/persona?             no·che/per·so·na

**Does it include breakfast?**
¿Incluye el                     een·kloo·ye el
desayuno?                     de·sa·yoo·no

## KICHWA

Most indigenous groups are bilingual, with Kichwa as their mother tongue and Spanish as second language. The Kichwa spoken in Ecuador is quite different from that of Peru and Bolivia.

The following phrases could be useful in areas where Ecuadorian Kichwa is spoken. Pronounce them as you would a Spanish word. The apostrophe ( ' ) represents a glottal stop, ie the sound that occurs in the middle of 'uh-oh'.

| | |
|---|---|
| Hello. | Napaykullayki. |
| Please. | Allichu. |
| Thank you. | Yusulipayki. |
| Yes./No. | Ari./Mana. |
| How do you say ...? | Imainata nincha chaita ...? |
| It is called ... | Chaipa'g sutin'ha ... |
| Please repeat. | Ua'manta niway. |
| How much? | Maik'ata'g? |
| father | tayta |
| food | mikíuy |
| mother | mama |
| river | mayu |
| snowy peak | riti-orko |
| water | yacu |

| | |
|---|---|
| 1 | u' |
| 2 | iskai |
| 3 | quinsa |
| 4 | tahua |
| 5 | phiska |
| 6 | so'gta |
| 7 | khanchis |
| 8 | pusa'g |
| 9 | iskon |
| 10 | chunca |

| | | |
|---|---|---|
| campsite | terreno de cámping | te·re·no de kam·peeng |
| hotel | hotel | o·tel |
| guesthouse | pensión | pen·syon |
| (small) hotel/ country inn | hostal/ hostería | os·tal/ os·te·ree·a |
| youth hostel | albergue juvenil | al·ber·ge khoo·ve·neel |
| air-con | aire acondi- cionado | ai·re a·kon·dee· syo·na·do |
| bathroom | baño | ba·nyo |
| bed | cama | ka·ma |
| window | ventana | ven·ta·na |

# DIRECTIONS

**Where's ...?**
¿Dónde está ...?    don·de es·ta ...

**What's the address?**
¿Cuál es la dirección?    kwal es la dee·rek·syon

**Could you please write it down?**
¿Puede escribirlo, por favor?    pwe·de es·kree·beer·lo por fa·vor

**Can you show me (on the map)?**
¿Me lo puede indicar (en el mapa)?    me lo pwe·de een·dee·kar (en el ma·pa)

| | | |
|---|---|---|
| at the corner | en la esquina | en la es·kee·na |
| at the traffic lights | en el semáforo | en el se·ma·fo·ro |
| behind ... | detrás de ... | de·tras de ... |
| far | lejos | le·khos |
| in front of ... | enfrente de ... | en·fren·te de ... |
| left | izquierda | ees·kyer·da |
| near | cerca | ser·ka |
| next to ... | al lado de ... | al la·do de ... |
| opposite ... | frente a ... | fren·te a ... |
| right | derecha | de·re·cha |
| straight ahead | todo recto | to·do rek·to |

# EATING & DRINKING

**Can I see the menu, please?**
¿Puedo ver el menú, por favor?    pwe·do ver el me·noo por fa·vor

**What would you recommend?**
¿Qué recomienda?    ke re·ko·myen·da

**Do you have vegetarian food?**
¿Tienen comida vegetariana?    tye·nen ko·mee·da ve·khe·ta·rya·na

**I don't eat (red meat).**
No como (carne roja).    no ko·mo (kar·ne ro·kha)

**That was delicious!**
¡Estaba buenísimo!    es·ta·ba bwe·nee·see·mo

**Cheers!**
¡Salud!    sa·loo

**The bill, please.**
La cuenta, por favor.    la kwen·ta por fa·vor

| | | |
|---|---|---|
| I'd like a table for ... | Quisiera una mesa para ... | kee·sye·ra oo·na me·sa pa·ra ... |
| (eight) o'clock | las (ocho) | las (o·cho) |
| (two) people | (dos) personas | (dos) per·so·nas |

## Key Words

| | | |
|---|---|---|
| bottle | botella | bo·te·ya |
| bowl | bol | bol |

| breakfast | desayuno | de·sa·yoo·no |
|---|---|---|
| children's menu | menú infantil | me·noo een·fan·teel |
| (too) cold | (muy) frío | (mooy) free·o |
| dinner | cena | se·na |
| fork | tenedor | te·ne·dor |
| glass | vaso | va·so |
| highchair | trona | tro·na |
| hot (warm) | caliente | kal·yen·te |
| knife | cuchillo | koo·chee·yo |
| lunch | almuerzo | al·mwer·so |
| plate | plato | pla·to |
| restaurant | restaurante | res·tow·ran·te |
| spoon | cuchara | koo·cha·ra |
| with/without | con/sin | kon/seen |

## Meat & Fish

| beef | carne de vaca | kar·ne de va·ka |
|---|---|---|
| chicken | pollo | po·yo |
| fish | pescado | pes·ka·do |
| lamb | cordero | kor·de·ro |
| pork | cerdo | ser·do |
| turkey | pavo | pa·vo |
| veal | ternera | ter·ne·ra |

## Fruit & Vegetables

| apple | manzana | man·sa·na |
|---|---|---|
| apricot | damasco | da·mas·ko |
| artichoke | alcaucil | al·kow·seel |
| asparagus | espárragos | es·pa·ra·gos |
| banana | banana | ba·na·na |
| beans | chauchas | chow·chas |
| beetroot | remolacha | re·mo·la·cha |
| cabbage | repollo | re·po·yo |
| carrot | zanahoria | sa·na·o·rya |
| celery | apio | a·pyo |
| cherry | cereza | se·re·sa |
| corn | choclo | cho·klo |
| cucumber | pepino | pe·pee·no |
| fruit | fruta | froo·ta |
| grape | uvas | oo·vas |
| lemon | limón | lee·mon |
| lentils | lentejas | len·te·khas |
| lettuce | lechuga | le·choo·ga |
| mushroom | champiñón | cham·pee·nyon |
| nuts | nueces | nwe·ses |
| onion | cebolla | se·bo·ya |

| orange | naranja | na·ran·kha |
|---|---|---|
| peach | melocotón | me·lo·ko·ton |
| peas | arvejas | ar·ve·khas |
| (red/green) pepper | pimiento (rojo/verde) | pee·myen·to (ro·kho/ver·de) |
| pineapple | ananá | a·na·na |
| plum | ciruela | seer·we·la |
| potato | papa | pa·pa |
| pumpkin | zapallo | sa·pa·yo |
| spinach | espinacas | es·pee·na·kas |
| strawberry | frutilla | froo·tee·ya |
| tomato | tomate | to·ma·te |
| vegetable | verdura | ver·doo·ra |
| watermelon | sandía | san·dee·a |

## Other

| bread | pan | pan |
|---|---|---|
| butter | manteca | man·te·ka |
| cheese | queso | ke·so |
| egg | huevo | we·vo |
| honey | miel | myel |
| jam | mermelada | mer·me·la·da |
| oil | aceite | a·sey·te |
| pepper | pimienta | pee·myen·ta |
| rice | arroz | a·ros |
| salt | sal | sal |
| sugar | azúcar | a·soo·kar |
| vinegar | vinagre | vee·na·gre |

## Drinks

| beer | cerveza | ser·ve·sa |
|---|---|---|
| coffee | café | ka·fe |
| (orange) juice | jugo (de naranja) | khoo·go (de na·ran·kha) |
| milk | leche | le·che |
| tea | té | te |

### Signs

| Abierto | Open |
|---|---|
| Cerrado | Closed |
| Entrada | Entrance |
| Hombres/Varones | Men |
| Mujeres/Damas | Women |
| Prohibido | Prohibited |
| Salida | Exit |
| Servicios/Baños | Toilets |

| (mineral) water | agua (mineral) | a·gwa (mee·ne·ral) |
| (red/white) wine | vino (tinto/ blanco) | vee·no (teen·to/ blan·ko) |

## EMERGENCIES

| Help! | ¡Socorro! | so·ko·ro |
| Go away! | ¡Vete! | ve·te |

| Call ...! | ¡Llame a ...! | ya·me a ... |
| a doctor | un médico | oon me·dee·ko |
| the police | la policía | la po·lee·see·a |

**I'm lost.**
Estoy perdido/a.   es·toy per·dee·do/a (m/f)

**I'm ill.**
Estoy enfermo/a.   es·toy en·fer·mo/a (m/f)

**It hurts here.**
Me duele aquí.   me dwe·le a·kee

**I'm allergic to (antibiotics).**
Soy alérgico/a a   soy a·ler·khee·ko/a a
(los antibióticos).   (los an·tee·byo·tee·kos) (m/f)

**Where are the toilets?**
¿Dónde están los   don·de es·tan los
baños?   ba·nyos

## SHOPPING & SERVICES

**I'd like to buy ...**
Quisiera comprar ...   kee·sye·ra kom·prar ...

**I'm just looking.**
Sólo estoy mirando.   so·lo es·toy mee·ran·do

**Can I look at it?**
¿Puedo verlo?   pwe·do ver·lo

**I don't like it.**
No me gusta.   no me goos·ta

**How much is it?**
¿Cuánto cuesta?   kwan·to kwes·ta

**That's too expensive.**
Es muy caro.   es mooy ka·ro

**Can you lower the price?**
¿Podría bajar un   po·dree·a ba·khar oon
poco el precio?   po·ko el pre·syo

**There's a mistake in the bill.**
Hay un error   ai oon e·ror
en la cuenta.   en la kwen·ta

### Question Words

| How? | ¿Cómo? | ko·mo |
| What? | ¿Qué? | ke |
| When? | ¿Cuándo? | kwan·do |
| Where? | ¿Dónde? | don·de |
| Who? | ¿Quién? | kyen |
| Why? | ¿Por qué? | por ke |

| ATM | cajero automático | ka·khe·ro ow·to·ma·tee·ko |
| credit card | tarjeta de crédito | tar·khe·ta de kre·dee·to |
| internet cafe | cibercafé | see·ber·ka·fe |
| market | mercado | mer·ka·do |
| post office | correos | ko·re·os |
| tourist office | oficina de turismo | o·fee·see·na de too·rees·mo |

## TIME & DATES

| What time is it? | ¿Qué hora es? | ke o·ra es |
| It's (10) o'clock. | Son (las diez). | son (las dyes) |
| Half past ... | ... y media. | ... ee me·dya |

| morning | mañana | ma·nya·na |
| afternoon | tarde | tar·de |
| evening | noche | no·che |
| yesterday | ayer | a·yer |
| today | hoy | oy |
| tomorrow | mañana | ma·nya·na |

| Monday | lunes | loo·nes |
| Tuesday | martes | mar·tes |
| Wednesday | miércoles | myer·ko·les |
| Thursday | jueves | khwe·ves |
| Friday | viernes | vyer·nes |
| Saturday | sábado | sa·ba·do |
| Sunday | domingo | do·meen·go |

| January | enero | e·ne·ro |
| February | febrero | fe·bre·ro |
| March | marzo | mar·so |
| April | abril | a·breel |
| May | mayo | ma·yo |
| June | junio | khoon·yo |
| July | julio | khool·yo |
| August | agosto | a·gos·to |
| September | septiembre | sep·tyem·bre |
| October | octubre | ok·too·bre |
| November | noviembre | no·vyem·bre |
| December | diciembre | dee·syem·bre |

## TRANSPORTATION

| boat | barco | bar·ko |
| bus | autobús | ow·to·boos |
| (basic) bus | chiva/ ranchera | chee·va/ ran·che·ra |
| plane | avión | a·vyon |
| (shared) taxi | colectivo | ko·lek·tee·vo |
| train | tren | tren |
| truck/pickup | camioneta | ka·myo·ne·ta |

| first | primero | pree·*me*·ro |
| last | último | *ool*·tee·mo |
| next | próximo | *prok*·see·mo |

| A ... ticket, please. | Un boleto de ..., por favor. | oon bo·*le*·to de ... por fa·*vor* |
| 1st-class | primera clase | pree·*me*·ra *kla*·se |
| 2nd-class | segunda clase | se·*goon*·da *kla*·se |
| one-way | ida | *ee*·da |
| return | ida y vuelta | *ee*·da ee *vwel*·ta |

**I want to go to ...**
Quisiera ir a ...          kee·*sye*·ra eer a ...

**Does it stop at ...?**
¿Para en ...?          *pa*·ra en ...

**What stop is this?**
¿Cuál es esta parada?          kwal es es·ta pa·*ra*·da

**What time does it arrive/leave?**
¿A qué hora llega/sale?          a ke o·ra ye·ga/*sa*·le

**Please tell me when we get to ...**
¿Puede avisarme          pwe·de a·vee·*sar*·me
cuando lleguemos          kwan·do ye·*ge*·mos
a ...?          a ...

**I want to get off here.**
Quiero bajarme aquí.          kye·ro ba·*khar*·me a·*kee*

| airport | aeropuerto | a·e·ro·*pwer*·to |
| aisle seat | asiento de pasillo | a·*syen*·to de pa·*see*·yo |
| bus stop | parada de autobuses | pa·*ra*·da de ow·to·*boo*·ses |
| bus station | terminal terrestre | ter·mee·*nal* te·*res*·tre |
| cancelled | cancelado | kan·se·*la*·do |
| delayed | retrasado | re·tra·*sa*·do |
| platform | plataforma | pla·ta·*for*·ma |
| ticket office | taquilla | ta·*kee*·ya |
| timetable | horario | o·*ra*·ryo |
| train station | estación de trenes | es·ta·*syon* de *tre*·nes |
| window seat | asiento junto a la ventana | a·*syen*·to *khoon*·to a la ven·*ta*·na |

| I'd like to hire a ... | Quisiera alquilar ... | kee·*sye*·ra al·kee·*lar* ... |
| 4WD | un todo-terreno | oon to·do-te·*re*·no |
| bicycle | una bicicleta | oo·na bee·see·*kle*·ta |
| car | un coche | oon *ko*·che |
| motorcycle | una moto | *oo*·na *mo*·to |

## Numbers

| 1 | uno | *oo*·no |
| --- | --- | --- |
| 2 | dos | dos |
| 3 | tres | tres |
| 4 | cuatro | *kwa*·tro |
| 5 | cinco | *seen*·ko |
| 6 | seis | seys |
| 7 | siete | *sye*·te |
| 8 | ocho | *o*·cho |
| 9 | nueve | *nwe*·ve |
| 10 | diez | dyes |
| 20 | veinte | *veyn*·te |
| 30 | treinta | *treyn*·ta |
| 40 | cuarenta | kwa·*ren*·ta |
| 50 | cincuenta | seen·*kwen*·ta |
| 60 | sesenta | se·*sen*·ta |
| 70 | setenta | se·*ten*·ta |
| 80 | ochenta | o·*chen*·ta |
| 90 | noventa | no·*ven*·ta |
| 100 | cien | syen |
| 1000 | mil | meel |

| child seat | asiento de seguridad para niños | a·*syen*·to de se·goo·ree·*da* pa·ra *nee*·nyos |
| diesel | petróleo | pet·ro·le·o |
| helmet | casco | *kas*·ko |
| hitchhike | hacer botella | a·ser bo·*te*·ya |
| mechanic | mecánico | me·ka·nee·ko |
| petrol/gas | gasolina | ga·so·*lee*·na |
| service station | gasolinera | ga·so·lee·*ne*·ra |
| truck | camion | ka·*myon* |

**Is this the road to ...?**
¿Se va a ... por          se va a ... por
esta carretera?          es·ta ka·re·*te*·ra

**(How long) Can I park here?**
¿(Cuánto tiempo)          (kwan·to tyem·po)
Puedo aparcar aquí?          pwe·do a·par·*kar* a·*kee*

**The car has broken down (at ...).**
El coche se ha averiado          el ko·che se a a·ve·*rya*·do
(en ...).          (en ...)

**I had an accident.**
He tenido un          e te·*nee*·do oon
accidente.          ak·see·*den*·te

**I've run out of petrol.**
Me he quedado sin          me e ke·*da*·do seen
gasolina.          ga·so·*lee*·na

**I have a flat tyre.**
Se me pinchó          se me peen·*cho*
una rueda.          *oo*·na *rwe*·da

# GLOSSARY

**AGAR** – Asociación de Guías de Águas Rápidas del Ecuador (Ecuadorian White-Water Guides Association)

**aguardiente** – sugarcane alcohol

**ASEGUIM** – Asociación Ecuatoriana de Guías de Montaña (Ecuadorian Mountain Guides Association)

**balneario** – literally 'spa', but any place where you can swim or soak

**cabaña** – cabin, found both on the coast and in the Oriente

**camioneta** – pickup or light truck

**campesino** – peasant

**capitanía** – port captain

**casa de cambio** – currency-exchange bureau

**centro comercial** – shopping center; often abbreviated to 'CC'

**chifa** – Chinese restaurant

**chiva** – open-sided bus, or truck mounted with uncomfortably narrow bench seats; also called *ranchera*

**colectivo** – shared taxi

**comedore** – cheap restaurant

**comida típica** – traditional Ecuadorian food

**cuencano** – person from Cuenca

**curandero** – medicine man

**ejecutivo** – 1st class, on buses

**folklórica** – traditional Andean folk music

**guayaquileño** – person from Guayaquil

**hostal** – small and reasonably priced hotel; not a youth hostel

**hostería** – small hotel, which tends to be a midpriced country inn; often, but not always, found in rural areas

**IGM** – Instituto Geográfico Militar, the Ecuadorian government agency that produces topographic and other maps

**indígena** – indigenous person

**lavandería** – laundry

**malecón** – waterfront

**mestizo** – person of mixed indigenous and Spanish descent

**otavaleño** – person from Otavalo

**paja toquilla** – straw from the *toquilla* (a small palm), used in crafts and hat making

**Panamericana** – Pan-American Hwy, which is the main route joining Latin American countries to one another; known as the Interamericana in some countries

**panga** – small boat used to ferry passengers, especially in the Galápagos Islands,

but also on the rivers and lakes of the Oriente and along the coast

**páramo** – high-altitude Andean grasslands of Ecuador, which continue north into Colombia with relicts in the highest parts of Costa Rica

**parque nacional** – national park

**pasillo** – Ecuador's national music

**peña** – bar or club featuring live folkloric music

**playa** – beach

**puente** – bridge

**quinta** – fine house or villa found in the countryside

**quiteño** – person from Quito

**ranchera** – see *chiva*

**refugio** – simple mountain shelters for spending the night

**residencial** – cheap hotel

**río** – river

**salsateca** – (also *salsoteca*) nightclub where dancing to salsa music is the main attraction

**serranos** – people from the highlands

**shigra** – small string bag

**tagua nut** – from a palm tree grown in local forest; the 'nuts' are actually hard seeds, which are carved into a variety of ornaments

**terminal terrestre** – central bus terminal for many different companies

**tzantza** – shrunken head

# behind the scenes

## SEND US YOUR FEEDBACK

We love to hear from travelers – your comments keep us on our toes and help make our books better. Our well-traveled team reads every word on what you loved or loathed about this book. Although we cannot reply individually to postal submissions, we always guarantee that your feedback goes straight to the appropriate authors, in time for the next edition. Each person who sends us information is thanked in the next edition – the most useful submissions are rewarded with a selection of digital PDF chapters.

Visit **lonelyplanet.com/contact** to submit your updates and suggestions or to ask for help. Our award-winning website also features inspirational travel stories, news and discussions.

Note: We may edit, reproduce and incorporate your comments in Lonely Planet products such as guidebooks, websites and digital products, so let us know if you don't want your comments reproduced or your name acknowledged. For a copy of our privacy policy visit lonelyplanet.com/privacy.

## OUR READERS

**Many thanks to the travelers who used the last edition and wrote to us with helpful hints, useful advice and interesting anecdotes:**

Steve Bray, Lauren Burns, Aoife Byrne, Lani V Cox, Asa Cusack, Renate De Jonge, Nicolas Dubois, Lukasz Duda, Andrew Duniec, Caroline Evenden, Diego Torres Garzón, Mathias Gerth, Marshall Goldberg, Ricia Gordon, Desmond Graal Cullen, Markus Hauk, Katja Heijnen, Brent Helmkamp, Esther Hermans, Wally Johnson, Cleo Kale, Thomas Knoblauch, Dietmar Krumpl, Cathrin Kurz, Jake Ling, Marcus Loane, Carl Lobitz, Vanessa Mcintyre, Elizabeth Meyrick, Greg Miier, Leslie Moore, Dan Morris, Eric Neemann, Darshan Neubauer, Lukas Nigg, Amber Novak, William Olvera, Maxime Peeters, Natalia Platonova, Daniel Richter, Thomas Schetty, Sonja Schoentag, Stefanie Schuster, Keela Shackell, Kati Sivula, Shelly Skaug, Agnethe Spangberg, Gera Stout, Mariët Struijk, Sebastián Pablo Taboada, Matt Van Der Peet, Erwin Van Liempd, Ray L Vansickle, Margaret Vile, Olivia Watson, Mark Weisbrot, Reto Westermann, Annie White, Brian White, Jason White, Daan Wijsman, Barbara Wilson, Elaine Wiltshire, Louisa Wood, Marie-louise Zimmermann

## AUTHOR THANKS

### Regis St Louis

Big thanks to the countless *quiteños* and expats for tips and insight: Dominic Hamilton at Metropolitan Touring; Patricio Gaybor and Luz Elena Coloma at Quito Turismo; Adriana and Fernando at Casa Gangotena; Santiago at Vibes; John and Eva at Happy Gringo; Silvia Garcia and Ritmo Salvaje for the salsa instruction; and Paul Parreno at CarpeDM for all his help in Quito (and a great run!). As always, thanks to Cassandra and our daughters Magdalena and Genevieve for continued love and support despite sometimes long absences.

### Greg Benchwick

The biggest and boldest of thanks goes to my wife and daughter who traveled with me through the central highlands on the first stage of my research trip... you are the best travel companions a man could ask for. The people of Ecuador were amazingly gracious and kind, as were the tour operators, guides and street rascals that set me on my way. And to my Cotopaxi climbing companions, Julian and James, thanks for the best summit of my life!

## Michael Grosberg

First and foremost, thanks to the warmth and kindness of Ecuadorian strangers I met along the way. And to Christopher Jimenez in Guayaquil for all his advice; Xavier 'Tito' Burbano for sharing his political and social insight; Alan Smith for his travel thoughts; Jascivan Carvalho for his experience with environmental issues; Fabrizio Prado in the Galápagos; Aline Louvet in Puerto Baquerizo Moreno; and to Carly Neidorf, for being there for me, both on the road and stateside.

## Tom Masters

Many thanks to my friend Alexandra Tampa-kopoulos, who accompanied me for much of my journey through Ecuador, for her great company and unfailing sense of humor, even when things didn't turn out as planned. I'm indebted to many people all over Ecuador who helped me throughout my trip, but thanks especially to the staff and guides of the Lower Río Napo who made sure than my journey went like clockwork, to the very kind owners of the Ali Shungu Mountaintop Lodge in Otavalo, and to the friendly staff at Casa de Amigos in Same for making me feel at home on the road.

# ACKNOWLEDGMENTS

Climate map data adapted from Peel MC, Finlayson BL & McMahon TA (2007) 'Updated World Map of the Köppen-Geiger Climate Classification', *Hydrology and Earth System Sciences*, 11, 163344.

Cover photograph: Blue-footed booby, Galápagos Islands, John Freeman, LPI.

Many of the images in this guide are available for licensing from Lonely Planet Images: www.lonelyplanetimages.com.

# THIS BOOK

This 9th edition of Lonely Planet's *Ecuador & the Galápagos Islands* guidebook was researched and written by Regis St Louis (Coordinating Author), Greg Benchwick, Michael Grosberg and Tom Masters. The previous edition was researched and written by Regis St Louis, Lucy Burningham, Aimée Dowl and Michael Grosberg. This guidebook was commissioned in Lonely Planet's Oakland office, and produced by the following:

**Commissioning Editor**
Kathleen Munnelly

**Coordinating Editors**
Nigel Chin, Amanda Williamson
**Coordinating Cartographers** Karusha Ganga, Andy Rojas
**Coordinating Layout Designer** Juan Winata
**Managing Editors** Barbara Delissen, Bruce Evans, Annelies Mertens, Martine Power
**Managing Cartographers** Shahara Ahmed, Alison Lyall
**Managing Layout Designer** Jane Hart
**Assisting Editors** Amy Karafin, Kate Mathews, Joanne Newell, Karyn Noble, Sophie Splatt

**Assisting Cartographer** James Leversha
**Cover Research** Naomi Parker
**Internal Image Research** Nicholas Colicchia
**Language Content** Branislava Vladisavljevic

**Thanks to** Anita Banh, Sasha Baskett, Elin Berglund, Lucy Birchley, Ryan Evans, Larissa Frost, Chris Girdler, Paul Iacono, Sally Morgan, Mardi O'Connor, Trent Paton, Kirsten Rawlings, Wibowo Rusli, Gerard Walker, Simon Williamson

NOTES

# how to use this book

These symbols will help you find the listings you want:

| | | | | | |
|---|---|---|---|---|---|
| ◉ | Sights | ☞ | Tours | 🍷 | Drinking |
| 🏖 | Beaches | 🎊 | Festivals & Events | ☆ | Entertainment |
| 🏃 | Activities | 📋 | Sleeping | 🛍 | Shopping |
| 🥢 | Courses | ✕ | Eating | ❶ | Information/Transport |

**Look out for these icons:**

| | |
|---|---|
| TOP | Our author's recommendation |
| FREE | No payment required |
| 🌿 | A green or sustainable option |

Our authors have nominated these places as demonstrating a strong commitment to sustainability – for example by supporting local communities and producers, operating in an environmentally friendly way, or supporting conservation projects.

These symbols give you the vital information for each listing:

| | | | | | |
|---|---|---|---|---|---|
| ☎ | Telephone Numbers | 🛜 | Wi-Fi Access | 🚌 | Bus |
| ☺ | Opening Hours | 🏊 | Swimming Pool | 🚢 | Ferry |
| Ⓟ | Parking | 🥗 | Vegetarian Selection | Ⓜ | Metro |
| ⊖ | Nonsmoking | 📋 | English-Language Menu | Ⓢ | Subway |
| ❄ | Air-Conditioning | 👪 | Family-Friendly | 🚋 | Tram |
| @ | Internet Access | 🐾 | Pet-Friendly | 🚆 | Train |

Reviews are organised by author preference.

## Map Legend

**Sights**

- 🏖 Beach
- 🛐 Buddhist
- 🏰 Castle
- ✝ Christian
- ☪ Hindu
- ☪ Islamic
- ✡ Jewish
- ❶ Monument
- 🏛 Museum/Gallery
- ⊗ Ruin
- 🍷 Winery/Vineyard
- 🐘 Zoo
- ◉ Other Sight

**Activities, Courses & Tours**

- Diving/Snorkelling
- Canoeing/Kayaking
- Skiing
- Surfing
- Swimming/Pool
- Walking
- Windsurfing
- Other Activity/Course/Tour

**Sleeping**

- Sleeping
- Camping

**Eating**

- ✕ Eating

**Drinking**

- Drinking
- Cafe

**Entertainment**

- Entertainment

**Shopping**

- Shopping

**Information**

- Post Office
- Tourist Information

**Transport**

- Airport
- Border Crossing
- Bus
- Cable Car/Funicular
- Cycling
- Ferry
- Metro
- Monorail
- Parking
- S-Bahn
- Taxi
- Train/Railway
- Tram
- Tube Station
- U-Bahn
- Other Transport

**Routes**

- Tollway
- Freeway
- Primary
- Secondary
- Tertiary
- Lane
- Unsealed Road
- Plaza/Mall
- Steps
- Tunnel
- Pedestrian Overpass
- Walking Tour
- Walking Tour Detour
- Path

**Boundaries**

- International
- State/Province
- Disputed
- Regional/Suburb
- Marine Park
- Cliff
- Wall

**Population**

- Capital (National)
- Capital (State/Province)
- City/Large Town
- Town/Village

**Geographic**

- Hut/Shelter
- Lighthouse
- Lookout
- Mountain/Volcano
- Oasis
- Park
- Pass
- Picnic Area
- Waterfall

**Hydrography**

- River/Creek
- Intermittent River
- Swamp/Mangrove
- Reef
- Canal
- Water
- Dry/Salt/Intermittent Lake
- Glacier

**Areas**

- Beach/Desert
- Cemetery (Christian)
- Cemetery (Other)
- Park/Forest
- Sportsground
- Sight (Building)
- Top Sight (Building)

# OUR STORY

A beat-up old car, a few dollars in the pocket and a sense of adventure. In 1972 that's all Tony and Maureen Wheeler needed for the trip of a lifetime – across Europe and Asia overland to Australia. It took several months, and at the end – broke but inspired – they sat at their kitchen table writing and stapling together their first travel guide, *Across Asia on the Cheap*. Within a week they'd sold 1500 copies. Lonely Planet was born.

Today, Lonely Planet has offices in Melbourne, London and Oakland, with more than 600 staff and writers. We share Tony's belief that 'a great guidebook should do three things: inform, educate and amuse'.

# OUR WRITERS

### Regis St Louis

Coordinating Author, Quito After Regis' first journey to the Andes in 1999, he returned home, sold all his belongings and set off on a classic journey across South America. Since then, he's returned numerous times, traveling dodgy roads by truck, horse and bicycle, scaling Andean peaks (small ones) and flailing away at Spanish and Portuguese. On his most recent trip he dined his way through countless *cevicherías*, joined the night ride through Quito's old town and finally learned some salsa moves. Regis is the coordinating author of *South America on a Shoestring*, and he has contributed to more than 30 Lonely Planet titles. He lives in Brooklyn, New York.

Read more about Regis at:
lonelyplanet.com/members/regisstlouis

### Greg Benchwick

Central Highlands, Southern Highlands Greg has been writing about Latin America for the past 10 years. He's rumbled through the jungles of Central America, met with heads of state while working for the UN and trekked along ancient Inca roads in Ecuador, Bolivia and Peru. To cap off his research for the central and southern highlands, Greg huffed and puffed his way to the top of Cotopaxi.

### Michael Grosberg

South Coast, The Galápagos Islands This is the third edition of *Ecuador & the Galápagos Islands* Michael has worked on. In addition to his Lonely Planet assignments, he's visited Ecuador on a number of other occasions, including a long-ago summer spent teaching in Quito. During his graduate school days he focused on the literature and culture of Latin America. Michael, a reformed academic, is based in Brooklyn, New York and has worked on more than 17 Lonely Planet books.

### Tom Masters

Northern Highlands, The Oriente, North Coast & Lowlands Tom first went to Ecuador as a student backpacker and immediately loved this fascinating corner of South America. Since then, he's covered all corners of Latin America for Lonely Planet, including Mexico, Cuba and Venezuela. Covering the vast Oriente, the stunning northern highlands and the super-relaxed north coast for this book was a real adventure that involved fording surprisingly large rivers in a tiny car, anaconda sightings, a laptop breakdown in the rainforest and one shamanic soul cleansing. You can find Tom online at www.tommasters.net.

Read more about Tom at:
lonelyplanet.com/members/tommasters

OVER PAGE / MORE WRITERS

Published by Lonely Planet Publications Pty Ltd
ABN 36 005 607 983
9th edition – May 2012
ISBN 978 1 74179 809 8
© Lonely Planet 2012    Photographs © as indicated 2012
10 9 8 7 6 5 4 3 2 1
Printed in China

Although the authors and Lonely Planet have taken all reasonable care in preparing this book, we make no warranty about the accuracy or completeness of its content and, to the maximum extent permitted, disclaim all liability arising from its use.

Bestselling guide to Ecuador – source: Nielsen BookScan, Australia, UK and USA, May 2011 to April 2012